THE SETTING OF THE
SERMON ON THE MOUNT

THE SETTING OF THE SERMON ON THE MOUNT

BY

W. D. DAVIES
M.A., D.D.

Edward Robinson Professor of Biblical Theology,
Union Theological Seminary
Adjunct Professor of Religion, Columbia University

CAMBRIDGE
AT THE UNIVERSITY PRESS
1966

PUBLISHED BY
THE SYNDICS OF THE CAMBRIDGE UNIVERSITY PRESS
Bentley House, 200 Euston Road, London, N.W. 1
American Branch: 32 East 57th Street, New York, N.Y. 10022
West African Office: P.M.B. 5181, Ibadan, Nigeria

©

CAMBRIDGE UNIVERSITY PRESS

1963

First published 1963
Reprinted 1966

Printed in Great Britain at the University Printing House, Cambridge
(Brooke Crutchley, University Printer)

CONTENTS

Preface   *page* ix

Abbreviations   xiii

I   Introductory   1

II   The Setting in Matthew   14

    1 Pentateuchal motifs   14

    2 New Exodus and New Moses   25

       (*a*) The treatment of Mark and Q   26

       (*b*) Material peculiar to Matthew   61

       (*c*) Miracles   86

    3 Mosaic categories transcended   93

       (*a*) The Christian life   94

       (*b*) Terminology   99

III   The Setting in Jewish Messianic Expectation   109

    1 The Old Testament   122

    2 The Apocrypha, Pseudepigrapha and Dead Sea Scrolls   139

    3 The Rabbinical sources   156

IV   The Setting in the Contemporary Judaism   191

    1 Gnosticism   192

    2 The Dead Sea Sect   208

    3 Jamnia   256

CONTENTS

V   The Setting in the Early Church   *page* 316

    1 Anti-Paulinism   316

    2 Paul and Tradition   341

    3 Q and Crisis; Catechesis; the Pastorals   366

    4 M and *Gemara*   387

    5 The Epistle of James and the Johannine Sources   401

VI The Setting in the Ministry of Jesus   415

    1 Transmission of his words   415

    2 The Teacher   418

    3 The Eschatological Preacher   419

    4 The Rabbi   422

    5 The demand of Jesus in its setting   425

VII Conclusion   436

APPENDICES

  I   Mekilta on Exod. xiv. 13–15   441

 II   Mekilta on Exod. xv. 1–2   442

III   The Character of Matt. i and ii   443

 IV   Isa. xli. 2 and the Pre-existent Messiah   445

  V   '¿ Cesará la Tora en la Edad Messiánica?'   446

 VI   The Role of Torah in the Messiánic Age   447

VII   Galilean and Judaean Judaism   450

VIII   The Doxology in Matt. vi. 13   451

 IX   The Use of the Term ἱστορῆσαι in Gal. i. 18   453

  X   Rabbis and their Pupils   455

 XI   'Wisdom' Sayings of Jesus   457

XII   The Influence of Catechisms on the Gospels   460

CONTENTS

XIII The Textual Problem of Mark x. 12 *page* 462

XIV Echoes of Synoptic Words in John 463

XV Reflections on a Scandinavian Approach to 'the Gospel
Tradition' 464

Bibliography 481

Indices

I *Index of Quotations* 505

   A The Old Testament 505

   B The Apocrypha and Pseudepigrapha of the Old
Testament 509

   C The New Testament 510

   D The Targums 526

   E The Dead Sea Scrolls 526

   F Rabbinical Sources 527

II *Index of References to Classical and Hellenistic Authors and
Extra-Canonical Christian Writings* 532

III *Index of Authors* 533

IV *Index of Subjects* 540

PREFACE

This volume grew out of the Syr D. Owen Evans's Lectures which I was honoured to communicate to the University of Wales, at Aberystwyth, in 1957, and it is indissolubly linked with the memory of my friend, the late Vice-Chancellor, R. M. Davies, and with the courtesy of Acting-Principal Morton. I am grateful to the University authorities for their patience in waiting for the publication of the lectures in their present form. Different parts of the work were also delivered as the Duncan Lectures, at the Candler School of Theology, Emory University, Atlanta, Georgia; as the Chancellor's Lectures, Queen's University, Kingston, Ontario; as the Annual Lectures, Louisville Presbyterian Seminary, Kentucky; and at Münster and Cambridge Universities.

Part of a wider attempt to understand the interaction of Christianity and Judaism in the first century, the work is limited to an examination of influences, within and without the Church, which led to the concentrated presentation of moral teaching known as the Sermon on the Mount. It is not directly concerned with the content of that teaching, nor its significance for Christian doctrine or ethical theory, but only with the circumstances of its emergence and formulation. That such a historical theme can have theological significance I have ventured to suggest, without elaboration, in the conclusion.

Owing to the exigencies of printing, much material has been assigned to appendices. The reader is asked not to treat this as secondary but as integral to the argument. This applies especially to Appendix xv, which deals with recent Scandinavian studies. I thank Professors Van Unnik and Bo Reicke, who edited the *Freundesgabe* for Dr Cullmann in which the material presented there first appeared, for permission to reprint it.[1] I particularly regret that Dr Birger Gerhardsson's significant volume, *Memory and Manuscript*, appeared too late for detailed use in the body of this work, as did also the important works *Überlieferung und Auslegung im Matthäus-Evangelium*, by G. Bornkamm, G. Barth, and H. J. Held (1960) and *Das wahre Israel*, by W. Trilling (1959).

It is a pleasure to express my gratitude: to the Research Council of Princeton University for making it possible for me to enjoy and profit from consultations with Professors E. Stauffer, G. Friedrich and

---

[1] *Neotestamentica et Patristica* (Leiden, 1962).

H. J. Schoeps at the University of Erlangen before this study had taken shape; and to the John Simon Memorial Guggenheim Foundation, New York City, for honouring me with a fellowship, in the summer of 1959, which enabled me to enlarge my understanding of the theme in talks with Professors C. H. Dodd and David Daube in England and Professors Joachim Jeremias and K. H. Rengstorf in Germany. My colleagues at Princeton University and Union Seminary have provided much stimulus. Professor James Muilenburg especially shared with me his deep knowledge and insight in Old Testament matters, and, on the Rabbinic side, I have been highly privileged in the ready helpfulness of President Louis Finkelstein, Professor Saul Lieberman and Rabbi Neil Gillman of the Jewish Theological Seminary of America, and Professor S. W. Baron of Columbia University. This privilege has to be experienced to be appreciated and has reinforced my awareness of the need for still greater co-operation between Jewish and Gentile students in an area where much, not only in the background of primitive Christianity, but in its very structure, can only be adequately revealed by Jewish scholarship.

If, despite my concern to pay due attention to the role of Law in primitive Christianity, it should prove that I have succeeded in avoiding tendentiousness and in maintaining, to some degree, a proper balance between Gospel and Law, this will be largely due to Dr Reinhold Niebuhr. His profound awareness of the ambiguity of all human conduct has continually reasserted for me the primacy of Grace. And yet at no time have I been more confirmed in the concern of this volume than when listening, during the last four years, to moving sermons in which he has wrestled with the relation between Gospel and Law and compelled the conclusion that Law cannot only be the instrument of Justice, but the expression of Grace. To this last I have also been recalled by Dr Abraham Heschel. Unfortunately his work on the Haggadah (*Torah min ha shamaim*, Soncino Press, London, 1962), appeared too late for my use. It should, however, be noted that his high estimate of the theological significance of Haggadah, which contrasts with the view mentioned on p. 185 herein, adds force to the material presented in the third chapter and should now be taken into consideration in the assessment of it.

To Dr M. S. Enslin, editor of the *Journal of Biblical Literature*, and to Dr Moshe Greenberg, editor of the monograph series of the Society of Biblical Literature and Exegesis, I am thankful for permission to use, in the third chapter, material from a previous study, published by the Society as Number VII in the series mentioned, entitled *Torah in the*

Messianic Age and/or the Age to Come (Philadelphia, 1952). I was much instructed by reviews of this by Dr Morton Smith and Father D. Barthélemy and, especially, by a prolonged and enriching critique of it by Professor Díez Macho of Barcelona, from which I was able to profit by the translation of a former student, the Reverend Dr José Míguez, now President of the Union Theological Seminary of Buenos Aires. (See pp. 446 f.)

I was helped in the reading of proofs especially by my former pupils Professor Arthur Bellinzoni, Jr, of Wells College, Aurora, New York, who checked the biblical references and prepared the biblical indexes, and Professor Robin Scroggs, of Dartmouth College, who helped with these and prepared the index of subjects. Both made valuable criticisms and suggestions. The bibliography was prepared by the Reverend Howard Newton, and other indices by Mr Donald Williams, graduate students at Union Seminary. To all these I tender my most grateful acknowledgements, as also to Mrs Newton Todd who typed most of the manuscript. On the bibliographical side I found the librarians and their staffs at Union, the Jewish Theological Seminary and Pusey House, Oxford, of the greatest possible help. The skill of the readers and printers of the Cambridge University Press it would be an impertinence to praise: suffice that it evoked my keenest, and sometimes amazed, admiration. And, finally, what the volume owes to my wife must remain unexpressed.

W. D. D.

UNION THEOLOGICAL SEMINARY,
NEW YORK
3 February 1963

ABBREVIATIONS

B.A.S.O.R.	*Bulletin of the American School of Oriental Research*
B.T.Z.	*Theologische Zeitschrift* (Basle)
D.S.S.	*The Dead Sea Scrolls*
E.T.	*The Expository Times*
H.D.B.	*Hasting's Dictionary of the Bible*
H.T.R.	*The Harvard Theological Review*
I.C.C.	*The International Critical Commentary*
J.B.L.	*The Journal of Biblical Literature*
J.E.	*The Jewish Encyclopedia*
J.J.S.	*The Journal of Jewish Studies*
J.Q.R.	*The Jewish Quarterly Review*
J.T.S.	*The Journal of Theological Studies*
M.T.Z.	*Theologische Zeitschrift* (Munich)
N.E.B.	*The New English Bible*
N.T.S.	*New Testament Studies*
P.A.A.J.R.	*Proceedings of the American Academy for Jewish Research*
P.C.	*Peake's Commentary on the Bible*, 1962
P.R.J.²*	Davies, W. D., *Paul and Rabbinic Judaism²*, 1955
R.B.	*Revue Biblique*
R.E.J.	*Revue des Études Juives*
R.S.R.	*Recherches de Science Religieuse*
R.S.V.	*The Revised Standard Version of the Bible*
S.–B.	Strack, H. L. und Billerbeck, P., *Kommentar zum Neuen Testament aus Talmud und Midrasch*
S.J.T.	*The Scottish Journal of Theology*
T.L.	*Theologische Literaturzeitung*
T.M.	W. D. Davies, *Torah in the Messianic Age and/or the Age to Come*
T.W.Z.N.T.	*Theologisches Wörterbuch zum Neuen Testament*, ed. G. Kittel, G. Friedrich
Z.N.W.	*Zeitschrift für die neutestamentliche Wissenschaft*
Z.R.G.	*Zeitschrift für Religions- und Geistesgeschichte*
Z.T.K.	*Zeitschrift für Theologie und Kirche*

The following abbreviations are used in connexion with the Dead Sea Scrolls:

CDC   *The Zadokite Documents.* Ed. Chaim Rabin (Oxford, 1954)

DJD I   D. Barthélemy, O.P., J. T. Milik, *et al.*, *Qumrân Cave I. Discoveries in the Judaean Desert I* (Oxford, 1955).

ABBREVIATIONS

DSD or 1QS The sectarian Rule of the Community, exemplar from Cave I, Qumran. Published in DSS II.

DSS I M. Burrows, John C. Trever and W. H. Brownlee, eds., *The Dead Sea Scrolls of St Mark's Monastery*, vol. I (New Haven, 1950).

DSS II M. Burrows, John C. Trever and W. H. Brownlee, eds., *The Dead Sea Scrolls of St Mark's Monastery*, vol. II, 2 (New Haven, 1951).

OMG E. L. Sukenik and N. Avigad, *'ôṣar hamměgillôt haggěnûẓôt* (Jerusalem, 1954).

1QH [*hôdāyôt*] The sectarian roll of Psalms of Thanksgiving from Cave I. Published in OMG.

1QpHab and 1QpH [*péšer Habakkuk*] The commentary on Habakkuk from Cave I. Published in DSS I.

1QIsa^a A scroll of Isaiah from Cave I, Qumran, exemplar a. Published in DSS I.

1QM [*milḥāmāh*] The sectarian War of the Children of Light against the Children of Darkness. Published in OMG.

1QSa, 1QSb Adjuncts to the Rule of the Community (1QS). Published in DJD I as 1Q28a and 1Q28b.

4Q Flor (ilegium) A document published by Allegro in *J.B.L.* LXXV (1956), 176–7; and *J.B.L.* LXXVII (1958), 350–4.

4Q Testimonia The sheet of testimonia from Cave IV. Published by Allegro in *J.B.L.* LXXV (1956), 174–87.

All other abbreviations are customary or self-explanatory. Scriptural references denoted only by figures are from The Gospel according to St Matthew: for example, x. 1 refers to Matt. x. 1. Complete consistency in the transliteration of Rabbinic names has not been possible: for example, the form 'R. Johannan ben Zakkai' is used of the Jamnian figure and 'R. Joḥanan' of the third-century figure. But in quotations the usage of the various translators has been followed.

Δεῦτε πρός με πάντες οἱ κοπιῶντες καὶ πεφορτισμένοι, κἀγὼ ἀναπαύσω ὑμᾶς. ἄρατε τὸν 3υγόν μου ἐφ᾽ ὑμᾶς καὶ μάθετε ἀπ᾽ ἐμοῦ, ὅτι πραΰς εἰμι καὶ ταπεινὸς τῇ καρδίᾳ, καὶ εὑρήσετε ἀνάπαυσιν ταῖς ψυχαῖς ὑμῶν· ὁ γὰρ 3υγός μου χρηστὸς καὶ τὸ φορτίον μου ἐλαφρόν ἐστιν.

XI. 28–30. *The quintessence of the Matthaean interpretation of Christianity as Gospel and Law.*

Through throats where many rivers meet, the curlews cry

From *In the white giant's thigh,* by DYLAN THOMAS

I. INTRODUCTORY

Matthew v–vii, usually referred to as the Sermon on the Mount (*SM*), with which we are to be concerned in the following pages, has been variously assessed. Some have found it a pernicious document, which, by presenting an utterly impossible ethic, has wrought incalculable harm in personal, social and international life. An exceptional English jurist in the last century claimed it to be 'not only imprudent but unjust'.[1] Others have seen in it the finest statement of the highest ethic that mankind has known. The words of a recent commentator, that 'These chapters have won universal recognition as the supreme statement of the ethical duties of man', are typical.[2] Different as are these estimates, however, they share one common assumption, namely, that Matt. v–vii can be regarded as a single entity, which has its own unified secret to reveal, and that this secret is the ethical teaching of Jesus of Nazareth. But it is precisely this assumption that modern critical studies have made dubious. The views propounded by scholars in our day about the contents and structure of Matt. v–vii seem to compel the conclusion that the whole section is merely a collection of unrelated sayings of diverse origins, a patchwork, which cannot possibly retain the pre-eminence once accorded to it as the authoritative source for the teaching of Jesus. To embark critically on the interpretation of the *SM* is inevitably to encounter the 'frustration' of that honest dissection which, in New Testament scholarship, as in other spheres, so often seems to end in murder. Three disciplines are mainly responsible for this.

First, there is the influence of the source-criticism of the Synoptic Gospels. Protestant scholars have generally held that behind the *SM*, as behind the rest of Matthew, there are three main sources upon which Matthew has drawn for his material. These are Mark, probably written in Rome after A.D. 65; another written or oral collection of the sayings of Jesus, usually dated about A.D. 50, and referred to as Q; and, thirdly, a source named M, probably derived from the Church at Jerusalem. Materials from all three, Mark, Q and M, have been combined in the *SM* as elsewhere in Matthew. A typical Protestant study is that of Marriott. A considerable part of his work is devoted to source-criticism, that is, the disentangling of what in Matt. v–vii is to be derived from Mark, Q and M.

[1] See *The Times Literary Supplement*, November 1948, N. 662. The jurist was Sir James Fitzjames Stephen.
[2] T. H. Robinson, *The Moffatt New Testament Commentary on Matthew* (1928), p. 25.

It is not surprising that he is particularly dissatisfying in his exegesis of the Sermon.[1] And not only is the multiplicity of sources to be reckoned with. There are also different views as to the priority ascribed by Matthew to those which he employed. While most have allowed that Matthew has fitted material from M into the order of the material from Q, Perry[2] has urged that the Q material has been fitted into an order derived from M. But in any case it is the patchwork character of the Sermon that most forcibly emerges. The same is true of W. L. Knox's recent work on the Synoptics.[3] He deals with Matt. v–vii as a unit, under the title of 'The New Law', but the result of his work is certainly to accentuate that fissiparous impact of critical studies to which we refer.

Roman Catholic scholarship has also experienced this impact. Even if we retain the priority of Matthew, as do Roman Catholic scholars, the impression is not easy to escape that the *SM* is so artificial a construction that it cannot have any essential integrity in the sense that it is a well-knit unit, governed throughout by an overruling purpose. Thus the Roman Catholic scholar Soiron[4] found two principles governing the arrangement of material in Matthew, as also in Mark and, to a lesser degree, Luke: namely, the agglomeration of material dealing with common or related themes (*systematische Gesichtspunkte*) and the association of material in accordance with convenient key words (*Stichwortdisposition*). In the *SM* the former principle determines the proximity of the following passages: v. 1–12, 13–16, 17–48; vi. 1–18, 19–34; vii. 1–12, 13 f. But the *Stichwortdisposition* Soiron finds in (1) v. 14–16, where the words φῶς (light), λύχνον (lamp), λυχνία (stand), and λάμπειν (shine) suggested the association of the material; (2) v. 24–5, where verse 25 is drawn by association of ideas to the word διαλλάγηθι (be reconciled) in verse 24; (3) v. 28–30, where verses 29–30 are attracted to verse 28 by the key word βλέπων (seeing) in verse 28; (4) vi. 21–3, where the sequence of material is determined by the occurrence of the associated terms καρδία (heart), σῶμα (body), ὀφθαλμός (eye); (5) vi. 25–34 where the key words are λύχνος

---

[1] H. Marriott, *The Sermon on the Mount* (London, 1925). Out of 274 pages, literary and source problems largely occupy 140.

[2] C. Perry, 'The Framework of the Sermon on the Mount', in *J.B.L.* LIV, 103–5. See G. D. Kilpatrick, *The Origins of the Gospel According to St Matthew* (1946), p. 24.

[3] *Sources of the Synoptic Gospels*, vol. II, *St Luke and St Matthew* (Cambridge, 1957), pp. 7–36.

[4] Th. Soiron, *Die Logia Jesu, Neutestamentliche Abhandlungen* (Münster i. W., 1916). The two principles indicated are accepted as in the main correct by Morton Smith, *Tannaitic Parallels to the Gospels* (1951), p. 115; he also suggests other parallels in types of association between the Gospels and the Tannaitic sources.

(lamp), ὀφθαλμός (eye), ἐμβλέπω (look at), καταμανθάνω (consider), and these again connect the whole section vi. 25–34 with vi. 22 f.; (6) vii. 21–3, where vii. 22, 23 begin with almost the same words. But, while Soiron's work richly illumines the literary devices employed by Matthew[1] in the arrangement of his materials, its immediate impression is to emphasize the fragmentary nature of the contents of the *SM*. In both Protestant and Roman Catholic scholarship the question is inevitable whether Matt. v–vii can be treated as a unity at all, when it is so clearly an agglomeration of sources and even of snippets of tradition. At least the section cannot be regarded as a sermon: at best it can only be a collection of sayings drawn from discourses uttered at diverse times and circumstances. That these discourses necessarily go back to Jesus himself has been questioned in the light of the next discipline which we have to notice.

Secondly, then, apart from the plague of source-criticism, there is the 'nightmare of form-criticism'.[2] Before the tradition about what Jesus did and said came to be written in documents, it circulated for over two decades at least in an oral form. And, as its name suggests, form-criticism has been concerned to examine the forms which the tradition about Jesus assumed in this period before it came to be recorded in writing. These forms have been variously classified, but a common conviction appears in most of the work of form-critics, namely, that the tradition about Jesus was preserved, moulded, and, therefore, influenced by the Christian community. It was the needs of the Church in preaching, teaching, catechetical instruction at baptism and other occasions, propaganda and apologetic that determined what was transmitted both in content and form. Some form-critics ascribe not only the preservation of the tradition but its very creation in large measure to the Church itself. In any case, it is only through the eyes of the early Christians that we can see Jesus of Nazareth and through their ears only can we hear him. Thus form-criticism, just as it has invaded the quest of the historical Jesus to produce frequently a deep-seated scepticism as to the possibility of finding out what actually happened in the life of Jesus, has also influenced—not to say vitiated—efforts to establish the exact content

[1] We here employ the name Matthew without prejudice for the author of the Gospel, or, if such existed, for the 'school' which produced the Gospel (see K. Stendahl, *The School of Matthew*, 1954).

[2] The best introduction to this is still Vincent Taylor, *The Formation of the Gospel Tradition* (London, 1933). The phrase the 'nightmare of form-criticism' I heard used in a lecture dealing with the works of R. H. Lightfoot, *History and Interpretation in the Gospels* (London, 1935) and *Locality and Doctrine in the Gospels* (London, 1938).

of the teaching of Jesus. For example, Bultmann, one of the leading practitioners of form-criticism, is compelled to reduce the *SM* to an arrangement of a multiplicity of pericopae or divisions of tradition which have assumed a certain form and whose contents are to be traced not to Jesus himself but to the early Church.[1] Thus, like source-criticism, form-criticism also has complicated any attempt at understanding Matt. v–vii as a totality by splitting it up into small sections, the authenticity of which is variously estimated.

And, thirdly, closely related to form-criticism is the work of those scholars who have emphasized the liturgical factors in the formation of the Gospel tradition. According to these, the tradition about Jesus took shape under the need to supply the Church with lectionary material, that is, material that could be used in the services of the Church for reading in public. The works and words of Jesus were thus forced into a calendrical mould to fit the needs of each Sunday in the year, and the *SM* was probably formed as a lesson to be read at a particular time in the Church year. Quite clearly, it follows from this, not only that it would be unwise to attach undue historicity to the sequence given to the life of Jesus in the Gospels, but, particularly for our purposes, that the material in the *SM* will have suffered considerable fashioning. It has been cut to size for use in public reading in the services of the Church.[2]

We have above indicated the three main disciplines—source-, form- and liturgical-criticism—which make the interpretation of Matt. v–vii, as a unit, very tortuous. We may sum up. Matt. v–vii *is* made up of material drawn from diverse sources, which can fairly easily be isolated and can be seen tabulated in any handbook on the Gospels. The needs of the Church have dictated, if not created, much of the form and possibly much of the content of the material. And while liturgical influences in the preservation of the tradition have been exaggerated, as we have indicated elsewhere, nevertheless, liturgical modifications have undoubtedly crept into the *SM*. By way of a single illustration, we need only compare the form of the Lord's Prayer as it occurs in Matthew and Luke. They read as follows:

Matt. vi. 9 ff.	Luke xi. 1 ff.
Our Father *which art in Heaven*,	And He was praying at a certain place
Hallowed be Thy Name,	and when he stopped, one of his

[1] *Die Geschichte der synoptischen Tradition*[2] (Göttingen, 1931) *ad rem.* It is fair to note, however, that Bultmann is not concerned to discuss Matt. v–vii as a totality.
[2] See P. Carrington, *The Primitive Christian Calendar* (Cambridge, 1952) and W. D. Davies, 'Reflections' on this in *The Background of the New Testament and its Eschatology*, ed. Davies and Daube (Cambridge, 1956), pp. 124–52.

Thy kingdom come,
Thy will be done,
On earth as it is in Heaven.
Give us this day our daily bread
And forgive us our trespasses
As we forgive those that trespass
   against us
And lead us not into temptation
But deliver us from evil.
For thine is the Kingdom and the Power
   and the Glory for ever and ever. Amen.

disciples said to him, 'Lord, teach us to pray as John taught his disciples.' He said to them, 'When you pray, say,
Father, hallowed be thy Name,
Thy Kingdom come,
Give us this day our daily bread,
And forgive us our trespasses
As we forgive those that trespass against us,
And lead us not into temptation'.

The difference in the setting of this material in the two Gospels makes it clear that a prayer taught by Jesus to the disciples in Luke has become a prayer for use by the Church in Matthew, and the words in italics are best understood as liturgical formulations designed to make the prayer appropriate for common worship.[1]

Thus the impact of recent criticism in all its forms is to cast doubt on the propriety of seeking to understand this section, Matt. v–vii, as an interrelated totality derived from the actual teaching of Jesus. And this impact must not be ignored. This is the error in two recent treatments of the *SM* which have sought to impose a unity of a 'literary' kind upon it. Morton Smith[2] has lamented the fact that most scholars have neglected to consider the sermons in the Gospels from the point of view of literary form. While he rightly rejects Schweitzer's[3] claim that Matt. x preserves for us the original words that Jesus preached, he also dismisses Bultmann's[4] view that the Gospels contain no passages of a unified structure. He asserts that 'even if the present sermons be not abbreviations of longer originals, it is yet possible to suppose that the editors of the Gospels, when writing the outline of an imaginary sermon, wrote it according to the customary form of the sermons known in their days'.[5] Whether the Synoptic sermons, which he finds in Matt. v–vii; Luke vi. 20–49; xii. 15–40; Matt. x. 5–42; Luke x. 2–16; Matt. xxiii. 2–39; xxiv. 4–25, 46; Mark xiii. 5–37; Luke xxi. 8–36, are not so much proper sermons as merely outlines of such or not, they each conform to what is almost a common pattern, which Morton Smith describes as follows: 'Most often (but not always...)

[1] On this process of applying to the Church what was first uttered to disciples, see J. Jeremias, *The Parables of Jesus* (New York, 1955). See Appendix VIII.
[2] *Op. cit.*
[3] *The Quest of the Historical Jesus*, Eng. trans. (1910), pp. 357 f.
[4] *Op. cit.* p. 87.　　　　　　[5] *Op. cit.* p. 88.

there is a short introduction. . . which generally contains either the thesis or the underlying principles of what is to be said in the body. The body itself is generally composed of a list or a story. Only in exceptional cases does it contain any important development of thought, but the completely simple form may be varied in any of several ways. . . and may be elaborated, of course, by such customary forms of rhetoric as antithesis, comparison, metaphor, and direct address to the listeners. . . . Conclusions sometimes state the consequences of what was said in the body, sometimes are exhortations to the listeners to act according to the rules laid down in the body, but almost always contain warnings, and especially warnings about punishment in store for the wicked, or promises of the pay destined for the Saints, on the day of judgment.'[1]

This pattern which Morton Smith discovers in the Synoptic sermons he also traces in the Tannaitic sources, except that there the sermons undergo such modifications as the differences between the nature of the Tannaitic and Synoptic sources demand. For example, they do not usually contain introductions and conclusions.[2] For our purpose we need merely indicate that pattern that Morton Smith finds in the *SM*. It is as follows:

I. Introduction to the Sermon: v. 1–2.

II. The Introduction of the Sermon: a challenge to the listener: v. 3–16.

III. The Body of the Sermon: concerning the Law.

   (*a*) v. 17–20: The Law is important.

   (*b*) v. 21–vii. 12: Principles of the Law, taught, as usual in Tannaitic literature, by reference to particular commandments.

      (1) v. 21–48: The purpose, rather than the letter, of the Law is to be obeyed.

      (2) vi. 1–18: Obedience must be motivated by proper intention.

      (3) vi. 19–33: Intention must be based on trust.

      (4) vii. 1–5: Against fault-finding (and, thence, on humility).

      (5) vii. 6: Against those who profane holy things.

      (6) vii. 7–9: Trust implies prayer.

      (7) vii. 12: Summary: definition of the Law of which the principles have thus been outlined.

IV. The Conclusion of the Sermon: salvation is given not for the acceptance of the Law, but for its practice: vii. 13–28.

V. Conclusion after the Sermon: vii. 28.

---

[1] *Op. cit.* p. 101.

[2] As we have implied above, Morton Smith is careful to note that because of the similarity of form between the Tannaitic and Synoptic sermons, as he understands these, we are not to conclude that any one of these sermons is in fact an outline of one actually preached: they may be the compositions of editors who followed in their sermons the prevailing rules for their construction.

Clearly Morton Smith finds a sequence of thought throughout the Sermon. But in two places, at vii. 6 and vii. 15, he himself has to note[1] that he is unable to find any connexion with the context, because these verses break the sequence of thought. He concludes that they were added after the Sermon as such was complete. He does not discuss when or by whom these additions were made. We may further question Morton Smith's assumption that v. 17–vii. 12 is all concerned with one theme, the Law. Thus it is difficult to believe that the connexion of the parts in vi. 19–24 a can all be subsumed under the one heading: 'Intention must be based on trust.' It seems far more natural to regard vi. 1 ff. as concerned not primarily with 'intention' as such, so much as with the nature of true worship. Indeed v. 48 seems to be not merely a summary of what precedes in v. 17 ff., but also its closure. In vi. 1 a new section on worship opens, so that vi. 1 ff. should not be treated as a continuation of the theme of v. 21–47, as is done by Morton Smith. It must be insisted that his assumption that there is one sequence of thought running through the *SM* is precarious. Other divisions of it than his are possible. In all such divisions there is inevitably a subjective element, and enough has been indicated to suggest that the divisions that Morton Smith proposes are largely his own imposed upon Matthew's work and not legitimately derived from it. The disjunctions in it, arising from the use of multiple sources and from the exigencies of the liturgical and lectionary needs of the Church, must not be ignored. Moreover, the words which introduce the Sermon in v. 1 probably preclude any strictly 'sermonic' approach to it—they read:

Ἰδὼν δὲ τοὺς ὄχλους ἀνέβη εἰς τὸ ὄρος· Καὶ καθίσαντος αὐτοῦ προσῆλθον αὐτῷ οἱ μαθηταὶ αὐτοῦ· Καὶ ἀνοίξας τὸ στόμα αὐτοῦ ἐδίδασκεν αὐτοὺς λέγων....

While didache and kerygma are not clearly differentiated in the life of the modern churches, and are not to be too sharply separated even in the primitive Church,[2] nevertheless ἐδίδασκεν in v. 1 must be given its full

---

[1] *Op. cit.* p. 111, n. 30; p. 112, n. 32.

[2] On the relation between kerygma and didache, see C. H. Dodd, *The Apostolic Preaching and its Developments* (1949), p. 7. For a criticism of this, see T. J. Vincent, 'Didactic Kerygma in the Synoptic Gospels', *S.J.T.* x (1957), 262–73; K. Stendahl, 'Kerygma und Kerygmatisch', in *T.L.* (December 1952), pp. 715 ff.; G. Friedrich, *T.W.Z.N.T.* III, 713. It may be noteworthy that following ἐδίδασκεν in v. 1 f. Matthew uses the form λέγων (so Luke vi. 20). Had he been thinking in terms of a sermonic or prophetic announcement, he would probably have used λαλεῖν which occurs elsewhere in Matthew 26 times (Luke has it 31 times and Mark 21). λαλεῖν is used regularly in the LXX in connexion with prophetic proclamations and in the Fourth Gospel there are 60 instances referring to the discourses and revelatory words of Jesus (e.g. viii. 26, 28, 38; xii. 49; xiii. 34; xiv. 10). See F. Gils, *Jésus Prophète* (1957), pp. 29f.

force and differentiated from ἐκήρυξεν. The ease with which Matthew changes the audience addressed, from the disciples in v. 1 to the crowds in vii. 28, bespeaks not a 'sermonic' understanding of the section but a general, didactic one, as does also the phrase 'when he had sat down' (καθίσαντος αὐτοῦ), which suggests a teaching rather than a proclamation. That sitting is the posture for teaching and learning appears clearly from such passages as M. Aboth i. 4 ('Let thy house be a meeting-house for the Sages and *sit amid the dust of their feet*...') and iii. 2 ('But if two *sit* together and words of the Law (are spoken) between them, the Divine Presence rests between them...') and iii. 6 ('If ten men *sit* together and occupy themselves in the Law...'). The pertinent part of Matt. v. 1 f. translated into Hebrew would read:

וַיַּעַל הָהָרָה וַיֵּשֶׁב שָׁם וַיִּגְּשׁוּ אֵלָיו תַּלְמִידָיו וַיִּפְתַּח אֶת־פִּיו וַיּוֹרֵם וַיֹּאמַר . . .

The two words underlined both point to a didactic function. יָשַׁב is the verb whence comes the later substantive, not found in the Old Testament, יְשִׁיבָה=scholar's session, council, academy, school. The parallel Lucan passage in vi. 17–20 is instructive. It has no reference either to sitting or teaching. Luke contemplates a kind of open air sermon or address. Billerbeck comments on Matt. v. 2 that not only synagogues and schools but also streets and free open places offered opportunities for teaching. He refers to Luke v. 1 in further illustration of this, where again before actually teaching 'Jesus sat down and taught the people from the boat'. The same reference to sitting to teach from a boat occurs in Mark iv. 1. These references to sitting are not accidental but probably preserve a memory of the way in which Jesus actually taught. On the other hand, the absence of a reference to sitting in Luke vi. 17–20 and the statements that 'he stood on a level place' (ἔστη ἐπὶ τόπου πεδινοῦ) (vi. 17) and that 'he lifted up his eyes on his disciples and said'...(καὶ αὐτὸς ἐπάρας τοὺς ὀφθαλμοὺς αὐτοῦ εἰς τοὺς μαθητάς) are not accidental. The Lucan account in vi. 17 ff. is probably closer to Q than the Matthaean, which is much more edited. Matthew has transformed what we may loosely call a 'sermonic scene' to a didactic one, in which Jesus suggests a rabbi giving his Torah to his *talmidim*.

Finally, Morton Smith himself recognizes that even in most of the Tannaitic sermons that he cites there is no sustained sequence of thought,[1] and the propriety of applying the term 'sermon' to the Tannaitic material he

[1] *Op. cit.* pp. 78–110.

adduces is itself open to question.[1] Seldom do the sources derived from a predominantly Jewish milieu in our period provide such a sequence as Morton Smith suggests, and it is certain that he has carried the unity of the *SM* too far in finding in it a more or less logical, sermonic sequence of thought.

Another scholar, Austin Farrer, has revolted against the difficulties created by problems of source in a highly personal way.[2] He understands the *SM* as a section where Matthew was composing freely, and where, as he puts it, neither Q or M nor 'any other shadowy anonymity' stood behind his shoulder. This position raises two questions. First, whether the generally held view that Matthew is dependent on the sources Q and M, as well as Mark, is still tenable; and secondly, whether, granted that this is not the case, the schematization which Farrer discovers in the *SM* is to be accepted as a legitimate interpretation of the material it contains. To embark on a defence of the view that Matthew used Q and M would take us too far afield. We must here at this point waive this question and examine Farrer's understanding of the structure of the Sermon on his own terms.

His position is as follows. The Sermon in Matt. v–vii is modelled on Exod. xx–xxiv, where the Decalogue of chapter xx finds an exposition in the Covenant Laws given in the rest of the section, Exod. xx. 22–xxiii. 19. The Beatitudes occupy a place in the Sermon corresponding to that of the Decalogue in Exod. xx–xxiv, the rest of the Sermon being an orderly exposition or application of the Beatitudes. Insisting that the Western and Syriac[3] texts supply us with the original Matthaean order for these last, Farrer takes that order to be as follows:

> Blessed (are) the poor in spirit, for theirs is the kingdom of heaven.
> Blessed (are) the meek, for they shall inherit the earth.
> Blessed (are) the mourners, for they shall be comforted....

The order usually, and rightly, followed is that found in the best manuscripts where the blessing on the mourners precedes that on the meek, but the above cited Western and Syriac order enables Farrer to claim that the *SM* can be divided into three couplets, 'the first simple, the second and

---

[1] See a review of Morton Smith in *J.B.L.* LXXII (1953), 64–6 by S. S. Cohon.

[2] *St Matthew and St Mark* (1954).

[3] The evidence, as given by Legg, *Evangelium secundum Matthaeum* (Oxford, 1940), is in favour of the traditional order. So Uncs. pler. Minus pler b f q r² vg Sy^s pesh hl hier Cop^{sa bo} Aeth Arm Geo Tert pat^{11}. In favour of putting 'Blessed are the meek...' before 'Blessed are those that mourn', he cites D 33 a c d ff¹ g¹² h k l m aur Syr^c Aph^{41} Eph^{62}. The weight of the evidence is clearly against Farrer, but we have above sought to argue on his own premisses.

third each having an additional line attached to them'.[1] The structure of the Beatitudes and of the whole Sermon is then interpreted as follows:

First couplet   The Beatitudes

(1) Blessed (are) the poor in Spirit, for theirs is the kingdom of heaven.

(2) Blessed (are) the meek, for they shall inherit the earth.

Second couplet

(1) Blessed (are) the mourners, for they shall be comforted.

(2) Blessed (are) they which do hunger and thirst after righteousness, for they shall be filled.

Additional line: Blessed (are) the merciful, for they shall obtain mercy.

Third couplet

(1) Blessed (are) the pure in heart, for they shall see God.

(2) Blessed (are) the peacemakers, for they shall be called the children of God.

Additional line: Blessed are they which are persecuted for righteousness' sake, for theirs is the kingdom of heaven.

Concluding line harking back to the form of the first: Blessed are ye when (men) shall revile you, and persecute you, and shall say all manner of evil against you falsely for my sake.

The above pattern of three couplets in the Beatitudes governs the structure of the rest of the Sermon. This is threefold:

(1) v. 17–48: Christ's interpretation of the commandments.

(2) vi. 1–18: Christ's interpretation of the three meritorious works.

(3) vi. 19–vii. 27: which culminates in the parable of the two houses built on the rock and the sand.

These three divisions are 'commentaries' on the three couplets of the Beatitudes, but, by a kind of chiasmus, the commentaries deal with the couplets in their reverse order, that is, v. 17–48 is a comment on the third couplet; vi. 1–18 on the second, and vi. 19–vii. 27 on the first. The comment on the Beatitudes begins immediately with v. 11.

We need not pursue Farrer's details further: they will be clarified as we point out difficulties in them, even if we dismiss source-criticism as he does. First, the antithesis to v. 11 is to be found not in v. 13 ff. but in v. 12. It is doubtful if v. 13 ff. are intended to look back to the phrase 'for righteousness' sake'. Were v. 12 missing we might then concede that this phrase might be taken to govern the whole complex down to v. 20, and even to v. 48, but its inclusion makes it more natural to take v. 13 as beginning a new theme, and v. 12 as the suitable climax to v. 1–11. Secondly, to claim that v. 21–4 is a comment on v. 8 (Blessed are the pure

[1] *Op. cit.* p. 165.

in heart), and v. 23–48 a comment on v. 9 (Blessed are the peacemakers. . .) means that the chiasmus, which Farrer is tracing, here breaks down, because on his principles we should expect v. 23–48 to precede v. 21–4. Thirdly, Farrer finds the comment on v. 7, which does not form part of one of the couplets, in vi. 2, ὅταν οὖν ποιῇς ἐλεημοσύνην, which recalls the ἐλεήμονες of v. 7, and the comment on v. 4, 6 in vi. 16–18. But, apart from the dubiety of taking those that 'do hunger and thirst after righteousness' to refer to those who fast, there is the added and more serious difficulty that vi. 5–14, the section dealing with prayer, finds no point of contact with the Beatitudes. It is true, as Farrer points out,[1] that v. 14 deals with mercy, and thus may be taken to recall v. 7, but this merely helps to undermine his contention that the Beatitudes are being commented on systematically by chiasmus, because his schema is thereby disrupted. Apart from this, however, this contention is very seriously shaken by the intrusion of the theme of prayer, which we have already noted. It is best to take alms-giving, prayer and fasting as a threefold illustration of the righteousness (δικαιοσύνη) mentioned in vi. 1. They constitute a triad frequently met with in Jewish sources, although not always in this order. Farrer demands that vi. 19–21 should form the comment on the first couplet of the *SM*, v. 3, 5. Not only does this imply the destruction of the unity of the section vi. 1–18, where ὅταν οὖν and ὅταν in vi. 2, 5, 16 seem obviously to constitute a triadic unity which, on Farrer's theory, would refer to *one* couplet in the Beatitudes, but it is doubtful whether we should connect μὴ θησαυρίζετε ὑμῖν θησαυροὺς ἐπὶ τῆς γῆς κ.τ.λ. as directly, as Farrer insists, with v. 5. If, as he holds, the earth which the meek are to inherit is a 'regenerated earth', then clearly the earth in vi. 19 has a different con-notation and should not be referred to v. 5. Further, in seeking to connect vi. 19–34 with v. 5 Farrer ignores the insertion of vi. 22–3 and vi. 24.

Fourthly, Farrer finds no difficulty in describing the whole of vii. 7–27, which has usually baffled attempts at any illuminating classification, as a natural peroration, but to account for vii. 1–7 he introduces a further complication into the schematization of the Sermon. It is determined by the influence of the Lord's Prayer, which has slipped in unobtrusively as an appendix to the section on prayer in vi. 7–15. This prayer, indeed, which, Farrer claims, had already been fixed in liturgical usage, determined also the arrangement of the Beatitudes. The promises made in these correspond to the petitions of the Lord's Prayer. The correspondence is not complete, but Farrer arrives at the curious position that a section

[1] *Op. cit.* p. 168.

which, as he has already admitted, has no direct point of contact with the Beatitudes determines their structures (what is clearly an addition to the prayer itself, vi. 14, 15, becomes the point at which the prayer is attached to the Beatitudes), and also that of what follows in vi. 19 ff. There are here wheels within wheels. Thus vi. 19–34 refers back both to the first couplet of the Beatitudes[1] and to the first clause of the prayer. But there is no near-chiasmus in the treatment of the material in vi. 19 ff. in its relation to the Lord's Prayer, as there is in its relation to the Beatitudes.

There are still further difficulties. Thus when Farrer asserts that vii. 1–5 is a variant form of the same idea that is found in vi. 14–15, he does not notice that vi. 14–15 is not strictly, on his theory, a part of the Lord's Prayer at all but merely a kind of connecting link with the Beatitudes. Farrer argues that the phrase in vi. 12 finds an appropriate comment in vii. 1–12. But here it is difficult to understand what the point is of his reference to vii. 6. He writes 'Pray (with reference to vii. 7 ff., which is one of the conditions which the use of the Lord's Prayer imposes upon us)—it is a divine principle that we ourselves should follow, not to throw holy things away to dogs...'. The connexion here is not clear. When this is still further complicated by the claim that Matthew here intends to draw upon Mark vi. 30–viii. 38 in dealing with God's providential care, and that this explains the allusion to dogs in vii. 6 and indeed the remainder of chapter vii, it will be readily admitted with Farrer that 'it is difficult in this type of investigation to know where to stop'.[2] Farrer confuses the way in which other portions of the New Testament naturally illumine the *SM* (and from this point of view his interpretation of the Sermon contains much that is illuminating) with the manner in which Matthew has worked on his materials. Parallelisms of thought between the Sermon and the rest of the New Testament do not necessarily imply conscious and highly intricate literary manipulation of the tradition under the direct influence of those materials where the parallelisms occur.

Finally, apart from the above specific difficulties, we can only state that our view of literary probability differs from that of Farrer as this is revealed in his treatment of Matt. v–vii. Those documents which, from the literary point of view, are most like it, collections such as the Didache, The Manual of Discipline, The Zadokite Fragment, that is, compilations of moral and religious teaching, show no such intricacy of structure as Farrer discovers in the *SM*, and it is only by procrustean methods that such a structure can be discovered in it at all.

[1] *Op. cit.* p. 171.   [2] *Op. cit.* p. 20.

Nevertheless, although Morton Smith has carried the unity of the *SM* too far by demanding of it a logical, sermonic sequence which it is not its intention to provide, and although Farrer also goes too far in imposing a literary subtlety on the section which is alien to its purpose, both these scholars have helped us to recover an awareness that too much criticism has failed to reveal.[1] We refer to the awareness that we should think of Matthew, and of other composers of the Gospels, not as mere editors, manipulating sources with scissors and paste, so to speak, to produce a mosaic of snippets, but as themselves in a real sense 'authors'. Dependent on a tradition they were, but not passive transmitters of it. By what they preserved, by the way they changed and, above all, arranged, the tradition, they left their impress upon it. This is particularly true of Matthew. No unimaginative compiler or slavish editor, he was a formulator of the tradition, concerned to present it in a specific way to meet the needs of his Church as he understood them. And in the light of this we must insist that Matthew, the final author of the Gospel, did himself regard v–vii as a unit. The section closes with the words: 'And it came to pass when Jesus had ended these sayings the people were astonished at his doctrine, for he taught them as one having authority and not as the scribes.' Matt. v–vii is not a sermon, but the author of it has used his sources for his own ends, so that v–vii do constitute for him an essential unity. We shall now be concerned to discover how he understood the material so monumentally concentrated and 'unified' in these chapters.

[1] The tide in favour of such an approach to the Gospel writers has already turned: see, for example, G. Bornkamm on 'Enderwartung und Kirche im Matthäusevangelium' in *The Background of the New Testament and its Eschatology*, cited above, pp. 222 ff. His first paragraph deserves quotation. 'Es gehört zu den gesicherten Ergebnissen der Synoptiker-Forschung, daß die ersten drei Evangelisten in erster Linie Sammler und Redaktoren überkommener Traditionen sind. Die stereotypen, historisch-pragmatisch durchaus unergiebigen redaktionellen Wendungen, mit denen Mk. Logien und Einzelperikopen rahmt und verknüpft, und die entsprechenden redaktionellen Mittel, deren Matt. und Lk. sich bedienen, speziell auch in der Verarbeitung und Gruppierung ihren Quellen, lassen an der Richtigkeit dieses Urteil keinen Zweifel. Gleichwohl sind auch die ersten drei Evangelien Dokumente einer bestimmten, in jedem Fall sehr verschiedenen Theologie, die jedem von ihnen, unbeschadet des ihnen Gemeinsamen, eine eigene mehr oder weniger Konsequent und planmäßig durchgeführte Thematik gibt...die Synoptiker...keineswegs nur Tradenten und Sammler, sondern auch Interpreten der Überlieferung sind.' H. Conzelmann has approached Luke in the same way in *Die Mitte der Zeit* (1954), which gives an excellent statement of the new emphasis to which we refer, and Willi Marxsen has so interpreted Mark in *Der Evangelist Markus* (1956). See also H. Riesenfeld, *The Gospel Tradition and its Beginnings: a study in the limits of Formgeschichte* (1957), p. 6. On Luke, see also C. K. Barrett, *Luke the Historian in Recent Study* (1961), pp. 24 f. *et passim.*

II. THE SETTING IN MATTHEW

1. PENTATEUCHAL MOTIFS

Certain documents are so loosely constructed that it is possible to treat their separate parts in isolation from the whole. Various sections in the early chapters of Mark, for example, have sometimes been so treated.[1] But there are other documents which are so closely knit that their parts can only be adequately understood in the light of the whole. Such is the Fourth Gospel,[2] and such also is Matthew. It reveals not only a meticulous concern, numerically and otherwise, in the arrangements of its details, but also an architectonic grandeur in its totality. Its different parts are inseparable, like those of a well-planned and well-built house.[3] Any attempt to understand the *SM* in stark separation from the rest of the Gospel (and many treatments of it have been such) must therefore be deemed inadequate: it must be approached in the light of its setting in Matthew.

First, then, how does the *SM* fit into the structure of the Gospel as a whole? The significance of this last for its understanding has been most emphasized by Bacon.[4] Following a tradition which he traced back possibly to the second century,[5] he pointed out that apart from the Prologue (Matt. i, ii), and the Epilogue (Matt. xxvi–xxviii), the remainder of the material in the Gospel falls into five 'books', each of which is terminated by a formula, which occurs in almost identical forms at vii. 28;

---

[1] Moffatt Commentaries, for example, B. H. Branscomb on St Mark.

[2] C. H. Dodd, *The Interpretation of the Fourth Gospel* (Cambridge, 1953), p. 3, 'with such a work as the Fourth Gospel.... At every step the exegete is faced with the necessity of considering his text in the light of the ultimate meaning of the work.'

[3] See, for example, W. C. Allen, *St Matthew*, I.C.C. (Edinburgh, 1907), p. lxiv.

[4] *Studies in Matthew* (New York, 1930).

[5] *Op. cit.* p. xv. See J. R. Harris, *Testimonies*, part II (1920), p. 110. A Greek fragment dated by Harris in early second century and by Bacon in the age of the Apologists refers to Matthew thus:

> 'Matthew curbs the audacity of the Jews
> Checking them in five books as it were with bridles....'

The reference Bacon thinks is to our Matthew: Harris finds here a reference to a book of testimonies in five books. See B. W. Bacon, *The Expositor*, vol. xv, 8th series (1918), pp. 56 ff. on 'The "Five Books" of Matthew against the Jews'. Bacon refers to non-Jewish works in five parts also—Irenaeus, *Against Heresies*, see p. 62.

xi. 1; xiii. 53; xix. 1; xxvi. 1. The Gospel thus presents the following structure:

Preamble or Prologue: i–ii: The birth narrative.

Book I: (*a*) iii. 1–iv. 25: Narrative material.
(*b*) v. 1–vii. 27: The Sermon on the Mount.
 Formula: vii. 28–9: '*And when Jesus finished these sayings*, the crowds were astonished at his teaching, for he taught them as one who had authority, and not as their scribes.'

Book II: (*a*) viii. 1–ix. 35: Narrative material.
(*b*) ix. 36–x. 42: Discourse on mission and martyrdom.
 Formula: xi. 1: '*And when Jesus had finished instructing his twelve disciples* . . . .'

Book III: (*a*) xi. 2–xii. 50: Narrative and debate material.
(*b*) xiii. 1–52: Teaching on the Kingdom of Heaven.
 Formula: xiii. 53: '*And when Jesus had finished these parables* . . . .'

Book IV: (*a*) xiii. 54–xvii. 21: Narrative and debate material.
(*b*) xvii. 22–xviii. 35: Discourse on church administration.
 Formula: xix. 1: '*Now when Jesus had finished these sayings* . . . .'

Book V: (*a*) xix. 2–xxii. 46: Narrative and debate material.
(*b*) xxiii. 1–xxv. 46: Discourse on eschatology: farewell address.
 Formula: xxvi. 1: ' *When Jesus finished all these sayings*, he said to his disciples . . . .'

Epilogue: xxvi. 3–xxviii. 20: From the Last Supper to the Resurrection.

With the above five blocks of material Bacon compared the Pentateuch. 'The Torah', he wrote, 'consists of five books of commandments of Moses, each body of law introduced by a narrative of considerable length, largely concerned with the "signs and wonders" by which Jehovah "with an outstretched hand and a mighty arm" redeemed his people from Egyptian bondage. Matthew is a "converted rabbi," a Christian legalist. Each of the "five books" of his "syntax of the logia" of Jesus begins with an introductory narrative and closes with a stereotyped formula linking its discourse to the next succeeding narrative section.'[1] Hawkins[2] had long since drawn attention to the fivefold arrangement of the sayings of Jesus. He referred to them as five *peraqim* or *chapters* of sayings, and compared them, not exclusively to the Pentateuch, but also to the five books of Psalms (i–xli; xlii–lxxii; lxxiii–lxxxix; xc–cvi; cvii–cl). Moreover,

---

[1] *Op. cit.* p. 81.
[2] *Horae Synopticae* (Oxford, 1899), pp. 132 f.

each of these 'books' ends with a formula of praise: which, though not identical in each case, is comparable. Thus:

xli. 13: Blessed be the Lord, the God of Israel, from everlasting to everlasting! Amen and Amen.

lxxii. 18–19: Blessed be the Lord, the God of Israel, who alone does wondrous things.

Blessed be his glorious name for ever; may his glory fill the whole earth! Amen and Amen!

lxxxix. 52: Blessed be the Lord for ever! Amen and Amen.

cvi. 48. Blessed be the Lord, the God of Israel, from everlasting to everlasting.

And let all the people say, 'Amen!' Praise the Lord.

cl: A psalm of praise closes the whole collection.

Comparable also are the five Megilloth,[1] the five divisions in Ecclesiasticus, the five divisions in Proverbs (i–ix; x–xxiv; xxv–xxix; xxx; xxxi: here there is no concluding formula repeated); Enoch (i–xxxvi; xxxvii–lxxi; lxxii–lxxxii; lxxxiii–xc; xci–cviii). (See R. H. Charles, *Apocrypha and Pseudepigrapha*, II, 168); and Pirqê Aboth (it is generally recognized that the sixth chapter, included in all modern editions of the Mishnah, was not originally part of it).[2] Hawkins does not explicitly state that the structure of Matthew should not of necessity be taken to point to the Pentateuch, but this seems to be implied in his presentation of the Gospel's fivefold division. Nevertheless, an emphasis similar to that of Bacon appears in Lagrange[3] and Schlatter[4] and in most British and American work on Matthew, as in Green,[5] Kilpatrick[6] and Stendahl.[7] The French scholar Godet,[8] who emphasized the pentateuchal element in Matthew, has been followed by his countrymen Benoit[9] and Feuillet.[10]

[1] The five books: Esther, Ruth, Song of Songs, Lamentations, Ecclesiastes.

[2] H. Danby, *The Mishnah* (1933), p. 446, n. 1. Professor Muilenburg pointed out to me the reference to 5 books by Jason of Cyrene, in 2 Macc. ii. 23.

[3] *Évangile selon St Matthieu* (Paris), p. lxxxv...: 'Comme le premier (discours) rappelle la promulgation de l'ancienne loi sur une montagne, on peut penser que les cinq discours rappellent les cinq livres du Pentateuque.'

[4] *Der Evangelist Matthäus* (Stuttgart, 1948), pp. 125 ff.

[5] *Saint Matthew*, The Clarendon Bible (Oxford, 1936).

[6] *The Origins of the Gospel According to Saint Matthew* (Oxford, 1946), pp. 135 ff.

[7] *The School of Matthew* (Uppsala, 1954), pp. 24 f., compare *P.C.* (1962), p. 770.

[8] *Introduction to the New Testament*, II, Eng. trans. (1899), p. 182. But Godet treated the fivefold division as a survival from an earlier composition—the Proto-Matthew supposed to have been attested by Papias.

[9] *L'Évangile selon St Matthieu* (Paris, 1950), pp. 7–12.

[10] *Biblica*, vol. XXXIX, fasc. 3 (1958), p. 292.

On the other hand, many scholars have been content either to ignore this fivefold arrangement on which Bacon so powerfully insisted or to ascribe to it no emphatic significance. Such is the case in the commentaries of Loisy (1907–8), B. Weiss (1910), Wellhausen (1914²), A. H. McNeile (1927²), M.-J. Lagrange (1941⁵), Montefiore (1927²), T. H. Robinson (1928), T. W. Manson (*The Sayings of Jesus*, 1937, 1949). The most recent German Protestant commentators Schniewind (*Das Neue Testament Deutsch*, Göttingen, 1950, p. 8) and Lohmeyer (*Meyer Kommentar*, Göttingen, 1956) do not accept the emphasis urged by Bacon; and the same is true of the Roman Catholic J. Schmid in the *Regensburger Neues Testament*, 1956. These scholars have all proposed their own analyses of the Gospel. For illustration, we note a recent treatment by Stonehouse. He is fully aware of the conspicuousness of the formulae with which Matthew concludes his five discourses, but these expressions, he holds, do not mark any definite stages in the ministry of Jesus. As in Mark, so in Matthew, it is the events at Caesarea Philippi that constitute the pivotal point of the history. 'Consequently, while the particular setting of each of these great discourses requires to be noted within the larger structure of the Gospel, these five expressions do not involve any significant modification of the divisions indicated by Matt. iv. 17 and xvi. 21.'[1] It is these last two references that denote the distinct turning points in the ministry. Stonehouse divides Matthew accordingly, and dismisses Bacon's view of the significance of the five discourses for Matthew's conception of his Gospel as an exaggeration. Similarly Behm[2] makes no use of the fivefold formulae in his analysis of the Gospel, and Michaelis ignores Bacon's work entirely.[3]

In view of all this dissent from, or refusal to deal seriously with, Bacon's position, it must be critically examined despite its immediate persuasiveness. Obvious objections to it present themselves.

First, is it legitimate to assume that the words occurring at the close of the five discourses constitute anything more than mere connecting formulae which, in the mind of the evangelist, were quite insignificant? Can they bear the structural strain imposed upon them by Bacon and others? Their exact nature has been disputed. Hawkins[4] compared them to the colophon, which closes the second book of Psalms, which reads: 'The

[1] *The Witness of Matthew and Mark to Christ* (Philadelphia, 1944), pp. 130 f.
[2] Feine–Behm, *Einleitung in das N.T.* (Heidelberg, 1950), pp. 46 ff.
[3] *Einleitung in das N.T.* (Bern, 1946).
[4] *Op. cit.* p. 132. More appropriate in comparison would have been a reference to the closing formulae we referred to above at the close of each book of the Psalms.

prayers of David the Son of Jesse are ended' (Ps. lxxii. 20). To this Streeter objected on two grounds, one of which was that 'the formula has really no resemblance to a colophon; its emphasis is not on "Here endeth" but on "Here beginneth"; it is a formula of transition from discourse to narrative'.[1] With this many have agreed, and have consequently, as we saw, ignored the formulae in their interpretation of the Gospel.[2] Bultmann includes them in his list of concluding formulae (*Abschlußbildungen*) employed by Matthew.[3] He treats them as intended merely to signify the transition from Q material to Marcan: they are no more than a kind of connecting 'particle', such as 'and' (καί, δέ), 'behold' (ἰδού), and the like, except that they are more elaborate.[4] Clearly such mere literary links cannot have been very significant. Should the formulae be such, Bacon's architectonic, pentateuchal analysis of Matthew would seem to appear incongruous, if not bizarre.

Secondly, it has been urged that the fivefold division of this material by Matthew is derived by him from the sources upon which he drew. Such a division, as we saw, was common in Jewish tradition, perhaps because of the influence of the 'five' books of Moses. It may, therefore, be that the division in Matthew, certainly if it was derivative, and possibly even if it was not, had no profound significance for the Evangelist. It was perhaps a literary convention and traditional convenience which had no theological intention. That the division was a derivative was the view of Godet,[5] who envisaged a proto-Matthew so divided. Hawkins[6] favoured this on three grounds, namely, that Luke vii. 1, at the close of the Sermon on the Plain, is so closely parallel to Matt. ̣vii. 28 in substance, if not in words, that a common origin is suggested for them both; that there is nothing distinctively Matthaean in the wording of the closing formulae concerned; and that Matt. vii. 28; xiii. 53; xix. 1 and, especially, xxvi. 1, convey the impression, as Hawkins expresses the matter, 'that the author regarded the preceding sayings as having been delivered at the time', which implies that the collection of the sayings had taken place 'before the blocks of sayings came into the hands of the writer of this formula and that he was, therefore, unaware of their having been so composed'. Nestle urged that the fact that Papias chose to arrange his *Expositions of*

---

[1] *The Four Gospels* (London, 1926), p. 262.
[2] McNeile, *op. cit.* p. 99; Klostermann, *Das Matthäus-evangelium* (1927), pp. 9 f., 'eine typische Schlußformel ohne chronologischen Wert'.
[3] *Die Geschichte der synoptischen Tradition* (Göttingen, 1931), p. 376.
[4] *Op. cit.* p. 359.   [5] *Op. cit.* p. 182.
[6] *Op. cit.* p. 132.

the Dominical Oracles[1] in five books points to a fivefold division of the *logia* used by Matthew, which, presumably, Papias imitated. While all this cannot be taken to prove that the fivefold division of Matthew is to be regarded merely as an unimportant derivative, it can at least be taken to suggest that the division, if it be a derivative, cannot be of dominant significance in deciphering the intention of the Evangelist.

Thirdly, the parallelism which Bacon draws between the structure of each 'book' in Matthew, as made up of a narrative section followed by a 'legal' one on the analogy of the books which constitute the Pentateuch, is precarious. It is not the case that each of the books of the Pentateuch consists of 'commandments of Moses, each body of law [being] introduced by a narrative of considerable length', and that this is an arrangement strictly paralleled in the five books of Matthew. Genesis presents no such division of narrative and legal material, so that the proposed parallelism breaks down in the first item. Moreover, while Genesis is almost entirely narrative, Leviticus is mostly legal. No neat division between narrative and legal material can be made in Numbers. Only in Exodus and Deuteronomy is this at all convincingly possible.[2] To approach the alleged parallelism from the Matthaean side, we note that it is illegitimate to envisage all the discourse material in the five Matthaean blocks as 'legal', even in remotest intention, as compared with the legal sections of the Pentateuch. Although it may be permissible to regard Bacon's first book, that is, v–vii, the *SM*, and his fourth book, that is, xvii. 22–xviii. 35, the section on church administration, as a statement of the moral and regulatory demands of the Gospel, much as the legal portions of the Pentateuch express the demands of the Old Covenant, nevertheless, Book III, xiii. 1–53 (Parables) and Book V, xxiii–xxv (Judgement), cannot be so interpreted. Furthermore, it is erroneous to confine 'legal' discussions in Matthew to the second half of the various 'books', for example, the discussion of things clean and unclean, a 'halakic' discussion, occurs in xv. 1–20, outside what Bacon would set in parallelism to the legal portions of the Pentateuch. To claim that this is explained by Matthew's adherence to the Marcan order is to miss the point. Indeed, it is to admit that it is not his pentateuchal intent, but his loyalty to his Marcan source, that governs Matthew's arrangement.[3] Matthew's adherence to Mark after

---

[1] *Z.N.W.* (1900), pp. 252 ff. For Papias, see Eusebius, *Hist. Eccl.*, cxi, 39.

[2] A glance at the contents of the pentateuchal books is necessary here.

[3] Bacon, *op. cit.* pp. 218 ff. Perhaps we should have emphasized this point even more in criticism. From xiii. 53 onwards Marcan items determine the Matthaean order: this, as stated in the text, is very surprising if we take Bacon's theory seriously.

xiii. 53 seems to demand that, not a pentateuchal schema, but the Marcan source, henceforth at least, governs Matthew's arrangement of his material. In sum, on examination, any rigid parallelism between the structure of Matthew and that of the Pentateuch breaks down. Had Matthew a strictly detailed, schematic parallelism with the five books of Moses in mind, it would surely have been far more obviously noticeable.

In the light of the above criticisms, can we endorse, on structural grounds, the interpretation of Matthew propounded by Bacon and others? Let us examine each criticism in turn.

First, it is not correct to hold that the concluding formula 'And it came to pass', etc. at vii. 28; xi. 1; xiii. 53; xix. 1; xxvi. 1 merely marks the transition to Marcan material. This is not so in xi. 1 where the formula occurs in the midst of Q material. In any case, to judge from Matthew's customary method of conflating his sources, over against Luke, who preserves them more intact, it is unlikely that at five specific points only, Matthew should have been so concerned to keep his sources distinct as to use so conspicuous a formula merely for this purpose. Again Streeter is justified in objecting to treating the formula as a colophon, as does Hawkins, and that not only because the formula does not obviously serve as a formal closure to the various discourses at xi. 1; xiii. 53; xix. 1; xxvi. 1 (it is surely a colophon at vii. 28), but also because, were the mere provision of such Matthew's intention, he would probably have used more fitting formulae, especially if he had the Pentateuch in mind, similar to those, for example, at the end of Leviticus (xxvii. 34, 'These are the commandments which the Lord commanded Moses for the people of Israel on Mount Sinai') and Numbers (xxxvi. 13, 'These are the commandments and the ordinances which the Lord commanded by Moses to the people of Israel in the plains of Moab by the Jordan at Jericho'). It is further possible to feel the force of Streeter's additional claim that the use of a formula as a colophon at the close of such short discourses as are found in Matt. x, xiii, xviii would be a trifle ridiculous. But this last thrust of Streeter's, against Hawkins, is double-edged. May we not also infer that the regular introduction of such a marked formula at the close of such short discourses must be of peculiar import? And, at the same time, we may add that the *omission* of a closing formula at the end of chapter xxiii, where we should expect it, were it merely a closing formula, again suggests a deliberate intention, perhaps, only to use the formulae five times. Apart from its length, the persistence of the formula and the unmistakable deliberateness of its fivefold use makes it difficult to accept the view of

Bultmann, Klostermann and others, that it is simply a connecting link like 'and' (καί), 'behold' (ἰδού), etc. Nor can we dismiss its significance as merely liturgical. Indeed, it is doubtful if Kilpatrick is right in regarding it as a liturgical formula at all. Neither at the close of discourses nor at the beginning of a new narrative does it seem to be liturgically appropriate. Neither as 'Here beginneth' nor, except in vii. 28, as 'Here endeth' is it fitting. The history of lectionary practice in the time when Matthew composed his Gospel is unknown to us. In the view of those most competent to judge, lectionaries as such did not emerge till much later. Although they may have been produced earlier, their main development was connected with the growth of the monastery[1] in the fourth century, in response to 'the need for orderly and uniform worship'.[2] Thus, despite Carrington's attempt to prove that Mark and Matthew were intended specifically as lectionaries, this remains exceedingly unlikely. And, although Kilpatrick's more modest claims for a 'liturgical' factor in the formation of the Matthaean material are plausible, nevertheless, it is only with great caution that we can certainly isolate liturgical formulae.[3]

From all this it follows that the significance of the formula lies neither in the marking of a transition from one source to another nor, most probably, in the demands of liturgy, but elsewhere. Possibly, those—Bacon and others—are right who have found its significance in the intention of Matthew to present a new Pentateuch.[4]

Secondly, let us examine the next criticism mentioned, namely, that the fivefold division of Matthew is merely an insignificant derivative from sources used in the compilation of the Gospel. Bacon[5] and Bussmann[6]

---

[1] Kirsopp and Silva Lake, 'The Text of Mark in Some Dated Gospel Lectionaries', in *Amicitiae Corolla*, ed. H. G. Wood (London, 1923), pp. 148–9.

[2] H. M. Buck, Jr., *The Johannine Lessons in the Greek Gospel Lectionary* (Chicago, 1958), p. 1.

[3] P. Carrington, *The Primitive Christian Calendar* (Cambridge, 1952); G. D. Kilpatrick, *The Origins of the Gospel According to St Matthew* (Oxford, 1946). See W. D. Davies, 'Reflections on Archbishop Carrington's "Primitive Christian Calendar"', in *Studies in Honour of C. H. Dodd* (Cambridge, 1955).

[4] It should be noted that the acceptance of the formula as a lectionary one is not decisive against Bacon's position. Thus Streeter accepts Bacon's pentateuchal view of Matthew, although he rejects Hawkins's view of the formula, and regards the formula as a mark of transition (and possibly therefore as liturgical, though he does not state this).

[5] *Op. cit.*; his sources are discussed by G. D. Kilpatrick, *op. cit.* pp. 8 ff.

[6] W. Bussmann, *Synoptische Studien*, i, ii. For a discussion of his theory, see T. W. Manson, *The Sayings of Jesus* (1949), pp. 15 ff., especially pp. 20–1; also Kilpatrick, *op. cit.* pp. 11 ff.

have severally re-examined the problem of the sources of Matthew in great detail. For our purpose, however, it is unnecessary to estimate the probability of their somewhat novel conclusions, not only because they have both failed to convince most scholars that, apart from editorial elements, we need to postulate sources other than Q, M, and Mark for Matthew, but also because, in any case, neither the sources called S, P, O, N nor the sources G, R, B, T, which are isolated by Bacon and Bussmann respectively, have been claimed to exhibit any fivefold division of their material. Thus, in view of the predominant weight of scholarship, it is with Q, M, and Mark that we are concerned; and Mark need not be further considered, because, quite clearly, it is not a source pentateuchally arranged. Do Q and M reveal any such arrangement?

One thing is certain, that the discourse material available to Matthew, in whatever form, was not regarded by him as rigidly associated with any specific order of the ministry of Jesus, because all his discourse material he fits into the Marcan sequence. Thus the *SM* is placed at Mark i. 22; the address to the Twelve in Matt. x fits into Mark vi. 1–8; Matt. xiii is centred around Mark iv. 1–20; in Matt. xviii both the content and context are determined by Mark ix. 33–53; Matt. xxiv is an expansion of Mark xiii. This it is that has led to the claim so often made that Matthew is a revised edition of Mark (a fact which, as we saw, has been insufficiently recognized in discussions of the possible pentateuchal structure of Matthew). Again, equally certain is it that the five groups of discourses in Matthew are so composite that they could not, in their present form, have stood in any previous source. Streeter's emphatic treatment of this makes his conclusion incontestable that 'an analysis of every one of the Great Discourses yields evidence that it is an agglomeration put together by the editor of the Gospel'.[1] This is so established that it need not be examined further.

But we have still to deal with the question with which we closed the previous paragraph. Did the Evangelist have precedents for arranging the discourse material in a fivefold manner, and, in particular, did Q and M offer a pentateuchal division or arrangement? To begin with, we must insist that the fact that Luke vii. 1 has a formula, almost identical in form with that used by Matthew five times, cannot be taken to imply that Q may have had the fivefold formula, because the repetition of formulae is a characteristic of Matthew.[2] All that Luke vii. 1 proves is that probably

---

[1] *Op. cit.* p. 265.
[2] See, for example, the repetition of the 'gnashing of teeth' in viii. 12; xiii. 42, 50; xxii. 13; xxiv. 51; xxv. 30. The full phrase is: 'there men will weep and gnash their

Matthew derived the formula from Q, not that Q had used the formula five times. Again, the argument that Papias modelled his *Expositions of the Dominical Oracles* upon the *logia* of Matthew, and that, therefore, we are justified in supposing that these had a fivefold division is quite gratuitous, because, whether the *logia*, which Papias ascribed to Matthew, represented Q or not, Papias himself understood by the term *logia* the Gospel of Matthew, so that, if we desire to derive Papias' predilection for the fivefold form from his sources, the Gospel itself will suffice.

An answer can only be found to our question by discovering from Q and M themselves, in so far as we can reconstruct them, how they were organized. T. W. Manson revealed a correspondence at four points between the order of the material in Q and M. (He prefers the Lucan order for Q, as do most scholars: the order, moreover, that he suggests would command general assent, because reconstructions of Q vary, not in broad outlines, but only in details.) The four points are:

> Jesus' preaching;
> The mission charge;
> The speech against Pharisaism;
> The eschatological speech.

Moreover there are coincidences in the internal structure of the speeches as follows:

In Jesus' preaching

With Luke vi. 20–3	compare Matt. v. 7–10.
With Luke vi. 27–36	compare Matt. v. 17–24, 27, 39a, (44a), (44b–8).
With Luke vi. 42–5	compare Matt. vi. 1–4, 5–8, (9–15), 16–18.
With Luke vi. 46	compare Matt. vii. 21–3.

In the mission charge

| With Luke x. 8 f. | compare Matt. x. 7 f. |
| With Luke x. 16 | compare Matt. x. 40 f. |

In the speech against Pharisaism

With Luke xi. 43	compare Matt. xxiii. 7b.
With Luke xi. 44	compare Matt. xxiii. 27 f.
With Luke xi. 47 f.	compare Matt. xxiii. 30.

In view of all this Manson writes: 'We should not attempt to build too much on these parallelisms, but such as they are they allow us to entertain

teeth'. Compare the reference to Gehenna in v. 22, 29, 30; x. 28; xviii. 9; xxiii. 15, 33. This is to be distinguished from Matthew's avoidance of repetition in his reproduction of his sources: see Allen, *op. cit.* pp. xxiv–xxvi.

the supposition that there was a rough outline of the essentials of the teaching at an earlier stage of the tradition than is represented by Q and M. This outline, if it had a separate existence, dealt with essentials: the substance of the Christian life, the principles of Christian missionary propaganda, the defence of the new religion against Jewish attacks, and the hope of the future.' This outline he finds largely followed by the Didache.[1] In all this it is significant that, although he is naturally aware of Matthew's use of such, Manson does not refer to any possible fivefold grouping or ordering that Q and M might have revealed: such has not emerged from his studies. Nor can such be found without violence to the material, as we can reconstruct it, from either. We must, therefore, conclude that there is no solid ground for assuming that the fivefold grouping of Matthew's material is a derivative: it is the Evangelist's own stamp that his Gospel bears. It may be, therefore, that that grouping is important.

It is when we come to the third objection that the admission is at once inevitable that Bacon has, at least, overemphasized the structural parallelism between Matthew and the Pentateuch of the Old Testament. Two difficulties in the parallelism are suggested. First, while in the second, third and fifth books the narrative material is clearly preparatory to the discourse material, as are Exod. i–xix to Exod. xx ff., this, it has been claimed, is not true of the first and fourth books of Matthew, as isolated by Bacon. This difficulty, however, is not serious. A close scrutiny of the material preceding the *SM*, and the discourse on church administration in xvii. 22–xviii. 35, reveals a preparation therein for both these discourses. Thus, as we shall note below, it has been possible to find the motif of a New Exodus in the birth narratives in Matt. i, ii and possibly in the story of John the Baptist, a New Exodus preceding and leading up to the *SM*, as the New Law of the New Sinai. And again the whole section in Matt. xiii. 54–xviii. 35 has been regarded as a unity, as a kind of church order. On this view the confession at Caesarea Philippi, the Feeding of the Multitudes, Peter's Walking on the Sea, the Transfiguration, the Temple Tax, are all integrally related to Matt. xviii, and are designed to lead on to it.[2] More important is the second difficulty. On any theory of a detailed parallelism between Matthew and the Pentateuch, the first chapter of Matthew should correspond to the first in Genesis. Similarly the institution of the Eucharist in xxvi. 17 ff. should correspond to the establishment of the Old Covenant at Sinai. Matt. i. 1 may in fact recall

[1] *Op. cit.* pp. 21 ff.
[2] See especially W. Vischer, *Die evangelische Gemeindeordnung* (Zürich, 1933).

Gen. i. 1, as we shall see below, pages 61 ff., but the position of the Eucharist cannot be made to correspond with the institution of the first covenant at Sinai. In any case, the real difficulty is that the birth narratives in Matt. i, ii, which constitute the Prologue of the Gospel, and the story of the Passion and Resurrection, which constitute its Epilogue, are placed outside the main structure of the Gospel. This would be grave enough did it only involve the birth narratives in the Prologue, but it might be considered almost fatal when surely the most basic elements in the preaching of the early Church, the Death and Resurrection of Jesus, are treated as a kind of 'afterthought' or 'addendum'. This has led some to prefer to think of Matthew as a Hexateuch rather than as a Pentateuch.[1]

Our examination of the alleged fivefold structure of Matthew is closed. Taken in isolation on its 'literary' merits, the pentateuchal approach to Matthew must remain questionable. But we have been concerned with its literary character only in so far as this has been claimed to have important theological implications, namely, that Matthew's intention was to present the Christian dispensation in terms of Judaism, the *SM* being presented as the counterpart of the Old Law, and Christ, as a New Moses, proclaiming it from a New Sinai. It is legitimate, therefore, in view of the inconclusiveness of the purely literary approach to Matthew's structure to inquire whether there are other non-literary elements in the Gospel which might be understood to support the pentateuchal theory. Are there factors in Matthew, which, apart from the possibly fivefold nature of its structure, point to Jesus as a New Moses on a New Sinai, and so confirm the pentateuchal approach?[2]

2. NEW EXODUS AND NEW MOSES

Before turning to the relevant texts, it must be strongly emphasized that we pursue our inquiry into Matthew's understanding of the Christian dispensation in terms of a New Exodus, with all that this implies, over

[1] A. M. Farrer, *St Matthew and St Mark* (1954), pp. 179 ff.; for other scholars, see E. P. Blair, *Jesus in the Gospel of Matthew* (1960), p. 133, n. 35.

[2] The usage of scholars in referring to Matthew as a New Pentateuch varies. Are we to take the whole Gospel as a New Pentateuch, or is the New Law, strictly speaking, merely the *SM*? W. L. Knox takes the latter to be the case, as does Bacon (see Knox, *Sources of the Synoptic Gospels*, II (1957), pp. 9 ff.). In view of the uncertainty of the pentateuchal structure of Matthew, it is best, if the phrase New Law be used at all, to think of it in terms of Matt. v–vii. Notice that there is danger of arguing in a circle in these matters, one assumption being used to prop another to produce a conviction and *vice versa*.

against a very rich complex of concepts or, better, patterns of thought, which were alive in Matthew's milieu, and which gave to the Exodus and to Moses a marked significance, not only in Israel's history, but also in its Messianic expectation. This significance was not merely homiletic, but also theological, in that, to a degree which we shall be concerned to examine in the next chapter, the first redemption from Egypt became the prototype of the future redemption. Before the discovery of the Dead Sea Scrolls, the enthusiasm with which the theme of a New Exodus was often discovered in pre-Christian Judaism,[1] and employed in the elucidation of the New Testament, may have been over-confident and slightly uncritical, in view of the sparse evidence for the motif in the sources available. But there can no longer be any doubt, since that event, that the ideal future of Jewish expectation was conceived, in some circles at least, in terms of a New Exodus. The history of the Dead Sea Sect no less than its documents reveal this (see chapter III, pages 111 ff.).[2] It is, therefore, *a priori* to be expected that these concepts may have influenced Matthew, as they did other New Testament writers. This climate of expectation in which Matthew wrote must be given due weight, and the real possibility reckoned with that it would have considerably influenced Matthew.

With this preliminary, let us now examine the Gospel in an attempt to answer the question we have posed above. Clarity demands that we deal with two questions in turn. First, does Matthew introduce the New Exodus motif into his treatment of the material that he derives from Mark and Q, by changing its contents or form, that is, by modifying its details or by rearranging its various pericopae? And, secondly, in the material peculiar to Matthew is this motif convincingly detectable?

(a) *Matthew's treatment of material from Mark and Q*

The pertinent passages are the following:

(i) *The Ministry of John the Baptist* (Matt. iii. 1–11; Mark i. 1–8; Luke iii. 1–18)

With minor variations, the view has been urged that the Baptist's ministry is to be understood in the light of the parallelism to which we

---

[1] Very salutary in this connexion is the essay by J. Giblet on 'Prophétisme et attente d'un Messie Prophète dans l'ancien Judaïsme' in *L'Attente du Messie* (1954), pp. 85–130.

[2] T. H. Gaster, *The Dead Sea Scriptures* (1956), p. 4: 'The members of the community conceived of themselves as repeating in a later age the experience of their remote fathers in the days of Moses.'

have referred. In Mark it has been customary to detect three factors that suggest this.

(1) The Baptist appeared on the scene when Jesus, then about thirty years old, had spent that length of time in obscurity in Galilee. This corresponds to the forty years spent by Moses, from his infancy to the beginning of his redemptive work, in the obscurity of Midian.[1]

(2) More frequently noted is the location of the Baptist's ministry 'in the wilderness'. No mere geographic accident, this was intended to recall the Exodus from Egypt in accordance with those Jewish expectations of a Messianic Age, which would reproduce the conditions of the Mosaic period to which we have referred.[2]

(3) In line with this also, the actual activity of John in the baptism to which he summoned Israel is to be understood as the eschatological counterpart of the passing through the Red Sea, that is, the 'baptism' which led to the emergence of the old Israel. This is the position most frequently urged. Levertoff's view that John's baptism is a parallel to the sanctification of Israel demanded before the receiving of the Law in Exod. xix. 10, a sanctification which is referred to as a baptism in Siphre on Numbers § 108, has not been found convincing.

In Matthew these motifs are preserved. Like Mark and Luke, it is claimed, he also emphasized 'the wilderness' as the scene of the Baptist's ministry, but he has enhanced the parallelism with the Exodus by making that ministry precede the establishment of a new Law (Matt. v–vii), and a New Covenant founded on the forgiveness of sins (Jer. xxxi. 31 ff.), just as, according to Levertoff, the 'sanctification' mentioned in Exod. xix. 10

[1] P. Levertoff, *A New Commentary*, ed. Gore, Goudge, Guillaume (1928), p. 133 *ad rem*. 'Between the infancy of Moses and the commencement of his redemptive work there is an interval of forty years spent in the obscurity of the Midian desert; and between the infancy of Jesus and His entry into Israel's history as the last Redeemer is an interval of thirty years spent in the obscurity of a Galilean village.'

[2] W. H. Brownlee, 'John the Baptist in the New Light of Ancient Scrolls', in *The Scrolls and the New Testament*, ed. K. Stendahl (1957), pp. 34–5. C. H. Kraeling, *John the Baptist* (1951), pp. 1 ff., makes no mention of this motif in the NT, despite his recognition of the parallels to his retreat to the wilderness in the first-century movements (p. 30) which others have associated with the concept of a New Exodus; see, for example, G. Vermès, 'La figure de Moïse au tournant des deux Testaments', in *Cahiers Sioniens*, viiie année, no. 2-3-4 (1954), p. 79. Kraeling's treatment is invaluable factually, but it would be richer had he discussed the possible theological motifs at work in the Baptist's ministry more thoroughly. John Marsh found in the honey in the Baptist's diet a further indication of a new Exodus motif in the light of Exod. xvi. 31 (so in a public lecture). But that verse merely states that the taste of the manna was 'like wafers made with honey'. For this, see Kraeling, *op. cit.*

('And the Lord said to Moses, "Go to the people and consecrate them today and tomorrow and let them wash their garments"'"), which was later called a 'baptism', preceded the Old Covenant on Sinai.[1] On this view, Matthew has emphasized the Exodus motif in the account of the Baptist not so much by making changes in the material from Mark as by his arrangement of it.

But how far can we be sure that this is the case? We have first to ascertain whether there was in Mark such a motif which Matthew *could* emphasize. Certain considerations make this less than certain. Clearly the first parallelism mentioned above—since thirty and forty do not too obviously correspond—we can dismiss. Before we deal with the exact meaning of John's baptism on pages 34 ff. below, the crux of the matter would seem to be whether 'the wilderness' was understood by Mark and Matthew to indicate specifically a New Exodus on the way. To form a judgement on this the following facts are pertinent: we begin with positive considerations.

(*a*) Matthew, like Mark and Luke, understood the Baptist to be Elijah, the expected herald of the Messiah.[2] While, on the one hand, there is no specific evidence that the Tishbite was to lead the people into the wilderness in preparation for the Messiah's advent, nevertheless, on the other hand, there may be detected signs that this was implied. In Mal. iii. 1: 'Behold, I send my messenger to prepare the way before me...' it is possible that the term 'the way', which looks back to Isa. xl. 3, may refer to a 'way' through the wilderness.[3] Although this cannot be pressed, it would seem to be confirmed in an early passage in the Mekilta on Exod. xvi. 33 which reads:

And Put an Omerful of Manna Therein, and Lay It Up Before the Lord to be Kept for Your Generations. R. Joshua says: For the generation of the forefathers themselves. R. Eleazer of Modi'im says: For subsequent generations. R. Eliezer says: For the time of the prophet Jeremiah. For when the prophet Jeremiah said to the Israelites: Why do you not busy yourselves with the Torah? they said to him: If we be kept busy with the words of the Torah, how will we get our sustenance? Then Jeremiah brought forth to them the bottle containing the manna, and said to them: 'O generation, see ye the thing of the Lord' [Jer. ii. 31].

---

[1] P. Levertoff, *op. cit.* p. 129*a*. But it is odd that while Levertoff throughout emphasizes the New Redemption as corresponding to the First in the ministry of the Baptist (pp. 128*b* f.), as elsewhere, he also insists that the emphasis is not on the scene of his preaching in any manner that would suggest that in *that* was the fulfilment of prophecy, but only on the content of John's message (p. 134*a*).

[2] Matt. xi. 14, Mark ix. 13 and parallels.

[3] Isa. xxxv. 8 may have this concept.

See with what your forefathers, who busied themselves with the words of the Torah, were provided. You, too, if you will busy yourselves with the words of the Torah, God will provide you with sustenance of this sort. And this is one of the three things which Elijah will, in the future, restore to Israel: The bottle of manna, the bottle of sprinkling water, and the bottle of anointing oil. And some say: Also the rod of Aaron with its ripe almonds and blossoms, for it is said: 'Bring back the rod of Aaron', etc. [Num. xvii. 25].

All the rabbis mentioned in this quotation flourished between A.D. 80 and 120. The 'manna' in the above context does not seem necessarily to demand a geographic wilderness as its background, as is clear from the passage dealing with Jeremiah. Thus the section falls short of a proof that, in the period when Matthew was being written, Elijah would be connected with the wilderness of a New Exodus. Nevertheless, it may be argued that, on the haggadic level, at least, although there is no direct reference to his preparing a way 'in the wilderness', this may have been implied of Elijah, that is, in some sense, he was to inaugurate an Exodus.

(*b*) The 'heretical' *Gospel of the Ebionites* may have understood the Baptist's ministry in terms of the Exodus. It reads:

John was baptizing, and there went out unto him Pharisees and were baptized, and all Jerusalem. And John had raiment of camel's hair and a leather girdle about his loins: and his meat (it saith) was wild honey, whereof the taste is the taste of manna, as a cake *dipped* in oil. That, forsooth, they may pervert the word of truth into a lie and for locusts put a cake *dipped* in honey.

Is the reference to manna here governed by an understanding of the Baptist as recreating the conditions of the first Exodus? We cannot be certain, because, as Epiphanius makes clear in his comment, the Ebionite Gospel was, at this point, concerned with vegetarianism, not theology proper,[1] and it is striking that, in the fragments of this Gospel available to us, the wilderness is not once specifically mentioned. The reference to the manna may merely be a haggadic titbit, for we know that there was much discussion of the taste of the manna.[2] Nevertheless, the possibility remains that the Ebionites did understand the Baptist in the terms referred to above.

(*c*) All the Synoptists make it clear that the Baptist prepared for the

[1] M. R. James, *The Apocryphal Gospels* (1953), p. 9: 'These Ebionites were vegetarians and objected to the idea of eating locusts. A locust in Greek is ἀκρίς, and the word they used for cake is ἐνκρίς, so the change is slight.'

[2] Mekilta on Exod. xvi. 16–27: 'If one liked to eat something baked, he could taste in the manna the taste of any kind of baked things in the world', etc.; see also L. Ginzberg, *The Legends of the Jews*, vol. III (1942), pp. 41–50.

Messiah and his Age, and, even at the risk of redundancy, it is necessary to repeat again that the climate of Jewish expectation would favour the emergence of the wilderness motif. The Baptist's ministry in the wilderness follows a pattern, dictated by this motif, most certainly in the case of the Dead Sea Sect, and, possibly, in that of certain individuals, such as Theudas and a certain Egyptian false prophet.[1]

But there are, on the other hand, strong considerations of a negative kind.

(a) The evidence of *The Gospel of the Ebionites* is offset by that of *The Gospel according to the Hebrews*. In the account of the Baptist in the fragments of it in our possession 'the wilderness' is not mentioned, and the theological motifs at work in it would seem to point away from any emphasis upon that phenomenon. No interest is shown in any symbolic meaning that the activity of the Baptist in the wilderness may have had, but rather a concentration on the problem constituted by the submission of Jesus, the sinless one, to a baptism designed for the forgiveness of sin. Thus the extra-canonical Gospel usually regarded as closest to Matthew does not support the detection of any recondite symbolism in the geography of the Baptist's work in Matthew's Gospel. As translated by M. R. James, *The Apocryphal Gospels*, p. 9, the pertinent words are:

[In the description of the baptism of Jesus]...and again *there was* a voice from heaven saying unto him: This is my beloved Son in whom I am well pleased. And then (it saith) John fell down before him and said: I beseech thee, Lord, baptize thou me. But he prevented them saying: Suffer it (or let it go): for thus it behoveth that all things should be fulfilled.

(b) Perhaps it is not without significance that Matthew's change of the generalized 'the wilderness' of Mark (and Luke) into the particularized 'the wilderness of Judea' suggests that he at least thought of it in strictly geographic, not merely symbolic, terms, even if the latter were more in Mark's mind.

(c) In discussions of this problem, insufficient attention has been paid to the precise use of the Old Testament in the Synoptics at this point. Mark introduces the activity of the Baptist with a quotation—a combination of Mal. iii. 1 (and Exod. xxiii. 20: MT 'Behold, I send an angel before you, to guard you on the way and to bring you to the place which I have prepared') and Isa. xl. 3—as follows:

As it is written in Isaiah the Prophet,
'Behold, I send my messenger before thy face,
Who shall prepare thy way;

[1] See below, pp. 111 ff.

The voice of one crying in the wilderness:
Prepare the way of the Lord,
    make his paths straight—.' (RSV.)

Matthew here omits the quotation from Mal. iii. 1, only to introduce it in
xi. 10, but retains Isa. xl. 3 in exactly the same form as it is found in Mark
(so also Luke, who, however, also quotes Isa. xl. 4, 5). All the Synoptics
use the translation of Isa. xl. 3 found in the LXX, except that they substitute 'his' (αὐτοῦ) for 'our God' in the last line. The LXX reads:

> The voice of one crying in the wilderness (ἐν τῇ ἐρήμῳ)
> Prepare ye the way of the Lord,
>   make straight the paths of our God.

This is syntactically different from the underlying Hebrew text. The MT
demands the following translation:

A voice cries:
'In the wilderness (בַּמִּדְבָּר) prepare the way of the Lord, make straight in the
desert (בָּעֲרָבָה) a highway for our God....'

The emphasis in the MT is on preparing a way in the wilderness as such,
that is, geographically. This was the interpretation placed on Isa. xl. 3 by
the Dead Sea Sect, which accordingly journeyed into the wilderness.
DSD viii. 14 reads:

When these exist in Israel, these are the provisions whereby they are to be kept
apart from any consort with froward men, to the end that they may indeed 'go
into the wilderness to prepare the way,' i.e., do what scripture enjoins when it
says, 'Prepare in the wilderness the way...make straight in the desert a highway for our God [Isa. xl. 3].' (Gaster's translation.)

Contrast with this the emphasis in the LXX, where, syntactically, the
'wilderness' of the first line is connected not with the verb 'prepare', but
with the term 'voice', while the 'desert' of the second line is omitted
altogether. It is this emphasis that is revealed in the Synoptics, both here
and at Matt. xi. 10, Luke vii. 27, and in John i. 23, where an explicit
identification of the Baptist and the 'voice' is made. To judge from
Justin's *Dialogue with Trypho*, L, 3 this was not questioned in the early
Church. It seems reasonable to suppose that, had early Christians been
particularly concerned to claim a symbolic significance for the wilderness,
where the Baptist laboured, as the scene of a New Exodus, they would
have been led to use the Hebrew text, in expounding his work, as did the
Dead Sea Sect in interpreting theirs. Instead, as we have seen, all the

Synoptics, like the Fourth Gospel, identify the Baptist with 'the voice' in the wilderness, but do not demand that the very preparation for the Coming One should be located there. Nor can this difficulty be explained away on the assumption that the evangelists, who wrote in Greek, were ignorant of the Hebrew text. We need not here decide whether the quotations from Mal. iii. 1 and Isa. xl. 3, in their exact form and combination, are to be understood in terms of a synagogal lectionary or targumic tradition,[1] which had already joined Mal. iii. 1 and Exod. xxiii. 20, or from a collection of testimonies, which would explain the ascription of a passage from Malachi to Isaiah.[2] Suffice it that the forms used in the Gospels from Mal. iii. 1 and Isa. xl. 3 presuppose, in the sources behind them and, we must assume, at least in the case of Matthew, in the evangelists themselves, a knowledge of Hebrew. Thus:

The LXX of Mal. iii. 1 reads

Behold, I send forth my messenger, and he shall survey the way before me. [shall survey=LXX ἐπιβλέψεται.]

The Synoptics read (Mark i. 2)

Behold, I send my messenger before thy face who shall prepare thy way [prepare thy way=κατασκευάσει= וּפִנָּה, the reading of the MT. In Matt. xi. 10 the ἔμπροσθέν σου, corresponding to לְפָנַי, 'before me', found in the MT, is added].

The NT quotation from Malachi thus presupposes, not the LXX, but the MT. This means that before the quotations were used by the evangelists, if they took them from existing sources, they were based on a knowledge of the Hebrew underlying the text. On the other hand, if the quotations are due to the evangelists, a less likely view, they themselves must be credited with a knowledge of Hebrew. It is, therefore, significant, that either sources earlier than the evangelists, or the evangelists themselves, did not use the Hebrew text to press the symbolic significance of the 'wilderness', when that text was admirably suited to their purpose.

(*d*) That no exact counterpart to the wilderness of the first Exodus is intended by Matthew is also clear, it may be argued, from another consideration, which can best be seen, however, in Luke's account of the Baptist's preaching in Luke iii. 10–14.

And the multitudes asked him, 'What then shall we do?' And he answered them, 'He who has two coats, let him share with him who has none; and he who has

---

[1] See K. Stendahl, *The School of Matthew* (1954), pp. 47 ff.
[2] C. H. Dodd, *According to the Scriptures* (1952), p. 40.

food, let him do likewise.' Tax collectors also came to be baptized, and said to him, 'Teacher, what shall we do?' And he said to them, 'Collect no more than is appointed you.' Soldiers also asked him, 'And we, what shall we do?' And he said to them, 'Rob no one by violence or by false accusation, and be content with your wages.' (RSV.)

Here there is no call to forsake the world for the wilderness, but to live in a new way in the old world. Essentially similar is Matthew's understanding of the Baptist's demand. John's preaching is a call to bear good fruit, presumably 'in the world' (iii. 7–10). Whatever may have been his previous affinities with it, this at once sets the Baptist apart from the Dead Sea Sect, which tried to 'repeat' the days of Moses. As Matthew seems to have understood it, the Baptist's work was to make a general appeal for repentance to the people of Israel. That his appeal was effective, at least in the immediate attention it drew, is clear from iii. 5 (note the emphatic 'all' in 'all Judea' and 'all the region about Jordan'), where it is not necessary to find a recondite eschatological reference based upon Isa. xlviii. 20; lii. 11, but a natural hyperbole.[1] To find the 'eschatological group' in the 'all' of iii. 5 is to miss the point that, not for the Baptist was it to call upon a select group to leave the world for the wilderness, as was the intent of the Teacher of Righteousness of the Dead Sea Sect, but to broadcast a challenge. The specialized task of forming the select group is left to a greater one to come 'who would clear his threshing floor and gather his wheat...', that is, who would establish the new Messianic community.[2] The most we can claim for any community that John himself brought into being is that it was anticipatory of another community of the one greater than he.[3]

The above assessment of the positive and negative considerations for deciding whether, for Matthew, the Baptist's activity in the wilderness as

---

[1] E. Lohmeyer, *Das Evangelium des Markus* (1958), p. 15; V. Taylor, *Commentary on Mark* (1953), p. 155 a. Possibly the reference to the numbers who came to John's baptism may be due to the desire to emphasize it as a baptism of readiness for a New Israel, the communal aspect of the event. Lohmeyer makes much of the difference between ἐκπορεύεσθαι and ἐξέρχεσθαι, the former suggesting a procession (*op. cit.* p. 15, n. 4), and sees in the reference in Mark i. 5 a parallel to the Exodus from Egypt. Such an 'exodus' he finds part of Jewish eschatological expectation on the basis of Isa. xlviii. 20; lii. 11. But he does not note that in both these passages the LXX has ἐξέρχεσθαι. His interpretation, therefore, must be regarded as forced. Note, however, that יצא is used of the exodus of the Dead Sea Sect in CDC iv. 3; vi. 5.

[2] The idea of community is implied in the 'gathering'.

[3] C. H. Dodd, *A Companion to the Bible*, ed. T. W. Manson (1939), p. 370.

such was governed by the New Exodus motif is weighted on the negative side. But there remains to add to the positive side two possibilities. First, the argument from Matthew's schematization (that is, the claim that the incidence of the Baptist's activity in Matthew between the flight from Egypt in Matt. ii, and the giving of the New Law from the New Sinai in Matt. v–vii, makes it correspond to the period of the wilderness in the first Exodus) must be given due weight. Full justice can be meted out to it, however, only after we have treated the birth narratives and other sections, so that at this stage it must merely be noted. But the frequency with which it has been reiterated points to its pertinence in this discussion even if not necessarily to its truth.[1]

Secondly, the significance of the act of baptism for John must now be considered. While in the above treatment we have dealt only with the interpretation of the Baptist in the evangelists, without raising the question as to the actual historical character of his ministry, the fact is to be seriously assessed that this historical character of the ministry, despite the incrustations of interpretation by the early community, may have continued to remain influential and significant. And the essential character of the Baptist's activity, as it happened as 'event', is indicated by the very title, 'the Baptist' or 'the Baptizer', that was given to John; that is, it consisted in the act of baptism which John himself administered.[2] The nature of that baptism has been much disputed. Pertinent to our discussion are two aspects of it on which there is much agreement.

(a) The possibility, which has most to be said for it, is that it was an adaptation of proselyte baptism.[3] And, if such was the case, then the Exodus motif was integral to all John's thinking, because proselyte baptism owes its imagery to the Exodus from Egypt, and we may assume that, if it was present in John's mind, this imagery was also in the minds of the evangelists when they reported the activity of the Baptist, even though they may have further developed their own interpretation of that activity. Proselyte baptism was part of that ceremony of dedication by which a Gentile was made a member of Israel. He did so by recapitulating in baptism, and other aspects of the ceremony, those historic acts whereby

[1] To anticipate the discussion on pp. 78 ff., it has to be stated that the Exodus motif in the Prologue is not sufficiently dominant to allow as much force to the argument as does Levertoff.

[2] E. Lohmeyer, op. cit. p. 13; M. Dibelius, Die Urchristliche Überlieferung von Johannes dem Täufer (1911), p. 47.

[3] W. F. Flemington, The New Testament Doctrine of Baptism (1948), pp. 15 ff who regards John's baptism as an adaptation of proselyte baptism.

Israel was constituted as a people. As W. L. Knox expressed it: 'The proselyte through circumcision and the proselytes' bath, was enabled to come out of Egypt and pass through the Red Sea into the promised land of Israel.' He was thus brought under 'the wings of the Shekinah', which is probably a reference to that cloud of the Divine Presence which accompanied Israel in its Exodus from Egypt.[1]

(b) Even more is it recognized that the baptism of John was thoroughly eschatological, that is, directed towards the time of the End, the coming of the Kingdom of God and of a 'greater one than he'.[2] But as we have already indicated, and shall attempt to show at length below, the eschatology of Israel was a protology, that is, the End was conceived in terms of the Beginning, of the creation of the universe itself and of the people of Israel at the Exodus. Thus the possibility is a very real one, in view of the climate of expectation within which John laboured, that 'baptism', no less than 'wilderness', was a term evocative of 'Exodus' associations. And in view of this, coupled with the other considerations enumerated above, we must be prepared to allow the existence of such associations in the ministry of the Baptist, both historically and in the interpretation of the Church. The extent to which Matthew may have emphasized these associations is bound up primarily with the argument from schematization we have mentioned above to which we shall turn later. Apart from this it can hardly be said that there is any such emphasis in Matthew.

Up to this point, leaving aside the quotation from Isa. xl. 3 in Matt. iii. 3 (the force of which, however, in view of its failure to emphasize the wilderness as such, is weakened as evidence for any exact correspondence intended between the first Exodus and the Christian dispensation inaugurated by the ministry of the Baptist, while nothing has emerged to indicate a New Moses motif), it will be recognized that we have come to a result which can only be regarded as implicit. By painstaking scrutiny of the possible unexpressed connotation and evocativeness of certain activities and terms we have thought it not impossible that the New Exodus motif is to be discovered in the ministry of the Baptist. Must we be content with this kind of result when we deal with the baptism of Jesus himself or do we find there an explicit reference to the New Exodus or New Moses motif?

If they are operative in the work of the evangelists at all, it is here that we might expect these concepts to assert themselves, because the ex-

[1] W. L. Knox, St Paul and the Church of the Gentiles (Cambridge, 1939), pp. 87 f.
[2] Flemington does not mention the Exodus motif in proselyte baptism.

perience of Jesus in baptism could lend itself so directly to a comparison with the events at the Red Sea. This can be stated somewhat categorically, because those events were seen by Paul as a type of Christian baptism,[1] and this, in turn, is most probably to be connected, in its origin, with the baptism of Jesus himself.[2] But do the concepts referred to emerge in this last? Three accompaniments of that event—the heavens opened, the Spirit descending like a dove, the voice from heaven—are emphasized. The opening of the heavens is used in apocalyptic sources only,[3] after the manner of Ezek. i. 1, so it is claimed, to describe an eschatological revelation; the 'voice from heaven' is a familiar phenomenon in rabbinic sources: it is not usually found in epiphanies, although it occurs in connexion with the Spirit of God in Rev. xiv. 13, and in a context similar to that in the Synoptics in Test. Lev. xviii. 6, 7.[4] It is the meaning of the descent of the dove and of the words of scripture uttered by the 'voice' that fall to be examined. In the main, three interpretations have been offered.

(1) The reference to the dove is usually understood in the light of Gen. i. 1 f., where the Spirit hovers, so we are probably to gather, like a dove over the face of the primeval waters, so that the beginning of Jesus' ministry is thus related to the cosmogonic myth of Gen. i. 1 f. and its parallels in surrounding cultures,[5] as a new creation comparable to the first. The inauguration of the Redemption is parallel to that of the created order. The association of the Spirit in Gen. i. 1 with the Messiah is found in Judaism in this period.[6] More important for our immediate purpose, however, is that in Judaism the act of creation had become linked with that of redemption from Egypt, the Exodus being regarded as an intervention of God in a new act of creation. In Isa. xliii. 16–20 the fusion of creation and Exodus motifs in the descriptions of the future salvation is evident.[7]

> Thus says the Lord,
>   who makes a way in the sea,
>   a path in the mighty waters,

[1] 1 Cor. x. 1 ff.
[2] Flemington, *op. cit.* p. 32.
[3] Apoc. Bar. xxii. 2; 2 Macc. vi. 18; Test. Lev. ii. 6; v. 1; xviii. 6; Test. Jud. xxiv. 2; Asc. Is. vi. 9; John i. 51; Acts vii. 56; Rev. iv. 1; xi. 19; xix. 11. See Taylor, *op. cit.* p. 160; Lohmeyer, *op. cit.* p. 21.
[4] But see p. 41.
[5] See Skinner, *Genesis*, I.C.C. (1930), *ad rem.* Dr Muilenburg reminded me that the term for hovering occurs in exodic contexts, Deut. xxxii. 10; Exod. xix. 3.
[6] See n. 1, p. 37 below.   [7] Taylor, *op. cit. ad rem.*

who brings forth chariot and horse,
army and warrior;
they lie down, they cannot rise,
they are extinguished, quenched like a wick:
'Remember not the former things,
nor consider the things of old.
Behold, I am doing a new thing;
now it springs forth, do you not perceive it?
I will make a way in the wilderness
and rivers in the desert. . . .'

It follows that the creation motif in the story of the baptism of Jesus may carry with it connotations of the Exodus. It must, however, be recognized that these can only be implied to be in the text: they are not made explicit.

(2) The words 'Thou art my beloved Son; with thee I am well pleased' recall several Old Testament passages (Ps. ii. 7; Isa. xlii. 1, 2; Gen. xxii. 2; lxii. 4).[1] Here, in Taylor's judgement, we have a 'striking and original combination of ideas', 'the idea of the Messianic Son is combined with that of the Servant', and this expresses 'a new and vital relationship to God which transcends Messiahship as it was understood in Jewish thought. . . . The fundamental note in the saying is the filial status of Jesus; and the words are best understood as an assurance, or confirmation, of this relationship, rather than a disclosure or revelation'.[2] It should be emphasized that Taylor is on explicit ground in this only if his interpretation of the Old Testament references are accepted and the same qualification must be added to the next point.

(3) But recently this combination of the Messianic and Servant motif has been set in the light of the kingship ideology of the Old Testament, where the fusion of these motifs had already at least partially been expressed.[3] In the Old Testament the king was the life-force of the nation

[1] C. K. Barrett, *The Holy Spirit in the Gospel Tradition*; E. Lohmeyer, *op. cit.* p. 21; Taylor, *op. cit.* p. 160. For Spirit and Messiah in Gen. i. 2, see the Jerusalem Targum; *P.R.J.*[2] p. 189.

[2] Taylor, *op. cit.* p. 160.

[3] See A. R. Johnson, 'The Role of the King in the Jerusalem Cultus', in *The Labyrinth*, ed. S. H. Hooke (New York, 1935), pp. 71–111; 'Living Issues in Biblical Scholarship; Divine Kingship in the O.T.', *Expository Times*, LXII (1950), 36–42; J. Morgenstern, 'A Chapter in the History of the High Priesthood', in *The American Journal of Semitic Languages and Literature*, LV (January–October 1938), 1–24, 183–97, 360–77; *Amos Studies*, I, II; 'The Sin of Uzziah, the Festival of Jeroboam and the Date of Amos', in *Hebrew Union College Annual*, XI, pp. 19 ff.; XII, pp. 1 ff. (1936–8), 1–53; C. R. North, 'The Religious Aspects of Hebrew Kingship', in *Zeitschrift für die Alttestamentliche Wissenschaft*, XLIX–L (1931–2), 8–38. For the

as a psychic whole and is presented as the Son of God, as, for example, in Ps. ii. 7, where the king says:

> I will tell of the decree of the Lord:
> He said to me, 'You are my son,
>   today I have begotten you'.

So also in Ps. lxxxix. 26–7 the intimacy of the relationship is thus expressed:

> He shall cry to me, 'Thou art my Father,
>   my God, and the Rock of my salvation'.
> And I will make him the first-born,
>   the highest of the kings of the earth.

And again in Ps. lxxxix. 49–52, where the figure of the Davidic King is one of humiliation comparable to that of the servant of the Lord in Deutero-Isaiah:

> Lord, where is thy steadfast love of old,
>   which by thy faithfulness thou didst swear
>   to David?
> Remember, O Lord, how thy servant is scorned;
>   how I bear in my bosom the insults of the peoples,
> with which thy enemies taunt, O Lord,
>   with which they mock the footsteps of thy
>   anointed.
> Blessed be the Lord for ever!
>   Amen and Amen.

A. R. Johnson[1] has commented thus on the combination of Messianic ideas in this psalm. 'The Davidic King is the Servant of Yahweh; but... at the New Year Festival he is the Suffering Servant. He is the Messiah of Yahweh; but on this occasion he is the humiliated Messiah. The fact is that we are here dealing with a ritual humiliation of the Davidic King which in principle is not unlike that suffered by the Babylonian king in the analogous New Year Festival....' It is in the light of such ideas of kingship, it has been suggested, that we are to understand the baptism of Jesus. John's baptism was one of 'repentance for the forgiveness of sins', but nowhere does Jesus in the New Testament reveal a consciousness of

Hebrew psychology which lies behind ideas of corporate personality, see Wheeler Robinson, 'Hebrew Psychology', in *The People and the Book*, ed. A. S. Peake (1925), pp. 375 ff.; Johs Pedersen, *Israel: Its Life and Culture*, I–II (1926), pp. 475, 99 ff., 106, 207 f., 178, 195, 338; A. R. Johnson, 'The Role of the King', in *The Labyrinth*, pp. 74–5 and *The One and the Many in the Israelite Conception of God* (1942).
[1] 'The Role of the King', in *The Labyrinth*, p. 100.

sin.[1] Nevertheless, in the role of King-Messiah Jesus 'accepted baptism as an act of self-identification with sinful Israel'. In a corporate sense, then, Jesus may have been conscious of sin, and possibly, as Taylor asserts, 'it is reasonable to infer that his sense of suffering destiny is lineally connected with the initial experience of baptism'.[2] 'As the old Israelite king', writes Bogard Dunn, 'was assured of the favour of Jahweh at the moment when the outlook was blackest, so too Jesus, when he came from the water of ritual humiliation, was given the assurance of his sonship: "Thou art my beloved Son; with thee I am well pleased."'[3]

Attempts to inquire whether another approach to this material is possible are far to seek. Lohmeyer,[4] however, cast out a suggestion, which he did not develop, but which is pertinent to our purpose and which carries the act of self-identification still farther, indeed which implies not only that Jesus identifies himself with Israel but that in the baptism he represents or is Israel. Pointing out that in an account of the dealings of Yahweh with Israel in Deutero-Isaiah lxiii. 14 the presence of the Spirit in the wandering in the desert is asserted, he suggests that the declaration of Jesus' sonship at his baptism recalls the adoption of Israel as Yahweh's son at the Exodus, that is, the birth of the nation. Certain considerations might be advanced in support of Lohmeyer's view. First, it has long become clear that the concepts of the Messiah and the Servant of the Lord, combined as they are here, were possibly fused, in varying degrees, in pre-Christian Judaism, with the figure of Moses. The evidence for this is given below on pages 130 ff. Secondly, the term 'Son' was applied not only to the Messiah, and to the King of Israel, and to the pious, but also to the people of Israel, as such. The Sonship of Israel was particularly connected with the Exodus; it was then that Israel truly became Yahweh's 'Son' (and in this connexion we repeat that the King-Messiah and the people were a corporate unity, the former representing the latter).

---

[1] Compare Flemington, *op. cit.* p. 27.

[2] *Ibid.* It should not be overlooked how central was suffering for Moses' vocation; this Dr Muilenburg pointed out to me.

[3] In a dissertation, unpublished, on the theme 'Some Mythological and Cosmological Motifs in the Gospel According to Mark' (Duke University, 1954), which gives full bibliographies and an acute discussion of the Marcan text. He refers to no 'New Exodus' motif in connexion with the Baptism. The qualification mentioned in the text acquires importance in the light of Cranfield's point, that it is unlikely, if Mark were looking back to Ps. ii. 7, that he should not have reproduced the LXX order υἱός μου εἶ σύ, as is done elsewhere in the NT when Ps. ii. 7 is quoted. See C. E. B. Cranfield, *The Gospel according to St Mark, ad rem.*

[4] *Das Evangelium des Markus, ad rem.*

Thirdly, contrary to the assertion that the symbolism in the baptismal account is purely apocalyptic, it emerges in a striking, though loose, parallel in the haggadic treatments of the crossing of the Red Sea in the Mekilta and Midrash Rabbah on Exodus. The fact that Moses was regarded as a prophet[1] and Miriam[2] as a prophetess prepares us to expect the Spirit to be present at the Exodus, because prophecy was the gift of the Spirit. And already in Isa. lxiii. 11 the Spirit is expressly connected with the actual passing through the Red Sea: before this event 'Yahweh put into the midst of (Israel) his holy spirit'. This emerges with emphasis in the Mekilta on Exod. xiv. 13.[3] There the interpretation deals with the moment before the Israelites actually cross the Red Sea. The Holy Spirit (רוח הקדש) then rested upon them, presumably to give them confidence in the presence and power of God. At the same moment, Israel is compared to a dove (a customary figure for the people). At the same moment also, although the express phrase 'the heavens were opened' is not used, this is what is implied to have happened, because squadrons of the heavenly hosts appear to the Israelites' sight, that is, they are granted a vision in which God reveals his power to save. We miss in Mekilta on Exod. xiv. 13 any reference to a 'heavenly voice', but this omission is supplied substantially, if not identically, in another passage which deals with the moment at which the Israelites leave the Sea on the far side. Thus in Mekilta on Exod. xv. 2 there is the same emphasis on the presence of the Spirit, but also references to the Holy Spirit calling aloud from heaven. Moreover, in both Mekilta on Exod. xiv. 14, 15 Yahweh's special love for Israel is evident, the Exodus marking in a real sense the adoption of Israel as Yahweh's son.[4] Note the care shown for Israel also in Mekilta on xv. 2.[5] The treatment of the passing through the Red Sea in Exodus Rabbah is comparatively free from these motifs that we have mentioned above. The Holy Spirit is mentioned once only and then is claimed to be a reward given to Israel for its faith in God before the crossing. Israel's condition is described in terms of a 'dove', but there is an emphasis on the immediacy of God's direct action in the crossing. Angelic hosts do not appear to strengthen Israel, rather the guardian angel of Egypt was

---

[1] Deut. xviii. 15; Hos. xii. 13; Deut. xxxiv. 10; Philo, *Life of Moses*, II, 188–245; II, 6; *De Somniis* II, 189; *De virtutibus* LI.

[2] Exod. xv. 20.

[3] See J. Z. Lauterbach, *Mekilta*, I (1949), pp. xiii ff.; Moore, *Judaism*, I, p. 136.

[4] See Appendix I.

[5] See Appendix II.

destroyed by God: he had first terrified Israel and then been overcome by the Lord.[1]

It is, therefore, the treatment of the Mekilta that is most pertinent to our purpose. The three elements, the coming of the Holy Spirit, the figure of the dove, the heavenly voice, in effect at least, and, in addition, the equivalent of the rending of the heavens all occur here, as part of the event in which Israel became the 'Son' of Yahweh. As far as we are aware this is the closest parallel, in all its details, to the baptism of Jesus. (Thus the passage usually quoted as such, that is, Test. Levi xviii. 5–12, although containing the substance of much of the story of Jesus' baptism, only offers a generalized parallel to the Voice, and no parallel at all to the dove, nor is there a scriptural passage as such applied to the *bath qôl*.) Are we then to assume that, like the Mekilta in the passages quoted above, Mark and the parallels in Matthew and Luke are concerned to describe how Jesus is the Messianic King who represents Israel, the new Israel that comes into being in him? This possibility is not to be too easily ruled out.

But two difficulties are to be noted.

(1) The date of the Mekilta is later than that of the Synoptics and it may be suggested, therefore, that it cannot be used in the interpretation of the Synoptics. But the Mekilta, nevertheless, and, in particular, the sections in it dealing with the crossing of the Red Sea, contains the oldest midrashic material known to us. Much, especially in Mekilta on Exod. xiv, xv, comes from a period after the fall of the temple in A.D. 70, when there was live discussion between the Church and the Synagogue.[2] It is, therefore, not inconceivable that the account of the crossing of the Red Sea has been

[1] Exodus Rabbah on xiv. 15 (Soncino translation, pp. 264 ff.). See also J. Daniélou, *Sacramentum Futuri* (1950), *ad rem*.

[2] A. Guttmann, *The Hebrew Union College Annual*, xx (1947), 363 ff., points out that there was a sudden change in the attitude taken towards the *bath qôl* in Judaism, probably as a reaction against Christian emphasis upon it. The famous halakic controversy between the Houses of Hillel and of Shammai was resolved by the advent of a *bath qôl*, probably shortly after A.D. 70. But this poses a problem. Why did the *bath qôl*, which immediately after A.D. 70 could play a crucial part in settling one of the most important problems of Jewish unity, cease to exert any further influence on the development of the Law? Guttmann, following Goodspeed, refers to the upsurge of Pauline influence between A.D. 90 and 100 as witnessed in the emergence of the Pauline corpus. He connects with this an awakening on the part of rabbinic leaders to the menace of Christianity. One result of this awakening was the rejection of the *bath qôl* in halakic discussions, in favour of majority decision, because of its popularity with Christians. One may question the necessity of connecting Pauline Christianity specifically with this rejection; Christian forces in general may have been responsible. That the Christian tradition was consciously opposed seems clear. See below, pp. 272 ff.

modelled in conscious opposition or parallelism to the baptism of Jesus—
the birth of the old Israel being set over against the birth of the new. This
parallelism is accentuated to the detriment of the latter. The figure of the
dove is confiscated for Israel as a people, what connotations of a new
creation it may have had being ignored. Instead of a comparatively simple
opening of the heavens, the whole angelic hosts, 'squadrons upon
squadrons of ministering angels' appear; no mere *bath qôl* or 'heavenly
voice' speaks but the Holy Spirit itself 'calls aloud from heaven'.[1] Moreover, a directly polemical note seems to be introduced in Mekilta on
Exod. xv. 2 which has not been noticed. It reads:

This is My God and I Will Glorify Him. R. Eliezer says: When can you say that
a maidservant saw at the sea what Isaiah and Ezekiel and all the prophets never
saw? It says about them: 'And by the ministry of the prophets have I used
similitudes' [Hos. xii. 11]. And it is also written: 'The heavens were opened
and I saw visions of God' [Ezek. i. 1]. To give a parable for this, to what is this
like? To the following: A king of flesh and blood enters a province surrounded
by a circle of guards: his heroes stand to the right of him and to the left of him;
his soldiers are before him and behind him. And all the people ask, saying:
'Which one is the king?' Because he is of flesh and blood like those who
surround him. But, when the Holy One, blessed be He, revealed Himself at the
sea, no one had to ask: 'Which one is the king?' But as soon as they saw Him
they recognized Him, and they all opened their mouths and said: 'This is my
God and I will glorify Him.'

In short, God himself was seen at work at the crossing of the sea. The
thought here applied to the Exodus is similar to that applied in Matt. xiii.
17 (=Luke x. 23–4) to the ministry of Jesus. 'Truly, I say to you, many
prophets and righteous men longed to see what you see, and did not see it,
and to hear what you hear, and did not hear it' (cf. 1 Pet. i. 10 f.). If we
set the above passage from the Mekilta over against Christian emphasis on
the fulfilment of prophecy in Jesus, which would naturally be contradicted
by Jewish leaders, we may well understand that R. Eliezer's dictum is
designed to belittle the argument from prophecy. Anything the prophets
ever saw was inferior to what the simplest maidservant saw at the Exodus,
that is, the presence of God himself. This rabbi we know had had relationships with Christians at least in his early days and was actually charged
with heresy on this account, while his wife could quote a saying of Jesus![2]

[1] Mekilta, *ad rem.*
[2] Tos. Hul. ii. 24; TB Abodah Zarah 16*b*; TB Shabbath 116*a–b*; R. T. Herford,
Christianity in Talmud and Midrash, pp. 338, 142; J. Klausner, *Jesus of Nazareth*,
pp. 37–44. Weiss, *Dor Dor*, 11, p. 87, suggests that it was perhaps their knowledge

In view of all this we need not cavil at using the Mekilta in the exposition of Matthew, as we have done above.

(2) A second difficulty in finding in the baptism of Jesus that of the representative of the New Israel may, at first sight at least, be found in the verses which seem to precede the actual baptism, although in fact Matthew intends them probably to be an actual part of the baptismal event. Peculiar to Matthew, they read:

Then Jesus came from Galilee to the Jordan to John, to be baptized by him. John would have prevented him, saying, 'I need to be baptized by you, and do you come to me?' But Jesus answered him, 'Let it be so now; for thus it is fitting for us to fulfil all righteousness.' Then he consented.... (Matt. iii. 13–15.) (RSV.)

Although it is entirely probable that it was the Baptist's custom, as it was of those who administered Jewish proselyte baptism,[1] to inquire of candidates their motives in presenting themselves and their readiness for baptism, and that, possibly, after such an inquiry in the case of Jesus, the Baptist should desire to exchange places with the baptized, nevertheless, most scholars, probably rightly, have preferred to see here a reflection of a Christological dilemma in the early Church. Why did the Sinless One undergo a baptism which required the confession of sin? It may be argued that, whether reflecting history or *Gemeindetheologie*, this question reveals an atomistic or individualistic approach to the baptism of Jesus which is incompatible with the concept of the solidarity of the Messiah with 'Israel', which the understanding of the baptism propounded above presupposes, and that it also follows that Matthew, who has preserved this section, was unaware of this 'solidarity', so that any thoughts of a New Exodus were far from his mind in his treatment of Jesus' baptism. But, while the Baptist's question reveals a context of 'individualism' alien to the milieu which conceived of the King-Messiah as one with his people, the answer to it reveals that Matthew was aware of the

of his associations with Christians that made other rabbis oppose R. Eliezer; A. Edersheim, *The Life and Times of Jesus of Nazareth*, vol. XI, pp. 193–4; H. J. Schoeps, *Theologie und Geschichte des Judenchristentums*, p. 24.

[1] TB Yebamoth 47 *ab*. Montefiore notes that since the commandments used as illustrations are mainly agricultural and precede even the sabbath 'one is inclined to assign an early date to the material contained in this passage', *A Rabbinic Anthology* (1938), pp. 578; see O. Cullmann, *Revue d'Histoire et de Philosophie Religieuses*, XVII (1937), pp. 424–34, and also in *The Earliest Christian Confessions* (1949), pp. 19 f.; J. Jeremias, *Die Kindertaufe in den ersten vier Jahrhunderten* (1958), pp. 34 ff.; D. Daube, *The New Testament and Rabbinic Judaism* (1956), pp. 106–40.

identification of the Messiah with his people, because the phrase 'to fulfil all righteousness' at least means the identification of Jesus with the New Israel, that John's baptism had proleptically inaugurated. In fulfilling the demand of God, which he himself expounded in Matt. v–vii, he had to know himself as one with his own.[1] In this Jesus is like Moses. Nothing is more clear in the Exodus story than the identification of Moses with the people of Israel and, at the same time, his moral transcendence over them, which, nevertheless, so far from securing for him a treatment different from theirs, demands of him the readiness to die on their behalf. Solidarity is of the essence of the Exodus story.[2] And it is that same 'solidarity' that informs those frequent discussions among the rabbis as to whether sinful Israelites were to participate in the benefits of the virtuous: 'solidarity' saw to it that they were.[3]

We can now draw our conclusions concerning the baptism of Jesus himself. They are similar to those on the rest of the activity of the Baptist. The last comparison with Moses must be regarded as strictly illustrative. The motif of a New Moses, it would seem, is not present either implicitly or explicitly. It may be argued that the New Exodus motif is implicit in the baptism of Jesus as in the whole of the Baptist's activity, Jesus as King-Messiah and Servant identified with, and representative of, a New Israel undergoes a New Baptism corresponding to that of the first Exodus. Explicit, however, this is not. It can be held to be present on the ground that the language used by the evangelists *evokes* such a motif. But this evocativeness cannot but be variously assessed, and by some it can, quite legitimately, be dismissed outright as an imposition on the text. Even for those who do find the language used in the baptismal account evocative, the suspicion is insidious that this evocativeness may not be indigenous to the Gospel, but, if we may so express it, epigonous. The wealth of Exodus motifs employed by the Church Fathers may have influenced the interpretation of subsequent exegetes and lent to the text of

---

[1] G. Bornkamm, 'Enderwartung und Kirche im Matthäusevangelium', in *Studies in Honour of C. H. Dodd* (1956), p. 246, connects iii. 15, 'to fulfil all righteousness', with xi. 29—'the meekness and lowliness' of Christ is expressed in his readiness to participate in John's baptism. With this agrees Jesus' interpretation of the Law, 'I desire mercy and not sacrifice' (ix. 13; xii. 7). 'Die πραΰτης des Messias und seine Barmherzigkeit gegenüber den Geringen, beides als Erfüllung aller Gerechtigkeit, durchzeicht das Evangelium des Matth. bis hin zu der Weltgerichtschilderung (xxv. 31 ff.), in der der Menschensohn die Geringsten seine Brüder nennt' (p. 247). C. E. B. Cranfield, *op. cit.* p. 52.

[2] Exod. xxxii. 30 ff.

[3] See *P.R.J.*[2] pp. 268 f.

the Gospels a spurious evocativeness foreign to the evangelists' intent.[1] In any case, there is nothing to indicate that Matthew has emphasized the Exodus motif in any way, if such was present.

(ii) *The Temptation of Jesus* (Mark i. 12–13; Matt. iv. 1–11; Luke iv. 1–13)

That Jesus is to be regarded in relation to the people of Israel, not with Moses as such, would appear to be the case also in this section. Here it has been claimed that Matthew has introduced the New Exodus motif. It is here noteworthy that while in the later treatment of the Exodus in Midrash Rabbah, the power of the demon of Egypt is destroyed at, or immediately before, the crossing of the Red Sea, a view which is reflected in the Church Fathers,[2] in the earlier Mekilta, which we have already found to be the most pertinent for our purpose, this is not mentioned. So too in the Synoptics Satan is very much alive after the baptism of Jesus.[3] And the first temptation to which he subjected Jesus in Matt. iv. 3 f. has been understood in the light of the giving of the manna in the wilderness in Exod. xvi. 4 ff. The Messianic Age, among other things, was expected to reproduce the characteristics of the time of Moses, which had been marked by the gift of the manna, and Jesus, who is at the same time Messiah and New Moses, is here tempted by Satan to reproduce the miracle of the giving of the manna by turning stones to bread. In confirmation of this Mosaic reference, it is pointed out that in Matt. iv. 2 Jesus is made to fast forty days and forty nights, as was the case with Moses on Mount Sinai in Exod. xxxiv. 28. The Mosaic motif, if it be proven, occurs only in Matthew. With the Marcan temptation narrative, which may reveal an Adamic motif,[4] Matthew has little in common. Similarly, while he shares with Luke in imaginative, midrashic expansions on the temptation, probably drawn from Q, Matthew goes his own way in introducing a clear reference to the manna. This is held on the basis of what is taken as

[1] The evidence of the Fathers is presented in J. Daniélou, *Sacramentum Futuri* (1950), pp. 131–76. It can certainly be said that the Exodus typology employed in the Old Testament (Daniélou, *ibid.* pp. 131 ff.) is much more *explicit* than anything found in Matthew's account of the baptism of John (see, for example, Hos. ii. 14–15; Isa. xliii. 16–20, etc.).

[2] Tertullian, *On Baptism*, chapter IX: 'The nations are set free from the world by means of *water*, to wit: and the devil, their old tyrant, they leave quite behind, overwhelmed in the *water*.' See Daniélou, *op. cit.* pp. 154 f.

[3] C. K. Barrett, *The Holy Spirit and the Gospel Tradition* (1947), p. 52.

[4] J. Jeremias, *T.W.Z.N.T.* I, 141; *P.R.J.*[2] pp. 42 f.; contrast Cranfield, *op. cit.* p. 60; compare P. Carrington, *According to St Mark* (1960), p. 36.

a significant difference between Matt. iv. 3 and Luke iv. 3, between 'If you are the Son of God, command these *stones*[1] (plural) to become loaves of bread', and '...this *stone* (singular) to become bread'. Whereas in Luke Jesus is merely asked to satisfy his own hunger, in Matthew, the plural form 'stones' implies that he is commanded to perform a miracle corresponding to the production of the manna in the wilderness, that is, to introduce the eschatological conditions on the pattern of the Mosaic.[2]

But the difficulties in this view are formidable.

(1) The fast for forty days and forty nights has other parallels in the Old Testament, for example, Elijah fasted thus on his way to Mount Horeb (1 Kings xix. 8). This is probably the meaning of the verse, although there is no explicit reference to a deliberate fast. Elijah's journey to Horeb was possibly in imitation of that of Moses.[3] But the number forty is a traditional stereotype for which there are many parallels, and need not be pinned down specifically to Moses' experience, which, in any case, occurred, not in the wilderness as such, but on Mount Sinai.

(2) While it should readily be admitted, in discussions of such a passage as this, that precision in the details of typology or exactitude in parallelism is not to be forced, nevertheless, to find in the turning of stones into bread by Jesus a counterpart to God's gift of the manna from heaven carries imprecision too far. While in the light of John vi. 32, where Jesus denies that it was Moses who gave the bread from heaven, and in other Jewish sources, it is clear that Judaism recognized Moses as the giver or creator of the manna, nevertheless, nowhere is there any suggestion that the manna was converted from stones. It was a gift *from above*, and the Mekilta[4] emphasizes its supra-terrestrial origin. Perhaps it should also be noted that had Matthew intended the temptation to be that of presenting a proof of Jesus' Messiahship by the repetition of the miracle of the

---

[1] J. Schniewind, *Das Evangelium nach Matthäus* (1956), pp. 28 f., especially emphasized the 'Messias-Zeit = Mose-Zeit' motif in the Temptation. The forty days in the wilderness correspond to the forty days of Moses on Sinai (Exod. xxxiv. 28). Note, however, that, although Moses is alone with God on Sinai for this length of time, there is no explicit reference to his fasting: Jesus' fast is specifically mentioned in Matthew and Luke. J. Schmid, *Das Evangelium nach Matthäus* (1956), p. 63, rejects the view that the plural 'stones' in Matthew is a clear reference to the 'reproduction' in the Messianic Age of the manna. [2] J. Schniewind, *ibid.*

[3] See M. Buber, *Moses* (New York, 1958), p. 112. So Professor Muilenburg, orally: Elijah renews the Covenant.

[4] The manna came down from above; see Mekilta on Exod. xvi. 11–15. J. Jeremias, *T.W.Z.N.T.* IV, 872, finds that Jesus' refusal to turn the stones to bread proves at least that he was himself aware of the Moses/Messiah typology in popular expectation.

manna, he would hardly have placed it in the wilderness in circumstances where there was no one to witness the miracle.[1] Matthew surely understands this temptation, as does Luke, who makes this clear by the use of the singular, 'stone', in terms of Jesus' hunger, not of his 'supernatural' power, as a New Moses. The quotation from Deut. viii. 3 in Matt. iv. 4 (and Luke iv. 4), as the other quotations from Deut. vi. 13, 16 and Ps. xci. 11, 12, and Deut. viii. 15–16 in the other temptations, suggest that, if there is symbolism in the narrative at all, Jesus is best understood as representing the Israel of God, who undergoes in his own experience, the trials of the Old Israel, to whom the words quoted are addressed in the Old Testament.[2] The designation of Jesus as the Son of God would reinforce this because that phrase is peculiarly rare in Judaism as applied to the Messiah, but frequent as applied to Israel.[3]

(3) If it be urged that the temptation narrative in Matthew as in all the Synoptics must be interpreted in close connexion with the activity of the Baptist, and that this last was determined by the expectation that the New Age, to be introduced by the stronger one, was inaugurated in a wilderness, meant to correspond to that which witnessed the activity of Moses, it still remains true that the emphasis in the Old Testament was not on the temptation of Moses but on that of the people. This is particularly so in the actual giving of the manna in Exod. xvi. 4 f.: 'that I may prove them, whether they will walk in my law or not'.

---

[1] Schmid, op. cit.

[2] Schniewind, op. cit. p. 29; contrast Schmid, op. cit. p. 65, 'Für den eigentlichen Inhalt der ganzen Versuchung dagegen bietet das A.T. kein wirkliches Vorbild', although he does refer the 'situation' to the influence of Exod. xxxiv. 28—the forty days of Moses on Sinai and the wandering in the wilderness for forty years. This last is insisted on strongly by J. Guillet, Thèmes Bibliques (1951), p. 23, who adds an additional point of comparison to those mentioned above. 'De même qu' Israël après avoir été choisi par Yahweh comme son fils [Exod. iv. 22], fut conduit au désert par une colonne de feu, c'est à dire, selon une interprétation consacrée en Israël, par l'esprit saint de Yahweh [Isa. lxiii. 11, 14] pour y être, durant quarante ans, tenté [Deut. viii. 2], de même aussi Jésus, le fils de Dieu bien aimé [Matt. xiii. 17] est poussé au désert par l'Esprit qui vient de se révéler au Jourdain, afin d'y subir sa tentation' (p. 23). But it is doubtful if the references to the Spirit in Isa. lxiii. 11, 14 can be understood in terms of a 'temptation': there the Spirit gives Israel 'rest' not 'temptation'. However, there can be no question that in Matt. iv. 1 ff. the temptation of Jesus is closely associated with the Spirit: the πειρασθῆναι is purposive (compare Deut. viii. 15–16). But the point of this is not to draw any parallel with the experience of the Old Israel but to designate the temptation as of divine origin; see M.-A. Chevalier, L'Esprit et le Messie (1958); so Schmid, op. cit. p. 62.

[3] See O. Cullmann, The Christology of the New Testament, Eng. trans. (1959), pp. 273 f.

In the light of all this it is precarious to find even in the Matthaean version of the Temptation any convincing parallel between Jesus and Moses, although Jesus does re-enact the experience of the 'Son of God', the Old Israel.[1]

(iii) *The Feeding of the Five Thousand* (Mark vi. 30–44; Matt. xiv. 13–21; Luke ix. 10–17)

Readiness to see in this a New Moses motif is natural, because in John vi. 25 ff. the event is explicitly understood, at the same time, as the counterpart of and as the antithesis to the gift of the manna under Moses, so that we might expect Matthew and the other Synoptics to reveal the same awareness of the theme: 'as the first redeemer, so the last'. But there is no explicit evidence for this and much that would suggest the opposite. Thus (1) the geographic vagueness of the Synoptics does not suggest any deliberate parallel between a feeding in the wilderness and the Exodus story of the manna. Luke is so careless in his details that he makes Jesus take the crowds into Bethsaida, as if that were the scene of the feeding (Luke ix. 10), and later refers to the place as 'a lonely place' (Luke ix. 12). Clearly the wilderness as such it is not his concern to emphasize. Mark and Matthew also do not speak of 'the desert' but only vaguely of 'a lonely place' (Mark vi. 32; Matt. xiv. 13). They are both apparently equally unconcerned to make plain any parallelism with the wilderness of the

---

[1] J. Daniélou, *Sacramentum Futuri*, pp. 135 ff., draws out the parallels that we have merely indicated above. The second temptation, Matt. iv. 7, is set in the light of Deut. vi. 16 and Exod. xvii. 1—the 'putting to the proof' of God at Massah and Meribah, an event which is also recalled in the quotation from Ps. xci. 11–13 in Matt. iv. 6. The third temptation, on the Mountain, to which Jesus replies in the words of the Decalogue from Exod. xx. 5; Deut. v. 9 (vi. 13), refers us directly to Mount Sinai. But this is hardly likely. D. Daube has more correctly pointed out the probable derivation of this scene from Jewish law, dealing with the transfer of land, see *Studies in Biblical Law* (1947), pp. 35 ff.: 'with the notion of transfer of ownership (of land) by one party offering and pointing out the object and the other accepting and seeing it'. If there is a parallel of any kind intended between Jesus and Moses on the Mountain of the third temptation, the reference is not to Moses on Sinai, but on Mount Nebo, Deut. xxxiv. 1 ff., compare iii. 7. We might then find here a contrast: Moses saw what he desired and could not possess it; Jesus did not desire what he saw and could possess it. There is, however, no suggestion of a temptation of Moses either on Sinai or Nebo or Pisgah (Daube, *op. cit.* pp. 24 ff.). The difficulty is that subjectivity plays such a great part in the interpretations mentioned above. Thus A. Schlatter, *Der Evangelist Matthäus* (1929), pp. 95–112, finds the motif of a second Adam, not of a New Moses, in the Temptation narratives. It is doubtful if the New Moses motif as such should be read into the Temptation narratives at all.

Exodus. Moreover (2) one point seems to be noted by the Synoptics, which directly opposes any exact correspondence with the manna. In the Old Testament strict injunctions were given that the manna was not to be hoarded (Exod. xvi. 19 f.), but in the Synoptics care is taken to gather up all the crumbs left after the feeding (Matt. xiv. 20 and parallels in Mark and Luke). And, (3) finally, there is no real parallel to the relation of Moses and Israel to that of Jesus and the crowds. Jesus has sought to escape the latter, who have followed him: there is here no deliberate exodus of the people to the wilderness under the leadership of a New Moses (the search for a place of rest for the weary disciples can hardly be called such) (Mark vi. 31). Nevertheless, these three factors are all present in John vi. 1–14—thus the feeding there takes place in the hills (vi. 3), the crumbs are picked up as in the Synoptics (vi. 12). Jesus is not a New Moses instigating an Exodus like the Moses of old, rather he suffers from the importunities of those whom he does not want to lead (vi. 15). And yet all these elements do not prevent John from presenting Jesus after the image of the first Moses, even though in contrast to him, and the same might well be true of the Synoptics. While there can be little doubt that the feeding of the five thousand in the Synoptics is an act anticipatory of the Eucharist and of the Messianic banquet to come,[1] this also has undertones of the New Exodus motifs since manna was food for the Messianic meal of the future in Jewish expectation along with Leviathan (which *may* be represented in the fishes of Matt. xiv. 17, etc.).[2] But certainly Matthew reveals no accentuation of any such motifs. In fact by omitting Mark vi. 34 at this point, which echoes passages such as Num. xxvii. 17; Ezek. xxxv. 4; Isa. lxiii. 11 (LXX), it might be argued that Matthew has rejected an element which might be taken to point to a New Moses (although the figure of a 'shepherd' is not exclusively, and not even mainly, Mosaic in Judaism: it is more often employed of God and the Messiah).[3]

[1] A. Schweitzer, *The Quest of the Historical Jesus, ad rem*; for bibliographical details, but with no reference to the problem of any possible Exodus motifs, see Taylor, *op. cit. ad rem.* pp. 321–6. Neither Schniewind, Schmid nor Lohmeyer dwells on Exodus motifs here.

[2] Mekilta on Exod. xvi. 33.

[3] *T.W.Z.N.T.* vi, 486 ff. The omission of Mark vi. 34 is the more striking because elsewhere Matthew makes use of the shepherd motif, for example x. 6; xv. 24; xviii. 12–14; xxv. 32; xxvi. 31 f.

(iv) *The Transfiguration* (Mark ix. 2–8; Matt. xvii. 1–8; Luke ix. 28–36)

Here we find a more tangible indication of Matthew's interest in the Exodus motif. All three of the Synoptic accounts have been claimed to present Jesus in the light of the Exodus and of the first Moses at this point. In the Marcan account, which lies behind Matthew, the following have been alleged as indications of this:[1]

(*a*) In ix. 2 the phrase 'after six days' is symbolic. As in Exod. xxiv. 16 Moses was commanded by the Lord to build the Tabernacle, so the three who accompany Jesus on the Mount of Transfiguration are led after six days to build tents (ix. 5).

(*b*) The voice of God is uttered from the midst of the cloud (Exod. xxiv. 15 ff. and Mark ix. 7), just as the command came to Moses on a mountain covered by 'the cloud'.

(*c*) Just as in Exod. xxiv. 1 f. Moses is accompanied by a small group, Aaron, Nadab, Abihu, and the seventy elders, while the people as a whole are kept at the foot of the mountain, so Jesus is accompanied by Peter, James and John, while the rest of the disciples and the crowds remain below. On Sinai, Moses alone, and on the Mount of Transfiguration, Jesus alone, holds converse with the Lord, or is in intimacy of fellowship with the Unseen.

(*d*) Noteworthy is it that the two figures, who appear along with Jesus on the Mount, are those of two men who had held discourse with God on Mount Sinai: Moses in Exod. xxxiii. 17 ff., and Elijah in 1 Kings xix. 9–13. They now appear, so we are perhaps meant to think, on a New Sinai.

(*e*) The radiance of Moses on his descent from Mount Sinai (Exod. xxxiv. 29 ff.) may be recalled in Mark ix. 2 'and he was transfigured before them and his garments became glistening, intensely white, as no fuller on earth could bleach them'.

(*f*) In Mark ix. 7 the command is issued to obey Jesus, even as Moses was obeyed. The verse may recall Deut. xviii. 15, Jesus being the prophet like unto Moses.

The emphasis in Mark does not lie there. The mere fact that Mark alone places Elijah before Moses indicates this. Briefly, the Transfiguration scene in Mark is probably best understood in relation to Mark's emphasis on the Passion, which has preceded it. Jesus, destined to suffer, neverthe-

[1] On all that follows, see A. Feuillet, *Biblica*, XXXIX (1958), 281–301; J. Daniélou, *op. cit.*; P. Dabeck, 'Siehe es erscheinen Moses und Elias', in *Biblica*, XXIII (1942); J. Jeremias, *T.W.Z.N.T.* IV, 868–78.

less, at the Transfiguration, is proclaimed as Messiah, Servant, Son of Man: the proclamation at the Baptism is now enhanced—Jesus is Son of Man after the manner of the Book of Daniel. Thus the Transfiguration looks forward in Mark both to the Passion and the Resurrection. This appears from the insistence on the Cross of the Son of Man (ix. 12); the priority given to Elijah, who is identified with the Baptist, whose death was a premonition of that of Jesus himself (ix. 12); the similarity between the Transfiguration and the Agony in Gethsemane, in that the witnesses of both are identical (ix. 2; xiv. 33); and the metamorphosis of Jesus in ix. 2 which looks forward to the glory of the Resurrection (xvi. 12) (cf. II Pet. i. 16–18). All this does not mean that the figure of Moses has not influenced Mark's account of the Transfiguration. Clearly Jesus is both distinguished from Moses, who along with Elijah testifies by his presence to him, and also set in parallelism to him, as the prophet like unto him. Nevertheless, even in this parallelism there may be a distinction: the content of the teaching of Jesus in Mark ix. 30–2 is the suffering of the Son of Man, not ethical commandments. (But these, though not expressly mentioned, should not perhaps be excluded from the provenance of 'Hear ye Him' so that this last point cannot be pressed.) In any case not as 'Mosaic' teacher but as suffering and triumphant Lord, does Mark present Jesus in the Transfiguration.

We may now ask how Matthew has dealt with Mark's account? We have to notice significant changes in details and in order.

(a) He alters Mark's order by referring to Moses before referring to Elijah (xvii. 3). This is not a triviality. It at least means that no priority of significance is given to Elijah, as in Mark, and, probably, that the reference to Moses is to be taken as emphatic.

(b) While Mark only refers to 'the garments of Jesus', which became glistening, intensely white 'as no fuller on earth could bleach them' (Mark ix. 3), Matthew adds: 'and his face shone like the sun' (xvii. 2). This recalls Exod. xxxiv. 29–35, where the Hebrew reads: 'the skin of [Moses'] face shone' because he had been talking to God (כִּי קָרַן עוֹר פָּנָיו). Matthew does not quote either the Massoretic text or the Septuagint exactly (the LXX reads: 'the appearance of the skin of his face was glorified', δεδόξα-σται ἡ ὄψις τοῦ χρώματος τοῦ προσώπου αὐτοῦ, which is an attempt at 'refinement' or 'spiritualization'), so that there is no direct verbal allusion to Exod. xxxiv. 29. It is difficult, for example, to understand why Matthew, did he have a direct reference to that passage in mind, has omitted all reference to the 'skin', unless he too is governed by a concern for an even greater refinement than the LXX. Nevertheless, Matthew does bring out the essential force of the Hebrew text. The shining on Moses' face was so unendurable, so the Exodus story implies, that Moses in his converse with the people had to put a veil over it. So Matthew probably intends us to understand the phrase 'like the sun' the vision of which is also unendurable. There is no midrashic or haggadic ornamentation of the phenomenon in Matthew, as in the rabbis.[1] One fact only concerns him, that on the face of Jesus is seen the glory of the mediator of the Law, Moses (and this in later rabbinic tradition is none other than the glory of the Law itself).

(c) In describing 'the cloud' that appears, Matthew uses the same verb as Mark and Luke, ἐπισκιάζειν. But he adds a significant adjective. The cloud is a 'bright' cloud (νεφέλη φωτεινὴ ἐπεσκίασεν αὐτούς): thus he expresses a paradox, a bright light *overshadows*. Can we detect why he adds this adjective? Is it not to make it beyond doubt that he has the Shekinah in mind, that presence of the Lord which used to fill the tabernacle in the wilderness, and which was often connected with depths of light 'more intense than the midsummer sun'?

(d) The climax of the story is particularly instructive in Matthew. First, the declaration 'This is my beloved (ὁ ἀγαπητός) son, with whom I am well pleased' (ἐν ᾧ εὐδόκησα) in Matt. xvii. 5 is significantly different from Mark ix. 35: 'This is my beloved Son', and from Luke: 'This is my Son, my Chosen' (ὁ ἐκλελεγμένος). Mark and Luke look back mainly to Ps. ii. 7, whereas Matthew here, as in the account of Jesus' baptism, refers both to Ps. ii. 7 and Isa. xlii. 1. 'Behold, my servant, whom I uphold, my chosen, in whom my soul delights...' (LXX: 'Israel is my chosen (ἐκλεκτός), my soul has accepted him' (προσεδέξατο αὐτὸν ἡ ψυχή μου)). Matthew seems to have added the phrase 'with whom I am well pleased' to signify Jesus as the one who was destined to bring his law to the nations (Isa. xlii. 4) (וּלְתוֹרָתוֹ אִיִּים יְיַחֵלוּ). Taken in isolation this suggestion cannot be pressed because the phrase 'with whom I am well pleased' is not a direct quotation of Isa. xlii. 1; but, on the other hand, other elements in the climax might support it. Thus, secondly, the final utterance of the Voice from heaven is a command to obey Jesus as God's Son. In Matthew there can be little doubt on *a priori* grounds that this points to Jesus as an ethical teacher, like Moses. Thus while the content of Jesus' teaching in Mark ix. 30–2 is explicitly stated as the suffering of the Son of Man, and this receives

---

[1] See Midrash Rabbah on Exod. xxxiv. 28 f. (Soncino translation, p. 541); and L. Ginzberg in *The Legends of the Jews, ad rem.*

adequate recognition in Luke ix. 43*b*–45, Matthew, although he knows of the significance of the Passion, has so softened and shortened his reference to it in xvii. 22–3, that he has robbed it of its total pre-eminence. A comparison of the passages puts this beyond doubt:

Matt. xvii. 22–3:

As they were gathering in Galilee, Jesus said to them, 'The Son of man is to be delivered into the hands of men, and they will kill him, and he will be raised on the third day.' And they were greatly distressed.

Mark ix. 30–2:

They went on from there and passed through Galilee. And he would not have any one know it; for he was teaching his disciples, saying to them, 'The Son of man will be delivered into the hands of men, and they will kill him; and when he is killed, after three days he will rise.' But they did not understand the saying, and they were afraid to ask him.

Luke ix. 43*b*–45:

But while they were all marvelling at everything he did, he said to his disciples, 'Let these words sink into your ears; for the Son of man is to be delivered into the hands of men.' But they did not understand this saying, and it was concealed from them, that they should not perceive it; and they were afraid to ask him about this saying. (RSV.)

In a similar spirit, it would seem that Matthew, after relating the Transfiguration, cannot quickly enough get to the discourse section, giving teaching of Jesus, in xvii. 24–xviii. 35: he is concerned not primarily with the Passion motif after the Transfiguration, but with the 'teaching' of Jesus (although he follows Mark too faithfully to omit that motif altogether, because it was too well fixed in the tradition here to be ignored). The 'Hear ye him' of xvii. 5 both looks backward to v–vii and forward to xvii. 5—xviii. 35. And it is possible, and even probable, that we should understand the phrase in the light of Deut. xviii. 15: 'The Lord shall raise up for you a prophet like me from among you, from your brethren—him shall ye heed' (compare xviii. 15) (LXX: αὐτοῦ ἀκούσεσθε); the future tense has become a present tense. But, thirdly, while Moses' figure informs so much in the Transfiguration scene, it is also no less surely being superseded. At the last, Moses and Elijah disappear and Jesus remains alone. This fact, common to all the Synoptics, is specifically emphasized by Matthew. The reading of ℵ, B, θ, 700 is to be accepted here, that is, αὐτὸν Ἰησοῦν μόνον, that is, Jesus himself alone, the 'himself' being emphatic in Matthew and absent in Mark and Luke. Jesus for Matthew has become the teacher unique, the 'New Moses'. And, finally, it is important to note a change that Matthew has introduced in the order of the material at this point, in a section far too summarily dismissed by most commentators. Mark places the 'awe' felt by the disciples early in the narrative, immediately after the transfiguration of Jesus and the vision vouchsafed to them of Elijah and Moses—in that order—with him. Not the fact that he was to command, but that he was 'transfigured', is emphasized. Luke makes the descent of 'the cloud' the cause for fear (ix. 34b). With Matthew it is otherwise. He reserves the expression of 'awe' in Peter and James and John till immediately after the words 'Hear ye him'. And it is such 'awe' as fells them to the ground: in token of their veneration they fall on their faces to the earth, as was customary in epiphanies (see Gen. xvii. 3, Abraham before God; 1 Sam. xxiv. 9, David before Saul; 2 Sam. ix. 6, Mephibosheth, son of Jonathan, before David; Dan. x. 9, Daniel before 'one in the likeness of the sons of men'). And the final item in the complex is that Jesus touches the disciples and says, 'Rise and have no fear'.

(This last is most frequently slurred over by commentators. The nearest linguistic parallels are between Dan. x. 7, 9 and xvii. 6. Dan. x. 6 (Theodotion) recalls xvii. 7,[1] and it may be that we should not emphasize the touching of the disciples as anything more than traditional in such scenes. But the total scene is not like that in Dan. x, where no 'cloud' is mentioned, but rather a vision. Perhaps in view of the descent of the 'bright cloud' upon them (the text of Luke ix. 34b makes it clear that the cloud overshadowed them all—Jesus, Elijah, Moses and the disciples— and this is implied in Matthew and Mark also) we should compare such scenes as Deut. xxxi. 1–8, 14 f., 23 and Deut. xxxiv. 9; Num. xxvii. 15 ff. (and possibly Num. xi. 16 ff.) where Moses ordained Joshua. There is an interesting distinction between the earlier and the later passages here. In Deut. xxxi. 1–8, 14 f., 23 Moses and Joshua convene in the 'tent of meeting'. In 14 f. and 23 we read:

And the Lord said to Moses, 'Behold, the days approach when you must die; call Joshua, and present yourselves in the tent of meeting, that I may commission him.' And Moses and Joshua went and presented themselves in the tent of meeting. And the Lord appeared in the tent in a pillar of cloud; and the pillar of cloud stood by the door of the tent.

---

[1] A. Feuillet, *op. cit.* p. 283, n. 1. At various points in the above I have followed Feuillet, whose article is most illuminating.

And the Lord commissioned Joshua the son of Nun and said, 'Be strong and of good courage; for you shall bring the children of Israel into the land which I swore to give them: I will be with you.' (RSV.)

The LXX in xxxi. 15 has 'And the Lord descended in a cloud' (καὶ κατέβη κύριος ἐν νεφέλη). The death of Moses is at hand, Joshua takes over his role. No mention is made of the precise method of 'ordination': Moses is not said to have laid his hand upon Joshua or to have touched him. But in Deut. xxxiv. 9 this is assumed:

And Joshua the Son of Nun was full of the spirit of wisdom for Moses *had laid his hands upon him*; so the people of Israel obeyed him, and did as the Lord had commanded Moses.

(The Hebrew for the words in italics is:

כִּי סָמַךְ מֹשֶׁה אֶת־יָדָיו עָלָיו

LXX=ἐπέθηκεν γὰρ Μωυσῆς τὰς χεῖρας αὐτοῦ ἐπ' αὐτόν.)

The process of 'ordination' is further elaborated in Num. xxvii. 18 ff. It is possible to suggest that Matt. xvii. 7, considered in the context of the Shekinah, and the proposed 'tents', may have undertones of a kind of 'ordination'.[1] Aware of his approaching death Jesus 'touches' his three disciples, transmits his authority to them, the authority they are allowed to exercise in Matt. xviii. 18 f., and all this takes place within the 'bright cloud'. In any case, nowhere else does Matthew have anything like a 'choice' or authorization of his disciples. There is no parallel to Mark iii. 13–19 and Luke vi. 12–16 in Matthew nor again to Luke x. 1 ff.: we only have a list of the Twelve introduced abruptly in x. 2–4. This can only be a very tentative suggestion, because to 'touch' (ἀψάμενος) cannot perhaps bear the weight that we have put upon it and is probably too generalized a term to be taken for 'the laying on of hands' even in intent.[2] Daube's treatment of 'ordination' (*op. cit.* pp. 224 ff.) makes it unlikely that this should be read into this passage, and we, therefore, bracket our discussion: but the possibility suggested has not been sufficiently noted.)

Our examination of the Transfiguration is over. Here more convincingly than in any other of the materials that we have so far examined

---

[1] E. Burrows in *The Labyrinth*, ed. S. H. Hooke (1935), pp. 43–70, and H. Riesenfeld, *Jésus Transfiguré* (1947), p. 276.

[2] On the question of ordination, see E. Lohse, *Die Ordination im Spätjudentum und im Neuen Testament* (1951). The idea associated with ἅπτω in such contexts as we are dealing with is that of healing and blessing (see Arndt–Gingrich, p. 102). In the 'call' of Isaiah ἅπτω (middle) is used of Isaiah's lips being '*touched*' to translate נגע.

Matthew seems to have altered and rearranged the material in Mark, not merely from motives of simple reverence (as in the use of 'Lord' in xvii. 4 rather than the *Rabbi* of Mark ix. 5, and the ἐπιστάτα, *Master*, of Luke ix. 33 and the addition of 'if you wish' in xvii. 4 instead of the less polite 'let us make' of Mark ix. 5), but with the deliberate purpose of presenting Jesus after the manner of Moses, albeit a Moses whom he supersedes as 'the unique and definitive teacher of mankind'. (It is this Mosaic, and yet more-than-Mosaic, character of Matthew's Jesus that lies behind the substitution of 'Lord' for 'rabbi' at xvii. 4).[1]

In addition to the passages dealt with above, there are others of lesser significance where the concept of a New Moses has been claimed to have influenced the tradition which Matthew has drawn from Q and Mark. Thus the scene in the wilderness in Matt. xi. 7 has been noted in this connexion. Just as the salvation wrought by Moses led through the wilderness, so that wrought by the New Moses, Jesus, is to take place there.[2] The force of this parallel, we reiterate, can be variously assessed.

[1] For a brief statement of attempts to understand the Transfiguration in terms of the Exodus, see H. Baltensweiler, *Die Verklärung Jesu* (1959), pp. 108 ff. He deals with D. F. Strauss's interpretation of the Transfiguration as a myth developed around Exod. xxiv and xxxiv. 29 f., 35: Strauss's position was furthered by E. Wendling in *Theologische Studien und Kritiken* (1911), pp. 117 f. Baltensweiler rightly allows an influence from the passages in Exodus but refuses to regard the Transfiguration as a pure invention, a myth concocted out of these. He treats the event in Mark ix. 2 f. as historical. His study of the Marcan material though subtle is convincing, but he does not seem to us to allow sufficient weight to the New Moses motif in the Matthaean presentation of the material. He does, however, make clear the Mosaic function which the Lord Jesus has in Matthew. In Matt. xvii. 4 Jesus is addressed as 'Lord': He stands over against the disciples (this explains the phrase 'if you wish' in xvii. 4 also), but he is Lord as the one who addresses them, whom they must hear as the New Moses. (See also Baltensweiler, *op. cit.* pp. 131 ff.)

[2] See P. Bonnard, 'La signification du désert selon le N.T.', in *Hommage à Karl Barth* (Neuchâtel, 1946), pp. 9 ff.; H. J. Schoeps, *Theologie und Geschichte des Judenchristentums* (1949), p. 94; J. Jeremias, *T.W.Z.N.T.* iv, 865; J. Daniélou, *op. cit.* pp. 131 ff. He compares Matt. xi. 4–6 with Isa. xxxv. 1–5; lxi. 1. Schoeps refers to R. Meyer, *Jesus, der Prophet aus Galilea* (Leipzig, 1940), pp. 27 f., but the reference to Lev. R. xviii. 4 on xv. 2 does not seem particularly pertinent. More convincing is a reference that Schoeps gives to Tanḥuma, *'Eqeb*, 7b. See also P. Dabeck, *op. cit.* Notice that G. Vermès, 'La figure de Moïse au tournant des deux Testaments', in *Cahiers Sioniens*, viiie année (1954), p. 79, finds an echo of this in Matt. xxiv. 25 f.: 'Lo, I have told you beforehand. So if they say to you, "Lo, he is in the wilderness"...', etc. This was the expected place for the appearance of a Messiah. Compare Kittel, *T.W.Z.N.T.* ii, p. 655. More important still is the work of McCown in 'The Scene of John's Ministry and its Relation to the Purpose and Outcome of his Mission', in *J.B.L.* LIX (1940), 122, and Funk, 'The Wilder-

That the term 'wilderness' must always surreptitiously, if not obviously, carry an undertone of the Exodus motif must surely be regarded as doubtful.[1] If this connotation does exist in Matt. xi. 7, Matthew certainly cannot be claimed to have emphasized it; he differs from Luke in no significant item, and is, primarily, if not wholly, concerned, while giving his due to the Baptist, to set him in true perspective, to honour him 'while he strikes him down'.[2]

Perhaps it is noteworthy that in the catena of 'signs' of the presence of the 'one who was to come' in Matt. xi. 5–6, while there is much that is reminiscent of Isa. xxxv. 5–6; lxi. 1, there is no reference to Isa. xxxv. 3–4; lxi. 2, both of which look forward to a future day of vengeance. This omission is deliberate: at this point the Jewish expectation is *not* fulfilled in Jesus. But there is no reference either to Isa. xxxv. 1–2, 6–7, where 'the wilderness and the dry land' are expected to become 'glad' in the days of the Messiah. Is the omission of such a reference also deliberate? Does it point to a rejection of the 'wilderness' as the necessary setting for the coming one, as John the Baptist may have thought it to have been? John, who had appeared in the wilderness, is declared to be less than the least in the new order (xi. 11 ff.). Certainly, if 'the wilderness' is treated with any emphasis at all here, in xi. 2–16, it is with a view to minimizing its significance. This understanding of the material is confirmed when we turn to xxiv. 26–8. The whole section xxiv. 23–8 reads as follows:

23 Then if any one (ἐάν τις) says to you (ὑμῖν), 'Lo, here is the Christ!' or 'There
24 he is!' do not believe it. For false Christs and false prophets will arise and show
25 great signs and wonders, so as to lead astray, if possible, even the elect. Lo, I

ness', in *J.B.L.* (1959), pp. 205–14. In both articles it is urged that ἔρημος stands for עֲרָבָה which had come to be the equivalent of מִדְבָּר, as used in Isa. xl. 3. Thus the wilderness around the Dead Sea could be identified with the wilderness of Sinai. 'That place, as actually *midhbar*, and as the end and climax of the long period of "wandering in the wilderness", would be taken as the surrogate of the whole' (McGown, *op. cit.* p. 127). See also W. H. Brownlee, *The Scrolls and the New Testament*, ed. K. Stendahl, p. 254, n. 2.

[1] Kittel in *T.W.Z.N.T. loc. cit.* sets the proper perspective. He recognizes both the necessity to treat the term ἔρημος naturally as a place where Jesus retired for peace and called his disciples to rest and as having, in some contexts, a Messianic significance. He rejects any parallelism between the Temptation of Jesus in the wilderness with Deut. viii. 2—the forty years of Israel in the wilderness—on the obvious ground that forty days and forty nights do not correspond to forty years (p. 655), though he recognizes that there *may* be a parallel to Moses' fast for forty days (Exod. xxxiv. 28; Deut. ix. 9, 18: but this was on Mount Sinai).

[2] See on this J. Jeremias, *Jesus' Promise to the Nations*, p. 45.

25–6 have told *you* (ὑμῖν) beforehand. So, if *they* say (εἴπωσιν) to *you* (ὑμῖν), 'Lo, he
is in the wilderness', do not go out; if *they* say, 'Lo, he is in the inner rooms'
27 (ἐν τοῖς ταμιείοις), do not believe it. For as the lightning comes from the east
28 and shines as far as the west, so will be the coming of the Son of man. Wherever
the body is, there the eagles will be gathered together. [Italics ours.]

Several significant factors emerge here. (1) Note the change in xxiv. 25–6
to the plural (they say) from the singular (any one says) in xxiv. 23,
and also the emphatic 'you' in xxiv. 25. '*They*' are set over against the
disciples, as a group. (2) This group is, by implication, characterized as
claiming that the Messiah is in the wilderness. This would fit the sect at
Qumran. The reference to the '*inner rooms*' (ἐν τοῖς ταμιείοις) is in parallelism with that to the wilderness. It has been variously interpreted, but
it may well be understood in terms of the caves and grottos surrounding
the headquarters at Qumran. (3) The assertion of the 'universal' nature
of the coming of the Son of Man in xxiv. 27, symbolized by the lightning
coming from the east to the west is a rebuttal of any 'localized' expectation
of the coming of the Messiah such as was cherished at Qumran. If there
be any validity in these points, then there is in Matthew a polemic against
the concentration in much of the contemporary Judaism on the 'wilderness' as the scene of the final salvation.[1]

Again reference is frequently made to Jesus' choice of 'Twelve'
disciples as evidence for a New Exodus motif.[2] The Twelve are noted in
all the Synoptics and in John and understood to symbolize the twelve
patriarchs of the Old Israel or its twelve tribes. But it is questionable
whether Matthew has in any way emphasized this symbolism. Thus
xix. 28 is not peculiar to Matthew, but has a parallel in Luke xxii. 28. The
absence of any parallel to the choice of the Twelve on a mountain in
Mark iii. 16 (=Luke vi. 12–16) might even suggest that Matthew was not
concerned to reveal a correspondence in this matter between the Old and
the New Israel, as does also his omission of any reference to the mission

---

[1] See B. Hjerl-Hansen, *Revue de Qumrân*, I, pp. 495 ff. (July 1959), on 'Did
Christ Know the Qumran Sect?'

[2] H. J. Schoeps, *Theologie und Geschichte des Judenchristentums*, p. 96; especially
A. M. Farrer, *A Study in St Mark*, who argues that the Exodus motif is very evident
in Mark; L. Rost, *Die Vorstufen von Kirche und Synagoge im Alten Testament*. On
the '70' in Luke and in the OT, see Schoeps, *ibid.* and G. Dix, in *The Apostolic
Ministry*, ed. by K. E. Kirk (New York, 1946). B. M. Metzger, *N.T.S.* (July 1959),
pp. 299–306, has exhaustively dealt with the textual problem in Luke: on the whole he
favours reading 72. On '70' and Moses, see especially pp. 303 ff.; S. Jellicoe (*N.T.S.*
(July 1960), p. 319), favours 72 also.

of the Seventy recorded in Luke x. 1, which has often been taken to recall the seventy elders chosen by Moses in the wilderness (Num. xi. 26). But, while this last is strange, if Matthew was concerned at all points to present a parallelism between the Old and the New Israel, the former point, namely, that there is no direct parallel to Mark iii. 16, must not be pressed, because Matt. x, although it introduces the Twelve without any solemn mountain scene, nevertheless does show that the Twelve were considered significant; their authorization is described in x. 2–4, and an express charge is given to them in x. 5–xi. 1, a long discourse which gives to the Twelve an important and dignified pre-eminence and the discussion on page 54 above is also to be recalled. It is doubtful, however, whether more can be claimed than that Matthew at least pays as much attention to the Twelve as do Mark and Luke; that he shows any peculiar emphasis on them is hardly proved.

Nor does Matthew's treatment of the Last Supper lend much support, if indeed any, to the view that he was concerned with the Exodus motif in a particular fashion. Whether that supper was a Passover meal or not, it is certain that Passover motifs entered into its understanding in the Church. And apart from certain liturgical improvements introduced by Matthew (for example, at xxvi. 26—τοῖς μαθηταῖς for αὐτοῖς; the change of καὶ ἔδωκεν αὐτοῖς καὶ εἶπεν· Λάβετε to καὶ δοὺς τοῖς μαθηταῖς εἶπεν Λάβετε, φάγετε; xxvi. 27 the addition of καί; the change of καὶ ἔπιον ἐξ αὐτοῦ πάντες to πίετε ἐξ αὐτοῦ πάντες; xxvi. 28 the addition of γάρ, etc.), Matthew has introduced a reference to 'the forgiveness of sins' in xxvi. 28, and the phrase 'with you' in xxvi. 29, and to the anticipation of the future feast in the Kingdom of God. The reference to 'the blood of the Covenant' in Mark xiv. 24 probably looks back to Exod. xxiv. 8; Matthew's addition of 'for the remission of sins' (a phrase which he omitted in describing the baptism of John) is probably intended to connect 'the blood of the covenant' with the New Covenant of Jer. xxxi. 31 f. But this both looks back in parallelism to the Exodus and also in distinction from it, so that the addition to Mark at this point does not necessarily point to an emphasis on the Exodus motif as such.

Other suggestions are also to be rejected. First, that in Matt. xxi. 1–9; Mark xi. 2–10; Luke xix. 30–8; John xii. 14–15 the ass on which Jesus rides into Jerusalem recalls not only Zech. ix. 9, but also Exod. iv. 20 ('So Moses took his wife and his sons and set them on an ass, and went back to the land of Egypt...'), that is, the Messianic ass of Zech. ix. 9 also signifies the Mosaic ass which took Moses to Egypt, so that the entry of

Jesus into Jerusalem suggests both Moses and Messiah.[1] But the rabbinic sources to which appeal is made in support of this, that is, Pirqe de Rabbi Eliezer 31; Yalqut, Zech. ix. 9, 575; Rashi on Exod. iv. 20 are too late to be convincing or pertinent evidence. The Septuagint does not indicate that any connexion was made between the two texts adduced. It renders Exod. iv. 20 thus: 'And Moses took his wife and his children, and mounted them on the beasts (ἐπὶ τὰ ὑποζύγια) and returned to Egypt'. On this passage Exod. R. comments: 'AND MOSES TOOK HIS WIFE AND HIS SONS (iv. 20). Why did he take them? To be with the Israelites when they received the Torah. AND SET THEM UPON AN ASS. This is one of the eighteen passages which the Sages changed [in their translation] for King Ptolemy.' Probably from motives of reverence, the translators wanted to avoid using the term 'ass'. But, surely, had this particular 'ass' acquired Messianic significance, squeamishness about the dignity of Moses on an ass would not have arisen. Moreover, had Matthew attached Messianic significance to the beast of Exod. iv. 20, we would have expected him to refer to it in ii. 20 f. where there is an echo of Exod. iv. 19. On the other hand, had he noticed any connexion between Zech. ix. 9 and Exod. iv. 20 he would not in xxi. 1–9 have misinterpreted the quotation from Zechariah, and out of one animal (a colt, the foal of an ass), made two, an ass and a colt (xxi. 2). But this use of the plural would be explicable if he was following the LXX, which, however, ascribed no Messianic significance to Exod. iv. 20.[2]

Again, secondly, a parallel has been drawn between the Beatitudes in Matt. v and the Woes in Matt. xxiii and the Blessings and Woes or Curses in Deut. xxvii, xxviii.[3] But neither in order, number, content nor audience is there here any real parallel. Curses and Blessings in Deuteronomy are invoked upon all Israel: in Matthew on the Pharisees and the 'New Israel' respectively; in Deuteronomy Curses and Blessings occur in close propinquity: in Matthew they are divided. Matt. vii. 24–7 does indeed offer a miniature parallel, of a loose kind, to Deut. xxvii, xxviii, but recourse to this parallelism is not necessary because Blessings and Curses were a common feature of first-century Judaism, rabbinic and sectarian.[4]

---

[1] H. J. Schoeps, *op. cit.* pp. 91 f.

[2] K. Stendahl, *The School of Matthew*, p. 119, thinks it unlikely that Matthew is 'the originator of the tradition of the two asses, verses 2 and 7, or that this was created on the basis of this quotation from Zechariah'. Do we need to go further than the LXX for Matthew's usage here?

[3] P. Dabeck, *op. cit.*

[4] See now DSD i. 16 ff.–ii. 18. The OT and rabbinic blessings are familiar.

The results of our survey of the material which Matthew shares with Mark and Q can now be drawn. Such New Exodus motifs as have been detected in these sources are preserved, though hardly emphasized, in Matthew. The 'New Moses' motif as such is more rare. In the baptism of Jesus and his temptation Jesus is not so much New Moses as the representative of the New Israel, who recapitulates in his experience that of the Old Israel. Nevertheless, in two places we are probably justified in detecting the lineaments of the New Moses, in the feeding of the thousands, where, however, his 'Mosaic' character is not particularly emphasized by Matthew, and in the Transfiguration scene, where this character can be regarded as deliberately developed by Matthew, Jesus being the one who replaces Moses as the one who is to be heard. The Mount of Transfiguration thus recalls the Mount from which Jesus proclaimed the Sermon in v–vii, and to this extent supports the interpretations of the Jesus of the Mount as a New Moses and a greater.

(b) The Material Peculiar to Matthew in Content and/or Arrangement

We now turn to those elements in his Gospel where Matthew has employed material peculiar to him or has so rearranged materials derived from Mark and Q, with which we have not dealt above, as to give to these, by their very rearrangement, a significance that they did not possess in the sources mentioned. Does Matthew, in this peculiar or rearranged material, reveal a concern with Jesus as a New Moses?

(i) The Prologue

Our obvious starting point is in the first two chapters, sometimes regarded as the Prologue to the Gospel, consisting of the genealogy, the account of 'The Virgin Birth', the visit of the Magi, the flight to Egypt, and the return thence.

As in the Old Testament so in the New the prologues to the various documents often illumine their contents.[1] This is true, for example, of the book of Job, where the Prologue is designed to make the reader aware of the reason for Job's suffering, even though it is hidden from the sufferer himself, and from those around him. So in the New Testament, the prologues of the Fourth Gospel and of Mark, on examination, explain the contents of the two Gospels as a whole, while the prologue of Luke explicitly states the author's aim. We might therefore expect this to be the

[1] R. H. Lightfoot, Locality and Doctrine in the Gospels, p. 113.

case with Matthew also. Indeed we might suspect that this would be pre-eminently true of this Gospel, because of its so emphatic schematic character. If so, it is likely that the Prologue may help us in seeking to understand the rest of the Gospel,[1] and in particular the nature of the *SM*: does the Prologue lend support to the view that the Mount is a New Sinai of a New Moses?

We shall here assume that the two chapters, Matt. i, ii, are an integral part of the Gospel, no mere patchwork of interpolated materials, but a unity wrought by the Evangelist.[2] On this assumption we are justified in looking for possible motifs which govern their contents. The Prologue may be approached in three ways: as a historical unity, concerned with strictly biographical data; or as a mythological unit, or, again, as a midrashic presentation of the birth of Jesus.

First, there have always been those who claim that Matt. i, ii are accurate factual accounts of the birth of Jesus. Thus Allen[3] was concerned to defend the historical validity of the narratives, not to mention Roman Catholic scholars like Lagrange.[4] But the difficulties against such an approach are real. First, there are internal ones. The genealogy itself is artificially divided into three avowedly equal parts (although, in fact, the divisions are unequal), and bears obvious marks of manipulation.[5] Leaving aside, for the moment, the account of the Virgin Birth, it surely cannot be claimed that 'the main story of the Magi is in many respects noteworthy for its historical probability'.[6] Herod's failure to discover the actual birthplace of his child-rival reveals an almost ridiculous naïveté, if the story is meant to be historical. The retarded mention of Bethlehem in ii. 1, when we should have expected it much sooner in the narrative, is also a difficulty in a strictly historical account. And, lastly, the constant introduction of quotations from scripture suggests at least the possible

---

[1] W. Michaelis, *Das Evangelium nach Matthäus*, I (1948), *ad rem.* The genealogy he regards as the very pivot of the Gospel.

[2] See J. Moffatt, *Introduction to the Literature of the New Testament* (1922), pp. 249 ff.; V. Taylor, *The Historical Evidence for the Virgin Birth* (1920). See also Appendix III.

[3] I.C.C., *The Gospel according to St Matthew, ad rem.* On the 'historical' improbability of Matthew i, ii, see Goguel, *Jesus and the Origins of Christianity*, II, pp. 253 ff.

[4] *Op. cit. ad rem.*

[5] If we count inclusively, there are given fourteen generations from Abraham to David and from David to the Exile, but, in the third section, from the Exile to Jesus, there are only thirteen generations. That the name David itself could suggest Messiah, appears from Jer. Berakoth ii. 4. 5 *a.*

[6] Allen, *op. cit.*

manipulation of events, and, according to some, their creation. Secondly, external difficulties arise from the existence of a distinct and very contrasted birth narrative in Luke i. 5–ii. 52. In Matt. i, ii and Luke i. 5–ii. 52 the genealogies, the circumstances attending the actual birth of Jesus, the activity of his parents, the point of view from which the birth narratives are related—all these are so different that most have claimed that they must be independent of one another. Both accounts cannot be factually true and their extreme divergence necessarily casts doubt on the strictly historical validity of both. But it is unnecessary to knock at open doors. Nor is it from such factors as we have mentioned that the merely historical approach to the Prologue breaks down. Rather is it from the nature of the narratives concerned, as we shall see below, that is, from the nature of the literary genre to which they belong.[1]

But before we enlarge upon this, we note that there are those who have found the clue to the Prologue in the mythological ideas of the first-century Hellenistic world. The work of Bultmann, who has predecessors, is a convenient starting point. Ignoring the genealogy, he asserts that the story of the Virgin Birth could not have arisen on Jewish soil; it belongs to the process of Hellenization which the primitive Gospel had to undergo. He finds traditional Old Testament motifs overlaid by Hellenistic forms in the story of the Virgin Birth; the homage of the Magi had its origin in an Arabic cult which centred in Petra, Hebron and, possibly, Bethlehem. As to the nature of ii. 13–19 (the Flight to Egypt and Return), Bultmann cannot decide whether they are the products of meditation upon prophecy or of traditional motifs.[2] But his assumption that the Virgin Birth cannot have arisen on Palestinian soil is by no means certain. The parallels adduced to it from Hellenistic mythology have not convinced, while Daube has suggested that a passage in Leviticus Rabbah has reference to a direct generation by Yahweh and connects the Virgin Birth, in this way, to the New Exodus motif.[3] To this we return below. In any case, what

---

[1] For a recent attempt to deal with the Birth Narratives in Matthew and Luke as historical, see E. Stauffer, *Jesus, Gestalt und Geschichte* (1957), pp. 21–42. For an approach more akin with the one adopted in the text see the suggestive work of Paul Minear, *Theology Today*, VII, 3 (October 1950), 358 ff. On the chronological value of the Nativity Narratives, see G. Ogg, *N.T.S.* (July 1959), 297 f. He does not value it highly.

[2] *Die Geschichte der synoptischen Tradition, ad rem.*

[3] *The New Testament and Rabbinic Judaism* (1956), pp. 5–9. The reference to 'our affliction' in Deut. xxvi. 7 was interpreted in the Midrash on the Passover to mean the enforced abstention from sexual intercourse, which Israel endured at the Exodus, and the phrase 'and God knew' to refer to generation by God himself, who thus secured

must always impress even the casual reader, the extreme Jewishness of the Prologue, forbids us from wandering into Hellenistic realms for their explanation. And this brings us to what is almost certainly the best approach to their understanding, that which regards the contents of the Prologue as specimens of Christian Midrash or Jewish-Christian Midrash.

Strack,[1] following Zunz, described this kind of exposition within Judaism in the following terms:

The Torah...meant to the Jews the sum and substance of all that is good and beautiful, of all that is worth knowing. Hence it ought to be possible to apply it to all conditions of life; it should comfort, exhort and edify, and it must be shown that it contained everything even though only germinally. It is through Midrash [that is, exposition] (as well as Halakah), that Holy Writ was made to do this service; but this midrashic activity is now ordinarily expressed by the word Haggadah. The Haggadah in part followed closely the biblical text; frequently, however, the latter served as a peg upon which to hang expositions of the most divergent sort. 'The Haggadah, which is to bring heaven nearer to the congregation and then to lift man heavenward, approves itself in this profession on the one side as glorification of God and on the other as consolation to Israel. Hence the chief contents of the addresses are made up of religious truths, maxims of morality, colloquies on just retribution, inculcation of the laws which mark off national coherence, descriptions of Israel's greatness in the past and future, scenes and legends from Jewish history, parallels drawn between the institutions of God and those of Israel, praises of the Holy Lord, edifying accounts and all kinds of consolation.' These addresses used to be delivered in synagogue or academy, feasibly also in private dwellings or in the open, principally on Sabbaths and festivals, but also on important public or private occasions (war, famine, circumcision, weddings, funerals, etc.).

The kind of midrashic activity here described grew up in the Church as well as in the Synagogue,[2] and perhaps particularly, if we are to follow

the birth of Moses. For a criticism of Daube's position see a review, signed by Z.W., in *J.J.S.* VII, 234 f. Z.W. recognizes, in the Midrash on Deut. xxxv. 7, a pun on ידע in Exod. iii. 25, but holds that this was never construed as implying a virgin birth or that the Midrash was subsequently suppressed because it was undesirable. If we here claim a supernatural birth for Moses, we do so also for the other six thousand Israelites whom he led out of Egypt. On these, and other grounds, Z.W. rejects Daube's view that the idea of a supernatural birth of the Messiah was conceivable in first-century Judaism. But the evidence produced by Daube is too striking to be dismissed.

[1] *Introduction to the Talmud and Midrash* (Philadelphia, 1931), p. 202. The quotation is from Zunz, *Die gottesdienstlichen Vorträge* (1832), pp. 349 f.

[2] That this was so has been held by Bacon, *op. cit.* pp. 20 ff. Zahn, Box and Loisy have all rightly regarded Matthew i and ii as Christian haggadic material which is to

Stendahl,[1] in the church or 'school' from which Matthew emerged, and it is best to regard the Matthaean Prologue as Christian haggadic material to be understood in the light of Jewish Haggadah. Apart from their undefinable 'atmosphere', which is unmistakably such, those elements in these chapters which have suggested their haggadic character are: the introduction of scriptural texts, which we shall note below; the expository element in the account of the Virgin Birth; the story of the Magi following the Star; the artificial arrangement of the genealogy at the beginning.[2] The significance of these factors will emerge as we proceed. We shall now, assuming the haggadic nature of the Prologue, seek to discover what the motifs are that underlie its various parts.

But before we so approach the Prologue, an alleged apologetic motive for its composition, urged by many scholars,[3] must be examined. Of the genealogy McNeile wrote that 'Matthew's whole object was to show, in the face of current calumnies, that the Messiah's genealogy was divinely ordered and legally correct...whilst the story of the Virgin Birth is designed to show that there was nothing new or extravagant in the thought of a miraculous birth'.[4] The same was claimed by Box[5] of the Virgin Birth: it was designed to meet Jewish calumny. According to Wright[6] the publication of the story of the Virgin Birth is directly related to the conflict with heresy. Taylor[7] follows Burkitt,[8] and points out the same motive of defence against Jewish calumny in the references to the 'undesirable' women in the genealogy, as in the Virgin Birth narrative.[9]

But did the aim of combating Jewish calumnies play a large, or indeed any, part in the formation of the birth narratives? Those calumnies belong to a later date than Matthew. Nor must the possibility be ruled out that it

be understood in the light of Jewish Haggadah, as indicated above. Zahn retains a basis in fact for i and ii as does Box: around this midrashic features have gathered.

[1] *The School of Matthew* (1954).

[2] The most convincing presentation of all this is that of G. H. Box, *The Virgin Birth of Jesus Christ*, pp. 12 ff. It should be noted that Bacon, *op. cit.* pp. 151 ff., while giving full weight to Hellenistic parallels to the Nativity Story, also finds the Jewish element dominant. His treatment is still enriching.

[3] So Allen, I.C.C. *op. cit.*; F. C. Burkitt, *The Gospel History and its Transmission*, *ad rem*, and others.

[4] *The Gospel according to St Matthew*, pp. 6, 11.

[5] *The Virgin Birth of Jesus Christ*, *ad rem*: so too of the genealogy.

[6] A. Wright, *A Synopsis of the Gospels in Greek*[3] (1906), p. xlii.

[7] *Historical Evidence for the Virgin Birth* (1920), *ad rem*.

[8] See Bultmann, *op. cit. ad rem*.

[9] See Michaelis, *Das Evangelium nach Matthäus, ad rem*.

was the birth narratives themselves that actually stimulated such calumnies. And were the genealogy aimed at supplying exact 'legal' correctness to the descent of Jesus, it is doubly unfortunate not merely that Luke should have so contradicted it, but also that illegitimacy should have been allowed to show its head at all. To remind Jewry that there was illegitimacy in their 'royal line' was no defence of the 'purity' or 'legality' of Jesus' birth. Polemic seldom creates poetry, and we can be sure that the motive of combating Jewish slanders against Mary's chastity is inadequate to account for the richness of the infancy narratives.[1]

So too when we pass to the story of the Magi and other events of Matt. ii, where similar attempts have been made to explain the material as aimed at enhancing the claims of Jesus in the Gentile world, that is, as apologetic.[2] This was the way in which some of the Fathers actually used the birth narratives.[3] But it has been insufficiently recognized that these last could and did occasion difficulty to the Church and served not as apologies but as 'scandals'.[4] Thus it is unlikely, for example, that a Church which had to combat astrological speculation would have presented the story of the Star as part of its apology. Justin makes it clear that, so far from being such, the birth narratives were a source of offence: they placed Jesus—or so they could be interpreted—under the domination of the stars, a fact which had to be explained away.[5]

In view of the above, it is well not to over-emphasize, and perhaps not to emphasize at all, any strictly apologetic or polemic motives in the birth narratives. Directed not to the world but to the Church, the product of Christian devotion to, love for and awe before Christ, they are aimed not so much at meeting calumnies and producing an impression on the pagan world, as at expounding the mystery of their Lord to the Church, through his birth. They are neither simply history, although they deal with a historic fact, the birth of Jesus, nor apologetic or polemic, but rather confessions of a faith, proclamations of the truth about the person

[1] C. K. Barrett, *The Holy Spirit and the Gospel Tradition* (1947), *ad rem.* A. Plummer finds the references to women in the genealogy of such a kind as to suggest that Jesus was a friend of sinners, commentary on Matthew, *ad rem.*

[2] Box, *op. cit.* p. 24; see Michaelis, *Das Evangelium nach Matthäus*, 1, 91 and other commentators.

[3] See the references to ii gathered in Harold Smith, *Ante-Nicene Exegesis of the Gospels* (London, 1925), 1, 258 ff.

[4] See Justin, *Apology*, 1, xxxiii: 'the Virgin Birth' recalled stories about the amours of Jupiter.

[5] See Harold Smith, *op. cit.* p. 261. 'Tertullian', he notes, '*On Idolatry*, ix, seeks to prevent the case of the magi being used to defend astrology.'

of Jesus adorned in tales about his birth. This means—to use a familiar distinction—that they are not primarily didactic but kerygmatic.[1]

From this point of view we shall now examine the Prologue. Instead of examining each of its pericopae separately, and disentangling their various emphases, a process which would prolong our discussion inordinately and repetitiously, we shall point out four motifs which seem chiefly to emerge in the infancy stories as a totality, presenting the evidence for each motif from all the Prologue as compactly as possible.

First, then, we notice an interest in asserting that the coming of Jesus of Nazareth inaugurates a new era, and, indeed, a new creation. While this is not explicitly stated, it is clearly implied. In Matt. i. 1 we read: βίβλος γενέσεως Ἰησοῦ Χριστοῦ υἱοῦ Δαυείδ, υἱοῦ Ἀβρααμ rendered in the RSV: 'The book of the genealogy of Jesus Christ, the son of David, the son of Abraham', and regarded by perhaps most scholars as the title to the genealogical table that follows in i. 2–16. In the Septuagint γένεσις frequently translates תולדות, and the phrase αὗται αἱ γενέσεις is the regular translation of אלה תולדות to introduce a genealogy. In Gen. v. 1 the term βίβλος γενέσεως in the LXX translates ספר תולדות and introduces the genealogical table of Adam. Thus the anarthrous phrase βίβλος γενέσεως in Matt. i. 1 would seem best understood as introducing the following genealogy only. On this view Ἰησοῦ Χριστοῦ would be an objective genitive.

But there are two difficulties. First in Gen. v. 1 the phrases βίβλος γενέσεως, and in other places αὗται αἱ γενέσεις, are followed, not as in Matt. i. 1 by a list of progenitors, but by a list of the descendants of the person whose genealogy is being given. Secondly, it is difficult to understand why, if his object was merely to introduce the genealogy, the Evangelist should not have preferred αὗται αἱ γενέσεις, the phrase most frequently found in such a context in the LXX. The precise phrase βίβλος γενέσεως is found twice only in the LXX at Gen. v. 1 to translate, as we saw, ספר תולדות, and at Gen. ii. 4a to render אלה תולדות. In the latter text it seems clear that the LXX has been assimilated to Gen. v. 1. Aquila and Symmachus render αὗται αἱ γενέσεις.[2] Moreover, in both Gen. v. 1 and ii. 4a the phrase βίβλος γενέσεως introduces not merely a genealogy.

---

[1] See on this also Paul Minear, *Theology Today*, VII, 3 (Oct. 1950), 358 ff.; K. Stendahl, on 'Quis et Unde? An analysis of Matt. i–ii', in 'Judentum, Urchristentum, Kirche', *ZNW*, Beiheft 26 (1960), 94 ff.

[2] See Field's *Hexapla*.

5-2

After Gen. v. 1 there is an account of the creation of Adam as male and female; the ages of Adam and his descendants are given and their names; details such as that Enoch walked with God (v. 24) are added. In Gen. ii. 4a the phrase under discussion constitutes a difficulty. It serves either as a closure to the account of creation in Gen. i. 1–ii. 3 or as a superscription to ii. 6 f. In any case the phrase βίβλος γενέσεως does not refer to a straightforward genealogy but either to the process of the creation (or generation) of the universe in Gen. i. 1–ii. 3 or that of man in Gen. ii. 4b ff. Fortunately we need not enter into the minutiae of pentateuchal criticism at this point, because the Evangelist was not aware of them. What we are concerned to point out is that βίβλος γενέσεως might suggest both the creation story and the genealogical table of Adam. The question is inevitable whether the Evangelist consciously began his Gospel with this phrase to suggest a parallel between Jesus and the first Adam and the creation of the universe: was his coming for Matthew, as for Paul, a 'new creation'?[1] This suggestion would be strengthened could we be sure that the title of the first book of the Old Testament in the LXX had already been fixed as Γένεσις in which case Matthew is introducing a new Genesis corresponding to, though transcending, the old.

Certain objections have been offered to this view. First, that to make Matt. i. 1 the title of all the Gospel would mean that Matt. i. 2 ff., the genealogy, would begin too abruptly and without a proper title. But it is doubtful if a first-century reader would feel this objection. Thus 1 Chronicles begins more abruptly than this and so does Pirqê Aboth which without introduction starts with 'Moses received the Law from Sinai...'.[2] The former reference, 1 Chron. i. 1 ff., makes it clear that no title was considered necessary for the introduction of a genealogy. More serious is the second claim that the use of γένεσις in Matt. i. 18, where it clearly refers to the birth of Jesus, demands a comparable meaning for the word in Matt. i. 1. Had it referred to more than the genealogy in this last verse, then the use of γένεσις in a different sense in Matt. i. 18 would have been avoided. On the other hand, if βίβλος γενέσεως in i. 1 refers to the genealogy only, then the use of γένεσις in i. 18 presents no difficulty. But two considerations are pertinent. First, the text is not certain at Matt. i.

---

[1] 2 Cor. v. 17; *P.R.J.*[2], pp. 36 ff.

[2] The phrase βίβλος γενέσεως was *not* customary for a genealogy. It is significant that S–B, 1, 1, do not consider βίβλος γενέσεως a translation of ספר תולדות: if it were it would be a title for the whole of the Gospel (*ibid.*). They prefer to regard it as a translation of סֵפֶר יוּחָסִין—that is, the title of the genealogy. On this, see J. Jeremias, *Jerusalem zur Zeit Jesu*, pp. 145 ff., 150 n. 55; M. Yebamoth iv. 13.

18. Most texts print τοῦ δὲ ᾿Ιησοῦ Χριστοῦ ἡ γένεσις οὖτως ἦν.[1] But the MS evidence is varied. Legg supplies the following lists:[2]

Ιησου Χριστου: Uncs pler Minusc pler Sy[pesh hl hier] Cop[sa bo] Aeth Arm Geo Iren.

Χριστου Ιησου: B.

Ιησου W. (R[m] Kilpatrick) Χριστου 71, vg, Sy[cs] Iren[bis].

The best-attested reading appears to be ᾿Ιησοῦ Χριστοῦ being probably due to assimilation to Matt. i. 1. In addition, there is confusion regarding γένεσις. The evidence is as follows:

γενεσις ℵ, B, C, P, S, W, Z, Δ, Θ, Σ, 1, 1582, 259, 372, 399, 482, 1604 al similiter Cop[bo], Eus.

γεννησις L Γ Π ℔ (exc S) 209, 124, 346, 543, 28, 33, 157, 700, 892, 1241 al Ir Or Epiph.

The MS evidence favours γένεσις, but if γέννησις were original, we could account for the change to γένεσις by assimilation to Matt. i. 1, as in the case of ᾿Ιησοῦ Χριστοῦ: this would be the reading which we should naturally perhaps expect especially in the light of the use of ἐγέννησεν in i. 2 ff.[3] The reading of Matt. i. 18 may, therefore, have been τοῦ δὲ ᾿Ιησοῦ Χριστοῦ ἡ γέννησις οὖτως ἦν[4] so that we need not understand Matt. i. 1 in the light of i. 18. But, secondly, even if the original reading in i. 18 were γένεσις it by no means necessarily follows that i. 1 should be confined to the genealogy. Thus many who have denied that Matt. i. 1 is a title for the whole book have found it possible to regard it as the title of the whole of the Prologue. It was quite possible for γένεσις in Matt. i. 1 and i. 18 to have a different connotation.

A third objection is more formidable. If Matt. i. 1 be taken to be the title of the whole Gospel, that is, for the Gospel events in their totality, as recorded by Matthew, as the inauguration of a New Creation which is understood over against that of the Old in Genesis, it follows that 'Jesus Christ' in Matt. i. 1 becomes the author of the process, that is, ᾿Ιησοῦ Χριστοῦ is a subjective genitive, Jesus being regarded as the agent of the

[1] So Nestle, Kilpatrick, Souter.

[2] *Novum Testamentum Graece, Evangelium Secundum Matthaeum* (Oxford, 1940).

[3] The reading in i. 16 is a famous difficulty; see the critical apparatus and the commentaries. Clearly the precise meaning of γένεσις was much discussed.

[4] So Allen, I.C.C. *op. cit.*: see the discussion in Westcott and Hort, *The New Testament in the Original Greek*, II (1882), 7 ff. in the Notes on Select Readings; they prefer the reading γένεσις in i. 18; γέννησις was suggested by ἐγεννήθη in i. 16.

New Creation. The title βίβλος γενέσεως 'Ιησοῦ Χριστοῦ would then
signify, 'The book of the "New" Creation being wrought by Jesus
Christ'. This, it can be urged, places a burden on the genitive, 'Ιησοῦ
Χριστοῦ, too heavy to be borne. Far more natural is it to regard that
genitive as an objective one, Jesus Christ being the object of the genealogical process that follows. The force of all this is clear. Nevertheless, it
is also to be acknowledged that the same ambiguity as to the character of
the genitive occurs in the opening of Mark at i. 1, in the phrase, 'The
beginning of the gospel of Jesus Christ, the Son of God', where 'Jesus
Christ' has been variously interpreted as the object of the Gospel or its
source (subjective genitive). Moreover, the concept of a whole Gospel
containing the work or creation of Christ emerges clearly in Acts i. 1, in
a reference which explains how Luke regarded his Gospel: while Jesus is
the object of the Gospel, he was also its subject.[1]

The objections noted above, and particularly the last mentioned, make
it exceedingly difficult, if we only consider Matt. i. 1 in isolation, to claim
with any degree of confidence that the Evangelist would have us see a
correspondence between the advent of Jesus into the world and the
creation in Gen. i, Matt. i. 1 recalling Gen. i. 1 or at least Gen. ii. 4a and
v. 1, and that there may even be a side-glance in Matt. i. 1 at the first
Adam (although this, apart from every other consideration, is probably to
read too much into Matt. i. 1). But it becomes less difficult to do so when
it is recognized that this correspondence occurs elsewhere in the Prologue,
as we shall now show.[2]

In Matt. i. 18–25 we find treated the 'Virgin Birth' of Jesus. 'Now the
birth of Jesus Christ took place in this way. When his mother Mary had
been betrothed to Joseph, before they came together she was found to be
with child of the Holy Spirit. . . that which is conceived in her is of the
Holy Spirit.' The concept of the Holy Spirit is seldom mentioned in the
Synoptic Gospels, but here it is very prominent. The very birth of Jesus
from Mary is due to the Holy Spirit. Why? The role of the Spirit in
creation in Gen. i. 1 and its activity in the created order elsewhere in the
Old Testament has been much exaggerated. After the first two verses in

[1] For a convenient presentation, see Cranfield on Mark i. 1, *St Mark* (1959),
pp. 34 f. He prefers to take Mark i. 1 as a title for Mark i. 2–13; see Lohmeyer's
commentaries on Matthew and Mark. Schniewind, *Das Neue Testament Deutsch*
(1956), p. 43, on Mark i. 1: 'Jesus ist zunächst der Verkünder der Freudenbotschaft.'
[2] It is also necessary to recall the whole emphasis on the coming of Christ as a new
creation in the New Testament to feel the force of the argument on Matt. i. 1.
Compare Giovanni Miegge, *The Virgin Mary*, Eng. trans. (Philadelphia, 1950), p. 29.

NEW EXODUS AND NEW MOSES

Gen. i the Spirit is not mentioned: in subsequent verses the 'word' of God rather than the Spirit is active.[1] Nevertheless the Spirit is clearly associated with the creation in Gen. i. 1, 2. 'In the beginning God created the heavens and the earth. The earth was without form and void, and darkness was upon the face of the deep and the Spirit of God was moving over the face of the waters.' Here the Spirit of God moves over material things, and it may be that we should not compare the activity of the Spirit in a living person with the same activity in inanimate nature. The Old Testament itself, however, does so and to refuse to do so here would be to be too precise. There can be little question that it is the thought of a new creation analogous with the first in which the Spirit of God was also active which governs the role of that same Spirit in Matt. i. 18–25.[2] We are emboldened in this view because John iii. 8 reveals possibly a pun on the second verse of Gen. i in a discussion on the 'new birth'.[3] And just as in John iii. 2 this is deemed to be only possible with the presence of God himself, so in Matt. i. 23 the birth of Christ is the birth of Emmanuel, 'God with us'. The coming of Jesus is the presence of God in the midst.

That the thought of Matthew turns to the creation of the world is again possibly suggested by a further parallelism which may be detected between Matt. i and Gen. i, ii. There are two separate accounts of the creation of man in Gen. i, ii, one in Gen. i belonging to the document P and the other to J. Gen. i. 1 ff. gives a catalogic account of the stages of the process of creation which culminates in man, created in the image of God (Gen. i. 26 ff.). Gen. ii. 4 ff., however, gives a different account of man's creation 'from the dust from the ground', not after the creation of the vegetable and animal world but before it: the actual formation of man at creation is here given in greater detail than in Gen. i. 26 ff. It is not fanciful to see some such distinction in Matt. i. 2–17 and i. 18–25. In the former we find a catalogic account of Jesus' ancestors culminating in him: the historical or what we may loosely call the 'earthly' Christ's generation

[1] Skinner, I.C.C., *Genesis, ad rem.*; *P.R.J.*[2] pp. 188 ff. But see C. E. Raven, *Natural Religion and Christian Theology*, Second Series (Cambridge, 1953), pp. 220 f.

[2] So C. K. Barrett, *The Holy Spirit and the Gospel Tradition*, p. 24.

[3] I owe this to Martin Buber: he enlarged upon it in a seminar at Princeton University. The Greek in John iii. 8: τὸ πνεῦμα ὅπου θέλει πνεῖ he took to be an exaggerated assonance to recall the Hebrew of Gen. i. 2 וְרוּחַ אֱלֹהִים מְרַחֶפֶת עַל־פְּנֵי הַמָּיִם. The 'water' and 'spirit' of John iii. 5 recalls Gen. i. 1 f. also. Again, as Dodd notes in *The Interpretation of the Fourth Gospel*, p. 305, 'the expression of [John] iii. 5, 6, 8 ἐκ πνεύματος γεννᾶσθαι echoes the expression ἐκ θεοῦ γεννᾶσθαι which is found in John i. 13', but this is in a context of 'creation' in the Prologue also.

is revealed: then in i. 18–25 a more concentrated treatment of the way in which he came into being: he proves to be the Son of God born of the Holy Spirit, his supernatural origin is stressed. Like Paul, and unlike Philo, who both speculated much on Gen. i, ii, Matthew places the earthly Christ first and then the man born directly of the creative activity of God.[1]

The evidence presented above exhausts those references which might be taken to refer to the inauguration of a new creation. But this, however, although traceable, is not the sole and not even the dominant concept in the birth narratives. Not only the ambiguity of the phrase 'book of the generation' in i. 1 makes this apparent, but also the simple fact that in the story of the Virgin Birth itself, where the new creation motif has been most emphatically claimed, it is the fulfilment of prophecy that is explicitly declared to be served. Primarily for Matthew, 'All this took place to fulfil what the Lord had spoken by the prophet: Behold a virgin shall conceive...' (Matt. i. 22 f.; Isa. vii. 14). There are no fewer than four direct allusions to such a fulfilment in Matt. i, ii, apart from other indirect allusions. While, therefore, the advent of Jesus is a new departure in history, a new creation by the Spirit, looked at from another point of view the same advent is not a new departure but the last stage in a long, though chequered, development. This is the meaning, in part at least, of the references to the fulfilment of prophecy to which we next turn.

But before we do so, as a preliminary, it is well to note that probably the mere insertion of a genealogy, stretching from Abraham to Jesus, in Matt. i. 1–17, had itself a theological significance, not in connecting the birth of Jesus with the act of creation necessarily, but at least in suggesting that one era was over and a new one begun.[2] Standing within a Jewish tradition, it was natural for Matthew to begin his account of the redeemer with his genealogy (compare Gen. v. 1 ff., 9 ff.; x. 1 ff.; xi. 10, 27; xxv. 12, 19). Indeed any biographical interest would usually demand this,

---

[1] On this see *P.R.J.*[2] pp. 47 ff.

[2] See S. Schechter, *J.Q.R.* XII, 418 ff.; Box, *op. cit.* p. 13; S–B on Matt. i. 17; also Exkurs II, p. 994, where rich material is gathered. Billerbeck opens his treatment of 'Vorzeichen und Berechnung der Tage des Messias' with the sentences: 'Der Weltplan Gottes ist seit Ewigkeit festgestellt. In den Büchern des Himmels sind seine Einzelheiten aufgezeichnet' (p. 977). The passage referred to in Exod. R. (ed. Soncino, p. 196) reads: 'Even before God brought Israel out of Egypt, He intimated to them that royalty would last for them only until the end of thirty generations...there were fifteen generations from Abraham to Solomon....' The passage is anonymous. See further Karl Bornhauser, *Die Geburts- und Kindheitsgeschichte Jesu* (Gütersloh, 1930), pp. 6 ff.; and p. 108 n. 2 below.

although Mark's Gospel should warn us that this was not always the case and that therefore a genealogy deserves attention. But another factor may also be operative. In Jewish apocalyptic, and this is not to be rigidly separated from rabbinic or pharisaic Judaism,[1] the concept of 'the End' was bound up with that of temporal fulfilment. The idea meets us explicitly in Paul, when he speaks of 'the fullness of time', and by implication it is ubiquitous in Matthew. Moreover 'the fullness of time' would naturally imply the fullness of certain generations, an idea which comes to the surface in 4 Ezra vi. 7, 8 (and in Exod. R. on xii. 2 it occurs, not in connexion with the End, but with the duration of the monarchy). Matthew clearly by his schematization intends to imply that the generations of Abraham, that is, the time of the Old Israel, whose father was Abraham, has issued in its fulfilment in the coming of Jesus. It is now over; the time of the New Israel has come. Such concepts we are probably justified in reading into Matthew's use of the genealogy. The New Age has dawned. The genealogy may be taken to declare that in Jesus the true seed of Abraham, in which the promises of God are fulfilled, has appeared, a thought familiar to Paul (Rom. iv. 10 ff.; Gal. iii. 6 ff.), and the claim has also been made that it contains the concept of the fulfilment of prophecy and of the hopes of the Psalms in a cryptic form. However, this rests on a conjecture that the Asaph referred to in i. 7, 8, when we should expect Asa, is designed to recall the psalmist (Ps. lxxiii. 1; lxxv. 1, etc.) and that Amos in i. 10 designates the prophet, when we should expect a king, Amon. The changes from Asa to Asaph and Amon to Amos may be accidental, but they may also be deliberate.[2] Be this as it may, the genealogy, as such, is an impressive witness to Matthew's conviction that the birth of Jesus was no unpremeditated accident but occurred in the fullness of time and in the providence of God, who overruled the generations to this end, to inaugurate in Jesus a new order, the time of fulfilment.

This is also the significance of the direct references to the fulfilment of scripture in the Prologue. This reveals a complexity of emphases, which we must examine for the sake of clarity, but which interpenetrate so closely that to dissect them is to distort. At the risk, in Montefiore's phrase, of applying critical hammers to the wings of a butterfly, we now note that the fulfilment referred to is conceived in a twofold way. In

---

[1] W. D. Davies, *The Expository Times*, LIX, 233 ff.; J. Bloch, *On the Apocalyptic in Judaism* (Philadelphia, 1952). See *P.R.J.*[2] p. 353. Add to all this that on the Day of Atonement the High-Priest had Daniel read to him (M. Yoma i. 6).

[2] J. Schniewind, *Das Neue Testament Deutsch, Das Matthäusevangelium*, p. 10.

addition to what we have previously asserted, it is the fulfilment of 'the Davidic hope' and of what we may call 'the Mosaic hope'.

First, then, Matt. i. 1 makes it clear that Jesus of Nazareth is to be regarded as the Son of David, and it is equally clear from i. 6 that in his genealogical history the point of supreme (though not sole) interest is the 'kingship' of David. To judge from i. 17 the loss of that 'Kingship' from Israel in the Exile, and its recovery in the advent of Jesus, constitute the decisive points. Attempts to subordinate the Davidic motif in the genealogy, on the ground that, were this primary, then i. 2–6 become redundant or irrelevant, so that the Abrahamic motif would have to be taken as the dominant one, cannot be regarded as convincing, because of the ubiquity of the Davidic motif in the Prologue.[1] Moreover, some have sought to buttress the Davidic interest of the Prologue by seeking to find an intricate numerical intent in the structure of Matt. i. 1–17. Gfrörer[2] suggested that, through *gematria*, the division of the genealogy into three compartments of avowedly fourteen generations each is to be connected with the name David, which has three consonants d, w, d (דוד) whose numerical value in Hebrew amounts to fourteen (d=4, w=6). Many English scholars have tentatively followed Gfrörer in finding the use of *gematria* here, but most German scholars seem to have ignored his view, while Guignebert[3] speaks vaguely of 'the symbolism of numbers' and 'that equality of parts which the Orientals of those days regarded as a form of perfection'. That *gematria* was practised in the first century is proved by the New Testament itself, as in Rev. xiii. 18. Matthew's fondness for arithmetical neatness is evident, nor should the fact that *gematria* was regarded as of secondary value for exegesis,[4] prejudice its

---

[1] It is important not to impose any one motif on the material.

[2] S–B accept *gematria* in i. 1 ff. *Gematria* has two meanings: (a) computation of the numeric value of letters, (b) secret alphabets or substitution of letters for other letters. For details, see W. Bacher, *Die Älteste Terminologie der Jüdischen Schriftauslegung* (Leipzig, 1899), p. 127 under *Notarikon*.

[3] *Jesus*, Eng. trans. (New York, 1935), pp. 109 f.

[4] See Mishnah Aboth, iii. 19. 'R. Eliazer Ḥisma (A.D. 120–140) [The rules about] bird-offerings and the onset of menstruation—these are essentials of the *Halakoth* (being difficult and complicated they must be accounted the most important subjects of study); but the calculations of the equinoxes and gematria are but the savoury dishes of wisdom.' The term for 'savoury dishes' is 'used in Mishnah Ber. vi. 5 and Shab. xxiii. 2 of the relish or savoury which begin or end a meal but are not the essential item of the meal' (see H. Danby, *The Mishnah*, p. 453, n. 2). Danby takes *gematria* here to refer to geometry (p. 453, n. 1) but in his note on Mishnah Uktzin iii. 12 (p. 789, n. 7) refers to it as *gematria* proper. In fact *gematria* is not to be connected with γεωμετρία (geometry) at all but is derived from γράμμα and γραμματεία;

use here in what was primarily a midrashic genealogy: it finds a place in the Mishnah itself (Mishnah Aboth, iii. 19; Mishnah Uktzin, iii. 12). That it was known to the Church further emerges in the Epistle of Barnabas, where the number 318, servants of Abraham, Gen. xiv. 14 is found to refer to the cross T = 300 and Jesus I H = 18.[1]

Nevertheless, there are difficulties that make its exercise here not certain. First, in those passages in Greek documents where *gematria* is employed it is usual to find an express statement to this effect. The one passage in the New Testament where it seems to occur, Rev. xiii. 18, is significant. It reads, 'This calls for wisdom: let him who has understanding reckon the number of the beast, for it is a human number, its number is six hundred and sixty-six'. Here the method whereby the beast is to be known is indicated—it is by the reckoning of his number, that is, the letters of his name. Possibly the figure of Nero the Emperor is indicated as the beast. The Greek Νέρων Καῖσαρ gives the numerical value of 666. (Thus: Ὧδε ἡ σοφία ἐστίν. ὁ ἔχων νοῦν ψηφισάτω τὸν ἀριθμὸν τοῦ θηρίου. ἀριθμὸς γὰρ ἀνθρώπου ἐστίν. καὶ ὁ ἀριθμὸς αὐτοῦ ἐξακόσιοι ἑξήκοντα ἕξ.)[2] The same is true in the *Sibylline Oracles* v, 12 ff. where *gematria* occurs. It reads: 'There shall be a king first of all who shall sum up twice ten with his initial letters. . . .' Even in rabbinic sources where the use of *gematria* is natural its occurrence does not need to be inferred because it is unmistakable, as, for example, in Numbers Rabbah on v. 18; xvi. 1. It follows that in the prologue to a Greek document such as Matthew it is unlikely that *gematria* should have been used without express mention. It is also noteworthy that in the many genealogies referred to in support of the view that genealogies are often to be understood midrashically,[3] there is no use made of *gematria* to explain the significance of genealogical details, so that they do not lend support to the view that considerations of *gematria* generally entered into genealogical speculations. Too much weight, however, should not be given to this: each genealogy has to be examined in its own light.

see Bächer, *op. cit.* The usage appears clearly in Mishnah Uktzin iii. 12 as follows: 'R. Joshua b. Levi (*c.* A.D. 250) said: The Holy One, blessed is He, will cause every saint to inherit hereafter three hundred and ten worlds, for it is written, *That I may cause those that love me to inherit yesh* (substance) *and that I may fill their treasuries.*' Here the consonants of *yesh* (yodh and shin) have the numerical number of 10 and 300.

[1] *The Epistle of Barnabas*, IX.

[2] See for the possibilities, Martin Rist, *Revelation*, in *The Interpreter's Bible*, XII, 466.

[3] See Box, *The Virgin Birth of Jesus Christ*, who cites Leviticus Rabbah i. 1 (Soncino translation, pp. 4 ff.).

And, secondly, more serious is it that the list of names given in Matt. i. 1–11 must probably be regarded as traditional. The only section in Matt. i. 1–16 for which we have no parallels is that from i. 13–16. Thus i. 2–6 are paralleled in 1 Chron. ii. 1–15; i. 3–6, in Ruth iv. 18–22 and i. 7–12 in 1 Chron. iii. 10–17. The list in Ruth iv. 18–22 occurs in Exod. R. on xii. 2 in a passage which is also otherwise instructive. There the period from Abraham (or Adam) to the Exile is divided into thirty generations, at the end of which the kingdom was to cease from Israel. Both the periods from Abraham (or Adam) to Solomon and from Solomon to Zedekiah (a period for which the genealogical scheme of 1 Chron. iii. 10–16 recurs in Exod. R.) were supposed to cover fifteen generations. This reconstruction of history was understood in the light of the phases of the moon. Thus:

THIS MONTH SHALL BE UNTO YOU THE BEGINNING OF MONTHS; just as the month has thirty days, so shall your kingdom last until thirty generations. The moon begins to shine on the first of Nisan and goes on shining till the fifteenth day, when her disc becomes full: from the fifteenth till the thirtieth day her light wanes, till on the thirtieth it is not seen at all. With Israel too, there were fifteen generations from Abraham to Solomon. Abraham began to shine. . . . When Solomon appeared, the moon's disc was full. . . . Henceforth the kings began to diminish in power. . . . With Zedekiah. . . the light of the moon failed entirely . . . .[1]

Here Solomon not David is the pivotal figure, and while we should not ascribe to this passage the kind of deliberate seriousness which is evident in Matt. i. 1–17, since it is in a lighter haggadic vein, nevertheless it does offer a rough parallel in schematization to what is found in Matt. i. 1–11, and the genealogical tables in this section are similar though not identical.[2] In view of all this traditional schematization of genealogical material it would be rash perhaps to discover *gematria* in Matt. i. 1–16. That the name David was thus numerically treated appears in Gen. R. xxxix. 11, in a section again giving a division of history, this time in terms of the descendants of Judah and of the building of the temple; but, if it were being so treated in Matt. i. 1 ff., since the *waw* in the middle of the name stands for 6 and the *daleth* at the beginning and the end of it only for 4, we might expect, if *gematria* were being employed, that the central section of the genealogy from David to the Exile would contain more generations than the other two sections, but this is not the case, each

[1] See the Soncino translation, pp. 196 ff.   [2] See Appendix IV.

76

section being claimed to have the same number of generations. Despite all the above objections, it must, however, be fully recognized that the numerical item 'fourteen' (=David) is explicitly given a marked place in Matt. i. 17, and that *gematria* may be so indicated.[1]

Nevertheless, attractive as it is, we cannot be sure that the theory of Gfrörer should be followed. But, this aside, that part of the aim of the genealogy in Matt. i. 1 is to emphasize the Davidic character of Jesus is clear. It is not merely that Jesus is of the stock of David, who is mentioned five times in Matt. i. 1–17, but that he is the counterpart of David as king. In the story of the Virgin Birth a reference to David is introduced in i. 20. It is so pointed that we must regard it as significant. Joseph is visited, by the angel of the Lord, as the son of David. Later in Matt. ii the Magi seek the *king* of the Jews, and this king whom they seek is clearly set over against another king, Herod. Schlatter[2] has found in the contrast between Jesus, the new king, and Herod, the reigning king, the clue to Matt. ii. Kings are meeting there. This certainly is one of the motifs in Matt. ii, because in ii. 1–12 the term 'king' occurs three times. The Messianic king must come to terms with the rulers of this world, and their encounter must be described. That the new king is a Messiah of the House of David is further reinforced by the addition to Micah v. 1 (quoted in Matt. ii. 6), which is a strictly Messianic passage, of words from 2 Sam. v. 2, which deals with the anointing of David as king over Israel. It is possible, however, to over-emphasize the parallel between David and Jesus in this section. Burkitt's suggestion that Herod's attack on Jesus echoes that of Saul on David is extremely unlikely, just as is the further claim that Jesus found a refuge in Egypt as David found a refuge among the Philistines.[3] In all this imagination has been allowed to run wild. The terms of such parallelism as have been mentioned are not compatible. Jesus was a child when Herod sought to destroy him in Matt. ii, not a full-grown rival as was David to Saul, nor is it likely that Egypt should be meant to suggest Philistia. All that can safely be said in this connexion in Matt. ii is that the emphasis on Herod adds significance to Jesus as a king meeting a king, and that he is a king in the line of David. But there is no justification in pressing any parallelism between David and Saul and Jesus and Herod.

---

[1] That the divisions of the genealogy are not *exactly* fourteenfold adds force to this, 'fourteen' being insisted upon despite this discrepancy.

[2] *Der Evangelist Matthäus* (1948), pp. 25 ff.

[3] V. Taylor, *op. cit.* p. 101.

This brings us to the second element of fulfilment set forth in Matt. i, ii. Jesus is a second Moses. Fortunately we are spared from speculation because a direct quotation guides us at once to the Exodus. In Matt. ii. 13 ff. the flight of Joseph, Mary and the infant Jesus to Egypt and their sojourn there is described, and in ii. 15 it is asserted that 'This was to fulfil what the Lord had spoken by the prophet, "Out of Egypt have I called my son"'. As in Exod. iv. 22 so in this verse quoted from Hos. xi. 1 the 'son' is a designation for 'Israel' as a people. Matthew sees in the history of Jesus a recapitulation of that of Israel. Can we go further and say that he also sees in it the history of Moses repeated? In ii. 16 ff. we may safely assume that Herod has taken on the role of Pharaoh: the slaughter of the innocents befits a New as an Old Exodus. Moreover, the terms in which Moses is described as leaving Midian to deliver Israel from bondage are recalled in Matt. ii. 19 ff. when Joseph takes Jesus back from his refuge in Egypt to Israel. No exact correspondence can be discerned nor is intended: rather the latter incident is couched in language that recalls the former. A glance at the passage reveals this:

Exod. iv. 18 ff.	Matt. ii. 19–21
Moses went back to Jethro his father-in-law and said to him, 'Let me go back, I pray, to my kinsmen in Egypt and see whether they are still alive.' And Jethro said to Moses, 'Go in peace.' And *the Lord said* to Moses in Midian, 'Go back to Egypt; *for all the men who were seeking your life are dead.*' So Moses took his wife and his sons and set them on an ass....	But when Herod died, behold, an *angel of the Lord* appeared in a dream to Joseph in Egypt, saying, 'Rise, take the child and his mother, and go to the land of Israel, *for those who sought the child's life are dead.*' And he rose and took the child and his mother, and went to the land of Israel.

Particularly noticeable is the use of the plural verb in Matt. ii. 20*b*. (τεθνήκασι) when only Herod has died. This is surely not here a plural of majesty but a reflection of the plural verb in the parallel in Exodus.

But, apart from these fairly direct indications of a New Moses motif, others *may* be present, though veiled. Let us begin with the Magi. While most modern commentators have been content with a historical note on these, it is seldom noticed that they may have a parallel in the Exodus story. The role of 'the wise men of Egypt and the sorcerers and charmers' in the Exodus tradition is a strongly marked characteristic of P. They are represented as in conflict with Moses, a conflict which increases in intensity until they are compelled to admit Moses' superiority. In Exod. vii. 11 f. they succeed in imitating the feat that Aaron performed with his rod, although finally the latter swallows up their rods. In Exod. vii. 22 they succeed, by sorcery, in turning water into blood, just as Moses and Aaron had done. So too in viii. 7 they brought up frogs on the land of Egypt, just as had Aaron. But after this the sorcerers fail. When Aaron had caused lice to be 'on men and quadrupeds and in all the dust of the earth' by stretching forth his rod and the charmers also tried, with their sorceries, to bring forth the lice, they could not (viii. 18). Their final discomfiture is such that the next struggle against 'boils and blains' finds them not only unable to repeat what Moses had done, but actually themselves involved in the calamity he wrought (ix. 11). Even before this final defeat they had come to confess that 'This is the finger of God' (viii. 19). By gradual means the supremacy of Moses comes to be acknowledged and vindicated.

The conflict of Moses and the magicians may be reflected in the Synoptic tradition at Luke xi. 20: 'But if it is by the finger of God that I cast out demons, then the kingdom of God has come upon you.' It is, therefore, not unnatural to look for it in a context where we have previously discovered the Exodus motif in the Prologue. Just as the magicians are led to see in the activity of Moses the finger of God, so the Magi from the East are led to kneel at the feet of the greater Moses. Note that in Matt. ii as in Exodus the Magi are intended to subserve the purpose of Herod and the Pharaoh respectively, but fail to do so. That the Magi could be regarded as having sinister powers appears in Ignatius, Tertullian and Origen.[1] Their power was broken at the advent of Christ, just as the sorcerers had been vanquished by Moses.

Certain obvious objections arise to all this. First, the term μάγος is not used in the LXX to describe the sorcerers, etc., in Egypt, although we should expect Matthew to use terms which occur in the Exodus story did he have it in mind. Against this it may be noted that Symmachus does use μάγος to translate one of the terms in Exodus, though not in Exodus itself but at Gen. xli. 8, 24. So Theodotion renders the הָאַשָּׁפִים as τοὺς μάγους in Dan. i. 20.[2] Secondly, it might be claimed that it is not at the

---

[1] A. Gelin, 'Moïse dans l'Ancien Testament', in *Cahiers Sioniens* (1954), no. 2–3–4, p. 37. 'Dans la plus ancienne représentation, la plus pathétique, Moïse est seul devant la puissance qui s'oppose à Yahweh comme une sorte d'anticipation de l'Épiphanie de Daniel ou de l'Hérode de Matthieu.'

[2] For details see the *Dictionnaire de la Bible: Supplément, ad rem*. In Dan. ii. 2 חַרְטֻמִּים is rendered by μάγους. (See Field's *Hexapla, ad rem*.)

birth of Moses but at his prime that the conflict with the magicians occurs in the Exodus story. To this two rejoinders are pertinent:

(*a*) The conflict with evil forces continues throughout the ministry of Jesus also, while, if any parallelism is to be drawn between Jesus and Moses at all, in view of the early incidence of the death of Jesus, much has to be concentrated into his early years which corresponds to what occurred in Moses' life at a later stage. For example, the flight from Egypt (ii. 19 ff.) anticipates a much later departure in Moses' life.

(*b*) The conflict with the magicians in the extra-Biblical tradition about Moses began early in his life. Thus, for example, in Josephus we read:

While the affairs of the Hebrews were in this condition, there was this occasion offered itself to the Egyptians, which made them more solicitous for the extinction of our nation. One of those sacred scribes (ἱερογραμματέων τις) who were very sagacious in foretelling future events truly, told the king that about this time there would be a child born to the Israelites, who, if he were reared, would bring the Egyptian dominion low, and would raise the Israelites; that he would excel all men in virtue, and obtain a glory that would be remembered through all ages.... (*Antiquities*, II, ix, 2; see also *ibid*. II, ix, 7.)

This resulted in the slaughter of the male children. The sacred scribes here fulfil the role of the Magi, like them they make the ruling monarch aware of the impending danger. The vitality of this element in the tradition is further demonstrated by the fact that the Targum of Jerusalem[1] as well as the New Testament preserves the very names of the antagonists of Moses,[2] as does also CDC v. 18–19.

The tradition preserved in Midrash Rabbah on Exodus is also relevant. While there is no specific mention of a star that accompanied the birth of Moses, we do read that his birthplace was flooded with light, a light associated with that which shone at creation.

The Sages (A.D. 150) say: When Moses was born the whole house became flooded with light: for here it says: AND SHE SAW HIM THAT IT WAS A GOODLY CHILD, and elsewhere it says [in the creation episode]: *And God saw the light, that it was good*. (Gen. i. 4.)[3]

---

[1] See Etheridge, *The Targums on the Pentateuch* (1862), I, 444. 'Immediately *Jannes* and *Jambres*, the chief of the magicians (רִישֵׁי חַרְשַׁיָּא) opened their mouth and said...'; these appear also in CDC v. 18.

[2] 2 Tim. iii. 8: 'As Jannes and Jambres opposed Moses, so these men also...'; on magic in Judaism, see M. Simon, *Verus Israel* (1948), pp. 394 ff. For a full bibliography and references to Jannes and Jambres in pagan sources, etc., see R. Bloch, *Moïse* in *Cahiers Sioniens* (1954), viiie année, no. 2–3–4, p. 105, n. 21.

[3] On the 'light', see also above, p. 445. The evidence for the association of 'light' with the birth of Moses is given in S–B, I, 78 on Matt. ii. 2. The passage

There is one further point of possible comparison between the Exodus story in the Old Testament and Matt. i. 18–25. Daube[1] has pointed out 'a trace of a Jewish legend of a conception without a human father, and the child in question may well be Moses. This would not be a virgin birth—both Miriam and Aaron were older than Moses. But it would be close enough to be of interest.' He refers to a passage in the Passover Haggadah which reads:

'*And He saw our affliction*' [Deut. xxvi. 7]. This means the abstention from sexual intercourse, as it is written (in Exodus [ii. 25]), '*And God saw the children of Israel, and God knew*'.

The view that at some stage in Egypt marital union did not take place appears in several rabbinic sources. Daube refers to Exod. R. on i. 15; ii. 25; TB Yoma. 74*b*; TB So. 11*b* f. The verb 'to afflict', he argues, would naturally be associated with this episode because it occurs 'in those statutes which enjoin fasting and—at least in rabbinic interpretation—abstention from sexual intercourse'. A problem arises, however, as to how they came to connect the verse 'And God saw the children of Israel, and God knew', as supporting this exegesis. 'The only satisfactory explanation seems to be that the author of the Midrash took "to know" in the sexual sense. The Israelites abstained from marital relations. God saw their affliction, and he knew. In other words, it may well be that, for the author of this Midrash, as natural propagation was impossible, the women—or perhaps only the mother of Moses—conceived from God himself.' The details of Daube's argument cannot be reproduced here. He notes that both the Targum of Jerusalem and the LXX introduce changes at the verse possibly to combat the interpretation of it as alluding to the Virgin Birth. There is some confirmation possibly for Daube's thesis in Josephus' treatment of the Exodus in *Antiquities*, II, ix, 3 ff. God promises

cited above is from TB Sotah 12*a*; see also Exod. R. i. 19–20 on ii. 2. The whole passage there shows how creation motives were associated with Moses' birth: it read: 'AND THE WOMAN CONCEIVED AND BORE A SON [11, 11]. R. Judah said: Her giving birth is compared to her pregnancy; just as her pregnancy was painless so was her giving birth—a proof that righteous women were not included in the decree pronounced on Eve. AND WHEN SHE SAW HIM THAT HE WAS A GOODLY CHILD–TOB. It was taught: R. Meir (A.D. 140–65) says: His name was "Tob". R. Josiah (third century) says: His name was Tobiah. R. Judah: He was fit for prophecy. Others say: He was born circumcised. The Sages say: When Moses was born...(as above).' A passage introduced by 'The Sages say' is likely to be early. Other parallels between Matthew and the Exodus are referred to in R. Bloch (*op. cit.* pp. 164 ff.), who works out a detailed comparison between Pharaoh and Herod.

[1] *The New Testament and Rabbinic Judaism* (1956), pp. 5 ff.

to safeguard the posterity of the young men of Israel, as he had done in the case of Abraham and Sarah. God enabled Sarah to conceive. The Midrash on this theme makes it clear that the intervention of God in the birth of the children of the righteous was easily understood. This is expressly stated in Josephus, *Antiquities*, II, ix, 5, where we read that 'God had taken such great care in the formation of Moses' and in the previous paragraph the easy labour at Moses' birth is referred to God's activity. Moreover, while Josephus does not explicitly or implicitly connect the birth of Moses with the act whereby God created the universe, it is interesting that in some midrashic texts the birth of Isaac is so connected.[1] It is not unlikely that the Virgin Birth motif—which looks back to the creation—was indigenous in Judaism in the time of Jesus and an element associated with the Exodus from Egypt, as, in Christian circles, it was connected with the New Exodus.[2]

After the above examination, we can now estimate the role of the New Exodus and New Moses motif in the Prologue. Assume its presence we may, though specific proof, in that there is no direct quotation from Exodus, is lacking, and a degree of subjectivity may enter into all interpretations which have this lack. But exaggerate its importance we must not. As the absence of any reference to Moses in the opening genealogy suggests, the lineaments of Moses in the Prologue are not so drawn that they obliterate or crowd out other emphases with which they coexist, that is, New Creation, Messiah, Son of David, Emmanuel, prophecy fulfilled. Thus their significance is not dominant: they constitute only one motif among others. Nevertheless, they are to be given their due weight.[3] Taken, as a whole, the Prologue presents two aspects of the coming of Jesus Christ. On the one hand, it is discontinuous with Judaism, a new act of creation, unprecedented as the creation of the universe itself. This is the import of the Virgin Birth story, which declares that his coming is

[1] S–B, I, 49.

[2] Contrast S–B, I, 48 who claim that the creative power of the Spirit does not appear in rabbinic sources, as it does in Matt. i. 18.

[3] The caution we have observed in our treatment may be excessive. For a more forthright recognition of the New Exodus and New Moses motif in the Prologue, see R. Bloch, *op. cit.*; R. V. G. Tasker, *The Old Testament in the New Testament* (1946), p. 35. One additional point may be noted. In Matt. ii. 14 Joseph is said to flee to Egypt by night. In the Exodus story the flight *from* Egypt was by night and great haggadic ingenuity was spent on the explanation of this: see the Passover Haggadah, and Midrash Rabbah on Exodus, Soncino translation, pp. 225 ff. Daube, *op. cit.* pp. 190 f. and *N.T.S.* v (1958–9), 189–92, finds the legend of Laban persecuting Jacob here. But this does not exclude the New Moses motif.

the presence of God in the midst, and possibly the title, though this is less certain, in Matt. i. 1 points to the same truth. On the other hand, the coming of the Christ is continuous with Judaism, the fulfilment of its Davidic and, if we may so express it, its 'Mosaic' hope. Because of this last, we seem to be justified in finding in the Prologue support for regarding the *SM* in the light of Sinai and the Christ of the Mount in the light of Moses, though we emphasize that this is never made explicit by Matthew. But just as the words in Jer. xxxi. 15, referring to the present distress of Israel, precede its future redemption and the expression of a hope for a New Covenant in xxxi. 31 ff., so in Matt. ii. 18, where they are cited, they precede a New Covenant and a New Sinai. (On the incidence of these in the reverse order in Matthew we have again to note that the fact of Jesus' death in inaugurating the New Covenant has necessitated a relocation of the terms of the Covenant to the early part of the ministry. The Fourth Gospel has solved this problem by inserting the farewell discourses at the Last Supper in xiii–xvii, these being modelled on Passover customs.)

(ii) *The Epilogue* (Matt. xxvi. 1–xxviii. 20)

If Matthew intended to emphasize them, we should expect the motifs of the New Exodus and New Moses to emerge particularly in his treatment of the Passion, because whether the Last Supper was a Passover meal or not, motifs drawn from that Festival became part and parcel of early Christian thinking. Nevertheless, traces of any emphasis on such motifs as we are concerned with are hard to find in the Epilogue. The following passages alone merely raise the possibility of the presence of such.

(1) In the account of the words which Jesus uttered at the Last Supper, Matthew has added to Mark's text, 'This is my blood of the covenant, which is poured out for many', the following phrase: 'for the forgiveness of sins', which he omitted from his account of the ministry of the Baptist in iii. 1 ff. (contrast Mark i. 4; Luke iii. 3). This assertion of the connexion between the death of Jesus and the forgiveness of sins cannot be laid down to any emphasis on a comparison between the death of Jesus and the Passover motif in Matthew, because the forgiveness of sin is not a main emphasis in the covenant formed at Sinai, even if we could be certain that the Marcan account in xiv. 24 does look back to Exod. xxiv. 8. Assuming that in fact there is a side-glance at the latter passage in Mark xiv. 24 and Matt. xxvi. 28, what Matthew has done by his addition is to combine with Mark's reference to Exod. xxiv. 8 one to Jer. xxxi. 31; but this last,

although it drew upon Exodus concepts, at the same time suggested a contrast to and not a parallel with the first covenant. In short, Matthew by inserting 'with you' in xxvi. 29 retains the communal emphasis proper to the covenantal concept, which is native to the Passover, but, at the same time, by introducing the reference to 'the forgiveness of sins' moves beyond paschal, that is, traditionally Exodus, motifs, because 'the paschal victim was not a sin-offering or regarded as a means of expiating or removing sins'.[1]

(2) It might be argued that in Matt. xxvi. 53 Jesus, facing his opponents, like Moses confronting the Red Sea in Exod. xiv. 19 ff., has the power of angels to draw upon; the theme is developed at length, as we saw above, in connexion with Moses, in the Mekilta. But to find a direct or indirect reference to the Exodus story here is impossible. The theme of Matt. xxvi. 53 might equally well recall 2 Kings vi. 15–17, the story of Elisha 'when the mountain was full of horses', etc., although the parallel with Mekilta on Exod. xiv is closer. But, in any case, it should be noted that there is here not a parallel to the latter but rather a contrast. Jesus refused to call the angelic hosts to his succour.

(3) In Matt. xxvii. 45–56 to the symbols accompanying the death of Jesus which Mark and Luke employ, that is, the darkness and the rending of the veil of the temple, Matthew has added the words in xxvii. 51b–52. Like Mark, and unlike Luke, who makes the two phenomena coincide, he separates the incidence of the darkness (xxvii. 45) from that of the rending of the veil (xxvii. 51). The darkness cannot here be compared with the darkness mentioned in the Exodus story in Exod. xiv: because that darkness was a beneficent, protective darkness, nor again does it obviously recall the plague of darkness called upon the land of Egypt by Moses in Exod. x. 21 ff., nor the thick cloud that descended on Sinai in Exod. xix. 16 and xx. 21, where the term σκότος (חֹשֶׁךְ) is not used but rather νεφέλη γνοφώδης (עָנָן כָּבֵד) and γνόφος (עֲרָפֶל). Were a comparison intended with Sinai at this point, we should expect more points of contact with Heb. xii. 18 ff., where the two Sinais of Judaism and Christianity are contrasted. More likely is it that the 'darkness' is intended to suggest either the return of that darkness which was at creation, the earth having, symbolically, returned to the first beginning or, more likely, the Day of the Lord depicted in Amos viii. 1–ix. 10. The rending of the veil of the temple, following the death of Jesus, signifying the destruction of the old order of worship, naturally recalls Exod. xxvi. 31, where the veil is

---

[1] See *P.R.J.*[2] pp. 250 ff.

described, but hardly invokes any specifically Exodus motif, while its incidence alongside that of the 'darkness' can be understood in terms of Amos ix. 1 f. Thus while at first sight the words in xxvii. 51 *b*–52, which are peculiar to Matthew, might be thought to recall the phenomena described on Mount Sinai at the giving of the Law, this is hardly likely because the parallels with Exod. xix. 16–20 are extremely tenuous as they are with Heb. xii. 18 ff. In fact the words in xxvii. 51 *b*–52 express that sympathy between nature and man which is a mark of the Old Testament and of Judaism, and which was particularly manifested at the Exodus, as at the crucifixion, at least symbolically. But the introduction by Matthew of the reference to the resurrection of the saints makes it clear that he is here concerned not with any Exodus motif but with eschatology of the time, which looked forward to a resurrection of the dead in the Messianic Age or Age to Come. This, too, has a point of contact with Amos viii. 1–ix. 10, by way of contrast with ix. 2 ff. Thus the verses xxvii. 51 *b*–52 belong to the general furniture of eschatology and need not be related to the Exodus.

(4) We are on more promising ground perhaps in Matt. xxviii. 16–20 where the New Moses motif has been claimed to emerge.[1] But that this is not indisputable emerges from the simple fact that other motifs have been claimed to govern the section. Thus the ascription of all authority in heaven and on earth to the living Lord has been understood as a mark of Matthew's sustained polemic against gnosticism.[2] Or, again, the whole scene described in these verses has rightly suggested the enthronement of the Son of Man in terms of Dan. vii.[3] The Risen Christ is the victorious and elevated Son of Man who once suffered. Thus warned of other possibilities for the interpretation of these words, can we with any degree of certainty claim that at least part of their purpose is to present Christ as a counterpart of the First Moses? Three factors may be urged in support of this view:

(1) The last verse of the Epilogue echoes Matt. i. 23 in the Prologue. If therefore we found the New Moses in the Prologue, we might expect it to re-emerge again in the Epilogue, as has the theme of 'Emmanuel'.

(2) The reference to 'the mountain' in xxviii. 16 recalls v. 1; xvii. 1. On the latter there is what we may safely regard as an implicit, if not explicit, presentation of Jesus as a New Moses, and, as we have seen, the same thing is true perhaps on the mountain in v. 1 (the antitheses at least would suggest this in v. 21–48).

---

[1] See, for example, A. M. Ramsey, *The Resurrection of Christ* (1945), p. 78; H. Holtzmann, *Hand-Kommentar* (1889), p. 301; K. Stendahl, *P.C.* (1962), p. 798.
[2] See below, pp. 192 ff.   [3] See below, pp. 196 ff.

(3) In xxviii. 16–20 the disciples are sent forth to teach those commandments given by Christ under which the Church is to live. The actual moral demands of Jesus have become the content of the disciples' teaching: this is probably the meaning in Matt. xvii. 1 ff. also, over against Mark ix. 2 ff. where the content of Jesus' teaching was more concentrated in his Cross and Resurrection. Here in Matt. xxviii. 16–20 Jesus surely is the Moses, a greater than the old, who is the source of a new tradition of a New Israel. The substance of such a figure is here if not the name.

All this in xxviii. 16–20, it has to be admitted, is persuasive. And yet it has to be noted, by way of a caveat, that at no point is there any specific reference to Moses, and it may be questioned whether, if the latter was in Matthew's mind as he drew his picture of the Risen Christ, he would not have been more explicit in his reference to him. As it is we have a plausible conjecture, not a certainty.

We must, therefore, conclude that in the Epilogue the New Moses motif cannot be regarded as in any way determinative or influential. Traces of it are uncertain and conjectural; such cogency as they possess is confined to xxviii. 16–20 and is no more than suggestive, and rests on indications of the New Moses motif which may have emerged elsewhere in the Gospel, not in its own right.

(c) *The Arrangement of Ten Miracles in Matt. viii. 1–ix. 34*

In the contents of the Prologue the New Moses motif is traceable; in those of the Epilogue far more doubtfully so. We have now to examine a section in which the arrangement, as well as some aspects of the content, of the material has been claimed to point to the same motif.

In Matt. viii. 1–ix. 34 we find the following ten miracles recorded:

(1) Healing the leper (viii. 2–4)	(= Mark i. 40–4).
(2) Healing the centurion's servant (viii. 5–13)	(Q).
(3) Healing Peter's mother-in-law (viii. 14–17)	(Mark i. 29–34).
(4) Quieting the storm (viii. 23–7)	(Mark iv. 36–41).
(5) Exorcisms of demons (viii. 28–34)	(Mark v. 1–20).
(6) Healing the palsy by the forgiveness of sins (ix. 2–8)	(Mark ii. 3–12).
(7) Raising the ruler's daughter (ix. 18–19, 23–6)	(Mark v. 22–4, 35–43).
(8) Healing the woman with the issue of blood (ix. 20–2)	(Mark v. 25–34).
(9) Healing two blind men (ix. 27–31)	(M).
(10) Healing a dumb man (ix. 32–4)	(M).

According to Schoeps, this series is intended by Matthew as a deliberate parallel to the ten wonders associated with the first Moses at the Exodus, in fulfilment of Mic. vii. 15, 'As in the days of thy coming forth out of the land of Egypt will I show unto him marvellous things'.[1] Before accepting this position let us ask three questions.

(i) Is the number ten a correct estimate of the miracles recorded in this section? Allen, like Michaelis more recently, found only nine miracles in it. These he divided into three triplets, thus:

(1) viii. 1–15: three miracles of healing;
(2) viii. 23–ix. 8: three miracles of power;
(3) ix. 18–34: three miracles of restoration.

This enumeration and division are only possible by the inclusion of the healing of the woman with the issue of blood (ix. 20–3) with the miracle of the healing of Jairus' daughter (ix. 18–26). This procedure Allen justifies by claiming that 'the fact that there are two previous series of three miracles suggests that the editor reckoned this last series as three not four'.[2] But this is to beg the question. To merge the healing of the woman with an issue of blood with the healing of Jairus' daughter is illegitimate. Moreover, the last group of miracles isolated by Allen does not form such a unity as he claims. They vary in degree of importance so much that the idea of restoration seems quite insufficient to distinguish them as a special class. And when we look at the order of the three items in this supposed class, there is a descent from 'life' to 'sight' and 'hearing', an anticlimax which we cannot possibly attribute to the compiler who *ex hypothesi* arranged the ascending scale of miracles in the second triplet (viii. 23–7 natural forces controlled; viii. 28–34 demons controlled; ix. 1–8 spiritual forces controlled). Klostermann[3] also rejects Allen, and we too must agree with Schoeps in his enumeration of ten miracles.

(ii) But this being so, does it necessarily follow that the section provides a deliberate parallel to the Mosaic wonders? Clearly the number ten has here a certain deliberateness. Matthew has drawn his material from Q, Mark and M, having radically departed from the Marcan order in doing so. The Marcan 'chronology' and 'sequence' he has ignored in order to provide a fairly consecutive series of ten miracles. Moreover, Bacon's

[1] H. J. Schoeps, *Theologie und Geschichte des Judenchristentums* (1948), p. 93. See especially p. 93, n. 3, where the performance of wonders is claimed to be a mark of the New Exodus motif. This is well documented.
[2] I.C.C. *St Matthew, ad rem.*
[3] H. Klostermann, *Matthäusevangelium, ad rem.*

argument at this point can be given a twist other than he intends. Although Bacon apparently finds here a deliberate parallel to the ten Mosaic wonders, he merely mentions this fact cursorily and does not regard it as relevant to the interpretation of the material. The appending in ix. 18–26, after the proper climax of the raising from the dead of Jairus' daughter, of two more briefly recorded and really duplicate miracles, for a numerical reason, is so curious and so belated that the effort to reach a total of ten miracles cannot be regarded as significant.[1] But this cuts both ways. May not this curious and belated appendage suggest that the number of miracles recorded did have a significance for the Evangelist? If so Loisy,[2] who saw no side-glance at Moses in the figure ten here and regarded the last two miracles recorded as pure invention, and Bultmann,[3] who regards the series as merely one of 'great wonders' (*die große Wunderserie*), may be wrong. But clearly there can be no certainty at this point. The number ten may be deliberate, but (although ten miracles were deemed to have been wrought at the Exodus) nevertheless a purely literary convenience. The popularity of the number ten, apart from all Exodus motifs, is apparent in the very passage in Aboth v. 1–6, where the ten plagues of Egypt are mentioned. The incidence of ten miracles cannot be assumed to point to the Exodus.

(iii) Can we find any indications in the contents of the miracles that would necessarily suggest this last? At two specific points it might be argued that Matthew recalls Moses. In viii. 4 there is a direct reference to him at the end of the healing of the paralytic: '...go show yourself to the priest, and offer the gift that Moses commanded, for a proof to the people' (RSV). Is this merely the presentation of Jesus in a light consistent with v. 17 ff., that is, showing respect to the Law, or is it something more, Moses, as Lohmeyer[4] holds, being here claimed as a direct witness to Christ? On this view, the phrase εἰς μαρτύριον αὐτοῖς 'for a proof for the people' is to be taken directly after the verb προσέταξεν, that is, Moses gave the specific command referred to with the direct purpose of supplying an offering which should be a witness to the Christ, so that Jesus here deliberately sets himself forward as the one to whom Moses pointed. This is subtle to a degree, however, and cannot be accepted. In another place, in viii. 24–7 in the story of the stilling of the storm, Christ, it has been claimed, recalls Moses' crossing of the Red Sea. But apart from the fact that this story has parallels elsewhere in that of Jonah in the

---

[1] *Op. cit.* [2] *Op. cit.* [3] *Op. cit.*
[4] *Kultus und Evangelium* (1942), *ad rem*, and his commentary on Matthew.

Old Testament and Paul (more loosely in Acts xxvii. 9 ff.) in the New, and in Jewish and pagan sources, the story offers no exact parallel to Moses' achievement at the Exodus. There a strong wind is not so much stilled as called up. Nothing corresponds to the Synoptic ship, just as nothing in the Synoptics corresponds to Moses' rod.[1] The motif of the stilling of the sea frequently occurs in the Old Testament in connexion with the figure of Yahweh, not with that of Moses. Supremacy over the sea was a mark of God's mighty power (Ps. xxix. 3, 10; lxxxix. 9; xciii. 3, 4: compare Nahum i. 14; Hab. iii. 15; Ps. xcvi. 11; xcviii. 7; xlii. 10). Creation itself was regarded as the binding or limiting of the sea by Yahweh (for example, Job xxxviii. 8–11; Prov. viii. 22–31; Jer. v. 22b; xxxi. 35; Ps. xxxiii. 6; lxv. 7 f.–civ. 5–9), an idea which shows the influence of old Babylonian mythology on Tiamat–Marduk. Moreover, the eschaton had come to be depicted in terms of Yahweh's victory over the cosmic sea. Victory over the nations is compared with victory over the sea in the last days (Isa. xvii. 12–14; Ps. xlvi). The future final conflict between Yahweh and 'the Adversary' comes to be expressed in similar terms (Isa. lix. 15b–20).[2] It is probably over against this tradition that we are to understand the description of the sea, the terror of the disciples and the action of Jesus in the passage in Matt. viii. 20–7 and its parallels. Taken in isolation the story suggests how cosmic forces of evil threaten the order of creation itself only to be brought under the control of one who has authority over them, and who exercises the sovereign power of God. Now it is true that the language of the creation myth has been taken up into the description of the Exodus in the Old Testament as in Ps. lxxvii. 16:

> When the waters saw thee, O God,
>> when the waters saw thee, they were afraid,
>> yea, the deep trembled,

and in lxxvii. 19, 20:

> 19 Thy way was through the sea,
>> thy path through the great waters;
>> yet thy footprints were unseen.
> 20 Thou didst lead thy people like a flock
>> by the hand of Moses and Aaron.

[1] See on this the very interesting *Anhang* in R. Mach, *Der Zaddik in Talmud und Midrasch* (1957), pp. 223 ff.; he refers to E. Peterson, 'Das Schiff als Symbol der Kirche', in *Theologische Zeitschrift*, VI (1950), 77–9.

[2] On this see H. Gunkel, *Schöpfung und Chaos* (1895), pp. 91 ff.; Alan Richardson, *The Miracle Stories of the Gospels* (1941), 189 ff.; S. A. Cook, *The 'Truth' of the Bible* (1938), pp. 127 ff.

So, too, in Ps. cvi. 9:

> He rebuked the Red Sea, and it became dry;
> and he led them through the deep as through a desert.

But apart from this indirect possibility of its being present in this way in the 'imagery' or 'symbolism' of Matt. viii. 23–7, the Exodus motif would seem to be absent. The light in which Matthew understood the story is probably revealed to us in the conclusion to which it leads, namely, the exclamation on the divine authority of him who stilled the storm in viii. 27, which in viii. 29 is followed by the demoniacs' recognition of Jesus as the Son of God. Whether a deliberate intention to draw a contrast between this divine figure, as Lord of creation, and Jesus, the Son of Man, in his humiliation which places him below the beasts of the field and the birds of the air, in the light of Ps. viii, or the desire to emphasize the nature of discipleship to him who is Lord of nature, but yet hath nowhere to lay his head, dictates the insertion of the whole section from viii. 18–22, we cannot surely decide but, in any case, it warns us again against treating viii. 1–ix. 34 as a catalogue of ten miracles only designed to recall ten plagues. Apart from the number ten, which itself may be a mere literary convenience, there is no indication that the shadow of Moses falls on viii. 1–ix. 34.

We may now draw our conclusion on the whole section. Probably viii. 1–ix. 34 is meant to correspond to v. 1–vii. 28: it expresses the infinite succour available in Christ in his deeds, just as v. 1–vii. 28 expresses his infinite demand. (viii. 18–22 may be regarded, in its emphasis on discipleship, as a loose link with v. 1–vii. 28.) The former expresses Christ's authority in action, the latter in word. This authority is exercised (1) in healing (in viii. 1 ff. a leper is healed, in viii. 5–13 a Gentile, and in viii. 14–17 a woman. These figures have been claimed to have a 'cultic' significance:[1] their healing may indicate that those types excluded from the benefits of religion in Judaism are made nigh by Christ); (2) in the right of Jesus to call whom he willed (viii. 19–22), the most sacred family ties being transcended; (3) over nature (viii. 23 ff.), over the demonic even in Gentile territory (viii. 28–34); (4) over the priesthood and the cultic enactments of Judaism (ix. 1–9 ff.); and, finally, over death and again over disease (ix. 18 ff.). The manner in which this authority, in almost all instances, is asserted suggests, not so much the Exodus, as the creative

---

[1] E. Lohmeyer, *Matthäusevangelium, ad rem,* and *Kultus und Evangelium, ad rem.* See below, p. 330, n. 3.

activity of God. The creativity of Christ's word appears in viii. 1–4, where the leper is healed, in viii. 9, 13 in the case of the centurion's son, and of Peter's mother-in-law, because 'the word' in viii. 16 probably includes the whole of viii. 14–17. The word of Jesus stills the seas (viii. 23–7), expels the demons from the Gadarene swine (viii. 28–34), brings forgiveness of sin (ix. 1–8) and heals (viii. 29). Only in ix. 18–34 in the story of Jairus' daughter is there no explicit reference to the 'word' of Jesus, the emphasis being on the faith of the woman with the issue of blood in ix. 22 and on that of the two blind men in ix. 29, the 'word' spoken being left perhaps to be implied in ix. 25, 33. Throughout the section, in almost all its parts, we are recalled not so much to the Exodus as to Gen. i, and confronted with the succour of one who reminds us of the activity of God, by his word, in creation itself, and who is at the same time Son of Man (especially in viii. 18 ff.). Moreover, the whole series of miracles is brought to a close with words which are hardly appropriate if the intention were to draw a parallel between Jesus and Moses: they read, 'Never was anything like this seen in Israel' (ix. 33). And the very last words in ix. 34 may further indirectly confirm our refusal to see an Exodus motif in viii. 1–ix. 34. As we saw above, the sorcerers, etc., at the Exodus are led to recognize in the activity of Moses the finger of God (Exod. viii. 19), but the Pharisees only see in that of Jesus a sign that he is the Prince of demons. Matthew does not here rebut the charge, but he does so elsewhere in terms which are, for our purpose, highly significant. Compare the following verses from Luke xi. 19 ff. and Matt. xii. 27 ff. where the rebuttal occurs:

Luke	Matthew
And if I cast out demons by Beelzebul, by whom do your sons cast them out? Therefore they shall be your judges. But if it is by *the finger of God* that I cast out demons, then the kingdom of God has come upon you.	And if I cast out demons by Beelzebul, by whom do your sons cast them out? Therefore they shall be your judges. But if it is by *the Spirit of God* that I cast out demons, then the kingdom of God has come upon you.

Luke's version is probably the more original.[1] In any case, whereas Luke understands the exorcistic work of Jesus in the light of the Exodus, Matthew, who may have deliberately altered Q, connects it with the spirit of God, that is, he thinks of it in terms of the creative activity of God in Gen. i. 1. This difference between Luke and Matthew at this point is a

---

[1] See T. W. Manson, *The Teaching of Jesus* (1945), pp. 82 f.

strong indication that creation motifs were at least as strong as those of the Exodus in Matthew and that the importance of the latter in the interpretation of his Gospel must not be over-emphasized.

Let us now assess the total significance of the above examination of Matthaean passages which have been claimed to present Jesus in the light of Moses. Parallelism can be urged, with some certainty, in the Transfiguration, provided it be recognized that, while Matthew has here deliberately emphasized reminiscences of Mount Sinai, Jesus is nevertheless, even here, not a second edition of Moses, as it were, on a grand scale, but one who supersedes him. In the Prologue the New Moses motif is probably to be detected, but, there again, it is neither neat nor predominant. Rather is it one element in a mosaic of motifs, one strand in a pattern, which equally, if not more, emphasized the Christ as a new creation, the Messianic King, who represents Israel and is Emmanuel. In the Feeding of the Multitudes, in the light of the Fourth Gospel particularly, it may be well to recognize the Exodus motif, although it is not peculiarly emphasized in Matthew. In the remainder of the passages examined, dealing with the ministry of the Baptist, the baptism and temptation of Jesus, despite the confident claims for the presence of the motif frequently made, it is more difficult to be convinced. In these sections the motif can only be found very precariously, if at all; certainly there is no more emphasis in it in Matthew than in Mark or Q. The degree of conviction which the discovery of the motif will carry in these sections will depend on the evocative power allowed to the terms employed in them, to the weight of 'New Exodus' connotation with which they are deemed to be charged in the first-century milieu.[1] But, and this we must emphasize, even where, on such grounds of evocativeness, as in the force of the term 'mountain' in xxviii. 16 ff. and the significance of the incidence of 'ten' miracles in viii. 1–ix. 34, the presence of the motif may be allowed, it is so intertwined with others, which are even more clearly detectable, that its significance cannot be too exclusively stressed. Thus in xxviii. 16 ff., if the New Moses be at all suggested, so is also the Son of Man, the exalted Lord of the Church; and in viii. 1–ix. 34 though it be granted, with doubtful justification, that the ten miracles do suggest the ten plagues of the Exodus, there is also present the activity of the creative word.

Our examination thus indicates that Matthew was well aware of that interpretation of Christ which found his prototype in Moses, and that, at

---

[1] Here Bloch, *op. cit.* and J. Jeremias, *T.W.Z.N.T.* IV, on Moses, are invaluable.

certain points, he may have allowed this to colour his Gospel. But the restraint with which the New Exodus and New Moses motifs are used is noticeable. Evidences for these two motifs are not sufficiently dominant to add any significant support to Bacon's pentateuchal hypothesis, which must, therefore, still remain questionable, though possible. While these motifs have influenced Matthew's Gospel, it is not clear that they have entirely fashioned or moulded it. This also appears when we consider Matt. v–vii. Those elements to which we referred above, especially in the Prologue and the Transfiguration and, less certainly, the Feeding of the Multitudes, do add force to the view that in the *SM* we are to detect a New Sinai. But the tentativeness and reserve of Matthew's use of the Exodus motif is striking. There is no explicit reference to Mount Sinai; no features from the account of the giving of the Law in Exod. xix, as they are developed, for example, in Heb. xii. 18 ff., appear in v. 1 f.; and at no point, apart from the express quotations from the Law in the antitheses, in v. 21 ff., are we directly referred to the events at Sinai. Any pointers to the latter are extremely hesitant, if they exist at all. Even though the writing of a Gospel did not allow the same freedom of elaboration as did that of an epistle, like Hebrews, we cannot but ask whether Matthew could not have been somewhat bolder in his 'Mosaism' had the idea of a New Moses played a great part in his purpose in writing the Gospel. The case would seem to be that, while the category of a New Moses and a New Sinai is present in v–vii, as elsewhere in Matthew, the strictly Mosaic traits in the figure of the Matthaean Christ, both there and in other parts of the Gospel, have been taken up into a deeper and higher context. He is not Moses come as Messiah, if we may so put it, so much as Messiah, Son of Man, Emmanuel, who has absorbed the Mosaic function. The Sermon on the Mount is therefore ambiguous: suggestive of the Law of a New Moses, it is also the authoritative word of the Lord, the Messiah: it is the Messianic Torah.

3. MOSAIC CATEGORIES TRANSCENDED

But an adequate appreciation of the Sermon as Mosaic and yet more than Mosaic, that is, as Messianic Torah, can only be achieved when we ask two further questions. First, what is its relation to the moral demand as Matthew presents it elsewhere in the Gospel; and, secondly, what precisely do the literary 'formulae' within the Sermon itself suggest as to its character or intent?

(a) The Christian Life

First, then, let us ask how Matthew, as a totality, conceives of the Christian life. To begin with, were it only in the light of the Sermon itself, that life is to be under the imperative of the words of Jesus. The title disciples (μαθηταί) applied to Christians in Matthew is not merely a derivative from the tradition, but indicative of a significant aspect of the nature of the Christian life. The relation of Christians to Jesus during his earthly ministry, and after his exaltation in the Resurrection, can be expressed in a terminology derived from Judaism, the religion of the Law. Christians are to learn of Christ and bear his yoke, a metaphor which suggests the existence of a Law of Christ (xi. 29). They constitute a brotherhood of disciples under one master (just as Judaism has its master in Moses?) (xxiii. 8); in xiii. 52 we may legitimately see them as 'taught or trained for the Kingdom of Heaven' (literally, if the phrase be permissible, 'discipled' unto it) and part of their final commission from the Risen Lord is to make disciples (xxviii. 20). Similarly the community of Christians has its prophets, wise men, scribes (xxiii. 34), and is to exercise its discipline of 'binding and loosing' in terms reminiscent of the 'legal' discipline in Judaism (xviii. 18). To judge from the evidence dealt with by Stendahl,[1] it constituted a school of interpretation, that is, it was a *beth midrash*. Thus the discovery of a Mosaic motif in the *SM* comports with an emphasis we discover elsewhere in the Gospel, as indeed, from another point of view we have previously recognized. Christians, for Matthew, do stand under the 'New Sinai' of a 'New Moses'.

But here precision is necessary, lest the ambiguity of the Sermon be neglected and the character of this New Sinai misunderstood.

In the first place, the words under which the disciple stands are most emphatically presented as the words of Jesus himself: the commandments of the Sermon are *his* to be obeyed (this is the least that can be said of the phrase 'But I say unto you' in the antitheses), and it is as *his* words that they constitute the standard of judgement on the Last Day (vii. 24, where the 'mine' is emphatic: πᾶς οὖν ὅστις ἀκούει μου τοὺς λόγους τούτους: the translation might be: 'Everyone then who hears me, in respect to these sayings...'). In this sense, the ethical teaching is not detached from the life of him who uttered it, and with whom it is congruous. It is personalized in him. It is not only given *through* or

[1] *The School of Matthew* (1954).

by means of Jesus but *in* him, if we may borrow a possibly Johannine distinction.[1]

And, in the second place, this personalization of the words of Jesus, that is, their inseparable attachment to him, so that they are not presented in isolation from his life, as are, for example, the sayings of rabbis in Pirqê Aboth and the sayings of Jesus himself among the Gnostics, occurs within a context in which all Christian activity is so personalized, that is, so related to Jesus himself.[2] Because coincident with the demands expressed in the words of Jesus is another demand, which is not another, that the disciple should be conformed to the person whose are the words. The demand for *imitatio Dei*, expressed in v. 48, becomes that for *imitatio Christi*. Not only does the insistence that the words are *his*, to which we have referred, suggest this, but the inclusion of '*faith*', along with 'judgement' and 'mercy', as the quintessence of the demand made upon Christians, is significant (xxiii. 23). This triad can be understood as the expression of Jesus' understanding of the essential or weighty matters of the Law, as are the Golden Rule (vii. 12) and the twofold commandment (xxii. 40). In this case 'faith', one element in the triad, stands for 'loyalty' to the will of God as revealed in the Law and the Prophets.[3] But, elsewhere in Matthew, faith means reliance upon the authority of Jesus (viii. 10; ix. 2; viii. 13; ix. 22, 28 f.); disciples are called upon to trust in him with whom nothing is impossible (xvii. 20; xxi. 21); the Marcan '*believe*' becomes '*believe in*' (compare Mark ix. 42; xv. 32 and Matt. xviii. 6 τῶν πιστευόντων εἰς ἐμέ and xxvii. 42 πιστεύσομεν ἐπ᾽ αὐτόν).[4] So too in xxiii. 23, therefore, 'faith' is probably to be understood not simply in the sense indicated above as loyalty to the Law and the Prophets, but as trust in Jesus, and the two other members of the triad 'mercy' and 'judgement' are thereby given a Christocentric direction. The demand of the Law and the Prophets is, at the same time, the demand to trust in Jesus. And this can be so because, in his every activity (iii. 15) and in his words (v. 17 ff.), Jesus has 'fulfilled' the demand for 'righteousness'.

Thus it is that, in the third place, the life which is under the judgement

---

[1] John i. 17, on which see E. C. Hoskyns and F. N. Davey, *The Fourth Gospel*.

[2] Gnostics isolated the words of Jesus in the way that Judaism isolated the words of rabbis: see, for example, R. M. Grant and D. N. Freedman, *The Secret Sayings of Thomas* (1960).

[3] See G. Bornkamm, *The Background of the New Testament and its Eschatology*, ed. W. D. Davies and D. Daube (1956), pp. 235 ff.

[4] Note that in Mark ix. 42 the reading usually accepted is simply τῶν πιστευόντων. The RV of 1881 adds εἰς ἐμέ, the reading of A B W θ f f 13 (the majority) Sa bo (most manuscripts). ℵ has τῶν πιστευόντων: πίστιν ἐχόντων is the reading of C* Da.

of the words of Jesus is, at the same time, a life of trust in him, which means, in turn, a life of following him. As we have seen, just as his words reveal the essence of the Law of God, so does his life, so that to obey the Law of God comes to mean, for Matthew, to follow Christ. This is clear in xix. 16–20, where the following of Jesus is the culmination of the perfect fulfilling of the Law. And this implies the *imitatio Christi*, not in a wooden, literalistic sense, but in that the marks of the life of Jesus are to be traceable in that of his followers. Thus, in his counsels to the Twelve in Matt. x, Jesus seems to predicate of the life of his apostles what became true of himself in the Passion. And other similar marks of his life, apart from the Passion, strictly so called, are to characterize Christians—readiness to suffer (x. 17 ff.; xvi. 24 ff.), to be poor (xix. 23 ff.; vi. 19 ff.), to be humble (xviii. 1 ff.), to love (xxiii. 31 ff.), to reject worldly honour (xxiii. 7 ff.), to serve (xx. 20 ff.). Thus the ethical norm for Christians is not only the words but the life also of him who uttered them. The shadow of Jesus' own life is over all the Sermon. To appreciate this fully the connexion of the Sermon has to be noted with what precedes it in chapter iv. Jesus came as a light to lighten those that sat in darkness (iv. 15 ff.), not only preaching but healing 'every disease and every infirmity among the people'. His fame was that of one who bore the pains of the afflicted (iv. 23 ff.), that of the Servant of the Lord (xii. 15). Jesus first appeared, not making a demand, but offering succour, his first concern, not the exaction of obedience, but the proclamation of blessing (iv. 23 ff.; v. 3–11). For Matthew, therefore, the Sermon is set within a framework of healing and pity. The proclamation of the higher righteousness in the Sermon (v. 20) is of a piece, as we saw, with his fulfilment of all righteousness in baptism (iii. 15). This last signifies at least a humble readiness in Jesus to be identified with his people, to be one with them. He thus fulfils the essential demand of God, as he himself expresses it in v. 21 ff., so that to obey his words is to imitate him.

And with this, in the fourth place, it agrees that the merely Mosaic character of Jesus' relation to his disciples has been transcended. This in two ways.

(i) In the terminology used by Matthew in reference to Jesus there is a significant development. While Christians always remain for him disciples of a teacher of righteousness, so that he uses the terms teacher and rabbi of Jesus, nevertheless, it is striking that, apart from Judas Iscariot, he allows none of the disciples to address him thus.[1] While Mark and Luke

---

[1] G. Bornkamm, *op. cit.* p. 250.

place these terms on the disciples' lips frequently, Matthew consistently avoids doing so, and prefers to make the disciples address Jesus as Lord. Nor is this merely a title of respect, a courtesy title; it is honorific. Despite its persistently didactic character in Matthew the relationship between Jesus and his disciples is also that between Lord and 'slave' or 'servant'; not only pedagogic, it is proprietary. Within the Sermon itself this is made clear, even though the mere recognition of Jesus' lordship as such avails nothing (vii. 21 ff.). And this insistence on the lordship of Jesus must be allowed to temper any interpretation of Matthew's conception of him as New Moses: Jesus commands as Lord; Moses commanded as mediator.[1] The two categories, of Lord and teacher, are coincident in x. 24 f., where Christ as teacher is in parallelism with Christ as Lord, and the disciples are in parallelism with 'slaves' or 'servants'. So too in xxviii. 16–20 the Risen Lord, who is worshipped, commands the making of disciples who are, however, to be more than disciples, because they are baptized in his name. Thus Christians, for Matthew, are disciples within a larger context of incorporation into their Lord.

(ii) And this last brings us to the second way in which the merely 'Mosaic' relationship of the Christian to his Lord is transcended in Matthew. In the two passages last referred to, that is, x. 24; xxviii. 16–20, it is clear that for Matthew the Christian disciple is so related to his Lord that there is a kind of identity between them. This also appears elsewhere. Although there is no phrase used in Matthew corresponding to the Pauline formula 'in Christ' to express the nature of the Christian's life, because the Evangelist prefers to emphasize explicitly that Christ is 'with' his own, as Emmanuel, nevertheless, the reality expressed in the Pauline formula is implicit in his Gospel. Particularly is this so in chapter x, where not only

---

[1] A glance at a concordance reveals how very frequently Matthew uses κύριος as compared with Mark: the usage of διδάσκαλος and διδαχή are equally revealing. The tables given by R. Morgenthaler, in *Statistik des Neutestamentlichen Wortschatzes* (1959), are as follows:

διδάσκαλος		διδαχή		κύριος	
Matt.	12	Matt.	3	Matt.	80
Mark	12	Mark	5	Mark	18
Luke	17	Luke	1	Luke	103
John	9	John	3	John	53
Acts	1	Acts	4	Acts	107
Paul	7	Paul	6	Paul	275

Neither διδάσκαλος nor διδαχή is included by Hawkins as typically Matthaean, *Horae Synopticae* (1899), pp. 3 ff. But that Matthew's 'Lord' was a teacher appears from the fact that the disciples are called μαθηταί 73 times in Matthew (compare 46 times in Mark, 38 in Luke, 78 in John, 28 in Acts).

is the experience of Jesus to be enacted in the lives of his apostles, as we saw above, but there is a real representation of the Lord by the apostles which amounts to a kind of identification, in terms of the Jewish *Shaliach*. x. 40 makes this utterly clear. 'He who receives you receives me, and he who receives me receives him who sent me' (compare Mark ix. 41; Luke x. 16; John xii. 44 f.; xiii. 20). If in xviii. 5 we take 'one such child' to refer to 'Church members' or Christians, the same truth emerges there. 'Whoever receives one such child in my name receives me; but whoever causes one of these little ones who believe in me to sin....' The last part of the verse confirms the interpretation of 'the child' suggested, as also does xviii. 10 ff. And in between xviii. 6 and xviii. 10 Matthew inserts a section which, though not explicitly, nevertheless by implication, in this context, reveals an awareness of the Christian community as the 'body' of Christ. The same relationship between Christ and Christians emerges in xxv. 31 ff., where service to the latter is service to the former, as it is expressed in xxv. 37 ff., 'Then the righteous will answer him, "Lord, when did we see thee hungry and feed thee, or thirsty and give thee drink?..." And the King will answer them, "Truly, I say to you, as you did it to one of the least of these my brethren, you did it to me."' There can be little doubt that 'the least of these my brethren' has reference to Christians. Elsewhere in Matthew a 'brother', except where a blood brother is meant, means a Christian (v. 22; xviii. 15, 21; v. 23 f.; v. 47; vii. 3–5). Matt. xxv. 31–46 should be interpreted in terms of Matt. x: those who do acts of kindness or neglect to do so in the former being identical with those who receive or reject those who proclaim the Gospel in the latter.[1] We need not further enlarge on this point except to recall that this intimacy of relation between Jesus and his own is rooted in Jewish conceptions of solidarity and eschatological expectations that the Messiah would bring with him his community.[2] What we are concerned to indicate is that Matthew understands the Christian life in the light of this relationship. If we may so express it, Christians are called upon 'to live out' their oneness 'in Christ', not only in their relations to the world, in the acceptance of suffering, but to one another, in the acceptance of mutual service. In other words, there is in Matthew the implication that

[1] See on this an unpublished dissertation by a former pupil, Dan O. Via, 'The Church in Matthew' (Duke University, 1955). See also C. H. Dodd, 'Matthew and Paul', *Expository Times*, LVIII, 296–7. On Matt. x see A. Schweitzer, *The Mysticism of Paul the Apostle, ad rem.*

[2] See A. R. Johnson, *The One and the Many in the Israelite Conception of God* (1942); on Matt. xxv, Theo Preiss, *Life in Christ* (1954); and literature cited by Via.

the imperative is based on an indicative. This familiar formulation is usually appealed to in connexion with the ethical teaching of Paul, but, though not so clearly expressed by him, it is equally true of that of Matthew. Nowhere does the latter explicitly urge Christians to be what they are in the sense indicated, and the explicit sanctions of his ethics, both secondary and primary,[1] are other than this; nevertheless, the above evidence makes clear the implicit sanction we have indicated. And while (apart possibly from v. 11, where 'on my account' may mean 'on account of your relationship to me', though this cannot be pressed) the *SM* does not appeal to Christians' oneness with their Lord and with one another as a ground for moral conduct, nevertheless it is directed to the Christian community, at least primarily, and for Matthew this was the community of the Son of Man, united with him, as we have seen. Thus the context of the Sermon in the totality of the Gospel's thought on the nature of the Christian life forbids any exclusive or even predominant 'Mosaic' approach to it. The Sermon is that of the Messiah, the Son of Man and the community addressed is incorporated in him.[2]

(b) Terminology

We can now turn to the second question posed above, namely, what indications are there in the circumstances, terminology and formulae of the Sermon itself as to its meaning? In the circumstances surrounding the actual delivery of the Sermon, as we saw previously, there is little, if indeed anything, to recall the giving of the Law on Mount Sinai. At first sight it might be argued that the location of the delivery on 'the Mountain' in v. 1 is very deliberate, and designed to suggest a counterpart to Sinai, because in Q, as is clear from Luke vi. 17, the Sermon was 'delivered' after Jesus had descended from the mountain and 'stood on a level place'. But it is equally arguable that the Lucan account is, if anything, more reminiscent of Exod. xix, where Moses descended from the mount to give the commandments he had received upon it. Taken in isolation, the circumstances described in v. 1 ff. cannot be made too much to suggest a New Sinai, a suggestion which, as we noted above, only acquires force from other elements in the Gospel which point to this.

That Matthew understands the teaching of Jesus as no revolutionary phenomenon appears immediately from two things. First, from a change

[1] See A. N. Wilder, *Eschatology and Ethics, ad rem.*
[2] On Messiah and Ecclesia, see Via, *op. cit. ad rem,* and literature there cited.

he makes in the Marcan material at this point. In Mark i. 21–8 Jesus appears in a synagogue at Capernaum, teaching with authority and healing a man with an unclean spirit (that is, the healing is here exorcism). Into the difficulties presented by the fact that the act of exorcism itself seems here to be characterized as a 'new teaching' (διδαχὴ καινή) we need not enter, except to assert that this phrase must be understood to include not only the exorcism but also the actual teaching, here undescribed (i. 21 ff.).[1] The point which concerns us is that Matthew has omitted the whole incident described in i. 21–8. Instead he has given, in iv. 23–5, a summary, generalized paragraph describing synagogal teaching, preaching, healing and exorcism throughout the whole of the country. This becomes for him the immediate prelude to the *SM* which he clearly intends to be understood as constituting the teaching with authority referred to in Mark i. 22, a verse which he quotes in vii. 28, at the close of the Sermon, almost verbatim. He has avoided giving the healing of the demoniac in the synagogue at Capernaum for reasons of arrangement, having preferred to concentrate the healing activity of Jesus into viii–ix, as we saw above. But one thing is striking. Had Matthew thought of the *SM* as a radically new teaching, he had to hand a phrase in Mark i. 27, which he could have used to describe it, and we should have expected in vii. 28 to read: 'And when Jesus finished these sayings, the crowds were astonished at his new teaching. ...' But this we do not find: this is significant evidence that the teaching of Jesus for Matthew was not radically 'new'.

This is confirmed, in the second place, by explicit statements in the Sermon and outside it. First, in v. 17–20. The verb 'to fulfil' in v. 17, variously interpreted, is best taken, in the light of its total context, to mean 'to complete' or 'to bring to its destined end'. From v. 18, 19, 20,

---

[1] The text of Mark i. 27 has caused much discussion. τί ἐστιν τοῦτο is absent from D W b c e ff sy⁸ geo aeth arm. Many MSS have τίς ἡ διδαχὴ ἡ καινὴ αὕτη ὅτι κατ' ἐξουσίαν, with variations in the position of καινή. D W and other Western MSS read ἐκείνη ἡ καινὴ αὕτη. Taylor rightly regards the Western reading as conflate. Couchoud, *J.T.S.* xxxiv, 116, and Lohmeyer, *Matthäusevangelium*, p. 34, have urged that the original text was τίς ἐστιν ἡ διδαχὴ ἐκείνη, in which case the point we make above, that Matthew has significantly omitted any reference to a *new* teaching as such, is invalidated. Couchoud finds support for his argument in e, the Old Latin Palatinus from the fifth century, *quaenam esset doctrina haec*, and from the fact that Luke iv. 36, τίς ὁ λόγος οὗτος, has nothing corresponding to καινή, but has a parallel to καινή in οὗτος (see Taylor, *The Gospel according to St Mark*, p. 176, n. 2). But καινή is attested in all MSS save the Western: a confusion of καινή and ἐκείνη has taken place. The Lucan reading is a smooth version of the Marcan. The difficulty of the reading in אBL, τί ἐστιν τοῦτο; διδαχὴ καινή, explains the rise of variants.

this would seem to allow of the continuance of the Old Law in force, since it is not abolished (v. 17) but remains in every jot and tittle. On the other hand, while certain of the so-called 'antitheses', in v. 21–48, have been claimed to enhance the Law, others have been claimed to annul it. Thus Albertz[1] distinguished two kinds of antitheses within the complex v. 21 ff. In the first group, which consists of verses 21, 22*a*, 27 f., 33, 34*a*, 37, the antitheses take the form of a deepening of the demand of the Law, as it were, to the *n*th degree. In the second group, in verses 31–2, 38 f., 43, we have not a radicalizing of the pertinent demands of the Law, as in the first group, but what at first sight seems a contravention of them.[2]

But Daube has helped us to understand the nature of these so-called antitheses better. The forms in which the antitheses are couched all follow more or less the pattern: 'Ye have heard that it was said by them of old time, Thou shalt not kill. But I say unto you, That whosoever is angry with his brother shall be in danger of the judgement.' There are two parts to this form: (*a*) *Ye have heard*', etc.; (*b*) '*But I say unto you*', etc. In the light of the rabbinic evidence produced by Daube, the part (*a*) is to be interpreted as meaning, in the case of the first group of antitheses isolated by Albertz, 'You have understood the meaning of the Law to have been'; and in the case of the second group so isolated, 'You have understood literally'. Similarly, behind the part (*b*) lies a rabbinic form expressing a contrast between 'hearing', the literal understanding of a rule, and what we must 'say' it actually signifies. (There is a difference between the rabbinic formula and that employed by Jesus, as we shall note

---

[1] *Die synoptischen Streitgespräche* (Berlin, 1931), *ad rem*; and *Botschaft des Neuen Testaments* (Zürich, 1947–52), *ad rem*. On 'fulfil', see the bibliographical note in *Mélanges Bibliques rédigés en l'honneur d'André Robert* (Paris, 1956), pp. 429, n. 1. I there argued (pp. 428–55) that the ambiguity which our sources reveal in the attitude of Jesus to the Law, namely, that he appears to uphold it and to annul it at the same time, is to be understood in terms of a distinction which Jesus himself drew between the time before and the time after his death. While in principle the Law had passed away during his ministry, it was not until Jesus had sealed the New Covenant in his death that it could openly be declared to have done so. Hence the ambiguity to which we referred. The assumption was there made that, as Albertz claimed, some of the antitheses were intended to annul the Law. As far as the antitheses are concerned this may be an error and in the text above I follow Professor Daube in the view that no annulment of the Law is intended in any of them but rather its completion. But this does not remove the ambiguity in the attitude of Jesus elsewhere in the Synoptic tradition, so that my thesis in the work cited still deserves consideration. For criticisms of it, see J. Dupont, *Les Béatitudes* (1958), pp. 116 n., 134 n., 132 n.

[2] D. Daube, *The New Testament and Rabbinic Judaism* (1956), pp. 55–62. It is impossible to summarize the subtle turns of this chapter.

below, but at this juncture this is not relevant.)[1] The point is that in none of the antitheses is there an intention to annul the provisions of the Law but only to carry them to their ultimate meaning. This has been expressed so convincingly by Daube that his words deserve quotation: 'the Matthaean form is far milder, less revolutionary, than one might incline to believe...these declarations, "Ye have heard–But I say unto you", are intended to prove Jesus the Law's upholder, not destroyer. The relationship between the two members of the form is not one of pure contrast; the demand that you must not be angry with your brother is not thought of as utterly irreconcilable with the prohibition of killing. On the contrary, wider and deeper though it may be, it is thought of as, in a sense, resulting from and certainly including the old rule; it is the revelation of a fuller meaning for a new age. The second member unfolds rather than sweeps away the first.' To interpret on the side of stringency is not to annul the Law, but to change it in accordance with its own intention. From this point of view, as Daube shows, we cannot speak of the Law being annulled in the antitheses, but only of its being intensified in its demand, or reinterpreted in a higher key.

One caveat alone needs to be issued here. The fact that the so-called 'antitheses' are to be regarded more accurately as exegesis than as strict antitheses, must not be allowed to depress their significance. Nor is it correct to isolate the phrase 'but I say unto you', which in itself probably merely means that Jesus is here offering his own interpretation of the Law, from its total context in the Sermon, and in the Gospel. It surely has a peculiar force here, as the occurrence of 'verily' (ἀμήν) in v. 18, before the first incidence of 'I say unto you' indicates. The use of ἀμήν in this way by Jesus *may*, indeed, be unique.[2] The phrase 'I say unto you' occurs on the lips of him who is Messiah and Lord, and the overwhelmingly solemn nature of the setting of the pronouncements must be given its full force. Matthew has draped his Lord in the mantle of a teacher of righteousness,

---

[1] D. Daube, *op. cit.* p. 60.

[2] The use of 'Amen' by Jesus is discussed by Daube, *op. cit.* pp. 388–93; and by J. Jeremias, in *Synoptische Studien* (München, 1953), pp. 89–93 under the title 'Kennzeichen der *ipsissima vox* Jesu'. Jeremias writes: 'Auch bei den 'Amen-Sprüchen haben wir also das Auftauchen eines neuen, völlig singulären Sprachgebrauches festzustellen'; with this he also connects 'ein göttliche Vollmacht beanspruchendes Hoheitsbewußtsein' (p. 92). Daube, on the other hand, finds possible an anticipation of this in Judaism, despite the late character of the sources to which he appeals. He suggests that because the 'Amen' was mainly employed in eschatological contexts it was disliked by rabbis: for the same reason it is frequent in the New Testament. On the 'I', see A. Schweitzer, *The Quest of the Historical Jesus*, Eng. trans. (1910), pp. 370 ff.

like Moses, even though no explicit comparison between the two figures is drawn.[1]

Secondly, in three passages the question of Jesus' attitude to the Law arises with special force, that is, in Matt. xii. 1–14; xv. 1–20; xix. 1–9. While Schoeps,[2] in particular, has argued that, even in their Marcan form, these passages afford no evidence that Jesus was concerned to abrogate the Law itself but merely to criticize the tradition of the fathers, that is, the oral Law, most Christian scholars have referred all three passages to Jesus' rejection of the written Law itself. But if there is ambiguity in Mark's treatment of Jesus' attitude in the parallels he offers to the above sections, there is none in that of Matthew himself. In each case he has so changed or added to the Marcan material as to make it perfectly clear that not the validity of the Law as such is in dispute but its interpretation in the tradition. The following are the passages with their parallels:

(i) *The observance of the Sabbath* (Matt. xii. 1–14; Mark ii. 23–iii. 6; Luke vi. 1–11). Matthew adds to the Marcan account of the Plucking of the Corn on the Sabbath (Mark ii. 23–8) another verse (Matt. xii. 5). As Daube has made brilliantly clear,[3] this serves to provide a precedent for the action of the disciples in the Law itself (Num. xxviii. 9, 10). Matthew further employs a familiar rabbinic argument called 'the light and weighty'. His intention is clear. Useful as was the reference to the conduct of David (1 Sam. xxvii. 1–7) referred to in Mark, it had no strict relevance to the question of the sabbath and was, in any case, of merely haggadic significance. To produce a strong argument such as Matthew desiderated for Jesus' justification of his disciples' conduct, more was needed. 'It

---

[1] See also E. Percy, *Die Botschaft Jesu* (Lund, 1953), pp. 123 ff. Morton Smith's work on the antitheses also deserves special attention in *Tannaitic Parallels to the Gospels* (Philadelphia, 1951), pp. 28 f., 43. Percy finds a real antithesis intended between the demand of Jesus and that of the Mosaic Law. He severely criticizes Smith's position that there is no such antithesis intended (see *Die Botschaft Jesu*, pp. 309, 123 n.). Percy urges that in none of Smith's evidence 'handelt es sich aber wie in Matt. v. 21 ff. darum, daß der betreffende Lehrer seine Lehre den Geboten des Gesetzes als solchen entgegenstellt'. He also adds 'kommt bei dem ἐρρέθη τοῖς ἀρχαίοις der große Abstand in sprachlicher Hinsicht von der vermeintlichen rabbinischen Parallele'. Percy refers 'those of old' to the generation in the wilderness.

[2] In *Revue d'Histoire et de Philosophie Religieuses*, xxxiii (1953), 15 f., 'Jésus et la loi juive'; see Davies, *Mélanges Bibliques*, pp. 433 ff. The most trenchant statement of Jesus' extreme criticism of the Law itself is in E. Stauffer, *Die Botschaft Jesu* (1959), pp. 13 ff.

[3] D. Daube, *op. cit.* pp. 67 ff.; see also Davies, *Mélanges Bibliques*, p. 435.

was of the essence of the rabbinic system that any detailed rule, any halakha, must rest, directly or indirectly, on an actual precept promulgated in scripture. It must rest on it directly or indirectly: that is to say, there was no need for a halakha to be laid down in so many words, so long as it could be derived from some precept by means of the recognized norms of hermeneutics. One of these norms, for example, was the inference *a fortiori*, or as the rabbis termed it *qal waḥomer*, " the light and the weighty ".' [1] This explains Matthew's addition to Mark: it fulfils the requirements enumerated, and, in addition, is peculiarly pertinent because it refers to the temple service and the argument from the temple service on a sabbath rests on a definite precept. Its force is to place Jesus securely within the Law.

Strikingly enough Matthew introduces a similar addition to Mark iii. 1–6, which deals with healing on the sabbath. In Matt. xii. 11 we have again the *qal waḥomer* in reference to the healing also designed to place beyond any doubt that Jesus was within the Law, this time the oral law (Mishnah Yoma viii. 6; Shabbath xviii. 3).

(ii) *Laws of Purity* (Matt. xv. 1–20; Mark vii. 1–23). While dispute is possible over the Marcan formulation of the case here, and many have found, especially in Mark vii. 14–23, that Jesus annuls the written Law itself, since the laws of things clean and unclean were written, and not merely oral, there can be no dispute over Matthew's meaning. Not only does he omit the words, in Mark vii. 19, to the effect that Jesus intended to declare all foods clean, but his closure with the words 'but to eat with unwashed hands does not defile a man', a closure to which there is no parallel in Mark vii. 23, has the effect of making the whole discussion turn around the question of the oral tradition rather than the written Law, because the washing of hands before meals was not enjoined in the latter, but only in the former.[2]

(iii) *Divorce* (Matt. xix. 1–9; Mark x. 2–12). For our purposes we need note only that, by the addition of the phrase 'for any cause' to the Marcan version, Matthew has brought the question of divorce into the realm of strict legal discussion more clearly than has Mark. But his treatment, like that of Mark, in no way can be interpreted as a radical departure from the Law of Moses, but only as a radical interpretation of it, such indeed as Shammai gave. To forbid divorce was not to annul the law of divorce

[1] D. Daube, *op. cit.* p. 68.   [2] See B. W. Bacon, *op. cit. ad rem.*

but to intensify it. In any case, it should not be overlooked that Gen. i. 27, to which, like Mark, Matthew appeals, is itself a part of the written Law. Jesus is, therefore, only appealing from one part of the Law to another. Daube further claims that the Matthaean prolongation of the Marcan quotation to include the words 'and he shall cleave to his wife', is designed to place all the emphasis in Matthew's understanding of divorce on the precept itself as drawn from Gen. i. 27.[1]

In all the three areas mentioned, therefore—that of the sabbath, things clean and unclean, divorce—Matthew makes it clear that the teaching of Jesus is not in antithesis to the written Law of Moses, though it is critical of the oral tradition: it is the full interpretation of the former, rather than its annulment.

And this Matthaean emphasis emerges thirdly in the way in which Matthew either directly or indirectly refers to Moses himself. To viii. 4; xvii. 3, 4 we have referred sufficiently above. In xv. 4 and xxii. 31 there are significant changes from Mark. Mark vii. 10 reads: 'For Moses said, "Honour your father and your mother...".' In xv. 4 Matthew changes this to 'For God commanded, "Honour your father and your mother"'.[2] The commandment of Moses is the commandment of God. A change similar, though perhaps less immediately noticeable, occurs in xxii. 31. In the parallel in Mark xii. 26 we read: 'And as for the dead being raised, have you not read in the book of Moses, in the passage about the bush, *how God said to him....*' Matthew, who incidentally accepts the Pharisaic position here, as does Mark, simply has: 'And as for the resurrection of the dead, have you not read *what was said to you by God....*' Here what was delivered to Moses is taken by Matthew as the direct word of God to his own generation. Greater eminence not even Moses could be accorded. It is hardly likely that Matthew's changes are merely dictated by the desire to produce a liturgically clearer text: the theological implication of these must be recognized. And we may further note that the anxiety not to place Jesus in direct antithesis to Moses may emerge, subtly, in the section on divorce. Here Matthew refuses to follow Mark in making Jesus introduce the reference to Moses but prefers to let the Pharisees first do so. Slight this change may be, but perhaps significant. The Matthaean Christ does not himself initiate a comparison which might suggest opposi-

---

[1] D. Daube, *op. cit.* p. 83.

[2] This should not be taken to mean that for Mark the Law of Moses was not also the Law of God (see C. E. B. Cranfield, Mark, *ad rem*), but the Matthaean change is none the less noteworthy.

tion to Moses, or rather criticism of him, whereas the Marcan Christ has no such scruples.[1]

Fourthly, the striking evidence of the attack on the Scribes and the Pharisees in xxiii must be considered. With the question whether there is here discernible an utterly radical criticism and rejection of Scribalism and Pharisaism we are not concerned.[2] The fact is that, as Matthew has fashioned his material, there is no such rejection. The Scribes and Pharisees in xxiii. 1–7 are condemned not for exercising their several functions but for doing so in the wrong way, that is, hypocritically. Their teaching is accepted, their practice alone being rejected. We cannot doubt that xxiii. 2 expresses Matthew's understanding of the Christian attitude to Pharisaism. 'The Scribes and the Pharisees sit on Moses' seat; so practise and observe whatever they tell you, but not what they do; for they preach and do not practise....' This point of view, set as a frontispiece to the whole of xxiii, governs the rest of the chapter; it emerges also elsewhere in a more radical form in xv. 3 ff. where the claim is made that Pharisees actually transgress the commandment of God for the sake of their tradition, and become blind guides of the blind (xv. 14). But, even so, their adherence to the Mosaic Law as such is not condemned, but only their misinterpretation of it. As we have previously seen, there are scribes in the Christian community itself (xxiii. 34) who are taught in the Kingdom of Heaven (xiii. 52). Such scribes, we may presume, would exercise their function both in relation to the words of Jesus, as the new interpretation of the Law of Moses, and with the latter itself. Similarly to take the yoke of Christ upon oneself would mean submission to the authority of his teaching, and implies, as we saw above, that there is a Law of Christ, but this Law of Christ we now see was for Matthew the true interpretation of the old Law, which is also thus subsumed under 'the yoke of Christ' for him. Thus our discussion suggests that the understanding of the Law of Moses both within and without the Sermon in Matthew forbids any emphasis on an antithesis to the Law of Moses and must be allowed, along with the other factors mentioned above, to temper our eagerness to see in Jesus a New Moses opposed to the first.

The threads of our treatment must now be drawn together. That we might the better understand it, we have sought, as pertinently as possible, to place the *SM* in its setting within the Gospel as a whole. Matthew has

---

[1] See G. Bornkamm in *The Background of the New Testament and its Eschatology*, ed. Davies and Daube, *ad rem.*

[2] E. Haenchen on 'Matthew 23', *Z.T.K.* XLVIII (1951), 38–63.

been shown to reveal the influence of the New Exodus and New Moses motif, but this has not been allowed to dictate his presentation of the Gospel to any serious degree. Thus its fivefold structure cannot certainly be held to have any theological significance, that is, it does not necessarily point to a deliberate interpretation of the Gospel in terms of a new Pentateuch as, in its totality, a counterpart to the five books of Moses. At this point, though certainly not at others, it might prove profitable to exorcize the awe-inspiring ghost of Bacon from Matthaean studies. Similarly the *SM* itself is not set forth as a 'new', revolutionary Law, in sharp antithesis to that given on Sinai. Matthew, indeed, seems pointedly to have avoided the use of the phrase 'new teaching' to describe the words of Jesus and presents them as the true interpretation of the Law of Judaism. Not antithesis but completion expresses the relationship between the Law of Moses and the teaching of Jesus.

But the mere recognition of this is not enough: its full force for the understanding of Matthew must be apprehended. One of completion (reformation is too weak a word) and not revolution, the above relationship may be for him, but, quite clearly, he has, with unmistakable deliberateness and with massive and majestic impressiveness, placed the teaching of Jesus in the forefront of his Gospel. His Christ is inevitably thought of as on the Mount, a teacher of righteousness. At the same time the demand that Matthew's Christ laid upon his disciples, elsewhere in the Gospel, had a personal reference to himself, which could not be exhausted in terms of the commandments of the Sermon, but which, combined with the latter, make of it an expression of the Lord's very being. Despite its didactic isolation, its setting in Matthew's interpretation of the Gospel as a whole gives to the Sermon a quality of 'personalism' 'in Christ'. We cannot doubt that Matthew intended it to represent the Messianic Torah. By this he meant not a new, that is, a different, Law, but a new interpretation of the Old Law. This new interpretation of Jesus we can justifiably designate as 'Torah', just as the interpretations of Hillel and Shammai are so designated (Tos. So. xiv. 9). But though strictly interpretation, the words of Jesus are authoritative in a new way (vii. 28). Daube, who more than any other has taught us caution in applying the term 'antitheses' to the demands of the *SM*, has also recognized the element of newness in the words of Jesus. 'The point is that, in Matthew, we have before us, not a scholarly working out by some rabbis of a progressive interpretation as against a conceivable narrow one, but a laying down by Jesus, supreme authority, of the proper demand as against a view, be it held by friends or enemies, which would still take the exact words of the scriptural precept as a standard of conduct. Jesus, supreme authority, lays down the proper demand: this accounts for "But I say unto you, That whosoever is angry, etc....". The demand is opposed to a view held among those addressed which would still take the exact words of a precept as a basis: this accounts for, "Ye have understood literally what was said", etc. The setting in life of the rabbinic form is dialectic exposition of the Law; that of the Matthaean is proclamation of the true Law...."[1]

We cannot then doubt that the *SM* is the 'law' of Jesus, the Messiah and Lord. Our treatment thus ends in an ambiguity. Matthew presents Jesus as giving a Messianic Law on a Mount, but he avoids the express concept of a New Torah and a New Sinai: he has cast around his Lord the mantle of a teacher of righteousness, but he avoids the express ascription to him of the honorific 'a New Moses'.[2] Can we understand this ambiguity? Why, in a Gospel, where there is much to evoke the use of these terms, where the *substance* of the New Law, the New Sinai, the New Moses, are present, is there an obvious hesitancy in giving explicit expression to them? Perhaps the eschatological expectations of and conditions within first-century Judaism can clarify this ambiguity and explain Matthew's caution: we shall explore them in this hope in the next two chapters.

[1] D. Daube, *op. cit.* p. 58; on the Torah of Hillel and Shammai, p. 214.

[2] That the interpretation of historical figures in terms of Moses was familiar in Judaism appears from the way in which Hillel and Akiba were treated. Thus the significance of Hillel was shown by setting his life over against that of Moses and dividing it into three parts accordingly. See I. Elbogen, 'Die Überlieferung von Hillel', in *Festschrift für Leo Baeck* (Berlin, 1938), pp. 68 ff. Hillel founded the Torah along with Moses and Ezra (TB Sukkah 20*a*). Akiba's life lasted 120 years as did those of Hillel and Moses (*op. cit.* p. 68, n. 5) in the tradition. This approach to the life of a significant individual finds a parallel in the genealogies of some peoples. Professor D. M. Emmet refers to the use of genealogies in a mythical way. She writes: 'Some peoples like the Bedouin Arabs present their membership system by retailing it in the form of a lineage story. Such a lineage system is drawn in terms of putative relationships to ancestors of former generations. It is not a realistic ancestral tree, but a tradition of descent *as believed in* by members of the group' (*Function, Purpose and Powers*, 1958, p. 20, cited by D. O. Thomas, in *Efrydiau Athronyddol*, XXVI, Cardiff, 1963, p. 21). The mythical genealogy subserves the needs of the group for unity and glory. I know of no study of genealogies in the Bible from this point of view.

III. THE SETTING IN JEWISH
MESSIANIC EXPECTATION

The issue raised by the non-observance of the Torah among Gentile Christians in the primitive Church was so central that the relation between the Torah and the Gospel could not but have commanded much attention among historians of primitive Christianity. What is surprising, however, is that one pivotal aspect of this relation has been little discussed. Early Christians believed that Jesus of Nazareth was the Messiah of Jewish expectations, and that they were living in that Age which had long been promised by the Hebrew scriptures. It would, therefore, seem natural that, in trying to understand the interactions between the Torah and the Gospel, scholars should have asked the question what role, if any, the Torah was expected to assume in the Messianic Age or in the Age to Come:[1] it could be assumed that this would illumine for us the impact of the Gospel on the Torah and thus best enlighten us on the various attitudes within the early Church towards Judaism and also within Judaism towards the Church. At the same time we might expect it to lead to a better appreciation of certain relevant elements in the Christian movement itself, and, especially for our purpose, on Matthew's presentation of the *SM* as the Law of the Messiah.

Nevertheless, obvious and important as is its necessity, those who have sought to clarify the role expected of the Torah in the Messianic Age, as was suggested, have been few. For any extended discussions of the problem we have to go to Christian controversialists of the Middle Ages, whose works are not easily accessible, and treatments of these by modern scholars such as Lieberman. But such discussions are late.[2] The following references to the problem are the only ones we have been able to trace in recent scholarship dealing strictly with the period of our interest. Edersheim published an appendix to his work, *The Life and Times of Jesus the Messiah* (1901), vol. II, appendix xiv, pp. 764 ff., entitled *The*

---

[1] The relation of the Messianic Age to the Age to Come need not, for the moment, concern us. In this chapter, except in the last sections where the distinction becomes important, both terms will be used to signify generally the ideal future of Jewish expectation. See chapter II in J. Klausner, *Die Messianischen Vorstellungen des Jüdischen Volkes im Zeitalter der Tannaïten* (1904).

[2] See Appendix V.

Law in Messianic Times: in this he also refers to Holdheim, *Das Ceremonialgesetz im Messias-Reich*.[1] Klausner dealt with the same problem in his book *Die Messianischen Vorstellungen des Jüdischen Volkes im Zeitalter der Tannaïten* (1904), pp. 52 f.; in addition Kohler allotted a paragraph to it in his article on Eschatology in the *Jewish Encyclopedia*, v, 216, a paragraph to which Abrahams referred with approval in his *Studies in Pharisaism and the Gospels* (1924), 2nd ser., pp. 125 ff. The most recent and thorough treatments are those of Strack–Billerbeck (Exkurs IV, pp. 1 ff.: 'Zur Bergpredigt Jesu' (1928)), and Aptowitzer in *Parteipolitik der Hasmonäerzeit im rabbinischen und pseudepigraphischen Schrifttum* (Vienna, 1927). Baeck has some interesting remarks on the question in his book, *The Pharisees* (Eng. trans. 1947), pp. 72 ff., and there are scattered references in Montefiore and Loewe, *A Rabbinic Anthology* (1928), pp. 157 ff., 558, and in the works of Moore and Bonsirven.

The material which has been written is not bulky, as is evident.[2] But it has already revealed the especial difficulties which the sources present. These are chiefly two. First, there is the dating of the various relevant passages. Thus most of the rabbinic material used is post-Christian and often reveals a marked tendentiousness: and it is the weakness of Edersheim's treatment of our problem, as that of Aptowitzer, for example, that they ignore the complications caused by these factors. The second difficulty arises from the precise interpretation of the Hebrew terms used in certain contexts: to note only one example, even the term *Torah* itself in different places may mean different things and is thus a constant source of confusion. This difficulty is brought out in Klausner's treatment of our theme and in that of Aptowitzer.[3] Both these difficulties will occupy

---

[1] No date. [2] See Appendix VI.

[3] V. Aptowitzer, *Parteipolitik der Hasmonäerzeit*, pp. 116 ff., held that it was the politico-religious rivalries of the Hasmonaean period that stimulated speculation on the role of the Torah in the future—whether in the Messianic Age or the Age to Come. The hands of the Hasmonaeans were stained with blood so that many of the pious objected to their High Priesthood: the Pharisees also objected to their kingship because they were not of the stock of David to whom (according to scripture and tradition) the kingship rightfully belonged. Out of this situation between Hasmonaeans and anti-Hasmonaeans there arose disputes over the perpetuity of the Law and its role in the Messianic Age and in the Age to Come. The radical anti-Hasmonaenists proposed the view that in the future the Messiah would be of the stock of David and also High Priest; there would be a Messiah-Priest: while the Hasmonaeans looked for a Priest-Messiah; but the views of both sides were only made possible by the manipulation of scripture. The Pharisaic expectation of a Davidic High Priest in particular implied that the copies of the Torah in the Messianic Age would have to be changed, at least in parts. This in turn raised the question of the perpetuity

us later, we mention them here merely to indicate beforehand the complexity of our task. Thus warned we can proceed to our examination of the sources, beginning with the Old Testament: and it should be noted at the outset that we are particularly concerned to discover whether or not Judaism contemplated a New Torah in the future, in the light of which we can approach the *SM*.

But before we examine the relevant texts, the first of the passages with which we shall deal (Jer. xxxi. 31–4) suggests a highly pertinent fact in the background of our quest, namely, the significance of the Exodus not only in Israel's history but also in its Messianic speculation. This was not merely homiletic, but also theological. Briefly we may assert that the memory of the Exodus comes to be of the essence of the Old Testament, because, just as behind the New Testament there is a kerygma centred in an event, the life, death and resurrection of Jesus of Nazareth, so in the Old the Exodus constitutes a kerygmatic core. This emerges clearly in passages where 'credal', confessional, material, older than the texts in which they now occur, break through. The oldest of these is probably Deut. xxvi. 5 ff.

5 And you shall make response before the Lord your God, 'A wandering Aramaean was my father; and he went down into Egypt and sojourned there, few in
6 number; and there he became a nation, great, mighty, and populous. And the

of the Torah. Within the Pharisaic party Aptowitzer found a struggle. The rigorists maintained that the Law was perpetually unchanged and unchangeable: others held that in the Messianic Age it would be modified and in the Age to Come abrogated; thus if the Messianic Age can be identified with the Age to Come it also would see the abrogation of Torah. This discussion within Pharisaism was possible because of differences over the question of the incidence of the Resurrection: did it occur at the close of the Messianic Age, then that Age could still have its Torah; did it occur at the beginning of the Messianic Age, then clearly the conditions would approximate those of the Age to Come when the Torah would be abrogated. Were there no Resurrection at all then the eternal validity of the Torah could be held, and this was the position of the Sadducees. According to Aptowitzer this explains why the Sadducean–Hasmonaean author of the *Book of Jubilees* is so insistent on the perpetuity of the Law: his insistence is not aimed at the antinomianism of Paul, as Singer had argued, but at his political opponents. Nevertheless much of the Christology of the New Testament in Matthew, Luke (the genealogies), Paul and Hebrews is to be understood in the light of the speculations to which the political struggle indicated gave rise. The value of Aptowitzer's treatment lies in the wealth of material which he commands, not in the interpretation he puts upon it. It is precarious to use rabbinic texts of a far later period to illumine the struggles of the Hasmonaean period: in the words of J. Bonsirven, 'ces divinations sont trop conjecturales pour qu'il soit prudent d'en faire état' (*Le Judaïsme Palestinien*, I, 47); compare A. Marmorstein, *Monatschrift für Geschichte und Wissenschaft des Judentums* (1929), 224–50, 440 f., 478–87.

Egyptians treated us harshly, and afflicted us, and laid upon us hard bondage.
7 Then we cried to the Lord the God of our fathers, and the Lord heard our voice,
8 and saw our affliction, our toil, and our oppression; and the Lord brought us
out of Egypt with a mighty hand and an outstretched arm, with great terror,
9 with signs and wonders; and he brought us into this place and gave us this land,
10 a land flowing with milk and honey. And behold, now I bring the first of
the fruit of the ground, which thou, O Lord, hast given me.' And you
shall set it down before the Lord your God, and worship before the Lord
11 your God; and you shall rejoice in all the good which the Lord your God has
given to you and to your house, you, and the Levite, and the sojourner who is
among you.

12 When you have finished paying all the tithe of your produce in the third year,
which is the year of tithing, giving it to the Levite, the sojourner, the fatherless,
13 and the widow, that they may eat within your towns and be filled, then you shall
say before the Lord your God, 'I have removed the sacred portion out of my
house, and moreover I have given it to the Levite, the sojourner, the fatherless,
and the widow, according to all thy commandment which thou hast commanded
me; I have not transgressed any of thy commandments, neither have I forgotten
14 them; I have not eaten of the tithe while I was mourning, or removed any of it
while I was unclean, or offered any of it to the dead; I have obeyed the voice
of the Lord my God, I have done according to all that thou hast commanded
15 me. Look down from thy holy habitation, from heaven, and bless thy people
Israel and the ground which thou hast given us, as thou didst swear to our
fathers, a land flowing with milk and honey.'

16 This day the Lord your God commands you to do these statutes and ordinances; you shall therefore be careful to do them with all your heart and with all
17 your soul. You have declared this day concerning the Lord that he is your God,
and that you will walk in his way, and keep his statutes and his commandments
18 and his ordinances, and will obey his voice; and the Lord has declared this day
concerning you that you are a people for his own possession, as he has promised
19 you, and that you are to keep all his commandments, that he will set you high
above all nations that he has made, in praise and in fame and in honour, and
that you shall be a people holy to the Lord your God, as he has spoken. (RSV.)

This amounts to a confession of Yahweh's saving acts in forming a nation
out of a number of aimless tribes; it recapitulates the mighty deeds which
gave birth to Israel. This 'credal' concentration on the Exodus also
emerges in Deut. vi. 20–4; Joshua xxiv. 26–31. The significance of the
Exodus is also illustrated in such passages as Deut. iv. 32–4:

32 For ask now of the days that are past, which were before you, since the day that
God created man upon the earth, and ask from one end of heaven to the

other, whether such a great thing as this has ever happened or was ever heard of.
33 Did any people ever hear the voice of a god speaking out of the midst of the
34 fire as you have heard, and still live? Or has any god ever attempted to go and
take a nation for himself from the midst of another nation, by trials, by signs, by
wonders, and by war, by a mighty hand and an outstretched arm, and by great
terrors, according to all that the Lord your God did for you in Egypt before
your eyes?

Throughout Israel's history the Exodus came to serve as a point of
reference for the elucidation of the present, as in such passages as 1 Sam.
x. 18; 2 Sam. vii. 6, 23; 1 Kings vi. 1; viii. 16, 21.[1] The story of Elijah may
be understood from this point of view; it is possible, though not certain,
that he deliberately relived the experience of Moses in making a pilgrimage,
lasting forty days, to Horeb, and, like Moses, hiding in a cave in the rock
while the Lord passed by (1 Kings xix. 9, compare Exod. xxxiii. 22).
Reference to the Exodus emerges clearly—in Amos iii. 1–2:

Hear this word that the Lord has spoken against you, O people of Israel, against
the whole family which I brought up out of the land of Egypt:
2 'You only have I known of all the families of the earth; therefore will I punish
you for all your iniquities.'

And in Hosea as follows:

Therefore, behold, I will allure her, and bring her into the wilderness, and
speak tenderly to her. And there I will give her her vineyards, and make the
valley of Achor a door of hope. And there she shall answer as in the days of
her youth, as at the time when she came out of the land of Egypt. (ii. 14–15.)
   Like grapes in the wilderness, I found Israel. Like the first fruit on the fig
tree, in its first season, I saw your fathers. (ix. 10.)
   When Israel was a child, I loved him, and out of Egypt I called my son. (xi. 10.)
   I am the Lord your God from the land of Egypt; you know no God but me,
and beside me there is no saviour. It was I who knew you in the wilderness,
in the land of drought. . . . (xiii. 4–5.)

Although Jeremiah contrasts the New Covenant with that ratified at the
Exodus, nevertheless, it was that same Exodus, which, were it only by
contrast, supplied him with the very categories with which to describe the
new redemption that he desired, and throughout he appeals to the
memory of the Exodus, as in ii. 1–3, 6; vii. 22–6; xvi. 14–15; xxxii. 17–23.

---

[1] Gerhard von Rad, *Das Formgeschichtliche Problem des Hexateuchs*, p. 4; also
H. Wheeler Robinson, *Inspiration and Revelation in the Old Testament*, p. 151.

Ezekiel also has the same motif, for example in xx. 5–13, 36 f., and Micah in vi. 3–4:

> O my people, what have I done to you?
> In what have I wearied you? Answer me!
> 4 For I brought you up from the land of Egypt,
> and redeemed you from the house of bondage;
> and I sent before you Moses, Aaron, and Miriam.

And, as is the witness of the prophets, so is that of the cultus. In much, if not all, of the liturgy of Judaism we are brought face to face with the deliverance from Egypt. Much of it was designed to re-enact that event. Thus, this was the purpose of the Feast of Passover, which is mentioned twice before the Exile in 2 Chron. xxx; 2 Kings xxiii. 21–3, and it is no accident that the major Festivals—Tabernacles and Pentecost—are all associated with the Exodus.[1]

Not only the present but the future also was placed in the light of the Exodus. We have indicated this in our reference to Jer. xxxi. 31 f., compare xvi. 14 f. The most striking example of it occurs in Deutero-Isaiah where a parallelism is drawn between the first and last redemption, which is described in terms, enhanced indeed, but, nevertheless, derived from the first. Long a commonplace, this has been forcibly presented in a recent commentary in which Isa. xlii. 14–xliv. 23 is entitled 'The New Exodus'. The thought is that Yahweh, who created Israel and redeemed her from Egypt, is about to intervene once more on her behalf (xlii. 23–xliii. 2). Just as his special relation to Israel led him to deliver her in the past, so will it involve his delivering her again in the future (xliii. 3–8). The Old Exodus became the guarantee of the New (xliii. 9–12), when Babylon would suffer as formerly did Pharaoh (xliii. 14–17), in an Exodus far more glorious than the Old (xliii. 18–21). The full extent to which Deutero-Isaiah is impregnated with the motif of the New Exodus can only be appreciated by the detailed study of passages such as the following: xl. 3; xli. 17–20; xlii. 10; xliv. 27; xlviii. 21; l. 2; li. 10, 11; lii. 3, 4, 12; lv. 3; lviii. 8; lxiii. 11–14. Ezekiel's vision of the future is also governed by the memory of the Exodus, the twelve tribes of the 'new' people that was to come recalling those of the desert of old.[2]

---

[1] See J. Pedersen, *Israel*, III–IV, 398–414; *P.R.J.*[2] pp. 102 ff.

[2] P. Volz, *Eschatologie der jüdischen Gemeinde*, p. 113. See E. J. Kissane, *The Book of Isaiah*, II, 39 ff.; J. Bright, *J.B.L.* LXX, 22; J. Muilenburg, *Interpreter's Bible*, V, compare p. 400 with p. 405. A. Bentzen finds here essentially the contrast later drawn between the two Ages, *Messias, Moses redivivus, Menschensohn*, p. 56:

Memory of a past Exodus, then, and anticipation of a new are the twin poles in much of the faith of the Old Testament. Nor did they cease to be such in Judaism. In the cultic life of Israel as revealed in its liturgy, especially in its festivals, the same notes of memory and anticipation, both rooted in the first Exodus, recur. The Dead Sea Scrolls in particular justify the claim that what we may call the Exodic current in Messianism deepened. Thus the community at Qumran was organized in terms of a New Exodus. This it was that determined the flight to the desert, the sojourning for about forty years around Damascus and the details of the organization of the camp. Thus we read in the Manual of Discipline:[1]

When these things come to pass for the community in Israel, by these regulations they shall be separated from the midst of the session of the men of error to go to the wilderness to prepare there the way of the Lord; as it is written, 'In the wilderness prepare the way of the Lord; make straight in the desert a highway for our God'. (Millar Burrows's translation.)

Nor were the sectarians apparently alone in being moved by such ideas. Josephus mentions Theudas, a Galilean, and another, an Egyptian prophet, who led their followers to the wilderness in force. The 'Messianic' character of these figures must not be too readily assumed. In both cases the wilderness may have had no 'typological' significance, that is, may not have been intended to recall the first wilderness of the Exodus: it may have been merely strategically convenient to gather in such a place or ascetically appropriate.[2] Moreover, the activity of Theudas in attempting to cleave the waters of Jordan suggests not Moses so much as Joshua or

'Dieser deuterojesajanische Gedanke vom "Neuen" hat—das sei nur kurz angedeutet—in der neutestamentlichen Eschatologie seine Entsprechung. Es sei nur erinnert an 2 Korinther 5. 17*b* und Apoc. Joh. 21. 5. Deuterojesaja arbeitet faktisch mit dem Gegensatz zwischen den beiden Aeonen den wir aus dem Spätjudentum so wohl kennen.' C. R. North in *Studies in Old Testament Prophecy*, ed. H. H. Rowley (Edinburgh, 1950), denies this (pp. 111 ff.). On the Mosaic character of the Messianic Age, see also H. Gressmann, *Der Messias* (1929), pp. 181 ff.

[1] See DSD viii. 12–16, the community lived in camps (CDC vii. 6; xix. 2–3; xiv. 3, 9); the division into units (CDC xiii. 1) compares with what we find in Exod. xviii. 25–6; J. Jeremias, *T.W.Z.N.T.* on Moses, p. 865; J. T. Milik, *Dix Ans de Découvertes dans le Désert de Juda*, pp. 63, 76; H. M. Teeple, *The Mosaic Eschatological Prophet*, p. 30; G. Vermès, on 'La Figure de Moïse au Tournant des Deux Testaments', in *Moïse l'Homme de l'Alliance*, p. 76; N. Wieder, 'The "Law-Interpreter" of the Sect of the Dead Sea Scrolls', in *J.J.S.* IV (1953); M. Black, *The Scottish Journal of Theology*, VI (1953), 5; T. H. Gaster, *The Dead Sea Scriptures*, p. 4; J. Schmitt, *Revue des Sciences Religieuses*, no. 4 (October 1955), 398; S–B, III, 812.

[2] For the caution necessary here, see Giblet, *L'Attente du Messie*, p. 107.

Elijah.[1] Nevertheless, it is difficult, in view of the other material to which we have referred, to exclude an Exodic motif from these movements to which Josephus refers. Theudas and the Egyptian were concerned probably to inaugurate a redemption on the analogy of the first. The ease with which New Testament writers interpreted the Christian dispensation in terms of the Exodus is explicable only on the supposition that such a procedure was readily comprehensible. This emerges most clearly in John vi. 30–4, even though by way of contrast as well as comparison.

30 So they said to him, 'Then what sign do you do, that we may see, and believe
31 you? What work do you perform? Our fathers ate the manna in the wilderness;
32 as it is written, "He gave them bread from heaven to eat".' Jesus then said to
them, 'Truly, truly, I say to you, it was not Moses who gave you the bread from
33 heaven; my Father gives you the true bread from heaven. For the bread of God
34 is that which comes down from heaven, and gives life to the world.' They said
to him, 'Lord, give us this bread always'.

In later rabbinic sources the motif to which we refer is quite explicit also. On this we refer to the work of R. Bloch, 'Moïse dans la Tradition Rabbinique', in *Moïse l'homme de l'Alliance* (Paris, 1955), pp. 92–167, especially pp. 150 ff., 156 ff. Giblet, in *L'Attente du Messie, ad rem*, pp. 113 f., appears excessively cautious but should be read as a corrective to Bloch. And we have already alluded to the presence of this motif in Matthew (see pages 25 ff. above).

But, we must press our examination of the Exodic motif still further. Two questions particularly concern us: first, whether within the complex of the Exodus, both as an event in the past and as the prototype of the final deliverance, the figure of Moses became prominent and, especially, whether it acquired Messianic proportions? And, secondly, whether within that complex, the giving of the Law, on which Judaism certainly came to concentrate in retrospect, also played a significant role in its anticipation of the future? Would the giving of Law mark the End as it had the Beginning of Yahweh's dealing with Israel?

As to the first question, in many of the relevant Old Testament passages, there is no marked concentration on Moses. The Exodus in its totality as 'deliverance' is the centre of interest. But there did develop in Israel and in Judaism a growing veneration for Moses himself as the divine instrument in that deliverance. Each period reflected in the Old Testament seems to have pictured Moses in its own image, so that he emerges as

---

[1] The river does suggest this; but this should not be pressed, because the Jordan could be a symbol of the Red Sea.

priest, sage and, possibly, as king, in addition to being humble mediator and intercessor.[1] But it is as prophet that he appears most clearly. He became the type of the prophet to come (Deut. xviii. 15), even though it is asserted that none after him could surpass him (Deut. xxxiv. 10–12). Is this 'prophet to come' associated particularly with the Messianic Age as constituting a new Exodus? There is nothing in Deut. xviii. 15 ff. to suggest this, but it is perhaps significant that in Deutero-Isaiah, where the motif of the New Exodus is most apparent, the instrument of deliverance, the Servant of the Lord, has long been connected with Moses, by Sellin.[2] And although his reasons for doing so were faulty, this identification, according to Bentzen,[3] was essentially sound. Criticizing Engnell's over-emphasis on the king motif in the Servant poems, Bentzen finds the prototype of the Servant in Moses; especially is this true in Isa. xlix. 5–6, 8–12, and in those passages depicting the vicarious suffering of the Servant which Bentzen thinks are best understood in the light of verses such as Exod. xxxii. 31 ff.; Deut. ix. 17–20, 25–9, and again Deut. i. 37; iii. 26; iv. 21. The following marks of the Servant recall Moses—his task is to regather the tribes of Israel (Isa. xlix. 6), to intercede on behalf of his people (Isa. liii. 12; compare Exod. xxxii. 32), to establish a covenant (Isa. xlii. 6; xlix. 8; compare Exod. xxxiv. 8), to bring his *Torah* and his word (Isa. l. 4; xlii. 4; compare Exod. xx. 1; xxxiv. 3; Deut. iv. 1, 13; vii. 11–12; x. 4). Like Moses he suffers contradiction (Isa. l. 7–8; compare Exod. xxxii). But both the figure of the Servant and the possible relation of such a figure to the Messiah in the view of many are highly problematic, and it is, therefore, precarious to ascribe to Moses an eschatological and Messianic function merely on the ground that the Servant of the Lord has been clothed in his mantle. To be convincing the ascription of such functions to Moses must rest on other evidence. Is there such?

Although direct references to Deut. xviii. 15 are rare in Judaism, owing probably, in later sources, to anti-Christian polemic, the expectation of a prophet, as a mark of the End, emerges clearly in 1 Maccabees. And, especially in 4 Ezra, it is reasonable to connect such an expectation with Deut. xviii. 15, even though no precise identification of the prophet with a New Moses occurs. In this connexion also the view has to be mentioned

---

[1] See, for example, A. Gelin, 'Moïse dans l'Ancien Testament', in *Moïse l'Homme de l'Alliance*, p. 47, *et passim*.

[2] For Sellin's position, see C. R. North, *The Suffering Servant in Deutero-Isaiah*, *ad rem*; H. Riesenfeld, *Jésus Transfiguré* (1948), pp. 81 ff.; C. Chavasse, *Theology*, LIV (August 1951), 295 ff.

[3] A. Bentzen, *op. cit.* pp. 64 ff. J. Muilenburg, *op. cit.* p. 409, is cautious.

that the figure of the 'Interpreter of the Law' in CDC, who is the Teacher of Righteousness, has been understood as a new Moses.[1]

There can be little doubt that the figure of Moses, then, had eschatological significance. But in the sources mentioned the function of the eschatological person concerned—'prophet', 'interpreter', like unto Moses—is preparatory rather than final. Can we go further and claim that the figure of the Messiah itself became a 'Mosaic' one? Although this should not be regarded as introducing a radical change in the character of the Messiah, because these offices are implicit in that figure from the first, it is significant that in the Testament of Levi the Messiah is not only king, but priest and prophet, that is, we may claim, a Mosaic figure. But can we go further still and hold that the Messiah is *identified* with a Second Moses? Jeremias urged that there was no such concept of a returned Moses who would be the Messiah in the older sources.[2] This would seem to be implied, it has been urged, in two passages in Josephus, where Theudas (*Antiquities*, xx, v, 1), the Messianic prophet, repeats the very deeds of Moses and where in the Slavonic version Jesus appears as a Moses returned from the dead. But the evidence of Josephus, it is to be admitted, is indirect. Theudas can be taken for other figures (see above), and the value of the Slavonic version of Josephus may be questioned. It is when we turn to the New Testament itself and to rabbinic sources that the full force of the comparison between the first Exodus and the last and the first Redeemer and the last appears. That the Redeemer would be the New Moses for contemporary Judaism is implicit in much of the New Testament, outside Matthew, and explicit in the rabbis. The evidence for this statement is plentiful.[3] While it cannot be held that first-century Judaism had a well defined doctrine of a New Exodus and a New Moses as Messiah and while the haggadic fluidity of these concepts must be recognized, so that no single pattern should be imposed upon them, it is also to be acknowledged that the Mosaic mantle, which we can discern wrapped around the Christ of Matthew, would not be alien to his contemporaries however startling. Not the mantle but its texture would be strange.[4]

And this brings us to the second question which we mentioned above.

[1] Test. Reub. vi. 7–12; see K. G. Kuhn, 'The Two Messiahs', in *The Scrolls and the New Testament*, ed. K. Stendahl, p. 57; see below pp. 151 ff.

[2] *Op. cit.* p. 861.

[3] See especially R. Bloch, *op. cit.* pp. 156–67. Contrast Giblet who denies that there is any Moses–Messiah typology in the pertinent sources, *op. cit.* pp. 113 f.

[4] On the whole, we may say *at least* that the concept of a Messiah like unto Moses was inchoate in the milieu of Matthew. Bloch, Vermès and others would be more

We are especially concerned to discover whether Messianic speculation, which found a correspondence, which we have above indicated, between the Mosaic and Messianic periods, made the attempt to carry this correspondence to its logical conclusion and thus came to demand a Messianic Torah, as a counterpart to the Mosaic Torah. Let us here recall that the event of the Exodus constituted a kerygmatic core for the faith of Israel. That event was an act of grace, but it is accompanied in the Old Testament by a demand, the Law. Indeed, we may go further, and claim that it becomes the ground of this demand. In Exodus and Deuteronomy succour goes before demand, the kerygmatic reference precedes the halakic.[1] There has been much discussion as to the precise historical relation between the events at the Red Sea and at Sinai. These, it has been urged, may have been unrelated. North[2] has claimed further that 'There is nothing in the prophets to indicate that the covenant was concluded at Sinai in particular, as distinct from the Exodus proper. This is not to say that the prophets were ignorant of the Sinai tradition.' He hesitatingly adds that 'it may well be that Galling [*Die Erwählungstraditionen Israels* (Giessen, 1928), pp. 26–37] is right in his surmise that for their religious consciousness the act of deliverance, the Exodus itself, was the immediate occasion of the covenant relation between Yahweh and Israel, rather than any deliverance of specific laws at Sinai.' It is difficult to accept Galling's position even for the prophets. Certain it is that for Judaism, which came increasingly to emphasize Moses as lawgiver and the Law itself as the

emphatic than this. If the world into which the New Testament came had not already produced this concept, it had already provided the raw materials out of which it could be produced. Jesus from this point of view was a catalyst. For the significance of Moses in the mind of Israel, see Johs. Pedersen, *Israel*, III–IV, 54 ff. This persisted in Hellenistic Judaism. See, for example, Philo, *On the Life of Moses*, Book I: Philo's desire is ἀναγράψαι τὸν βίον ἀνδρὸς τὰ πάντα μεγίστου καὶ τελειοτάτου. Later we meet the colossus in the murals at Dura-Europos: see M. Rostovtzeff, *Dura-Europos and its Art* (Oxford, 1938), p. 111. According to him, Moses is here almost deified: he is a counterpart to Christ. His importance for the rabbis cannot, of course, be exaggerated. See below, pp. 156 ff. P. Volz, *op. cit.* pp. 195 ff., 359 ff., 113 f. See also H. J. Schoeps, *Theologie und Geschichte des Judenchristentums* (Tübingen, 1949), pp. 87 ff., for much relevant material and references. Also H. Riesenfeld, *op. cit.*, index on Moses. On the whole subject of Moses in Palestinian and Hellenistic Judaism, see J. Jeremias, *T.W.Z.N.T.* IV, 852 ff.

[1] Exod. xx. 1 f.; Deut. v. 1 ff.

[2] *The Old Testament Interpretation of History*, pp. 52 f.; see further A. Gelin, *op. cit.* pp. 32 f. He cites, to refute him, M. Noth, *Histoire d'Israël* (1954), pp. 121 ff.: 'Moïse n'a historiquement rien à voir dans l'événement du Sinaï.' W. Beyerlin, *Herkunft und Geschichte der ältesten Sinaï-traditionen* (Tübingen, 1961), also connects the Exodus with Sinai historically.

revelation of God, it is false to separate the covenant relation from what North calls the 'deliverance of specific laws'. Whatever the precise chronological sequence of the passage through the Red Sea and the events connected with Sinai, the element of demand was integral to any covenant relationship, and it is safe to regard the Exodus, implicitly for the prophets, it may be, but explicitly for Judaism, as generally including the whole complex of events at Egypt, the Red Sea and Sinai. North's hesitancy in fully endorsing Galling's position is therefore justified. It is accordingly to be expected that, in its thought of a New Exodus, Judaism included speculation on the role of the Law, and it is this speculation which we shall attempt to trace in the following pages, particularly as it bears on the concept of a New Law.

Before we do so, however, two further preliminary considerations are noteworthy. First, full significance must be given in any inquiry into the role of the Law in the ideal future to the emphatic expectation in Judaism that the End would be marked by radical newness, and, in some sources, by the recreation of all things.[1] Here we must recall that no single eschatology had imposed itself on the whole of Judaism. The 'Mosaic' or 'Exodic' was only one strand in Jewish expectations, and this itself was not neat, but highly complex. Thus the Exodus had come to be connected in the Old Testament with the thought of creation.[2] That event had been made possible by a 'creative' act of God comparable to that which had brought all things into being, so that 'redemption' and 'creation' were inextricably bound. Thus it was that when the End came to be conceived as a New Exodus, it naturally took to itself also the marks of a New Creation. But, although it may have been primordial in the Old Testament, it was in the post-exilic period, owing largely to an increasing awareness of the exceeding sinfulness of sin, that the need for an expectation of a radical renewal of 'this world' became marked.[3] Already in Deutero-Isaiah a contrast between the Old and the New emerges clearly. This has been variously interpreted. The New was conceived by Deutero-Isaiah as a re-enactment of the Exodus and, *ipso facto*, of creation, and some have claimed that in the Isaianic contrast here

[1] This is emphasized by D. Barthélemy in a review in *R.B.* LX (1953), 316 ff. He cites Jub. i. 29; Apoc. Bar. xxxii. 6; xvii. 2; 4 Ezra vii. 75. Compare *P.R.J.*[2] pp. 38 f.

[2] Compare C. R. North, *op. cit.* pp. 48 ff.; A. Bentzen, *King and Messiah*, Eng. trans. p. 13. Isa. xxx. 7; li. 9–11; Ps. lxxiv. 12–15; lxxvii. 11 f.; lxxxvii. 4; Hab. iii. 8–15. See also H. G. May, *J.B.L.* LXXIV (1955), 5–21 on 'Some cosmic connotations of *mayim rabbim*, "Many Waters"'. [3] *P.R.J.*[2] *ibid.*

referred to we have a counterpart to or anticipation of the later one between 'this Age' and 'the Age to Come'.[1] In Daniel[2] certainly the End was a New Creation, and by the first century the Messianic idea had taken up into itself, along with many other elements, the expectation of a radical transformation of the existing order. The End was to be not only like the Exodus and like the ideal period of the wilderness, but also like the very creation itself. A new heaven and a new earth, a new Jerusalem, a new covenant, a new Temple, all these we meet in the sources.[3] It is, therefore, reasonable to expect that speculation on the Law may have taken an equally radical turn. At least, within the framework of such an eschatology, an inquiry into the possibility that Judaism may have looked forward to a renewal or recreation of the Law also is justifiable.

The other preliminary to note concerns the understanding of the Messiah himself in Judaism. The roots of Jewish Messianism were traced by Klausner to the Exodus, but Mowinckel[4] and others have grounded these in the kingship ideology of Israel, an ideology that was part of that of the Ancient Near East. Of necessity, the king in Israel, as in all ancient and modern societies, stood in a close relationship to Law. The evidence is clear that in pre-exilic Israel David, Solomon, Jeroboam, Uzziah and Josiah were priestly figures.[5] The king, moreover, was a Mosaic figure and, indeed, *verkörpertes Gesetz*, who possessed wisdom and the Spirit.[6]

[1] A. Bentzen, *op. cit.* (German ed.), p. 56. See T. H. Robinson, *A History of Israel*, I, 429; H. H. Rowley, *Studies in Old Testament Prophecy* (1950), pp. 157 ff.

[2] E. W. Heaton, 'Daniel', *Torch Commentaries* (1956), pp. 101 f.

[3] Isa. lxv. 17; lxvi. 22; Test. Dan. v (ἐπὶ τῆς νέας Ἱερουσαλήμ); Jer. xxxi. 31 ff. Into the New Temple in Ezek. xliv. 1 ff. only the Prince, who *may* be the Messiah, is allowed to enter. But it is Yahweh himself who gives the laws for the New Temple. Muilenburg, *P.C.* p. 589, speaks of these laws as a new Torah given within the solemnity of a theophany (xliv. 4). But we cannot speak of a Messianic Torah here.

[4] J. Klausner, *op. cit.*; S. Mowinckel, *He that Cometh*, Eng. trans. (1954).

[5] George Widengren, *Sakrales Königtum im Alten Testament und im Judentum* (Stuttgart, 1952), pp. 17–34. Note the following:

(*a*) David: is king and leader of the cultus (2 Sam. vi. 12–19, vii. 1–29).

(*b*) Solomon: fulfils priestly functions in 1 Kings viii. 1–6 (LXX), 7–11, 14. Both David and Solomon pronounced the High Priestly Blessing.

(*c*) Jeroboam: 1 Kings xii. 33.

(*d*) Uzziah: 2 Chron. xxvi. 16–20.

(*e*) Josiah: 2 Kings xxiii. 2 f.

In pre-exilic Israel the king exercised priestly functions: his clothing points to this also: he possessed Urim and Thummim, which means, according to Widengren, that he upheld the Law. Above all, for our purposes, the prototype of the king is Moses. See Deut. xvii. 18–19. In 2 Kings xxiii. 2 f. Joshua is a New Moses: clearest is Deut. xxxi. 10–13, where the King is the renewer of the Covenant.

[6] Deut. xvii. 18–19; compare Isa. xlii. 1–6, where the Servant is kingly.

Caution is necessary, however, lest the role of the king in relation to Law be misunderstood; the king certainly maintained Torah, but did he impart it, was he its source? This is not apparent. But this caveat being recognized, it is clear that, as a kingly figure, the Messiah also would have had to define his relationship to the Law and the role of the Law in the Messianic Age becomes at once not only an interesting object of inquiry, but also, in view of the problems of the early Church, a matter of crucial concern. This will emerge as our treatment proceeds. We merely note in concluding these preliminaries, that we pursue our quest into the Old Testament and other sources against a very rich complex of concepts which might perhaps be expected to contain, at least implicitly, that of a New Messianic Torah. The relevant passages are the following.

1. *The Old Testament*

The ground has been prepared for us in this matter by G. Ostborn, in his book, *Torā in the Old Testament* (Lund, 1945). There are passages which reveal clearly that in the ideal future, however conceived, the imparting of תורה, whatever its exact significance, would be a function of the Deity himself or of his agent. We shall examine the passages in what would seem to be that chronological order which is most generally adopted.

(a) *Jer. xxxi. 31–4*

This is the most crucial, perhaps, of the passages with which we have to deal (though it is also the most tantalizing). Even its authenticity has been denied and its significance consequently deemed to be trivial, if not banal. Thus Duhm[1] placed the passage in the Maccabean period. We need not enlarge upon his reasons, stylistic and other, for taking this position: here we are only concerned to recall that he strongly denied that the passage possessed that spiritual depth which Christian scholarship has usually read into it. To Duhm the verses merely pointed to the desire for a new covenant after the pattern of those previous covenants which had marked the Exodus and other events in Israel's history. This becomes clear from the fact that no new kind of Torah is mentioned in the passage, but merely a new covenant, formulated, it is implied, on the basis of the existing Torah. Under the new covenant contemplated, it is the demands of the old Torah, both moral and ceremonial, that are to be obeyed; and what the author desiderates is that every Israelite should know those demands by heart, without the necessity of any human teacher's insistent instruction. This

---

[1] B. Duhm, *Israels Propheten*[2] (1922), pp. 456 f.

was also the ideal of the Deuteronomist, who has often, and wrongly, been compared unfavourably with Jeremiah. Hence we should not regard these verses as introducing new conceptions of the nature of the covenant between Yahweh and his people; indeed, Duhm argued that there was no reason why, if the form of the old Torah was unsatisfactory, Yahweh should have introduced Israel to that particular form at all; surely, were it necessary, he would and could already at the Exodus have introduced the better form, which, it is claimed by Duhm's critics, is desiderated in these verses.

The glaring lack of historic perspective displayed in this last judgement of Duhm's need not detain us,[1] and the whole position he maintained has often been severely criticized,[2] and although some later scholars[3] have followed Duhm in regarding it as post-Jeremianic, the consensus of scholarship is in favour of accepting the authenticity of the passages concerned; and in the light of this consensus we must now examine its contents: it reads as follows:

31 Behold, the days are coming, says the Lord, when I will make a new covenant
32 with the house of Israel and the house of Judah, not like the covenant which

[1] See J. Skinner, *Prophecy and Religion, ad loc.*

[2] C. Cornill in particular argued against Duhm in *Einleitung in das A.T.* (1913). The following accept the authenticity of the passage: J. A. Bewer, *The Literature of the Old Testament in its Historical Development* (New York, 1922), p. 165; J. E. Binns, *The Book of the Prophet Jeremiah*, Westminster Commentaries (1919), pp. 241 ff.; A. Condamin, *Le Livre de Jérémie* (Paris, 1920), p. 237; S. R. Driver, *The Book of the Prophet Jeremiah* (1906), p. 1; F. Giesebrecht in *Handkommentar zum A.T.*, ed. W. Nowack (1907), *ad loc.*; G. B. Gray, *A Critical Introduction to the Old Testament* (1913), p. 196; W. F. Lofthouse, *Jeremiah and the New Covenant* (1925); F. Nötscher, *Das Buch Jeremias* (Bonn, 1934), pp. 234 f.; W. O. E. Oesterley and T. H. Robinson, *An Introduction to the Literature of the Old Testament* (1934), pp. 304, 309; A. S. Peake, *Jeremiah, Century Bible* (1929), p. 248; H. H. Rowley, *The Growth of the Old Testament* (1950), p. 102; Hans Schmidt, *Die Schriften des Alten Testaments*, Zweite Abteilung (1923), p. 372; E. Sellin, *Introduction to the Old Testament*, Eng. trans. W. Montgomery (1923), p. 150; J. Skinner, *op. cit. ad loc.*; G. A. Smith, *Jeremiah*, Baird Lectures (1922), pp. 375 ff.; P. Volz, 'Der Prophet Jeremia', in *Kommentar zum A.T.* (Leipzig, 1922), pp. xlvi, 279 f.; A. C. Welch, *Jeremiah: His Time and his Work* (Oxford, 1928)—but he confesses to a certain sympathy with Duhm—pp. 229 f.

[3] These are chiefly O. Eissfeldt, *Einleitung in das Alte Testament* (1934), p. 407 (but he admits that the thought of the New Covenant is consonant with that of Jeremiah); A. Bentzen also seems to favour classifying this passage with those revealing a background of later times and markedly Deutero-Isaianic diction, *Introduction to the Old Testament* (1949), pp. 117 f.; G. Hölscher (so W. O. E. Oesterley and T. H. Robinson, *op. cit.* p. 304, n. 1); S. Mowinckel, *Prophecy and Tradition, ad loc.* Two recent books I have not been able to consult: W. Rudolph's commentary (Tübingen, 1947), and H. Ortmann, *Der alte und der neue Bund bei Jeremia* (Berlin, 1940).

I made with their fathers when I took them by the hand to bring them out of the
land of Egypt, my covenant which they broke, though I was their husband, says
33 the Lord. But this is the covenant which I will make with the house of Israel
after those days, says the Lord: I will put my law within them, and I will write
34 it upon their hearts; and I will be their God, and they shall be my people. And
no longer shall each man teach his neighbour and each his brother, saying,
'Know the Lord,' for they shall all know me, from the least of them to the
greatest, says the Lord; for I will forgive their iniquity, and I will remember
their sin no more. (RSV.)

The significant factors are the following. For Jeremiah the relation
between Yahweh and his people in 'the days to come' will be covenantal:
the covenant which will then come into being will be a new one: one
element in it, as in all covenants, will be Torah. But, whereas in previous
covenants the Torah involved was written on some outward material, and,
in the particular covenant which Jeremiah had in mind, written on tablets
of stone, in the new covenant the Torah will be written 'in the heart', or
'in the inward parts'; and whereas the writing of the previous Torah was
accomplished by human means, the Torah in the new covenant will not
need to be taught by human teachers, because all who participate in the
new covenant will 'know' the Lord; and they will share in this knowledge
because the barrier to it, sin, has been forgiven by God. As a result of all
this Israel will become the people of Yahweh and he their God.

Our main concern is with the Torah which Yahweh will write in the
'inward parts', or 'in the hearts' of his people. G. A. Smith[1] insisted that
here, as so often elsewhere, the term תורה should be interpreted not as
'law' in the sense of legal codes, but as 'instruction' or 'revelation'.
Moreover, in view of the immediacy of Yahweh's activity in putting his
Torah in the 'inward parts' and in writing it 'in the hearts' of the members
of the New Covenant, and also in view of the emphasis on the knowledge
of Yahweh, which it would involve in the future envisaged by the
prophet, most Christian scholars have concluded that Jeremiah here
introduces a new conception of that covenantal relation between 'Israel'
and Yahweh which would ultimately prevail, a new conception which in
effect nullifies the necessity of all Torah in any external sense. A. S. Peake's
expression of this position will suffice as typical. 'The New Covenant is
new not in the sense that it introduces a new moral and religious code, but
that it confers a new and inward power of fulfilling the code already given.
The law ceases to be a standard external to the individual, it has become

[1] *Op. cit.* p. 377.

an integral part of his personality.'[1] And again, 'The law written on the heart implies an inner principle which can deal with each case of conscience sympathetically as it arises, and can ensure the fulfilment of its behests, because it has brought the inner life into perfect harmony with itself. The heart, and thus the whole life, has with the engraving of the law upon it, itself become new. The heart embraces not only the emotional and ethical but also the intellectual life. And thus, by being transformed from a foreign ruler into a native and inward impulse, the law gains the power of self-fulfilment.'[2] In agreement with this is G. Quell in the *Theologisches Wörterbuch zum Neuen Testament*. To him the New Covenant is really no covenant, the law in the heart no law. The categories of 'covenant' and 'law' have been transcended.[3]

In confirmation of the above, it has been claimed that the yearning for a covenant new in kind, in which there would apparently be no external Torah, is illuminated for us, and, therefore, reinforced in its historical probability, by the circumstances of Jeremiah's life. It was his poignant experience of the failure of the Deuteronomic reform movement that led Jeremiah to question the efficacy of the outward forms of religion and their necessity, and so created in him a distrust of written Torah in all its forms.[4] Ostborn[5] has conveniently summarized much of the discussion on this point. He refers to Volz's view that 'in the time of Jeremiah, Israel's leaders were investigating the *possibility* of fulfilling the divine commands' (our italics); this, so Volz suggests, because the people had so resisted the demands of the prophets: and it was this same resistance that compelled Jeremiah to speak of a new kind of covenant. Volz argues that Jer. vii. 7 ff. seems 'to warrant the inference that in the prophet's opinion the very circumstance that "the law" has been recorded in writing has come to thwart the realization of "the law" in agreement with those ideas the prophet expresses in Jer. xxxi. 31–4'. Similar to Volz's position is that of G. von Rad.[6]

If the scholars mentioned above are to be followed, then the concept of

[1] *Jeremiah, The Century Bible*, II, 103.
[2] *Ibid.* p. 106.   [3] Vol. II, pp. 126 f.
[4] See T. H. Robinson, *A History of Israel*, I, 429; H. H. Rowley, *Studies in Old Testament Prophecy* (1950), pp. 157 ff.
[5] *Op. cit.* pp. 152 ff. Johs. Pedersen, who is doubtful of the authenticity of the passage, takes it to demand 'a psychic transformation', 'an intense change of disposition, a conversion'. See *Israel*, III–IV, 556; compare P. Volz, *Der Prophet Jeremia*, pp. 293 ff., who thinks that Jeremiah wishes to see the earth peopled by godlike people.
[6] In 'Das Gottesvolk im Deuteronomium', in *Beiträge zur Wissenschaft vom Alten und Neuen Testament* (Stuttgart, 1929).

an outward Torah is really transcended and even annulled in the New Covenant envisaged by Jeremiah. There are certain considerations, however, which incline us to suspect this view as, at least, an overstatement. Let us begin with the last point made, namely, that Jeremiah was in sharp reaction against Deuteronomy. Ostborn[1] points out that von Rad, although agreeing in the main with Volz, nevertheless departs from him in claiming that none of Jeremiah's words suggest that he had rejected Deuteronomy. This was the position long since reached by Skinner. 'In spite of differences', he writes, 'there are close affinities between the school of Deuteronomy and the teaching of Jeremiah. The mere fact that the prophecies of Jeremiah were edited by the Deuteronomic school shows that there was no consciousness of antagonism between them. Deuteronomy as well as Jeremiah insists on the need of a circumcision of the heart (Jer. iv. 4; Deut. x. 16; xxx. 6); and the author of the principal edition of Deuteronomy...inculcates so earnestly the inwardness of true obedience as springing from love to God, that we can almost think of him as a disciple of the prophet, or a Melanchthon to his Luther. Moreover, the steadfast loyalty of the family of Shaphan till the end of Jeremiah's life suggests that he never broke openly with the reforming party, and certainly makes it extremely improbable that he had denounced them as a clique of forgers and deceivers.'[2] This is not to deny that Jeremiah was of a different spirit possibly to the Deuteronomists: but that difference can be grossly exaggerated. Recently this point of view has been maintained with much emphasis by Rowley.[3] He makes it clear that we can overemphasize the distrust of the written Torah, as of other outward forms of religion, in Jeremiah's mind. The prophet was probably not so much discontented with the written Torah as such, as with the Torah which was merely written in a book or on tablets of stone or any other outward material: he could express discontent with the written Torah without wishing to imply that it was necessarily evil in itself, and, therefore, had to be transcended.

---

[1] *Op. cit.* p. 154.　　　　　　　　[2] *Op. cit.* p. 107.

[3] *Op. cit.* p. 154. See, however, A. Bentzen, *op. cit.* pp. 118 ff., where he speaks of the process of 'deuteronomizing' that has gone into the reporting of Jeremiah's work (so also B. Duhm and S. Mowinckel). A. Bentzen speaks of the radicalism of Jeremiah 'breaking through the orthodox varnish', especially in his polemic against the cultus. This implies that H. H. Rowley's position does not sufficiently recognize the way in which Jeremiah's radicalism has been modified by deuteronomistic revision. Nevertheless H. H. Rowley has historical probability on his side and A. Bentzen does not meet J. Skinner's treatment of the theme.

From this we go on to point out that it was possible to speak of the *written* Torah as being 'in the heart'. This means that the express terms used by Jeremiah in connexion with Torah in the New Covenant do not necessarily exclude some form of written Torah. Ostborn[1] indeed refers to several passages—Deut. xvii. 19; Joshua i. 8; Ps. i. 2; xxxvii. 31; xl. 8— as containing the concept of the Law being written in the heart or in the inward parts. But of these only two are strictly permissible, namely, Ps. xxxvii. 31; xl. 8. The former reads:

> The law of his God is in his heart;
> his steps do not slip.

This passage is dated by C. A. Briggs[2] in the period of Nehemiah when the Torah was beginning to assume its subsequent dominance over Israel's life. W. F. Cobb[3] regarded Psalm xxxvii in its entirety as Messianic: it is those who now have the Law in their heart who will enjoy the Messianic blessings in the future. Psalm xl. 8 reads:

> I delight to do thy will, O my God;
> thy law is within my heart.

Cobb[4] here found a reference to Jer. xxxi. 31 ff., and it is possible that it is the influence of Jeremiah that accounts for the concept expressed, and the same applies to Ps. xxxvii. 31. It might, therefore, at first sight appear as though we should not use these passages to corroborate our interpretation of Jeremiah, because they themselves may be the product of Jeremiah's own influence. But this is not the case. If the passages were produced under the impact of Jeremiah, they merely prove that Jeremiah's thought of a New Covenant could be reconciled with the thought of a *written* Torah and was, in fact, interpreted in that light by his successors.

Moreover, there are other passages to be noted, especially Deut. xxx. 11–14; the whole passage reads:

11 For this commandment which I command you this day is not too hard for you,
12 neither is it far off. It is not in heaven, that you should say, 'Who will go up for
13 us to heaven, and bring it to us, that we may hear it and do it?' Neither is it
    beyond the sea, that you should say, 'Who will go over the sea for us, and bring
14 it to us, that we may hear it and do it?' But the word is very near you; it is in
    your mouth and in your heart, so that you can do it.

---

[1] *Torā in the Old Testament*, p. 151, n. 1.
[2] I.C.C., *Psalms*, vol. I, *ad loc.*
[3] *The Book of Psalms* (1905), *ad loc.*　　　　[4] *Op. cit., ad loc.*

The thought of verse 14 is also expressed in Deut. vi. 7 and xi. 19. In all these passages the Torah, that is, the written code of laws, can be regarded as having been so much impressed upon 'Israel' that it can be said to be upon or in their hearts.[1]

It is possible that our position can also be reinforced by another consideration. In the elucidation of Jer. xxxi. 31 ff., Ostborn, like others before him, refers to Ezek. xi. 9 and xxxvi. 26 ff. Without attempting to justify his procedure, he uses these passages to introduce the idea that it is Yahweh's spirit which teaches Torah in the New Covenant.[2] Now, if it be permissible to use Ezekiel in this manner, and if the passages referred to in Jeremiah and Ezekiel are 'Messianic',[3] then it will also follow that the Torah of the New Covenant will be the Old Torah. This is made clear in Ezek. xxxvi. 27 f., where the 'new heart' and the 'new spirit' are expressly connected with the written statutes and judgements of Yahweh.

It follows from all the above that the reference in Jer. xxxi. 31 ff. to a Law written 'in the heart' or 'in the inward parts' does not necessarily imply any rejection of the written Law as such. In a confused manner Ostborn has recognized this, but insufficiently; he merely concedes in a footnote that 'To judge from our previous findings, Torah "in the heart", "in the inner man", would appear to allude to the consciousness of Yahweh's "will" ("Law") felt by a man in whom the Spirit of Yahweh resides. However, this need not imply any opposition—not on principle, at least—to the written Law.'[4]

But before we draw our conclusions we have, finally, to meet G. A. Smith's contention that Torah in Jer. xxxi. 31 ff. should be translated by 'instruction' or 'revelation' in a general sense.[5] We must insist over against this that the context, that of a covenant, here seems to demand a translation which will somehow preserve for תּוֹרָה its connotation as the element of demand (both ethical and ceremonial) in the covenant, that is, the part played by the Law. The Targum does not help us at this point; it translates תּוֹרָתִי by אוֹרַיְתִי, which is ambiguous, like תּוֹרָה itself. But the LXX seems to corroborate our view. One manuscript translates תורתי by νόμον which is the obvious translation: but the majority of MSS have νόμους; and this, as the reading of B, was followed by Swete: it may be that it is used by the LXX so as to make it clear what the reference is—it

---

[1] Johs. Pedersen, *Israel*, III–IV, 581, calls the keeping of the Torah in the heart a fundamental idea of Deuteronomy.

[2] *Torā in the Old Testament*, p. 151. See *P.R.J.*[2] p. 224.

[3] The term is here used in a general sense as referring to the ideal future.

[4] *Op. cit.* p. 155, n. 3.   [5] *Op. cit.* p. 337.

is to the many demands of the Torah.[1] To all this G. A. Smith[2] has in effect replied that, in expressing new conceptions, Jeremiah, like all others, had to use old words: pointing out that the term 'covenant' was not 'unnatural to Jeremiah nor irrelevant to his experience and teaching'; that its associations as he had recalled them had been those 'not of law but of love', he claimed that covenant was only a metaphor to describe a relation which was really beyond the compass of any figure; and how else than by those terms that he used, asked Smith, 'could the prophet have described an inward and purely spiritual force?'[3] We cannot dissent from the view that the term 'covenant' came naturally to Jeremiah's lips: we may also admit that there is a fleshly screen in all language. But Smith's contrast of law and love would be alien to Jeremiah's thought. The giving of the Law was in itself, we cannot sufficiently emphasize, a mark of Yahweh's love, and at this point Smith is surely reading back into the Old Testament a false antithesis derived from later Christian theology.

We are now in a position to seek to assess the passage in Jer. xxxi anew. It is possible to argue that the covenant envisaged by Jeremiah in the future would be a new covenant demanding a new kind of Torah,

---

[1] See S. H. Blank, 'The Septuagint Renderings of Old Testament Terms for Law', in *Hebrew Union College Annual*, VII (1930), 278 f. In view of his treatment, the use of νόμους for תורתי hardly seems accidental. There seems to be no reading תורותי which could have underlain it. Where תורה is rendered by terms other than νόμος those terms are often in the plural. Here in Jer. xxxi. 33 only in B, and a scribal correction to א, do we find the plural νόμους for תורה (sing.). The plural νόμους for sing. תורה is very rare. Blank only refers, in addition, to B to 2 Kings xiv. 6; A to Jer. xxvi. 4, a marginal correction in Q to Jer. xliv. 10 and א to Prov. xxviii. 7. Usually even a plural תורות in the MT was rendered by νόμος (sing.). This difficulty of the text at Jer. xxxi. 33 is not mentioned by Λ. W. Streane, *The Double Text of Jeremiah* (Cambridge, 1896), pp. 218 f., nor by P. Volz, *Studien zum Text des Jeremia* (Leipzig, 1920), pp. 237 f. G. C. Workman, *The Text of Jeremiah* (Edinburgh, 1889), *ad loc.*, notes that the LXX translates תּוֹרָתִי while the Massoretic text has תּוֹרָתִי: but this may be due, he suggests, to the fact that the vowel letters י and ו were used very variably and often omitted. 'Had these letters', he writes, 'been always written in the translators' MS where they are now written in the Hebrew text many significant deviations could not have occurred.' He mentions 49 cases in Jeremiah where the ו was omitted and 32 where the י was omitted. If G. C. Workman is correct, we have in Jer. xxxi. 33 another instance of the LXX translator being confused by the omitted ו. See R. R. Ottley, *A Handbook to the Septuagint*, p. 113. (Compare S. R. Driver, *Hebrew Tenses*, p. xiii, to which he refers.) In this case the LXX has no theological bias in rendering תּוֹרָתִי of the MT by νόμους. On the other hand, S. H. Blank's study must be given full consideration and we have allowed for it in our treatment, that is, νόμους (pl.) for תּוֹרָתִי (sing.) is intended to make clear that it is the many demands of the Torah that Jeremiah has in mind.

[2] *Op. cit., ad loc.* [3] *Op. cit., ad loc.*

apparently of a kind which may best perhaps be called 'pneumatic' in the sense that it involved the activity of an inner, spontaneous principle. At the same time, however, we have seen reason to question that sharp antithesis to the old written Torah which this has been claimed to imply. We have had to recognize a certain tension in his thought between the written Torah and the Torah to be dispensed in the 'new covenant', and we have been unable to resolve this tension into a complete difference. It is Ostborn and Skinner who have perhaps best recognized this tension in Jeremiah's thinking, in which the old and the new stand in uneasy juxta-position. Ostborn,[1] as we saw, must be included among those for whom there is a Torah of a new kind involved in the New Covenant but a Torah which is called such only for want of a more adequate term. But he is uneasy about this interpretation. He is at pains to insist that the Torah in the heart need not imply any opposition in principle to the written Law and thus recognizes that it was possible to be conversant with 'the same religious and ethical ideas as characterize the inner, pneumatic Torah' and yet accept the book of the Law.[2] Skinner also reveals the same uneasiness: he is constrained to admit that the New Covenant involved a new Torah: for him the essence of the prophecy lies in the 'spiritual illumination of the individual mind and conscience, and the doing of the will of God from a spontaneous impulse of the renewed heart', and so the 'Torah of Yahweh is the living principle of religion which is ever new, which exists perfectly in the mind of God, and is therefore capable of being reproduced in the minds of men who "know Yahweh" in spirit and in truth'. But Skinner is also careful to insist that in the written Torah also the essential will of God had been at least partly expressed.[3] Both Ostborn and Skinner are struggling to preserve in their concept of the new Torah that duality which marks Jeremiah's thought of the Torah, as of nationalism, the desire to preserve and yet to fulfil. What we are concerned to emphasize is that Torah, new in some sense and yet not divorced utterly from the Old Torah, that is, an external Torah, is part of Jeremiah's hope for 'the latter days'. For Jeremiah the New Covenant would probably demand both the letter and the Spirit.

(b) The Servant of Yahweh and Torah

We now come to passages later than Jeremiah. We have already referred to some verses in the Psalms where it may be that we are to trace the prophet's influence. These we shall not need to discuss further, and we

---

[1] *Op. cit.*   [2] *Op. cit.*   [3] *Prophecy and Religion, ad loc.*

proceed to the so-called Servant passages in Deutero-Isaiah. These are variously understood but most scholars include among them the following: Isa. xlii. 1–4; xlix. 1–6; l. 4–11; lii. 13–liii. 12.[1]

Before we deal with them it is necessary at the outset to recall that the very legitimacy of isolating the Servant passages from the rest of Deutero-Isaiah has often been questioned, and especially, recently, by Miss M. H. Hooker.[2] In a work which demands serious attention, she emphasizes the continuity of the Servant passages not only with the remainder of Deutero-Isaiah but with Hebrew prophecy in general. The term 'servant' refers to no separate figure: it merely designates that quality of life which was to characterize anyone in Israel who was obedient to Yahweh: it is a collective term for 'Israel' itself. The individual traits that emerge in the Servant are explicable in terms of the theory of 'corporate personality' made familiar to us by Wheeler Robinson, Aubrey Johnson and others, and of the solidarity of king and people in the Ancient Near East. The reason why Isaiah liii has been understood in so much scholarly work in isolation from its total context is that it contains the apparently unique idea of vicarious suffering. But there is no such isolation of it in later Judaism, where the Servant does not emerge as a distinct figure. Attempts to trace the influence of the 'Servant' figure as such in the New Testament are therefore misguided, since no such figure existed. In Hooker's judgement, in dealing with the Servant we are merely dealing with Israel; thus she returns to a view which has a long history.

On the other hand, many recent scholars have understood the Servant in individual terms, and have felt justified in isolating the Servant passages. And even though, as North[3] has concluded, it is not possible to prove that the Servant was originally conceived as the Messiah, nevertheless, that figure is highly pertinent in any discussion of Old Testament Messianism. From New Testament to modern times there has been a constant stream of Messianic interpretations of the Servant;[4] and recently this has been

---

[1] For an exhaustive survey, see H. H. Rowley, *The Servant of the Lord* (London, 1952), pp. 1–89; N. H. Snaith's treatment 'The Servant of the Lord in Deutero-Isaiah' is a clear critique of Duhm's position, see *Studies in Old Testament Prophecy*, ed. H. H. Rowley (Edinburgh, 1950), pp. 187 ff.

[2] *Jesus and the Servant* (London, 1959); see review by J. Jeremias, *J.T.S.* New Series, XI (April 1960), 140 ff. (he rejects Hooker's position); and a critique by L. S. Mudge, on 'The Servant Christology in the New Testament' (unpublished dissertation, Princeton University, 1961).

[3] *The Suffering Servant of Deutero-Isaiah*, ad rem.

[4] In the Targum of Jonathan ben Uzziel, the Talmud, the Fathers, the Reformation; and since J. C. Döderlein's work in 1771 up to B. Duhm, the majority of scholars

reinforced by the Scandinavian School.[1] I. Engnell,[2] H. S. Nyberg,[3] A. Bentzen have all, in different but related ways, interpreted the Suffering Servant as the Messiah. A most convenient discussion is that of Bentzen, *Messias, Moses redivivus, Menschensohn* (Zürich, 1948), where, beginning with the now familiar interpretation of many Psalms as cultic material connected with the Jewish New Year Festival when the drama of creation was re-enacted, he proceeds to show how the figure of the king in these Psalms is Messianic, but is also to be identified with the *Urmensch* and, finally, with the Suffering Servant, and the Son of Man, all figures which were originally elements in a great cosmic myth whose pattern is traceable all over the Ancient East.[4]

There is, therefore, impressive support for the Messianic interpretation of the Servant. But, as North's survey shows, there are also other interpretations with massive support. Nevertheless, even if the direct Messianic interpretation of the Servant be rejected and the mythological one be not convincing, as most British scholars seem to judge,[5] we have further to consider William Manson's[6] suggestion that in the pre-Christian era the figure of the Servant came to be closely related to, if not actually merged or identified with, the Son of Man and the Messiah. Rowley[7] strongly dissents from any such identification, but it is favourably received by Black[8] (apparently) and by J. Jeremias.[9] We need only refer

both Roman Catholic and Protestant; all these witness to the possibly Messianic character of the Servant. Since B. Duhm the Messianic interpretation has found support from both Protestant and Roman Catholic scholars, namely, Julius Ley, L. Laue, G. Füllkrug (though he speaks of the Servant as a soteriological rather than as a Messianic figure), A. van der Flier, A. Mäcklenburg, E. Ziemer, H. Gressmann, J. Schelhaas, A. H. Edelkoort, O. Procksch among Protestants; and F. Feldmann, A. Condamin, A. van Hoonacker, J. Fischer, J. S. van der Ploeg, among Roman Catholics. (For bibliographical details see C. R. North, *op. cit.*, whom we have followed.)

[1] The most enriching volume now is S. Mowinckel, *He That Cometh*, Eng. trans. (Oxford, 1956).

[2] See *The Bulletin of the John Rylands Library*, vol. XXXI, no. 1 (1948).

[3] A summary of his position is given by C. R. North, *op. cit.*, *ad loc.*

[4] For criticism of the Scandinavian position, see N. H. Snaith, *The Jewish New Year Festival* (1948). A. R. Johnson, *E.T.* (November 1950), p. 39, n. 7, rejects Snaith's position.

[5] C. R. North, *op. cit.*

[6] *Jesus the Messiah*, pp. 171 ff.

[7] *The Relevance of Apocalyptic*, p. 57; *The Biblical Doctrine of Election*, and fully in *Oudtestamentische Studien*, Deel viii, ed. by P. A. H. de Boer, *ad loc.*, where the relevant literature is surveyed; compare T. W. Manson, *J.T.S.* (April 1950).

[8] *E.T.* (October 1948).

[9] *Nuntius* (Uppsala), vol. I, no. 1; see H. H. Rowley, *op. cit.* for other references.

to our discussion of this elsewhere.[1] In any case, however, whether the identification in pre-Christian times be accepted or not, although we have been taught greater caution in claiming that Jesus himself was controlled by a 'Servant motif' derived from Isa. liii, the Messianic significance given to the Servant by the Church at least in Acts viii. 32–33 and 1 Pet. ii. 21–5 makes the consideration of the relation of the Servant to the Torah necessary here.[2]

And from our point of view it is highly significant that many scholars have been led to see in the Servant a teacher of the Law, this especially on the basis of the first of the Servant poems, Isa. xlii. 1–4. North renders it as follows:

1 Behold! My Servant whom I uphold,
  My chosen in whom I delight!
  I have endowed him with my spirit,

2 He shall announce judgement (מִשְׁפָּט) to the nations,
  He shall not cry nor make any clamour,
  Nor let his voice be heard in the street;

3 A reed that is bruised he shall not break,
  And the wick that burns dimly he shall not quench,
  Faithfully shall he announce judgement,

4 Not burning dimly nor himself being bruised,
  Until he have established judgement in the earth.
  And for his instruction (וּלְתוֹרָתוֹ) the far coasts
    wait eagerly.

The first scholar to emphasize the Servant as a *Toralehrer*[3] was Duhm. His position rests, first, on his interpretation of the term מִשְׁפָּט in xlii. 2. He takes it to be a kind of summary term for the total 'law' of Israel, and thus he regards xlii. 2 as a support for his view that the mission of the Servant is the giving of the 'Law', which Israel already had received, to other nations.[4] In this interpretation of מִשְׁפָּט he was followed by Skinner,[5] who defined it to mean 'the religion of Jehovah regarded as a system of practical ordinances', and by G. W. Wade,[6] who writes of it as 'a collective expression for the divine requirements both ceremonial [2 Kings xvii. 26–7] and moral [Jer. v. 4]'. In this he is to be preferred to T. K. Cheyne[7]

---

[1] *P.R.J.*[2] pp. 279 ff.

[2] Contrast, for example, C. T. Craig, *The Journal of Religion*, XXIX (Chicago, 1944), 240–5.   [3] *Das Buch Jesaia* (1914), pp. 284 ff.

[4] E. J. Kissane, *The Book of Isaiah*, II, 36.

[5] Cambridge Bible for Schools, *Isaiah xl–lxvi* (1911), p. 27.

[6] *The Book of the Prophet Isaiah*, Westminster Commentaries, *ad loc.*

[7] *The Prophecies of Isaiah*, vol. I (1884), *ad loc.*

who quite unjustifiably confined מִשְׁפָּט here to moral demands. Duhm's interpretation of the Servant has been followed by Bertholet, details of whose position are given by North.[1]

Is this understanding of מִשְׁפָּט as a generalized term for law acceptable? North[2] discussed whether the Servant gives his מִשְׁפָּט as a travelling preacher or as a king, and concluded that 'the phrase suggests decisions uttered by someone vested with executive authority. His authority may be exercised mildly—"A bruised reed he shall not break"—but the implication is that he could be severe if he wished.'[3] This suggestion of North's agrees with the view of J. Begrich[4] that מִשְׁפָּט cannot be identified with law but should be translated as 'judgement'. This is its meaning, so Macho claims, throughout Isaiah.[5] In those Old Testament passages where מִשְׁפָּט does have the connotation of 'law' it occurs only in the plural and in historical not prophetical contexts.[6] But the evidence on the whole is against understanding מִשְׁפָּט (=κρίσις) in Isa. xlii. 2 f. in terms of 'judgement'. Mowinckel is surely right against Begrich and Snaith here. 'It is clear that in xlii. 3, the metaphors do not point to any action of the Servant as a judge, but to his preaching as a prophet, preaching which is for edification, not condemnation. The "judgement" and "instruction", which he "brings forth" and establishes denote (......) the true religion.'[7] Thus in the LXX κρίσις is parallel to ἔλεος and ἐλεημοσύνη and ἀλήθεια (Ps. ci. 11; xxxiii. 5; cxi. 7) and so in the New Testament passages,

---

[1] Op. cit. p. 49. [2] Op. cit. pp. 141 ff.

[3] R. Marcus in H.T.R. xxx, 4 (October 1937), 249 ff., translates Isaiah xlii. 3 freely as follows: 'A crushed reed he may be, but one that no one shall break; a dimly burning wick he may be, but no one shall quench its light; in spite of everything he shall bring justice to the nations.' Like C. R. North and N. H. Snaith he sees severity in the Servant. He takes תּוֹרָתוֹ to mean 'teaching'; and מִשְׁפָּט 'the suppression of immorality and idolatry and so salvation for mankind' (p. 251). He writes: 'The meaning of (xlii. 4) is that when the servant has finished his task the nations will have a knowledge of the true God, and in consequence will desire to know his law.'

[4] J. Begrich, Studien zu Deuterojesaja (Stuttgart, 1938), pp. 161–3. He translates מִשְׁפָּט by Urteil.

[5] Alejandro Díez Macho, Estudios Bíblicos, XII, 2 (1953), 115–58. He refers to Isa. i. 17; iii. 17; v. 7, 16; x. 1; xxvi. 4, 8; xxviii. 6; xxviii. 17; xli. 1; xlix. 4; liii. 8; liv. 17; lix. 8, 9, 14; vi. 8.

[6] See Lev. xviii. 4, 5, 26; xix. 37; xx. 22; Ezek. xx. 11; Lev. xxvi. 15; Deut. xxxiii. 10; Josh. xxv. 25. On מִשְׁפָּט, see N. H. Snaith, The Distinctive Ideas of the Old Testament (1944), pp. 74 ff. He writes: '[Torah and mishpat] are synonymous to the extent that both are the declared word of God. They are different in that torah, at this early stage, meant an original pronouncement, while mishpaṭ meant a decision according to a precedent' (p. 75).

[7] Op. cit. p. 219, nn. 4 f., where bibliographical details are given.

Matt. xxiii. 23 (ἀφήκατε τὰ βαρύτερα τοῦ νόμου, τὴν κρίσιν καὶ τὸ ἔλεος καὶ τὴν πίστιν) and Luke xi. 42 (παρέρχεσθε τὴν κρίσιν καὶ τὴν ἀγάπην τοῦ θεοῦ). So in Matt. xii. 18–21 where the מִשְׁפָּט of Isa. xlii. 4 is rendered by κρίσις the meaning demanded is 'justice' or some kind of 'salvation' rather than 'judgement'. On the whole, therefore, Duhm was justified in finding in xlii. 2 support for the view that the Servant was a teacher of the Law.[1]

In any case, in Isa. xlii. 4 the reference to the Torah of the Servant is clear. The only question to be raised is whether the possessive pronoun is to be emphasized, that is, do the isles wait specifically for the Servant's own Torah which is set over against the Mosaic Law. The term לְתוֹרָתוֹ obviously created difficulty—perhaps for this reason. The LXX renders καὶ ἐπὶ τῷ ὀνόματι αὐτοῦ ἔθνη ἐλπιοῦσιν (this is followed in Matt. xii. 21 in the Greek and Syriac, τῷ ὀνόματι and ܣܡܗ). Later Judaism came to distinguish between the 'laws' placed upon Israel and those demanded of Gentiles.[2] Is there a premonition of this in xlii. 4? And again is the לְמִשְׁפָּטוֹ of the Isaiah Scroll due to a desire to avoid any suggestion, which might arise, that the Servant had a special Torah for the Gentiles?

Be this as it may the Servant of Deutero-Isaiah will bring his Torah. Ostborn[3] would see in this Torah of the Servant a mark of his kingship. But he seems to do violence to the evidence when he makes the king in Israel too much the imparter of Torah.[4] The passages he quotes as well as those indicated by us on the pages above show that the king was expected to maintain Torah, but not necessarily that he mediated Torah.[5] The

[1] See V. Herntrich, *T.W.Z.N.T.* III, 932: 'Das Hinausbringen des מִשְׁפָּט bedeutet Heil für die Völker, Barmherzigkeit für den Unterdrückten, es ist die gnadenreiche Willensoffenbarung Jahwes, die einst den Bund mit Israel begründet hatte. Daß der מִשְׁפָּט den Völkern gebracht wird, bedeutet die Ausweitung des Bundes auf die Welt.' North, *op. cit.* pp. 140 ff., shows how difficult it is to understand precisely. In the Targum on Isaiah in xlii. 1 מִשְׁפָּט is rendered by דִינִי 'my judgement'. The Servant is the instrument of God's judgement, but דִין has the connotation of 'religion and justice' probably, as in Arabic, see Herntrich, *ibid.* though J. F. Stenning, *The Targum of Isaiah*, edited and translated, 1949, renders it in Isa. xlii. 1 by 'judgement'.

[2] *P.R.J.*[2] *ad rem.* 　　　　[3] *Op. cit.* pp. 56 ff.

[4] See on this Mowinckel, *He That Cometh*, pp. 219 ff.

[5] This problem has again come to the fore through I. Engnell's insistence on the character of the Servant as King. The term '*ebed* he regards as, originally, a royal cultic title (*Bulletin of John Rylands Library*, vol. XXXI, no. 1, p. 69, n. 4). This concept he applies to all the Servant passages. On Isa. xlii. 1 ff., he writes that 'it looks most like an oracular assertion in which the royal qualifications of the Servant are accumulated: he is upheld, chosen, beloved, possessing the spirit; he also has his own תּוֹרָה or מִשְׁפָּט, his royal judicial function, the discharging and extending of

fairest conclusion may be that the Servant is both a kingly and prophetic figure; and in view of his kingly character, Skinner's[1] comment is apt that the best commentary on Isa. xlii. 1–4 is Isa. ii. 1–5, which shall occupy us next. Before we turn to this, however, we repeat that the imparting of Torah is a central function of the Servant of Yahweh: this Torah will be directed to the world. It agrees with this that the traits of a 'teacher' emerge clearly in the Servant. The following are the main indications of this: like the prophets, the Servant is endowed with the Spirit (xlii. 1); he delivers Torah (xlii. 4); he is a disciple either of another prophet or of one endowed with the Spirit of God (l. 4); he has been called from his mother's womb to his task, as were other prophets (Jer. i. 5); he opens his ears daily for revelations (l. 4) and it is by his message,[2] as well as by his suffering, that he works salvation (Isa. xlii. 4).

It may not be possible, on the basis of their subsequent identification, to ascribe the teaching or prophetic function of the Servant to the Messiah, but in any case, the function of the Servant, be he the people, the individual, Messiah or other, is to impart מִשְׁפָּט and תּוֹרָה. Should Jeremias and others, who have claimed that Servant and Messianic ideas were already fused in pre-Christian Judaism, be correct, then the Messiah

which is his special task'. He refers in comparison to J. Begrich, and E. Burrows, who defines מִשְׁפָּט as 'the right of the Messianic House of David, as in Ezekiel'. Similarly in Isa. xlix. 2, I. Engnell refers the words 'and he made my mouth like a sharp sword', not to the prophetic art of speaking but to the royal pronouncement of judgements. Again l. 4–5 depicts the Servant as a diviner, 'which tallies with the fact that the King was in principle the only oracle-receiver' (*ibid.* p. 71). And l. 10 is translated, 'Whosoever of you feareth Yahweh should listen to the voice of His Servant, who walketh in darkness having no light, but trusteth in the name of Yahweh and stayeth upon his God'. A. Bentzen has joined issue with I. Engnell in all this, even though he recognizes the mythological background for the Servant passages which Engnell assumes. It is as a prophet that the Servant is conceived in xlii. 1 ff.; in xlix. 1–13 he regards the Servant as a New Moses; in l. 4–5 A. Bentzen urges that in lii. 13; liii. 12 the author has a contemporary prophet or even himself in view. (See *Bulletin of John Rylands Library, ibid.*; A. Bentzen, *op. cit.* pp. 46 ff.)

[1] Cambridge Bible for Schools, *Isaiah xl–lxvi*, p. 27.

[2] S. Mowinckel, *op. cit.* p. 208. But Mowinckel gets rid of the saving 'knowledge' of the Servant. He renders liii. 11 as

> When the purpose of Yahweh is fulfilled through him,
> (He will deliver) his soul from distress,
> he will see (light and live long)
> And be satisfied with what he desires.

He takes *bᵉdaʿtô* as *birᵉūto*. North retains *bᵉdaʿtô* but connects it with the words 'he shall be satisfied'. Thus both North and Mowinckel do not ascribe saving value to the Servant's 'knowledge' as do some other scholars.

as Servant, not merely as king, would not only have had to define his attitude to the Law but also, in the light of Isa. xlii. 1 ff., to bring his own Law.

(c) *Isa. ii. 1–5* (with parallel, offering from our point of view only unimportant variation, in Mic. iv. 1–5).

The word which Isaiah the son of Amoz saw concerning Judah and Jerusalem.

2 It shall come to pass in the latter days
    that the mountain of the house of the LORD
  shall be established as the highest of the mountains,
    and shall be raised above the hills;
  and all the nations shall flow to it,
3   and many peoples shall come, and say:
  'Come, let us go up to the mountain of the LORD,
    to the house of the God of Jacob;
  that he may teach us his ways
    and that we may walk in his paths.'
  For out of Zion shall go forth the law (MT תּוֹרָה, LXX νόμος),
    and the word of the LORD from Jerusalem.
4 He shall judge between the nations. . . . (RSV.)

The phrase בְּאַחֲרִית הַיָּמִים, 'in the end of the days', is ambiguous. S. R. Driver defines it as 'the final period of the future so far as it falls within the range of the speaker's perspective'.[1] It is, therefore, not strictly Messianic and is not regarded as such by Wade.[2] Other scholars, the vast majority, however, take it so in this context; we mention Cheyne, Driver, Duhm, Gray, Peake. In any case the passage clearly refers to that final aeon, when God's will should be done, and in that sense we may broadly term it Messianic, even if it has no explicit reference to the Messiah. In Messianic times, then, Jerusalem is here pictured as the religious centre of the world, whence Yahweh himself will instruct people in his ways. Torah shall go forth from Zion, and his word from Jerusalem.[3]

But the exact significance of the term תּוֹרָה here, as so often, is difficult to assess. The LXX renders it by νόμος, 'law', but this means little because the LXX often uses νόμος for תּוֹרָה where we should rightly expect such words as διδαχή, διδασκαλία or some other derivatives of verbs used to

[1] I.C.C., *Deuteronomy*, p. 74.
[2] *The Book of the Prophet Isaiah*, Westminster Commentaries, p. 15.
[3] See further B. Gerhardsson, *Memory and Manuscript* (1961), pp. 274 ff.

translate הורה.[1] And most scholars have concluded that because of the absence of the article, the parallelism with 'the word of Yahweh', and the fact that it is non-Israelites who utter the words under discussion, the term is more akin to 'instruction' in a general sense than to 'law' either written or oral. It is so taken by Gray, Wade, Powis-Smith,[2] Duhm, and Ostborn. But two things should be said in this connexion.

First, the date of this passage has been variously assessed. Wade, Peake, Powis-Smith all point out that its ideology is post-exilic: the conversion of the nations, the pilgrimage to Zion, these are ideas typical of the post-exilic prophets. The phrase בְּאַחֲרִית הַיָּמִים itself is first applied Messianically in Ezek. xxxviii. 16. Gray also inclines to a late date in view of all this. Duhm's view that the section was by Isaiah himself makes its position in Micah and its title in Isa. ii. 1, which shows that it has no connexion with what preceded, sources of difficulty.[3] On the other hand, its context in Micah does not suggest the authorship of that prophet, the transition from iii. 9-12 being too abrupt; and Jer. xxvi. 18 makes the ascription of iv. 1-5 to Micah very improbable. But, although its meaning is 'instruction' in a general sense, if the passage is post-exilic we must beware of emptying the term תּוֹרָה here of all reference to the Law. In the post-exilic period it would naturally draw to itself a more legal connotation, because the instruction of Yahweh was increasingly being thought of in terms of 'the Law' which was principally expounded at the sanctuary by prophet and priest. The homiletic reflection found in verse 5, which unites verses 1-4 with what follows in verses 6 ff., shows that the instruction referred to is 'the light of the Lord', which, as Gray points out, refers to the path lighted by the Law. We can be certain that the persons who incorporated this poem in Isaiah and Micah, while they might have thought of the תּוֹרָה referred to in Isa. ii. 3 (=Mic. iv. 2) as general instruction, would not in the least have regarded this as in any way incompatible with the legal tradition in Israel. Thus Cheyne is most emphatically to be rejected when he suggests that there is a contrast implied here between the Jerusalem of the future and the Sinai of the past 'whence the earlier and more limited

[1] C. H. Dodd, *The Bible and the Greeks*, p. 32.
[2] I.C.C., *Micah, ad loc.*
[3] O. Procksch, *Jesaia*, 1 (Leipzig, 1930), *ad loc.*, thinks that the question of its Isaianic authorship cannot be decided. The best treatment of the thought of the passage is by E. J. Kissane, *The Book of Isaiah* (1941), 1, 26. He accepts its authenticity. Note that G. B. Gray does not take בְּאַחֲרִית הַיָּמִים to be necessarily late in its Messianic sense, I.C.C., *Isaiah, i–xxxix*, p. 44; R. B. Y. Scott takes it to be late in that sense (*The Interpreter's Bible*, vol. v, *ad rem*).

revelation proceeded'. The 'instruction' of the future Jerusalem would be, we cannot doubt, in line with the Torah of Sinai.

The second factor to be noted is that we here meet with Yahweh himself as a teacher, and we are possibly to think of him as teacher in virtue of his kingship; certainly he will judge in virtue of this. Ostborn[1] claims that part of Yahweh's kingly rule in 'the latter days' would be the imparting of Torah. He cites Robertson Smith who has familiarized us with the view that from the first the divine king of the Israelites had to give counsel by oracles or soothsayers in matters of national difficulty, and a sentence of justice when a case was too hard for ordinary decision. We have above questioned Ostborn's view; and North seems to differ from him: the latter denies that the king *gives* Torah.[2] Nevertheless, Ostborn[3] and North[4] would agree that the Servant of Yahweh can be both prophetic and kingly in Isa. xlii. 1 (he can give מִשְׁפָּט and תּוֹרָה), and we may also think of Yahweh himself in the ideal future as both exercising the kingly function of giving מִשְׁפָּט and the 'prophetic' function of giving תּוֹרָה.

2. *The Apocrypha, Pseudepigrapha and Dead Sea Scrolls*

We have now examined the evidence of the Old Testament. Next we shall turn to the Apocrypha and Pseudepigrapha, which introduces us to the relevant apocalyptic literature. Ever since R. H. Charles'[5] brilliant presentation of it, the view has been all too easily accepted that apocalyptic was the only true development of the prophetic tradition, a development which had perforce to assert its rights within Judaism, and that under the cloak of pseudonymity, against the crippling tyranny of the Law. Referring to the process whereby the Law came to be regarded as the final word of God to Israel, Charles wrote: 'By such drastic measures prophecy was driven forth from the bosom of Judaism, and has never since been suffered to return. The task of leading the people into more spiritual conceptions, alike as regards the present life and that which is to come, devolved henceforth on apocalyptic, and that a pseudonymous apocalyptic.'[6] But Charles' presentation of the relation between Pharisaism and

---

[1] *Op. cit.* p. 150.　　　　[2] In a private communication.
[3] *Op. cit. ad rem.*　　　　[4] *Op. cit. ad rem.*
[5] See *Apocrypha and Pseudepigrapha* (1913), II, vii ff. See also F. C. Burkitt, Schweich Lectures (1913), *Jewish and Christian Apocalypses*, pp. 14 ff.
[6] *Op. cit.* p. viii, n. 1. For a penetrating analysis of the relation of Apocalyptic with Law and Prophecy, see T. W. Manson, 'Some reflections on Apocalyptic', in *Aux Sources de la Tradition Chrétienne, Mélanges offerts à M. Maurice Goguel* (Paris, 1950), pp. 139 ff.

apocalyptic no longer satisfies. We have argued elsewhere[1] that between these two factors in the life of Jewry no great gulf was fixed, and that while there is a difference of emphasis in apocalyptic and Pharisaic circles, nevertheless, there was no cleavage between them; and in their attitude to the Law they were at one; indeed, some of the apocalyptists were probably as strict in their adherence to the Law as were the Pharisees themselves, and we can be fairly sure that what the former would have to say about the Law would, usually at least, command the assent of the latter.

What then does this literature reveal as to the function of the Law in the ideal future? Here again the material relevant to our purpose is scanty.[2] The following are the only passages that we have been able to glean.

(i) We first turn to 1 Enoch. We have to recognize that the Similitudes of Enoch, from which we draw our material, like other parts of 1 Enoch, have been very variously dated.[3] Here, however, we must accept the general consensus of opinion that they are pre-Christian, and thus assume that we can use them for our purpose, with full awareness, however, of the strictures of J. Y. Campbell[4] and others on those who follow this practice.

In a vision, which he calls a vision of wisdom, Enoch is granted to see that which is to come. To him is revealed the coming judgement of the wicked (chapter xxxviii), the abode of the Elect One, who is marked by righteousness (chapter xxxix); and later it is revealed to him that this Elect One or the Son of Man is very closely associated not only with righteousness but also with wisdom. Thus in xlviii. 1 we read:

And in that place I saw the fountain of righteousness
Which was inexhaustible:
And around it were many fountains of wisdom:
And all the thirsty drank of them,
And they were filled with wisdom,
And their dwellings were with the righteous and holy and elect.
And at that hour the Son of Man was named
In the presence of the Lord of Spirits,
And his name before the Head of Days.

[1] 'Apocalyptic and Pharisaism', E.T. (July 1948); also P.R.J.[2] pp. 9 f.; J. Giblet, L'Attente du Messie, pp. 110, 117; E. Schürer, op. cit. III, 185; also J. Bloch, On the Apocalyptic in Judaism (1952).

[2] Thus there is no passage cited by R. Marcus, Law in the Apocrypha (1927), which is immediately relevant to our purpose.

[3] See H. H. Rowley, The Relevance of Apocalyptic, pp. 52 f., 75 f.

[4] J.T.S. XLVIII (1947), 146: it may be that the recently discovered Dead Sea Scrolls can settle the date of 1 Enoch; see Père Milik, R.B. LXIII (1953), 60.

Further on there is mention again of the power and wisdom of the Elect One who is to be the judge of the righteous and the wicked 'in those days' that are to come. Chapter xlix. 1 f. reads:

> For wisdom is poured out like water,
> And glory faileth not before him for evermore.
> For he is mighty in all the secrets of righteousness,
> And unrighteousness shall disappear as a shadow,
> And have no continuance. . ...

And in li. 3 we read:

> And the Elect One shall in those days sit on My throne,
> And his mouth shall pour forth all the secrets of wisdom and counsel:
> For the Lord of Spirits hath given (them) to him. . ...

There is in all the above, it is true, no specific reference to the Torah. But we cannot doubt that for the author of the Similitudes the righteous are those who have been faithful to the Torah and it is in accordance with the Torah, we can be sure, that the Elect One shall judge (see xxxviii. 2; xxxix. 6; xlvi. 2; liii. 6). The association of the Elect One with wisdom may also be significant because from early times wisdom had been associated with Torah, as in Deut. iv. 6, and as early as Ecclesiasticus was actually identified with the Torah. The passage concerned from Ecclesiasticus is interesting; it reads (xxiv. 3 ff.):

> 3 I came forth from the mouth of the Most High
>   And as a mist I covered the earth. . ...
> 5 Alone I compassed the circuit of heaven,
>   And in the depth of the abyss I walked.
> 6 Over the waves of the sea, and over all the earth,
>   And over every people and nation I held sway.
> 7 With all these I sought a resting place
>   And (said) In whose inheritance shall I lodge?
> 8 Then the Creator of all things gave me commandment,
>   And he that created me fixed my dwelling place (for me),
>   And he said: Let thy dwelling place be in Jacob
>   And in Israel take up thine inheritance.

In verse 23 the identification of Wisdom with the Torah is made explicit:

> All these things are the book of the Covenant of God Most High,
> The Law which Moses commanded (as) an heritage for the assemblies
>   of Jacob.

Here Wisdom has found the completely satisfying home in the Torah on earth. Now in 1 Enoch this view is not found. Instead we have a curious passage, which looks like an interpolation in its present context, where the view is expressed that Wisdom searched the earth in vain for a satisfactory home and failing to find such returned to heaven. The passage (1 Enoch xlii. 1 ff.) reads:

> Wisdom found no place where she might dwell;
> Then a dwelling place was assigned her in the heavens.
> Wisdom went forth to make her dwelling among the children of men
> And found no dwelling place:
> Wisdom returned to her place,
> And took her seat among the angels....

It agrees with this that there are several passages where it is claimed that Wisdom in its fullness is the mark of the Messianic existence, see xlviii. 1; xlix. 1 f.; compare v. 8; xci. 10; 2 Bar. xliv. 14; Charles comments on Wisdom in xlii. 1 f. that 'she will return in Messianic times'; and with Wisdom, we may confidently repeat, goes the Torah in its fullness. The Son of Man, when he should come, would therefore be accompanied by or endowed with wisdom. But, while 1 Enoch would seem certainly to emphasize the character of this wisdom as knowledge of divine mysteries hidden since the creation and of the purpose of God for the world, we may assume that it also connoted knowledge of the Law, because the Son of Man was 'mighty in all the secrets of righteousness'. We need not, with Giblet,[1] regard the Son of Man as exclusively concerned with 'revelations', although his connexion with the Law can only be an implied one.

(ii) Next we refer to the Psalms of Solomon which are generally dated in the first century B.C. In the famous Psalm contained in chapter xvii the Messiah is endowed with wisdom and understanding (29 f., 42): he is claimed to be taught of God (34); his word will be powerful in judgement (41); and it is implied that his judgement will not only be powerful, but penetrating (48). There is nothing in the context to suggest, however, that he will bring a new Law but merely that he will establish a condition when the life of righteousness in accordance with the Torah will prevail.[2]

---

[1] Giblet, 'Le Messianisme Prophétique', in *L'Attente du Messie*, p. 108, takes the Son of Man in 1 Enoch to be the Messiah, but denies that he bears prophetic marks. Charles takes 'wisdom' in xlix. 1 to mean 'the knowledge and fear of God': *The Book of Enoch or 1 Enoch* (1912), p. 96 n.

[2] See H. E. Ryle and M. R. James, *The Psalms of Solomon*, p. 143, n. on verse 37 (in their text).

(iii) Next there are two more significant passages to be noted in
1 Maccabees, where it is made clear that it was expected that certain
difficulties which beset the interpretation of the Law in the present would
be made plain at some future date. The first is in 1 Macc. iv. 41–6:

Then Judas appointed certain men to fight against those that were in the fortress,
until he had cleansed the sanctuary. And he chose blameless priests, such as had
delight in the Law; and they cleansed the Holy Place, and bare out the stones of
defilement into an unclean place. And they took counsel concerning the altar
of burnt offerings, which had been profaned, what they should do with it. And
a good idea occurred to them (namely) to pull it down, lest it should be a
reproach unto them because the Gentiles had defiled it; so they pulled down the
altar and laid down the stones until a prophet should come and decide (as to
what should be done) concerning them. (μέχρι τοῦ παραγενηθῆναι προφήτην
τοῦ ἀποκριθῆναι περὶ αὐτῶν.)

There are no textual points of note. The passage belongs to a section
which describes how Judas Maccabaeus purified the Temple after he had
taken the city of Jerusalem. The altar of burnt offerings still stood, but it
had been profaned by the Gentiles. The discussion which arose concerning
the altar suggests not the 'casuistry' and exegetical subtlety of Pharisaism
but either the rigid literalism of the Sadducees, who were at a loss to find
any pertinent direction in scripture, or a more unsophisticated legalism
which was simply puzzled and led to a convenient compromise until a
prophet should appear. The belief that prophecy belonged to the past
appears elsewhere in 1 Macc. ix. 27,[1] where it is clear that its cessation was
regarded as epochal. Here the authorities fall back on the expectation of a
prophet who should speak authoritatively in the name of the Lord. But
note: he would, in fact, be concerned with the interpretation of the Law:
he would have to pronounce on a specific matter of law. There is, however,
no suggestion that this prophet should be regarded as the Messiah: the
reference may merely be to any prophet who might appear in the future.
The absence of the definite article before προφήτην is to be given its full
significance. No manuscript inserts it.

[1] The precise point at which prophecy was deemed to have ceased varied. Some regarded Malachi as the last of the prophets: Josephus traced the end of prophecy to the
exile itself (*Against Apion*, 1, viii, 41). The phrase ἀφ' ἧς ἡμέρας οὐκ ὤφθη προφήτης
αὐτοῖς, in the words of Abel, 'demeure dans le vague qui convient à ce genre de
chronologie populaire' (*Les Livres des Maccabées*, Paris, 1949, p. 165). See also
J. C. Dancy, *A Commentary on 1 Maccabees* (Oxford: Blackwell, 1954), p. 2. What
justifies us in claiming that the cessation of prophecy was epochal is the fact that it
provides a specific historical point of comparison with the present evil times. 'La
disparition du prophétisme', as Giblet puts it, 'est une date' (*op. cit.* p. 95).

The reference to a prophet also emerges in 1 Macc. xiv. 25–49. The specific words which concern us are:

And the Jews and the priests were well pleased that Simon should be their leader and high priest for ever, until a faithful prophet should arise. (ἕως τοῦ ἀναστῆναι προφήτην πιστόν.)

The Simon referred to became High Priest after the death of Jonathan and had undertaken to fulfil the necessary important functions of leadership, both political and sacerdotal. His accession to power was welcomed warmly—he was to be leader (ἡγούμενον) and priest *for ever*, εἰς τὸν αἰῶνα. Nevertheless, those who installed him had scruples. He had been instituted as leader and priest by merely human hands: the belief that the throne belonged to the descendants of David and the priesthood to the sons of Zadok was a living one. It was natural, therefore, that the phrase 'for ever' should be adequately qualified. Used absolutely it suggested that Simon's hegemony and priesthood were irrevocable. This could not be contemplated even in the enthusiasm of his accession, and so the addendum occurs: ἕως τοῦ ἀναστῆναι προφήτην πιστόν. His leadership and priesthood are 'for ever' in the sense that they are to continue until a divine revelation is given which might demand their supersession.

Here again there is no definite article before the term prophet, and though the adjective πιστός may be an allusion to Moses, as in Num. xii. 7; Eccles. xliv. 4, while the verb ἀναστῆναι may recall Deut. xviii. 15 (προφήτην ἐκ τῶν ἀδελφῶν σου ὡς ἐμὲ ἀναστήσει σοι κύριος ὁ θεός σου), it is safer to take the reference here also to be a general one. Present arrangements are to hold until the Spirit, in prophecy, again visits Israel. No Messianic undertones emerge here. The hope for a prophet 'is vague and almost formal: we have not yet progressed to the confident expectation of a Messiah'.[1] Moreover, a further point is to be noticed here: the term 'prophet' is used to describe one to whom difficulties of a specific and legal kind are referred with the expectation that he should have a communication from God which would solve these difficulties; the specific prophetic function, as generally understood, of interpreting the purpose of God in a broad way is here, perhaps, replaced by one that is more circumscribed and 'legal'. But this should not be pressed.[2]

In sum, both passages from 1 Maccabees refer difficulties in the interpretation of the Law to a coming prophet who should have a communication

---

[1] Dancy, *op. cit.* p. 2; Abel, *op. cit.* pp. 260 ff.
[2] Giblet, *op. cit.* p. 106.

from God which would solve these. The reference to a coming prophet may be based on Deut. xviii. 15, but nothing demands that 'the prophet' in these texts should be interpreted messianically. Nevertheless, they may be cited as confirming the view that the Torah would at least be better understood in the future than in the present, and that prophetic revelation was part of the hope of Judaism.

A passage from the Old Testament has been appealed to in discussions of this problem as expressing the hope, not for a prophet in the future, but for a priest in the Messianic Age. Ezra ii. 61–3 reads as follows (parallel in Neh. vii. 61–5):

61 Also, of the sons of the priests: the sons of Habaiah, the sons of Hakkoz, and the sons of Barzillai (who had taken a wife from the daughters of Barzillai the
62 Gileadite, and was called by their name). These sought their registration among those enrolled in the genealogies, but they were not found there, and so they
63 were excluded from the priesthood as unclean; the governor told them that they were not to partake of the most holy food, until there should be a priest to consult Urim and Thummim.

Here 'priests' without proper genealogical accreditation were denied the right of fulfilling their priestly functions until one should arise qualified to use Urim and Thummim. In the light of 1 Sam. xiv. 41, Urim and Thummim would seem to be two objects drawn out of some place by the priest, one meaning 'Yes' and the other 'No'. The usage was early, but in the post-exilic period it has ceased because either the objects themselves had disappeared or the technique for using them had become unknown. Here the expectation of a priest—and by this is meant probably a High Priest—capable of obtaining divine guidance by the manipulation of Urim and Thummim emerges. This hope has been claimed to be Messianic; that is, there was expected to arise in the Messianic Age a priest to gain divine guidance by the use of Urim and Thummim. The verb עָמַד may be taken pregnantly, as referring to a Messianic appearance.

There is a reference to the cessation of Urim and Thummim in Mishnah Sotah ix. 12. It reads:

מִשֶּׁמֵּתוּ נְבִיאִים הָרִאשׁוֹנִים בָּטְלוּ אוּרִים וְתֻמִּים

that is, 'When the first prophets died Urim and Thummim ceased'. Danby[1] understands by this that they ceased, not to exist, so he implies at least, but 'to have power to indicate God's will'. But to judge from the use of בטל in the parallel passage in the Tosefta such a view cannot be

---

[1] *The Mishnah*, p. 305, n. 9.

held. The expansion of this in Tosefta Sotah xiii. 2, taken literally, might suggest a hope for their return or reapplication in the Messianic Age. There the phrase is cited from Ezra ii. 63 and is equated with 'until Elijah comes' or 'until the dead shall live'.

משחרב בית הראשון בטל מלכות מבית דוד ובטלו אורים ותומים ופסקו ערי
מגרש שנ׳ ויאמר התרשתא להם אשר לא יאכלו מק׳ הק׳ עד ע׳ כ׳ לאורים
ותומים כאדם שאומ׳ לחבירו עד שיבא אליהו או עד שיחיו המתים משמת
חגי זכריה ומלאכי נביאים האחרונים פסקה רוח הקדש מישראל ואף על פי
כן היו משמיעין להן בבת קול:

The phrases referred to are best not taken seriously in a Messianic sense, but simply as customary expressions for 'never'. This is brought out in the Soncino translation of the *gemara* on the passage in TB Sotah 48 *b*.

Come and hear: When the first Temple was destroyed, the cities with pasture land were abolished, the *Urim* and *Thummim* ceased, there was no more King from the House of David; and if anyone incites you to quote, *And the governor said unto them that they should not eat of the most holy things till there stood up a priest with Urim and Thummim,*[6] reply to them: [It is only a phrase for the very remote future] as when one man says to another, 'Until the dead revive and the Messiah, the Son of David, comes!' (n. 6 is from Ezra ii. 63).

This means that 'until the Messiah comes' is here merely a synonym for 'never'.

Kennedy contrasted the desire for a prophet in the passages quoted above from 1 Maccabees, with that for a priest to use Urim and Thummim in Ezra–Nehemiah, and saw in this a sign of the deepening of Israel's understanding of God's ways of revealing himself.[1] That this view may be correct would seem to be supported by TB Sotah 48 *b*, which makes it clear that later rabbis were accustomed to drawing a contrast between revelation by Urim and Thummim and through the prophets. It reads:

WHEN THE FORMER PROPHETS DIED. Who are the former prophets? R. Huna said: They are David, Samuel and Solomon. R. Nahman said: During the days of David, they were sometimes successful (that is, in obtaining knowledge of the future by consulting Urim and Thummim); for behold, Zadok consulted it and succeeded, whereas Abiathar consulted and was not successful, as it is said, And *Abiathar went up* (2 Sam. xv. 24). [This, notes the translator, is explained by the Rabbis: he retired from the priesthood because he received no

---

[1] *H.D.B.* pp. 838 ff.

reply from the Urim and Thummim.] Samuel objected: (It is written), *And he set himself to seek God all the days of Zechariah who had understanding in the vision o, God* [that is, Uzziah, King of Judah]. Was this not by means of Urim and Thummim? No, it was through the prophets.

It is, however, precarious to illumine a passage from Ezra from such a late source as this. Moreover, prophecy itself gradually fell into disrepute in the post-exilic period[1] and the contrast drawn by Kennedy should not accordingly be pressed. More likely is it that the growing veneration for the Law, as the means of divine revelation, meant that interest turned away from Urim and Thummim and it is unlikely that these were re-introduced at any period after their cessation. We must conclude that no Messianic significance can be read into Ezra ii. 63.

(iv) Next we turn to the DSS (including CDC), the pre-Christian dating of which has been accepted by the majority of scholars. They reveal a group of people who, as they await the End, constitute themselves as the people of the New Covenant.[2] We have previously emphasized how their activity seems to have been governed by the concept of a New Exodus parallel to the first. Their preoccupation with the Law of Moses shines clear. What we are here concerned to discover is whether they reveal an awareness of a need or hope for changes in the Law or for a New Law. The following passages are pertinent.

DSD ix. 9–11:

They shall not depart from any counsel of the Law, walking in all the stubbornness of their hearts; but they shall judge by the first judgements by which the men of the community began to be disciplined, until there shall come a prophet and the Messiahs of Aaron and Israel. (Burrows's translation.)

Thus the community, which, from DSD viii. 13–14, we know was formed on the basis of Isa. xl. 3, was to be governed by the rules laid down in the Manual until a prophet and 'Messiahs', one of Aaron and one of David, should arise. While there is nothing in the text to suggest

---

[1] Israel Abrahams, *Studies in Pharisaism and the Gospels*, 2nd ser., pp. 120 f.; *P.R.J.*[2] pp. 208 ff.

[2] By the term 'New Covenant' the Sect did not understand that the Old Covenant was annulled. The reverence for Moses excludes any such idea. (DSD i. 1; v. 8; the aim of the sect is to return to the Law of Moses, CDC iii. 13, 19; xv. 8–10.) Probably the community had its own regulations received through the insight of or revelations to the Teacher of Righteousness. (See H. Teeple, *op. cit.* pp. 20, 24; G. Vermès, *op. cit.* p. 75; J. T. Milik, *Dix Ans de Découvertes dans le Désert de Juda*, pp. 63, 76. The latter fully recognizes the interim character of the regulations of the Sect to which we allude below.)

that the prophet to come would bring a New Law, the very clear implication is that the rules governing the life of the community would be open to change on his coming. Thus the rules of the Manual constitute an interim programme.[1]

The same concept of an interim programme emerges in CDC. In the opening of this document, in i. 10–12, after a statement about the original members of the community (who, though earnest in their ways, 'were like the blind and like them that grope *their* way' for twenty years) we read:

And God considered their works for 'with a perfect heart' did they seek Him; | and He raised for them 'a teacher of righteousness' (מורה צדק) to lead them in 'the way of His heart' and to make known | to the last generations that which He ⌐would do⌐ to the last generation, the congregation of the faithless. (Rabin's translation.)

We are probably to understand that the instructions for 'the Way' given by this figure, the Teacher of Righteousness, are contained in CDC. Are these regarded as eternally binding? Words in CDC vi. 14 suggest that they were not. They constituted rather an interim ethic. Here the sectarians are to take care 'to do according to the exact statement of the Law for the epoch of wickedness (לעשות כפרוש התורה לקץ הרשע).'[2] Here פרוש means 'the detailed manner in which a general prescription is to be applied'. Beyond 'the epoch of wickedness' the present writ, it is implied, did not run.

A Dutch scholar, Dr A. S. Van der Woude,[3] by giving a chronological sequence to DSD and CDC, placing the former first in time, has been able to suggest that the prophet, who was expected in DSD ix. 9–11, had

[1] Not the Mosaic Law itself but the regulations of the Sect which, in turn, rest upon its interpretation of the Law, are to be changed. See H. Teeple, *op. cit.* p. 26; T. H. Gaster, *The Dead Sea Scriptures*, p. 4.

[2] C. Rabin, *The Zadokite Documents*[2] (1958), p. 22, n. 14: 2. The next note on the same page deserves quotation in full, even though it anticipates our discussion: 'Some medieval Jewish mystics believed the Law would receive a different meaning in messianic times, cf. Scholem, *Major Trends in Jewish Mysticism* (2nd ed.), p. 175. The phraseology seems to exclude the supposition that the sect believed the entire Law as such would cease to be applicable, though this view is put forward authoritatively ("from the academy of Elijah") in b. Sanhedrin 97a and by R. Simeon b. Eleazar (2nd cent.), b. Shabbath 151b; cf. L. Baeck in *J.J.S.* III (1952), p. 106, who ascribes this view also to Paul. But they certainly did not, like Samuel (3rd cent.), b. Sh. *ib.*, believe the Messianic coming to be a mere political event.'

[3] Dr A. S. Van der Woude, *Die Messianischen Vorstellungen der Gemeinde von Qumran* (Assen, 1957), *passim*. A brief but very balanced statement of the material appears in F. M. Cross, *The Ancient Library of Qumran, ad rem.*

appeared in the Teacher of Righteousness who appears in CDC i. 16. On this view, for the sectarians in CDC only the coming of the Messiahs of Aaron and Israel lies in the future. We may gather, therefore, that there are three clearly differentiated periods: (1) that before the coming of the prophet (DSD); (2) that from the prophet (= Teacher of Righteousness) to the advent of the Messiahs (CDC); (3) that after the latter, that is, the Messianic Age. Each period had its appropriate laws.[1] We are to find in DSD and CDC the laws pertaining to the first two stages respectively.[2] Attractive as is this schematization, it should not be uncritically endorsed. The chronological sequence presented above cannot be regarded as certainly established: the priority of DSD can be neither proved nor disproved, nor can the Teacher of Righteousness be identified beyond doubt with the prophet expected in DSD. Unified and coherent interpretations in this field are *ipso facto* suspect.[3]

But one thing is certain. In both DSD and CDC a future is envisaged in which a change in the laws governing the community is expected. The phraseology employed does not make it clear how the Law was conceived to operate in the Messianic Age: certainly we are not permitted to claim that at that time it would cease or that there would be a New Law, but only that the current interpretations would be obsolete. This means, however, that 'the Law' for the sect (whether we postulate the stages, as indicated above, or not) was not completely adequate. There was an intense awareness that the days of the Messiah would introduce changes in the laws governing the community.

Can we go further? There is one extended passage which suggests perhaps a radical break in the Messianic Age in DSD iv. 18–26. The pertinent words are in iv. 25:

כיא בד בבד שמן אל עד קץ נחרצה <u>ועשות חדשה</u>.

For in equal measure God has established the two spirits until the period which has been decreed and *the making new....* (M. Burrows's translation.)

Is the 'making new', referred to in the above passage, to include the Law itself? This is a real possibility; because the Sect was aware of tension

---

[1] Van der Woude, *op. cit.* pp. 84 f. He refers to CDC xx. 8 f.

[2] See Van der Woude, *op. cit.* pp. 97 f., on the relation of DSD, 1QSa, CDC which he places in that order. I suggested that DSD was earlier in parts than in others in *The Scrolls and the N.T.*, ed. K. Stendahl, p. 165; but see Flusser, *Scripta Hierosolymitana* (Jerusalem, 1958), p. 253.

[3] On this see Morton Smith, *J.B.L.* LXXVIII (March 1959), 66–72, on 'What is implied by the variety of Messianic figures?'

under the Law. The concentration, relentless and rigid, on obedience to the Law and the intense awareness of sin which accompanied this tension shine equally clear. In no other sources in first-century Judaism is failure to achieve the righteousness of the Law more recognized and at the same time its demands pressed with greater ruthlessness. May it be that this condition may have led to the hope that the Messianic Age would bring relief? This possibility is perhaps further to be discerned in the yearning expressed in the above passage for fullness of knowledge in the Messianic Age. The chief end of man is here defined in terms of the knowledge of God: it is to share in the wisdom of the angelic hosts. How is this knowledge to be understood? Is it more knowledge in and through the Law or is it knowledge beyond the Law? There is evidence that in the Scrolls the 'knowledge' which marks the final time is eschatological not only in the sense that it belongs to the final time, but in the sense that it gives insight into the meaning of the events of that time. Should we go further and find among the sectarians a yearning for a knowledge which itself constitutes 'eternal life', which transcends the knowledge supplied by the 'Law' as known in this present age? We can at least claim that Judaism is here straining at the leash of the Law: the Scrolls reveal it at 'boiling point'.[1]

In the last passage quoted, the attempt has been made to discover a strictly Messianic note in the reference to the 'man' in DSD iv. 20 f.[2] This is to be rejected, but it prompts the question how the anticipated changes in the Law in the future, to which we have referred, are to be achieved. The agent of the 'New Order' described in DSD iv. 18 ff. (when the destruction of evil from man's flesh, the purification by the sprinkling of Holy Spirit, the gift of knowledge and the restoration of man's lost glory are to be achieved) is God Himself. But by what agencies are the new משפטים (regulations) to be given? The following figures have been distinguished as eschatological.

[1] For all the above compare my work in *The Scrolls and the N.T.*, ed. K. Stendahl, p. 281, n. 86. It is in this light that we are doubtless to understand those anticipations of the Pauline emphasis on justification by faith or trust alone which have been found in the DSS; see K. Stendahl, *op. cit.* p. 9; S. E. Johnson, *H.T.R.* XLVIII (1955), 157 ff. on 'Paul and the Manual of Discipline'; W. Grundmann, *Revue de Qumran*, VI (February 1960), 237–59; W. Grossouw, *Studia Catholica*, XXVII (1952), 1–18. On 'Knowledge', see my work in *H.T.R.* XLVI (1953), 113–39.

[2] W. H. Brownlee, *B.A.S.O.R.* (October 1954), 35–8. Refuted by Yigael Yadin, *J.B.L.* LXXIV (1955), 40–3. Brownlee is more cautious in *The Scrolls and the N.T.*, ed. K. Stendahl, p. 43. See the treatment by Van der Woude, *op. cit.* pp. 91 ff.

(1) *The prophet*: DSD ix. 9–11:

They shall not depart from any counsel of the Law, walking in all the stubbornness of their hearts; but they shall judge by the first judgements by which the men of the community began to be disciplined, until there shall come a prophet and the Messiahs of Aaron and Israel (עד בוא נָבָא ומשיחי אהרון וישראל). (Burrows's translation.)

(2) *Either One or Two Messiahs*
DSD ix. 9–11 *may* have two Messiahs.
CDC xiv. 19:

And this is the exact statement of the rulings (משפטים) in which [they shall walk during the epoch | of wickedness, until there shall arise the Messi]ah of Aaron and Israel and he will make conciliation for their trespass[. . .] (Rabin's translation and reconstruction).

Here one Messiah is contemplated.
A single Messiah would seem also to be contemplated in the following:

(*a*) A *pesher* from Cave IV on Isa. x. 22–xi. 4 mentions the Messiah as such (4QpIsa).

(*b*) A collection of blessings in the same Cave IV containing an interpretation of Gen. xlix. 10 (see J. M. Allegro, *R.B.* LXIII (1956), 62 f.; *J.B.L.* LXXV (1956), 175 f.) (4QFlor; 1QSb).

(*c*) CDC vii. 18–20 refers to the 'Prince' (נשיא):

And the Star is the searcher of the Law (דורש תורה) | who came (or: shall come) (הבא) to Damascus, as it is written: 'A star shall step forth out of Jacob and a sceptre shall rise | out of Israel'—the Sceptre is the prince (נשיא) of all the congregation, and when he arises 'he shall strike violently | all sons of Seth'. . . . (Rabin's translation.)

Compare Ezek. xxxiv. 24; xxxvii. 25 where the Prince may be the Messiah. (But see p. 121, n. 3.)

(*d*) There is a blessing for the Prince of the Congregation among a series of blessings found in Cave I (Qumran Cave 1, pp. 127 f.) (1QSb).

(*e*) In Qumran Cave 1, p. 110, we find the Messiah present at an assembly of the whole congregation. This envisages one Messiah only but according to others two (1QSa ii. 11–22).

(*f*) Qumran Cave 1, p. 132, line 2 refers to 'the holy [M]essiah'.[1]

[1] Accordingly E. F. Sutcliffe argues in favour of a single Messiah: see *The Monks of Qumran* (London, 1960), pp. 84 ff. He fully recognizes the role of the High Priest in the Messianic Age but insists that, although he is anointed (מָשִׁיחַ), he is still to be clearly distinguished from the Messiah.

But on the basis of DSD ix. 9–11 and 1 QSa ii. 12 ff., Kuhn,[1] in particular, has argued that, like the Testaments of the Twelve Patriarchs, the Sect
looked forward to two Messianic figures: (i) the Messiah of Aaron, who
is given priority; and (ii) the Messiah of Israel, the Davidic Messiah; the
first a High Priest, the second a political leader subordinate to the former.
Kuhn explains the fact that the phrase 'The Messiah (singular) of Aaron
and Israel' occurs at CDC xii. 23; xiv. 19; xix. 10; xx. 1, by urging that
originally the formula was in the plural, but that the unfamiliarity of the
concept caused scribes to change it to the singular. He finds confirmation
for this view in CDC ii. 12–vi. 1 where also an original plural has become
singular. Most scholars have followed Kuhn.

(3) The 'Star' referred to in CDC vii. 18 has been referred to as the
Messiah of Aaron who was to come, on the assumption that there were
two Messiahs. It reads:

and the Star is the searcher of the Law (דורש תורה) who came (or: shall come) to
Damascus, as it is written: 'A Star shall step forth out of Jacob and a sceptre
shall rise out of Israel'—the Sceptre is the prince of all the congregation....
(Rabin's translation.)

Those who have translated the phrase 'and the Star is the searcher of the
Law *who came*' (הבא) have been able to find here a reference to the
Teacher of Righteousness, who was a searcher of the Law. But more
probably the tense is future, הבא referring as in the phrase העולם הבא to
a future event. In this case, the Star refers to a Messianic figure and fits in
well with the Aaronic Messiah expected by the Sect. Similarly the Sceptre
(השבט) is a reference to the Davidic Messiah to come.[2]

(4) The figure of the Teacher of Righteousness himself has been
claimed to be eschatological not merely in the sense that he is a participant
in the events *leading to the End*, but also as *appearing at the End*. The basis
for this claim is CDC vi. 8 ff.:

And the Nobles of the People are | they that have come to dig the Well with the
staff which the Staff instituted | to walk ⌐in them⌐ during the whole epoch of
wickedness and without which they (or: and others than they) will not grasp
⟨instruction⟩ 'until there shall arise | he who teaches righteousness' in the end
of the days. (עד עמד יורה הצדק באחרית הימים.)

Moreover, the Teacher of Righteousness already as a figure in history
had, like Moses, taught righteousness, so that he is to appear as a kind of

---

[1] *The Scrolls and the N.T.*, ed. K. Stendahl, pp. 54–64.
[2] Van der Woude, *op. cit.* p. 58 for a full discussion.

New Moses again at the End. But this view rests on two faulty pillars. First, the term 'arise' cannot bear the weight of Resurrection;[1] and, secondly, it is inadmissable to equate the יורה הצדק of the above passage with the Teacher of Righteousness (מורה צדק). Only the similarity in the two Hebrew phrases lends any support to this, and this is negated by the fact that it was possible for Judaism to think of many teachers of righteousness without identifying such with the Teacher of Righteousness of history. Full justice, however, should be given to the Mosaic traits in the latter. He is rightly equated with the Staff in CDC vi. 4 ff.:

The Well is the Law. And those that digged it are | 'they that turned (from impiety) of Israel', who went out from the land of Judah and sojourned in the land of Damascus |—inasmuch as God called all of them Princes, for they sought him, and their ⌜fame⌝ was not rejected by the mouth of anyone—and the Staff is the Searcher of the Law (והמחוקק הוא דורש התורה), as Isaiah said: | 'who bringeth forth a tool for his work.' (Rabin's translation.)

And in view of the Exodic conceptions which governed the community, that the Teacher of Righteousness should be like Moses is to be expected. This means that he is concerned with the Law though not necessarily a 'Lawgiver'.[2] Like Moses, the Teacher of Righteousness had given rules by which his community was to live (1QpH ii. 2–3); the community consisted of those who had faith in him (1QpH viii. 1–3). Nevertheless, caution is necessary: the relation of the Teacher of Righteousness to the Sect was not quite like that of Moses to Israel. He was not *founder*, as was Moses, but rather the guide of his people *after* it had set forth on its way (CDC i. 1 ff.). The utmost we can certainly say is that the Teacher of Righteousness, as a figure in history, reveals certain Mosaic traits;[3] but

[1] Compare E. F. Sutcliffe, *op. cit.* pp. 86 ff.; contrast C. Rabin, *op. cit.* p. 23, who finds the term to mean 'to be revealed'.

[2] See C. Rabin, *op. cit.*, *ad rem*, who rejects the translation 'lawgiver' for מחוקק; according to him, the term is not attested thus before the fourteenth and fifteenth centuries. Teeple, *op. cit.* p. 52, favours 'lawgiver'; W. H. Brownlee, 'Messianic Motifs of Qumran and the New Testament', *N.T.S.* III (1956), 17, is not emphatic. G. Vermès, however, 'La Figure de Moïse au Tournant des deux Testaments', in *Moïse l'Homme de l'Alliance* (1954), p. 81, argues strongly that מחוקק refers to a religious authority, a doctor of the Law, and finds that the Teacher of Righteousness, with whom he identifies this figure, is here a New Moses. He provides evidence from the ancient versions and the Targumim for rendering 'une personne ayant le pouvoir de porter un décret (ḥoq)'. He cites the Peshitta and the Vulgate in support and Sirach x. 5, where it is rendered by γραμματεύς.

[3] See G. Vermès, *op. cit.* pp. 80 ff. Among those who have favoured finding in the Teacher of Righteousness a New Moses are: W. H. Brownlee, *op. cit.* p. 17; M. Black, *Scottish Journal of Theology*, VI (1953), 5, on 'The Servant of the Law and the Son of

that he was regarded as 'one to come', to be raised from the dead as New Moses (by the equation of the Star in CDC vii. 18, with the Teacher of Righteousness) is only a possibility.[1]

However, there can be little doubt that, at least, the first item mentioned above, 'the Prophet' to come, was understood in terms of a New Moses, in the light of Deut. xviii. 15–18. It is no objection to this that the term 'prophet' in DSD ix. 9–11 is anarthrous; so is it in Deut. xviii. 15. Moreover, the fact that the latter passage has appeared in the so-called Testimonia[2] of the Sect lends added justification for connecting it with the expectation of the Prophet in DSD ix. 9–11. If so, one of the main eschatological figures in the sectarian expectation was to be like Moses.

Can we go further than this? Van der Woude, as we saw, identified the prophet as having come in the Teacher of Righteousness, and equated the Searcher of the Law in CDC vii. 18 with the Aaronic Messiah who was to come. He then proceeds to claim that this Searcher of the Law, the Aaronic Messiah, is none other than Elijah, returned as Messianic High Priest.[3] In this case, one of the two strictly Messianic figures of the Sect was to be concerned with the interpretation of the Law.[4] In this way, the eschatology of the Sect is connected with features which are familiar to us elsewhere in Judaism. The latter looked forward to the coming of Elijah in particular because he was to unravel points in the Law,[5] which occasioned difficulty and obscurity (and there was a parallel expectation of a

Man'; J. Jeremias, *T.W.Z.N.T.*, on Moses, p. 865; H. Teeple, *op. cit.* p. 52; G. Vermès, *op. cit.* pp. 81 ff.; N. Wieder, *J.J.S.* IV (1953), on 'The Law-Interpreter of the Sect of the Dead Sea Scrolls: the Second Moses', pp. 158 ff.; *et alia*.

[1] Contrast C. Rabin, *ibid.* Compare Van der Woude, *op. cit.* p. 73; M. Black, 'Theological Conceptions in the Dead Sea Scrolls', *Svensk Exegetisk Årsbok*, XVIII–XIX (1953–4), 86.

[2] 4Q Testimonia.

[3] Van der Woude, *op. cit.* pp. 55–60: he notes that Elijah was of priestly descent. See Molin, *Judaica*, VIII (1952), 82–4.

[4] L. Ginzberg, *Eine Unbekannte Jüdische Sekte* (1922), pp. 311 ff., interpreted the יורה הצדק of CDC vi. 11 of Elijah, but distinguishes between Elijah, as forerunner of the Messiah, and the latter. (Contrast Van der Woude who equates the Aaronic Messiah with the returned Elijah.) The whole section, pp. 303–24, is important. Note his claim that הצדק after יורה rather than צדק as in CDC i. 11 denotes a special kind of teacher of righteousness, not any kind of teacher—'dieser Unterschied zwischen Elija und den anderen Gesetzlehrern wird durch יורה הצדק im Gegensatz zum sonstigen מורה צדק in unserer Schrift angedeutet' (pp. 314–15). Any teacher might be called מורה צדק but יורה הצדק is Elijah. (Is there a misprint on p. 315, that is, הצדק for צדק after מורה?)

[5] See below, pp. 158 ff.

New Moses in Samaritanism).[1] The equation of the Searcher of the Law with the future Elijah, however, must remain conjectural.

We may now draw the threads of this brief treatment together. One thing is quite certain: the sectarians expected the Messianic Age to remove the inadequacies of their understanding of the Law. While there is no suggestion that they anticipated any New Law (unless such be implicit in DSD iv. 18 ff., which is unlikely), in the 'making of the New' the Law itself was not to escape attention: it too required redemption, at least in its interpretation. And one eschatological figure, at least, the Prophet, as New Moses,[2] was to provide a new understanding of it. But this Prophet, while he accompanies the Messiahs, is not himself a Messiah. Can the Messianic figures strictly so called be connected with the re-interpretation of the Law? It should be fully recognized that the Aaronic Messiah in virtue of his priesthood might be expected to be concerned with the Law, although this cannot be too much pressed. This apart, it seems that, unless we are prepared to accept the view that the Messiah of Aaron is Elijah *redivivus*, especially concerned with the interpretation of the Law (a view which cannot but be conjectural and tentative), then the function of interpreting the Law is mainly connected with a figure, the Prophet, as New Moses, who accompanies the Messiahs, but is not to be confused with them: the new interpretation of the Law is a mark of the Messianic Age but apparently not particularly of the Messiahs as such.

Our survey of the Old Testament, the Apocrypha and Pseudepigrapha is now complete. When we ask what evidence it supplies for the role which the Torah would play in the Messianic Age, we can assert that that Age was expected to be a period when the rebelliousness of 'Israel' would be undone and righteousness enthroned. We have had no reason to believe that in most, if not in all cases, this righteousness would differ from that which was demanded by the Torah; and we may endorse the words of Moore as far as the Old Testament, the Apocrypha and Pseudepigrapha are concerned, at least that 'inasmuch as the days of the Messiah are the religious as well as the political consummation of the national history, and, however idealized, belong to the world we live in, it is natural that

---

[1] For the Moses *redivivus* among the Samaritans, see P. Volz, *op. cit.* p. 62.

[2] If the יורה הצדק of CDC vi. 10–11 should be equated with the 'Prophet' to come then he might also conceivably be 'Elijah *redivivus*'. C. Rabin, *op. cit.* p. 23, n. 11: 2, refers to Elijah in this connexion but does not identify 'the Teacher of Righteousness' in vi. 10–11 with Elijah. He accepts the future Resurrection of the Teacher of Righteousness there. See M. Black, *op. cit.* pp. 160 ff.

the law should not only be in force in the Messianic Age, but should be better studied and better observed than ever before; and this was indubitably the common belief'.[1] Nevertheless, we have encountered noteworthy features of the Messianic hope as it touches upon our quest. The belief was obviously cherished that the Torah would be interpreted in a more satisfactory and glorious fashion and would also come to include the Gentiles in its sway. We failed to decide definitely whether Jeremiah's hope that there would be a new covenant implied a New Torah or whether it merely involved better obedience to the Old Torah, or again whether Jeremiah expected a condition of affairs in which no external Torah of any kind would be necessary. We suggested, however, that a certain tension between the written Torah and that Torah which would mark the New Covenant was probably not resolved by Jeremiah, although those who succeeded him appear to have understood his words as still referring to the Old Torah. It is clear, moreover, that the hope of a new covenant[2] persisted as a dynamic element in Judaism as is witnessed to by the Dead Sea Scrolls, where especially changes in the interpretation of the Law in the Messianic Age are anticipated, and it is well to remind ourselves again of the rich complex of concepts—covenantal, Mosaic and Exodic— which informed the eschatological hope of Judaism, against which we make our way in this search.

3. *The Rabbinical Sources*

When we turn to the rabbinical sources in our attempt to discover what role the Torah was expected to play in the Messianic Age, we must begin by recognizing certain commonplaces. First, it is always dangerous to impose any one mode of thought on Judaism: it could tolerate the widest varieties and even contradictions of beliefs. Moreover, it must be recognized that our rabbinic sources represent the triumph of only one stream within Judaism, the Pharisaic, and even of only one current within that one stream, that of R. Johannan ben Zakkai.[3] Hence the possibility is to be reckoned with that many emphases or tendencies in Judaism in the first century are not represented in our rabbinic sources; and this is a possibility which, in view of the antagonism which arose between the Old Israel and its Torah and the New Israel with its new commandment, is not

[1] G. F. Moore, *Judaism*, I, 271.
[2] See Baruch ii. 35 where the covenant of the future probably looks back to the New Covenant of Jeremiah and Ezekiel. See R. Marcus, *Law in the Apocrypha* (1927), p. 13.   [3] H. Danby, *op. cit.* pp. xiv f.

negligible in the present inquiry. Possibly much in the tradition about the nature and role of Torah in the Messianic Age has been either ignored or deliberately suppressed or modified. We have elsewhere emphasized the heterogeneity of first-century Judaism. This has been amply insisted upon in the works of Daube, Goodenough, Lieberman and Morton Smith, and it cannot be overlooked in this quest.

On the other hand, it has to be recognized also that by the first century that movement which received its greatest impulse from Ezra and which was designed to make Jewry a people of the Torah had come to fruition: Pharisaism had become well established even if its first-century significance has often been over-emphasized.[1] And for many Jews the Torah had become the cornerstone of life. How true this was can be grasped not only from those episodes in Jewish history where loyalty to the Torah was the crucial factor governing religious activity in politics and other spheres, but also from the glorification of Torah in much Jewish thought. As Moore has made so clear, so central was the Torah for Judaism that it could conceive neither of the present nor of the past and future except in terms of Torah. The significance of the Torah in the present is demonstrated by that regulation of all life in its minutest details in accordance with the Torah which ultimately led to the codification of the Mishnah, a codification which was not a mushroom growth, but the fruit of much previous codification which goes back at least to the first century.[2] The significance of the Torah in the past was secured by the development of the belief that the Torah was not only pre-existent—as were certain other pivots of Jewish life—but also, and more vitally, instrumental in the creation of the world.[3] The evidence for this need not be repeated here, because it is only with the Torah in the future that we are concerned, and the place of the Torah in the future was guaranteed by the development of the 'doctrine' which we know as that of the immutability of the Torah.

This 'doctrine' we may briefly characterize as follows. The Torah, whether written or oral, had been given to Moses by Yahweh. As the gift of Yahweh and as the ground plan of the Universe it could not but be perfect and unchangeable; it was impossible that it should ever be forgotten; no prophet could ever arise who would change it, and no new

[1] See Morton Smith on 'Palestinian Judaism in the First Century', in *Israel*, ed. M. Davis (New York, 1956), pp. 74 ff.

[2] H. L. Strack, *Introduction to the Talmud and Midrash*, pp. 20 ff.

[3] See G. F. Moore, *op. cit.* I, 263 ff. See also on the above P. Volz, *op. cit.* especially pp. 113 ff. and p. 101.

Moses should ever appear to introduce another Law to replace it.[1] This was not only Palestinian belief but also that of Hellenistic Judaism. Philo in a passage where he contrasts the unchanging Torah with the ever-changing laws of other nations writes: 'The provisions of this law alone, stable, unmoved, unshaken, as it were stamped with the seal of nature itself, remain in fixity from the day they were written until now, and for the future we expect them to abide through all time as immortal, so long as the sun and moon and the whole heaven and the world exist.'[2] Moore suggested that the association of the Torah with Wisdom helped in the development of this view.[3] We are also tempted to find, as we shall point out later, that a certain polemic motive entered into the insistence on the 'doctrine'. But whatever be the contributory factors in its rise, and it is far too pronounced and early merely to be a polemic reaction against Christian teaching, we can be certain that the words in Matt. v. 18a adequately express what came to be the dominant 'doctrine' of rabbinic Judaism.

Thus the developed (rabbinic) Judaism revealed to us in our sources was not a soil in which the belief in any radical changes in the existing Torah was likely to grow nor a soil which would welcome a new Torah. On the one hand, a preliminary consideration—the hospitable comprehensiveness of Judaism—should make us prepared for variety in the treatment of the Torah, while, on the other hand, another preliminary consideration—the dominance even in pre-Christian times of the 'doctrine' of the immutability of the Torah—should make us hesitate before accepting any other view too easily. With these two preliminaries recognized we can now proceed with our task. The following factors are relevant.

(i) *The eschatological role of the rabbinic Elijah.* We begin with the rabbinic treatment of the prophet Elijah. Perhaps because of the vividness of the stories about him in the Old Testament, but, more probably, because of the last words of that volume, Mal. iv. 5: 'Behold, I will send you Elijah the prophet before the great and terrible day of the LORD

---

[1] See G. F. Moore, *loc. cit.*; J. Bonsirven, *Le Judaïsme Palestinien*, I, 301 ff., 452 ff.
[2] G. F. Moore's translation, in *Judaism*, I, 269, of Philo, *Vita Mosis*, II, 3, §§14–16.
[3] See also V. Aptowitzer, *Parteipolitik der Hasmonäerzeit*, pp. 116 ff. (Notice that the individual commandments, like the Law as a totality, are said to be eternal; see R. Marcus, *op. cit.* p. 53; cf. S–B, I, 244 ff.)

comes', already in pre-Christian Judaism he had become a figure of the End: while not strictly a Messianic figure himself, he was a Messianic 'forerunner'. In the Old Testament, the LXX and the New Testament, three things were connected with him in that capacity—repentance, restoration and resurrection. Although the first of these, repentance, is not a prominent characteristic of the work of *Elias redivivus* in the rabbinic materials, the other two reappear in them also. What concerns us, however, is that the figure of Elijah underwent a process of 'rabbinization'. In the rabbinic sources he appears especially as one who would explain points in the Torah which had baffled the Rabbis. This has been made clear by Ginzberg in his work *Eine unbekannte jüdische Sekte* (New York, 1922), pp. 303 ff.[1] He notes no less than seventeen places where this emerges. These are: TB Berakoth 35 *b*; TB Shabbath 108 *a*; TB Pesaḥim 13 *a*; TB Pesahim 70 *a*; Mishnah Shekalim ii. 5; TB Chagigah 25 *a*; TB Yebamoth 35 *b*, 41 *b*, 102 *a*; TB Gittin 42 *b*; Mishnah Baba Metziah i. 8; iii. 4, 5; TB Menahoth 45 *a*; ARN 98, 101 (ed. Schechter); TB Taanith viii. 1; Jer. Berakoth 1 *c*; Mishnah Eduyoth viii. 7. This last passage reveals not only that the significance of Elijah was a living issue in first-century Judaism but that possibly it was a living issue in its dialogue with Christianity. It reads as follows:

7 R. Joshua said: I have received as a tradition from Rabban Johanan b. Zakkai, who heard from his teacher, and his teacher from his teacher, as a *Halakah* given to Moses from Sinai, that Elijah will not come to declare unclean or clean, to remove afar or to bring nigh, but to remove afar those [families] that were brought nigh by violence and to bring nigh those [families] that were removed afar by violence. The family of Beth Zerepha was in the land beyond Jordan and Ben Zion removed it afar by force. And yet another [family] was there, and Ben Zion brought it nigh by force. The like of these Elijah will come to declare unclean or clean, to remove afar or to bring nigh. R. Judah says: To bring nigh but not to remove afar. R. Simeon says: To bring agreement where there is matter for dispute. And the Sages say: Neither to remove afar nor to bring nigh, but to make peace in the world, as it is written, *Behold I will send you Elijah the prophet...and he shall turn the heart of the fathers to the children and the heart of the children to their fathers.*

Two tasks are assigned to Elijah by the various rabbis mentioned in this passage. He is to pronounce on questions of legitimate Israelitish descent, that is, declare what is clean and unclean, and to create peace. All the

[1] On Elijah, see also R. B. Y. Scott, *The Canadian Journal of Religious Thought*, III (1926), 490–502 on 'The Expectation of Elijah'.

scholars mentioned are entitled 'rabbis', so that the situation which called forth this discussion prevailed after A.D. 70. Since the tradition about Elijah to which appeal is made goes back to an earlier date, Allen[1] is perhaps to be followed in his suggestion that the words, 'God is able of these stones to raise up children unto Abraham' (that is, purity, not blood, is the criterion for inclusion in the Kingdom), may refer to M. Eduyoth viii. 7; Rabban Johannan ben Zakkai's words would agree with such a point of view. But more probably it was the dissension among scholars after A.D. 70, which threatened the unity of Judaism, that called forth this emphasis on the importance of reconciliation. Elijah would come not to engage in legal niceties, but to reconcile the differences among scholars, that is, by implication, to give the true interpretation of the Law. Danby comments on the passage that '[Elijah] will make no change in the Law but only make an end to injustice'. Is the Christian claim to have had its 'Elijah' and his interpretation of the Law, reflected in this insistence on the part of the rabbis that this was not what mattered so much as 'peace'?

Before we leave this section reference must also be made to Ginzberg's emphasis in the volume already cited that, among the rabbis, the Messiah or Messiahs, as such, were not expected to exercise a didactic function. Instead in the Messianic Age this was to be concentrated in the figure of Elijah. On this ground, Ginzberg argued that no new strictly Messianic Torah was anticipated. Although we are fully aware of the danger of presumption in this matter, his position prompts two questions. First, as we have previously implied, may not the 'rabbinization' of Elijah, that is, the concentration of the didactic function in him, have been due to a reaction against Christian claims that their Messiah was the teacher, who had authority? And, secondly, does not the evidence, which we shall adduce below, make Ginzberg's radical rejection of the conception of a New Torah at least dubious? Certainly in such passages as Test. Benj. xi. 2; Test. Levi xviii. 9 the Messiah is the source of new knowledge, and the total evidence is more ambiguous, it seems to us, than Ginzberg allows. Jeremias[2] has even urged that Elijah himself was conceived as the Messiah. This must be regarded as questionable. But as precursor of the Messianic Age, Elijah is a 'Messianic' or 'eschatological' figure, who, in his work of reconciliation, prepares for the Messianic unity. Part of this work had to do with new interpretations of the Law. This justifies our reference to him here: he would be the instrument of changes in the

---

[1] In the I.C.C. on Matt. xi. 14.
[2] *T.W.Z.N.T.* on Elijah. He is opposed by Giblet, *op. cit.* p. 112.

understanding of the Law in Messianic times. This leads us on naturally to the next section.[1]

(ii) Our sources do reveal an awareness that, even though the Torah was immutable, nevertheless modifications of various kinds, at least in certain details, would be necessary.[2] We shall group the material as follows:

(a) *Passages suggesting the cessation of certain enactments concerning Festivals, etc.*[3] There were some who held the view that in the Messianic Age sin would not exist, and it followed that the vast majority of sacrifices, which naturally dealt with the taint of sin, would be irrelevant.[4] A passage in Leviticus Rabbah ix. 7 reads:

R. Phinehas and R. Levi and R. Johanan said in the name of R. Menaḥem of Gallia: In the time to come all sacrifices will be annulled, but that of thanksgiving will not be annulled, and all prayers will be annulled, but [that of] thanksgiving will not be annulled. This is [indicated by] what is written: Jer. xxxiii. 11. (Soncino translation.)

The text is:

ר׳ פנחס ור׳ לוי ור׳ יוחנן בשם ר׳ מנחם דגליא לע״ל כל הקרבנות בטלין
וקרבן תודה אינו בטל כל התפילות בטילות התודה אינה בטילה הה״ד....

Here the phrase referring to the future is לע״ל = לעתיד לבא : its meaning is fluid. Sometimes it refers to the final Age to Come, but at other times it is

---

[1] So too we cannot follow G. Friedrich in his implication that for Judaism the teaching of the Messiah would be insignificant (*T.W.Z.N.T.* II, 723).

[2] It is important to recognize what is meant by the Torah when we refer to its perpetuity. There are passages which claim that only the Torah in the strict sense would persist into the future: the prophets and the hagiographa would cease. See V. Aptowitzer, *op. cit.* p. 261, n. 133, who refers to Jerusalem Meg. 1, 70*d*; also Sh. Spiegel, *H.T.R.* XXIV, 245 ff. The passage in J. Meg. 1, 70, runs:

הנביאים והכתובים עתידין ליבטל וחמשת סיפרי תורה אינן עתידין ליבטל...

(See the translation of the whole section in M. Schwab, *Le Talmud de Jérusalem*, 1882, tome 6, 207.) The words cited only give the view of R. Johanan (A.D. 279–320). R. Simeon b. Laḳish (A.D. 279–320) gives an opposite view—not even the festival of Esther, which, because it had not been ordained by Moses, caused great difficulty, would cease; because it was only the ordinances of Moses himself that Lev. xxvii. 34 declared to be eternal. Doubtless for most the Pentateuch, the prophets and the hagiographa were 'eternal'.

[3] Translations of the Babylonian Talmud and Midrash Rabbah, unless otherwise stated, are derived from those of the Soncino Press.

[4] On the place of the cultus generally in the eschatological thinking of Israel see E. Lohmeyer, *Kultus und Evangelium* (Göttingen, 1942), pp. 19 ff.; also pp. 48, 49 ff.

equivalent to the Messianic era.[1] The context, therefore, must decide the particular meaning it may have: and here we are justified in referring it to the Messianic Age; the sense of the passage demands this and the verse from Jer. xxxiii. 11, by which the view is supported, comes from a Messianic prophecy. Notice, however, that the date of the view expressed must be late. Some scholars understand here Menahem of Galilee, reading גלילא. Israelstam[2] reads גליא, and renders as above: the term גליא he takes to refer to a place in Asia Minor. Wünsche[3] and Loewe[4] prefer to read גלילא. Even if we read the latter the date of the passage is A.D. 165–200—the period when Menahem of Galilee flourished.

Another passage refers to the festivals: it comes from Yalqut on Prov. ix. 2 and reads:[5]

All the festivals will cease but not Purim since it is said (Esther ix. 28) '...these days shall be...throughout every generation...and...should not fail from among the Jews...'. R. Eleazar said: The Day of Atonement too will not cease since it is said (Lev. xvi. 34) 'And this shall be unto you an everlasting statute'.

The text runs:

כל המועדים עתידין ליבטל וימי הפורים אינן בטלים לעולם,...א״ר אלעזר
אף יום הכפורים לא יבטל לעולם שנאמר והיתה זאת לכם לחקת עולם:

The date of the passage is uncertain, but it is probably early second century (A.D. 80–120). Here Purim and the Day of Atonement alone among the festivals are to survive into the Messianic Age. The justification for saying that the Day of Atonement would survive is that it is called in Lev. xvi. 34 'an everlasting statute' (חקת עולם). The same phrase is applied elsewhere to other festivals, for example, the Passover (Exod. xii. 17), the Feast of Weeks (Lev. xxiii. 21), Tabernacles (Lev. xxiii. 41). It is arguable therefore that we should not take this passage at its face value, and that it is merely designed to emphasize the importance of Purim and the Day of Atonement. But there is a significant difference between passages dealing with Purim and the Day of Atonement and those dealing with the other festivals. Thus in Exod. xii. 17 on the Passover the full temporal reference is: 'therefore you shall observe this day, *throughout your generations*, as an ordinance for ever'. Similarly on the Feast of

---

[1] See M. Jastrow, *Dictionary of the Talmud*, p. 1129; J. Bonsirven, *op. cit.* I, 319 f.
[2] Soncino translation: Midrash Rabbah, Leviticus, *ad loc.*
[3] *Bibliotheca Rabbinica, ad loc.*   [4] *A Rabbinic Anthology, ad rem.*
[5] See Midrash Mishle, ix. 2; J. Klausner, *From Jesus to Paul*, Eng. trans. by W. F. Stinespring, p. 321, n. 13.

Weeks in Lev. xxiii. 21 we read: 'it is a statute for ever in all your dwellings *throughout your generations*'. And again in Lev. xxiii. 41 we read on the Feast of Tabernacles, 'it is a statute for ever *throughout your generations...*'. The words in italics are missing in Lev. xvi. 34 on the Day of Atonement, where we only have '*an everlasting statute*', while in Esther ix. 28 on Purim we have the fulsome statement which follows: '*that these days should be remembered and kept throughout every generation, in every family, province, and city, and that these days of Purim should never fall into disuse among the Jews, nor should the commemoration of these days cease among their descendants*'. Thus while at first the claim that Purim and the Day of Atonement alone should be 'eternal festivals' might seem fanciful, it was well grounded by the rabbis in the text of scripture. On the same basis they had to recognize that radical changes in the festivals in the Messianic Age were contemplated. As such this passage is significant for our purpose.[1]

(*b*) *Passages which seem to suggest changes in the laws concerning things clean and unclean, etc.* We begin with a passage from Midrash Tehillim on Ps. cxlvi. 7. This is translated by Braude as follows:[2]

The Lord will loose the bonds (Ps. cxlvi. 7). What does the verse mean by the words *loose the bonds*? Some say that of every animal whose flesh it is forbidden to eat in this world, the Holy One, blessed be He, will declare in the time-to-come that the eating of its flesh is permitted. Thus in the verse *That which hath been is that which shall be, and that which hath been given is that which shall be given* (Eccles. i. 9), the words *that which hath been given* refer to the animals that were given as food before the time of the sons of Noah, for God said: 'Every moving thing that liveth shall be food for you; as the green herb have I given you all' (Gen. ix. 3). That is to say, 'As I give the green herb as food to all, so once I gave both beasts and cattle as food to all'. But why did God declare the flesh of some animals forbidden? In order to see who would accept His commandments and who would not accept them. In the time-to-come, however, God will again permit the eating of that flesh which He has forbidden.

Others say that in the time-to-come, God will not permit this, for it is said *They that...eat swine's flesh, and the detestable thing, and the mouse, shall be*

---

[1] I owe the details in the above to a private communication from Professor Daube.
[2] *Yale Judaica Series*, vol. XIII, *The Midrash on Psalms* (1959), *ad rem.* See also Montefiore and Loewe, *A Rabbinic Anthology*, p. 583. The date of this anonymous passage cannot be fixed. P. R. Weis, of the University of Manchester, in a private note, suggests that in view of the context the passage refers to the 'Final Age' not to the Messianic Age. The phrase לעתיד לבוא שהשכינה ביניהם, which occurs below the above passage, he thinks points to this. But the conditions implied seem to us to be Messianic.

consumed together, saith the Lord (Isa. lxvi. 17). Now if God will cut off and destroy men who eat forbidden flesh, surely he will do the same to the forbidden animals themselves. To what, otherwise, do the words *will loose the bonds* refer? Though nothing is more strongly forbidden than intercourse with a menstruous woman—for when a woman sees blood the Holy One, blessed be He, forbids her to her husband—in the time-to-come, God will permit such intercourse. As Scripture says, *It shall come to pass in that day, saith the Lord of hosts, that...I will cause the prophets and the unclean spirit to pass out of the land* (Zech. xiii. 2), the *unclean* clearly denoting a menstruous woman, and of such it is said '*And thou shalt not approach a woman to uncover her nakedness, as long as she is impure by her uncleanness*' (Lev. xviii. 19).

Still others say that in the time-to-come sexual intercourse will be entirely forbidden. You can see for yourself why it will be. On the day that the Holy One, blessed be He, revealed Himself on Mount Sinai to give the Torah to the children of Israel, He forbade intercourse for three days, as it is said *Be ready against the third day; come not at your wives* (Exod. xix. 15). Now since God, when He revealed Himself for only one day, forbade intercourse for three days, in the time-to-come, when the presence of God dwells continuously in Israel's midst, will not intercourse be entirely forbidden?

What, otherwise, is meant by *bonds* in *will loose the bonds*? The bonds of death and the bonds of the netherworld.

The pertinent Hebrew reads:

ה׳ מתיר אסורים. מהו מתיר אסורים יש אומרים כל הבהמה שנטמאה בעולם הזה מטהר אותה הקב״ה לעתיד לבוא... ומה שנעשה טהורים היו מקודם לבני נח...ולמה אסר אותה, לראות מי שמקבל דבריו, ומי אינו מקבל, ולעתיד לבוא הוא מתיר את כל מה שאסר:

Here distinctions between clean and unclean animals are to be abrogated in the Messianic Age, which is pictured as a return to the primitive or original condition of the world before the disaster of the flood: the idea that the End corresponds to the Beginning is a commonplace of apocalyptic and the principle would seem to be operative here. But there have been objections to the acceptance of this passage and others as rabbinic opinion.[1]

---

[1] Dr Finkelstein writes (19 June 1961): (1) on Gen. Rabbah (see below p. 179), 'Professor Chanoch Albeck, who completed the edition of Theodor, considers chapters xcv–cvi as not part of the original Genesis Rabba. The chapters, in the ordinary editions, do not all correspond to those in the manuscript used by Theodor, and even those included in that manuscript are not considered a part of Genesis Rabba, but of another book. This is on the basis apparently, of internal evidence.' (2) On Midrash Tehillim cxlvi he gives Buber's views. 'Buber's note [in his edition of Tehillim] is, in substance, as follows: "Reitmann has remarked in *Bet Talmud*, III, p. 332 that in Midrash Tehilim, chapter cxlvi there is a very strange passage. This

We notice further that there is an attempt in the passage immediately following to offset the view expressed; and not only so, but it is made clear that in the time to come some of the demands of the Law would be even more severe: thus marital relations would become stricter. Nevertheless this last in itself suggests the possibility of change in the Torah, and as such is again instructive for our purposes.

It is at this point that we can best deal with a passage which is usually cited in favour not merely of the view that the Messianic Age would see changes in the Torah but also that it would bring with it a New Torah. The passage from Leviticus Rabbah xiii. 3 reads as follows:

R. Judan b. R. Simeon said: Behemoth and the Leviathan are to engage in a wild beast contest before the righteous in the Time to Come, and whoever has not been a spectator at the wild beast contests of the heathen nations in this world will be accorded the boon of seeing one in the World to Come. How will they be slaughtered? Behemoth will, with its horns, pull Leviathan down and rend it, and Leviathan will, with its fins, pull Behemoth down and pierce it through. The Sages said: And is this a valid method of slaughter? Have we not learnt the following in a Mishnah: All may slaughter, and one may slaughter at all times (of the day), and with any instrument except with a scythe, or with a saw, or with teeth (in a jaw cut out of a dead animal), because they cause pain as if by choking, or with a nail (of a living body)? R. Abin b. Kahana said: The Holy One, blessed be He, said: Instruction [Torah] shall go forth from Me (Isa. li. 4) [that is, an exceptional temporary ruling will go forth from Me]. (Israelstam's Soncino translation.)[1]

is the passage to which he refers. According to him (Reifmann) this passage was added to the Midrash by someone who was quite confused. I (that is, Buber) have discussed this in *Bet Talmud*, IV, p. 54, at length, trying to show that this is not an addition to the text, but is part of the Midrash which was added at a later time, and is not of the original Midrash Tehilim. The original Midrash was completed only up to the end of Psalm cxviii. This passage also belongs to the later homilist who arranged the passages dealing with these later psalms. However, the question concerning whom the homilist referred to when he said, 'there are those who say', and where he found this passage, I just discovered in the book *Yeshuot Meshiho*, Rabbi Isaac Abravanel, part 4, chapter 3, who states that an opponent wanted to prove the ultimate nullification of the Torah from a homily which he said occurs in Genesis Rabba of Rabbi Moses Hadarshan in chapter Mikez, which begins with a verse in this very psalm, and according to which all animals which are impure in this world will be purified by God in the future world. Accordingly, the passage which the editor has added in his own supplement to the Midrash Tehilim is taken from the Midrash of Rabbi Moses Hadarshan. The intent of the passage has been very well explained by Rabbi Abravanel, and can be found by the reader in the place quoted."' Rabbi Moses Hadarshan flourished in the eleventh century A.D.

[1] V. Aptowitzer points out a parallel passage. See Jellinek, Beth ha-Midrash iii. 80; iii. 76, which reads, 'In the days of the Messiah Israel will live for 2000 years in

The text of the last sentence according to the Wilna and Warsaw editions is:[1]

א״ר אבין בר כהנא אמר הקב״ה תורה ²חדשה מאתי תצא חדוש תורה מאתי
תצא...

Now Edersheim, like Strack–Billerbeck, who, however, qualify their acceptance of this interpretation, took this to refer to a new (Messianic) Torah. Israelstam, however, as we saw, rejects this, and the context favours his interpretation. In his view, the point of the passage is that even though according to the Torah of this world it was not permissible to slay anything with a saw, because this would necessarily involve pain, nevertheless, in the Messianic Age the Leviathan would be permitted to pull down the Behemoth with its fins, which are like saws, in that they have serrated edges. Thus in the contest between Leviathan and Behe-

security, eat from Behemoth, Leviathan, and Ziz. The Ziz and Behemoth will be slaughtered. The Ziz will rend Leviathan and the Behemoth.' Here there is a specific reference to the days of the Messiah when a slaughtering involving pain will be allowed, whereas in the passage quoted in the text a painless slaughtering only will be allowed—this because, V. Aptowitzer argues, it refers not to the Messianic Age but to the Age to Come. But the picture of the wild beast contest probably refers to a Messianic Age on earth, not to the final Age to Come, in both passages, although the possibility is not to be ruled out that the Age to Come itself might be on earth.

[1] In translating Isa. li. 4 J. Israelstam follows the Massoretic text. It is better to understand his translation thus than to suppose that the text of the Midrash gives the text of Isa. li. 4 last, after the comment, and that Israelstam has reversed this by giving the quotation first, then the comment. In the 1890 Warsaw edition and reprints, where there is an error by printer or editor, the reference ישעיה נא is inserted, but in the wrong place. It should come in front of the first תורה not the second תורה. It is also found in some texts between תצא and חדוש, that is, at the end of the verse. Usually, however, the biblical reference is placed in front of the verse, and it is thus that J. Israelstam takes it here. He should, however, have pointed out that he is following the Massoretic text and not that given by the Midrash, which has the adjective חדשה. Professor A. Guttmann thinks that R. Abin bar Kahana may have had an original text, which read חדשה. However this may be, J. Israelstam goes on to translate חדוש תורה מאתי תצא by 'an exceptional temporary ruling will go forth from me' (A. Wünsche renders 'die Erneuerung des Gesetzes wird von mir ausgehen'). But this, as we saw above, is hardly to be accepted. Professor A. Guttmann informs me that J. Israelstam is following David Luria who held that תורה חדשה in the given context means 'temporary ruling' (that is, a ruling for the לבוא עתיד only) הוראת שעה: giving of biblical references, Professor A. Guttmann notes, was not customary in the original texts of the Midrashim. Some editions do not have them, for example the *editio princeps*, Constantinople, 1512. The second complete edition, Venice, 1545, gives the references in the margin. Yet for our passage, as in the Wilna edition, no reference is given. (The details from Professor Guttmann I gained by correspondence.)

[2] חדשה is read only by the MSS. of London and Paris: see the edition of *Wayyikra Rabbah*, by M. Margulies (Jerusalem, 1954).

moth, which would take place in the presence of the righteous in the Messianic Age, the use of an instrument prohibited in this world by the Torah would be allowed. This would seem to be a possible understanding of the passage: the term חדש is often used of promulgating a new law (not Law) or establishing a new interpretation of a biblical law. But it is desirable that the element of newness in the phrase תורה חדשה should be better preserved than in Israelstam's translation. Israelstam's diminution of the force of the adjective חדשה and his translation of חדוש תורה by 'an exceptional temporary ruling' has been called 'une pirouette d'apologé-tique juive, comme savent en accomplir les apologètes de tous les temps'. Barthélemy insists that since, as we fully recognize, Judaism became increasingly opposed to any suggestion of a New Torah, the reading תורה חדשה in Isa. li. 4 must be early, although he also suggests that it possibly emanated from unorthodox, peripheral circles.[1] So too, Díez Macho has insisted that here we encounter the concept of a New Torah for the Messianic Age.[2] Only by exercising an excess of caution, perhaps, can we favour Israelstam's interpretation over that of Barthélemy and Macho.

(c) *Other passages which seem to imply or actually express the expectation of changes in the Torah.* Bonsirven refers to one passage in Siphre on Deut. xvii. 18, §160, where it is explicitly stated, he thinks, that the Torah will be changed.[3]

The English would roughly be as follows:

He shall write him a copy of this Law (MISHNEH HA-TORAH) for himself (that is), for his own name (person): he should not be content with that of his fathers. MISHNEH (TORAH) (From this) I have no (proof) except for MISHNEH TORAH (that is, Deuteronomy). (As to) the rest of the words of the Torah, Whence (do we know that these too are intended)? Scripture teaches this by

---

[1] In a review in *RB*, LX (1953), 316–18. Barthélemy makes also an important point in the following words: 'Or, dans le Judaïsme du début de l'ère chrétienne, le substantif *ḥiddush* et le verbe *ḥaddesh* ont une signification eschatologique bien établie de "renouvellement apocalyptique", une "transmutation radicale". La première mention formelle d'un tel renouvellement se rencontre dans Jub. 1, 29 où il est dit que "cieux et terre *seront renouvelés*" et que "les luminaires seront renouvelés pour la guérison, la paix et la bénédiction de tous les élus d'Israël". Dans l'hébreu original, il y a très vraisemblablement des formes *hitpaël* du verbe.' He refers also to Apoc. Baruch xxxii. 6; xvii. 2; 4 Ezra vii. 75.

[2] *Op. cit.*

[3] *Op. cit.* I, 453, n. 9. J. Klausner, *op. cit.* p. 54, interprets 'wohl kann sie theilweise andern (שעתידה להשתנות) aber sie kann nicht abrogirt und durch andere ersetzt werden'.

saying (later in this passage) TO KEEP ALL THE WORDS OF THIS LAW, etc. Why then (does it say) MISHNEH TORAH? Because it was destined to be changed (le-Hishtannoth) [Hithpa'ēl of *shanah*, to change; also, to repeat, to copy—the root of *Mishneh*].

The text reads:

וכתב לו את משנה התורה הזאת על ספר לשמו שלא יהא נאות בשל אבותיו: משנה אין לי אלא משנה תורה שאר ד״ת מנין ת״ל לשמור את כל דברי התורה הזאת א״כ למה נאמר משנה תורה שעתידה להשתנות....

Bonsirven takes the term להשתנות to refer to a changing of the Torah itself, and this is a perfectly legitimate possibility. The Hithpa'ēl of שנה does mean '*to be changed*': moreover, the masculine gender of משנה makes it impossible to take להשתנות to refer to the copy. Bonsirven's interpretation is therefore, as stated, fully justified from the language of this passage taken alone. Unfortunately for our thesis, in the parallel passage in Tosefta, Sanhedrin iv. 4 ff., the phrase שעתידה להשתנות is referred, quite specifically, to the change in the *script* which was to be used in the writing of the Torah. The Hebrew in Tosefta, Sanhedrin iv. 7 reads:

וכתב לו את משנה התורה הזאת וג' תורה עתידה להשתנות ולמה נקרא שמה¹ אשורי על שום שעלה עמהן מאשור ר' אומר בכתב אשורי ניתנה תורה לישראל, וכשחטאו נהפכה להן לרועץ וכשזכו בימי עזרא חזרה להן אשורית:

The English of this would run somewhat as follows:

And he shall for himself write the copy of this law, etc. The Torah is destined to be changed. And why was it called Assyrian script? because it went up with them from Assyria. R. (Meir) said: When the Torah was given to Israel it was given in Assyrian script; and when they sinned it was changed for them into the form of the Samaritan type, and when they were worthy in the days of Ezra it went back for them into [or, came back to them in] Assyrian script.

The Tosefta, we may probably safely assume, preserves the oldest tradition of the meaning of the term להשתנות in this context, and is therefore to be followed. Hence we must reject Bonsirven's use of the passage as referring to a change in the Torah itself.

---

¹ The reading שְׁמָהּ is accepted by Professor A. Guttmann rather than שָׁמָּה If we read שָׁמָּה the translation is 'and why was it read there in Assyrian script?' The Codex Vienna and the *ed. princeps* read שְׁמוֹ, of which שְׁמָהּ is a corruption; so Professor Lieberman.

There are two other passages to be discussed here. One, in TB San-hedrin 51*b*, is sometimes wrongly interpreted to mean that much of the Torah which does not apply to this world will be applicable in the Messianic Age. But the actual meaning is that much of the Torah, meaning sacrifices, temporarily discontinued in this world, owing to adverse conditions, will again be practised in the Messianic Age.[1] It reads:

R. Nahman (A.D. 275–320) said in the name of Rabbah b. Abbuha (A.D. 257–320) in the name of Rab: The *Halachah* is in accordance with the message sent by Rabin in the name of R. Jose b. Hanina. R. Joseph queried: (Do we need) to fix a *halachah* for the days of the Messiah?—Abaye answered: If so, we should not study the laws of sacrifices, as they are also only for the Messianic era. But we say, Study and receive reward; i.e. Learning has its own merit quite apart from any practical utility that may be derived therefrom.

A more important and more often quoted passage occurs in TB Shabbath 151*b* where we find opposing views set in sharp juxtaposition. The passage reads as follows:

R. Simeon b. Eleazar (A.D. 165–200) said: ...*And the years draw nigh, when thou shalt say, I have no pleasure in them*[7]—this refers to the Messianic era, wherein there is neither merit nor guilt. Now, he disagrees with Samuel, who said: The only difference between this world and the Messianic era is in respect of servitude to [foreign] powers, for it is said, *For the poor shall never cease out of the land.*[8] (Note 7 is from Eccles. xii. 1; n. 8 from Deut. xv. 11.)

The context shows that the question as to when the Torah was obligatory and when it was not is the theme of the passage. Samuel apparently regards the Torah as obligatory in the Messianic Age which, he holds, would not differ in this respect from the present age. The meaning of R. Simeon b. Eleazar's (A.D. 165–200) dictum is difficult. Bonsirven[2] would seem to take the words to mean that in the Messianic Age the capacity to sin is obliterated, although he does not state this explicitly, and his meaning is not clear. It seems to us that there are two possibilities as to the interpretation of the phrase לא זכות ולא חובה, which is rendered by Bonsirven, very neatly, 'ni mérite ni démérite', but is better translated as 'no merit and no guilt'. First, the meaning may be that in the Messianic Age the Torah will be so fully obeyed that there will be no guilt, and so spontaneously or easily fulfilled that there will be no merit, a condition of affairs such as Jeremiah, perhaps, may have envisaged and desiderated. This interpretation, it will be agreed, involves a high degree of subtlety.

---

[1] So A. Guttmann in a private note.   [2] *Le Judaïsme Palestinien*, I, 452.

The second meaning is the one that seems to us perhaps most satisfying, namely, that the Torah no longer holds in the Messianic Age, so that questions of reward for observing it and guilt or punishment for refusing to do so do not arise. This would make the condition of those who live in the Messianic Age, in this respect, similar to that of the dead who, according to R. Joḥanan, in the passage immediately preceding, are free from religious duties (see below p. 181, on TB Niddah 61 b). The preceding passage in TB Shabbath 151 b reads:

It was taught, R. Simeon b. Gamaliel said: For a day-old infant the Sabbath is desecrated; For David, King of Israel, dead, the Sabbath must not be desecrated. 'For a day-old infant the Sabbath is desecrated': the Torah ordered, Desecrate one Sabbath on his account so that he may keep many Sabbaths. 'For David, King of Israel, dead, the Sabbath must not be desecrated': Once man dies he is free from [all] obligations, and thus, R. Joḥanan interpreted: *Among the dead I am free*:[5] once a man is dead he is free from religious duties. (Soncino translation, p. 772; n. 5 refers to Ps. lxxxviii. 6.)

It also implies, as we shall indicate below, that the Messianic Age is like the Age to Come in this matter (see below, pp. 181 ff.).

The evidence presented above sufficiently justifies the claim that despite the 'doctrine' of the immutability of Torah, there were also occasional expressions of expectations that Torah would suffer modification in the Messianic Age. There were some Halakoth which would cease to be applicable in that Age; others, by contrast, would acquire a new relevance. It is important, however, to recognize explicitly that most, if not all, the changes envisaged were deemed to occur within the context of the existing Torah and presuppose the continuance of its validity. Moreover, the changes contemplated imply no necessary diminution in what we may be allowed to term the severity of the yoke of the Torah. On the contrary, that yoke, in some passages, was expected to become even heavier than in this age (see especially Midrash Tehillim cxlvi. 7). In addition we have to point out that much of the traditional Christian interpretation of some of the passages cited does violence to the text and has to be rejected. It may also be helpful to state at this point that in all the passages so far quoted the reference probably is to the Messianic Age as such.

(iii) The third significant factor which we have to notice, is that the Messianic Age, as indeed we might expect, is presented as an era in which certain difficulties or incomprehensibilities which the Torah presented in this Age would be adequately explained and comprehended: now we see in a glass darkly, but then obscurities will be removed. Strack–Billerbeck have dealt with this, and for our purpose the briefest treatment will suffice.[1]

Many of the demands of the Torah seemed inexplicable and irrational: the reasons why certain things had been forbidden or commanded were obscure, and the fact that Jewry could not always give a satisfying apology for much in their practice laid them open to the attacks of Gentile cynicism and criticism. Hence there necessarily developed a considerable activity in the Tannaitic period, and earlier probably, in an attempt to explain why certain things had been commanded which at first seemed even merely stupid. So eager were some to explain the טעמי תורה, 'the grounds or reasons for the Torah's demands', that they were in danger of manipulating their texts, and consequently incurred suspicion. The normative position arrived at was that in this world the demands of Torah were to be obeyed because they were commanded: this was sufficient reason for their observance. This is made clear in the words of R. Joḥanan b. Zakkai (we quote the passage from Numbers Rabbah xix. 8 on xix. 2 because it illustrates the kind of criticism which was made of the demands of the Torah):

An idolater asked R. Joḥanan b. Zakkai: These rites that you perform look like a kind of witchcraft. You bring a heifer, burn it, pound it, and take its ashes. If one of you is defiled by a dead body you sprinkle upon him two or three drops and you say to him: 'Thou art clean.' R. Joḥanan asked him: 'Has the demon of madness ever possessed you?' 'No!' he replied. 'Have you ever seen a man entered by this demon of madness?' 'Yes,' said he. 'And what do you do in such a case?' 'We bring roots,' he replied, 'and make them smoke under him, then we sprinkle water upon the demon and it flees.' Said R. Joḥanan to him: 'Let your ears hear what you utter with your mouth: Precisely so is this spirit a spirit of uncleanness: as it is written, *And also I will cause the prophets and the unclean spirit to pass out of the land* (Zech. xiii. 2). Water of purification is sprinkled upon the unclean and the spirit flees.' When the idolater had gone R. Joḥanan's disciples said to their master: 'Master! This man you have put off with a mere makeshift but what explanation will you give to us?' Said he to them: 'By your life! It is not the dead that defiles nor the water that purifies! The Holy One, blessed be He, merely says: "I have laid down a statute (חקה),[2] I have issued a decree. You are not allowed to transgress My decree"; as it is written, *This is the statute of the law*' (Num. xix. 2).

---

[1] *Op. cit.* IV, 2, n. 9: Pesikta, ed. Mandelbaum, p. 71; Mekilta in Siphra, ed. Weiss, p. 86a; also M. Waxman, *J.Q.R.* vol. XLII (October 1951).

[2] This term denotes a command demanding implicit obedience, though the human mind may not comprehend its reason.

But although theirs was not to reason why in this world, the rabbis were convinced that the Messianic Age would bring with it an explanation of the inexplicable demands that the Torah made in this world: the טעמי תורה would be revealed. We have previously quoted passages from the Old Testament where the Messianic Age was depicted as a time when God himself would teach his people. This was the firm conviction of the rabbis also. In illustration we shall again quote a passage from Numbers Rabbah xix. 6 on xix. 2, despite its late date, where the reference is not strictly to the Messianic Age, however, but to the final Age to Come:

THAT THEY BRING THEE A RED HEIFER (xix. 2). R. Jose b. Ḥanina (the second half of the third century) expounded: The Holy One, blessed be He, said to Moses: 'To thee I shall disclose the reason for the Heifer, but to anybody else it is a statute.' For R. Huna said: It is written, *When I take the appointed time* [i.e., in the World to Come], *I Myself will judge with equity* (Ps. lxxv. 3) [i.e., reveal the reasons for My Laws], and it is also written, *And it shall come to pass in that day, that there shall not be light, but heavy clouds and thick*—weḳippa'on (Zech. xiv. 6). The written form is 'yeḳippa'on', as much as to say: The things that are concealed from you in this world, you will see in the World to Come, like a blind man who regains his sight, as it is written (Isa. xlii. 16), *And I will bring the blind by a way that they know not*.... (Soncino translation, Numbers, vol. II, 756.)[1]

We pass on to the next group of material.[2]

(iv) Despite the changes both in the substance and interpretation of the Torah which they contemplate, those passages which we have so far examined have afforded little if any evidence for the expectation of a New

---

[1] Sh. Spiegel, *H.T.R.* (October 1931), 261, points out that part of the significance of the predicted coming of Elijah on the threshold of the Messianic Age was that he should settle legal and ritual doubts 'to set straight all dissension, and to compose differences of opinion which could threaten to make of the one law two laws'. He relates this function of Elijah to the doctrine of the perpetual validity of the Law: the difficulties of the existing Law had to be explained because there could be no other Law. Hence the great joy of the rabbis at being able to resolve contradictions between Ezekiel and the Torah: they feared the danger of having to admit the existence of two laws in the canon should these contradictions not be resolved. Compare H. Danby, *op. cit.* p. 12, n. 4, on M. Eduyoth viii. 7.

[2] Professor Muilenburg emphasizes that in the Old Testament, as over against Judaism, the reasons for obedience were given, see *The Way of Israel* (1961), pp. 66 ff. He refers to Exod. xxiii. 8; Deut. v. 12–15; xxv. 3, 15–16; *Hebrew Union College Annual*, XXXII (1961), on 'The Linguistic and Rhetorical Usages of the particle כִּי in the Old Testament', pp. 135 ff. See also B. Gemser, *Congress Volume Copenhagen 1953* (Leiden, 1953), pp. 50–66, on 'The importance of the motive clause in Old Testament law'.

Torah in the Messianic Age. Changes in details and an increase in understanding there would be, but no substitution of the old Torah by a new one was envisaged.[1] In this section we must deal with passages where it has been claimed that it is possible that a New Torah is expressly indicated.

(1) *The Targum on Isa.* xii. 3. The MT reads: וּשְׁאַבְתֶּם־מַיִם בְּשָׂשׂוֹן מִמַּעַיְנֵי הַיְשׁוּעָה, that is, 'And you shall draw water in joy from the wells of salvation'. The whole context of the passage is Messianic: xii. 1–3 reads in its entirety:

> 1 You will say in that day:
>   'I will give thanks to thee, O LORD,
>   for though thou wast angry with me,
>   thy anger turned away,
>   and thou didst comfort me.
> 2 'Behold, God is my salvation;
>   I will trust, and will not be afraid;
>   for the LORD GOD is my strength and my song,
>   and he has become my salvation.'
> 3 With joy you will draw water from the wells of salvation. (RSV.)

The Targum renders xii. 3 as follows:

ותקבלין אולפן חדת בחדוא מבחירי צדיקיא

which is rendered by Stenning:[2] 'And ye shall receive new instruction with joy from the chosen of righteousness.'

The total passage in the Targum reads:

1 And thou shalt say at that time, I will give thanks before thee, O Lord; for because I had sinned before thee, thine anger was upon me; now let thine anger turn from me, and have pity upon me.

2 Behold, in the Memra of the God of my salvation do I trust, and shall not be dismayed; because my strength and my glory is the Terrible One, the Lord: he has spoken by his Memra, and has become my Saviour.

3 And ye shall receive new instruction with joy from the chosen of righteousness.

4 And ye shall say in that time, Give thanks before the Lord; pray in his name; proclaim among the nations his deeds; make mention that his name is mighty.

Israelstam[3] takes אולפן to refer to exposition: he contrasts it sharply with תורה, for which, he claims, usually אוריתא is used: the reference to the

---

[1] The one possible exception would be Leviticus Rabbah xiii. 3, see above, pp. 165 ff.

[2] J. F. Stenning, *The Targum of Isaiah.*

[3] In a private communication.

newness of the exposition is prompted by the thought of well-water, that is, fresh or new water (compare M. Aboth ii. 8). But something more than new exposition is expressed here. Daube[1] accepts אולפן in this context as the equivalent of תורה: thus the drawing of water out of the wells of salvation means not only the reception of new teaching or instruction (as in Stenning's translation), but the reception of a New Law. Daube accordingly translates: 'Ye shall receive a new Law from those chosen in righteousness.' He refers this to the Messianic Age. What precisely is understood by 'those chosen in righteousness' is not clear.[2]

(2) *Midrash Qoheleth on* ii. 1 and *on* xi. 8. In the passage, Midrash Qoheleth xi. 8, we read:

תורה שאדם למד בעוה"ז
הבל הוא לפני תורתו של משיח

The Torah which a man learns in this world is vanity compared with the Torah of the Messiah.

This passage carries no date; a somewhat similar passage, slightly more involved, which is given in the name of R. Simon b. Zabdai, is that on ii. 1, which is as follows:

ר' חזקיה בש"ר סימון בר זבדי אמר
כל התורה שאת למד בעוה"ז הבל הוא
לפני תורה שבעוה"ב . לפני שבעוה"ז אדם
לומד תורה ושוכח אבל לעתיד לבא מה
כתיב תמן ... : נתתי את תורתי בקרבבם:

R. Hezekiah said in the name of Rabbi Simon bar Zabdai: All the Torah which you learn in this world is 'vanity' compared with the Torah in The world to Come. For in This world a man learns and forgets but, as for The time to come, what is written there (Jer. xxxi. 33)? *I will put my Law in their inward parts.*

---

[1] *J.T.S.* xxxix (1938). To this M. Jastrow lends support, *op. cit.* p. 26. In the Targum on Isa. ii. 3 and xxxii. 6 אולפן and אורייתא are parallel. Dr Daube takes the phrase אולפן חדת of this passage to mean 'that Israel will be given a better Law, a new and final revelation' (*ibid.* p. 55). It is equivalent to תורה חדשה, but this term, he thinks, was probably 'used much more loosely in colloquial speech than it would seem from that particular passage in Targum'. He refers to Tos. Sotah xiv. 9 to prove that 'תורה does not necessarily signify the unique, ideal Law laid down by God. It may mean the Law as understood by one of the various sects; any of them might claim to have the true Torah, in contrast to the Torah of the opponents. It follows that when Jesus added yet another doctrine to those already in existence, he may well have been regarded as founder of a תורה חדשה.' Daube takes διδαχὴ καινή in Mark i. 27 to mean תלמוד חדש or הורייה חדשה or again הלכה חדשה. The whole article is of first-rate importance.

[2] Water is a familiar figure for the Torah, see S–B, *op. cit.* II, 433.

The date of R. Simon b. Zabdai is late (*c.* A.D. 300). But the passage is interesting on more grounds than one. Not only does it help us to understand how the Rabbis understood the Law of the New Covenant of Jeremiah, that is, as referring to the Mosaic Torah, but its context also reveals the background against which we are to place discussions of the problem of the future role of the Torah; because it is noteworthy that in the previous section R. Phinehas (fourth century A.D.) had referred both to the words of the Torah and to the words of מינות (heresy), that is, of sectaries, probably Jewish Christians. Then follows the passage quoted above, the contrast between Torah in this world and that of the world to come: whereas in this world men learn and forget Torah, in the world to come they will learn and not forget; the Torah of God will be in their hearts. The polemic background of the saying is significant, and will occupy us in due course. Now, at first sight, it would appear that the phrase תורה של משיח in xi. 8 implies a contrast between the תורה of this world and that of the world to come, but as Professor A. Guttmann noted to the author, xi. 8 is to be interpreted in the light of ii. 1. The תורה של משיח, he thinks, is to be understood as 'the Torah of the days of the Messiah'. And even if this be not admitted, it is not the Torah that is to be changed in the Age to Come (=the Messianic Age here), but the relation of man to the Torah: that is, the Torah will then be differently and more satisfactorily studied. This is brought out in the Soncino translation: 'in comparison with Torah [which will be learnt] in the World to Come'. Our rendering above is literal.

(3) *Targum on Song of Songs* v. 10:

דודי בכן שריאת כנשתא דישראל למשתעי בשבחא למרי עלמא וכן אמרת
לההוא אלהא רעותי למפלח דעטיף ביממא באצטלא חור כתלגא וזיו יקרא
דיי דאנפוהי זהרין כנורא מסגיאות חוכמתא וסברא דהוא מחדת שמעון חדתין
בכל יומא ועתיד לפרסמנון לעמיה ביומא רבא וטקסיה על רבוא רבון
מלאכין דמשמשין קדמוי:

The English would run somewhat as follows:

My beloved (Cant. v. 10). Then Kenesseth Israel commences to engage in the praise of the Master of the Universe and speaks thus: 'It is my delight to worship God who wraps Himself by day in a robe white as snow and the glorious divine splendour, whose countenance shines like a flame by reason of the greatness of [His] wisdom and thought, who delivers anew every day new traditions (or decisions) which He is to make known to His people on the Great Day, and whose array (or royal authority) extends over a myriad myriads of angels who serve before Him.'

Here Strack–Billerbeck refer, in a paraphrase of the above, to new Halakoth which God will give *by the hand* of the Messiah. But the text does not include a reference to the Messiah. The thought expressed is that new interpretations showing a new ingenuity in exegesis of the Torah will be given in 'the great day' by God himself.

(4) *Yalqut on Isa.* xxvi. 2. Isa. xxvi. 2 in the RSV reads: 'Open the gates, that the righteous nation which keeps faith may enter in.' The Hebrew is: פִּתְחוּ שְׁעָרִים וְיָבֹא גוֹי־צַדִּיק שֹׁמֵר אֱמֻנִים. The comment in Yalqut takes 'which keep faith' to be the equivalent of *'who say Amen'*. That is, they take *Shomer 'emunim* to be *She'omer 'amenim*. On the basis of this the following is developed. We give the translation of Loewe:[1]

For the sake of one single Amen which the wicked respond from Gehinnom, they are rescued therefrom. How so? In time to come, the Holy One, Blessed be He, will take His seat in Eden and expound. All the righteous will sit before Him: all the retinue on high will stand on their feet. The sun and the Zodiac [or, constellations] will be at His right hand and the moon and the stars on His left; *God will sit and expound a new Torah which He will, one day, give by the Messiah's hand* (my italics). When God has finished the recital [Haggadah], Zerubbabel, son of Shealtiel, will rise to his feet and say 'Be His Great Name magnified and sanctified' (that is, the prayer after study, PB p. 86). His voice will reach from one end of the universe to the other and all the inhabitants of the universe will respond 'Amen'. Also the sinners of Israel and the righteous of the Gentiles, who have remained in Gehinnom, will respond 'Amen' out of the midst of Gehinnom. Then the universe will quake, till the sound of their cry is heard by God. He will ask 'What is this sound of great rushing (Ezek. iii. 12, 13) that I hear?' Then the angels of the service make answer, 'Lord of the Universe, these are the sinners of Israel and the righteous of the Gentiles, who remain in Gehinnom. They answer "Amen", and they declare that Thy judgement of them was just.' Immediately God's mercy will be aroused towards them in exceptional measure (*be-yoter*) and He will say: 'What can I do unto them, over and above this judgement, or, what can I do unto them exceptionally, in view of this judgement? For it was but the evil inclination that brought them to this.' At that moment God will take the keys of Gehinnom in His hand and give them to Michael and to Gabriel, in the presence of all the righteous, and say to them, 'Go ye, open the gates of the Gehinnom and bring them up'. Straightway they go with the keys and open the eight thousand gates of Gehinnom. Each single Gehinnom is 300 [parasangs?] long and 300 wide: its thickness is 1000 parasangs and its height 1000 parasangs, so that no single sinner who has fallen therein, can ever get forth. What do Michael and Gabriel do? Immediately they take each sinner by the hand and bring him up, as a man

[1] *A Rabbinic Anthology*, p. 558.

raises his fellow from a pit and brings him up by a rope, as it says: 'And he raised me from the horrible pit' (Ps. xl. 3, 2 in EV). Then the angels stand over them, they wash and anoint them; they heal them from the smitings of Gehinnom, clothe them in fair raiment, and bring them into the presence of the Holy One, Blessed be He, and into the presence of all the righteous, when they, the sinners, have been clad as priests and honoured, as it says: 'Let Thy priests be clothed with righteousness and let Thy saints shout for joy' (Ps. cxxxii. 9). 'Thy priests', these are the righteous of the Gentiles, who are God's priests in this world, such as Antoninus and his associates. . . .

The Hebrew of the pertinent words in italics in the above quotation is: והקב"ה דורש להם טעמי תורה חדשה שעתיד הקב"ה ליתן להם על יד מלך המשיח. This seems the most unambiguous reference to a new Messianic Torah. Jewish scholars, such as Israelstam, in correspondence, however, have pointed out that Abarbanel's reading apparently was: טעמי מצוות ע"י מלך המשיה, that is, 'expound the grounds of commands by the hand of king Messiah'. But we can easily see why such an explicit reference to a new Messianic Torah would naturally lead to uneasiness, and possibly give rise to a modified and safer reading. The further attempt to interpret the phrase טעמי תורה חדשה as if it meant טעמי תורה החדשים, that is, 'new grounds of Torah', is suspect for the same reason, although it may be grammatically possible (Gesenius–Kautzsch (1892 ed.), p. 492; see especially 1 Sam. ii. 4; 1 Kings i. 41; Isa. ii. 11; xvi. 8).[1] It is, therefore, to be recognized that we find in this passage an explicit reference to a Messianic Torah new in kind. Notice particularly that this Messianic Torah and the divine exposition of it is in a context of universalism. It is destined not only for Israel, but for 'All the righteous' including those among the Gentiles. And not only so but even the righteous dead among the Gentiles and the unrighteous dead of Israel are brought into the sphere of this new Law. It should, however, be noted that Yalqut as a compilation or thesaurus is not earlier than the thirteenth century, although its component parts are variously dated before this. In fact, the pertinent section above, dealing with the New Torah, comes from the Othiyyoth of R. Akiba, where the reading is טעמי תורה חדשה.[2]

---

[1] So Israelstam in a private communication.

[2] On these, see Strack, op. cit. pp. 229, 347. See also L. Ginzberg, op. cit. p. 305. He recognized here a New Torah but emphasizes that the source is late, that is, the Alphabet of Akiba. The passage from Midrash Tehillim cxlvi, see above, p. 163, he refers not to the Messianic Age but to the time after the Resurrection (p. 305, n. 5). He writes: 'die alten Quellen kennen weder eine neue Thorah noch die Lehrtätigkeit des Messias' (p. 306). He regards the supposition of Christian influences in this matter as questionable.

(5) *Song of Songs Rabbah* ii. 29 *on* ii. 13. This is a comment on the words in ii. 13: 'The fig tree putteth forth her green figs.' The whole passage reads, in a literal translation, as follows:

R. Joḥanan said: As for the seven years in which the Son of David comes: the first year will see established what is written (Amos iv) '*And I caused it to rain upon one city*' etc. In the second arrows of hunger shall be sent upon it: in the third a great famine and men and women and children will die, and the pious and the men of 'good works' will be diminished: and the Torah will be forgotten from Israel: in the fourth there will be hunger and no hunger: plenty and no plenty: in the fifth a great plenty: and they shall eat and drink and rejoice and the Torah shall return to its renewal and it will be renewed to Israel. (The Soncino translation gives: 'the Torah will be renewed and restored to Israel': p. 126.)

א"ר יוחנן שבוע שבן דוד בא שנה ראשונה מתקיים מה שנאמ' (עמוס ד)
והמטרתי על עיר אחת וגו'. בשנייה חצי רעב משתלחין בה. בשלישית רעב
גדול ומתים בו אנשים ונשים וטף, וחסדים ואנשי מעשה מתמעטים. והתורה
משתכחת מישראל. ברביעית רעב ולא רעב. שובע ולא שובע. בחמישית שובע
גדול. ואוכלין ושותין ושמחין. התורה חוזרת לחדושה ומתחדשת לישראל.

In his discussion of this Klausner insists that the idea that the Torah would be forgotten from Israel in the days preceding the advent of the Messiah is familiar and early, and that the phrase והתורה חוזרת לחדושה ומתחדשת לישראל is really a late alteration of words which originally meant that in the days of the Messiah the Torah, which had been forgotten, would return to those learning it.[1] This is the force of TB Sanhedrin 97*a* (Soncino translation, p. 654):

Our Rabbis taught: In the seven-year cycle at the end of which the son of David will come—in the first year, this verse will be fulfilled: *And I will cause it to rain upon one city and cause it not to rain upon another city*; in the second, the arrows of hunger will be sent forth; in the third, a great famine, in the course of which men, women, and children, pious men and saints will die, and the Torah will be forgotten by its students; in the fourth, partial plenty; in the fifth, great plenty, when men will eat, drink and rejoice, and the Torah will return to its disciples; in the sixth, [Heavenly] sounds; in the seventh, wars, and at the conclusion of the septennate the son of David will come.

---

[1] *Op. cit.* p. 53. J. Klausner points out that in the parallel passage Pesiqta R. 75 *a* (ed. M. Friedmann), the words ומתחדשת לישראל are missing. He rejects Weiss's view that the change from והתורה חוזרת ללומדיה to והתורה חוזרת לחידושה is early. R. Joḥanan died in A.D. 279. In Pesiqta the passage is cited in the name of רבנן: the partial parallel in Sanhedrin 97 *a* is anonymous.

Passages beginning with 'Our rabbis taught' [ת"ר] are usually regarded as early. On the other hand, it is easier to understand why the phrase 'The Torah shall return to its renewal...' which *may* be taken to imply a New Torah would be changed to 'The Torah will return to its disciples' than the reverse. But, even if the reading in Song of Songs Rabbah should be the earlier, which is on the whole, however, unlikely, in view of the date of R. Joḥanan, the phrase חוזרת לחידושה may merely mean, as Klausner insists, 'will return to its original state'. Hence it does not refer to a New Torah which would replace the Old: this latter meaning can only be regarded as a most remote possibility.[1]

(v) There remains one other aspect of Torah in the Messianic Age which should be noted very briefly. There are passages which anticipate that the Gentiles will come to share in the blessings of the Torah in the Messianic Age. This was expressed in the Old Testament passages which we discussed and it is taken up by the rabbis. The chief passage is in Genesis Rabbah xcviii. 9 on Gen. xlix. 11 [But see above p. 164, n. 1]:

HE WASHETH HIS GARMENTS IN WINE, intimates that he [the Messiah] will compose for them words of Torah; AND HIS VESTURE IN THE BLOOD OF GRAPES—that he will restore to them their errors. R. Hanin said: Israel will not require the teaching of the royal Messiah in the future, for it says, *Unto him shall the nations seek* (Isa. xi. 10), but not Israel. If so, for what purpose will the royal Messiah come, and what will he do? He will come to assemble the exiles of Israel and to give them [the Gentiles] thirty precepts, as it says, *And I said unto them: If ye think good, give me my hire; and if not, forbear. So they weighed for my hire thirty pieces of silver* (Zech. xi. 12). Rab said: This alludes to thirty mighty men. R. Johanan said: It alludes to thirty precepts. R. Johanan's disciples said to him: Does not Rab hold that the verse refers only to the nations of the world?—In Rab's view, '*And I said unto them*' means unto Israel, while in R. Johanan's view '*And I said unto them*' means unto the nations of the world.

So Genesis Rabbah xcviii. 8 on Gen. xlix. 10 reads:

UNTIL SHILOH COMETH: this alludes to the royal Messiah. AND UNTO HIM SHALL THE OBEDIENCE (YIKHATH) OF THE PEOPLE BE: he [the Messiah] will come and set on edge (*makkeh*) the teeth of the nations of the world.

The first passage seems to imply both that the Messiah will bring his teaching and that he will propound new meanings and interpretations of

---

[1] V. Aptowitzer, *op. cit. ad rem*, compares the phrase with that used to describe the new moon, לבנה בחידושה, Sanhedrin 42 a.

Torah, but that he will direct all this to the nations not to Israel, because the latter, presumably, will receive its teaching directly from God, or already had received the requisite teaching.

There were different views as to what demands would be made on the Gentiles: according to some all the minute details of the Torah would be imposed upon them: according to others only three ordinances would be binding upon them: according to still others the Noachian commandments would be placed upon them. We need not here enlarge on the details: it is the fact that is significant: that in the opinion of some rabbis at least the Gentiles would submit to the yoke of the Torah in the Messianic Age.[1]

(vi) So far we have discussed what role the Torah was expected to play in the Messianic Age in a strict sense, and in particular whether Jewish speculation contemplated a New Torah in that Age. We have dealt with the relevant material in the light of the 'doctrine' of the immutability of the Torah which almost dominated Judaism. Next we have to refer to passages which have been held to suggest, not merely that there would be changes in the Torah in the Messianic Age, but that it would be completely abrogated.

The chief passage comes from TB Sanhedrin 97 a (end) and Abodah Zarah 9 a (middle). The Soncino translation of the former is:

The Tanna debe Eliyyahu taught: The world is to exist six thousand years. In the first two thousand years there was desolation; two thousand years the Torah flourished; and the next two thousand years is the Messianic era [97b] but through our many iniquities all these years have been lost.

The meaning of The Tanna debe Eliyyahu in this connexion is defined by Mishcon[2] as 'a Midrash containing chiefly Baraithas compiled by R. Anan, Bab. Amora of the 3rd cent.' We may therefore conclude that the evidence it supplies is fairly early. Baeck[3] on the strength of this, and other passages of lesser importance, has concluded that 'At that time (that is, the first century), the belief was widespread among the Jews that world history consisted of three epochs: first, the period of chaos—tohubohu; then the period of the Torah, beginning with the revelation

---

[1] See A. Edersheim, *The Life and Times of Jesus the Messiah*, II, 764 ff.; unfortunately there is no attempt made to date the various passages listed.

[2] Soncino translation of TB Abodah Zarah, *ad loc*. The translation of *tohu* may be 'anarchy'; so Morton Smith, *J.B.L.* LXXII (1953), 193.

[3] *The Pharisees*, Eng. trans. (1947), pp. 72 f.

on Mount Sinai; and finally, the hoped-for period of the Messiah....In conformity with this, the Gospels say: "Till heaven and earth pass, one jot or one tittle shall in no wise pass from the law, till all be fulfilled" (Matt. v. 18). When all is fulfilled, and the Messiah has come, the period of the law will have come to its close.' The same position is maintained by Silver.[1] Freedman,[2] however, rejects this interpretation of the passage from *The Tanna debe Eliyyahu*, and comments on the reference to the period of the Torah that 'this does not mean that the Torah shall cease thereafter, but is mentioned merely to distinguish it from the next era'. Mishcon makes no reference to the problem posed by the passage.

But we have seen that there is a passage in TB Shabbath 151 *b*, which possibly offers some support for Baeck's interpretation, where it is stated that in the Messianic Age there would be neither merit nor guilt (לא זכות ולא חובה). Baeck also refers to TB Niddah 61 *b* to confirm his position. It reads: אמר רב יוסף זאת אומרת מצוות בטלות לעתיד לבא, that is, R. Joseph (A.D. 320–75) said: 'This means the commandments shall be abrogated in the time to come.' Baeck refers this passage to the Messianic Age, but the context makes it clear that the reference is to the condition of the dead, who, as we nave seen before, are not subject to the Torah. The point at issue in TB Niddah 61 *b* is that of the use of *sha'atnez*, that is, a mixture of wool and linen, which was prohibited to the living but, because death brings exemption from מצות, was, nevertheless, permitted as shrouds for the dead. It seems clear, therefore, that in this passage the phrase לעתיד לבא merely means 'in death', and it is difficult to agree either with Klausner[3] that the context of TB Niddah 61 *b* supports the view that the saying does not merely refer to life in the next world but also, by implication, to the Messianic Age, or with Baeck who refers it expressly to the Messianic Age. But that the idea contained in TB Niddah 61 *b* may refer to the Age to Come and not merely to the life after death is highly probable, if not certain. It may be permissible for us to refer here to our argument in *Paul and Rabbinic Judaism*[4] that the Age to Come was regarded both as an event, which came into being in time, and also as an eternally existing reality in the heavens, as it were. Hence, in one sense, one entered the Age to Come at death when one became free from the

---

[1] *The History of Messianic Speculation in Israel* (1927), p. 9.

[2] Soncino translation of TB Sanhedrin, II, p. 657, n. 9.

[3] *Jesus of Nazareth*, Eng. trans. p. 275; Klausner regards the passage as earlier than R. Joseph.

[4] Pp. 314 ff.

obligation to obey the מצות. It is to this that TB Niddah 61 *b* explicitly refers. But in another sense the Age to Come was to *come* into history and when this would happen the commandments, that is, the מצות, would also cease then, and by implication TB Niddah 61 *b* can be referred to this Age to Come that is to *come*. We can only refer TB Niddah 61 *b* to the Messianic Age if we can equate or identify this, that is, the Messianic Age, with the Age to Come. That this is a justifiable equation would seem reasonable in many passages: we have seen above that the phrase לעתיד לבא was very fluid and could refer both to the Messianic Age and to the final Age to Come, that is, the post-Messianic period. The distinction between the Age to Come and the Messianic Age is a comparatively late development, and it follows that they were often synonymous terms in early apocalyptic.[1] On the other hand, however, there are passages where the Messianic Age and the Age to Come are sharply distinguished: of the former it was possible to prophesy, but of the latter it was thought that it transcended all human conception. A passage in TB Shabbath 63 *a* (middle) makes this clear:

Samuel said, This world differs from the Messianic Era only in respect to servitude of the exiled; for it is said, *For the poor shall never cease out of the land*. This supports R. Hiyya b. Abba (A.D. 320–59), who said, All the prophets prophesied only for the Messianic Age, but as for The world to come, the eye hath not seen, O Lord, beside thee what he hath prepared for him that waiteth for him....[2]

In view, therefore, of the distinction between the Messianic Age and the Age to Come implied and explicitly stated in such passages as this, it is probably highly precarious to apply TB Niddah 61 *b* too surely to the Messianic Age as such.[3] We can only be sure from this passage that in the Age to Come, that Age that both IS and COMES, the מצות will cease, but we can only regard this as a possibility for the Messianic Age. This point is important for the understanding of the New Testament; and the

---

[1] See R. H. Charles, *Eschatology*, pp. 200 f., and especially J. Klausner, *Die Messianischen Vorstellungen des jüdischen Volkes im Zeitalter der Tannaïten*, pp. 17 ff.

[2] See T. W. Manson, *The Teaching of Jesus*[2], p. 277, n. 2: compare 1 Cor. ii. 9.

[3] L. Ginzberg, *op. cit.* p. 306, n. 1, does not refer it to the Messianic Age but to the time after the Resurrection. S. Lieberman, *Historia Judaica*, v, 2 (October 1943), 91, refers to Tosaphoth Niddah 61 *b* and asserts that 'the abolition of the Law in the future world is a genuine Jewish idea'. He does not define the future world as the Messianic Age, however. On the other hand, J. Z. Lauterbach refers TB Niddah 61 *b* to the Messianic Age, *Rabbinic Essays*, p. 267 n. On the idea that prophecy, which was regarded as the continuation of the voice heard on Sinai, would cease in Messianic times, see S. Schechter, *Some Aspects of Rabbinic Theology*, p. 123. Schechter emphasizes the completeness and finality of the Torah given on Sinai (p. 134).

question forces itself whether the distinction of this age and the Age to Come had come to clear expression in the time of Jesus. This is discussed by Volz, *op. cit.* pp. 63 ff. He concludes that the idea of the Two Ages, in any case, is older than the terms used to express it; we may safely assume that the distinction was a real one in the time of Jesus.[1] Bonsirven[2] thinks that the expressions העולם הזה and העולם הבא appeared at that time.[3]

In the passages treated above we have sought to discover what part the Torah was expected to play in the ideal future whether conceived as a Messianic Age or as the ultimate Age to Come. To recapitulate, we found in the Old Testament, the Apocrypha and Pseudepigrapha and in the rabbinical sources the profound conviction that obedience to the Torah would be a dominating mark of the Messianic Age, and in the prophet Jeremiah a certain tension as to whether this obedience would be spontaneous, in the sense that it would not be directed to, nor governed by, any external code, or whether some form of external Torah would still be

---

[1] See Mark x. 30; Luke xviii. 30; Matt. xii. 32, *et al.* The significance of this will be clear when we recognize that the difficulty of deciding whether Paul, for example, believed that in the Resurrection of Jesus the final Age to Come had arrived or whether that event merely inaugurated the Messianic Age has an important bearing on the Apostle's attitude to the Law. See *P.R.J.*[2] pp. 297 f.; H. J. Schoeps in *Aus Früh-christlicher Zeit: Religionsgeschichtliche Untersuchungen* (Tübingen, 1950) (also *Paulus* (1959), pp. 177 ff.) has dealt with this in 'Paulus als rabbinischer Exeget, 1, Χριστὸς τέλος νόμου', pp. 221 ff. He applies some of the passages which we have examined above to the phrase in Rom. x. 4. 'Die Geltung des Gesetzes als göttlichen Heilsweges ist seit der Auferstehung Jesu von den Toten, die seine Messianität sowohl wie auch den Anbruch der Endzeit beweist, beendigt. Denn das Gesetz ist Herr über den Menschen, solange er lebt' (Rom. vii. 1) (p. 223). In view of our treatment, Schoeps' conclusions would seem to be too bold. The same difficulty must influence our interpretation of Matt. v. 18, on which see my article in *Mélanges bibliques en l'honneur d'A. Robert* (Paris, 1957), pp. 428–46. Leo Baeck in *Judaism and Christianity* (1958), in an essay on *The Faith of Paul*, pp. 139 ff., takes very seriously the need to understand Paul's attitude to the Law in terms of strictly Messianic speculation. The Law was to cease in the Messianic Age. 'The primary question which Paul's faith had to face was: which "period" was it, that of the Torah or that of the Messiah?' (p. 162). As is the case with H. J. Schoeps, Baeck seems to be too confident in his claim that the Law was to cease in the Messianic Age. On the other hand, D. Barthélemy, *RB*, LX (1953), 317, argues that, had the concept of the cessation of the Law been a marked element in Pharisaic Judaism in the first century, Paul would have made use of it in Rom. vii. 1–6. Instead he appeals to the principle that the Law was not binding after death.   [2] *Op. cit.* 1, 312.

[3] N. Messel, in *Die Einheitlichkeit der jüdischen Eschatologie* (1915), disputed that Jewish eschatology contained the distinction between *This (earthly) Age* and *the (supernatural) Age to Come*. The terms refer always, he claimed, to a purely this-worldly and earthly conception. See P. Volz, *op. cit.* p. 66.

operative. Generally, however, our sources revealed the expectation that the Torah in its existing form would persist into the Messianic Age, when its obscurities would be made plain, and when there would be certain natural adaptations and changes and, according to some, the inclusion of the Gentiles among those who accepted the yoke of the Torah. The most conscious and general recognition of the need for legal changes in the Messianic Age emerged in the DSS. It turned out to be difficult always to distinguish the Messianic Age from the Age to Come in the final sense, but we found evidence for the belief that this last would transcend all human thought and see the cessation of מצות: but, since the Holy One himself was conceived to be occupied with the study of the Torah in the eternal world, we must not preclude the Torah even from the Age to Come in too radical a fashion.[1]

The evidence for the expectation of a New Torah which the Messiah should bring was not sufficiently definite and unambiguous to make us as certain as were Edersheim and Dalman[2] that this was a well defined and accepted element in the Messianic hope, but neither was it inconsiderable and questionable enough for us to dismiss it, as does Klausner, as merely a late development in a Judaism influenced by Christianity, a point to which we shall return later. Strack–Billerbeck's claim that the Torah of the Messiah would be new merely in the sense that it would expound the Old Torah more fully than was possible in this age probably errs on the side of caution. We can at least affirm that there were elements inchoate in the Messianic hope of Judaism, which could make it possible for some to regard the Messianic Age as marked by a New Torah, new indeed, as Strack–Billerbeck maintain, not in the sense that it contravened the old, but yet not merely in the sense that it affirmed the old on a new level, but in such a way as to justify the adjective חדשה that was applied to it. (Possibly Jeremiah would have thought of a Torah new in kind, but even he, as we suggested, did not exclude the possibility of this new kind of Torah having at the same time an element of *gramma* in it like that of the Old Torah.)

It is perilously easy, however, to systematize what was varied, vague and amorphous. Moreover, the isolation of passages dealing with one theme and their presentation in a concentrated, consecutive manner can too easily create an erroneous impression of their significance: to isolate in this context is to magnify, and to view the passages with which we have dealt in true perspective it is necessary to set them over against the vast

[1] G. F. Moore, *Judaism*, I, 273.   [2] *Jesus-Jeshua*, Eng. trans. (1929), p. 85.

continent of the rabbinical sources; only then can they be rightly assessed. Nor must it be forgotten that the passages which we have cited are all haggadic, so that they must lack a certain seriousness which more halakic passages would afford.[1] [But see the preface.]

In addition to all this, there is one difficulty, which we mentioned at the beginning of our discussion, which we have not yet met. Those passages which specifically use the term תורה חדשה are late; and Klausner, who apparently accepts this term as referring to a New Torah, claims that the passages concerned are the result of Christian influence, by way of reaction, of course, upon Judaism. At a date earlier than these passages what we usually find is the belief that, before the Messianic Age, Torah would almost fail in Israel but that it would later return. This late date of the passages, it is clear, is a real difficulty, no less than the paucity of their number, but we can submit certain considerations which may serve to offset these two factors.

First, we must emphasize again that the silence of our sources as to an early belief in a New Torah may be due to deliberate surgery. We have previously pointed out that our rabbinic sources represent merely the Pharisaic element in Judaism and that certain polemic tendencies are traceable in them. We do know that the question of the New Torah agitated Judaism. There is a passage in Deuteronomy Rabbah viii. 6 which reads thus:

It is written, '*For this commandment is not in heaven*' (Deut. xxx. 11, 12). Moses said to the Israelites, Lest you should say, Another Moses is to arise, and to bring us another Law from heaven, therefore I make it known to you now that it is not in heaven: nothing of it is left in heaven....

The polemical intention is obvious. Paul had used the same kind of midrash on Deut. xxx in Rom. x. 6 ff. in support of the view that God's word had drawn near to men in Christ. Again in Baruch iii. 29 ff. we hear another undertone of controversy where Wisdom is claimed to be inaccessible in the following terms:

Who hath gone up into heaven, and taken her (that is, Wisdom)
And brought her down from the clouds?
Who hath gone over the sea, and found her
And will bring her for choice gold?[2]

[1] G. F. Moore, *op. cit.* I, 162. Dr Lieberman insists on this strongly (so orally).
[2] On this see M. Jack Suggs, 'The Word is near you: Note on Rom. x. 6–10', *Report of Society of Biblical Literature and Exegesis* (New York, 1960), p. 8. Paul, he claims, follows a well-established tradition in which the word of Deut. xxx. 12–14 is Wisdom's 'incarnation' in the Torah.

But in Baruch iv. 1 it is asserted that Wisdom has appeared on earth in the Torah. Justin's *Dialogue with Trypho* makes the same controversy clear: he goes so far as to claim that he has read that there will be a final Law.[1]

Weiss[2] also regarded a complicated passage from TB Shabbath 104*a*, which deals with variant forms of the Hebrew letters and claims that the text of the Torah can suffer no innovations from any prophet, as directed against Paul's attitude towards the Torah. The phrase 'these are the commandments', derived from Lev. xxvii. 34, was taken to teach that 'a prophet may henceforth (that is, after Moses) make no innovations'; and Strack–Billerbeck[3] cite R. Johannan b. Zakkai's famous dictum, which we cited above, as a direct polemic comment on Mark vii. 14 ff. (and parallels). In view of all the above, we may safely claim that the early presentation of Christianity as involving a New Law in the *SM* or in the καινὴ ἐντολή of the Fourth Gospel produced counter-claims within Judaism such as we see in Deuteronomy Rabbah viii. 6. But this may also, perhaps, account for the absence in our rabbinic sources of any specific early references to a New Torah, such as may possibly have been once contemplated. By the time that the passages which actually speak of a New Torah are found the separation of Church and Synagogue had become such that speculation among Jews and Christians could be mutually stimulating without being dangerous. It is arguable, at least, that this might account for the greater readiness of later Judaism to speak of a New Torah.[4]

Secondly, a further similar consideration illustrates the kind of situation which may account for the absence of early references to any New Torah. It has been pointed out by Bonsirven that despite the fact that the idea of

---

[1] *Ante-Nicene Christian Library*, II, see pp. 99 f. Justin here claims that he has read 'that there shall be a final law (and an eternal one)'. νυνὶ δὲ ἀνέγνων γάρ, ὦ Τρύφων, ὅτι ἔσοιτο καὶ τελευταῖος νόμος καὶ Διαθήκη κυριωτάτη πασῶν... Αἰώνιός τε ἡμῖν νόμος (Isa. lv. 3; lxi. 8; Jer. xxxii. 40) καὶ τελευταῖος ὁ Χριστὸς ἐδόθη καὶ ἡ διαθήκη πιστή. Text from G. Archambault, *Justin: Dialogue avec Tryphon* (Paris, 1909), I, 51 ff. See especially n. 2.

[2] Cited in Soncino translation of TB Shabbath, p. 499, n. 5.

[3] S–B, *Kommentar*, I, 719.

[4] I have here followed J. Klausner, but I do so with hesitation. I am not quite sure that he is correct in thinking that it would be easier for later Judaism to contemplate a New Torah than it would have been for first-century Judaism. The antipathy to Christianity had become greater, not less. The concept of a New Torah might perhaps have been indigenous and not merely the outcome of Christian influences. Within Christianity the concept of a New Law developed coincidentally with that of the Church as a New Israel. See on this, M. Simon, *Verus Israel* (1948), pp. 100 ff.

the Covenant dominates Jewish thought, surprisingly enough the idea is relatively little exploited in the rabbinical sources. Bonsirven gives a reason for this: he rightly suggests that the Law had replaced it as the centre of Jewish life and thought;[1] but an additional reason for the fact mentioned surely may be that the covenantal idea was so prominent in Christianity that it became, if not exactly distasteful to Judaism, nevertheless deliberately disused because of its marked Christian associations. It is the same kind of reaction against the New Law preached by early Christians which may have caused the comparative silence of the rabbinic sources on the concept of a New Law.

We are now in a position to turn again to the Matthaean approach to the words of Jesus with which we were concerned in the preceding chapter: how do Jewish expectations illuminate this? It must be recognized at the

---

[1] *Op. cit.* 1, 79 f. His words deserve quotation: 'Cette idée de l'alliance domine toute la pensée juive: nous sommes d'autant plus surpris de constater que la littérature rabbinique a relativement peu exploité cette donnée biblique primordiale.' J. Bonsirven asserts that there are very few places where rabbis speculate on the covenantal idea: in the Midrashim comments on the biblical texts dealing with the Covenant are few. He also points out how sectarian movements remained far truer to the Old Testament in this; for example, the Dead Sea Sect governed its life on the covenantal principle. Thus not only Christian concentration on covenantal ideas, but other sectarian tendencies also would tend to reinforce the surprising neglect of the explicit treatment of such texts in the rabbinic sources. To judge from the extant works of Philo the same neglect of the covenantal idea might be found in Hellenistic Judaism, but G. F. Moore pointed out that Philo wrote two lost treatises on the Covenants (see R. Marcus (citing G. F. Moore), *op. cit.* p. 14 n.). (The view expressed by H. J. Schoeps in *Aus frühchristlicher Zeit*, p. 228, that Diaspora Judaism or Septuagint-Judaism, as he describes it, had a false conception of the covenantal relation between Yahweh and Israel, as did also Paul, to speak very mildly, is to be very seriously questioned.) In his *Theologie und Geschichte des Judenchristentums*, p. 90, the same scholar offers parallels to the above mentioned neglect of the covenant concept in the rabbis, parallels which are illuminating. Schoeps is concerned to show the way in which Judaism reacted to the Jewish-Christian emphasis on Christ as the New Moses. He writes: 'Welchen Rang und welche Verbreitung dieses Dogma, vielleicht auf essäische Ursprünge zurückgehend, Christus Jesus–Novus Moses in der jüdischen Christenheit gehabt haben muß, lassen uns auch zwei weitere Umstände erkennen. . . . Zum anderen der auffällige Verzicht der Tannaiten und frühen Amoräer, Deut. xviii. 15 und 18 auszulegen [see especially p. 90, n. 3, for evidence]. Es begegnet uns hier dieselbe Erscheinung wie bei der Auslegungsgeschichte von Jes. liii; Ps. ii. 7; cx. 1; Jer. xxxi. 31 f.; Hos. ii. 25 usw. *Die jüdische Theologie der ersten Jahrhunderte n. Chr. fand diese Schriftsteller bereits durch die christliche Auslegung präokkupiert und verzichtete daher auf ihre Verwendung innerhalb messianischer Diskussionen oder legte sie betont unescatologisch aus.*' (Our italics.) Compare also G. Quell, *T.W.Z.N.T.* 11, *ad loc.* For the way in which Judaism closed its ranks against Christianity, see S. W. Baron, *A social and religious history of the Jews*[2], 11, 2 (Philadelphia, 1952), 130 ff., and the bibliographical details he supplies.

outset that the evidence that we have been able to adduce in favour of a *new* Messianic Torah, when set over against the totality of the eschatological expectation of Judaism, is not impressive. In one respect—apart from the comparative paucity of the material—it must appear negative. As we wrote at the beginning of this chapter, could we clearly distinguish the role expected of the Torah in the Messianic Age and in the Age to Come we would be able to set the early Christian attitude to the Law in true perspective. Thus, for example, by determining how the various elements in the New Testament conceived the Resurrection, whether it was regarded as the inauguration of the Messianic Age or of the Age to Come proper, in its ultimate manifestation, we could then discover what attitude to the Law would be natural to them. But this our Jewish sources will not allow us to do, except in the most ambiguous way. Not only was the distinction between the Age to Come and Messianic Age not always clear, so that we had constant difficulty in deciding to which Age a particular passage referred, but it would not be correct to speak of any one generally accepted Jewish expectation as to the role of the Torah in either of these periods. The result of our survey is not in any sense decisive.

On the other hand, the material presented above is sufficiently cogent to illumine for us the Matthaean understanding of the *SM*. Matthew was conscious, as were other early Christians, of living in the Messianic Age: the role of the Law, therefore, inevitably occupied him. We saw that for him the Christian Dispensation, among other things, denies the Old Law on one level, but affirms and fulfils it on another; this is the meaning of the *SM*. Matthew does not explicitly claim to have received a *New* Torah, although the substance of a New Messianic Torah is clearly present to his mind. As the rabbis, and especially as the Dead Sea Sectarians, anticipated, the Messianic Age had brought for Matthew a teaching (תורה, אולפן) with eschatological authority (vii. 28). In his emphasis on the Messianic teaching in the *SM*, Matthew reveals especial affinity, perhaps, with the sectarians, who had very unequivocally contrasted the 'judgements' by which they were to be ruled after the Prophet and the Messiahs of Aaron and Israel had come, with the interim ones to which, until then, they were subject. But, unless the Messiah of Aaron be equated with *Elias redivivus*, which is unlikely, the sectarians had ascribed the giving of these anticipated new judgements to the Prophet, that is, the Messianic function was not strictly connected with the promulgation of new laws. In connecting Jesus, as Messiah, especially with the giving of teaching, Matthew differs from the Sectarians: that is, the teaching in the *SM* is more specifically that of the Messiah in Matthew's view, than would have been the case had the Sectarians found that their Messiahs had come. In his awareness of the significance of the moral teaching of Jesus, as belonging to the Messianic Age, Matthew has Sectarian affinities, but in pinning this down to Jesus as *the Messiah himself* he departs from the Sectarian anticipation.

Does he, at this very point, attach himself to the rabbinic anticipation? Ginzberg would have denied this: he insisted strongly that the Messiah of Jewish expectation was not concerned with interpreting the Law. The marks of the Messianic Age in rabbinic tradition would be repentance, liberation from Gentile domination (by the Ephraimitic Messiah), the appearance of Elijah as forerunner of the Davidic Messiah, and finally, the coming of the latter. The 'teaching' of the Age would be in the hands of Elijah.[1] But the passages to which we have appealed justify the view that in some rabbinic circles the Messiah had a didactic function. And it is this emphasis that Matthew found congenial. His is, in this sense, in part a rabbinic Christ, whose words were for him *halakah* and the ground for *halakah* both for Israel and for the Gentile world: both Israel and the latter are addressed in these words of Jesus. At this point again it is impossible to claim Matthew for any single milieu: he reveals both sectarian and rabbinic affinities. One thing is clear: even if the concept of a New Torah in the Messianic Age had not become explicit in Judaism before Christ (which is not at all sure), his figure was a catalyst[2] which gave life to what was inchoate: with him came also a νόμος Χριστοῦ.

---

[1] *Op. cit. ad rem.*

[2] The situation revealed in Matthew recalls that in the Fourth Gospel. In xvi. 13–16 Jesus is denied to be one of the prophets, nor can xi. 2 be certainly regarded as referring to the expected 'Prophet' rather than to the Messiah himself. The crowds take Jesus to be a prophet in xxi. 46 and, almost certainly, in xxi. 11, but such a generalized concept of a prophet is to be distinguished from that of an eschatological figure 'the Prophet': this emerges from pp. 143 ff. above, and this is rightly emphasized by Bultmann, *Das Evangelium des Johannes* (Göttingen, 1953), p. 61. But the characteristics of 'the Prophet' to come are ascribed by Matthew to Jesus as Messiah. The Matthaean Messiah reminds us also of the Teacher of Righteousness and the Interpreter of the Law of the Scrolls. With the Messianic, Matthew has fused prophetic and rabbinic traits. The same ambiguity emerges in John. In John i. 22 'the Prophet' is distinguished from the Messiah. But in John vi. 14 Jesus is taken by the people to be 'the Prophet' and is, in turn, interpreted as a Messianic figure because they immediately want to make him a king (compare C. H. Dodd, *The Interpretation of the Fourth Gospel*, 1953, p. 345); this is a more natural explanation of John vi. 15 than that an ancient belief in the magic power of the king emerges here (H. Windisch, *Paulus und Christus*, 1934, p. 79). This understanding of the Messiah as 'the Prophet' Bultmann (*op. cit.* p. 61) takes to be a specifically Christian development (Acts iii. 22, vii. 37). Deut. xviii. 15 was not, he claims, Messianically

But despite his sense of the didactic significance of Jesus, the Messiah, Matthew, nevertheless, remains sensitive to the niceties of the expectations of Judaism. It was this sensitivity, in part at least, that may have made him hesitate to use the phrase 'new teaching' or 'new Law of the Messiah'. The ambiguity of Jewish expectation has invaded the Evangelist's presentation of the Messianic era. Nevertheless, the phrase 'New Torah' did emerge in Judaism and *may* have already emerged in the first century within Pharisaic Judaism; Paul did not hesitate to speak of 'the Law of Christ' (תורה של משיח) and John of 'the New Commandment', καινὴ ἐντολή, and of ἐντολαὶ τοῦ Χριστοῦ.[1] It is, therefore, probable that it was not only his sensitivity to the niceties of rabbinic and sectarian eschatological anticipations that caused Matthew to change the 'new teaching' of Mark i. 27 to the 'teaching' of vii. 28. There must have been other factors in his world which caused him to temper his language in this way. These we shall explore in the next chapter.

applied in pre-Christian Judaism (*ibid.*), and although he recognizes the Moses-Messiah, New Exodus motif therein (*op. cit.* p. 61, n. 8), he rejects Jeremias's view (*Golgotha*, 1926, p. 83) that 'the Prophet' is a returned Moses (Bultmann, *op. cit.* p. 158, n. 2). As far as the DSS are concerned our examination confirmed Bultmann's separation of 'the Prophet' from the Messiah, but, while the former was not to be a returned Moses, he was a New Moses, that is, a figure like the first Moses. The complexity of Messianic expectation does not allow us to be as unequivocal as Bultmann. We may claim, with some certainty, in the light of Matthew and John that eschatological figures which in Judaism were often distinct, even if they sometimes tended to merge, become identified in primitive Christianity. Is it unreasonable to suggest that this is so because the figure of Jesus historically suggested that he was all these—Messiah, 'the Prophet', Rabbi: it is in this sense that we use the term 'catalyst' of Jesus above. On John vi, see C. K. Barrett, *The Gospel according to St John* (London, 1958), p. 231: 'Several features of this chapter suggest that Jesus was the prophet "like unto Moses"'; and C. H. Dodd, *The Interpretation of the Fourth Gospel, ibid.* and p. 339. He takes 'the Prophet' to be a quasi-Messianic designation. Jesus in John vi is New Moses and infinitely more. On the influence of the belief in 'the Prophet', see F. W. Young, *J.B.L.* lxxv (1956), 285 ff.

[1] John xiii. 34; xiv. 15; compare 1 John ii. 7 ff.; 2 John v. In the Epistle to the Hebrews the failure of the old cultus necessarily demands the emergence of a new or, at least, changed Law; see Heb. vii. 12. The New Commandment of John is dealt with in *J.B.L.* lxxiv (1955), 69–79, by Harrisville. He rejects the view that the New Commandment is merely a radicalizing of the old, and Bultmann's claim that it is not new historically, and insists that the 'new commandment' is new in *content* and *historically*—because it belongs to a new aeon that has dawned and is to be practised 'in the light of that love which Jesus is about to show in his death' (p. 79). 'What gives Jesus' words their gravity in John xiii. 34 and their seriousness is that the one who delivers the commandment is about to be sacrificed in order to establish the new eschatological covenant, a covenant by which God orders his relationship to men in a new and final way' (*ibid.*).

IV. THE SETTING IN THE CONTEMPORARY JUDAISM

In a play dealing with complex domestic issues, T. S. Eliot asserts that to understand any situation we must know its *total* setting. As O'Reilly the psychiatrist puts it:

> It is often the case
> that my patients
> Are only pieces of a total situation
> Which I have to explore.[1]

This is also true of any document we have to study, and it is especially true of the documents of the New Testament. Because these were created to serve the needs of the Church, a community not enclosed within itself but ever concerned to present its faith to the world. Hence recent scholarship has rightly insisted that the various elements in the New Testament must be placed over against their 'setting in life'. This last can be conceived in a narrow and broad sense. In the narrow sense the 'setting in life' of any document in the New Testament is its foreground in the life of the Church or Churches within which it emerged, its worship, catechesis, preaching, peculiar needs and circumstances. In the broad sense the 'setting in life' has reference to the total environment of a document, to the whole range of circumstances, ecclesiastical, ideological, social and political within or under the pressure of which it came into being, that is, the fullness of its background in the contemporary world.

This holds true of the *SM*. Its foreground we assume, on grounds indicated elsewhere,[2] is the life of the Church in Syria or Palestine sometime between A.D. 70 and 100; its background the total circumstances of that place and period. And it is with this last, the 'setting in life' of the *SM* in the broad sense that we are to be concerned in this chapter. Were there forces at work which would demand the elevation of the moral teaching of Jesus to its dominating position in the *SM* in the second edition of Mark which we call Matthew? What occasioned or necessitated this concentrated and architectonic presentation of the sayings of Jesus?

---

[1] *The Cocktail Party*, in *The Complete Plays and Poems of T. S. Eliot* (New York, 1950), p. 350.
[2] See 'Matthew', in *H.D.B.*, eds. F. C. Grant, H. H. Rowley (1963).

The period indicated was marked by the rise and fall of certain 'movements': on the one hand, by the development of Gnosticism, and rabbinic Judaism, strictly so called, and, on the other, by the decline of Essenism, as well as other less significant aspects of early first-century Judaism. Can all this be connected either directly or indirectly with the generation and formation of the *SM*?

1. *Gnosticism*

There is first the possibility that what is termed Gnosticism was a force to be reckoned with in the presentation of the Gospel by Matthew. But before we can examine the claims made for the presence in Matthew's work of both Gnostic and anti-Gnostic motifs, it is necessary to define what is meant by Gnosticism in this connexion. The term is used, rather loosely, in two ways. First, to denote a Christian phenomenon, an aberrant movement within the Church in the second century. Thus Casey, for example, urged that 'there is no trace in early Christianity of gnosticism as a broad historical category, and the modern usage of gnostic and gnosticism to describe a large but ill-defined religious movement having a special scope and character is wholly unknown in the early Christian period'.[1] Like F. C. Burkitt,[2] therefore, Casey treated Gnosticism as 'Christian'. He confined the term 'to a group of theologians and sects in the second century characterized (*a*) by their obligations to Christianity; (*b*) by the autonomous quality of their systems which made them rivals of Christianity rather than modifiers of it in point of detail; and (*c*) by a demand for theological novelty which their frequent appeals to a remote antiquity have obscured but not concealed'.[3] If we relegate Gnosticism to the second century in this way, there can be no question of its influence upon Matthew. But there is a looser sense in which the term is used, that is, to denote a widespread movement of the human spirit, born out of that fusion of East and West which began with Alexander the Great and came to concentrate on some form of *gnôsis* (knowledge) as the means of redemption.[4] The marks of this gnosis are difficult to define: it was essentially concerned with knowledge of the nature and origin of three things—of the heavenly aeons, of this world and its rulers, of man himself.

---

[1] *J.T.S.* xxxvi (1935), 45 ff.
[2] *The Church and Gnosis* (1932).   [3] *Loc. cit.*
[4] For this, see Hans Jonas, *The Gnostic Religion* (Boston, 1958); on the whole field also, R. McL. Wilson, *The Gnostic Problem* (1958); in Paul, J. Dupont, *Gnosis* (1949); C. Colpe, *Die religionsgeschichtliche Schule* (Göttingen, 1961).

He who knew what he was and whence he came could by this very knowledge find his way home from this material world to the higher world, past the enslaving powers that constituted a barrier between these two worlds. Thus gnosis spelt power and redemption, deliverance from matter, fate and death into immortality. In later systems this saving knowledge came to be imparted by a Redeemer, but there is no evidence for such a figure in pre-Christian sources,[1] and it seems that it was contact with Judaism and Christianity which gave to the loose 'gnosis' we have indicated a quickened vitality. This, at the end of the first century and later, produced the developed Gnosticism described in the Church Fathers. The claim to a saving knowledge, decked out in abstruse mythological terms, and, owing to its interpretation of man and nature, often conducive to licence, could not but arouse the suspicion and, finally, the opposition of the Church. Can we trace such already in Matthew?

Syria, where we are probably to locate Matthew, was open to influences both Oriental and Hellenistic such as gave birth to Gnosticism.[2] Not far away was Samaria where Simon Magus,[3] whom the Church Fathers regarded as the father of Gnosticism, appeared, and in the neighbouring Tyre in Phoenicia he had found his Helena. Galilee of the Gentiles,[4] nearer still, was notoriously syncretistic and given to enthusiasms. Antioch and other Syrian centres were seed-beds for the kind of growth and crossbreeding which lie behind Gnosticism. Nor had Judaism in its purer forms escaped 'Gnostic' infiltrations.[5] It is legitimate, therefore, to ask whether Matthew shows an awareness of Gnostic tendencies which led him to a concentration on the moral teaching of Jesus.

Bacon[6] traced the very origin of the Gospel of Matthew in part at least to an anti-Gnostic motif: the ease with which Mark, because it lacked any treatment of the infancy of Jesus, could be exploited by docetists was one of the factors which created a demand for a revised version of Mark which

[1] Edwyn Bevan, *Hellenism and Christianity* (1921), Essay V, on 'The Gnostic Redeemer'.

[2] H. Jonas uses the term Syrio-Egyptian to designate a certain kind of gnosis originating with Simon Magus (*op. cit.* p. 112).

[3] For Simon Magus, see Irenaeus, *Against Heresies*, XXIII; H. Jonas, *op. cit.* pp. 103 ff.; and literature cited above.   [4] See Appendix VII.

[5] A. Altmann, 'Gnostic Themes in Rabbinic Cosmology', in *Essays in Honour of J. H. Hertz* (London, 1942), pp. 19 ff.: 'The early stages of Tannaitic thought are already under the spell of Gnostic ideas' (p. 20). See also H. J. Schoeps, *Urgemeinde, Judenchristentum, Gnosis* (1956); J. Daniélou, *Théologie du Judéo-Christianisme*, I (1958), 82 ff.; G. G. Scholem, *Jewish Gnosticism, Merkabah Mysticism, and Talmudic Tradition* (New York, 5720–1960), *passim*.   [6] *Op. cit.* p. 149.

eventually called forth Matthew. By way of illustration, Bacon refers to Cerinthus, who flourished about A.D. 100, and who 'according to Irenaeus, rested his docetism ("apparition" doctrine) on the Gospel of Mark, admitting no other'. It is legitimate to regard Cerinthus as a 'Gnostic', but in the passages in Irenaeus[1] dealing with Cerinthus there is no explicit reference to Mark. Indeed, 'with respect to the Lord' the opinions of Cerinthus are declared to be similar to those of the Ebionites and they are declared to use only the Gospel of Matthew. All that is stated directly concerning Cerinthus and the infancy narrative is that 'he represented Jesus as having not been born of a virgin'. But such a view may quite as much presuppose Matthew as be counteracted by it. It should also be noted that Irenaeus connects Cerinthus not with Syria or Palestine but with Ephesus.[2]

But it is Schlatter who has most emphasized Gnosticism as a factor for the understanding of Matthew.[3] His use of the term gnosis is exceedingly loose: it is hard to determine whether he meant by it merely immorality associated with 'gnosis' in a vague way or a fully developed system or type of thought. This will appear as we examine his statements. To begin with, he found in the very structure of the Gospel,[4] in which he recognized a fivefold schema of addresses, an anti-Gnostic intent, the moral demand of the Gospel, not emphasized by gnosis, being given precedence by Matthew in v–vii. We have seen, however, that theological interests centring in the understanding of Jesus as a New Moses can best account for any pentateuchal structure there may be in Matthew, and, taken alone, Schlatter's discovery of anti-Gnosticism in the structure of the Gospel cannot be regarded seriously. But he adduces other evidence. The relevant passages are the following:

(a) iv. 3 f.:

And the tempter came and said to him, 'If you are the Son of God, command these stones to become loaves of bread.' But he answered, 'It is written, "Man shall not live by bread alone, but by every word that proceeds from the mouth of God."' (RSV.)

Schlatter[5] contrasts Matthew's description of a temptation in terms of a conflict in the will of Jesus in iv. 3 with the elaborate mythological

---

[1] *Against Heresies*, I, 26, 1 f.
[2] *Op. cit. ibid.* and III, 3, 4. Hippolytus, *Refutations of All Heresies*, VII, 21, connects him with the learning of the Egyptians.
[3] *Der Evangelist Matthäus* (1948).
[4] *Op. cit.* pp. 424 f.   [5] *Op. cit. ad rem.*

descriptions of conflicts with Satan such as the Gnostics indulged in. Unfortunately, however, because he supplies no references to any passages portraying such Gnostic conflicts, Schlatter does not clarify what he has in mind at this point. But certain comments are pertinent. First, it is probably rash to dismiss mythological influences too easily from the temptation narrative in Matthew, as in the other Gospels. A side-glance at the myth of the fall of Adam may be detectable in the Marcan narrative of the temptation,[1] and in view of the first two chapters where, as we saw above in pages 70 ff., the first creation is possibly in the Evangelist's mind, it is not to be ruled out entirely from Matthew. That the temptation narrative is not consciously designed to avoid misinterpretations of it in the interests of Gnostic mythology becomes apparent, moreover, not merely from the possible presence of myth in it, although the Temptation itself was not a myth, but also from the simple fact that the Fathers found it so easy to interpret it mythologically, in terms of the Fall of Adam,[2] and what they could do in the interests of orthodoxy the Gnostics could have done in the interests of heresy.

But apart from this (and it must be strongly emphasized that the presence of a mythological motif can only be regarded as a bare possibility), in the second place, the citation of Deut. viii. 3, as well as the whole development of the temptation narrative in Matthew, as in Luke, show that it is governed by reference to Deuteronomy, and is designed largely to suggest how the experience of the people of God under the Old Covenant is being recapitulated in that of Jesus, the author of a new covenant, who constitutes in himself the People of God.[3] Along with this, it is aimed not at the rejection of Gnostic mythology so much as at the rejection of the traditional Jewish Messianism: what polemic there is in the Temptation narrative was called forth not by the exigencies of anti-Gnostic controversy, but by the necessity, which Jesus himself recognized, of enlightening the disciples on the nature of the Messiahship of Jesus and of the methods appropriate to such a Messiahship.[4]

(*b*) v. 16:

Let your light so shine before men, that they may see your good works, and glorify your Father which is in heaven.

---

[1] *P.R.J.*[2], p. 42; V. Taylor, *The Gospel According to St Mark, ad rem*; P. Carrington, *According to St Mark* (1961), pp. 36–42.

[2] Irenaeus, *Against Heresies*, v, 21, 2.

[3] See above, p. 48.

[4] T. W. Manson, *The Servant-Messiah* (1953), pp. 55–8.

Here Schlatter,[1] in pointing out that the Christian disciples are to impress men by their good works, again drags in a contrast with the Gnostics who emphasized not works but ideas as the media of the revelation of God. Moreover, in the Valentinian system we do find that the emphasis in v. 16 on good works is side-stepped in the interests of the system, 'let your light so shine' being by implication interpreted to refer to 'spiritual substance' (τὸ πνευματικόν).[2] But although the contrast which Schlatter draws with the Gnostics is, in itself, justified, and while the amoralism and even the immorality of much in Gnosticism could well be rebuked by the citation of such a verse as v. 16, it is unnecessary to find an anti-Gnostic motif in the insertion of the *logion* here. Throughout the *SM*, beginning with the Beatitudes, the Christian community is mainly set in antithesis to the Jewish: generally where the Gentiles are in mind this is explicitly stated.[3] It is the intense awareness of the Christian community as distinct from Judaism as well as from the world, a community called to a higher righteousness by which it is to impress the world, it is this that emerges in v. 16: it casts no side-glance at Gnosticism. The terminology employed does not depart in any way from that employed in the Old Testament to describe the function of Israel in the world: this is here applied to the New Israel, the Church, which has taken over the functions of the Old Israel.[4]

(c) xxviii. 18:

And Jesus came and spake unto them, saying, All power is given unto me in heaven and in earth. . . .

The phrase ἐδόθη μοι πᾶσα ἐξουσία prompts Schlatter to comment that 'nochmals kommt die antignostische Haltung des Evangelisten mächtig zum Ausdruck'.[5] Here again he is tantalizingly vague: he does not explain

---

[1] *Op. cit. ad rem.*

[2] Irenaeus, *Against Heresies*, 1, 6, 1. Verse v. 16 itself is not cited directly in the treatment in Irenaeus on the Valentinians but he offers his own understanding of it in IV, 37, 2. It has no direct parallel in *The Gospel according to Thomas*; see B. Gärtner, *The Theology of the Gospel of Thomas* (1961). In a list supplied by R. M. Grant and D. N. Freedman, *The Secret Sayings of Jesus* (1960), pp. 108 f., no parallel is given to v. 16, though parallels to material in Matthew are more frequent than to that in the other Gospels. Possibly the obviousness of the reference to 'good works' in v. 16 made the verse itself unpopular with Gnostics. In Clement of Alexandria's *Excerpta ex Theodoto*, 3, 1, the verse v. 16 is interpreted to mean that the Saviour came to awaken the soul and to kindle the spark, the element of deity enclosed within it. The Gnostic must cultivate the light within him: the first examples of this are the apostles (3, 2).

[3] vi. 7.   [4] See p. 290.   [5] *Op. cit.* p. 797.

exactly how this is anti-Gnostic. But so abundant is the evidence for the claim to ἐξουσία among Hellenistic groups making pretensions to gnosis that we can perhaps follow the unexpressed train of his thought.[1] Possibly Schlatter finds in xxviii. 18 a polemic reference to the kind of ἐξουσία which it has been customary to discover in Hellenistic religion, a kind of supernatural force, born of an immediate vision of the divine: Matthew is concerned to assert that to Jesus alone has such ἐξουσία been granted: he alone has the gnosis which confers this. This interpretation of Schlatter's comment can only be taken as conjectural. But fortunately it is not necessary to inquire further into his meaning, because, apart from the precise definition of the ἐξουσία which has been uncovered in Hellenistic sources of a 'Gnostic' kind, there is a far more probable explanation of xxviii. 18.

The thought of Matthew at that passage, as in xxvi. 64b ('Hereafter shall ye see the Son of Man sitting on the right hand of power and coming in the clouds of heaven'), reverts to Dan. vii. 14 where the future victory of the (suffering) Son of Man is described. The Greek of the LXX reads:

καὶ ἐδόθη αὐτῷ ἐξουσία [καὶ τιμὴ βασιλικὴ] καὶ πάντα τὰ ἔθνη τῆς γῆς κατὰ γένη καὶ πᾶσα δόξα αὐτῷ λατρεύουσα· καὶ ἡ ἐξουσία αὐτοῦ ἐξουσία αἰώνιος ἥτις οὐ μὴ ἀρθῇ, καὶ ἡ βασιλεία αὐτοῦ, ἥτις οὐ μὴ φθαρῇ.

There can be little question that in xxviii. 16 ff. we are to recognize the scene of a proleptic parousia or more precisely the description of the enthronement of the Son of Man, in which he sends forth envoys to summon the nations to his obedience.[2]

The precise definition of ἐξουσία is probably to be subsumed under two heads. First, the term translates the Hebrew שָׁלְטָן in Dan. vii. 14. In Dan. vii. 6, 12 it is used of the authority possessed on earth by the various beasts, that is, the empires or kingdoms of history referred to by the author.[3] This authority was not theirs absolutely: it was contingent upon the will of God, who both gave it to them and, at his pleasure, took it

---

[1] The term ἐξουσία rarely occurs in the work of Christian Gnostics, see J. Behm, *T.W.Z.N.T.* II, 568; but J. Dupont, *Gnosis* (1949), pp. 282 ff., finds it frequent in Hellenistic sources; see especially pp. 291 ff. *et al.* It occurs in the Apocryphal Acts of the Apostles and in magical papyri.

[2] See R. H. Lightfoot, *Locality and Doctrine in the Gospels* (1938), pp. 71 f.; so J. Behm, *op. cit.* p. 565. The words in brackets are in Symmachus and 88.

[3] In vii. 6 the LXX reads γλῶσσα, לשׁוּן being mistaken for שׁלטן. Theodotion translates ἐξουσία, and this is followed by AV, RSV. Possibly the error arose by a kind of onomatopoeia, especially if the scribe read the pointing שִׁלְטוּן, as in later Hebrew. See Jastrow, *Dictionary of the Talmud.*

away again. The authority wielded by the kingdoms of history are mere derivatives of the absolute authority which God exercises over nature and history. In vii. 1–13 the authority ascribed to the various beasts is described as שָׁלְטָן, which is rendered in vii. 6 by Theodotion as ἐξουσία, and in vii. 12 as ἀρχή, whereas the LXX renders γλῶσσα in vii. 6 and ἐξουσία in vii. 12. After vii. 13 this is related to the idea of a kingdom (מלכו): in the MT the שָׁלְטָן of the Son of Man is used, apparently, in parallelism with his kingdom (מלכו). The same term (מלכו) is used in vii. 23 of the fourth beast explicitly, and by implication of the other beasts. ('Thus he said, The fourth beast shall be the fourth kingdom upon earth, which shall be diverse from all kingdoms....') But their kingdom (מלכו) and their dominion (שלטנה) (vii. 26) was taken away from each of the beasts in turn and, finally, from the king, who rises after the other ten kings, who first arose out of the fourth kingdom (vii. 24 ff.). In vii. 26 this dominion (שלטנה), which we are perhaps to equate with the kingdom, is utterly destroyed, and in vii. 27 a different kind of kingdom (מלכותא) and dominion (שלטנא) is given to the saints of the Most High, who now are revealed as the equivalent of the Son of Man of vii. 14. It is still a kingdom 'under the whole heaven' (תחות כל שמיא) (vii. 27), that is, an earthly kingdom, but it is marked by two things, first, as the phrase 'under the whole heaven' suggests, it is universal in its scope (vii. 27), and, secondly, it is a מלכות עולם, which is rendered in Theodotion, as in the LXX, by βασιλεία αἰώνιος.

It is in the light of all this that xxviii. 18 is to be understood. Through the Resurrection, Jesus of Nazareth who, although he had had no place whereon to lay his head and had suffered death on the Cross, had nevertheless already revealed authority in word and deed, in the healing of the sick and in the forgiveness of sin, has now been given the authority of the Son of Man triumphant: in short, he has become Lord and Christ.

But how far the concept of ἐξουσία here is removed from any anti-Gnostic purpose is still further clear. Daube,[1] in his very important treatment of this term, established that it was used in a quasi-technical sense to distinguish those teachers in Judaism who were qualified to pronounce upon matters of *halakah*: such teachers exercized ἐξουσία. That this nuance is to be preserved in our understanding of xxviii. 18 is made evident by the following verses, where Jesus emerges as the teacher of the nations. Schlatter[2] himself only partly understands the Resurrec-

---

[1] *The New Testament and Rabbinic Judaism* (1956), pp. 206–23.
[2] *Op. cit.* p. 797.

tion when, in a succinct phrase, he writes: 'Mit stärkster Energie spricht Mat. aus, daß das Ziel des Verkehrs Jesu mit den Jüngern die Erneuerung ihrer Sendung war'; he does not go on to note that an important purpose of their 'sending' is that they should *teach*. The Risen Lord continues his authoritative teaching through his emissaries. It is not impossible that Matthew's final insistence at the very end of his Gospel upon this fact is directed against 'Gnostics', who regarded the commandments lightly, but it is equally understandable as part of Matthew's essential understanding of the Christian message, which did not need any polemic incentive to call it forth. The authority of the Risen Lord is of a kind with that of the historical Jesus. That this is so has been recognized not only by those who have traced the concept of authority throughout the whole of Matthew, but also by those who have connected xxviii. 18 particularly with xi. 25 ff., where, as we shall indicate below, there is no need to trace Gnostic undertones, and where, significantly, Schlatter himself finds none.

On the evidence adduced by Schlatter, therefore, the anti-Gnostic character of Matthew cannot be urged. But is there other evidence to make this credible? Do the references to the false Christs and false teachers in the Gospel justify Schlatter's position?[1] The false prophets are mentioned in the following:

(*a*) Matt. vii. 15 ff.:

Beware of false prophets, who come to you in sheep's clothing but inwardly are ravenous wolves. You will know them by their fruits. Are grapes gathered from thorns, or figs from thistles? So, every sound tree bears good fruit, but the bad tree bears evil fruit. A sound tree cannot bear evil fruit, nor can a bad tree bear good fruit. Every tree that does not bear good fruit is cut down and thrown into the fire. Thus you will know them by their fruits.

The verse vii. 15 is probably from M or is the work of the Evangelist. The verses following have parallels in Luke and Q where they are concerned with reality in personal religion. Matthew has used them for ecclesiastical purposes to suggest criteria for the false prophets. Who are the false prophets? There are three possibilities. Roman Catholic scholars find in them either a reference to Pharisees or to some other 'false' Jewish teachers contemporary with Jesus. Thus Lagrange[2] points out that Jesus often reproached the Pharisees for their hypocrisy, etc., as in xxiii. 26 ff. He rejects the objection to his view that the Pharisees could not be accused of offering a broad and easy way (vii. 13 f.), by claiming, rightly,

---

[1] So also Bacon, Weiss. 　　　　　　　 [2] *Op. cit. ad rem.*

that vii. 13–14 do not govern vii. 15 ff. To the objection that the Pharisees did not pose as prophets, he rejoins that the term 'false prophets' does not necessarily retain here its Old Testament significance, and that the Pharisees contemporary with Jesus might well play the role of the false prophets of the Old Testament.

But this last is not convincing. That the role of prophet could be assumed by Pharisees, in any sense, is unlikely: Pharisaism was too aware of the historic cessation of prophecy for this to be the case. In Matt. xxiii. 29 where they are set over against prophets and just men, the Pharisees are not termed false prophets, but 'hypocrites'. (Failing the term ὑποκριταί in this connexion surely Matthew would have used ψευδοδι-δάσκαλοι not ψευδοπροφῆται of them.)[1] What makes Lagrange's view even more difficult is that the false prophets concerned can easily be taken for good teachers: they are like lambs. This deception more befits a false Christian than either a Pharisee or any other kind of Jewish 'false prophet', who could not so easily deceive. We have to deal here with false *Christian* prophets, whose outward conduct belies their nature, which is one of lawlessness (ἀνομία) and unrighteousness (ἀδικία). This appears more likely still if we identify the false prophets of vii. 15 with those who cry 'Lord, Lord' in vii. 21 ff. This identification is probably correct in view of the total context and especially of the use of προεφητεύ-σαμεν in vii. 22. Matthew has taken the Q material and used it for an ecclesiastical end. Verse vii. 15 was suggested to him by M as a fitting introduction to teaching on false prophets in the Church.

But allowing this to be so, is there any justification for seeing Gnostic heretics behind such false prophets? Hardly, because it is the quality of the life of the false prophets and their pretensions, not so much their gnosis, which would be referred to perhaps as teaching, that is condemned. There is no reason for finding any specifically Gnostic reference here.

(b) We meet false prophets again in xxiv. 11, 24. In xxiv. 11 the term occurs in isolation: the false prophets are a mark of the End. McNeile finds here 'a Divinely intended' raising up of false prophets.[2] The appearance of these may here reflect the actual situation of the Church with which Matthew is concerned or may merely be part of the furniture of apocalyptic, a stock-in-trade of eschatological prediction. That the

---

[1] Pharisaism tended to frown on prophecy, see *P.R.J.*[2] pp. 211–13; also E. Urbach, 'Law and Prophecy', *Tarbiz*, XXIII (1958), 1–25; N. N. Glatzer, 'A Study of Talmudic Interpretation of Prophecy', *Journal of Religion* (January 1946), pp. 115–37.

[2] Commentary on *The Gospel according to St Matthew*, ad rem.

former is more probably the case appears from the fact that the passage is found only in Matt. xxiv. 9–13, and is inserted here in Matthew with the specific needs of his Church in view. That he is thinking of false prophets within the Church would seem to be substantiated by xxiv. 24 not only by the fact that it is the elect who are led astray by them, although this might also be the work of non-Christian false prophets, but also by the juxtaposition of false prophets with false Christs: false Christs, unlike Antichrist, could only arise within the Church. But both in xxiv. 11 and xxiv. 24 the indications are too vague to pin down the false prophets precisely to Gnostics.[1]

(c) Equally difficult is it to identify precisely who are meant in xxiv. 5: 'For many will come in my name, saying, "I am the Christ", and they will lead many astray.' The parallels in Mark xiii. 6 and Luke xxi. 8 omit the reference to 'the Christ'. Matthew we may accordingly assume is particularly concerned with some claims to Messiahship. Is it possible to connect Gnostics with such claims? To judge by Simon Magus this cannot have been the case. Acts deals with him very briefly and reports no Messianic claim that he made. The bitterness expressed towards him, however, is so deep that we must assume that Simon's influence was more than our Jewish and Christian sources suggest. But we cannot connect him with the false Christs of Matthew. Irenaeus' account of him, like that in Acts, does not suggest this in any way. No claim made by Simon suggests that he thought of himself as the Christ, nor does he appear in the name of Christ. Had Matthew been directly concerned with Simon Magus in such a passage as xxiv. 5 his reference would have been more explicit. Irenaeus does make use of vii. 15 and x. 26 in his discussion of the Gnostics, as he does of the parable of the Lost Sheep, but never of xxiv. 5.[2] The nature of Gnosticism, if the understanding of it as a kind of compensation for the failure of eschatology be anywhere near the truth, would further make it immune to Messianic claims.[3] Certainly there is not sufficient ground for tracing to it the 'false Christs' of Matthew.

It is a familiar fact that until the rise of Bar Kokba in the reign of Hadrian (117–38) there is no known claim to Messiahship in our period. The Theudas and Judas mentioned in Acts v. 36 ff., v. 37 respectively may have been Messianic claimants, but we have no evidence for this. This

---

[1] Compare now F. V. Filson, *The Gospel According to St Matthew* (1960), pp. 12 ff.

[2] *Against Heresies*, I, 2.

[3] See, for example, F. C. Burkitt, *op. cit. ad rem*; R. M. Grant, *Gnosticism and Early Christianity* (1959).

it was that led Graetz[1] to connect Matt. xxiv. 4 ff. directly with the rising of Bar Kokba, a position which well agrees with the heightened Apocalypticism of Matthew, and gives added relevance to the emphasis in Matthew on peace as in the *SM* and xxvi. 52 ('Then Jesus said to him, "Put your sword back in its place; for all who take the sword will perish by the sword"'). The whole section xxvi. 52–4 is peculiar to Matthew, and it acquires special pertinence had Matthew opposition to Bar Kokba in view. That there was bitterness, which led to violence, between the latter and Jewish Christians appears from Justin Martyr, *Apology*, xxxi: 'For in the Jewish war which lately raged, Barchochebas, the leader of the revolt of the Jews, gave orders that Christians alone should be led to cruel punishments, unless they would deny Jesus Christ and utter blasphemy.' But it is hardly necessary to wait till Bar Kokba's appearance to account for warnings against 'false Christs'. Thus, for example, expectation of Messianic figures in Qumran, as elsewhere, would necessitate such warnings. Some have found a point of contact with Essene expectations in the use of ταμιεῖα ('inner rooms') in Matt. xxiv. 26 ('So if they say to you, "Lo, he is in the wilderness", do not go out; if they say, "Lo, he is in the inner rooms", do not believe it') where the reference is claimed to be to the caves in the area surrounding Qumran.[2] But be this as it may, what must be recognized is that warnings against false Christs should not be interpreted as anti-Gnostic.

This conclusion is confirmed when we consider the meaning of the 'lawlessness' to which Matthew so often refers in connexion with them. Does this suggest the immorality or the amorality usually associated with Gnosticism? The term lawlessness (ἀνομία) occurs in the following passages:

(i) vii. 23:

And then will I profess unto them, I never knew you: depart from me ye that work iniquity (οἱ ἐργαζόμενοι τὴν ἀνομίαν).

[1] *History of the Jews*, Eng. trans. II (1893), 412 ff.; this position has recently been endorsed by F. C. Grant, *The Gospels* (1959), pp. 137 ff. He makes much of the change made by Matthew in the Marcan reference to the 'desolating sacrilege set up where it ought not to be', that is, to 'standing in a holy place'. He takes 'in a holy place' to refer to the holy *land*, compare Dan. xi. 16, 41. 'No longer is it the Fall of Jerusalem (as in Luke xxi. 20) or the Roman armies in Palestine—but *Antichrist*, standing in the midst of the holy land.' But it is doubtful if 'holy place' can be given such a meaning: the reference is probably to the temple in Mark and Matthew, see V. Taylor, *St Mark*, p. 512.

[2] Børge Hjerl-Hansen, 'Did Christ Know the Qumran Sect?', *Revue de Qumrân*, II (July 1959), 495 ff.

The people here condemned are Christians: they cry 'Lord, Lord'. We have previously identified them with false prophets, who are here shown to have prophesied, exorcized demons, performed miracles, in the name of Christ. Nevertheless they are workers of 'lawlessness'. That it is not their attitude to the Jewish Law that is in question appears not only from the fact that they are Christians, but also from the reading in the Lucan parallel which has ἀδικία. Even though it may be admitted that Luke, writing for Gentiles, may have preferred ἀδικία as a more natural term for such readers, nevertheless, the strictly legal undertone of ἀνομία should not be pressed here, as it cannot be elsewhere in the New Testament. What constitutes the lawlessness of the false prophets is their failure to do the will of God, to obey the demands (τοὺς λόγους τούτους: vii. 24) of the Father revealed by Jesus (vii. 21). There is a law other than the Jewish to which Christians are to submit and obedience to which alone is the condition of entry into the Kingdom: it is the law of ἀγάπη. (Note in xxiv. 12 the decline of this is explicitly connected with ἀνομία.)

The problem which emerges here is clear. It can be illustrated from Paul. At the close of a passage dealing with his work as a preacher of the Gospel, Paul recognized that it was possible for him to preach to others and yet himself be found wanting. And this dread possibility, which re-echoes the warnings of Matt. vii. 15 ff., spurs the Apostle on to greater efforts in self-discipline (1 Cor. ix. 27). Similarly the interest shown in the vicissitudes of Peter's career,[1] as a Christian, point to the same concern, which was only accentuated, but not created, by the problem of the lapsed Christians at a later date. Doubtless in the earliest days of the Church, as ever since, the conditions of entry into the Kingdom would be much discussed in the light of the manifold discrepancy between the *essential* nature of those who outwardly performed Christian service in preaching, exorcism, miracle, etc., and the faith they professed. This problem became extremely acute with the emergence of Gnosticism, but it marked the more orthodox life of the Church also,[2] and it had emerged at a very early date in the early Pauline and Palestinian churches, so that there is no need to call in the Gnostic menace to account for it. Benoit has compared this section of Matthew with 1 Cor. xiii.[3] But it is significant

---

[1] See J. Wagenmann, *Die Stellung des Paulus neben den Zwölf* (1926), *ad rem.*

[2] Compare J. Schniewind, *Das Evangelium nach Matthäus* (1956), p. 104.

[3] See, for example, P. P. Benoit, *La Sainte Bible, Saint Matthieu* (1950), p. 137 nn.

that there is no reference to the knowledge which puffeth up in Matthew, a reference which might easily have been introduced had Matthew been specifically concerned with Gnosticism.

There is, moreover, a further point to notice. As in Luke, so in Matthew, but in a more emphatic form, owing to the introduction of the phrase ἐν ἐκείνη τῇ ἡμέρᾳ, the reference to false prophets is eschatological: they are a mark of the End, and, since this is a common bit of apocalyptic furniture,[1] they need not be taken to apply necessarily to any specific brand of false prophets such as the Gnostics might be understood to be. This eschatological reference also occurs in the next two passages we note.

(ii) xiii. 41:

The Son of Man shall send forth his angels, and they shall gather out of his Kingdom all things that offend, and them which do iniquity (πάντα τὰ σκάνδαλα καὶ τοὺς ποιοῦντας τὴν ἀνομίαν).

This forms part of Matthew's interpretation of the Parable of the Wheat and the Tares. The tares he equates with 'the children of the wicked one', sown by the enemy, the devil, and these are further defined as σκάνδαλα and as τοὺς ποιοῦντας τὴν ἀνομίαν. The intention of Matthew is clear: it is to point out that the Church contains good and bad members, but that no attempt is to be made at their separation before the final judgement. Here again is a mark of the End, as is usually the case in Jewish apocalyptic, but it is not necessarily to be connected with Gnosticism.

(iii) xxiv. 12:

And because iniquity (τὴν ἀνομίαν) shall abound, the love of many shall wax cold (ψυγήσεται ἡ ἀγάπη τῶν πολλῶν).

Here again the reference is eschatological. The 'lawlessness' is to break out among many in the Church: it is connected with the emergence of false prophets and results in the cooling of ἀγάπη, that is, of that obedience to the will of the Father revealed in the words of Christ. But, as was

---

[1] See, for example, the signs of the coming of the Messiah in M. Sotah ix. 15. Where R. Eliezer (A.D. 80–120), a contemporary of Matthew probably, declares: 'Since the day that the Temple was destroyed the Sages began to be like school teachers.... On whom can we stay ourselves?—on our Father in heaven. With the footprints of the Messiah presumption shall increase and dearth reach its height;... the empire shall fall into heresy and there shall be none to utter reproof. The council-chamber shall be given to fornication.... The wisdom of the Scribes shall become insipid and they that shun sin shall be deemed contemptible, and truth shall nowhere be found....'

previously pointed out, there is nothing to connect this specifically with Gnosticism, nor again, it must be emphasized, does ἀνομία have a strictly legal connotation: it is rather, as we saw, connected with a decline in ἀγάπη. Does it, like ἀγάπη, refer to an inner disposition of the will rather than to some failure in outward observances? This would seem to be the case in our next passage.

(iv) xxiii. 28:

Even so ye also outwardly appear righteous unto men, but within ye are full of hypocrisy (ὑποκρίσεως) and iniquity (ἀνομίας).

Notice particularly that the charge of lawlessness (ἀνομία) is here laid against Scribes and Pharisees who are exceedingly zealous for the observance of the Law. (The charge of ἀνομία against such—if ἀνομία has any legal connotation—could not but be slightly paradoxical.) But although their outward acts make them appear to be righteous (δίκαιοι), like tombs washed white outside but hiding inside the putrid decay of death, their inward state is one of hypocrisy and 'lawlessness' (ἀνομία). Here again, then, ἀνομία refers not to any outward conduct but to an inner state, a condition of the will, as in xxiv. 12. Here, in the nature of the case, there can be no question either of a polemic against Gnosticism or against anti-legalism in any strict sense. Those guilty of ἀνομία here, as in xxiv. 12; xiii. 41, are contrasted with those who are δίκαιοι (and the same contrast emerges by implication in xxiii. 29), much as the ἄδικοι are contrasted with the δίκαιοι in v. 45, where the ἄδικοι and the δίκαιοι are parallel to the πονηροί and the ἀγαθοί.

Our survey of passages dealing with ἀνομία is now complete. For Matthew the term does not seem, primarily at least, to have reference to the Jewish Law. It may, indeed, be completely devoid of any 'legal' connotation and merely signifies sin in a general sense. It may be that the use of the term indicates that Matthew regards such sin as a breaking of a law—not the Jewish Law—but the Law which is God's will revealed in the words of Jesus. This, as we saw, seems to be the sense in vii. 23 and the close relation between ἀνομία and ἀγάπη (xxiv. 12) supports this. Matthew may have recognized a kind of Christian 'law' of love which constituted God's will, inner and outward disobedience to which is ἀδικία. But there is no indication that he is thereby combating any Gnostic denial of all legal restraint. Failure to recognize and obey the true will of God is ἀνομία for Matthew both among the Scribes and Pharisees and in the Church, and such failure in the Church, which meant a decline in ἀγάπη, he interpreted as a sign of the End. His understanding of it is rooted in apocalyptic tradition not in anti-Gnostic polemic.[1]

Before we leave the discussion of Matthew and Gnosis, a final passage, Matt. xi. 25–30, has to be considered:

At that time Jesus declared, 'I thank thee, Father, Lord of heaven and earth, that thou hast hidden these things from the wise and understanding and revealed them to babes; yea, Father, for such was thy gracious will. All things have been delivered to me by my Father; and no one knows the Son except the Father, and no one knows the Father except the Son and any one to whom the Son chooses to reveal him. Come to me, all who labour and are heavy-laden, and I will give you rest. Take my yoke upon you, and learn from me; for I am gentle and lowly in heart, and you will find rest for your souls. For my yoke is easy, and my burden is light.

---

[1] A survey of the passages where ἀνομία occurs elsewhere in the New Testament confirms that its strictly 'legal' connotation should not be pressed. In Rom. iv. 7 ἀνομίαι, which seem to refer to sins in a broad sense, are in parallelism with ἁμαρτίαι. In Rom. vi. 19 ἀνομία is set over against ἁγιασμόν: here it is comparable to ἀκαθαρσία, there being no legal nuance to it except in so far as it designates the violation of the moral law. So too in Titus ii. 14 the words ἵνα λυτρώσηται ἡμᾶς ἀπὸ πάσης ἀνομίας καὶ καθαρίσῃ ἑαυτῷ λαὸν περιούσιον, ζηλωτὴν καλῶν ἔργων suggest by implication that ἀνομία is ἀκαθαρσία: the necessity for cleansing (is it by baptism?) from ἀνομία either points to a kind of inner state of corruption or to the need to be purified from the stains of the unredeemed life. It is the Christian as such, not any Gnostics or similar heretics, who need to be thus purified: there is no trace of Jewish legalism in the use of ἀνομία here: the cleansing achieved by Christ issues in active moral earnestness. There may indeed be a contrast intended between ζηλωτὴς καλῶν ἔργων and the Judaizers who were ζηλωταὶ τοῦ νόμου (Acts xxi. 20; compare Gal. i. 14). In any case ἀνομία refers not to the Law but to failure to perform καλὰ ἔργα. Similarly in 2 Cor. vi. 14 and Heb. i. 9 ἀνομία is opposed to δικαιοσύνη in general, while in Heb. x. 17 ἀνομιῶν and ἁμαρτιῶν are probably roughly synonymous. Of particular interest, in view of our treatment of ἀνομία in Matthew, is its occurrence in 2 Thessalonians. Associated with the rebellion (ἀποστασία, 2 Thess. ii. 3) which precedes the End, an apocalyptic event whose precise nature eludes us, is the expectation of the revealing of the Lawless One (καὶ ἀποκαλυφθῇ ὁ ἄνθρωπος τῆς ἁμαρτίας [ἀνομίας], ὁ υἱὸς τῆς ἀπωλείας...). The manuscripts are divided here. Frame, in the I.C.C., accepts the reading ἀνομίας as does Neil, in the Moffatt Commentary, but the simple fact that ἀνομίας in itself could be changed to ἁμαρτίας shows that the two terms are largely interchangeable (compare 1 John iii. 4). There is a close connexion between the advent of the Lawless One and the Advent of the Christ, but we need not, for our purposes, decide exactly who or what is meant by the Lawless One. Sufficiently significant is it for us that ἀνομία in some form or other is a well defined element in New Testament apocalyptic speculation. The Matthaean usage conforms to that of the New Testament in general: it was not aimed at Gnosticism but rooted in a tradition of apocalyptic speculation (compare with our conclusion, C. Ryder Smith, *The Biblical Doctrine of Sin* (1953), ad rem).

This has been claimed to reflect a Hellenistic milieu, similar to that whence the Johannine literature emerged, and to present Jesus as a Mystagogue, the purveyor of a new gnosis. Matthew meets Gnosticism, therefore, on its own terms.[1] But such an approach to Matt. xi. 25–30 is unnecessary. Attempts to connect it with elements in Judaism have been rewarding, that is, with Ecclus. li. 17, 51 and with Daniel,[2] and it is not necessary to go outside the tradition of Judaism to account for its form and content. While full recognition must be given to the emphasis on the filial relationship between Jesus and the Father,[3] the nature of the knowledge in which this issues can only be fully apprehended when the pericope is treated, not as an isolated passage, but as an integral part of its context. The clue to it rests on the interpretation of ταῦτα 'these things', which have been revealed in xi. 25. They refer, not to an esoteric 'gnosis', but to those events and their significance dealt with in xi. 2 ff., that is, with the ἔργα τοῦ Χριστοῦ.[4] What has been revealed to the Son is the significance of his activity as eschatological. This makes it clear that we have to deal in Matt. xi. 25–30 not with Hellenistic gnosis but with the kind of 'gnosis' revealed in the DSS.[5] If this be the case, then we can safely conclude that at no point in Matthew is a direct encounter with Gnosticism reflected. The circles within which Matthew emerged were not particularly faced with the problems of syncretism, such as lie behind Gnosticism, and its attendant dangers, but with typical Jewish eschatological expectations, albeit in a Christian key. This is another way of claiming that the concern of Matthew is not with peripheral, esoteric movements in Judaism and

[1] For bibliographical details, see my article '"Knowledge" in the Dead Sea Scrolls and Matt. xi. 25–30', in *H.T.R.* XLVI (1953), 113–29; C. Colpe, *op. cit.* p. 28.

[2] *P.R.J.*[2] pp. 156 ff.; A. Feuillet, *R.B.* LXII (1955), 161 ff. on 'Jésus et la Sagesse Divine d'après les Évangiles Synoptiques'; L. Cerfaux, *Ephemerides Theologicae Lovanienses*, XXX (1954), 740–6; XXXI (1955), 331–42, on 'Les Sources Scripturaires de Matt. xi. 25–30', and *N.T.S.* II (May 1956), 238 ff., on 'La Connaissance des Secrets du Royaume d'après Matt. xiii. 11 et parallèles'; W. Grundmann, *N.T.S.* V (April 1959), 188 ff.

[3] *P.R.J.*[2] *ibid.*

[4] *H.T.R.* XLVI, 113–29, at the end; so F. V. Filson, *op. cit.* (1953), pp. 140 ff.

[5] See further on this Bo Reicke, 'Traces of Gnosticism in the DSS', in *N.T.S.* I, 2 (1954). I should recognize more strongly a proto-Gnostic element in the DSS, if I could be persuaded that the material in DSD iv. 2 ff. is concerned with man's origin and nature. But Iranian influences are clearly more present here than strictly Gnostic ones. It should be recognized, however, that by the first century Iranian and Hellenistic concepts had been so assimilated by Judaism that they had fused and cannot be split: they had become the common property of a 'syncretistic' Judaism. See on this P. P. Benoit on 'Qumrân et le Nouveau Testament', *N.T.S.* VII (July 1961), 276 ff., an excellently balanced statement. On the specific point referred to, see p. 278.

Christianity, characterized by incipient Gnosticism, expressed in 'myths and endless genealogies' (1 Tim. i. 4), but with the Gospel as it confronted the main currents of Judaism in rabbinism and apocalyptic and Essenism.

2. *The Dead Sea Sect*

The possible influence of the sectarians on Matthew raises questions of eschatology, ecclesiology, Christology and ethics, all of which are inter-related and so cannot strictly be isolated the one from the other.

Our treatment may begin with the work of Stendahl,[1] who concentrated his attention on the so-called formula quotations of the Gospel, which occur in i. 23; ii. 6, 15, 18, 23; iv. 15–16; viii. 17; xii. 18–21; xiii. 35. They all contain the formula ἵνα πληρωθῇ τὸ ῥηθὲν ὑπὸ κυρίου διὰ τοῦ προφήτου κ.τ.λ., whence their designation. An examination of these leads Stendahl to the conclusion that 'Matthew wrote Greek and rendered the Old Testament quotations along the lines of various traditions and methods of interpretation. This gives proof of a targumizing procedure which demands much of the knowledge and outlook of the Scribes. In distinc-tion from the rest of the Synoptics and the Epistles, with what seems to be their self-evident use of the LXX, Matthew was capable of having, and did have, the authority to create a rendering of his own.'[2] Following particularly on the work of Brownlee[3] and Roberts,[4] Stendahl claims that Matthew emerged from a school of interpreters who employed methods of interpretation very similar to those followed by the sect at Qumran. Without a detailed presentation of the evidence brought forward in its favour, it is not legitimate to criticize this position.[5] But we may ask two questions. First, whether the method of interpretation revealed in the formula quotation is to be so sharply distinguished from that found in the rest of the New Testament as to constitute a special peculiarity of Matthew. And, secondly, whether there is not a considerable difference between the formula quotations and the *pesher* in use at Qumran. In the former, the 'historical' event seems to determine the incidence and nature

---

[1] *The School of Matthew* (1954).   [2] *Ibid.* p. 127.

[3] W. H. Brownlee, *The Dead Sea Habakkuk Midrash and the Targum Jonathan* (Duke Divinity School, 1953).

[4] B. J. Roberts, 'The Dead Sea Scrolls and the Old Testament', *Bulletin of John Rylands Library*, XXXIV (1951/2), 366–87; XXXVI (1953/4), 75–96.

[5] For this see B. Gärtner, *Studia Theologica*, on 'The Habakkuk Commentary (DSH) and the Gospel of Matthew', VIII (1954), 1–24; S. Kistemaker, *The Psalms Citations in the Epistle to the Hebrews* (Amsterdam, 1961), p. 71; J. A. Fitzmyer, *N.T.S.* VII (July 1961), 297 ff., especially p. 331.

of the quotation, which serves as a closure to a pericope, that is, the scriptural quotation subserves the event. In the latter, the opposite is the case: the scriptural text is normative for the event, not a commentary upon this, but its ground.[1] As in all spheres, it was its Christological orientation that governed or rather stimulated the exegesis of the Christian community. Nevertheless, Stendahl has helped us to understand the scriptural methodology of Matthew in its proper setting. This means that he has brought into prominence the essentially eschatological climate which the Sect at Qumran and the Christian sect shared. However much they differed from each other, their immediately eschatological concern set the Essenes at Qumran and Christians apart from Pharisees and Sadducees and constituted them strictly as 'sects'.[2] Does the eschatological sect at Qumran illumine Matthew in any way? This question can be answered only by facing three questions, two of which are broad and one more specific. For convenience, we arrange these as follows. First, are there elements in the Matthaean ecclesiology which suggest influences from Qumran or, at least, similar to those at work there? Secondly, does the figure of Jesus in Matthew recall the Teacher of Righteousness and that intentionally? And, thirdly, can we point to specific points of contact between the sectarian sources and Matthew?

(i) Let us begin with the first question. Allowing for inevitable differences caused by the necessarily Christological orientation of Matthew, can it be held that its ecclesiology is parallel to the understanding of itself cherished by the Sect? Setting aside those elements in the Matthaean doctrine of the Church which are largely common to the rest of the New Testament,[3] three emphases emerge in Matthew which might suggest this, namely: on 'perfection' as the goal of the community, on 'knowledge' as the means to this goal, and, finally, on a 'true' interpretation of the Law as its ground.

First, in two passages the term 'perfect' (τέλειος) appears. Thus v. 48 reads 'You, therefore, must be perfect, as your heavenly Father is

[1] It is not always easy to affirm this, as, for example, in DSD viii. 13–15, but on the whole the position indicated in the text seems justified: the separation and departure into the wilderness seem, even here, to be dictated by the text, though the meaning of the text is given in 15 as 'studying the Torah'.

[2] This is well brought out by K. Stendahl in *The Scrolls and the New Testament*, pp. 7 ff.

[3] What these are will be apparent from R. N. Flew, *Jesus and His Church* (1938); G. Johnston, *The Doctrine of the Church in the New Testament* (1943), *et al.*

perfect', where the term for perfect is τέλειος. This recurs in xix. 21 where, in reply to the rich young man's question, 'What do I still lack?' Jesus said to him, 'If you would be perfect, go, sell what you possess and give to the poor, and you will have treasure in heaven; and come, follow me'. In both instances, the introduction of the term 'perfect' is peculiar to Matthew. Thus in the parallel to v. 48 in Luke vi. 36 we have οἰκτίρμονες, so that τέλειοι in v. 48 is a deliberate change.[1] So too in both the Marcan and Lucan parallels to xix. 21 the term 'perfect' is not introduced. Are we then to assume that Matthew has a peculiar interest in this term? Here caution is necessary. Such a peculiar interest could only be established if it were proved that 'perfect' in v. 48 and xix. 21 has the same connotation. If it differs in meaning in the two places, then the significance of the term for Matthew cannot be so much pressed.

The following are the possible positions:

(1) To regard the concept of perfection in v. 48 and xix. 21 as Greek, xix. 21 denoting two grades of achievement. In this case it is superfluous to attempt to connect these verses with Qumran (Wellhausen).[2]

(2) To distinguish the meanings of 'perfect' in v. 48 and xix. 21, but nevertheless to regard both as Semitic. Such is the position of Rigaux.[3] He interprets v. 48 in the light of Deut. xviii. 13 and Lev. xix. 22. The main emphasis in v. 48 is on whole-hearted devotion to the imitation of God, not in the perfection of his being, but of his ways. It is implied that there is a parallel here to the concept of 'perfection' at Qumran, although Rigaux does not make this explicit. In xix. 21 the same scholar finds a distinction between two grades of Christian commitment, an ordinary one and one of 'perfection' which implies giving away all and following Jesus ('faire partie du groupe qui suit Jésus partout').[4] Such a distinction he does not find in Qumran,[5] where all the community are perfect. On this view, only in one instance does the Matthaean treatment of perfection suggest Qumran and this can be explained in terms of the Old Testament without calling in Qumran influence at all.

(3) It is possible to go further than Rigaux and connect both v. 48 and

---

[1] See Julius Wellhausen, *Das Evangelium Matthaei* (1904), and other commentaries.

[2] Wellhausen, *ad rem.*

[3] *N.T.S.* iv (July 1958), 237–62 on 'Révélation des Mystères et Perfection à Qumrân et dans le Nouveau Testament'.

[4] *Ibid.* p. 248.

[5] *Ibid.* p. 261, 'on ne peut suffisamment souligner que tous les moines à Qumrân sont des parfaits'.

xix. 21 with a milieu like that at Qumran.[1] There are parallels to the idea of
perfection as the aim of the community in v. 48 in DSD i. 9, 13; xi. 2;
viii. 1, 10*b*, 26; ix. 2, 5, 6, 8, 9, 19; x. 21 and in DSD viii. 9 the Sect is
described as 'a house of perfection'. Is there, however, a parallel to xix. 21
where two orders of commitment have been differentiated? Certainly
degrees of perfection are recognized in the Scrolls. Thus DSD v. 24
implies that there is a yearly examination to ascertain the degree of
perfection achieved by the various members: 'And so that they shall have
an examination of their spirit and their works year by year, so as to
elevate each one according to his understanding and the perfection of his
way' (Burrows's translation).

ולהיות פוקדם את רוחם ומעשיהם שנה בשנה להעלות איש לפי שכלו ותום)

(....דרכו.

Compare with this DSD ix. 2; x. 21. But these passages do not imply a
twofold order, as in v. 48 all the members of the Sect, not only a few, are
called to perfection. However, there is another possibility. It is noteworthy that in the DSS distinctions are drawn between the novitiates in
the community and those who have actually professed membership (see
DSD i. 11–12; v. 2). The change from the novitiate to full profession
coincided with the abandoning of all property, not to the literally poor,
but to the community, which, in another sense, constituted 'the poor'
and also 'the perfect'. Is Matthew thinking of some such distinction in
xix. 21? The interpretation of perfection in xix. 21 we described cannot be
regarded as convincing because the distinction which Matthew introduces
is that between the merely good and the perfect, which is not necessarily
the same as that between the novitiate[2] and the professed, unless the latter
is suggested in the words 'and come, follow me'. The crucial question is
whether, as has been most commonly assumed, Matthew does contemplate
two orders of Christians here. This is at first sight the natural way in
which to take xix. 21, especially since it follows xix. 17, where the phrase
'*if you would enter life*' is contrasted with '*if you would be perfect*' in xix. 21.
But this 'natural' interpretation has recently been very forcibly challenged
in the position to which we turn next.

(4) The term τέλειος in xix. 21 is to be understood in the light of v. 48.
Not two orders of morality are to be understood in xix. 16 ff., but the
radicalizing of the moral demand in xix. 17. Just as the command to love
one's neighbour in v. 43 f. is radicalized in v. 48 in terms of perfection, so

---

[1] See my article in *H.T.R.* xlvi (1953).   [2] *Ibid.*

it occurs in xix. 19 to be radicalized in xix. 21 also in the same terms. Perfection in both passages is rooted in the new interpretation of the Law which Jesus has brought. Thus there is a certain similarity between the emphasis on perfection in Qumran and in Matthew. In the former also the community as a whole is called to a perfection rooted in a particular interpretation of the Law; the difference between the perfection demanded by Matthew and that at Qumran, was rooted in Jesus' interpretation of the Law in terms of ἀγάπη. Qumran demanded more obedience, Matthew deeper.[1]

Two difficulties to this understanding of xix. 21 might be thought to present themselves. First, the immediate context of τέλειος in v. 48 suggests not so much perfection in terms of a new interpretation of the Law as of the imitation of God, while it is difficult to think of 'Go sell all that thou hast and give to the poor', a counsel of abandon far removed from the caution of the Law, as intended as an interpretation of the latter; it far exceeds any possible legal calculation of less or more.[2] But this objection cannot be pressed, because the keeping of the Law in the tradition of Judaism is itself rooted in the concept of the imitation of God,[3] and the kind of 'abandon' demanded in xix. 21 is in fact congruous with the 'enthusiasm' of Jesus' demand in v. 22 ff., where it is presented as an interpretation of the Law. A second objection is that this view isolates xix. 21 too much from its context in the whole of chapter xix. As we have suggested elsewhere, xix. 3–9, 10–12, 13–15 are concerned with reducing what was radical to the regulatory or possible. If xix. 21 be interpreted as recognizing two grades of morality, as it is by most commentators, then it falls naturally into the total context of chapter xix. On the other hand, if it be understood as radicalizing the demand of Jesus, it strikes an incongruous note in that chapter. Against this objection is it that while the passages referred to from xix do effect a softening of the demand of Jesus, and while xix. 23–30 do suggest that the disciples, who have left all, do constitute a special category and are to receive a special reward, none of the pericopae necessarily imply a twofold standard of morality, one ordinary and the other 'perfect', so that the difference between the radicalism of xix. 21 and the rest of the chapter should not be pressed. On the other hand, full force must be given to the fact that

---

[1] See Bornkamm, Barth and Held, *Auslegung und Überlieferung im Matthäus-evangelium* (1960), pp. 54–154, the most profound of recent works on Matthew.

[2] This is part of the 'enthusiasm' of the Early Christian movement and of Jesus.

[3] *H.T.R.* XLVI (1953), 115.

nowhere does Matthew elsewhere lend support to the view that there are two types of Christians. Nowhere does Matthew reveal any emphasis on poverty and ascetic rejection of wealth, while it is clear from v. 48 that he uses the term 'perfect' with reference to the whole community rather than to a special group within it.[1]

On the basis of v. 48 and xix. 21, therefore, it is possible to claim that, as Matthew understood it, the Christian community as a totality was called to be perfect, a 'house of perfection', in the sense that it was to conform to the interpretation of the Law given by Jesus, as were the Sectarians to that of the Teacher of Righteousness. But two factors make it difficult to allow such an emphasis in Matthaean ecclesiology. First, the possibility is not to be ruled out that any Matthaean emphasis on perfection is in conscious opposition to that urged on the Sectarians. This is not only because v. 48 follows on v. 43 which may cast, as we shall note below, a critical side-glance towards Qumran. More generally than this, whereas the Sectarians were *all* asked to obey *all* the commandments as interpreted by the Teacher of Righteousness,[2] so that a rigid uniformity could not but result, the demands issued by Jesus allowed for individual differences of endowment, as is clear from chapter xix. Moreover, these were finally understood not only in terms of obedience to the Law, as interpreted by Jesus, but in terms of following him.[3] Matthaean perfection was Christified. Only with a full awareness of these deep differences should we pass from perfection at Qumran to that in Matthew. Secondly, and this must be pressed, were the motif of perfection in any way as significant for Matthew as this suggested, and as it was at Qumran,[4] we should expect far more references to it. The occurrence of a term in two passages does not by itself enable us to reconstruct a substantial element in Matthaean ecclesiology. The term 'perfect' was not common in first-century religious usage in Judaism as applied to God;[5] but, nevertheless, unless it be particularly frequent or prominent, as it is in the Sectarian sources, but not in Matthew, it cannot be accorded any special importance.

---

[1] Rigaux recognizes a twofold morality in xix. 21, but does not note that this contradicts v. 48: *op. cit.* pp. 248 f.

[2] There are about 73 instances of 'all' in the DSD alone; compare H. Braun, *T.L.* LXXIX (1954), cols. 347 ff.

[3] This emerges in xix. 21 ff. See the emphasis in viii. 19–22 also. On ἀκολουθέω, see G. Kittel, *T.W.Z.N.T.* I, 210–15.

[4] Rigaux, *op. cit.* p. 237, finds in the DSS 'une préoccupation qui semble à première vue commune: procurer aux adeptes la perfection'.

[5] See J. Dupont, *Les Béatitudes*, p. 153, n. 2.

Unless, therefore, there be other evidence to support the claim that Matthew's understanding of the Church is especially illumined by Qumran, the references in v. 48 and xix. 21 to perfection must be regarded as insufficient to justify it. Is there such evidence?

This question may be answered in the affirmative on the ground that throughout Matthew there is emphasis on the Church as a community which possesses understanding, which, among many other things, included knowledge of the *true* demands of the Law. In xi. 27–30, with which we have previously dealt, Jesus in virtue of his Sonship possesses a unique knowledge of God which he teaches to those who bear his yoke. These are therefore blessed with understanding.[1] This understanding on the part of the disciples is emphasized in three ways: first, by the contrast drawn between their receptiveness and the obtuseness of the multitudes,[2] secondly, by the removal of references to failure on their part to understand Jesus, which dot the pages of Mark,[3] and, thirdly, by the insistence that understanding is a necessary prelude to faith.[4] The Church of Matthew emerges as a community called to 'perfection' through its understanding or knowledge. The nature of this knowledge, transmitted by Jesus to his disciples, has to be carefully examined. It is defined in xiii. 10 ff. as knowledge of the mysteries of the Kingdom of Heaven. The phrase τὰ μυστήρια τῆς βασιλείας τῶν οὐρανῶν is to be understood in the light of the apocalyptic tradition. The eschatological purposes of God are made known to the disciples in the work and words of Jesus. As in xi. 27–30, so in xiii. 10 ff., the terminology is best understood in terms of the book of Daniel.[5] The disciples, the νήπιοι,[6] correspond to the young men in that volume who, set over against the uncomprehending wise men, are given understanding of God's purposes. But, their illumination has come not through the interpretation of visions given in the night, but through Jesus. Moreover, this understanding, as is the case with the young men of Daniel, is a gift of divine origin. Not the result of what we should call

---

[1] Bornkamm, Barth and Held, *op. cit.*   [2] *Ibid.*   [3] *Ibid.*   [4] *Ibid.*

[5] See L. Cerfaux on 'Les Sources Scripturaires de Matt. xi. 25–30', in *Ephemerides Theologicae Lovanienses*, XXX (1954), 740–6; XXXI (1955), 331–42 and in *N.T.S.* II (May 1956), 238 ff. on 'La Connaissance des Secrets du Royaume d'après Matt. xiii. 11 et parallèles'. Contrast A. Feuillet in *R.B. ibid.*; W. Grundmann, *N.T.S.* V (April 1959), 188 ff.; Légasse, *R.B.* LXVII (1960), p. 338.

[6] On the νήπιοι, see Cerfaux, the first item cited above. E. Werner, *The Sacred Bridge* (1959), takes νήπιος here and in xxi. 15, 16 as the equivalent of the 'ammei-haaretz'. To him the contrast here would seem to be between the scholars of Jerusalem and the ignorant Galileans—'the hill-billies', as he calls them, see pp. 18 and 42, n. 3. F. Gils, *Jésus Prophète* (1957), pp. 78–9, follows Cerfaux.

intellectual comprehension, as such, although this is not precluded, this means openness to the meaning of the deeds and words of Jesus.[1] The content of the 'knowledge' demanded of the disciples—the value of the Kingdom as the pearl of great price (xiii. 44–5), the significance of the Person of Jesus, as Messiah, for that Kingdom (xiv. 33; xvi. 16), the process of inclusion in and exclusion from it (xiii. 37–43; xxv. 31–46), the suffering of the Son of Man—on all this we need not enlarge.

The question which concerns us is whether the emphasis on under-standing connects Matthew with the Sectarians. Only in connexion with moral obedience does the term 'perfect' explicitly occur in Matthew, but it is implied that this rests on the true understanding of the Law as given by Jesus. The same collocation of intense moral earnestness with an emphasis on knowledge occurs in the Scrolls. Rigaux's description of perfection at Qumran is significant: 'En résumé,' he writes, 'nous avons rencontré dans les constituantes de la perfection qumrânienne un élément moral, l'obéissance et la marche dans la voie, un élément mystique, c'est-à-dire dépassant les catégories humaines du savoir, du vouloir et des actes, la purification et le don de l'esprit saint, enfin un élément gnostique, la con-naissance du plan de Dieu et de la Loi de Dieu, aboutissant à une révéla-tion de l'activité de Dieu et des destinées éternelles de l'homme. L'esprit saint est médiateur de connaissance des mystères.'[2] There can be little doubt that we are confronted with similar conceptions in Matthew. The perfection it demands is obedience to the true interpretation of the Law. But such a true interpretation has only been made available by a revelation of the mysteries of the Kingdom and of the Law to the disciples by Jesus. Thus, while on the basis of v. 48 and xix. 21 alone, it would be erroneous to detect any peculiarly marked similarity between the ecclesiology of Matthew and the understanding of itself entertained by the Sect, in the light of the total emphases in Matthew on the combination of under-standing, obedience and perfection this may not be so. The Church in Matthew is an eschatological community dedicated to a perfection based on a revealed knowledge of the purposes of God and of his true intent in the Law, as was the Sect at Qumran, except that Jesus was even more central for the former than was the Teacher of Righteousness for the latter.

(ii) This brings us to the second question posed above on the similarity which has been detected between the figure of Jesus in Matthew and the

---

[1] See my article, *H.T.R.* XLVI (1953).   [2] *Op. cit.* pp. 240–1.

Teacher of Righteousness, also called the Interpreter of the Law, in the Qumran sect. The latter defined the demands of the Law more exhaustively and more stringently than did even the Pharisees and urged upon the Sect radical obedience to them *all*.[1] Comparison with the Matthaean Jesus, who set before his followers a righteousness higher than that of the Pharisees, is inevitable. True, the Teacher of Righteousness did not interpret the Law in the same way as did Jesus, so that the commandments which were set before the Sect and the Church respectively were very different. Nevertheless, those commandments were marked by one common feature: they were radical, except that, if we may so put it, this radicalism was expressed in a demand for more and more obedience by Qumran (that is, it was quantitative), and for deeper and deeper obedience by Jesus (that is, his demand was qualitatively different). To determine precisely whether the Matthaean Jesus, as Messiah, has merely taken on the didactic lineaments which Judaism always expected in such an eschatological figure or whether the specific shadow of the Teacher of Righteousness has fallen on Matthew's pages as he delineated his Lord is difficult.

In any case, this last should not be over-emphasized if it is present at all. Any enlargement of the sectarian Teacher of Righteousness to the stature of Christ must be avoided: any reduction of the Matthaean Jesus to a Teacher of Righteousness rejected. The Teacher of Righteousness does emerge in certain passages as an eschatological figure with a quasi-soteriological significance.[2] But it must not be forgotten that any Messianic role assigned to him must be regarded as extremely dubious.[3] Concentration on the person and work of the Teacher of Righteousness, along with his teaching, such as we find placed by Matthew on Jesus, who is given full Messianic status, is lacking in the Sect. That means that the elements in the Matthaean figure, which recall the Teacher of Righteousness, are taken up into a larger complex in which Jesus, as the Christ, is not merely interpreter, but Saviour.

Certain factors make this clear. First, the relation of Jesus to the Christian community was very different from that of the Teacher of Righteousness to the Sect. The latter was not the *founder* of his community as was Jesus of his. The Teacher of Righteousness came to a group of people already broken in penitence and separated from the world.[4] He informed and guided this group farther in the way on which it was

---

[1] See above, p. 428, n. 1.
[3] *Ibid.*
[2] See above, pp. 152 f.
[4] CDC i. 1–12.

already set. On the other hand, Jesus called a new group into being from the people at large and in Galilee of the Gentiles. He was a founder as the Teacher of Righteousness was not. Secondly, although he can be understood in prophetic terms and even as having improved upon the prophetic message, the Teacher of Righteousness first appeared within the community as an Interpreter of the Law and his primary function seems to have remained that of expounding the Law and the mysteries of God and the prophets.[1] On the other hand, the Matthaean Jesus first appeared as an eschatological figure not in an already segregated 'sect' but among the multitudes, calling them to repentance and, even more, proclaiming good news before he taught them. For Matthew the title 'teacher' is not a central one:[2] not as the interpreter of the Law is Jesus most emphasized but as its fulfilment: not the substantive *pesher*, but the verbal πληρῶσαι is natural to the Evangelist's pen in connexion with Jesus, both in his words and deeds.[3] Thirdly, the difference between the Teacher of Righteousness and the Matthaean Christ can be illustrated in terms of 'faith'. The concept of faith does not expressly emerge with any frequency in the DSS. The significant passage is 1 QpHab. viii. 1–3:

פשרו על כול עושי התורה בבית יהודה אשר יצילם אל מבית המשפט בעבור
עמלם ואמנתם במורה הצדק...

At first sight this text suggests that salvation is by 'faith' in the Teacher of Righteousness[4] as a person: the claim is frequently made that האמין ב, which has as its equivalent in the New Testament πιστεύειν εἰς, implies a personal relationship. But it is clear that the members of the Sect are to be rescued by God as the 'doers of the law', because of their own labours. Thus 'faith in the Teacher of Righteousness' may here mean no more than faithfulness to his teaching, that is, to the Law as interpreted by him. There is no indication that a saving efficacy is ascribed to faith in the person of the Teacher as such. The precise nuance to be given to faith is

---

[1] See 1QpHab. vii. 4–5. The Teacher of Righteousness possesses a knowledge which surpasses that of the prophets. He knows the purposes of God in history (CDC i. 11), his words are to be received as those of the Lord (1QpH ii. 2–3). He is able to point the true way to the community. By means of *pesher* there is given a new revelation. See Rigaux, *op. cit.* pp. 246–8.

[2] See above, p. 97.

[3] iii. 15; v. 17 ff. The differences between Qumran and Jesus are strikingly listed by E. Stauffer, *Die Botschaft Jesu, Damals und Heute* (1959), pp. 13 ff. However exaggerated, his position is a corrective to any undue haste in drawing together Qumran and the Christian movement.

[4] See S. E. Johnson, *H.T.R.* xlviii, no. 3 (July 1955), 157–65.

perhaps illumined for us in CDC iii. 18–21 and vi. 2–11. The former reads:

But God in His wonderful mysteries made conciliation for their trespass and pardoned their impiety, | 'and He built them a sure house' in Israel, the like of which has not stood from ancient times even until | now. They that hold fast to it are *destined* for eternal life and all the glory of man is theirs; as | God swore to them by the hand of the prophet Ezekiel, saying 'The priests and the Levites....' (Rabin's translation.)

And vi. 2–11 reads:

'But God remembered the covenant of the forefathers', and He raised from Aaron 'men of understanding' and from Israel | 'men of wisdom', 'and He caused them to hear'; and they digged the well: 'the well which princes digged, which the nobles of the people delved | with the staff'. The Well is the Law. And those that digged it are | 'they that turned (from impiety) of Israel', who went out from the land of Judah and sojourned in the land of Damascus, | —inasmuch as God called all of them Princes, for they sought him, and their ⌐fame¬ was not rejected | by the mouth of anyone—and the Staff is the Searcher of the Law, as Isaiah said: | 'who bringeth forth a tool for his work'. And the Nobles of the People are | they that have come to dig the Well with the staffs which the Staff instituted | to walk ⌐in them¬ during the whole epoch of wickedness and without which they (or: and others than they) will not grasp ⟨instruction⟩ 'until there shall arise | he who teaches righteousness' in the end of days. (Rabin's translation.)

It is clear that the Teacher of Righteousness had an important, even essential role in the establishment of the covenant between God and the Sect. But apparently in CDC iii. 18–21 loyalty to the 'sure house' established on the work of the Teacher of Righteousness is the condition of salvation, not so much faith in his person. Through him they belong to a 'sure house'.

Such an understanding of faith recalls much in the New Testament both by way of contrast and comparison. Hab. ii was probably a focus of discussion both at Qumran and in the primitive Church.[1] In Matthew, where the concept of faith is given a significant place in the interpretation of the Church, there is much to recall the understanding of it that we find in the above sectarian passages. Thus 'faith' is an act of the will, so that πιστεύειν can be associated with θέλειν (viii. 13; xv. 28; compare ix. 29),

---

[1] Rom. i. 17; Gal. iii. 11; Heb. x. 38; Jas. ii. 14 ff. On faith in a person, see C. H. Dodd, *The Interpretation of the Fourth Gospel*, pp. 180 ff.

and denote loyalty to the revealed will of God (xxi. 32; xxiii. 23). To a considerable extent 'faith' in Matthew coincides with the אמונה of the Scrolls. But it departs from the latter also, because it becomes trust in Jesus, that is, dependence upon the person of Jesus, to which there is nothing that quite corresponds, at least in intensity, in the references to the Teacher of Righteousness in the Scrolls.[1]

Fourthly, the difference between the ethic of Qumran—the ethic of more and more obedience—and that of the *SM*—the ethic of deeper and deeper obedience—points us to the difference in status ascribed to the Teacher of Righteousness and to Jesus by Qumran and Matthew respectively. We noted above that the Teacher of Righteousness was at best only conceived as a future Messiah: and even his future Messianic status is problematic. Certainly the historical Teacher of Righteousness as such was not regarded as the Messiah, although he was an eschatological figure. But this meant that, however immediate the End was deemed to be by the Sect, it was still future.[2] Its ethic accordingly looked *to* the End but was not *of* the End: it belonged to this aeon, although it prepared for the coming aeon. Intense it was—terribly so—but, nevertheless, preparatory. On the other hand, Jesus, as Messiah, was for Matthew the One to Come who had come. In him the Messianic Age had begun. Accordingly, the moral demands of Jesus are *of* the new order: he summoned men in a *new* way. Buber has expressed this with typical force. 'Jesus...as represented by Matthew, means to summon the elect in the catastrophe of humanity to come as near to God as is made possible to it only in the catastrophe.'[3] What we find in the *SM* is not an ethic for those who expect the speedy end of the world but for those who have experienced the end of this world and the coming of the Kingdom of God.[4] Thus whatever reminiscences of the Teacher of Righteousness may be detected in Matthew they are transformed in the light of him who was the Messiah not merely the Interpreter.

We may now consider the outcome of our discussion of the first two broad questions which we posed above. Matthaean ecclesiology and Christology (in its didactic aspects) have revealed a considerable similarity to what appears in the sectarian sources. That these shared a common world of thought with Matthew is clear. Despite the differences in

---

[1] G. Barth, *Auslegung und Überlieferung*, pp. 105 ff.
[2] See K. Stendahl, *The Scrolls and the New Testament*, p. 10.
[3] *Two Types of Faith*, Eng. trans. (1951), p. 61.
[4] C. H. Dodd has made this emphasis in his many works.

details to which we drew attention, the structures of the Evangelist's thought are like theirs. But need we go further? Is the similarity to which we have referred above due merely to participation in a common milieu or must we postulate a direct sectarian influence on Matthew? In the material dealt with so far it is doubtful whether any direct connexion with the sectarians need be assumed. The common eschatological tradition, going back particularly to Daniel, and much in Jewish eschatological speculation about the Messiah as a teacher of some kind, which Matthew shared with Qumran, are sufficient to account for the similarities dealt with above. Undoubtedly Matthew shared the thought-forms of the Essenes in many ways but this need not mean that he *owed* these to them. Moreover, it cannot be sufficiently emphasized that while the thought-forms of Matthew are similar to those of Qumran, the content of his thought differs fundamentally from that of the latter, owing to the infusion of a specifically Christian element. This emerged clearly in our discussion of perfection, knowledge and ethics.

(iii) We now come to the third question which was asked above. Can we trace specific points of contact between the sectarian sources and Matthew? In the preceding pages we have emphasized the difference between the 'realized eschatology' of Matthew, that is, his conviction that the Messiah had appeared in Jesus, and the 'expectant eschatology' of the sectarians. And we can best seek to answer the question posed above by recalling that within this difference there was also a similarity between the Sect and the Church: they both lived, despite their different eschatology, in anticipation. At two stages the Essenes had had to live in terms of an interim-ethic. They had, therefore, developed a tradition of adaptation as they awaited the future. As Daube[1] has shown, the necessity for adaptation emerges elsewhere in the Old Testament and Judaism, but that among the sectarians is of peculiar interest for our purposes. Not only did it arise within the life of a Sect contemporary with and like the early Church, but, as we saw, it was also governed by eschatological conditions similar to, though not identical with, those at work within the latter. True, the dominant conviction of the early Church differed in degree from that of the Essenes. The latter had experienced the advent of an expected prophet, but not of its anticipated Messiah. On the other hand, the Church looked back to a Messiah who had already come in Jesus, in whom it discovered prophet, priest and king. This means that

[1] *J.J.S.* x, 1, 2 (1959), 1–12, on 'Concessions to sinfulness in Jewish Law'.

we should not expect always to find exact parallels in the literature of the two communities. That of the primitive Church inevitably has a Christological reference which that of the Sect lacked. And this creates differences, which will be emphasized in the course of our treatment. Nevertheless, the Christian community did not merely look to a past event: they, as did the Essenes, also looked forward to a consummation. And Matthew, who reveals a marked concentration on eschatology, seems particularly to have emphasized the immediacy of its expectations.[1] Thus the necessity to come to terms with life as it awaited a future consummation also faced the Church of Matthew. Like the Essenes, before the End came, the Church had to introduce regulations to meet the actualities of its present existence. It had, in short, to develop an interim-ethic. As we shall show in the next chapter, one way in which Matthew did this was to modify the absolute demands of Jesus by means of gemaric additions to these, which reduced what was originally radical to the regulatory. Here our concern is to inquire whether the Gospel of Matthew shows the influence of the interim-ethic and 'interim-paraenesis' revealed in the Dead Sea Scrolls. In providing guidance for his Church did Matthew draw upon a tradition similar to and even identical with that found in these documents?

It is natural to examine first those 'ecclesiastical' passages where Bultmann[2] has claimed that Matthew's peculiar understanding of the Church emerges, namely, xiii. 24–30, 47–50; xvi. 17–19; xviii. 15–20; xxviii. 18–20. We shall deal with these in an inverse order. In view of what we wrote in the preceding paragraph, the first passage xxviii. 18–20 cannot be expected to yield any exact parallel, because it is so specifically a Christian construction; so we pass on to xviii. 15–17. This reads as follows:

15 If your brother sins against you, go and tell him his fault, between you and him
16 alone. If he listens to you, you have gained your brother. But if he does not listen, take one or two others along with you, that every word may be con-
17 firmed by the evidence of two or three witnesses. If he refuses to listen to them, tell it to the church; and if he refuses to listen even to the church, let him be to you as a Gentile and a tax collector. (RSV.)

The following are the pertinent passages from the Manual of Discipline and the Zadokite Fragment. From the former, v. 25–vi. 1:

One shall not speak to his brother in anger or in resentment, or with a stiff neck or a hard heart or a wicked spirit; one shall not hate him in the folly of his heart.

[1] See, for example, F. C. Grant, *The Gospels* (1957), p. 137.
[2] *Die Synoptische Tradition*, p. 218.

In his days (Brownlee: though he shall reprove him on the very day) he shall reprove him and shall not bring upon him iniquity; and also a man shall not bring against his neighbour a word before the masters without having rebuked him before witnesses. (Translation by Millar Burrows.)

From the Zadokite Fragment, ix. 2 f.:

And as to that which He said: 'Thou shalt not take vengeance nor bear rancour against the children of thy people'—⌐every⌐ | man of the ⌐members⌐ | of the covenant who brings against his neighbour an accusation (lit.: word) without reproving before witnesses | and brings it up when he grows angry or tells his elders to make him contemptible, he is one who takes vengeance and bears rancour | —although it is expressly written (lit.: not is written but): 'HE taketh vengeance on HIS adversaries, and HE reserveth wrath to HIS enemies' |—*namely*, if he held his peace at him from one day to the next, and spoke about him when he got angry with him, ⌐and⌐ it was in a capital matter | that he testified against him; because he did not carry out the commandment of God, who said to him, 'Thou shalt surely | reprove thy neighbour and not bear sin because of him.' (Rabin's translation.)

xiv. 21:

[And he that bears rancour to his neighbour with]out justification [shall be punished] for [one] year (...). (Rabin's translation.)

The most pertinent passage is the first given above from the Manual of Discipline v. 25–vi. 1. There are obvious differences between this and xviii. 15–17. The Matthaean passage is in the second person singular, that of the Manual in the third. The number of witnesses required is not specified in the latter, nor the treatment finally to be meted out to an unrepentant neighbour: there is no parallel to the Matthaean 'let him be to thee as a Gentile and a tax collector'. Here Matthew seems to contemplate a worse treatment for the offender than does the Manual. Again, that Matthew does not insist on approaching the offender on the very day of his trespass, as does the Manual, might be claimed to indicate greater rigidity in the sectarian pericope than in the Evangelist. But other passages make it clear that the motive behind the demand for the immediate delivery of a reproach is to reduce the harbouring of evil thoughts to a minimum, such thoughts constituting sin and causing him who harboured them to be guilty.[1] The desire to avoid such guilt is emphasized

---

[1] K. Stendahl, *op. cit.* p. 8, finds 'a note of ultimate seriousness in the New Testament which does not leave room for the gracious casuistry and second chance which the Qumran sect practised in all cases except those of downright apostasy or disloyalty'.

in the Manual, while Matthew shows greater concern to gain the erring brother, and in this the Gospel is more 'Christian'. Nevertheless, the essentials of the procedure for dealing with an offender are the same in both passages, personal reproof is to be followed by that before witnesses, and further, if necessary, before the community (the Ecclesia or 'the Many') as a whole.

The closeness of the parallel cannot be denied, but does this necessarily imply that we have in xviii. 15 ff. what is a direct importation, although possibly Christianized, of a bit of discipline from the Sect into the Christian tradition? The change from the third to the second person is easily understandable. Unlike the Manual, which issues 'rules' in a statutory form, Matthew purports to give the words of Jesus where the direct personal form of address would be appropriate. The absence of an exact parallel to 'let him be to thee as a Gentile and a tax collector' can be explained by the fact that the procedure in such cases is dealt with elsewhere in the Manual (DSD vi. 24–vii. 25; viii. 23, 26). The omission of the exact number of witnesses in the Manual is no insuperable barrier to dependence of the Matthaean form upon it, because the tradition of two or three witnesses being employed in such cases would be taken for granted on the ground of Deut. xix. 15; although it should be noted that the Deuteronomic passage describes more what we should call the procedure in secular cases, whereas the Manual, like Matthew, is dealing with the life of a religious community. This caution holds despite the fact that the secular community in Israel was the religious community. Moreover, the distinction between the exact nature of the Church with which Matthew is concerned and the Dead Sea Sect is also instructive in this connexion. The phrase 'let him be to thee as a Gentile and a tax collector' suggests a Jewish-Christian community, sharply distinguished from 'the world', as was the Dead Sea Sect. On the other hand, Matthew's understanding of the Church as under commission to go to the Gentiles, as revealed, for example, in viii. 11; xxviii. 16 ff., points to a concern for the latter which was absent or, at best, secondary in the days of Jesus' flesh, as in x. 5. The developed regulations for conduct in the Manual of Discipline and CDC have no parallels in Matthew apart from those few which we shall indicate below. We have only to read CDC ix–xvi to realize that the legislative element was far less developed in the Matthaean Church than in the Dead Sea Sect, however much elements in Matthew suggest a separation from Gentiles.

The reference to Deuteronomy above reminds us that the procedure mentioned in Matt. xviii. 15 ff. has parallels elsewhere than in DSD. Reference to 1 Cor. v. 1 ff. comes naturally. There is, however, there no detailed parallel in the procedure described so much as a common climate of thought. Paul demands that the incestuous man should 'be removed from among you', which is like Matt. xviii. 17; we should not expect the precise Matthaean terminology to reappear. Absent in body but present in spirit in the Church at Corinth, Paul has for himself judged the person guilty of incest. He demands that, gathered together in the name of Christ and with his own spirit, the Church should condemn the offender and deliver him over 'to Satan for the destruction of the flesh'. What is recalled in this section are the verses in xviii. 18 ff.:

18 Truly, I say to you, whatever you bind on earth shall be bound in heaven, and
19 whatever you loose on earth shall be loosed in heaven. Again I say to you, if
   two of you agree on earth about anything they ask, it will be done for them by
20 my Father in heaven. For where two or three are gathered in my name, there
   am I in the midst of them. (RSV.)

We have here the same assertion of the authority of the community to act 'on every matter', which refers back to the offender in xviii. 15 ff., and the declaration of the presence of Christ with his own when they are gathered together in his Name. There can be no parallel in the DSS to this Christological orientation of the Matthaean and Pauline material, because a Messianic presence had not yet been realized by the Sect: the interim-regulations of the Church, therefore, necessarily differed from those of the latter; and that xviii. 18 ff. have no strict parallel in the DSS should not surprise us. One conclusion seems justifiable, that the procedure prescribed for dealing with the offender in xviii. 15 ff. is closer to that found in the Manual of Discipline than in rabbinic sources. The precise usage of the Synagogue in dealing with offenders is difficult to establish because of the complexity of the sources. It seems, however, that in the first century a ban termed נדוי was proclaimed on such, not by the community concerned, but by the Sanhedrin. This was imposed for a minimum of thirty days and could only be lifted on the initiative of the Sanhedrin. Thus the legislation in xviii. 15 ff. is more sectarian in its affinities than rabbinic.[1]

On the other hand, it has to be recognized that the way in which the Messianic presence is expressed in xviii. 19 f. is more reminiscent of the

---

[1] C. H. Hunzinger, *T.L.* (1955), pp. 114 f., on 'Die jüdische Bannpraxis im neutestamentlichen Zeitalter'.

rabbis than of the Sect. Verse 20 'For where two or three are gathered in my name, there am I in the midst of them' especially recalls a saying in Pirqe Aboth iii. 2 recorded in the name of R. Hananiah b. Teradion, the father-in-law of R. Meir; he was killed at the time of the Bar Kokba revolt. 'But if two sit together and words of the Law (are spoken) between them, the Divine Presence rests between them. . . .' In Aboth iii. 3 we find R. Simeon ben Yohai, A.D. 100–70, saying: 'If three have eaten at one table and have spoken over it words of the Law, it is as if they had eaten from the table of God (Ezek. xli. 22).' It is possible that the saying of R. Hananiah b. Teradion was called forth by xviii. 20 as a kind of counterblast, but more probably it expresses what was a rabbinic commonplace.[1] Matt. xviii. 20 is a Christified bit of rabbinism. It agrees with this that the phraseology of Matt. xviii. 18 is also more rabbinic than sectarian at this point. The text reads:

Ἀμὴν λέγω ὑμῖν, ὅσα ἐὰν δήσητε ἐπὶ τῆς γῆς, ἔσται δεδεμένα ἐν τῷ οὐρανῷ· καὶ ὅσα ἐὰν λύσητε ἐπὶ τῆς γῆς, ἔσται λελυμένα ἐν οὐρανῷ. . . .

The rabbinic parallels to δέω and λύω here, that is, 'binding' and 'loosing', are אָסַר [אָסַר]='to interdict', to declare a thing forbidden according to ritual law or simply 'to forbid', and the Hiphil of נתר, that is, הִתִּיר='to permit', to declare permitted (הִתִּיר is the more probable Hebrew underlying λύω, though a form שְׁרָא would also be possible). It is a striking fact that the terms אָסַר and הִתִּיר do not occur in DSD or CDC (נתר is found in the latter, but only in a quotation from Isa. lviii. 6 at CDC xiii. 10). This is so although CDC, particularly, offers many occasions where this terminology might be employed as in the section from ix onwards. But it prefers such a phrase as וכן המשפט. Thus CDC xvi. 13 reads: וכן המשפט לאביה, that is, 'Likewise is the rule for her father' where we might have found 'It is permitted for her father also', for example התירו לאביה, 'They permitted it to her father'. The rabbinic tone of Matt. xviii. 15 is further emphasized by the parallels to the demand for witnesses in cases of reproof which occur in the Mishnah in certain cases.

We find, therefore, in xviii. 15–20 the collocation of sectarian and rabbinic usage. As compared with the Synagogue which had already refined the 'ban' and the Essenes, the Church in Matthew had not developed a fully articulated system. The regulations it imposed are the bare minimum. This lack of 'refinement' leads to the impression that

---

[1] C. H. Dodd, *E.T.* (1953), 60. He also draws attention to the similarity between xv. 15 ff. and much in Paul, in Gal. vi. 1 f.; 1 Cor. v. 1–13.

Matthew is more rigid than the sectarians,[1] but this conclusion has to be tempered in the light not only of xviii. 21–2 but of the preceding section xviii. 10–14. Both passages emphasize the element of 'grace' in the Christian life, that is, of love towards the lost and undeserving.

One other point is noteworthy in the section Matt. xviii. 1–15. This contains a discussion on those little ones, like children, who believe on Christ. Such 'Church members' are not to be scandalized or despised, and the motive for avoiding such conduct is given in Matt. xviii. 10 which reads as follows: 'Take heed that ye despise not one of these little ones, for I say unto you, that in heaven their angels do always behold the face of my Father which is in heaven.' This verse is peculiar to Matthew. While the belief in angels, and that every person has his 'angel', is well attested, Strack–Billerbeck[2] point out that the view that angels see God is not rabbinic: it is the contrary that is frequently emphasized by the rabbis, namely, that even the angels cannot see God and live. In the New Testament, however, angels do emerge in discussions of Church activity. Thus Paul demands that women should continue to be veiled in Church services 'on account of the angels';[3] Timothy is given a charge 'before God and the Lord Jesus Christ and the elect angels';[4] and in 1 Tim. iii. 16 'angels' are appealed to as witnesses of the mystery of godliness manifested in Christ, that is, as if they 'belonged' to the witnessing Christian community and shared its functions. The passage in Matt. xviii. 10, therefore, which introduces a reference to angels into a discussion of Church membership, is not altogether strange. It is worth pointing out that there are striking parallels to this association of angels with 'churchly' activity and with the communion of the saints in worship in the sectarian sources.

The passages are as follows:

DSD xi. 8 f.:

To those whom God chose He has given them as an eternal possession;
And He has given to them an inheritance in the lot of | the Holy Ones;
And with the Sons of heaven He has associated their assembly [or Conclave]
    for a community Council;
Their assembly will be in the Holy Abode as an eternal planting,
During every | period that will be. (Brownlee's translation.)

The word, קדושים, translated 'holy ones', Brownlee[5] understands as 'angels', as he also does the phrase בני שמים: the phrase וסוד מבנית קודש he

---

[1] See above, p. 222.   [2] Vol. I, *ad rem.*
[3] See H. J. Cadbury, *H.T.R.* no. 1 (January 1958), 1 ff.; J. A. Fitzmyer, *N.T.S.* IV (October 1957), 48–58.   [4] 1 Tim. v. 21.   [5] *B.A.S.O.R. ad rem.*

refers to 'the heavenly abode of angels and sanctified spirits who belong to the same eternal society'. In the above passage the hymn celebrates that fellowship which the author certainly, and possibly, if we take the 'I' of the Psalm here to be collective, the whole Sect, enjoys with the angels.[1] The Sect or at least one particular member of it already knows communion here and now with the heavenly hosts above. It is probably in this sense also that we are to understand the passage in 1QSa i. 25–ii. 10: the reference is not to the future but to the present experience of the community in worship. Barthélemy and Milik write on 1QSa xi. 8, 1QSb iv. 25–6 and 1QSa ii. 8, containing כי מלאכי קודש בעדתם (= for the holy angels are (present) in their congregations) as follows: 'qui ne doivent pas être compris au futur mais en un présent mystique, la liturgie terrestre se déroulant *en même temps* dans le "Temple du Royaume"'.[2] Particularly interesting is it that whereas in 1QSa ii. 8–9 the disabled or mutilated are apparently excluded from the congregation because 'the

---

[1] See *The Scrolls and the New Testament*, ed. K. Stendahl, p. 278, n. 34.

[2] Barthélemy and Milik, *Qumrân Cave I* (1955), 117. In their comments on this section (on line 6) Barthélemy and Milik, *op. cit.* p. 116, write as follows: '"Boiteux et aveugles" n'avaient pas accès au Temple (2 Sam. v. 8). Le jour de son entrée solennelle au Temple, Jésus y guérit "boiteux et aveugles" qui y avaient pénétré avec lui (Matt. xxi. 14). Le Maître du festin messianique, voyant que les "invités" avaient dédaigné la convocation, fait entrer à leur place "estropiés, aveugles et boiteux" (Luke xiv. 21). L'auteur de notre Règle ne soupçonne pas la possibilité d'un tel renversement et se contente d'insister sur les vieux interdits.' It is tempting to suggest that Matt. xviii. 8–9 finds some illumination from this quarter. With minor variations the same verses occur in Matt. v. 29–30 where they refer to the necessity of personal discipline: they are clearly an insertion in xviii. 8–9 because xviii. 10 would follow very naturally on xviii. 7 or xviii. 6. What does Matthew intend to convey in Matt. xviii. 8–9? Is the meaning the same as in Matt. v. 29–30? But in this case there would be no need for the repetition of the words. Do we find here the conception of the Church as a Body, such as we find in Paul? Against this is the use of the singular (εἰ δὲ ἡ χείρ σου. . . σκανδαλίζει σε): moreover, in Matt. v. 29–30 the express term σῶμα is used: it is not employed in the complex xviii. 8–9 which seems to suggest that the idea of the Church as a Body in the Pauline sense is not to the fore here. It is impossible precisely to penetrate to the meaning of xviii. 8–9 and it may be that they are inserted here merely on the principle of *Stichwortdisposition* which Soiron emphasized. But it has to be still more recognized in the light of the sectarian documents, that physical disabilities had serious spiritual consequences in first-century Judaism. The rabbinic sources do not much point to this as the evidence suggested by S–B makes clear, but among the sectarians it is clear that physical handicaps were very seriously regarded. Did Jesus owe his simile about entering into life blind or lame and having only one hand, from ideas on these subjects entertained by sectarians? This possibility is at least worth mentioning, and it is probably to be recognized that a passage such as xviii. 8–9 would have undertones for the first-century reader which we probably miss.

angels' of men of renown in the congregation would be present and thereby offended, it is the angels of 'little ones', present before God, who make it wrong to offend or despise such in the Church.

It should also be noted that the opening question of the chapter, in xviii. 1, 'Who is the greatest in the kingdom of heaven?', introduces a theme which agitated the Church of Matthew, as it did the primitive Church generally, that is, that of rank. The approach to this is in direct contrast to that of the Essenes, who treated gradations of rank with marked seriousness.[1] Is there a deliberate opposition to the Essenes' emphasis in Matthew? The other sectarian undertones in chapter xviii make this not impossible and the urgency with which rank was regarded in the Essene movement lends a new pertinence to this question. But any answer to it must be guarded. While in xviii. 18 authority in the ecclesia is vested in the community, as a totality, in the presence of the Christ, in xix. 28 we read: 'Truly, I say to you, in the new world (ἐν τῇ παλιγγενεσίᾳ), when the Son of Man shall sit on his glorious throne, you who have followed me will also sit on twelve thrones, judging the twelve tribes of Israel.' Does this verse envisage a future order when 'the Twelve' would have a special rank in judgement? This has usually been the interpretation of the verse.[2] Taken precisely, it is not simply the Twelve who are to sit on the Twelve thrones but 'you who have followed me'; but it seems clear, none the less, that the Twelve or the Disciples are meant by these, because in xix. 29 a distinction is implied between them, in particular, and 'everyone who has left houses', etc. who are promised a hundredfold reward. If such a peculiar significance is given to the Twelve by Matthew, he does not wholly annul distinctions of rank. That the point of view is not peculiar to Matthew appears from Luke xviii. 29–30.

Again it appears that within the Matthaean community a special priority was given to Peter. He is the foundation member and is given a judiciary function ascribed in xviii. 15 ff. to the community as a whole (xvi. 13–20). This seems to go beyond the more generalized priority which Peter enjoys in all the Synoptics. This judiciary role of Peter seems to be recognized not only in the Christian community but by outsiders (xvii. 24).

Thus three elements enter into the Matthaean regulations for the Church —the rule of the community, the priority of Peter, the future role of the Twelve. Can this be connected with Essene sources? It will be well to

---

[1] See, for example, CDC xvii. 3 ff. Are passages such as Mark x. 35 ff. to be understood over against such an emphasis?

[2] See the various commentaries.

deal with this question in connexion with the next passage mentioned by Bultmann, namely, xvi. 17–19:

And Jesus answered him, 'Blessed are you, Simon Bar-Jona! For flesh and blood has not revealed this to you, but my Father who is in heaven. And I tell you, you are Peter, and on this rock I will build my church, and the powers of death shall not prevail against it. I will give you the keys of the kingdom of heaven, and whatever you bind on earth shall be bound in heaven, and whatever you loose on earth shall be loosed in heaven.'

Two sectarian passages have been claimed to offer parallels to this. Assuming that the Manual of Discipline is the earlier, we note the following from viii. 4–8 included in a larger passage viii. 1 ff.:

When these things come to pass in Israel, the council of the community will be established in the truth for an eternal planting, a holy house for Israel, a foundation of the holy of holies for Aaron, true witnesses for justice and the elect by God's will, to make atonement for the land and to render for the wicked their recompense—this is the tested wall, a precious cornerstone; its foundations will not tremble or flee from their place—a most holy dwelling for Aaron....
(M. Burrows's translation.)

Here twelve men and three priests constitute the foundation (יסוד) of the community (in viii. 5); in viii. 10 they are said to be prepared 'in the foundation' (ביסוד). Terms applied to the council are—eternal planting, a holy house, foundation, true witnesses, tested wall, precious cornerstone. In Matt. xvi. 18 Peter is given, as the Rock-Man, the significance in the Church corresponding to that of the Council in the Community in DSD viii. Among other things the Council has the function of judging in DSD viii. 9 (לחרוץ משפט רשעה) as Peter has in xvi. 19, and, as with Peter, so with the Council nothing is to prevail against it. In xviii. 18, as we saw above, the functions ascribed to Peter in xvi. 19 are given to the Church as a whole. But in xix. 28 the function of judgement in the future is in the hands of the Twelve. Do these correspond to the Council of the Sect? They are equal in number and it has been maintained that in the light of all the above—the role of the ecclesia, of the Twelve and of the later episcopos (fulfilled in Matthew by Peter)—we have repeated in the Church the pattern of community organization among the Essenes. We may be justified in finding in Peter, perhaps, a kind of Matthaean ἐπίσκοπος, =פקיד=מבקר, and the role of the community is found in Matthew, as in the sectarian sources. But the Twelve have only a future, eschatological role in Matthew, that is, beyond 'the End', 'in the new world': but in the Manual the Council prepares for that 'new world', and thus has only a preparatory eschatological significance. Any strict transference of a sectarian order to the Church, therefore, is ruled out. The most we can say is that the organizational data presented by the Matthaean Church are reminiscent of those of the sectarians.

In the passage cited from the Manual the term 'Rock' for the Council does not appear. In DSD xi. 4 the Rock (סלע) on which either the community or the Teacher of Righteousness stands is God's faithfulness. But in 1QH vii. 8–9 we read:

> Thou hast made me like a strong tower, like a high wall;
> Thou has established my building on a rock,
> With eternal bases as my foundation.... (M. Burrows's translation.)

Here the rock of the community is either the Teacher of Righteousness himself or his teaching: it is not the council. Probably in DSD xi. 4 the Teacher refers to God's faithfulness as the Rock on which he himself stands. All this suggests that the image of a Rock is too generalized even in the usage of the sectarians to enable us to find any direct contact between these and Matt. xvi. 18 ff.

To sum up our discussion so far, we may claim a sectarian colouring for much in chapter xviii; and a terminology similar to that of the Sect in xvi. 18 ff. But in both there emerges also a rabbinic element. In xviii. 15 f. Matthew may have applied to the Church as it awaited the Parousia a discipline similar to that found among the Essenes but in a less elaborated form. He has also Christianized his material and combined with Essene strands or terminology elements drawn from Pharisaic Judaism. The details of his Church Order are not sufficiently clear for us to trace it with any certainty to the Essenes. That the Matthaean world was closely related to the sectarian in some way seems clear, that it directly borrowed its forms from the latter on the evidence presented above cannot be established.

We next note the passage first mentioned above, namely, xiii. 24–30, the parable of the wheat and the tares (which has a loose parallel in xiii. 47–50, the parable of the net). It is not our concern here to discover what the parable was intended to convey on the lips of Jesus. It is the explanation of it offered by Matthew which chiefly attracts us: it occurs in xiii. 36–43:

Then he left the crowds and went into the house. And his disciples came to him, saying, 'Explain to us the parable of the weeds of the field'. He answered, 'He who sows the good seed is the Son of man; the field is the world, and the good seed means the sons of the kingdom; the weeds are the sons of the evil one, and the enemy who sowed them is the devil; the harvest is the close of the age, and the reapers are angels. Just as the weeds are gathered and burned with fire, so will it be at the close of the age. The Son of man will send his angels, and they will gather out of his kingdom all causes of sin and all evildoers, and throw them into the furnace of fire; there men will weep and gnash their teeth. Then the righteous will shine like the sun in the kingdom of their Father. He who has ears, let him hear....' (RSV.)

This explanation recalls the following passages from DSD:

(a) DSD iii. 17 f.:

Under His [God's] control are the laws of all; and He sustains them in all their pursuits. Now, He created man for dominion over | the world and assigned him two spirits by which to walk until the *season of His visitation* (עד מועד פקודתו). They are the spirits of | truth and perversion. From a spring of light [issue] the generations of truth; but from a foundation of darkness [issue] the generations of perverseness. In the hands of the prince of lights is the rule over all the *sons of righteousness* (בני צדק); in the ways of light they walk. But in the hand of | the angel of darkness is all the rule over the sons of perversion; and in the ways of darkness they walk. And it is because of the *angel of darkness* (מלאך חשך) | that all the sons of righteousness go astray; so all their sin and their iniquities and their guilt and the transgressions of their deeds are under his dominion | (according to God's mysteries), until his *end-time* (קצו); while their afflictions and their seasons of distress are under the dominion of his hostility. | And all the spirits allotted him [strive] to trip the sons of light; but the God of Israel and His angel of truth have helped | all the sons of light.... (Brownlee's translation.)

(b) DSD iv. 17–19:

For God has set them [that is, the two spirits] in equal parts until the | *last period* (קץ אחרון); and He has put eternal enmity between their divisions; an abomination to truth are acts of wrongdoing; an abomination to wrongdoing are all ways of truth. And passionate | strife pertains to all their practices, for they do not walk together. Now God through the mysteries of His understanding and through His glorious wisdom has appointed a *period for the existence of wrongdoing* (קץ להיות עולה); but at the *season of* | *visitation* (ובמועד פקודה), He will destroy it forever; and then the truth of the world will appear forever.... (Brownlee's translation.)

(c) DSD iv. 24–6:

Until now the spirits of truth and perversion strive within men's heart; | they walk in wisdom and folly [respectively]; and according as man's inheritance is in truth and righteousness, so he hates evil; but in so far as his heritage is in the portion of perversity and wickedness in him, so | he abominates truth. For God has set them [that is, the two spirits] in equal parts until the *period of the decree* (עד קץ נחרצה) and the making of the New (ועשות חדשה); and He knows the action of their deeds for all the periods of | their [striving]; and He apportions them to mankind that man may know good [and evil, and that He may al]lot the portions to every living being according to his spirit within [him until the season of] visitation. (Brownlee's translation.)

Certain passages in CDC are also relevant, as emerges below.

In xiii. 47–50 Matthew applies to the Church, as it awaits the Parousia, concepts that are somewhat parallel to those applied in the above passages to the Sect, as it awaits its Messiahs. It is possible to see in the children of the kingdom (xiii. 38) a parallel to the sons of righteousness (DSD iii. 17 ff.); in the children of the wicked one (xiii. 38) a parallel to the sons of perversion (DSD iii. 17 ff.); in the enemy, the devil (xiii. 39), a parallel to the angel of darkness (DSD iii. 17 ff.); in the end of the world (xiii. 39) a parallel to 'the season of His visitation' (DSD iii. 18; iv. 26) or 'the last period' (DSD iv. 17) or the period of the decree (DSD iv. 25). In both xiii. 36–43 and the DSS we find that good and evil are allowed to co-exist by God until 'the End'. Moreover, although the exact terminology of the sons of light and of darkness does not occur here, xiii. 43 may be taken to imply that the children of the Kingdom are the sons of light, because 'then shall the righteous shine forth as the sun in the Kingdom of their father'. The phrase 'furnace of fire' in xiii. 42 recalls the 'flames of fire' of CDC ii. 6, as does the 'angels' of xiii. 41 the angels of destruction (מלאכי חבל) of CDC ii. 6: those that do iniquity (τοὺς ποιοῦντας τὴν ἀνομίαν) may correspond in xiii. 41 to those that abhor the ordinance (מתעבי חק) in CDC ii. 6.

It should also be noted that the same thought as that found in xiii. 24 ff. recurs in xiii. 47 f.—the parable of the Net. Perhaps it should be noted further that in CDC iv. 13 ff. on the ground of Isa. xxiv. 17 the figure of a net is used of Belial's activity during the period when evil and good are allowed, although there is no real parallel here to what is found in xiii. 47 f. The passage reads:

And during all those years shall | Belial be let loose upon Israel, and He spoke by the hand of the prophet Isaiah son of Amoz, saying: 'Fear, and the pit, and the snare are upon thee, O inhabitant of the land'. Its explanation (פשרו): | the three nets of Belial, about which Levi son of Jacob said | that he 'catches in them ⌐the heart⌐ (or: ⌐the house⌐) of Israel' and has made them appear

ᒥto themᒧ as three kinds of righteousness. The first is whoredom, the second is wealth, the third is conveying uncleanness to the sanctuary.... (Rabin's translation.)

And before we leave this section the warning should be uttered that the parallelism between xiii. 24 ff. and the DSS should not be pressed even though the identity of thought concerning the coexistence of good and evil in the community of the New Covenant in both cases is clear. The terminology of xiii. 24 ff. can be paralleled in other sources, the figure of the net in xiii. 47 ff. is given by implication in the disciples' call to be fishermen (Mark i. 16–20, etc.). The parallels merely point to the similarity of the milieu in which the early Christian movement and the Dead Sea Sect found themselves. On the other hand, full force should be given to xiii. 52, which closes the section in which we have found these parallels and which reads as follows: 'Therefore every scribe which is instructed into the kingdom of heaven is like unto a man that is an householder, which bringeth forth out of his treasury things new and old.' It is tempting to see, in xiii. 51 especially, the influence of one who had given thought to the problems of lapsed and lapsing members and who has added his comment, we may be allowed to call it his 'gemara', on the parable of the Wheat and the Tares, thus combining things new and old; and it is not impossible that his gemara reflects the experience and thought of the Dead Sea Sect. But here again caution is salutary. The term 'scribe' perhaps suggests a rabbinic milieu; and it should be recalled that among the rabbis it was a commonplace that the evil yetzer would not be subdued until the Messianic Age. R. Tarfon's dictum in Aboth ii. 19, 'It is not thy part to finish the task, yet thou art not free to desist from it', probably refers to this conviction: evil is never completely overcome, nor, indeed, should the disappearance of the evil yetzer be desired because then 'no man would build a house nor marry a wife'. Only in the End was there discharge from the battle against the evil yetzer.[1] Thus the ideas behind xiii. 36–43 are in line with rabbinic thought, and terms occur in the section which are familiar in rabbinic sources also, although it is to be recognized that the affinities of the passage on the whole suggest more a sectarian than a rabbinic milieu, and recall Daniel.[2]

[1] See *P.R.J.*[2] p. 23.
[2] On the affinities between Daniel and the DSS, see K. Elliger, *Studien zum Habakuk-Kommentar vom Toten Meer* (1953), p. 157; B. J. Roberts, 'The DSS and Apocalyptic Literature', Oxford Society of Historical Theology: *Abstracts of Proceedings*, 1953, pp. 29–35; H. H. Rowley, *Jewish Apocalyptic and the DSS* (London, 1957).

But not only is the way in which the section xiii. 36–50 closes with xiii. 51–2 significant. Preceding it in xiii. 34 f. we have one of the formula quotations. The whole passage reads as follows: 'All these things spake Jesus unto the multitudes in parables; and without a parable spake he not unto them: That it might be fulfilled which was spoken by the prophet, saying, I will open my mouth in parables; I will utter things which have been kept secret from the foundation of the world.' There follows that material in xiii. 36 ff. and xiii. 47 (along with other parables) where we have traced possible sectarian parallels. In the sentence

ἀνοίξω ἐν παραβολαῖς τὸ στόμα μου,
ἐρεύξομαι κεκρυμμένα ἀπὸ καταβολῆς (κόσμου)

we have a reference to Ps. lxxviii. 2 which reads in the LXX

ἀνοίξω ἐν παραβολαῖς τὸ στόμα μου,
φθέγξομαι προβλήματα ἀπ᾽ ἀρχῆς

and in the MT

אֶפְתְּחָה בְמָשָׁל פִּי
אַבִּיעָה חִידוֹת מִנִּי־קֶדֶם

Like the LXX, Matthew translates בְמָשָׁל by the plural (Aquila has the singular ἐν παραβολῇ, Symmachus διὰ παροιμίας). But here the similarity between Matthew and the LXX ceases: אַבִּיעָה being rendered by the LXX as φθέγξομαι and חִידוֹת by κεκρυμμένα rather than by προβλήματα as in the LXX, and מִנִּי־קֶדֶם by ἀπὸ καταβολῆς (κόσμου) rather than the simpler LXX ἀπ᾽ ἀρχῆς. The use of ἐρεύγεσθαι, 'to belch forth', shows Matthew's direct dependence at this point on the Hebrew: the term אַבִּיעָה is rendered by ἐρεύγεσθαι also in Ps. xix. 3 in the LXX. Stendahl is therefore right in seeing here 'an *ad hoc* Christian interpretation'.[1] He also states that this interpretation is closely bound up with its context. He does not enlarge on this context: it is not his concern to do so. But he seems to mean by the context the fact that the parables are signs of the Messiah. He writes: 'Both the participle (κεκρυμμένα) and ἀπὸ καταβολῆς (κόσμου) express the aspect of sacred history more concretely than the LXX translation. The verbal significance in the participle is made full use of, a possibility permitted by the Greek. It is not the eternal mysteries which are pronounced, but it is the Messiah who has come and who reveals what had been hidden up to that time.'[2] This is correct; but the addition of the following verses in xiii. 36 should also be connected with xiii. 35. The meaning of the

---

[1] *Op. cit.* p. 117.   [2] *Ibid.*

parable of the Tares is explained privately and the explanation turns out
to be an interpretation of history similar to that granted to the initiates of
the Dead Sea Sect, as we have seen. The κεκρυμμένα announced previously
in the parables are now expounded. Jesus as Messiah *reveals*: he performs
the function ascribed in IQpH vii. 4 f., as Stendahl points out, to the
Teacher of Righteousness. Schniewind's comment on xiii. 34, 35 is as
follows: 'Dieser erste Abschluß ist nur so zu erklären, daß eine Überlieferung, das Matth. bis jetzt folgte, hier abschloß, während er im folgenden
Eigenes bringt',[1] and in much of what he himself brings, as we saw, there
is to be traced, if not sectarian influence, at least sectarian parallels.

But, in addition to the material that we have already adduced, we have
still another possibility to note. Bultmann not only isolated those
passages with which we dealt above which reveal the Matthaean understanding of the Church, but also claimed that the hand which shaped
them also fashioned the *SM* as a catechism.[2] Leaving aside the question
as to the propriety of thinking of the Sermon as a catechism, are there
elements in it which are illumined by being placed over against the
Qumran sources? It is our suggestion that this is the case. The Sermon
reveals an awareness of the Sect and perhaps a polemic against it.

First, let us look at the unit v. 21–6 which reads:

You have heard that it was said to the men of old, 'You shall not kill; and whoever kills shall be liable to judgment' (ἔνοχος ἔσται τῇ κρίσει). But I say to you
that every one who is angry with his brother shall be liable to judgment;
whoever insults his brother (ὃς δ’ ἂν εἴπῃ τῷ ἀδελφῷ αὐτοῦ, 'Ρακά) shall be liable
to the council (τῷ συνεδρίῳ), and whoever says, 'You fool!' (Μωρέ) shall be
liable to the hell of fire. So if you are offering your gift at the altar, and there
remember that your brother has something against you, leave your gift there
before the altar and go; first be reconciled to your brother, and then come and
offer your gift. Make friends quickly with your accuser, while you are going
with him to court, lest your accuser hand you over to the judge (τῷ κριτῇ), and
the judge to the guard (ὑπηρέτῃ), and you be put in prison; truly, I say to you,
you will never get out till you have paid the last penny. (RSV.)

There is some reason for thinking that the original unit here was formed
by v. 21, 22 *a*. The change from πᾶς ὁ in v. 22 to ὃς δ’ ἂν in the middle of
the verse suggests a change of material, as does again the change to the
second person in v. 23, ἐὰν οὖν προσφέρῃς. Thus v. 22*b*–24 would appear
to be a kind of gemaric addition, explanatory of v. 21, 22*a*. Moreover,
they introduce the notion of degrees of anger and of punishment for such:

---

[1] *Op. cit. ad rem.*   [2] *Ibid.*

anger with one's brother is worthy of the judgement (ἡ κρίσις); to call a brother ῥακά leads to the sanhedrin (συνέδριον) and μωρέ to τὴν γέενναν τοῦ πυρός. Finally, in v. 23, to have anything wrong in relation to one's brother (τι κατὰ σοῦ) makes a mockery of one's offering and must first be removed.

The material found in v. 21 can be set over against rabbinic usages. Thus Bornhauser[1] understood the passage in the light of the practice of excommunication in the Synagogue. It is the anger which leads to the excommunication of one rabbi by other rabbis that is here condemned: the terms ῥακά and μωρέ are equivalents of ריקא and מורה respectively, and are retained in the text in this form because they are technical formulae of excommunication. This interpretation of ῥακά is supported by appeal to Neh. v. 13 which reads: 'Also I shook out my lap, and said, So God shake out every man from his house, and from his labour, that performeth not this promise; even thus be he shaken out, and emptied . . .' (RV) (MT נָעַר; LXX κενός). Bornhauser supplies no evidence for the technical use of מורה. In the passage he adduces, Mishnah Eduyoth v. 6: 'Akabya b. Mahalel testified to four opinions. They answered: Akabya, retract these four opinions that thou hast given and we will make thee Father of the Court in Israel (that is, President). He said to them: Better that I be called a fool all my days than that I be made a godless man before God even for an hour; for they shall not say of me, He retracted for the sake of office.' The term translated 'fool' is שוטה not מורה. Bornhauser's attempt, therefore, to connect ῥακά with the formula for excommunication for seven days and μωρέ with that for thirty or more days is to be questioned. Similarly it is precarious to find in the term μωρέ (מורה) a reference to Shammai's violent habits as against Hillel's gentleness, as does Hüber.[2]

But, turning from the treatment meted out by rabbis to rabbis, is the passage to be understood in terms of legal procedures in Judaism? To what does the term κρίσις refer in v. 21 and v. 22? To what does συνέδριον in v. 22? Hüber[3] refers the κρίσις of v. 22 to the council of twenty-three members called the בת דין; the term συνέδριον naturally refers to the Sanhedrin and the γέεννα τοῦ πυρός to the final judgement of God. Thus the triadic form here emerging in Matthew is typically rabbinic. This is substantially the view of Lagrange,[4] although he suggests that the terms 'judgement' and 'sanhedrin' should not be too literally interpreted. The fact that the whole of the material is set in a context of contrast to the

[1] *Die Bergpredigt* (Gütersloh, 1923), p. 63.
[2] *Die Bergpredigt, ad rem.*   [3] *Ibid.*   [4] *Op. cit. ad rem.*

Scribes and Pharisees also demands full consideration. The rabbinic undertones of our passage must, therefore, be admitted. Particularly is the presence of the word συνέδριον significant.

Nevertheless, there is one weakness in any such rigid parallelism as is referred to by Hüber. Mishnah Sanhedrin does not note any punishment for anger or for speech that is unseemly. As Hüber himself remarks: 'Über den Zornigen gabs damals so wenig wie heute ein menschliches Gericht, weil das faktisch nur die greifbare Tat strafen kann.'[1] Should we then conclude that the point of v. 21 lies just in this, that matters which previously were taken so lightly by Judaism as to find no part in their legal system are now raised by Jesus to a new significance? Percy[2] emphasizes this in his recent discussion. This enables him to decide that the whole section v. 21–3 is a word of Jesus, as does also Hüber.

But, if it be argued that the intention of Jesus in Matt. v. 21–2a was to remove the nice calculation of less and more in the matter of anger and hatred in human relationships, at least within the community of Christians, by placing murder and anger on the same level of significance, then the reintroduction of degrees of anger and retribution in v. 22b, c is a contradiction of his intention. For him murder and anger incur the same retribution: they are both ἔνοχος τῇ κρίσει. The verses v. 22b f. do seem to be some kind of addition.

And it is just at this point that the DSS become pertinent. Note the following passages from DSD vi. 24 ff. where rigid rules are applied to personal relations within the Sect:

Now these are the laws by which they shall judge in the communal investigation (במדרש יחד) according to the [following] provisions: If there be found among them a man who lies | in the matter of wealth, and it become known, they shall exclude him from the Purity of the Many for one year, and he shall be fined one-fourth his food allowance; and he who answers | his fellow (רעהו) with stiff neck (בקשי עורף), or speaks with a quick temper (בקוצר אפים) so as to reject the instruction of his comrade, by disobeying his fellow who is enrolled before him, | [has] taken the law into his own hands; so he shall be fined for on[e] year [and be excluded; . . . .] (Brownlee's translation.)

Here there emerge regulations concerning words uttered in wrath and vilification between members of a religious community and the punishments deemed appropriate for such. The terms, the use of which is con-

---

[1] *Op. cit. ad rem.*

[2] E. Percy, *Die Botschaft Jesu. Eine traditionskritische und exegetische Untersuchung* (Lund, 1953), *ad rem.*

demned, are not specifically mentioned so that we do not find here the words ῥακά (ריקא) and μωρέ (מורה). But the following phrases from other passages are noteworthy: vii. 3, דבר בחמה=to speak in anger. The reference here is to speaking in anger against the priests: the fine is for one year and excommunication. There follow modifications of this to which we refer below. vii. 5, ואשר ידבר את רעהו במרים; Brownlee renders this: 'whoever speaks haughtily': Burrows: 'craftily'. The fine is for six months, and there follow modifications. vii, 4 והאיש אשר יצחה בלי משפט, that is, 'The man who vilifies unjustly his fellow': the fine is for one year and exclusion from the community. vii. 9, ואשר ידבר בפיהו דבר נבל, 'And whoever utters with his mouth a word of folly'—he is to be fined for three months. vii. 14, ואשר ישחק בסכלת להשמיע קולו, 'Whoever laughs foolishly with audible voice': he is to be fined for thirty days.

It will be objected that there is no equivalent in the passages cited to the distinction between κρίσις and συνέδριον which is found in Matthew. The investigation in DSD vi. 24 is called a 'communal investigation' (מדרש יחד), and while it is possible that in the Messianic period investigation would be by the priests, as we have previously seen, who would form a holy of holies within the community, a council, there is no evidence that συνέδριον would be a translation of עֵצָה. In view of this we cannot regard Matt. v. 21 f. as a close parallel to what we find in DSD. Nevertheless, the possibility must be recognized that a former sectarian may have formulated v. 22 b, c. The kind of *gemara* we find in v. 22 b would come very naturally to a person brought up in or influenced by the Dead Sea Sect. Johannes Weiss[1] saw in 22 b and 22 c a Jewish-Christian addition to the words of Jesus—an addition which arose out of a new casuistry which arose around the sayings of Jesus: was the Jewish Christian aware of the Dead Sea Sect and did he know their casuistry?

The difficulties in the way of this view must not be overlooked. To many, as we have seen, the stark forcefulness of v. 22 b f., no less than v. 21–2 a, points to Jesus as their author. It is possible that he has both the rabbis and the Sect and similar movements in view: the gradations of anger and speech would point to the Sect, the use of συνέδριον (unless the term is used freely to denote any council, such, for example, as the one mentioned in DSD) points to the Synagogue. Here again we note that juxtaposition of the rabbinic and the sectarian which we have previously isolated.

Perhaps it is not irrelevant before leaving this to mention two related matters. A reference to an 'idle word' occurs elsewhere in Matt. xii. 36

---

[1] *Op. cit. ad rem.*

(πᾶν ῥῆμα ἀργόν, ὃ ἐὰν λαλήσωσιν οἱ ἄνθρωποι κ.τ.λ.). Hüber[1] connects this with v. 21 f.: 'Steht hinter Jesu Urteil vielleicht Matt. xii. 36 wonach jedes unnützte Wort dem Gericht verfällt, wie vielmehr das absprecherische, schimpfende, zürnende?' But he does not note that Matt. xii. 36 f. is peculiar to Matthew and constitutes a bit of *gemara* on the preceding section: does it come from a person influenced by the Sect? The term ῥῆμα ἀργόν might be a translation of the terms דבר רק (though this is rendered in Deut. xxxii. 47 by λόγος κενός). The term רקים occurs in DSD x. 24, where it is rendered by Brownlee as 'vanities': is this the plural equivalent of ῥακά in v. 22 and ῥῆμα ἀργόν in xii. 36? The emphasis on the necessity for purity of speech emerges clearly in DSD x. 22 ff. But again it is also a rabbinic commonplace as is clear, for example, from Mishnah Aboth i. 17; iii. 14.

Another passage dealing with slanderous and similar words may illumine another passage in Matthew, as in its parallels, dealing with blasphemy. In DSD vii. 16 ff. we read as follows:

The man who slanders his fellow (ואיש אשר ילך רכיל ברעהו) | shall be excluded for one year from the Purity of the Many, and he shall be fined; but anyone who slanders the Many shall be banished from them | to return no more. They shall also banish never to return the man who murmurs against the institution of the Community (יסוד היחד); but if his murmuring be against his fellow | who has not been convicted, he shall be fined for six months. (Brownlee's translation.)

Here a distinction is rigidly drawn between a sin against the community in slander and a sin against an individual member of the community. Let us here recall two things: first, that the community is a community in Holy Spirit (DSD ix. 4), so that to sin against the community is to sin against Holy Spirit, and, secondly, that to be cast out of the community for ever was to be damned both in this world and in the Age to Come. Compare this with Matt. xii. 31–2:

Therefore I say unto you, Every sin and every blasphemy shall be forgiven unto men; but the blasphemy against the Spirit shall not be forgiven. And whosoever shall speak a word against the Son of Man, it shall be forgiven him; but whosoever shall speak against the Holy Spirit, it shall not be forgiven him, neither in this world, nor in that which is to come.

Let us turn now to another section of the antitheses, namely, Matt. v. 33–7:

Again you have heard that it was said to the men of old, 'You shall not swear falsely (οὐκ ἐπιορκήσεις, ἀποδώσεις δὲ τῷ Κυρίῳ τοὺς ὅρκους σου), but shall

[1] *Op. cit. ad rem.*

perform to the Lord what you have sworn (ὀμόσαι)'. But I say to you, Do not swear (ὀμόσαι) at all, either by heaven, for it is the throne of God, or by the earth, for it is his footstool, or by Jerusalem, for it is the city of the great King. And do not swear (ὀμόσῃς) by your head, for you cannot make one hair white or black. Let what you say be simply 'Yes' or 'No'; anything more than this comes from evil. (RSV.)

T. W. Manson[1] has urged that in its original form the passage was throughout concerned with oaths, that is, with relations between men in which the name of God or some substitute therefor was invoked. The context favours this view, as do the parallels in Matt. xxiii. 16 ff. and Jas. v. 12; moreover this gives to the passage a natural sense. On these grounds Manson regards the phrase ἀποδώσεις δὲ τῷ Κυρίῳ τοὺς ὅρκους σου as an addition to the original complex which, designed to clarify the passage, in fact, by introducing the matter of vows to God, merely complicates it. Kilpatrick[2] has rejected this view on the ground that ὅρκος cannot mean the same as εὐχή='vow' and that ἀποδιδόναι ὅρκον means 'to take an oath, to swear'. But it is far better to treat ὅρκους here as a misunderstanding for εὐχάς. Lieberman[3] has shown how there was a widespread popular confusion of ὅρκοι and εὐχαί, as in this passage, and it is best to understand the phrase ἀποδώσεις δὲ τῷ Κυρίῳ τοὺς ὅρκους σου in the light of passages like Num. xxx. 3, Deut. xxiii. 22 ff. and refer it to 'vows', although the exact term εὐχή does not occur in it. Both 33 *b* and 34 *b*–6 are best seen as additions to an original unit consisting of 33 *a*, 34 *a* and 37. The prohibition of oaths and vows on the part of Jesus is easily understandable in the light of the contemporary misuse of both among Jews as well as Gentiles. Indeed, it is not impossible that the introduction of the reference to vows here may have been suggested by the section on divorce in v. 31–2, which immediately precedes that on swearing, etc., in v. 33–7, since vows in marriage were a great source of difficulty and consequent legislation. To whom is the prohibition of vows and oaths directed?

The rabbis attempted to control the use of oaths and vows in various ways, as a whole tractate in the Mishnah makes clear.[4] Rabin[5] claims that the rabbis were against all vows, but it is difficult to see how this could be so. The passage cited in support of this view is in TB Nedarim 22 *a*, the words italicized in the following quotation being adduced:

[1] *The Sayings of Jesus*, p. 158.
[2] *The Origins of the Gospel according to St Matthew*, pp. 19 f.
[3] S. Lieberman, *Greek in Jewish Palestine* (1942), pp. 115 ff.
[4] Nedarim; also Arakhin.
[5] *The Zadokite Documents* (1954), p. 76, note on viii. 3.

R. Nathan said: *One who vows is as though he built a high place* (that is, for sacrifice: this being forbidden since the building of Solomon's temple), *and he who fulfils it is as though he sacrificed thereon.* (Our italics.)

But the whole context does not support this view: the pertinent section reads as follows:

Nor do we suggest the following, viz., what was taught, R. Nathan said: One who vows is as though, etc. [as cited above]. Now the first [half] (that is, 'merely building a high place without sacrificing is not so heinous an offence, and therefore the suggestion is not so terrifying', Soncino trans. p. 63, n. 5) may be given as an opening, but as for the second,—Abaye maintained: We suggest [it]; Raba said: We do not suggest [it]. This is the version of the discussion as recited by R. Kahana. R. Tabyomi reported it thus: We may not suggest the latter half ('All agreeing that it is too frightening', Soncino trans. *ibid.* n. 6); but as for the first,—Abaye maintained: We suggest [it]; Raba said: We do not. The law is that neither the first [half] nor the second may be proposed.

What the sources suggest is a regretful acceptance of vows by the rabbis. The same would seem to be the case also with oaths. While the House of Hillel allowed the remittance of a binding oath, the House of Shammai did not. The whole discussion in TB Nedarim 28 *a* should be consulted. Its substance is summed up in a comment by R. Ashi: 'This is what is taught: Beth Shammai say, There is no absolution for an oath; and Beth Hillel say, There is absolution for an oath' (TB Nedarim 28 *a*). In view of this the words of Jesus in v. 33–7 are pertinent to Pharisaic circles. But one thing should not be overlooked, the emphatic ὅλως. Here *all* oaths are forbidden. And at this point the usage of the sectarians may have particular relevance. The evidence for this usage is conflicting. In Josephus' account of the Essenes in *The Jewish War*, II, viii, 6 we read:

They dispense their anger after a just manner and restrain their passion. They are eminent for fidelity, and are the ministers of peace, whatsoever they say also is firmer than an oath; but swearing is avoided by them, and they esteem it worse than perjury; for they say, that he who cannot be believed, without (swearing by) God, is already condemned.

On the other hand in II, viii, 7 we read (of those who are to enter the sect):

Before touching the common food they swear dread oaths (ὅρκους αὐτοῖς ὄμνυσι φρικώδεις) first of all to revere God, then to act justly towards men and not to harm anyone deliberately or in obedience to an order, but always to hate the wicked (τοὺς ἀδίκους) and to take part in the cause of the just....

There seems to be a contradiction here. Oaths of a terrible kind are *demanded* on entry into the Sect, but all oaths are avoided (it is not expressly stated that they are forbidden) by those within the Sect. Sutcliffe[1] attempts to do away with this contradiction by claiming that 'there is a distinction between the two cases. The oaths repudiated are appeals to God in confirmation of some statement. The oaths taken on admission are vows, solemn promises made to God faithfully to observe certain practices.' But it is doubtful if such a distinction should be maintained. The situation is further confused when we turn to the Manual of Discipline and the Zadokite Fragment. Oaths corresponding to the 'dread oaths' mentioned by Josephus clearly emerge. Thus in DSD v. 8:

When they are gathered together, every one who comes into the council of the community shall enter into the covenant of God in the sight of all who have offered themselves; and *he shall take it upon himself by a binding oath to turn to the law of Moses* (ויקם על נפשו בשבועת אסר לשוב אל תורת מושה) .... (M. Burrows's translation; our italics.)

(In DSD v. 10 we have the phrase יקום בברית על נפשו, that is, 'he will take it upon himself in the covenant'.) If we take DSD vi. 27, however, to refer to oaths of some kind, then it would appear that within the Sect such were not allowed. The Hebrew text is broken: thus [ר יזכיר דבר בשם הנכד על כול ה]. Burrows translates: 'Any man who mentions anything by the Name which is honoured above all *shall be set apart.*' The italicized words, in the light of the context, are a justified conjecture (see vii. 1). Are we to conclude that the Sect as reflected in DSD prohibited all vows and oaths among its members, while, as Josephus held, demanding oaths on entry? We shall return to this question after dealing with CDC. There is reference to the oath demanded on entry into the Sect in CDC xv. 1–13 as well as a prohibition of swearing. It reads:

⌜swear⌝, not by Aleph and Lamedh (that is, El, ELOHIM), nor by Aleph and Daleth (that is, ADHONAI), but with an oath of ⌜agreement⌝ | by the curses of the covenant. Even the Law of Moses let him not mention, for (......) and if he were to swear, and then transgressed *his oath*, he would profane the name. But if he ⌜swears⌝ by the curses of the covenant ⌜before⌝ | the judges, if he transgresses *his oath*, he becomes guilty and confesses, and makes restitution, but does not bear ⌜sin and shall not⌝ | die. (Rabin's translation.)

The oath of the covenant in the above passage, xv. 6, is probably the same as the binding oath of DSD v. 8 and also the oath mentioned in CDC

---

[1] E. F. Sutcliffe, *The Monks of Qumran* (1960), p. 236, n. 2.

xv. 9, 12 and CDC vii. 8, that is, they all refer to what Josephus calls the ὅρκους φρικώδεις, 'the dread oaths', made on entry into the Sect. This is denied by Rabin who contrasts the oath mentioned in the passages cited, which suggests a vow to keep the Law of Moses, with the terrible oaths of secrecy in Josephus. But the latter were not only concerned with secrecy as the above quotations show, and we are probably justified in equating them with what we have isolated in DSD and CDC. But did the Sect according to DSD and CDC forbid all vows and oaths among its members, once they had given the oath on entry? This is difficult to answer. In two sections in CDC oaths are dealt with. These are:

ix. 9:

As to that which | He said: 'Thou shalt not find redress for thyself with thine own hand': a man who causes *another* to make oath in the open field, | not before the judges or at their decree, has found redress for himself with his own hand. (Rabin's translation.)

Here the imposing of oath is forbidden except in a legal manner. But ix. 11 seems to contemplate the use of an oath, although the phraseology is difficult. The passage reads:

And everything that is lost | without it being known who stole it from the property of the camp in which it has been stolen, let its owner 'charge with an oath of the curse', and anyone who hears *it*, 'if he knows and does not tell', is guilty. | (Rabin's translation.)

The phrase 'charge with an oath of the curse' (ישביע בשבועת האלה) looks back to Num. v. 21 where the same construction exactly occurs. The phrase seems then to mean to invoke a specific curse. The question of an oath strictly so called does not here arise, although the curse did involve the invocation of the Lord. It cannot be claimed therefore that CDC ix. 11 permits an oath except in the sense of curse. The other section in CDC to be considered is xv–xvi. The pertinent passages are:

xv. 1:

(swear) not by Aleph and Lamedh [that is, El, Elohim], nor by Aleph and Daleth [that is, Adhonai], but with an oath of ⌜agreement⌝ (שבועת ה[ס]כ[ם]) | by the curses of the covenant. Even the Law of Moses let him not mention, for (......) and if he were to swear and then transgressed *his oath*, 'he would profane the name'. But if he ⌜swears⌝ by the curses of the covenant ⌜before⌝ | the judges (השפטים), if he transgresses *his oath*, he becomes guilty and confesses and makes restitution, but does not bear ⌜sin and shall not⌝ | die. (Rabin's translation.)

16-2

Here the use of substitute oaths is prohibited and only a specifically defined oath sworn before the properly constituted judges is allowed— that by the curses of the Covenant. This seems to allow oaths only in terms of those sworn on entry into the Sect. In xv. 6–19 it is oaths of the Covenant that are in view. There remain to consider the references to oaths in xvi. In xvi. 1–6 we are dealing with the oath at the entry to the Sect. In xvi. 13–19 vows of a certain kind are forbidden. What of the material in xvi. 6b–13? We are tempted to suggest that the rules enunciated on oaths in this section deal with those which one who was entering into the Sect might have undertaken before he did so. How were such oaths to be dealt with? The answer given was that only those involving no conflict with the Law (as understood by the Sect) were not to be annulled; this held for oaths concerning husbands and wives.

Owing to the uncertain meaning of the pertinent texts, any conclusions we draw concerning oaths in the Sect must be tentative. The impression gained is that Josephus's evidence is in the main confirmed. There were highly emphasized oaths administered on entry into the Sect, the attitude towards oaths undertaken prior to this was defined, in terms of loyalty to this entry or to the Law of Moses as understood by the Sect; for members, oaths were forbidden or discouraged, certainly indiscriminate oaths or substitute formulae for these. If we could take the Sect to have condemned all oaths except the Oath of the Covenant, Jesus' dismissal of *all* oaths—including any sacroscant, entrance oaths—would have had a direct bearing on the practice of the sectarians. The prohibition μὴ ὀμόσαι ὅλως would have excluded the Oath of the Covenant itself. But unfortunately the evidence does not allow us certainly to claim this, although it is probable.

The section v. 35–6 'or by the earth, for it is his footstool, or by Jerusalem, for it is the city of the great King. And do not swear by your head, for you cannot make one hair white or black', would have no direct pertinence to the Sect. Once the complete prohibition of oaths has been expressed in v. 34a, its intention is to clarify still further the intention of Jesus: He will allow no such oaths as employ a substitute for the divine Name. As Schneider[1] puts it: 'Dem absoluten Verbot des Schwörens folgen Matt. v. 34b–36 vier Sätze, die jedes Mißverständnis des Grundsatzes μὴ ὀμόσαι ὅλως beseitigen. Jesus schließt das im Judentum übliche Verfahren aus, daß man zwar den Gottesnamen um seiner Heiligkeit willen meidet, dafür aber Umschreibungen einsetzt, die gleichwertig an die Stelle des Gottesnamens treten. Jesus deckt die Unwahr-

[1] *T.W.Z.N.T.* v, 180.

haftigkeit der jüdischen Praxis auf. Er zeigt daß man es auch da wo man den Gottesnamen meidet, mit Gott zu tun hat.' The section has direct relevance to Pharisaic practice when it is recognized that the rabbis, in attempts to check the too frequent and erroneous use of oaths, did allow and even encourage certain substitute oaths. Perhaps Jesus in rejecting substitutes stands nearer to the sectarians at this point. That the prohibition of swearing had particular pertinence in communities where Jewish influences were strong is established by the fact that, whereas the prohibition of false swearing is unusual in early Christian catechism, it is found in the Didache ii. 3, which, we have good reason to claim, is to be connected with traditions typical of the sectarians.[1] The quotation on the lips of Jesus in v. 33, οὐκ ἐπιορκήσεις, recalls Lev. xix. 12, the LXX of which reads: καὶ οὐκ ὀμεῖσθε τῷ ὀνόματί μου ἐπ' ἀδικίᾳ, but it is clearly not dependent on it nor on Exod. xx. 7 nor Num. xxx. 3 nor Deut. xxiii. 22. It probably comes from a catechetical tradition presumably used in circles where sectarian influences were strong.

This prompts the question whether elsewhere in the antitheses a specifically anti-sectarian tendency can be traced. At one point this has been strongly urged,[2] namely, at v. 43–8. It begins with the words ἠκούσατε ὅτι ἐρρέθη, ἀγαπήσεις τὸν πλησίον σου, καὶ μισήσεις τὸν ἐχθρόν σου. This refers back to Lev. xix. 18 (MT: ואהבת לרעך כמוך, LXX: καὶ ἀγαπήσεις τὸν πλησίον σου ὡς σεαυτόν). But there is no exact quotation of the verse in Leviticus where also the words καὶ μισήσεις τὸν ἐχθρόν σου are wholly lacking. These last have no parallel in the Old Testament. Daube[3] regards the whole verse v. 43 as not intended to be a quotation from the Old Testament at all, but as a presentation of a particular understanding of it. He would render: 'You have heard, i.e. you have literally understood that, it has been said, Thou shalt love thy neighbour and hate thine enemy.' In what circles was this understanding of the Law prevalent? We have seen that it is not found in the Old Testament: the rabbis also have no such view. But it has been urged that hatred of enemies was enjoined among the sectarians and that Jesus is here presented as specifically rejecting their position. The following passages from DSD i. 7 ff. are pertinent:

All those who devote themselves to do the ordinances of God, shall be brought into the covenant of mercy for the community, into the council of God. He

---

[1] See Audet, *La Didachè, Instructions des Apôtres* (Paris, 1958), pp. 159 ff.

[2] Morton Smith, *H.T.R.* xlv (1952), 71 ff. on 'Matt. v. 43: "Hate Thine Enemy"'. But he thinks that there may have been a Targum to this effect.

[3] *The New Testament and Rabbinic Judaism*, p. 56.

shall walk perfectly before Him according to all the things which have been revealed at the times fixed for their revelations. He shall love each one of the sons of light according to his lot in the council of God, and hate each one of the sons of darkness according to his guilt at the time of God's vengeance.

Curses on all the men of Belial's lot are uttered by those who enter the community, DSD ii. 5–9; separation from them is urged in DSD v. 10–14; ix. 15 f., 21 f.; iv. 12; 1QM iv. 1 f.; xv. 6; iii. 7; 1QH v. 4.

At first encounter this approach to v. 43 is attractive. But before we endorse it, certain considerations deserve notice. First, the evidence, outside the literature of the Sect itself, points away from any emphasis upon hatred among its members. Although Josephus mentions that among the oaths taken by the Essenes was one 'to hate the wicked', the overwhelming impression left by the accounts of them by Josephus himself, Philo and Pliny is that of a community exceptionally committed to virtue in all its forms. Josephus[1] explicitly states that 'they are Jews by race, but with greater mutual love than the others'. According to Philo[2] they lived by a triple canon—the love of God, the love of virtue, the love of man: this last he defines as 'friendliness, a spirit of equality, a communal mode of life that surpasses description...'. Secondly, the Essenes were highly attractive to those among whom they lived, which is unlikely had their conduct been marked by 'hatred' of outsiders. Thus Pliny[3] mentions the amazing fact that, despite the austerity of their lives, they found no difficulty in recruiting members, Philo[4] that no rulers had cause to complain against them, while Josephus[5] points to an awed and interested curiosity among outsiders as to the Essene way. Thirdly, this external evidence is in certain particulars reinforced by the internal evidence of the sectarian documents. Among the members of the Sect themselves it is clear that great emphasis was placed on love. Moreover, their separation from 'the world' was not absolute because rules were laid down to regulate trade with it. In what sense then was hate inculcated?

[1] *Jewish War*, II, viii, 2.

[2] *Quod omnis probus liber sit*, chapter 83.

[3] *Naturalis Historia*, v, xv, 73: 'As time goes on [the Essenes]...[are] reborn in equal numbers by the accession of numerous men weary of life whom the waves of fortune bring to their manner of life....'

[4] *Quod omnis probus liber sit*, chapters 89–91: 'In the course of time there have arisen in the country many rulers of different characters and policies, but no one, either of the very cruel or of the guileful and hypocritical, has been able to accuse the body of those called Essenes or "holy men"....'

[5] *Op. cit.* chapter 11. The tenets of the Essenes 'lay a bait irresistible by those who have once had a taste of their wisdom'.

This is the crux of the matter. Sutcliffe[1] has urged that just as Yahweh in the Old Testament is slow to anger and plenteous in mercy and, at the same time, angry against and the avenger of those that work iniquity, so the sectarians were full of hatred against the enemies of God while, at the same time, they were marked in their conduct by love. The hatred mentioned in their documents is not of a personal kind at all: it expresses the attitude of the total community to the sons of darkness. It is of the same quality as the hatred of God to all such and can co-exist with mercy. Sutcliffe[2] makes further claims:

(1) That the hatred inculcated is not indiscriminate: all the sons of darkness are to be hated but not to the same degree; each is to be hated according to his guilt with the vengeance of God.

(2) While the sectarians are to participate in the work of vengeance which God will ultimately wreak on the sons of darkness, their co-operation belongs exclusively to the time appointed for vengeance. Before that time is manifested by God it would be wrong to harm even the sons of darkness.

(3) Although it would be erroneous to claim anything like propaganda among the sectarians to gain recruits, there was among them an openness to receive such from the world.[3] Sutcliffe[4] compares the sectarian attitude to the sons of darkness with that of the early Church and finds certain points of difference. Thus the sectarians are to judge carefully the sons of darkness and to punish them accordingly, whereas in vii. 1 there is a total prohibition of judging; by implication there is to be hatred of sin among Christians, though hatred of the brethren is explicitly forbidden, and love of all men is inculcated, while the participation of Christians in the final vengeance of God is not asserted—except that in Rev. vi. 10 the martyrs pray God to avenge their blood. It is nowhere asserted in the New Testament that Christians are to hate the wicked, and Sutcliffe accordingly finds a great difference in emphasis between this attitude and that considered proper at Qumran. He refuses, however, to think that Matt. v. 43 is a rejection of Qumran teaching because the sectarians not only forbade hatred and rancour against fellow members of the community but insisted on repaying evil with good. But he does not do full justice to the evidence at two points:

[1] *Op. cit.* pp. 81 ff.
[2] *Op. cit.* p. 236.
[3] See on these three points DSD i. 7 f., 10 f., 24 f.; 1QpH vi. 12; CDC xix. 16, etc.
[4] *Op. cit.* p. 116.

(i) His interpretation of 1QS i. 10 f. is open to question. The Hebrew is:

ולשנוא כול בני חושך איש כאשמתו בנקמת אל ...

Sutcliffe renders this:

to hate all the sons of darkness each according to his guilt (deserving) God's vengeance.

This is forced, however, and Wernberg-Møller[1] is to be followed in translating

And hate each one of the sons of darkness according to his guilt at the time of God's vengeance.

בנקמת is best taken as a note of time. Thus one ameliorating feature of the sectarian hatred as understood by Sutcliffe is removed.

(ii) The other extenuating note in his treatment is that the sectarian hatred is postponed to a future day of judgement. Until that day dawns there is to be only good treatment of the sons of darkness. It is true that in 1QS x. 18 we read: 'I will repay no man with evil's due, with good will I pursue a man', but the motive for doing so is simply that at last God's vengeance, in which the Sect is to participate, is sure. Non-resistance is the strategy of the Sect as it awaits the End. But consider the spirit revealed behind this in DSD ix. 21 ff. Here, despite the non-violence and non-resistance, a suppressed, secret hatred is cherished. The non-resistance advocated in v. 43 is of a different order, inspired not as in DSD x. 19, etc., by hope for a future day of vengeance and submission to God's command but by the imitation of God's love. The interim-ethic of non-resistance at Qumran is only outwardly like that advocated in Matthew. It is overshadowed and robbed of its moral grandeur by an eschatology of vengeance which Jesus, if not the primitive Church, seems to have rejected.[2]

Full attention must be given to the significance of v. 46–8. The material in chapter v now stands in Matthew within the context of a dialogue between the Church and the Synagogue. But there are not wanting sayings among the rabbis which urge the saluting of all men. We note the words of R. Ishmael (a contemporary of R. Akiba): 'Be swift [to do service] to a superior, and kindly to the young, *and receive all men cheerfully*' (Aboth iii. 13) (והוי מקבל את כל אדם בשמחה); and again those of R. Matti-

---

[1] *The Manual of Discipline translated and annotated with an Introduction* (Leiden, 1957), *ad rem.*

[2] On this, see J. Jeremias, *Jesus' Promise to the Nations*, pp. 45 ff.

thiah b. Heresh (A.D. 150, that is, one who belongs to a period when Judaism had become increasingly withdrawn), 'Be first in greeting every man' (מקדים בשלום כל אדם). The sayings in v. 46–8 best fit a confrontation with the sectarians, in their initial vows at least, who as we saw above emphasized hatred of those without. The term 'brethren' in v. 47 should probably be given a specific religious connotation, that is, they indicate members of a religious brotherhood. This is the most frequent usage in Matthew. Except where the term refers to brothers by blood, it seems to denote fellow members of a (religious) group: see v. 22 f.; vii. 3–5; xviii. 15–21; xxv. 40. A comparison of Mark iii. 34 with xii. 49 is illuminating at this point. In Mark those sitting around Jesus who do the will of His Father are his brethren: in Matthew these are specifically designated as the disciples. 'Brethren' in v. 47 probably stands not for אחים, the usual term for a blood brother, but for רעים, the term used in the Manual for members of the Sect, as does the brother in xviii. 15 ff. for רֵעַ. These verses may perhaps be best understood as having been originally directed at the sectarians. There is demanded of the followers of Jesus a perfection other than the perfection aimed at in Qumran (v. 48).

This approach to v. 47 f. is perhaps enforced by a consideration of v. 13–16. The disciples are described in v. 13 as 'the salt of the earth' (τὸ ἅλας τῆς γῆς); in v. 14 as 'the light of the world' (τὸ φῶς τοῦ κόσμου) and in Matt. v. 16 they are to 'shine before men' (οὕτω λαμψάτω τὸ φῶς ὑμῶν ἔμπροσθεν τῶν ἀνθρώπων). The three sections emphasize the task of the disciples as universal in character, and this is also implied perhaps in the reference to 'all that are in the house' (πᾶσι τοῖς ἐν τῇ οἰκίᾳ) in v. 15. It is legitimate to see here a contrast drawn by Matthew between Jesus' understanding of the mission of the New Israel and that of the Scribes and Pharisees of theirs. The ὑμεῖς of v. 13, 14 is emphatic: the disciples rather than the Scribes are to be the light of the world, the salt of the earth. The present setting of the section favours this. It occurs between verses (v. 11, 12) referring to the enmity of the Old Israel to the New and a section, v. 17–20, dealing with the righteousness demanded of the new community as compared with that demanded of the old. In their setting in Matthew, then, the verses in v. 13–16 clearly transfer to the New Israel the functions demanded of the Old. But it is clear that their original context has been lost both in Matthew and in Luke. Thus v. 14 has no parallel in Luke, but v. 15 has a parallel in Luke xi. 33. It is difficult to relate Luke xi. 33 directly to its context: because the section Luke xi. 33–6 seems to be determined by *Stichwortdisposition*. And although in the section immediately following (Luke ix. 37 ff.) we find the story of the Pharisee, who invited Jesus to his home, it is legitimate to claim that neither Matthew nor Luke supplies a clue to the original reference of v. 14, 15. The same is also true of Matt. v. 13 which has a partial parallel in Luke xiv. 34, where the verse follows the description by Jesus to the multitudes, in xiv. 25 ff., of the austere demands placed upon his disciples. xiv. 33 reads 'So therefore whosoever he be of you that renounceth not all that he hath, he cannot be my disciple'. Hauck[1] considers Luke to have best preserved the context of the saying: it was uttered to multitudes. The phrase, 'that renounceth not all', we cannot doubt would be rich in all sorts of connotations. Would it not recall the demand of the Sect that those who desired to join would have to renounce all? It is not impossible that in its general context the saying in Luke xiv. 34 had, as Hauck pointed out, some reference to conditions in Palestine where the salt of the Dead Sea area was deemed to have peculiar qualities, in which case it is not stretching the matter too far to suggest that in its original setting the salt-saying partook of a criticism of the Dead Sea Sect over against which the disciples are set. The fact that Matthew has arranged his material so that the Christian community is opposed as salt to the Scribes and Pharisees does not exclude the possibility that historically it was the salt of the new community as over against the 'salt' of the Dead Sea community that was emphasized. No more is claimed here than that we should at least consider the possibility that there may have been a side-glance at our Sect in v. 13. This may also be true of v. 14 where a contrast is drawn between the new eschatological community, whose light is for the world, and that other withdrawn community, whose light was confined to its own members. The sectarians called themselves the sons of light but forsook the darkness of the world, whereas the new community 'in Christ' is to shine to the world. It may indeed be that the material in v. 13–16 was originally designed to set forth the universal, because eschatological, nature of the New Israel over against the 'sons of light', who hid their light under a bushel at Qumran and in enclosed communities. Matthew has given it a new orientation over against Pharisaism. This may help to explain what has often been pointed out as a contradiction between v. 16 and vi. 2 ff. If we can take v. 16, like v. 13, 14, to have been originally a critique of the withdrawn piety of the Sect then what we have is not a contradiction. While the New Israel as a community is to shine forth among men by

[1] F. Hauck, *Das Lukasevangelium* (*Theologischer Handkommentar*) (Leipzig, 1934), *ad rem.*

their 'good deeds', and not to withdraw under a bushel, individual Christians are, at the same time, not to be ostentatious in their piety, as were so many Pharisees. It is noteworthy that while in v. 16 the total context in Matthew demands a contrast between Christians and Scribes and Pharisees, which may not have preserved the original *Sitz im Leben* of the saying, vi. 2 ff. expressly name the ὑποκριταὶ ποιοῦσιν ἐν ταῖς συναγωγαῖς, that is, the reference is unmistakably to individual Pharisees.

Attempts have been made to show that the *SM* reveals a concern with Qumran in other passages. Schubert[1] claimed that the first beatitude, v. 3, 'Blessed are the poor in spirit...', indicates 'an awareness of Essene thought and an intention by Jesus to make clear his stand against their Sect', only because, apparently, the members of the Sect were called 'the poor'. The statement of Schubert's case is confused: he asserts that this indicates how Jesus was both aligned with and opposed to the Essenes. But it must be insisted that to pin down the phrase 'the poor in spirit' to the sectarians is unwarranted. True, its exact equivalent in Hebrew has only appeared in the Scrolls, but this merely proves its Palestinian origin.[2] The phrase is not to be distinguished from 'the poor' to which Isa. lxi. 1, cited in xi. 5, refers. The term 'the poor', rightly understood in v. 3 as 'poor in spirit', had a religious even more than a social and economic connotation in Judaism which need not be confined to the Essenes. Thus v. 3 indicates not a confrontation with the Sect either in opposition or confirmation but the recognition that the Kingdom was a miracle of grace: it was for 'the poor'.[3]

Again Schubert's[4] interpretation of v. 12 ('...for so men persecuted the prophets who were before you') against an Essene background is forced. With the details of his argument that the members of the Sect were regarded as prophets 'not in the sense of Old Testament prophecy, but as heralds of the Kingdom of God members of which they already were, in a certain sense, because they are no more mere "sons of men" but are

---

[1] In *The Scrolls and the New Testament*, ed. K. Stendahl, p. 122.

[2] The phrase 'the poor in spirit' is the exact equivalent of ענוי רוח (1QM xiv. 7), compare רוח ענוה in 1QS iv. 3. Thus the Lucan 'poor' need not be regarded as necessarily more primitive than the Matthaean 'poor in spirit'. But it is still more likely that Matthew made the term 'the poor' more precise by the addition of 'in spirit' than that Luke deleted the latter, although, as we indicate in the text, 'the poor' and 'the poor in spirit' have the same connotation. For a full treatment and documentation, see J. Dupont, *Les Béatitudes* (1958), pp. 209–17. Catechetical clarity, not hostility to Qumran, prompted Matthew to add 'in spirit'.

[3] On 'the poor' see E. Bammel in *T.W.Z.N.T.* vi, 888–915.

[4] In *The Scrolls and the New Testament*, ed. K. Stendahl, pp. 122 ff.

already reckoned to the "sons of heaven"' and that they were persecuted, we need not stay.[1] The reference to v. 12 is to be understood in terms of a well-established tradition that prophets had been persecuted.[2] No more recondite specifically Essene connotation need be given to the phrase. Other claims by Schubert are equally unconvincing. There are parallels to v. 28 in Essene sources, but it is not legitimate on this ground to assert that it is a sharpening of Exod. xx. 14 particularly 'in the spirit of the Essene ideal of self denial', because the same emphasis is found elsewhere in Judaism and indeed appears as early as Job.[3] Moreover, the similarity of the parallel in terminology between xix. 4 ff. and CDC iv. 21 merely proves that such terminology was employed in exegesis and in discussions of marriage, not that there was necessarily any dependence of Jesus on sectarian exegesis.

We are now in a position to assess the traces of Essene influences which have been claimed to be present in Matthew. While taken individually many items may appear dubious, their cumulative force is considerable. Two types of material should be distinguished.

First, there is that which points to an original *Sitz im Leben* in the relationships between Jesus himself and the Essenes. Such material has been taken by the Evangelist from the tradition and given a new setting, so that its pertinence for the dialogue between Jesus and the Essenes can only be tentatively disentangled. What originally arose out of a confrontation of Jesus and the Essenes serves in Matthew the purposes of a confrontation of Church and Synagogue, and is designed, as we hope to indicate later, to clarify the relationships between the Gospel and Pharisaic Judaism. To such material, we suggest, belong most of the material with an Essene undertone in the *SM*, for example v. 13–15, 22*b*, 34, 43 ff., 48 and xix. 21. In such passages we cannot think of any conscious borrowing from the Essenes. They constitute rather part of an undifferentiated tradition that Matthew, without raising the question as to its original significance, manipulated for his own ends. Its Essene coloration as far as Matthew is concerned is accidental.

But is this the case with the second group of materials which we distinguished? In the strictly 'ecclesiastical' material with Essene under-

---

[1] *Ibid.*

[2] A. Descamps, *Les Justes et la Justice* (1950), pp. 47–53; Félix Gils, *Jésus Prophète d'après les Évangiles Synoptiques* (1957), p. 19.

[3] xxxi. 9.

tones, which we discussed above, is there a *conscious* application of specifically Essene custom? To set this question in its proper context, we recall that the emergence of 'Catholicism' in the second century and subsequently, as a highly organized institution, has puzzled historians. The period between the primitive Church and 'the Great Church' has remained a dark tunnel; and to this belongs the 'ecclesiasticism' of Matthew. Protestant historians have sometimes thought of it as an unfortunate fall from the pristine purity of the pneumatic, free community of the first century. Roman Catholic and other Catholic historians have sought to explain and justify what happened in terms of development.

The pith of the problem may be put as follows. Were the impulses to organization revealed in Matthew indigenous or secondary? Or again, did they co-exist with a pneumatic emphasis from the beginning or emerge at a later date under specific pressures? The 'incipient Catholicism' or ecclesiasticism of Matthew has been traced back to Jewish-Christian influences. According to Karl Holl,[1] two types of churches are to be seen in the New Testament, the Pauline, charismatic in ethos and presbyteral in government, and the Jewish-Christian or Palestinian, which was authoritarian. Vischer[2] claimed that Matthew has consciously depicted the Jewish-Christian conception of the Church. Since Jewish-Christianity did not constitute the main stream in the Christian movement, whence the Great Church emerged, this means that Matthaean ecclesiasticism does not belong organically to the later Great Church. But Matthew became the chief Gospel of that Church, so that any view of primitive Christianity which relegates Matthew to a secondary stream within it, by over-emphasizing its affinities with Jewish-Christianity, must be suspect.

The literature of the Essenes uncovered recently has given a new turn to the discussion. Two factors emerge. First, if we could postulate that the early Christian community co-existed from the first with a charismatic, eschatological sect, far more developed than the חבורות of the Pharisees, then we should have a precedent for and possible explanation of the ecclesiasticism revealed in Matthew. We could then plead that spirit and form, ardour and order could have dwelt together in the Church also from the beginning and that the ecclesiasticism of Matthew could have been primitive. The existence of the Essenes, as they are now revealed to

[1] 'Der Kirchenbegriff des Paulus in seinem Verhältnis zu dem der Urgemeinde', in *Gesammelte Aufsätze* (1927); compare H. Lietzmann, *Beginnings of the Christian Church*, pp. 84 f.

[2] W. Vischer, *Die evangelische Gemeindeordnung: Matthäus xvi. 13–20* (Zürich, 1946).

us more fully, enables us to make just such a postulate, because they reveal charismatic and organizational characteristics. There is, therefore, precedent for the combination of charisma and order such as we find in Matthew: the ecclesiasticism of Matthew need not be regarded as necessarily an 'alien' development.

But, secondly, a further possibility has to be faced. Does the evidence sifted above support the view that the sectarian order was deliberately exploited by the Matthaean Church in formulating its own procedures? In addition to admitting that the ecclesiasticism of Matthew was not alien can we also claim that it reveals, on the institutional level, a 'Qumranizing'—if such a word be permitted—of the Christian movement? The claim has been made that Syria, when and where Matthew emerged, was especially open to Essene influences. The converted priests, termed Hellenists in Acts, were originally Essenes, who, owing to the persecution of the Church described in Acts, first spread to Samaria and later to Damascus and Syria. After A.D. 68, when Qumran was destroyed by Roman forces, they were joined by refugees from there, some of whom became Christians. An Essenic-Christianity, therefore, developed in Syria which produced its own peculiar forms and literature. If such, indeed, was the case, Essene influence on Christianity in the milieu to which Matthew belonged must have been very deep. This would help to explain those ecclesiastical reminiscences of Qumran which are found so often.[1]

Without prolonging our discussion inordinately, we cannot enter into the validity of this claim here. We only insist that, even if it should be granted, and there is much to make us question it,[2] two things are noteworthy. First, the ecclesiasticism of Matthew can be grossly exaggerated. It rests mainly on chapter xviii. Thus the ecclesiastical forms which may suggest the sectarians as their source are few in number. Strict exactitude demands that we refer not to the ecclesiasticism of Matthew but to traces of this. Secondly, the sectarian parallels do not usually occur neat but in

---

[1] See especially O. Cullmann, 'The Significance of the Qumran Texts for Research into the Beginnings of Christianity', in *The Scrolls and the New Testament*, ed. K. Stendahl, pp. 18 ff.; E. P. Blair, *Jesus in the Gospel of Matthew* (1960), pp. 142 ff.

[2] It is difficult to accept Cullmann's view that Christian universalism owes much to the sectarians or that the term Hellenists (however Hellenized we may allow the Sect to have been) is likely to point to representatives of anything like what we find at Qumran. The question, however, is still to be examined. But see now M. Black, *The Scrolls and Christian Origins* (New York, 1961), pp. 75 ff. He favours the position that we do and is critical of that of Cullmann.

juxtaposition with specifically rabbinic forms. The total impression gained is that while the Matthaean Church was open to sectarian influences of an organizational kind, there is little evidence that it succumbed more easily to these than to synagogal ones. It exploited both for its purposes. To claim that there was anything like a capture of the Matthaean Church by Qumran so that it thereby became institutionalized under the peculiarly potent impact of the Essenes after A.D. 68 is to outrun the evidence.[1]

The relevance of this prolonged discussion of the relationship between Matthew and Qumran for the understanding of the *SM* has now to be noted. We have seen that much material in the tradition upon which Matthew drew in the *SM* was probably concerned with a dialogue between Jesus, the disciples and Qumran. But this material was utilized by the Evangelist in the dialogue which particularly concerned the Church of his day, that between Pharisaism and Christianity. Thus the original *Sitz im Leben* of much in the *SM* involved the Essenes: the *Sitz im Leben* which he gave to this involved particularly the Pharisees. This explains the collocation of sectarian and rabbinic forms in Matthew. Material dealing with the confrontation with Qumran has become embedded in that dealing with Pharisaic Judaism and given a different relevance. This emerges clearly in the *SM*. The sectarians had been given a rigid interpretation of the Law, by the Teacher of Righteousness, which was designed to lead to perfection. There is every reason to believe that Jesus offered an interpretation of the Law which was set over against this, his radicalism standing over against that of Qumran. But when Matthew constructed his 'Sermon' he utilized the tradition of the teaching for his own purposes—to set the Christian ethic not over against Qumran but over against Pharisaic Judaism, the ethic of the New Israel over against that of the Old.

This helps us to understand an aspect of Matthew that has always been puzzling. One of its most characteristic marks has long been recognized to be its ambiguity. It reveals particularly the juxtaposition of a kind of 'Jewish' particularism and 'universalism'. May it be that this juxtaposition is stressed partly because in the background of Matthew is a Church ready to absorb sectarian, and thus particularistic, influences but only on its own universalist terms. This is merely to assert that whatever the sectarian influences on Matthew may have been it would be unwise to look in their direction for the key to Matthew and, especially, the *SM*.

---

[1] See J. Daniélou, *Les Manuscrits de la Mer Morte et les Origines du Christianisme* (Paris, 1957).

For this we have to look elsewhere. Much of the content of the *SM* originally emerged in the encounter of sectarians and Jesus: its present form and purpose are dictated by the Pharisaic–Christian encounter after A.D. 70 to which, therefore, we now turn.

3. *Jamnia*

Previously we have sought to set the *SM* over against Gnosticism and Essenism. Since we have assumed that the Gospel is to be dated somewhere between A.D. 70 and 100, we must now further inquire whether developments within Pharisaism itself in that period can illumine its emergence and formulation. The events that culminated in the fall of Jerusalem in A.D. 70 and those that ensued therefrom were of crucial significance in the history of Judaism. The shattering of the Jewish state made possible the emergence of the Pharisaic party, which had hitherto only been one among many others, as the leading force in Judaism. Under the initial leadership of Rabbi Johannan ben Zakkai, it was the Pharisees at Jamnia who laid the foundations for the more concentrated and homogeneous rabbinic Judaism of later history. It is, therefore, difficult to exaggerate the significance for Jewish history of the events that followed the fall of the city. But, strangely enough, their possible relevance for the life of the Christian Church has been little exploited, and it will be now our task to ask whether Matthew, and the *SM* in particular, owe anything to the impact of what we shall call the Jamnian period.

Chronologically that period cannot be precisely charted. Our sources do not allow us to date with exactitude any of those items, such, for example, as the *Birkath ha-minim*, with which we shall be concerned below. Nevertheless, the essential characteristic, activity and achievement, of the period are clear. They are symbolized in the character and work of R. Johannan ben Zakkai, who first gathered the scholars who survived the war at Jamnia. Owing to the paucity and confusion of our sources, there can be no complete biography of this key figure. But three forces seem to have moulded him. First, under the influence of the great and gentle Hillel, his teacher, he became, like him, in a positive, almost aggressive, way, a man of peace. He opposed the policy of armed revolt against Rome from the beginning; and when war finally came his experience of it merely confirmed Johannan in his pacifism. At the appropriate moment, he decided to leave the doomed city to found a school in Jamnia where

Judaism could preserve its continuity. His attitude to the war had set Johannan over against all the apocalyptic–zealot visionaries who had plunged his people into destruction. Not fiery zeal, inspired by apocalyptic hopes, but patient attention to the immediate task had always been his aim. It continued to be such after A.D. 70, when he sought to lead his people away from fiery, futuristic fantasies to the actualities of the present. Thus the study and application of the Torah with a view to defining the task next to be *done* was his policy. Secondly,[1] the earthly, rabbinic sobriety of R. Johannan had been probably reinforced by his early experience in Galilee, which was prone to the charismatic and the apocalyptic. Reaction against unrealistic, uninformed enthusiasm, which he encountered in Galilee, had increased Johannan's reverence for the learning of the schools. But there remains to note a third factor[2] in his development. The relationship between Pharisaism and the priesthood in first-century Judaism can be easily misunderstood: it was one of both acceptance and rejection. On the one hand, the sacrificial system and the priesthood were ordained in the Law and, therefore, to be honoured. The Jerusalem priesthood was famous for its devotion to the Temple and for its discipline in fulfilling its obligations punctiliously. This had been proved and admired in the last days of the temple.[3] Moreover, while many priests were doubtless ignorant, their leaders, some of whom were Pharisees, often were not. It is not surprising, therefore, that Pharisees accepted and sometimes even admired the priesthood, mourned the loss of the temple and prayed for its restoration. But, on the other hand, there was much in the priesthood that Pharisees could not but condemn: the fact that political considerations so influenced appointments to priestly offices, the extortion of greedy priests and even their violence, the frequent concern of the priesthood, because of its political affiliations, to maintain an unjust *status quo*—all these considerations created friction between the priests and the Pharisees, who were essentially purists. This was aggravated because Pharisees sometimes presumed in their interpre-

---

[1] See below, pp. 450 f. Add to the note on Galilee references made by the way in L. Finkelstein's *Akiba* (1936), pp. 13 f. ('thus the faith which moved the plebeian of Jerusalem to live, moved the Galilean peasant to die'), LXII, 250.

[2] On the indissoluble connexion between the priesthood and the Law, see Heb. vii. 11–14.

[3] TB Yoma, 23 a. See Morton Smith, on 'The Dead Sea Sect in Relation to Ancient Judaism', in *N.T.S.* VII, 14 (July 1961), 347–60, especially p. 353. He emphasizes, among other things, 'the identification of the individual learned in the Law as, in the last analysis, the final religious authority' (p. 359) as an element in the growth of sects in Judaism. Compare fissiparous Protestantism.

tation of the Law to instruct the priesthood. It is not surprising, therefore, that a predominantly lay Pharisaism found itself opposed to the priesthood in fact, although it accepted it in principle.[1] In this opposition Johannan b. Zakkai shared. Over against charisma, apocalyptic-vision and priesthood, he set the Sage and the Torah; alongside, if not over against, the temple, the House of Study; and he carried these emphases with him to Jamnia.

Thus both nurture and experience had determined that the leader of Judaism at Jamnia should be a man of the Law and the Synagogue and of peace, of the present duty rather than the future hope, of 'study' more than 'sacrifice'. It was he who placed his stamp on the deliberations of the Sages at Jamnia as they faced the problems of reconstruction. By the time that he was followed as leader by Gamaliel II the foundations had been truly laid for the triumph of Pharisaic Judaism, and they were reinforced by the latter.[2] It would, perhaps, be possible to distinguish at length the distinctive contributions to the emerging Judaism of R. Johannan ben Zakkai and Gamaliel II, but this would not be directly pertinent to our purpose. Conditions immediately after the war were such as to enable the former to concentrate more on strictly liturgical measures, while by the time of Gamaliel II external pressures were demanding ever more attention.[3] But while recognizing the fluctuations in the immediate significance of different pressures at different times, we can here only enlarge upon the two inextricable dangers which confronted the Pharisaic leaders at Jamnia, namely, disintegration within Judaism itself and the contemporaneous, insidious attraction of forces from without, that is, of paganism in general and, especially, of Christianity and Gnosticism in some form or other.[4] Under these circumstances a policy of consolidation and exclusion was the only sane one, and, in the light of what we have written above, it was to be expected that this was the policy which their rabbinic sobriety dictated to both Johannan and Gamaliel. Rejecting apocalyptic fervour, priestly pretensions and also all unrealistic quietism or romanticism, they faced the present with the realism of the Law to be applied.

[1] On the lay character of Pharisaism, see L. Finkelstein, *The Pharisees*.

[2] H. Graetz, *The History of the Jews*, Eng. trans. II, 330 ff., is particularly helpful at this point.

[3] How much concentration on liturgical matters there was at Jamnia appears with special force in E. Werner, *The Sacred Bridge* (1959), pp. 24 ff.

[4] A. Marmorstein, *Studies in Jewish Theology* (1950), pp. 75 ff., convincingly rejected the view that after the advent of Christianity Judaism only played a secondary part in the struggle with paganism. See also J. Bergman, *Jüdische Apologetik im neutestamentlichen Zeitalter* (Berlin, 1908).

As always, the process of consolidation demanded certain 'pruning'.

(i) In the first place, serious rivals to the dominant Pharisaic elements within Jewry itself had to be eliminated. The Zealots, in any case discredited because of the failure of their policy, had been largely 'liquidated'—to use a modern euphemism—by the war; so too the Essenes were decimated, and although Essenism did not die in A.D. 70, it was not subsequently sufficiently aggressive to constitute a menace. It was, however, necessary to deal with the Sadducees. Many things would have disqualified them for leadership after A.D. 70. At a time when this life offered little comfort to Jews, their denial of the resurrection hope struck cold: their historic emphasis on the Temple and its services had become otiose: the wealthy and powerful priestly and political forces, with which they had been closely identified, had fallen, but the alienation from the masses of the people, which this identification had engendered, remained and had even been enhanced by the war. And, finally, the rigidity with which they adhered to the letter of the Law and resisted change unfitted them for a period which, above all else, demanded adaptability. But apart from their inherent disqualifications for the times, unity had now become a necessity for Judaism. The leaders at Jamnia saw to it that Sadduceanism was discredited: they made a 'dogma' of the resurrection from the dead, and thus the Sadducees automatically became heretics.[1] Mishnah Sanhedrin x. 1 reads:

All Israelites have a share in the world to come, for it is written, *Thy people also shall be all righteous, they shall inherit the land for ever; the branch of my planting, the work of my hands, that I may be glorified* [Isa. lx. 21]. And these are they that have no share in the world to come: he that says that there is no resurrection of the dead prescribed in the Law, [the words that follow show how this is aimed at one of the disruptive and dangerous elements. They read:] and (he that says)

---

[1] On the above see the illuminating treatment by B. Z. Bokser, *Pharisaic Judaism in Transition* (1935), pp. 1–6. That the influence of the Sadducees did not disappear overnight is clear, as Baron (*op. cit.* p. 129) has shown. But that they are classified with the Epicureans is highly significant. This term is rendered by H. Danby, *The Mishnah*, p. 449, in Aboth ii. 14, by 'unbeliever', and on Sanhedrin x. 1, p. 397, n. 4, he comments on it: 'A frequent epithet applied both to Gentiles and Jews opposed to the rabbinical teachings. It is in no way associated with teachings supposed by the Jews to emanate from the philosopher Epicurus; to Jewish ears it conveys the sense of the root *pakar*, "be free from restraint" and so licentious and sceptical.' But Jastrow gives the meaning 'Epicurean'. J. Bergman (*op. cit.* p. 2, n. 1), who finds points of contact between the Stoics and the rabbis, finds it also significant that the 'opponents' of the Stoics, 'the Epicureans', have lent their name to the 'opponents' of the rabbis: that is, the influence of the Epicureans is not to be ruled out of the term. On the 'heretical books', see below, p. 272.

that the Law is not from Heaven, and an Epicurean. R. Akiba says: Also he that reads the heretical books, or that utters charms over a wound and says, *I will put none of the diseases upon thee which I have put on the Egyptians: for I am the Lord that healeth thee* [Exod. xv. 26]. Abba Saul says: Also he that pronounces the Name with its proper letters.

Related to the treatment of the Sadducees, though not so drastic, was that of the priesthood. Priests were sufficiently influential after A.D. 70 to constitute both a challenge to the authority of the Pharisees at Jamnia, because of their ancient hereditary privileges, and a hindrance to reconstruction, because they might divert the activity of the people from national renewal in terms of obedience to the Torah to rebuilding the Temple and the reconstitution of their prerogatives. To deny their authority, based as it was on the Scriptures, was impossible for the Sages; nor was this desirable, because the Pharisees too shared in the hope that some day the Temple would be restored.[1] But to control priestly claims was necessary in view of the needs of the hour. And this necessity partly explains Johannan's concentration on liturgical questions in the first years at Jamnia. What was his policy? It was twofold—to concentrate authority previously vested in the Temple in the Sages and the Synagogue and to modify the importance of the priesthood. This policy was implemented by the proclamation of a series of decrees (*takkanot*) which made

---

[1] That Pharisees shared in the hope for a restoration appears in the Tefillah as revised. W. Bacher, *Die Agada der Tannaiten*, I, 94, claims that a special prayer for the restoration of Jerusalem was included in the Eighteen Benedictions after A.D. 70 (see Benediction 14). This is dated by C. W. Dugmore (*The Influence of the Synagogue on the Divine Office* (1944), p. 121) in 168–165 B.C. That there was a very strong hope for the restoration of Jerusalem after A.D. 70 is clear. Constant remembrance of Jerusalem was enjoined: see TB Baba Bathra 60 *b*. A rabbi, probably R. Joshua, held: 'One may whitewash his house and leave merely a spot not whitewashed in memory of Jerusalem; one may prepare everything for a dinner and leave one thing out in memory of Jerusalem; a woman may adorn herself and leave one ornament in memory of Jerusalem' (see A. Büchler, *The Economic Conditions of Judaea after the Destruction of the Second Temple* (1912), pp. 51 f.). A factor in this memory and hope was the survival of influential priests and High Priests after A.D. 70; for details see A. Büchler, *op. cit.* pp. 10 ff. In that period priests were especially anxious to guard the purity of their blood (p. 11). The exact condition of Jerusalem after A.D. 70 requires reconsideration, as K. W. Clark (see below, p. 321, n. 1) has shown; but Büchler brings forward little early support for Clark's position. Thus he cites a passage from TB Makkoth 24 *b* reporting how R. Gamaliel II, R. Eleazar b. Azariah, R. Joshua and R. Akiba visited the ruins of the temple and were grieved to see a fox coming out from the ruins of the Holy of Holies. But he notes that the tithe laws concerning Jerusalem still persisted in force after A.D. 70, and provides late evidence for the continuance of pilgrimages to Jerusalem: see pp. 15–18.

it clear that in everything, except the offering of sacrifice, Jamnia was to enjoy the prerogatives of Jerusalem.

(a) The necessity soon arose to assert the authority of the Sages in calendrical matters. Shortly after A.D. 70 the New Year fell on the Sabbath. The regulations governing the proclamation of such a year are given in Mishnah Rosh Hashanah iv. 1 as follows:

If a Festival-day of the New Year fell on a Sabbath they might blow the *shofar* in the Holy City but not in the provinces. After the Temple was destroyed Rabban Johanan b. Zakkai ordained that they might blow it wheresoever there was a court. R. Eliezer said: Rabban Johanan b. Zakkai ordained it so only for Jabneh. They replied: It is all one whether it was Jabneh or any other place wherein was a court.

In the *gemara* in TB Rosh Hashanah 29*b* we read:

AFTER THE DESTRUCTION OF THE TEMPLE RABBAN JOHANAN BEN ZACCAI ORDAINED, etc. Our Rabbis taught: Once New Year fell on a Sabbath [and all the towns assembled], and Rabban Johanan said to the Bene Bathyra,[1] Let us blow the *shofar*. They said to him, Let us discuss the matter. He said to them, Let us blow and afterwards discuss. After they had blown they said to him, Let us now discuss the question. He replied: The horn has already been heard in Jabneh, and what has been done is no longer open to discussion.

By insisting that the New Year, which occurred on a Sabbath, could be proclaimed by rabbinical courts, Johannan claimed for the latter one of the prerogatives of the Temple authorities. This was not in order to reject the Temple as such, because he himself desired its restoration, but to constitute a *valid* equivalent (not a substitute) for the Temple and the priests in the academy and the Sages respectively.

In the same way, Johannan ordained the proclamation of the New Moon in new terms:

Beforetime they used to admit evidence about the new moon throughout the day. Once the witnesses tarried so long in coming that the levites were disordered in their singing; so it was ordained that evidence could be admitted only until the afternoon offering. And if witnesses came from the time of the afternoon offering onwards, then this day was kept holy and also the morrow was kept holy. After the Temple was destroyed Rabban Johanan b. Zakkai ordained that they might admit evidence about the new moon throughout the day.

---

[1] On these, see *J.E. ad rem.* They survived the fall of Jerusalem probably as a family according to A. Büchler (*op. cit.* p. 12); but S. B. Hoenig (*The Great Sanhedrin* (1953), p. 199) takes them to stand for an 'opposition group in matters of law' at any time, not for a family.

R. Joshua b. Karha said: Rabban Joḥanan b. Zakkai ordained this also that wheresoever the chief of the court might be, witnesses should go only to the place of assembly. (Mishnah Rosh Hashanah iv. 4.)

WHEN THE TEMPLE WAS STANDING THEY USED TO PROFANE SABBATH FOR ALL THE MONTHS, IN ORDER THAT THE SACRIFICE MIGHT BE OFFERED ON THE RIGHT DAY. Our Rabbis taught: Originally the Sabbath could be profaned for all of them. When the Temple was destroyed, Rabban Joḥanan b. Zakkai said to them [the Beth Din], Is there then a sacrifice [waiting to be brought]? They therefore ordained that Sabbath should not be profaned save for Nisan and Tishri alone. (TB Rosh Hashanah 21 b.)

Johannan's regulations not only asserted the right of the Sages in calendrical matters, but emphasized that the Beth Din at Jamnia had taken over the function of the Great Sanhedrin at Jerusalem, whose prerogative it had previously been to announce the New Moon.[1] By thus controlling the calendar Jamnia claimed to have the prestige and authority of the national centre. In this connexion, it should not be overlooked that for a religion based upon the observance of Law, control of the calendar was of crucial significance, because a faulty calendar threw observance of the festivals and other requirements wholly out of joint. The seriousness with which calendrical matters were dealt with both at Jamnia and at Qumran can only be appreciated in this light.[2]

(b) Another way in which R. Johannan ben Zakkai sought to curtail priestly privileges emerges in TB Rosh Hashanah 31 b, where the priests are not permitted to go up (to bless the people with the priestly blessing) on to the platform with their shoes on (but rather, barefooted, as in the Temple).

The passage reads:

Our Rabbis have taught: 'The priests are not permitted to ascend the *duchan* in their sandals, and this is one of the nine regulations laid down by Rabban Johanan ben Zaccai.'

Here Johannan has transferred to the Synagogue a part of the ritual of the Temple. Why? This was a way of showing his right to regulate the conduct of the priests in worship, and also of insisting that an act which showed respect to the congregation in the Temple should be continued

---

[1] S. B. Hoenig, *op. cit.* pp. 100 f.

[2] DSD i. 14; x. 1–8; CDC iii. 13–16; compare Col. ii. 16 ff.; this was made doubly clear to me in a lecture by E. Stauffer. On DSD x. 1–8, see E. Ettisch, *Revue de Qumrân*, no. 5 (November 1959), 3 ff., on 'Eschatologisch-astrologische Vorstellungen in der Gemeinderegel, x. 1–8'.

outside the Temple. Thus the dignity of the congregations outside the Temple was to be honoured: the priests had to approach the congregation as did Moses the burning bush. In short, any pretensions to priestly superiority over the congregation are denied.

(c) Thirdly, Johannan assumed the right to legislate concerning gifts and offerings normally due to the Temple which, owing to its destruction, now constituted a problem. To enter into the technicalities involved is not possible here. We need only refer to the pertinent sources in TP Shekalim viii. 4; TP Hallah i. 1; Mishnah Maaser Sheni v. 2:

Fruit of a Fourth Year Vineyard was taken up to Jerusalem (from any place) one day's journey in any direction. And what was the (farthest) limit? Elath to the south, Akrabah to the north, Lydda to the west, and the Jordan to the east. When the fruits became too many it was ordained that they might be redeemed even though (the vineyard was) near to the (city) wall. And this was with the understanding that when they wished, the matter might be restored as before-time. R. Jose says: This was the understanding after the Temple was destroyed, and the understanding was that when the Temple should be rebuilt the matter would be restored as beforetime.

In these ways the authority of the Sages over the priests, who might have been a very disruptive influence, was asserted.[1] That the reason for the ordinances referred to above, however, was not exhausted by the anti-priestly concern of the Sages will appear below.

(ii) But, in the second place, there was deep disunity among the Pharisees themselves. In referring to those who emerged dominant in the period of Jamnia we used the term 'party'. But those Pharisees who survived the war were no more a unified, monolithic group than had been those who lived in pre-war days and during the war. They too had shared in the שִׂנְאַת חִנָּם (hatred without cause) among Jews to which the Talmud traced the downfall of Jerusalem.[2] Disunity among the Pharisees had been particularly caused by the differences between the Houses of Hillel and Shammai. These went back to Hillel and Shammai themselves

---

[1] The strength of the priestly element in the period after A.D. 70 must be recognized. This was increased by the fact that many of the leading rabbis may have been priests. Thus R. Johannan b. Zakkai himself was possibly the son of a priest; R. Ishmael, a priest, was the son of a High Priest (TB Hullin 49a); R. Zadok was a priest (TB Bekhoroth 36a); Jôse, a disciple of R. Johannan b. Zakkai, was a priest; R. Tarfon had been a priest. For details, see A. Büchler, op. cit. pp. 10–12. E. Werner, op. cit. p. 24, holds that R. Joshua ben Hananiah was a Levite priest who helped to transfer the tradition of the Temple to the Synagogue.

[2] TB Shabbath 32b.

and were deep-rooted in the different social strata which they represented, the former coming from the lower or artisan classes, the latter from the patricians. These social differences may have been largely responsible for the different attitudes which they took towards the Law, the Hillelites, in the interests of the people, being ready to adapt the Law, on the basis of Scripture, to new conditions, the Shammaites, who saw less need of adaptation, accepting, as true tradition, only what had been delivered to them by their teachers. In addition, the Shammaites opposed a rigid, militant fanaticism to the pacifism of the Hillelites.[1] These differences led to much personal acrimony and even broke out into physical violence in the notorious occasion of the 'Eighteen Issues', when the Shammaites attempted to impose a general boycott on the Gentile world and, on being opposed by the Hillelites, attacked them.[2] The same situation between the two groups continued after A.D. 70. This meant that there was a diversity of opinion between two major groups among the Pharisees, which occasioned deep personal bitterness. There was also a real danger that the view should be encouraged that there could be two 'Laws', a conception which would insinuate a divided loyalty at the very heart of Judaism. The following passages are illuminating: TB Berakoth 11 a which reads:

Our Rabbis taught: Beth Hillel say that one may recite the *Shemaʿ* standing, one may recite it sitting, one may recite it reclining, one may recite it walking on the road, one may recite it at one's work. Once R. Ishmael and R. Eleazar b. Azariah were dining at the same place, and R. Ishmael was reclining while R. Eleazar was standing upright. When the time came for reciting the *Shemaʿ*, R. Eleazar reclined and R. Ishmael stood upright. Said R. Eleazar b. Azariah to R. Ishmael: Brother Ishmael, I will tell you a parable. To what is this [our conduct] like? It is like that of a man to whom people say, You have a fine beard, and he replies, Let this go to meet the destroyers. So now, with you: as long as I was upright you were reclining, and now that I recline you stand upright! He replied: I have acted according to the rule of Beth Hillel and you have acted according to the rule of Beth Shammai.

---

[1] See Nahum Glatzer, *Hillel the Elder* (New York, 1956), pp. 64 f., who holds that over against the Hasmonean priestly tradition of wars of defence and conquest, Hillel tried to reassert the 'old prophetic image' of the priest as a man of peace (G. F. Moore, *Judaism*, I, *ad rem*; H. Graetz, *op. cit.* pp. 130 ff.).

[2] TB Abodah Zarah 36 a; TB Shabbath 17 a; see especially H. Graetz, *op. cit.* p. 270. In this connexion Rabban Simeon ben Gamaliel urged that no ordinance which the majority of the people could not endure should be imposed (see above, p. 266): Tosefta Sanhedrin ii. 13, p. 418; TB Abodah Zarah 36 b.

In the Mishnah itself there is an effort to minimize the differences between the two houses in some passages. But even so, behind these is revealed, even by their protests, a very deep cleavage. In this connexion Mishnah Eduyoth iv is illuminating and iv. 8 particularly pertinent:

The School of Shammai permit levirate marriage between the co-wives and the surviving brothers. And the School of Hillel forbid it. If they performed *halitzah*[1] the School of Shammai declare them eligible to marry a priest, but the School of Hillel declare them ineligible. If they had been taken in levirate marriage, the School of Shammai declare them eligible but the School of Hillel ineligible. Notwithstanding that these declare ineligible whom the others declare eligible, yet (the men of) the School of Shammai did not refrain from marrying women from (the families of) the School of Hillel, nor (the men of) the School of Hillel from marrying women from (the families of) the School of Shammai; and despite all the disputes about what is clean and unclean, wherein these declare clean what the others declare unclean, neither scrupled to use aught that pertained to the others in matters concerned with cleanness.

But apart from the notorious disputes between these two main Pharisaic groups, the interpretation of the Law in general was in a chaotic state. There were in existence manuals to guide priests in the intricacies of the Temple services and also handbooks of court decisions for the benefit of judges. But, apart from this, the oral law was not codified in matters ritual or other. Thus a unified regulation of practice—and orthopraxy was then as always the life-blood of Judaism—was impossible. Personal animosities and a fissiparous fertility in the interpretation of the Law could supply no ground for unity. Thus it became imperative for the Pharisees to put their own house in order. At what exact date it is not certain, but the conflict between the House of Hillel and that of Shammai was eventually resolved in favour of the former. The relevant passage in TB 'Erubin 13*b* gives a legendary account of this as follows:

R. Abba stated in the name of Samuel: For three years there was a dispute between Beth Shammai and Beth Hillel, the former asserting, 'The *halachah* is in agreement with our views' and the latter contending, 'The *halachah* is in agreement with our views.' Then a *bath kol* issued announcing, '[The utterances of] both are the words of the living God, but the *halachah* is in agreement with the rulings of Beth Hillel.' Since, however, 'both are the words of the living God' what was it that entitled Beth Hillel to have the *halachah* fixed in agreement with

---

[1] Lit: drawing off (*sc.* of the shoe). The ceremony prescribed (in Deut. xxv. 7–9, compare Yebamoth xii. 1 ff.) when a man refuses to marry the widow of his brother who has died childless (Danby, *op. cit.* p. 794).

their rulings?—Because they were kindly and modest, they studied their own rulings and those of Beth Shammai, and were even so [humble] as to mention the actions of Beth Shammai before theirs.... (Soncino translation, pp. 85 f.)

The actual course of events is obscure. It has been argued that these schools—the Hillelite and the Shammaite—terminated their existence shortly after the destruction of the Temple and that 'Beth Shammai, having been outlawed, vanished from the history of Judaism'.[1] If we follow the view of the majority of scholars, however, many of the views of Shammaites are preserved for us in the Mishnah, along with those of the Hillelites, as in Mishnah Eduyoth. It is significant, however, that the very preservation of views different from those of the Hillelites is made to serve the ends of unity. The pertinent passage is the following, where, after references to differences of view between Hillel and Shammai, we read in Mishnah Eduyoth i. 4, 5:

And why do they record the opinions of Shammai and Hillel when these do not prevail? To teach the generations that come after that none should persist in his opinion, for lo, 'the fathers of the world' did not persist in their opinion.

And why do they record the opinion of the individual against that of the majority, whereas the *Halakah* may be only according to the opinion of the majority? That if a court approves the opinion of the individual it may rely upon him, since a court cannot annul the opinion of another court unless it exceeds it both in wisdom and in number; if it exceeds it in wisdom but not in number, or in number but not in wisdom, it cannot annul its opinion; but only if it exceeds it both in wisdom and in number.

Immediately important as was the settling of this controversy, however, it was only part of a larger problem already indicated, namely, the need for the codification of the Oral Law. Unfortunately, we cannot establish with any definiteness what were the exact codifications which came into being in the period of Jamnia. But one thing has emerged clearly from the significant studies of this problem, namely, that the development which culminated in the codification of the Mishnah of Rabbi Judah the Patriarch, about A.D. 220 had very insistent beginnings in the period of Jamnia, which, although it did not produce the Mishnah, was, nevertheless, a period of mishnaic activity. It must be emphasized that codification was in the air of Jamnia.[2]

---

[1] See A. Guttmann in *Hebrew Union College Annual*, xxviii (1957), 115 ff., on 'Hillelites and Shammaites—a Clarification'.

[2] See on the above H. L. Strack, *Introduction to the Talmud and Midrash* (Philadelphia, 1931), pp. 20 ff.; D. Hoffmann, *Die erste Mischna und die Controversen der*

This assertion can be supported in two ways. First, there is considerable evidence that collections of the oral tradition in Mishnah form took place in the period. According to TB Nedarim 41 *a*:

כי הוה גמיר רבי תלת עשרי אפי הילכתא אגמריה לר' חייא שבעה מנהון

that is,

When Rabbi had studied his teaching in thirteen different interpretations, he taught R. Hiyya only seven of them.[1]

This is taken by Danby to mean that Rabbi, 'in drawing up his Mishnah, made use of thirteen separate collections of *Halakoth*; that is to say, he had a knowledge of that number of varying systems by which the bulk or selections of the *Halakoth* had been transmitted in the names of the earlier authorities and by which they were taught in the schools of the disciples of these authorities'.[2] There are references to a Mishnah of Rabbi Meir (*c.* A.D. 140–65) which was based upon the teaching of R. Akiba (A.D. 40(?)–134) in TB Sanhedrin 86 *a*. In Mishnah Sanhedrin iii. 4 we read of a Mishnah of R. Akiba and of an earlier 'First Mishnah'. The term 'First Mishnah' occurs also in Mishnah Ketuboth v. 3; Gittin v. 6; Nazir vi. 1; Eduyoth vii. 2. In all these passages the meaning is ambiguous: the term 'First Mishnah' may merely refer to a previous specific ruling on the particular point under discussion. Nevertheless, the impression is hard to resist that it points to 'a complete compilation of tradition, like the extant Mishnah of R. Judah the Patriarch'. Danby finds references to earlier collections in the formula: 'Beforetime they used to say...but afterward...' at Mishnah Nedarim ix. 6; xi. 12; Gittin vi. 5; Niddah x. 6; Tebul Yom iv. 5. That the tractates Kelim and Uktzin had probably been arranged by the end of the first century appears from TB Baba Kamma 82 *a*, TB Megillah 31 *b*. Certain tractates go back before A.D. 70, for example, Middoth, Tamid and Yoma, while Kinnim has been traced to R. Joshua ben Hananiah, a contemporary of Johannan ben Zakkai at Jamnia, and Taanith to Rabban Simeon ben Gamaliel II, who took over the leadership at Jamnia from Johannan. Finkelstein considers that the maxims preserved in the name of Rabbi Johannan ben Zakkai in Mishnah Aboth are from a collection made by him or by his disciples during his

---

Tannaïm (Berlin, 1882); C. Albeck, *Untersuchungen über die Redaktion der Mischna* (1923) (there is a valuable review of his Hebrew work, *Mavo' la Mishnah* (Jerusalem, 1950), in *J.J.S.* x, 3, 4 (1959), 173–81 by B. de Vries); H. Danby, *The Mishnah*, translation (1933), pp. xiii–xxxii. On mishnaic as over against midrashic activity, see S. Lauterbach, *Rabbinic Essays* (1951), p. 166*a*.

[1] The rendering is that in the Soncino translation.   [2] *Op. cit.* p. xxi.

lifetime and possibly before the Sage took up his residence at Jamnia.[1] The activity in codification which we are justified, therefore, in connecting with the Jamnian period, was precisely what was to be expected. The essential task of the Sages at Jamnia has been described as follows by Danby: '(Upon them) fell the duty of administering and interpreting the religious law and, most important of all, the urgent task of conserving the body of traditional laws and solving the new and confusing problems which arose in the numerous observances dependent on the Temple and the priesthood.'[2] Codification had become a necessity.

But, secondly, a new twist has been given to the discussions of the origins of the Mishnah by Finkelstein. Here we can only refer to his convincing theory. He writes as follows:

We may therefore take it that the change in the arrangement of the Orders (of the Mishnah) was made by either Rabbi Akiba, or one of his successors, Rabbi Meir or Rabbi Judah the Patriarch. The purpose of the change was of course to introduce the student to those parts of the Mishna applicable to his own life. It was still considered appropriate to study the laws of sacrifices, but they were what we would call 'graduate studies', and could not serve as the beginning of the Mishna. The laws of purity were observed by many scholars, but not by all; and certainly did not have the universality of application of the laws of agricultural gifts and the festivals. The future teacher and scholar, who would be called upon to render decisions for the community, required these much more than the theoretical discussions regarding sacrifices and ritualistic purity; and hence they were taught first.

In this rearrangement of the Mishna, the former introduction to the Order 'Sacrifices' followed immediately on the old treatise Abot, and was added to it.[3]

The force of Finkelstein's contention is that the destruction of the Temple necessitated a reformulation of the traditional or existing mishnaic order. He assumes that a sixfold Mishnah existed in the first century, but that, after A.D. 70, it was rearranged in the light of new circumstances. In short, the Jamnian period was one of intense codification and modification of the legal tradition. This was part of the response of Judaism to the need for unity and for adaptation to changed conditions.

[1] *Mabo le Massekot Abot ve Abot d'Rabbi Nathan*, Introduction to the Treatises Abot and Abot of Rabbi Nathan (New York, 5711–1950), pp. xiii ff. See M. Aboth i. 8–16.   [2] *Op. cit.* p. xx.

[3] *Op. cit.* p. xx. On p. xviii he gives the original order of the Mishnah, which he takes to have been: Kodashim ('Sacrifices'), Toharot ('Purity'), Zeraim ('Agriculture'), Moed ('Festivals'), Nashim ('Women'), Nezikin ('Civil Law'). This order (beginning with 'Sacrifices') is logical, but not suitable for the period after A.D. 70, when 'sacrifice' had ceased; hence the rearrangement.

(iii) Mutual harmony and codification of the Law were not the only necessities for unity. The value of uniformity in religious practice was not unknown to the Sages at Jamnia. And, since the institution upon which scattered Jewry had most come to rely for its coherence was the ubiquitous Synagogue, it is not surprising that they made serious attempts at the regulation of its worship in the interests of unification. Exact dates cannot be given for the specific changes they introduced. In view of the conservatism of most religious bodies in modifying their ritual and usage, it is a fair assumption that the changes made in Jamnia were a long time brewing before they finally came to the boil. That the process involved was probably prolonged and much debated holds even though it was consummated by the somewhat volcanic Rabbi Gamaliel II, who did not suffer fools gladly.[1] Nevertheless, as we saw above, the situation immediately after the Fall of Jerusalem demanded 'a reformation without tarrying for any', and some immediate changes were introduced by R. Johannan ben Zakkai. We shall first consider these, although we have already dealt with some of them.

Although its spiritual impact on the nation could be exaggerated,[2] the Sages were aware of the unifying significance of the Temple before A.D. 70. Thus it was that Rabbi Johannan ben Zakkai was anxious to forge links between the Synagogue services and the now defunct Temple services. And some of the changes in the ritual of Judaism, which were governed by the desire to curb priestly power in the interests of national unity, as we noted above, reveal also this aim. More fully expressed, this aim was to concentrate in the Synagogue, when this was possible, forms previously associated with the Temple, so that they could continue to evoke memories of the Temple through the Synagogue, and thus still exercise their unifying power.[3] This, not only an anti-priestly concern, prompted the change in the use of the *lulab*[4] in the Feast of Tabernacles

---

[1] This is well brought out by Joshua Podro, *The Last Pharisee, The Life and Times of Rabbi Joshua ben Hananyah: A first century idealist* (London, 1959), pp. 68–82. For a less sympathetic treatment: Jost, *Geschichte der Israeliten* (Berlin, 1822), III, 193 ff. The pertinent passages are: TB Baba Metzia 59*b*; Siphre Debarim 1, chapter 16; Mishnah Rosh Ha-Shanah ii. 8–9; T. B. Rosh Ha-Shanah 5*a*; T. B. Bekhoroth 36*a*; T. B. Berakoth 27*b*, 28*a*, 29*a*.

[2] *P.R.J.*[2] pp. 254 ff.

[3] See J. Neusner, in an unpublished Ph.D. dissertation on *Rabbi Johannan ben Zakkai* (Columbia-Union, New York, 1961).

[4] '*Lulab*'—literally 'a palm branch'. The *lulab* stands for the branches of palm, myrtle and willow, bound together and carried with a citron, during the Feast of Tabernacles as prescribed by Lev. xxiii. 40. See *J.E. ad rem.*

and the introduction of the priestly blessing into the liturgy of the Synagogue. To use psychological terms, these were designed to create a 'sentiment' for and around the Synagogue, which, while it provided a substitute for the Temple, also recalled it. These changes were immediately necessary and were effected at an early date by Johannan. But the same motif was at work later in the policy of Rabban Gamaliel II. In his revision of the Passover Haggadah, he included references to the Passover sacrifice at Jerusalem and prayers for the restoration of the city and its sacrificial system. These evoked the Temple which had always been a living centre for Jewry, a symbol of their unity.[1]

But apart from innovations aimed at constituting the Synagogue as a substitute for the Temple, designed to recall it, the Fall of the Sanctuary, which had been the liturgical centre, also made necessary the unification and standardization of the traditional Synagogue service.[2] This led to the rearrangement of the most prominent element of prayer in the synagogal liturgy, the Tefillah or Amidah. The following account, the essential reliability of which is not to be doubted, comes from TB Berakoth 28 *b*:

ת״ר שמעון הפקולי הסדיר י״ח ברכות לפני ר״ג על הסדר ביבנה...

Our Rabbis taught: Simeon ha-Paḳuli arranged the eighteen benedictions in order before Rabban Gamaliel in Jabneh.

The verb סדר is used of systematizing material, and is frequently found in contexts dealing with proper arrangements for worship in its various forms.[3] The implication is that these benedictions had previously been used, but that, at Jamnia, they were given a standardized order. The Tefillah was an old prayer; it was now authorized in a definitive eighteen-fold form. To go into further details on this point is not necessary.[4] Nor can we here pursue the question whether other elements in the liturgy of the Synagogue point to Jamnia. The recital of the Shema goes back to the Temple and was almost certainly carried over into the worship of the Synagogue in pre-Christian times.[5] As to the four benedictions, Yotzer,

---

[1] See, for example, A. A. Green, *The Revised Haggada* (London, 1897).

[2] S. W. Baron, *A Social and Religious History of the Jews, ad rem.*

[3] Is τάσσω the Greek equivalent of סדר? Compare Papias' οὐ μέντοι τάξει, in Eusebius, *H.E.* iii, 39, 15.

[4] See I. Elbogen, *Jüdischer Gottesdienst* (1913), pp. 27–60; S–B, Exkurs iv. 1, pp. 208–49.

[5] On this see L. Blau, *R.E.J.* xxx–xxxi (1895), 179 ff. on 'Origine et Histoire de la lecture du Schema'.

Ahabah, Geullah, Hashkibenu, which are connected with the Shema, it is difficult to claim that they are to be peculiarly connected with our period. Since the discussion of these liturgical matters involve possible polemic interests, it will be best to deal with them at a later stage.

For the same reason also, we shall at this point merely refer to the concern for unity which is revealed in the concentration on the problem of the Canon which characterized the period of Jamnia. To judge from TB Sanhedrin 100*b* the prohibition to read 'external' books was not absolute: it referred, not to the private reading of such documents, but to their public reading, including public study and liturgical recitation. Here we merely emphasize that the attempt at the fixation of the Canon at Jamnia was part of the larger consolidating process with which we are concerned.[1]

Finally, this same process is revealed in the institution of the rabbinate which probably goes back to Johannan ben Zakkai. While Gamaliel I had been called Rabban, the title Rabbi had not been used even of great leaders such as Hillel and Shammai. But with the triumph of Pharisaism at Jamnia, the Law, and the student of the Law, came into their own. Johannan b. Zakkai considered that he and his fellow Sages had inherited the authority over Israel previously vested in the Great Sanhedrin. He, therefore, took upon himself the right to ordain his disciples, that is, to give them a formal status as authorities in their realm. Goldin[2] expresses the matter thus: '(The granting of the title "Rabbi") apparently was part of the large, new program of Talmud Torah. Every one must study Torah, and henceforth the man of authority, not just of influence but of authority, is the rabbi, the sage who goes through the discipline of a student of the sages and becomes a master of Torah.' We should add, perhaps, that to the desire to give the Sage his proper place, through 'ordination' by the laying on of hands, there was also added the concern to regularize the interpretation of the Law in the interests of unity by delivering it from 'charismatics'. The Jerusalem Talmud, Sanhedrin i. 2, reads:

At first each one would appoint (ordained) his own students, as Rabban Johannan ben Zakkai ordained Rabbi Eliezer, Rabbi Joshua, and Rabbi Joshua appointed Rabbi Akiba, and Rabbi Akiba, Rabbis Meir and Simeon.

---

[1] See O. Eissfeldt, *Einleitung in das Alte Testament* (1934), p. 624.
[2] J. Goldin on 'The Three Pillars of Simeon the Righteous', in *P.A.A.J.R.* XXVII (1957), 55.

The Sages at Jamnia were legitimized as the guarantors of the tradition, given an official status with a title. A rabbinical succession was established as an authoritative cohesive force.[1]

In addition to consolidating Judaism internally, the Sages at Jamnia were called upon to preserve it from enemies without. Consolidation was inseparable from exclusion. We are now concerned with the fear of the subversive influence of Christianity which may have influenced the rabbinic leaders. Some have sought to minimize, if not to deny, any such thing, on the ground that Judaism was so engrossed in its internal problems that it overlooked or deliberately ignored the incipient menace of Christianity.[2] Others have contrasted the active opposition to the latter, which Judaism offered in the second century, with its comparative unconcern with it in the first.[3] Thus, for example, although Christians had already in the first century interpreted the Fall of the Temple as a punishment on Jewry for their rejection of Christ, it is only in the second that the rabbis reveal a polemic interest in that event.[4] But, while it is true that bitterness increased as the second century came, there was conflict obviously before this, and there are unmistakable signs that what happened at Jamnia was not uninfluenced by the rising significance of Christianity.

Interest in the Canon was, partly at least, a reaction to Christianity. It is clear that the dispute as to whether the Scriptures 'rendered the hands unclean', that is, were to be treated as 'holy', went back to the period before the war, as appears from Mishnah Yadaim iv. 6:

The Sadducees say, We cry against you, O ye Pharisees, for ye say, 'The Holy Scriptures render the hands unclean', [and] 'The writings of Hamiram do not render the hands unclean'. Rabban Joḥanan b. Zakkai said, Have we naught against the Pharisees save this!—for lo, they say, 'The bones of an ass are clean,

---

[1] The parallel with the emergence of Canon and episcopate in the Church under similar influences is obvious. Probably, so Daube (*op. cit.* p. 232) thinks (and such is the view of Bacher and S–B), the increasing use of ordination in Christianity is one reason for the decline of its significance in later Judaism. Daube understands ordination as having as its object 'the pouring of the ordaining scholar's personality into the scholar to be ordained' (*op. cit.* p. 231). See S–B, II, 655 f.

[2] L. Ginzberg, *J.B.L.* XLI, 115–36. On the Canon, see also S. Zeitlin, 'An Historical Study of the Canonization of the Hebrew Scriptures', in *P.A.A.J.R.* (1932), 152 ff. See my *Christian Origins and Judaism, ad rem.*

[3] S. W. Baron, *op. cit.*

[4] See M. Simon on 'Retour du Christ et reconstruction du Temple...', in *Aux Sources de la Tradition Chrétienne* (Neuchâtel, 1950), pp. 247 ff.; and H. J. Schoeps, *Aus frühchristlicher Zeit, ad rem.*

and the bones of Johanan the High Priest are unclean'. They said to him, As is our love for them so is their uncleanness—that no man make spoons of the bones of his father or mother. He said to them, Even so the Holy Scriptures: as is our love for them so is their uncleanness; [whereas] the writings of Hamiram (these are variously explained as 'books of the heretics (Minim) or the books of Homer', Danby, *op. cit.* p. 784, n. 7), which are held in no account do not render the hands unclean.

Over against the Sadducees, the Pharisees virtually claimed that so sacred were the Scriptures that it was necessary to wash the hands after using them, just as the priests did after participating in the Temple rites.[1] Thus the 'status' of the Scriptures constituted a problem within Judaism itself. And, especially after A.D 70, the time had come to define what defiled, and the Pharisees at Jamnia were in a strong position to do so. Even though the authority of the Law and the Prophets had long been recognized and these distinguished from the other writings, it is significant that R. Gamaliel II is the first attested to have expressly used the division of the Scriptures into Torah, Prophets and Writings; and we know that there were many books disputed at Jamnia, because they were of doubtful authority, for reasons which were of import only to Judaism.[2]

But the attempts at fixing a canon have also been claimed to reflect the need to counteract certain influences, the futuristic fantasies of Apocalyptists, the speculative aberrations of Gnosticism, and, from the Pharisaic point of view, the equally dangerous quietistic illusions of Christianity. As Christianity produced a literature, Judaism had to look more guardedly to its own. Certain passages have suggested this last. First, those which refer to 'the outside books' and 'the books of the *minim*'. Thus in Mishnah Sanhedrin x. 1 we read:

All Israelites have a share in the world to come, for it is written, *Thy people also shall all be righteous, they shall inherit the land for ever....* And these are they that have no share in the world to come: he that says that there is no resurrection of the dead prescribed in the Law, and [he that says] that the Law is not from Heaven and an Epicurean. R. Akiba says: Also he that reads the heretical books, or that utters charms over a wound.... [Danby's translation: 'heretical books' are literally הספרים החיצונים, that is, outside books.]

Here the 'external books' (הספרים החיצונים), the prohibition of which occurs in a context dealing with heresy, have been interpreted as 'heretical'

---

[1] J. Neusner, unpublished dissertation on *R. Johannan ben Zakkai*.
[2] See my article in *The Interpreter's Dictionary of the Bible* on 'Law in first-century Judaism', vol. III, pp. 89–95.

and, particularly, early Christian writings. But Ginzberg[1] urged that 'external' here did not mean 'heretical', but merely non-canonical, and that the prohibition intended applied not to private but to public reading. It is exceedingly unlikely that Jewish synagogues would have been in danger of reading Christian writings in public, so that the prohibition can hardly have applied to them. Similarly the predominant view that 'the books of the *minim*' in such passages as Tos. Shabbath xiii. 5; TB Gittin 45 *b*, etc., can be regarded as Christian has been challenged. The pith of the argument for the customary view is twofold. (*a*) The term 'minim' can include Jewish Christians; (*b*) in TB Shabbath 116*a*, apparently an early passage, there is a specific reference to the Gospels, in the phrase און גליון, and in Tos. Yadaim ii. 13 and Tos. Shabbath xiii. 5 the term גיליונים again suggests the Gospels. But Kuhn's[2] arguments are convincing that the 'books of the *minim*' refer to Scriptural, that is, Old Testament, texts written and used by heterodox Jewish groups such as that at Qumran. The term '*minim*' used of such groups included Jewish Christians; it came to denote groups outside Jews and especially Gentile Christians only later. Moreover, גיליון refers quite simply to the margins of Torah-scrolls, while און גליון cannot be a transliteration of εὐαγγέλιον, a plural in ים, as in גליונים, hardly having been formed out of εὐαγγέλιον which has as its plural εὐαγγέλια. And TB Shabbath 116*a* is too late, despite its mention of early authorities, to be used for the Jamnian period. The outcome of Kuhn's work is to make us more cautious in connecting the fixation of the canon at Jamnia directly with the Christian gospels and writings, despite the impressive list of scholars who have urged this.[3]

Nevertheless, Kuhn's understanding of the '*minim*' as including Jewish Christians leaves the door open for the view that the fixation of the canon at Jamnia was not unrelated to the awareness of a growing Christianity, as was the later codification of the Mishnah with the growing authority of the New Testament.[4] The changes in liturgy and religious practice

[1] *J.B.L.* XLI, 115 ff.; for references see my *Christian Origins and Judaism*, pp. 25 ff.

[2] K. G. Kuhn, on 'Giljonim und sifre minim' in *Judentum, Urchristentum, Kirche: Festschrift für Joachim Jeremias*, Z.N.W. XXVI (1960), 24–61. He gives the pertinent texts and the bibliography.

[3] See, for example, K. G. Kuhn, *op. cit.* p. 33.

[4] See especially H. Graetz, *op. cit.* pp. 344, 364–80. H. L. Strack, *op. cit.* p. 12, writes: 'The conjecture may be advanced that the Jews were led to codify in a definitive form and thus also to commit to writing their oral traditions with a view, in part at least, to the New Testament canon then in process of formation.'

introduced at Jamnia make this clear. While the deliberate attention paid to these matters was largely stimulated by the need for liturgical and other unity within Judaism, it also revealed anti-Christian concern.

One of the liturgical developments was the reformulation of the chief prayer of the Synagogue called the Tefillah or Amidah, so that it came to constitute the Eighteen Benedictions. In the present Prayer Book, the 12th Benediction, which especially concerns us, reads:

And for slanderers let there be no hope, and let all wickedness perish as in a moment; let all thine enemies be speedily cut off, and the dominion of arrogance do thou uproot and crush, cast down and humble speedily in our days. Blessed art thou O Lord, who breakest the enemies and humblest the arrogant.

But this form is the result of much change inspired by the fear of censorship over many centuries. Fortunately we can go back to an early form discovered in a Cairo Genizah by Schechter.[1] Generally regarded as Palestinian in origin, it reads:

למשמדים אל תהי תקוה
ומלכות זדון מהרה תעקר בימינו
[והנוצרים והמינים כרגע
יאבדו ימחו
מספר החיים
ועם צדיקים אל
יכתבון]

For persecutors let there be no hope, and the dominion of arrogance do Thou speedily root out in our days; and let Christians and *minim* perish in a moment, let them be blotted out of the book of the living and let them not be written with the righteous.

Certain facts can be regarded as established. First, the 12th Benediction in its main structure, existed in the early part of the first century. Secondly, the last two lines in the Palestinian version, bracketed above, did not belong to the original Benediction but were an addition. Thirdly, the specific Talmudic evidence that the Birkath ha Minim (the name given to these lines) was composed in the time of Rabban Gamaliel II by Samuel the Small need not be questioned, and is confirmed by the fact that the rhyme in its two verses differs from that found in the rest of the Tefillah.[2]

---

[1] See C. W. Dugmore, *The Influence of the Synagogue upon the Divine Office* (1944), pp. 114–25; *Berakot* (*Die Mischna*), ed. O. Holtzmann, (Giessen, 1912), pp. 10 ff. whom I follow.

[2] See K. G. Kuhn, *Achtzehngebet und Vater Unser, ad rem.*

But there have been differences of view over the terms 'Christians or Nazoreans and heretics', והנוצרים והמינים. In the light of the Talmudic passage, we must assume that the term 'minim' stood in the text as supplemented by Samuel the Small. But on the ground that 'minim', a general term for heretics, includes Jewish Christians, so that the addition of the Nazoreans is tautologous, some have urged that הנוצרים, the Nazoreans, was not present in Samuel the Small's benediction. It was added by a later synagogue that knew not the meaning of 'minim'. But this must be regarded as dubious. If הנוצרים be removed from Samuel's prayer, its structure is seriously disturbed, whereas its inclusion gives a balanced form to the whole of his innovation. In any case, a petition, either against heretics, including Jewish Christians, or against heretics and specifically Jewish Christians, was introduced into the Tefillah at Jamnia, at what date exactly we cannot ascertain. It was probably somewhere around A.D. 85.[1]

The Birkath ha Minim makes it unmistakably clear that the Sages at Jamnia regarded Jewish Christians as a menace sufficiently serious to warrant a liturgical innovation. It worked simply, but effectively, as follows. In the Synagogue service a man was designated to lead in the reciting of the Tefillah. As he approached the platform, where stood the ark containing the Scrolls of the Law, the congregation rose. The leader would recite the Benedictions and the congregation, finally, responded to these with the Amen. Any one called upon to recite the Tefillah who stumbled on the 12th Benediction could easily be detected. Thus the Birkath ha Minim served the purpose of making any Christian, who might be present in a synagogal service, conspicuous by the way in which he recited or glossed over this Benediction.[2]

Largely similar in its intent to isolate Jewish Christians was the use of the ban at Jamnia. This again involved the assumption that the Beth Din in that place had taken to itself the status of the Sanhedrin, because it meant the reintroduction of a usage which, before the war, had been

---

[1] On the 'minim', see Jakob Jocz, The Jewish People and Jesus Christ (London, 1949), pp. 178 ff., where various interpretations are surveyed; M. Goldstein, Jesus in the Jewish Tradition (1950), ad rem; and especially now, K. G. Kuhn, ZNW, xxvi (1960), 24 ff. on 'Giljonim und sifre minim'.

[2] According to Elbogen, Jüdische Gottesdienst, the Tefillah from the first was regarded as congregational in its intent, as the congregational response in the 'Amen' at the end of each Benediction indicated. In order to ensure full individual participation in it R. Gamaliel II decided that every person should also utter the prayer for himself, even though the leader said it (that is, the שליח צבור). K. G. Kuhn, op. cit. thinks of the Tefillah as individual in its intent (p. 40).

controlled by that body. Significant is it that one of the most illuminating passages illustrating the practice of the ban concerns R. Eliezer b. Hyrkanos, who during the anti-Christian persecutions in the time of Domitian or Trajan was suspected of heresy by a Roman court. Probably all that lay behind the charge of the Romans was that, at that time, they were finding it difficult to distinguish Christians and Jews.[1] There is no ground for believing that R. Eliezer had actually been guilty of heresy. The reason for the ban upon him, passed with great heart-searching by Rabban Gamaliel, his brother-in-law, whose very irascibility was born of his passion for the unity of his people, was the need for solidarity in the understanding of the Law.[2] But there can be no doubt that R. Eliezer, one of the most important figures at Jamnia after the withdrawal of Rabbi Johannan ben Zakkai, had, either before or after his banishment, been in such communication with Christians that their tradition was known to him. And it is also clear that the reason for the frequent use of the ban by Rabban Gamaliel was his fear of dissentients, among whom were Jewish Christians, against whom he instigated the Birkath ha Minim.[3] In this connexion, it cannot be sufficiently emphasized that the Sages were frequently in contact with Jewish Christians. Despite the Birkath ha Minim, traffic between even the leaders of Jewry and Jewish Christians continued well into the second century. In illustration of this we may refer to a list of persons, who had been in contact with Christianity, which may be gleaned from Ecclesiastes Rabbah on vii. 26. Ecclesiastes Rabbah belongs to the seventh century, but the passage concerned is transmitted in the name of Rabbi Issi of Caesarea from the fourth century, and its substance is largely attested in earlier sources:

3. WHOSE HEART IS SNARE AND NETS:
...R. Issi of Caesarea interpreted the verse as applying to heresy. WHOSO PLEASETH: i.e. R. Eleazar, BUT THE SINNER: i.e. Jacob of Kefar-Nibbuyara. Another illustration of WHOSO PLEASETH: i.e. Eleazar b. Dama,* BUT THE SINNER: i.e. Jacob of Kefar-Sama. Another illustration of WHOSO PLEASETH: i.e. Hananiah* the nephew of R. Joshua, BUT THE SINNER: i.e. the inhabitants of Capernaum. Another illustration of WHOSO PLEASETH: i.e. Judah b.

---

[1] M. Goldstein, op. cit. pp. 48 ff.; see TB Abodah Zarah 16b, 17a; Tos. Hullin xi. 24.

[2] For the ban, see S–B, Exkurs iv. 1, pp. 293–333, and a different point of view in Cl.-H. Hunzinger, T.L. (1955), 114 f., on 'Die jüdische Bannpraxis im neutestamentlichen Zeitalter'.

[3] H. Graetz, op. cit. p. 339: the whole chapter is important still. No subsequent treatment gives the atmosphere of the Jamnian period in the same way.

Nakosa,* BUT THE SINNER: i.e. the *minim*. Another illustration of WHOSO PLEASETH: i.e. R. Nathan,* BUT THE SINNER: i.e. his disciple. Another illustration of WHOSO PLEASETH: i.e. R. Eliezer* and R. Joshua, BUT THE SINNER: i.e. Elisha. (Soncino translation, pp. 209 f.)

Stories connecting the five figures marked by an asterisk with heresy are reported in Ecclesiastes Rabbah on i. 8. Of these Ben Damah and Hananiah, the nephew of Rabbi Joshua, belong to the first half of the second century; Rabbi Judah b. Nakosa and Nathan to the mid-second century. Rabbi Eliezer we have dealt with above. We need not labour the obvious; from this and other plentiful evidence we can be certain that the Pharisaic leaders, throughout the period of Jamnia and later, were liable to encounter Christians. On the popular level this would probably be even more the case.[1]

On the other hand, such encounters occurred contrary to the desire of the Synagogue. Not only the Birkath ha Minim makes this clear, but also passages from Justin Martyr's *Dialogue with Trypho*, which is probably to be dated between A.D. 155 and 160.[2] Having first referred to the destruction of Jerusalem, Justin accuses Jewry thus (*Dialogue with Trypho*, XVI, 4):

Accordingly these things have happened to you in fairness and justice, for you have slain the Just One and His prophets before Him; and now you reject those who hope in Him and in Him who sent Him—God the Almighty and maker of all things—*cursing in your synagogues those that believe in Christ. For you have not the power to lay hands upon us, on account of those who now have the mastery.* But as often as you could, you did so (καταρώμενοι ἐν ταῖς συναγωγαῖς ὑμῶν τοὺς πιστεύοντας ἐπὶ τὸν Χριστόν. Οὐ γὰρ ἐξουσίαν ἔχετε αὐτόχειρες γενέσθαι ἡμῶν διὰ τοὺς νῦν ἐπικρατοῦντας, ὁσάκις δὲ ἂν ἐδυνήθητε, καὶ τοῦτο ἐπράξατε).

Here the reference to the Birkath ha Minim is clear. But it is also claimed that the Synagogue had laid hands on Christians. So too in the following pages Justin refers to discrimination on a wide scale:

For other nations have not inflicted on us and on Christ this wrong to such an extent as you have, who in very deed are the authors of the wicked prejudice against the Just One, and us who hold by Him. For after that you had crucified Him, the only blameless and righteous Man,—through whose stripes those who approach the Father by Him are healed,—when you knew that He had risen

[1] On this, see A. Schlatter, 'Die Kirche Jerusalems vom Jahre 70 bis 130', in *Beiträge zur Förderung christlicher Theologie* (II, 3, Gütersloh, 1898), pp. 90 ff.
[2] For Justin Martyr's *Dialogue with Trypho*, I have used G. Archambault, *Justin: Dialogue avec Tryphon* (2 vols., 1909).

from the dead and ascended to heaven, as the prophets foretold He would, you not only did not repent of the wickedness which you had committed, but at that time you selected and sent out from Jerusalem chosen men through all the land to tell that the godless heresy of the Christians had sprung up, and to publish those things which all they who knew us not speak against us. So that you are the cause not only of your own unrighteousness, but in fact of that of all other men. . . .

Accordingly, you displayed great zeal in publishing throughout all the land bitter and dark and unjust things against the only blameless and righteous Light sent by God. (*Dialogue with Trypho*, XVII, 1–3.) (See also CXVII, 3.)

The same accusation is made later in chapter CVIII, 2:

. . .you have sent chosen and ordained men throughout all the world to proclaim that a godless and lawless heresy had sprung from one Jesus, a Galilaean deceiver, whom we crucified, but his disciples stole him by night from the tomb, where he was laid when unfastened from the cross, and now deceive men by asserting that he has risen from the dead and ascended to heaven. Moreover, you accuse Him of having taught those godless, lawless, and unholy doctrines which you mention to the condemnation of those who confess Him to be Christ, and a Teacher from and Son of God. Besides this, even when your city is captured, and your land ravaged, you do not repent, but dare to utter imprecations on Him and all who believe in Him.

And again Trypho himself refers to a Jewish decree forbidding intercourse with Christians:

And Trypho said, 'Sir, it were good for us if we obeyed our teachers, *who laid down a law that we should have no intercourse with any of you, and that we should not have even any communication with you on these questions*' (νομοθετήσασι μηδενὶ ἐξ ὑμῶν ὁμιλεῖν, μηδέ σοι τούτων κοινωνῆσαι τῶν λόγων). (*Dialogue with Trypho*, CXXXVIII, 1.)

The reference here cannot simply be to the Birkath ha Minim, which was not strictly a law. But we have no other evidence for such a law. However, the main point is clear: by the end of the first century the Synagogue had adopted an attitude of isolation in the interests of its own integrity: it did this by a significant liturgical change, by the use of the ban and, possibly, by a legal enactment whose precise date and character is lost to us.

Can we trace a concern to combat Christianity elsewhere in the liturgy? Certain bare possibilities may be mentioned. The centrality of the Shema in the life of Jewry and in the synagogal service is clear, as is the reason for this. Because it was so exposed to the opposition of the world and to misunderstanding within Judaism itself, the unity of God, which the

Shema expresses, more than any other teaching needed emphasis.[1] Enemies in the Jamnian period, the heathen Gnostics, Jewish heretics and Christians made this obvious. It is not always possible to decide when the Sages were combating Gnostics and when Christians. Most, if not all, of the evidence pointing to criticism of the specifically Christian menace to the unity of God, as Judaism understood it, belongs to the second century and later. To carry this criticism back to Jamnia may be precarious.[2] While, however, the claim that, before Christianity demanded an emphasis upon it, the Shema was not present in the liturgy of the Synagogue, but only in that of the Temple, is highly improbable,[3] it is justifiable to assert that as the Church spread Judaism increasingly felt the necessity to define its faith. But caution is required at this point. Was the Shema originally summary in its intent,[4] that is, designed to present the quint-essence of the Law, so that we can speak of its assuming a confessional, polemic, significance at Jamnia, or did it have a confessional or credal significance as far back as the Exile?[5] This latter may be suggested by the wording of the first blessing introductory to the Shema, which is an adaptation of Isa. xlv. 7 and reads: 'Blessed art thou, O Lord our God, King of the universe, who formest light and createst darkness, who makest peace and createst all things.' In the latter case all that can be claimed is that the menace of Christianity increased a credal significance which the Shema already possessed. By the time of Akiba we know that it had become the *sine qua non* of Judaism, with a profound confessional but also polemic nuance.[6] The detailed and loving regulations on the recital of the Shema discussed by Rabban Gamaliel, Rabbi Eliezer, Rabbi Joshua in the very first lines of the Mishnah are significant. In their day, we may rightly conclude, the Shema had a marked significance as a bulwark of their faith. There can be little doubt that not only the prominence given to the Shema but to the Tefillin (phylacteries) and the Mezuzah (doorpost text) at Jamnia had a polemic intent. These last items were

[1] See A. Marmorstein, *op. cit.* p. 73; the whole chapter on 'The Unity of God in Rabbinic Literature' is illuminating.

[2] *Ibid.* pp. 72–105; where the evidence is frequently late. Nevertheless, that the Jamnian leaders were involved seems clear, see pp. 104–5; see also pp. 179 ff. on 'Judaism and Christianity in the Middle of the Third Century'.

[3] P. Levertoff on 'Synagogue Worship in the First Century', in *Liturgy and Worship*, ed. K. W. Lowther Clarke (1932), p. 67.

[4] See C. W. Dugmore, *The Influence of the Synagogue on the Divine Office*, pp. 16 ff., and references there given.

[5] See I. Elbogen, *op. cit. ad rem*; C. W. Dugmore, *op. cit.* p. 20.

[6] TB Berakoth 61 *b*. On all this see the discussion by O. Holtzman, *op. cit.* pp. 5–10.

standardized in the interests of orthodoxy and unity. The phylacteries discovered at Qumran, which differ from the rabbinic, illustrate this.[1] At this point also we note the discussions on the Decalogue. In the present Mezuzah there are two passages (Deut. vi. 4–9; xi. 13–21) and in the present Tefillin (Exod. xiii. 1–10 and 11–16; Deut. vi. 4–9; xi. 13–21). But there is evidence that at one time they included the Decalogue, as did the Synagogue service.[2] But the Decalogue was withdrawn from all these items. When did this happen? Loewe[3] implies that it was while the Temple was still standing that the Decalogue was removed from the Synagogue service. But he supplies no evidence for this. The first name in which the tradition comes to us is R. Nathan, who flourished A.D. 140–65. A passage in TB Berakoth 12a deals with Temple practice as follows:

They recited the Ten Commandments, the *Shema'*, the sections '*And it shall come to pass if ye diligently hearken,*' and '*And the Lord said,*' 'True and firm,' the '*Abodah* and the priestly benediction'. Rab Judah said in the name of Samuel: Outside the Temple also people wanted to do the same (that is, to say the Ten Commandments before the Shema), but they were stopped on account of the insinuations of the *Minim* (מפני תרעומת המינים) [that is, that the Ten Commandments were the only valid part of the Torah]. Similarly it has been taught: R. Nathan says, They sought to do the same outside the Temple, but it had long been abolished on account of the insinuations of the *Minim*.

It is clear from a passage in the Jerusalem Talmud, Berakoth 1. 8. 3c, that the Samuel referred to was a Palestinian Tanna of the period A.D. 320–59, that is, R. Shemuel bar Nahman. R. Nathan's words may be taken to imply that the discontinuance of the Decalogue in the Synagogue service *may* have been started in the Jamnia period. But the only certainty is that this took place when *minim* still frequented the Synagogue. Was Christian emphasis on the Decalogue sufficiently early to have influenced the Sages during the last quarter of the first century? This has been urged, but the evidence adduced for it comes from Pliny, the Didache, Irenaeus and other later material, so that we cannot over-emphasize concentration on the

---

[1] See K. G. Kuhn, *Phylakterien aus Höhle 4 von Qumran* (Heidelberg, 1957), pp. 24 ff. These differed in *form* and *content* from the rabbinic phylacteries. Kuhn makes it clear that after A.D. 70, more strictly in the period A.D. 90–100, Pharisaic Judaism imposed uniformity in the Tefillin (p. 31). On Tefillin, see S–B, Exkurs iv. 1, pp. 250–76.

[2] Siphre Deuteronomy, Waethanan, f. 74a, line 20, f. 74b, line 15, makes it clear that there was discussion as to whether the Decalogue should be included in the phylacteries and mezuzah.

[3] *A Rabbinic Anthology*, p. 641, n [1].

Decalogue in our period.[1] On the other hand, the depreciation of the oral law in the Christian tradition would tend to accentuate the significance of the written Law and, especially, the Decalogue in the Church.[2] On the whole, there is a real possibility that the suspension of the Decalogue, as a defensive measure against Christian influence, occurred in the Jamnian period.

For the sake of completeness, reference must be made to the treatment of the Old Testament in Judaism under Christian influences. The view that the lectionary of the Haftaroth in the Synagogue came into being as a polemic against Christianity need not detain us.[3] The need to familiarize Jews with their own documents sufficiently accounts for the development of lectionaries.[4] But were the forces leading ultimately to the translation of Aquila which may be dated about A.D. 140, and which was designed to counteract the Christian exploitation of the LXX, already at work at Jamnia?[5] This is likely, but we have no direct evidence for it. The words of Justin in his *Dialogue with Trypho*, however, presuppose a long discussion on points of translation. He tells Trypho: 'For some statements in the Scriptures, which appear explicitly to convict them (the Jews) of a foolish and vain opinion, these they venture to assert have not been so written.' And again on Isa. vii. 14 where the LXX had rendered עַלְמָה by παρθένος where, it was contended, νεᾶνις would have given the true meaning, he asserts that Jewish teachers 'venture to assert that the explanation which your seventy elders that were with Ptolemy the King of the Egyptians gave, is untrue in certain respects'.[6] Doubtless the Sages at Jamnia were not unaware of such linguistic points, and were prepared to meet Christians on their own ground in such matters.

Lastly, on the liturgical side, the history of the four benedictions connected with the Shema, to which reference was made above, that is, the Yotzer, Ahabah, Geullah, Hashkibenu, is too little known to warrant any certain judgement on their original intent. On the basis of fragments from

---

[1] R. M. Grant, *H.T.R.* xl (January 1947), 1–18, on 'The Decalogue in Early Christianity'.

[2] On the general relation between these in Judaism, see my article on 'Law in first-century Judaism' in *The Interpreter's Bible Dictionary*, vol. iii, pp. 89–95.

[3] Jacob Mann, *The Bible as Read and Preached in the Old Synagogue* (1940), p. 4, n. 4, dismisses this view cursorily: it was proposed by Venetianer; Mann refers to the latter's article 'Ursprung u. Bedeutung der Propheten-Lektionen', published in a reprint, 1909.   [4] Jacob Mann, *ibid.*

[5] For Aquila, see R. R. Ottley, *Handbook to the Septuagint* (1920), pp. 38 ff.; *J.E. ad rem.*

[6] *Dialogue with Trypho*, LXXI, 1 f.; see also XLIII, 7; LXVIII, 1; LXXXIV, 3.

the Cairo Genizah, it has been held that the Ahabah and the Geullah were not part of the liturgy before A.D. 150–200.[1] The utmost that can be suggested is that, while their themes are commonplaces to Judaism at all times, it was in reaction to Christianity that the Ahabah places such emphasis on the unchangeable love of God and the gift of the Law, and the Geullah on God, not only as King, but as Redeemer, Creator, Rock of our Salvation, Saviour from everlasting. But clearly such emphases are found outside our period also, so that their anti-Christian intent should not be pressed.

We next ask whether Jewish observance outside the Synagogue liturgy, as such, reveals an awareness of the Church. At an early date, even though Jesus himself had not fasted, Christians began to do so. The discussion of fasting in Mark ii. 18–20 is aimed at justifying the practice of the Church.[2] Matt. vi. 1 ff. presupposes private fasting at least as legitimate for Christians. At first, Christian usage in this matter was probably indistinguishable from Jewish. A late rabbi, Joḥanan (A.D. 279–320), claimed that Jews did not fast on Sundays because of Jewish Christians.[3] But this evidence is far too late for our purpose. We have evidence from the Didache, viii. 1, that Christians were to avoid fasting

---

[1] The dating of the Benedictions depends on the answer to two questions. First, is there evidence that they existed in pre-Christian times? In Mishnah Berakoth i. 14 they are assumed to be long established elements in the liturgy of the Synagogue: W. O. E. Oesterley in *The Jewish Background to the Christian Liturgy* (Oxford, 1925), p. 47, traced all except the Hashkibenu to the Temple liturgy whence they entered the Synagogue liturgy. A similar position was taken by Blau (L. Blau, 'Origine et histoire de la lecture du Schema', *R.E.J.* XXXI (1895), 181–201) who referred particularly to Mishnah Tamid v. 1. But by itself evidence from the Mishnah on historical matters is always uncertain, because of the possibility that it is imaginatively coloured and creates a past which never existed. This uncertainty compels the second question. Is there evidence that the Benedictions were post-Christian? Finkelstein, on the basis of fragments from the Cairo Genizah, maintained that there is no evidence for the Ahabah and Geullah before A.D. 150–200. They may, therefore, reflect Christian influences. But Finkelstein traced the Yotzer in a much simpler form than that now found in the *Authorized Jewish Prayer Book*, Eng. trans. S. Singer (London, 1918), p. 37, to the liturgy of the Temple. Yet it is in the Yotzer especially that Levertoff found anti-Christian motifs and references to v. 48 and John v. 10–18. Our knowledge of the Benedictions is not such as can be used with any confidence. See L. Blau, *ibid.*; L. Finkelstein, 'La Kedouscha et les Bénédictions du Schema', in *R.E.J.* XCIII (1932); Paul Levertoff on 'Synagogue Worship in the First Century', in W. K. Lowther Clarke (ed.), *Liturgy and Worship* (1932); C. W. Dugmore, *The Influence of the Synagogue on the Divine Office* (1944), pp. 13 ff.

[2] V. Taylor, *Mark, ad rem*; but see C. F. D. Moule, *New Testament Essays: Studies in Memory of T. W. Manson*, p. 174.

[3] TB Taanith 27*b*. See Aptowitzer, 'Bemerkungen zur Liturgie und Geschichte der Liturgie', *M.G.W.J.* LXXIV, 110 ff. It is easy to confuse this R. Joḥannan with R. Johannan b. Zakkai.

on the same days as Jews. 'Let not your fasts be with the hypocrites, for they fast on Mondays and Thursdays, but do you fast on Wednesdays and Fridays.' The Didache—according to the latest treatment of it—was contemporaneous with 1 Corinthians, Romans and 1 Timothy and the first written Gospels.[1] There is no such early evidence that Jewish fasting was in any way dictated by Christian usage nor is this at all likely. The designation of Mondays and Thursdays as Jewish fast days was earlier than Jamnia. On the other hand, there is considerable evidence that sorrow after the Fall of Jerusalem led, especially among the more charismatic, to an increase of fasting. So much was this the case that the more sober rabbis had to advise against excessive fasts. The attitude of R. Joshua ben Hananiah is instructive at this point. Like R. Johannan ben Zakkai, he too stood out against all unreasonable extremes of piety and practice (see the quotation on page 313 below).[2]

Finally, does the theology which emerged in rabbinic Judaism during the Jamnian period reveal anti-Christian emphases? We have referred to the sobriety of rabbinic thought. This was doubtless accentuated by contact with Christianity. Much of the ethical teaching of the Church would often appear extreme. Contrast, for example, the quotation on page 313 with vi. 25–34, which expresses the precise attitude belittled by R. Joshua ben Hananiah. Christian enthusiasm was part of the *Schwärmerei* against which Jamnia set its face. Related to this also is the growing distrust of the miraculous which characterized some of the rabbinic leaders. The passage depicting the pronouncement of a ban on R. Eliezer b. Hyrkanos is illuminating:[3]

It has been taught: On that day R. Eliezer brought forward every imaginable argument, but they did not accept them. Said he to them: 'If the *halachah* agrees with me, let this carob-tree prove it!' Thereupon the carob-tree was torn a hundred cubits out of its place—others affirm, four hundred cubits. 'No proof can be brought from a carob-tree,' they retorted. Again he said to them: 'If

[1] J. P. Audet, *La Didachè* (1958), p. 199. He dates the Didache between A.D. 50 and 70, that is, at a time earlier than we are prone to date Matthew, and connects it with tradition lying behind Matthew (p. 197).

[2] See TB Baba Bathra 60b cited on p. 313; Tos. Sotah xv. 10. Such an attitude is to be distinguished from the spontaneous and temporary expression of grief at the fall of the city in the case of R. Johannan b. Zakkai, *A.R.N.* 4: 'When Rabban Johanan ben Zakkai heard that Jerusalem was destroyed and the Temple was up in flames, he tore his clothing, and his disciples tore their clothing, and they wept, crying aloud and mourning' (Goldin's translation, p. 37).

[3] TB Baba Metziah 59a. Antipathy to the emphasis on the Spirit by Christians may lie behind TB Yoma 9b. See *P.R.J.*[2] p. 216.

the *halachah* agrees with me, let the stream of water prove it!' Whereupon the stream of water flowed backwards. 'No proof can be brought from a stream of water,' they rejoined. Again he urged: 'If the *halachah* agrees with me, let the walls of the schoolhouse prove it,' whereupon the walls inclined to fall. But R. Joshua rebuked them, saying: 'When scholars are engaged in a *halachic* dispute, what have ye to interfere?' Hence they did not fall, in honour of R. Joshua, nor did they resume the upright, in honour of R. Eliezer; and they are still standing thus inclined. Again he said to them: 'If the *halachah* agrees with me, let it be proved from Heaven!' Whereupon a Heavenly Voice cried out: 'Why do ye dispute with R. Eliezer, seeing that in all matters the *halachah* agrees with him!' But R. Joshua arose and exclaimed: '*It is not in heaven.*' What did he mean by this?—Said R. Jeremiah: That the Torah had already been given at Mount Sinai; we pay no attention to a Heavenly Voice, because Thou hast long since written in the Torah at Mount Sinai, *After the majority must one incline.* (Soncino translation.)

Neither miracles nor *bath qôl* were to be allowed to supersede the Torah. Even a Heavenly Voice in favour of the House of Hillel was to be rejected. There can be little question that part of the reason for the emphatic rejection of these two media of revelation was the weight placed upon them in Christianity. The evidence for this need not be repeated here.[1]

But can we go further? Do the understanding of the Law and of Israel itself which emerged in rabbinic Judaism reflect its reaction to Christianity? The doctrine of election in Tannaitic sources has been claimed to suggest this[2] and, in discussions on the Law, polemic against Paul emerges.[3] Judaism was not impervious to Christian influences despite its

---

[1] On this see A. Guttmann, *Hebrew Union College Annual*, xx (1947), 363 ff.

[2] See B. W. Helfgott, *The Doctrine of Election in Tannaitic Literature* (1954). He argues that the utterances in the Tannaitic Midrashim which emphasize God's love for Israel are better understood when seen as an indirect polemic against the Church's claim to be the true Israel of God (p. 135). Jewish scholars have preferred to find these as growing naturally within Jewish soil (see the review, signed Z.W., *J.J.S.* VII (1956), 238), but the evidence that Helfgott supplies is impressive. See also J. Bergmann, *op. cit.* pp. 130 ff.

[3] Allusions to Paul in Rabbinic sources have long been canvassed. H. J. Hertz, following I. Epstein, finds a possible polemic against Paul in the epilogue to Mishnah Aboth i taken from the end of Mishnah Makkoth iii. 16: 'R. Hananiah b. Akashya (A.D. 140–65) says: The Holy One, blessed is he, was minded to grant merit to Israel; therefore hath he multiplied for them the Law and commandments, as it is written, *It pleased the Lord for his righteousness' sake to magnify the Law and make it honourable*' (H. J. Hertz, *The Sayings of the Fathers* (London, 1952)). In *R.A.* p. 126, H. Loewe finds Siphre Deuteronomy, Ekeb, chapter 45 f. 82*b* to be directed against Paul: compare TB Kiddushin 30*b*. Mishnah Aboth iii. 15 has been referred

opposition to them. But into these vast questions we cannot enter here: the examination of them takes us too far from the Jamnian period.

We have above sought to describe briefly certain pertinent aspects of the Judaism which emerged after the fall of Jerusalem in the period when Matthew was written. One caveat needs to be issued. It is a safe principle to understand a movement, wherever possible, within its own terms. The reconstruction at Jamnia should first be understood as the giant self-assertion of a faith determined to survive, as the outcome of its concern simply to preserve its own integrity and identity. Extraneous factors impinging upon it there were, but the extent to which they deeply affected its forms, theology and life must be cautiously assessed. Some have claimed, as we saw, that the Jamnian Sages were largely unconcerned with the religious movement around them.[1] It is certainly dangerously tempting to discover Christian influences, when we are so inclined, where none existed. Nevertheless, while we have exercised as much circumspection as possible, there is sufficient evidence to justify the claim that Jamnian Judaism was consciously confronting Christianity. Given the solid ground of the Birkath ha Minim for such a statement, other less certain evidence gains in possibility, if not probability, and this is why we have included this. Cumulatively it suggests that it is reasonable to inquire whether Matthew was also consciously confronting Jamnian Judaism.

Matthew reveals not a single, clearly defined attitude towards Judaism but one that is highly complex and varied. At the risk of simplification the evidence can be sifted as follows.

(1) There are passages where apparently a great gulf is fixed between the Christian community and the Synagogue. Let us begin with the explicit reference to Jewish criticism in xxviii. 15. This is the conclusion

---

to Paul: R. Eleazar of Modiim (A.D. 80–120) said: 'If a man profanes the Hallowed Things [that is, the laws concerning offerings] and despises the set feasts and puts his fellow to shame publicly and makes void the covenant of Abraham our father, and discloses meanings in the Law which are not according to the Halakah, even though a knowledge of the Law and good works are his, he has no share in the world to come' (see J. Klausner, *From Jesus to Paul*, Engl. trans. p. 600). See also J. Bergmann, *op. cit.* pp. 110 ff. He refers to TB Menahoth 43 b; Mekilta on Exodus xxii. 30. M. Radin discovered anti-Pauline polemic in M. Aboth iii. 6: *Jews among the Greeks and Romans* (Philadelphia, 1915), p. 320.

[1] In addition to references given above, p. 272, see also M. Friedländer, *Der vorchristliche jüdische Gnosticismus* (Göttingen, 1898), pp. 71–94; *Der Antichrist*, pp. xix–xx, pp. 191–2, 206 f., 215–21.

of the section beginning at xxvii. 62 ff., which describes the safeguard taken by the High Priests and Pharisees (a strange collocation) against deception by the disciples of Jesus, who is called ὁ πλάνος[1] (RSV and NEB: Impostor), and the plot to claim that his body had been stolen by the disciples. 'And this story has been spread abroad among Jews (παρὰ 'Ιουδαίοις) to this day.' The use of the term 'the Jews' here implies, so it has been claimed, that Matthew sets them over against Christians, as does John.[2] But this cannot be pressed. This is the *only* occurrence of 'the Jews' in this manner on the Evangelist's own part: elsewhere only non-Jews use the expression 'the Jews'. Moreover, it must not be too certainly assumed that the use of 'the Jews' does imply disassociation. To judge from Pauline usage, this is not the case, as, for example, in 1 Cor. ix. 20 ('To the Jews I became as a Jew, in order to win Jews...') where 'the Jews' has no pejorative sense. What we can be certain of from xxviii. 15 is that Jewish opponents, while not denying the empty tomb as a fact, did try to discredit the evidence for it and to explain it away.[3] It is in the context of such hostile discussion that Matthew wrote.

An intent to counteract Jewish calumny concerning the birth of Jesus has been traced in Matthew.[4] Such calumny has been claimed to lie behind the phrase 'a gluttonous man and a wine-bibber', the use of which implied a reflection on the birth of Jesus as an illegitimate one (Matt. xi. 19; Luke vii. 34), but this cannot be substantiated.[5] More probable is it that the birth narratives in i, ii contain a defence against Jewish slander. The evidence for such slander in Tannaitic sources, however, is very meagre. The one pertinent passage is from Tosefta Hullin ii. 22, 23

[1] It is tempting to suggest that this was a *terminus technicus* for Jesus among Jews. See TB Sanhedrin 43 a.

[2] See N. Smith, *Jesus in the Gospel of John* (Nashville, 1959), pp. 6 f. He finds it possible to think that John was aimed at 'Jews' though he used that term no less than 25 times (out of just over 60) in a hostile sense.

[3] On this see, E. Stauffer, *Jesus and His Story*, Eng. trans. (London, 1960).

[4] See above, p. 65.

[5] E. Stauffer, *op. cit. ad rem.* It is his substantial contribution that polemics against Jesus are of great significance for the understanding of the Jesus of History. He takes the phrase a 'gluttonous man and a winebibber' to refer to a bastard: it is a kind of technical term of abuse. He refers to Deut. xxi. 18 ff. and to the Targum on this. But it is difficult to think that the latter supports Stauffer's claim. For Jewish law concerning apostasy and illegitimate birth, see E. Stauffer, *Jerusalem und Rom im Zeitalter Jesu Christi*, pp. 717 ff. The genealogy of Matthew is designed, according to Stauffer, to counteract such calumny as lies behind Mishnah Yebamoth iv. 13. See also E. Stauffer in *Wissenschaftliche Zeitschrift der Martin-Luther-Universität Halle-Wittenberg* (March, 1958), pp. 451–76.

(compare TB Abodah Zarah 27*b*; Jer. Shabbath 14*d*; Jer. Abodah Zarah 40*d*, 41*a*):

It happened with R. Eleazar ben Damah, whom a serpent bit, that Jacob, a man of Kefar Sama, came to heal him in the name of Yeshua ben Pantera, but R. Ishmael [about A.D. 130] did not let him. He said, 'You are not permitted, Ben Daniah'. He answered, 'I will bring you proof that he may heal me'. But he had no opportunity to bring proof, for he died.

Ben Pantera has been understood as a transliteration or corruption of παρθένος and so to contain an allusion to the Virgin Birth. But this cannot be regarded as certain. The context does not employ the name of Yeshua ben Pantera in a pejorative sense.[1] The attitude to Jesus revealed here on the part of R. Eleazar is even one of deep trust, although this is not shared by R. Ishmael. However, the inclusion of Tamar, Rahab, Ruth and Bathsheba in the genealogy in i. 1 ff. gains point if Jewish calumny was at work. Justin Martyr presupposes considerable discussion of Isa. vii. 14 among Jews and Christians, and we may perhaps carry this back to the Jamnian period. But apart from a polemic aim against Jewish slander, the Prologue in its presentation of Jesus as the Son of David and a New Moses was apologetic in its purpose.[2] This is not incompatible with the claim made previously that it was the Church itself that was being addressed in the Prologue.

In addition to explicit or nearly explicit references to the encounter with Judaism, throughout the Gospel Christians emerge as very markedly set over against the Jewish community. Within the *SM* itself, the Beatitudes suggest this. In their Lucan form, these are predominantly futuristic. The repeated contrast between the present and the future in vi. 20, 21 makes this clear and there is no need to regard the 'now' (νῦν) in these verses as secondary.[3] Luke, as Professor Dodd[4] has shown, is concerned in his Beatitudes and Woes to present a 'sublimated or etherialized kind of περιπέτεια', whereas Matthew presents in his Beatitudes 'types of character which have God's approval', and it is there, essentially, that is, in what they now are, that their blessedness lies, even though different aspects of the divine approval are represented in terms of

---

[1] See M. Goldstein, *op. cit.* pp. 32 ff.; he dates this story at the turn of the first century; the various possible interpretations are discussed by him.

[2] See above, pp. 65 ff.

[3] J. M. Creed, *The Gospel According to St Luke, ad rem.*

[4] In *Mélanges Bibliques: rédigés en l'honneur d'André Robert* (Paris, no date), pp. 404 ff.

the 'eschatological' blessings of the Kingdom of Heaven. The Matthaean emphasis falls on those who are blessed, as constituting a peculiar people. The repeated αὐτοί in the second clause in each part of the Beatitudes in v. 3, 4, 5, 6, 7, 8, 10 has an antithetical effect. It is not reading too much into these verses to find that it is 'these' people rather than 'those' who are blessed. In v. 11 ff. these two groups emerge as Christians and Jews.[1]

It may be argued that, since the contrast between the blessed and the Jews is present in both Matthew and Luke, there can be no special conclusions drawn from it in Matthew. But certain considerations point to a Matthaean emphasis on this contrast which is absent in Luke. In varying degrees, the opposition between Christians and Jews would of necessity be ubiquitous in the early Church, but the inclusion of the Woes in Luke vi. 24 ff. has the effect there of weakening the contrast between the blessed and 'Jews', as such. In addition, careful attention should be given to the increase of the Beatitudes in Matthew. Luke has four Beatitudes, Matthew, nine. But the ninth Beatitude in Matthew reads:

Blessed are you when men revile you and persecute you and utter all kinds of evil against you falsely on my account. Rejoice and be glad, for your reward is great in heaven, for so men persecuted the prophets who were before you. (RSV.)

μακάριοί ἐστε, ὅταν ὀνειδίσωσιν ὑμᾶς καὶ διώξωσι, καὶ εἴπωσι πᾶν πονηρὸν καθ᾽ ὑμῶν ψευδόμενοι, ἕνεκεν ἐμοῦ. χαίρετε καὶ ἀγαλλιᾶσθε· ὅτι ὁ μισθὸς ὑμῶν πολὺς ἐν τοῖς οὐρανοῖς· οὕτως γὰρ ἐδίωξαν τοὺς προφήτας τοὺς πρὸ ὑμῶν.

This Beatitude differs from the other eight thus: (i) It is longer in form; (ii) it is in the second person rather than the third; and (iii) it seems to point to a specific situation facing 'the blessed'. The specific situation, as the RSV understands it, refers to a general situation of persecution. The introduction of 'men' into the translation deprives the Beatitude of any particular reference. The NEB is more faithful to the text: 'How blest are you, when you suffer insults and persecution and every kind of calumny for my sake. Accept it with gladness and exultation, for you have a rich reward in heaven; in the same way they persecuted the prophets before you.' This, as the reference to the persecution of the prophets suggests, is not a generalized reference to persecution but to the condition of the Church face to face with Judaism: the undefined 'they' refers to the

[1] J. Dupont, *Les Béatitudes* (1958), pp. 223 ff., deals with v. 10 as a transition to v. 11–12. In his treatment of v. 11–12 he does not seem to us to pay sufficient attention to the *Sitz im Leben* of the Matthaean Church.

Synagogue.[1] That a contrast between the latter and the Christian community is intended appears clearly in v. 13–16, to which v. 11–12 is best regarded as an introduction. In these verses the persecuted Christian community is the salt of the earth (v. 13) and the light of the world (v. 14–16). In v. 13, 14 the ὑμεῖς is emphatic. Christians constitute a peculiar people which is called upon to bring forth good works and thereby glorify God among men (v. 16). The remainder of the *SM* carries further this antithetic motif, which is not confined to the Antitheses so-called. In v. 20–vii. 12 the good works demanded of Christians are described: they are summed up in what is usually called the Golden Rule in vii. 12. Explicitly in the description of its blessedness in v. 1–11 and implicitly in that of the demands made upon it, the Christian community is set over against the Old Israel. As New Israel, though no such term is employed, it is to fulfil a function similar to that of the Old Israel in glorifying God in good works. Even more to be emphasized are those passages in which Matthew makes clear that the Old Israel has been rejected in favour of a new community. We have previously referred to some of these. Special attention should be given to xxi. 33–45, the Parable of the Vineyard, and to xxvii. 15–26, where the guilt of the people of Israel as such is prominent.[2]

The engagement of Matthew with Judaism and the Old Israel needs no further comment. The one question which will not be silenced is whether this engagement took place *intra muros*, that is, as a dialogue, however crucial, within Judaism or *extra muros*, that is, as an appeal or apologetic to the Synagogue from a church that was already outside it.[3] This question brings us to the next material to be examined.

(2) So far we have emphasized how Matthew places 'the Jews' as a totality over against the Church but among them he particularly isolates

[1] In the Lucan parallel in vi. 22–3 the presence of οἱ ἄνθρωποι, which is missing in Matthew, should be noted. There the NEB rightly preserves 'men' in the translation. On the different schematization in Matthew and Luke at this point see J. Dupont, *op. cit.* pp. 228 ff.

[2] On this see K. W. Clark, *J.B.L.* LXVI, 165 ff. on 'The Gentile Bias in Matthew'; W. Trilling, *Das wahre Israel* (Leipzig, 1959), especially pp. 37–138.

[3] G. Bornkamm and G. Barth, *Überlieferung und Auslegung im Matthäusevangelium*, pp. 28 ff., 36, 80 ff. The former takes the struggle to be *intra muros*, but though allowing that there is no attack in principle on the oral tradition (v. 21, 43; xii. 11; xxiii. 23), Barth holds that the Matthaean understanding of *agape* abandons the Pharisaic position in essence. Bornkamm is criticized by E. P. Blair, *Jesus in the Gospel of Matthew* (1960), pp. 112 f., 141. But is not the ambiguity in Matthew on Pharisaism and its tradition what we should expect if he was presenting the Christian Dispensation to Judaism and so within the framework of it?

the Pharisees as the significant group with which he is concerned. This emerges in the following ways:

(i) The Pharisees are explicitly mentioned in comparisons drawn between them and the new community and in condemnations of them.

(a) v. 20:

For I tell you, unless your righteousness exceeds that of the scribes and Pharisees, you will never enter the kingdom of heaven. (RSV.)

Here the Christian life on its moral side is understood in comparison with that of the Pharisees: the antitheses are designed to set forth the new demands of Jesus as compared with those made by Pharisaism. This is made explicit in vii. 29: '...for he taught them as one who had authority and not as their scribes'. Note that both these verses have no parallel in Luke.

(b) xvi. 11–12:

How is it that you fail to perceive that I did not speak about bread? Beware of the leaven of the Pharisees and Sadducees. Then they understood that he did not tell them to beware of the leaven of bread, but of the teaching of the Pharisees and Sadducees. (RSV.)

Warning is here given against the *teaching* of the Pharisees. Luke xii. 1 warns against the hypocrisy of the Pharisees. The Marcan parallel reads: 'Take heed, beware of the leaven of the Pharisees and the leaven of Herod (or the Herodians)' and supplies no clue to what is meant by 'leaven' in both cases.

(c) xxiii. 1–36 where, although there is a recognition of the Pharisees as sitting in Moses' seat,[1] there is a violent denunciation of them because of their hypocrisy.

(ii) There are passages where what seems to be a kind of personal animus against Pharisees emerges. The phrase 'generation of vipers' is applied to them;[2] especially in xxiii. 13–36 is this the case. Here Matthew pronounces woes upon the Pharisees. Note that the characteristics condemned in the Pharisees in xxiii are almost precisely those decried in the *SM*. Compare the following: vii. 15–21 and xxiii. 2–3; vii. 1 ff. and

---

[1] On chapter xxiii, see E. Haenchen, on 'Matthäus 23' in *Z.T.K.* XLVIII (1951), 38–63, who holds that the radicalism of Jesus is suppressed here. E. P. Blair, *op. cit.* pp. 113 f., thinks that here Matthew has drawn on a source more Judaistic than is he himself. 'In reproducing it, he was not careful to assimilate it to his own point of view.'

[2] iii. 7; xii. 34; xxiii. 33.

xxiii. 4; v. 14–16 and xxiii. 16 (cf. xv. 14); vi. 16–18 and xxiii. 25–8; v. 12 and xxiii. 34–6. The Woes on the Pharisees serve as a counterbalance to the Beatitudes. The yoke of Jesus, which is easy (xi. 27–30), is contrasted with that of the Pharisees, which is 'grievous to be borne' (xxiii. 4). The kind of criticism of the Pharisees which emerges in these passages is similar to those found in Paul.[1] Both Matthew and Paul may be following a common early tradition of such criticism. But the admission of this does not mean that the conflict between Pharisaism and the Gospel is merely a traditional one for Matthew. It has for him a quite special significance. Not only chapter xxiii, but the other material dealt with above is so consciously presented that it implies more than the implementation of a traditional motif. The juxtaposition of the Pharisees and the Church is born of a special, living Matthaean concern.

(3) Can we still further particularize the Jewish–Christian encounter in Matthew? Does it reveal a concern with the activity which we described above at Jamnia?[2] Before we attempt to answer this we must first face a preliminary problem. The implication of the question raised is that the Pharisaism with which Matthew was concerned was not only that which confronted his Church locally, but that wider Pharisaic movement led by the Sages, who sat in Moses' seat, at Jamnia. We have previously insisted that there is considerable evidence that the Sages encountered Christians and that they were concerned with the Christian revolt, as they would regard it.[3]

---

[1] On this, see C. H. Dodd in *E.T.* LVIII, no. 11 (1947), 293 ff., on 'Matthew and Paul'.

[2] On the instigation of Professor Joachim Jeremias, who kindly allowed me to see proofs of a forthcoming work dealing with place-names in S–B, I looked up how often specific references to Jamnia occur in S–B and found that they were surprisingly few and intrinsically of little significance. I am, therefore, fully aware that it is impossible to pin down the developments after A.D. 70 to the town of Jamnia and the Sages there too rigidly. By 'Jamnia' or such phrases as 'the Jamnian Period' I therefore mean that movement in its totality, which preserved Judaism after A.D. 70, which, while it was centred, according to the tradition, in Jamnia, should not be confined to that place. Various rabbis settled in other places than Jamnia, though not too far away. Thus Lydda had several schools (Jer. Betzah iii. 6. 62*a*) R. Eliezer the Great was the authority there (TB Sanhedrin 32*b*); see A. Büchler, *op. cit.* pp. 18 ff.; Akiba had a school in Bene-Berak (TB Sanhedrin 32*b*). For other places, see Büchler. It is surprising, as Büchler (*op. cit.* p. 20) points out, that very few details are given in the Talmud about Jamnia. But there can be little doubt, on the other hand, that it was the centre for Jewry. Thus 72 members of the school being sometimes present at the same time in the town (Mishnah Zebaḥim i. 3) on 'that day' does not preclude such a number being present at other days.

[3] 'Revolt' is the term used by L. Finkelstein, for example in his *Akiba* (1936), p. xvi.

But, if Matthew originated in Syria, at Antioch, or in Phoenicia, is it likely that the developments within Pharisaism at Jamnia were known to him and affected his Church? This question we have mentioned previously, but it has to be repeated. Were the Sages at Jamnia likely to have been influential in the development of Christianity? Did they work in comparative seclusion so that Christian leaders went their way uninformed about and therefore uninfluenced by them, or was their activity of necessity widely known among Christians, as among Jews?[1] The indications are clear that this latter was the case.

The phrase 'the vineyard of Yavneh' (where R. Johannan ben Zakkai met his students) has perhaps created in most students a vague impression that Jamnia was a small secluded town, removed from the main currents of first-century Palestine. The term 'vineyard', however, may be merely a figure of speech, denoting an assembly of students.[2] In any case, Jamnia itself was a pleasant, commercial city, in a rich part of the Judaean plain, to which refugees from Jerusalem naturally turned, and where, in the city itself and in surrounding places such as Lud, Gumzo, Bene Brak and Emmaus, a livelihood for scholars was offered. Its advantages as a refugee centre had previously been recognized by Vespasian. To be at

---

[1] The influence of the Jamnian Sages even on Jews has been questioned by E. R. Goodenough, *Jewish Symbols in the Greco-Roman World*, vol. I. He has argued forcibly against the ascription of any widespread authority to the rabbinic Sages (I (1953), 11 ff.). He postulates a widespread Hellenistic Judaism, represented particularly by Philo, which he sets over against rabbinic Judaism, which sought at first to control all Jewry. But it failed to do so. The Judaism of the rabbis did not become normative for all Jews. It would be impertinent to discuss Professor Goodenough's work here: we may be permitted a few comments. First, we should go further than Dr Goodenough in recognizing that first-century 'legalistic' or Pharisaic Judaism was itself Hellenized, so that the gulf between Hellenism and Judaism of a rabbinic kind is not so sharp as he proposes. Secondly, whatever the variety of Judaism in the first century and subsequently (and this Goodenough and others have established beyond doubt) the historically significant force in first-century Judaism was the Pharisaic. And it was this force that the Church, and especially Matthew, had to oppose. That the extent and depth of Pharisaic–Rabbinic authority has been exaggerated we may admit, but that it asserted itself we must also admit. For discussions of Goodenough's work, see the following: Morton Smith, 'The Image of God: Notes on the Hellenization of Judaism', with especial reference to Goodenough's work on Jewish symbols, *Bulletin of John Rylands Library* (Manchester, 1958), 473–512; Cecil Roth, *Judaism* (New York, Spring 1954), pp. 129–35; *ibid*. pp. 179–82; S. S. Kayser, *Review of Religion* (Columbia University, November 1956), 54–60; A. D. Nock reviewed volumes I–IV and volumes V–VI in *Gnomon*, XXVII (1955), 558–72 and XXIX (1957), 524–33. E. J. Bickerman, *H.T.R.* LVIII (January 1965), on 'Symbolism in the Dura Synagogue', pp. 127 ff.   [2] TB Yebamoth, Soncino translation, I, 276, n. 14.

Jamnia, therefore, was not to be tucked out of sight, but thrown into the stream of Palestinian life.[1]

Not only must we avoid minimizing the geographic significance of Jamnia. Misconceptions about the assembly of Sages there have to be corrected.[2] On the one hand, it is misleading to think of it as a Sanhedrin like the one that existed in Jerusalem before A.D. 70. The term 'Sanhedrin', up to that date, had political connotations which transcended any powers which the Sages at Jamnia could ever have claimed. But, on the other hand, the latter are not to be thought of merely as constituting a kind of school in a purely academic sense. Doubtless they did resemble such. But, at the risk of repetition, it must be recalled that despite their preoccupation with the study of the Torah, they could never have been tempted to forget that the Torah was given that men might *live* thereby. As we saw, conditions in their time were such that 'scholarship could not now be permitted to relax into scholasticism'.[3] The Sages at Jamnia are best seen in perspective when the full significance of the fact is grasped that they were Pharisees bent on applying the Torah to the concrete situations of their lives. Thus although they never called themselves a Sanhedrin, they exercised as many of the functions of that now extinct body as they could.[4] Their specific aim of providing Judaism with a new centre and the measures taken to ensure it could not but have repercussions throughout Jewry and outside their ranks. The *takannot* (decrees), the common calendar issued from Jamnia, and the liturgy formulated there would be known among Jews in almost all places, and that of necessity (see, for example, Mishnah Rosh ha Shanah i. 4):

Because of two New Moons may the Sabbath be profaned, (the New Moon) of Nisan and (the New Moon) of Tishri, for on them messengers used to go forth to Syria, and by them the set feasts were determined. And while the Temple still stood the Sabbath might also be profaned because of any of the New Moons, to determine aright the time of the offerings.[5]

---

[1] For details, see A. Büchler, *op. cit.* p. 6: Jamnia was a centre for imperial storage and commerce (*ibid.* pp. 57 ff.).

[2] See Moore, *Judaism*, 1, 85.

[3] J. Goldin, 'The Period of the Talmud', in *The Jews*[3], ed. L. Finkelstein (1960), 1, 147.

[4] J. Goldin, *ibid.*

[5] M. Rosh ha-Shanah i. 6 reads: 'Once more than forty pairs [of witnesses] came forward....' The numbers involved are significant: the activity at Jamnia was well known. TB Rosh ha-Shanah 29 *b* mentions that on the day when a New Year fell on a Sabbath all the towns gathered around R. Johannan b. Zakkai in Jamnia. But some MSS read only 'all' not 'all the towns'.

Scholars were expected not only to attend the meetings at Jamnia, but to submit to the decisions reached there by the court. To the end of making Jamnian Judaism supreme, rabbis travelled to various centres of Jewry throughout the known world. Thus R. Gamaliel II, along with others, journeyed to Rome possibly to secure the imperial recognition, although the expedition has been variously interpreted.[1] Other journeys were probably of frequent occurrence, for example that of R. Gamaliel II mentioned in Mishnah Eduyoth vii. 7:

Once Rabban Gamaliel went to have authority given him from the governor in Syria, and he was long in returning; so they declared the year a leap-year on the condition that Rabban Gamaliel should approve; and when he returned he said, 'I approve'; and so the year was reckoned a leap-year.

Above all there were officials, the שליחים (apostles), appointed to visit synagogues, wherever they were scattered.[2] Akiba and others, at a later date, travelled extensively to collect money for the training of future rabbis, and it is probably legitimate to assume that such journeying was not an innovation.[3] Various of the Jamnian Sages appear in different places, so that their views and news travelled. For example, Eliezer b. Hyrkanos appears at Caesarea, Abelia, Sepphoris, Tiberias, Antioch, Rome.[4] Moreover, the economic impact of the Jamnian legislation must not be overlooked. Conditions in Palestine after A.D. 70 were economically difficult. As a result there developed an increasing tendency for Jews to emigrate from Palestine to neighbouring countries, especially to Syria. So serious did this become that it threatened the depopulation of the Holy Land. From this period come those passages which extol life in Palestine as superior to that possible elsewhere: the root of the glorification of life in that country, which is still very much alive in Judaism, were thus, in part at least, economic.[5] Conservative Sages such as Rabbi Eliezer the Great or ben Hyrcanus in order to protect Palestinian agriculture wanted to subject Syrian agriculture to all the requirements of tithing and

---

[1] H. Graetz (*op. cit.* pp. 387 ff.) dates this journey in the reign of Domitian (A.D. 81–96); B. Z. Bokser (*Pharisaic Judaism in Transition* (1935), pp. 23 ff.) later, in A.D. 116–17; see his bibliography. J. Goldin (*op. cit.* p. 150) claims that R. Gamaliel II 'visited one community after another in order to see for himself how the population was faring'. But he does not mention the visit to Rome. We read of Akiba going with R. Eliezer and R. Joshua on a sea voyage, Jer. Pesaḥim ii. 7, 29c, cited by L. Finkelstein, *Akiba*, pp. 109, 329, n. 34; the latter refers to Akiba's frequent journeys, p. 157. See now J. Neusner, *P.A.A.J.R.* xxx (1962), 83 ff., on 'Studies on the Problem of Tannaim in Babylonia'.

[2] See *J.E.* on 'Apostles'.   [3] Jer. Horayoth, III, 48a, 44.
[4] B. Z. Bokser, *op. cit.* p. 23.   [5] On all this see B. Z. Bokser, *op. cit.* pp. 98 ff.

the sabbatical year so as to check the emigration of farmers to Syria.[1] R. Gamaliel II, while he opposed such extreme measures, also shared in this purpose. The following passage from Mishnah Hallah iv. 7–8 is instructive:

7 If Israelites leased a field from gentiles in Syria, R. Eliezer declares their produce liable to Tithes and subject to the Seventh Year law; but Rabban Gamaliel declares it exempt. Rabban Gamaliel says: Two Dough-offerings (are given) in Syria. But R. Eliezer says: One Dough-offering. (Beforetime) they accepted the more lenient ruling of Rabban Gamaliel and the more lenient ruling of R. Eliezer, but afterward they followed the rulings of Rabban Gamaliel in both things.

8 Rabban Gamaliel says: Three regions are distinguished in what concerns Dough-offering. In the Land of Israel as far as Chezib one Dough-offering (is given); from Chezib to the River and to Amanah, two Dough-offerings, one for the fire and one for the priest; that for the fire has the prescribed measure, but that for the priest has no prescribed measure. From the River and from Amanah, inwards, two Dough-offerings (are given), one for the fire and one for the priest; that for the fire has no prescribed measure; and one that had immersed himself the selfsame day (because of uncleanness) may eat of it.

Legislation thus affected Syria, where Matthew probably originated. Such regulations as those of R. Gamaliel II deciding the geographic incidence of certain rules must have created a lively awareness of Jamnian affairs. (See also Mishnah Demai vi. 11.) R. Akiba's rule, 'the like of whatsoever is permitted to be done in the Land of Israel may be done also in Syria', implies much discussion on this point (Mishnah Shebiith vi. 2, 5, 6; also Mishnah Orlah iii. 9; Baba Kamma vii. 7). The sale of houses in Syria among Jews was regulated probably from Jamnia. Thus according to R. Meir 'in Syria houses may be hired to them [to Gentiles] but not fields; while outside the land houses may be sold and fields hired to them...' (Mishnah Abodah Zarah i. 8). (See also Mishnah Oholoth xviii. 7.)

Our purpose in enlarging on all this has been to show how inevitably leading Christians and, indeed, all who were in contact with the Synagogue in any way, even at a considerable distance away, would feel the impact of Jamnia on the religious and economic level. Does the Gospel of Matthew reveal this? The following considerations are pertinent. We shall divide them into direct and indirect elements.

(a) Let us consider those which may point directly to Jamnia.

(i) Like the expression 'the Jews' in xxviii. 15, so 'their synagogues' in

[1] B. Z. Bokser, *op. cit.*

iv. 23; ix. 35; x. 17; xii. 9; xiii. 54, and 'your synagogues' in xxiii. 34, and 'their scribes' in vii. 29 have been taken to imply a radical separation of Church and Synagogue such as was intended in the Birkath ha Minim. The Matthaean use of αὐτῶν and ὑμῶν in these connexions, then, has direct reference to Jamnian legislation.[1]

(ii) It is possible to claim that references to the maltreatment of Christians are too numerous to be regarded as merely sporadic, and suggest a deliberate policy on Jewish-Christianity such as emanated from Jamnia. Thus v. 11 seems to imply the use of the ban on Christians;[2] xxiii. 34, cf. x. 17, points to flogging, and even crucifixion; x. 23 to pursuit from town to town, διώκειν having acquired for Matthew a special significance in describing 'persecution'.[3] But it is difficult to connect such uncontrolled hatred as is here implied with Jamnia, where the ban and the Birkath ha Minim prevailed. The passages referred to suggest more violent local outbursts than the sobriety of Jamnia. Nor should we too readily assume that predictions, within which all the above references, except v. 11, occur, are necessarily guides to actual events. Moreover, Paul's letters, like Acts, attest violence on the part of the Synagogue, and that frequent, so that there is no reason to connect the passages referred to in any way specifically with Jamnian affairs, unless other factors point to this.

(iii) It is tempting to see a side-glance at Jamnia in xxiii. 5–10:

Whatever they [the Pharisees] do is done for show...they like to be greeted respectfully in the street and to be addressed as 'rabbi'. But you must not be called 'rabbi'; for you have one Rabbi, and you are all brothers. Do not call any man on earth 'father'; for you have one Father, and he is in heaven. Nor must you be called 'teacher'; you have one Teacher, the Messiah. (NEB.)

The Greek is:

πάντα δὲ τὰ ἔργα αὐτῶν ποιοῦσι πρὸς τὸ θεαθῆναι τοῖς ἀνθρώποις...φιλοῦσι... τοὺς ἀσπασμοὺς ἐν ταῖς ἀγοραῖς, καὶ καλεῖσθαι ὑπὸ τῶν ἀνθρώπων ῥαββί. ὑμεῖς δὲ μὴ κληθῆτε ῥαββί· εἷς γάρ ἐστιν ὑμῶν ὁ διδάσκαλος· πάντες δὲ ὑμεῖς ἀδελφοί ἐστε. καὶ πατέρα μὴ καλέσητε ὑμῶν ἐπὶ τῆς γῆς· εἷς γάρ ἐστιν ὁ πατὴρ ὑμῶν ὁ οὐράνιος. μηδὲ κληθῆτε καθηγηταί, ὅτι καθηγητὴς ὑμῶν ἐστιν εἷς ὁ χριστός.

---

[1] G. D. Kilpatrick, *op. cit.* pp. 110 f.; W. Trilling, *Das wahre Israel*, p. 61.

[2] Hunzinger, *T.L. loc. cit.*

[3] See G. D. Kilpatrick, *op. cit.* p. 16; and especially W. Trilling, *op. cit.* p. 62. Kilpatrick, *op. cit.* pp. 13, 115, goes too far in finding severe persecution and the death penalty exercised by Rabbinic authorities after A.D. 70. Where is the evidence for this? See Douglas R. A. Hare, *The Theme of Jewish Persecution of Christians in the Gospel According to St Matthew* (unpublished dissertation, Union Seminary, 1963), p. 31, n. 62.

The term *rabbi* up to A.D. 70 was a mark of courtesy, like 'Sir' or 'Lord' in English.[1] It was at Jamnia that it became a title for ordained scholars authorized to teach. Hillel, Shammai and early Tannaim were not entitled 'rabbi'. The Jamnian usage is revealed in xxiii. 8, where rabbi (ῥαββί) is understood as 'teacher' (διδάσκαλος). Titular consequence being such a natural weakness, there was possibly much pretentious use of the title rabbi at Jamnia and elsewhere. Not all Sages were gentle as Hillel, and some, like the great Gamaliel II himself,[2] were clearly 'touchy' about their dignity. Such consequence as we have referred to seems to have impressed and, perhaps, invaded the Matthaean Church: some leading members of it may have been tempted to ape it (the aping of the 'Establishment' by the sectarian, it might be noted, is not an unfamiliar phenomenon).

(*b*) Taken in isolation the above elements cannot be regarded as certainly pointing to Jamnia. They only gain in credence when set over against certain general, indirect considerations.

First, the events which occasioned the removal of the Sages to Jamnia, that is, the fall of Jerusalem, particularly occupied Matthew. In two passages, he introduces what can hardly be other than direct references to these. In the parable of the wedding feast, in xxii. 1 ff., the anger of the king with the recalcitrant elect, that is, the Jews, is expressed in what is almost certainly a reference to the siege and fall of the city. 'The King was angry, and he sent his troops and destroyed those murderers and burned their city' (xxii. 7). That is, the rejection of Israel is discussed particularly in connexion with A.D. 70.[3] Equally significant, and consonant with this, is it that Matthew places the poignant cry of Jesus over Jerusalem at the close of his anti-Pharisaic discourse. The culmination of that indictment and its vindication he states in xxiii. 37 f.: 'O Jerusalem, Jerusalem...Behold, your house (temple) is forsaken and desolate' (RSV). The full force of this can be seen only in comparison with Luke xiii. 34 and 1 Kings ix. 7 f. The comparison makes it clear that the reference in οἶκος is to the Temple (so NEB). The change in the context from the Lucan is striking. In Luke xiii. 31–3 the Pharisees warn Jesus against the danger that threatens him from Herod, that is, they are friendly.[4] In Matthew this is not so: the Pharisees—who are now en-

---

[1] *J.E. ad rem.*   [2] TB Berakoth 27*b*.

[3] Not all scholars, however, see a reference to the fall of Jerusalem here: for example, F. V. Filson, *St Matthew* (1960), pp. 232 ff.

[4] See W. L. Knox, *Sources of the Synoptic Gospels* (1953), p. 16.

sconced in Jamnia mainly—have become the villains of the piece: the verses in xxiii. 37–9 have become a sad comment on the Pharisaic movement in Jerusalem. It is followed immediately in chapter xxiv by the discussion of the Parousia, which in Matthew has been interpreted by Feuillet as the divine judgement on Judaism in the fall of Jerusalem and which, in any case, includes that event (xxiv. 1–3).[1]

Apart from these fairly direct indications of the importance attached by Matthew to the fall of Jerusalem, there are minor indications of his concern with the city as such. In the first prediction of the Passion, he makes it plain that there is a divine necessity that Jesus should suffer in Jerusalem. Mark and Luke make no such explicit reference to the city.[2] As Jesus entered the city, Matthew is careful to note that the whole city was disturbed at his advent, while neither Mark nor Luke are concerned to refer to the reaction of the city as such.[3] In the account of the Resurrection the custodians at the tomb 'went into the city to report what had happened' (xxviii. 11), the dead raised at the time of the Crucifixion 'went into the holy city' (xxvii. 53), and appeared to many. The sin of that city is particularly real to the Evangelist: throughout his passion narrative even its crowds appear hostile, in marked contrast to those of Luke, who tend, at least on occasion, to sympathize with Christ in his hour of death.[4]

Matthew then reveals a marked awareness of Jerusalem and its fate. But along with this, complicating it, he reveals an emphasis on the Holy City as the guilty city, and on Galilee as the scene of redemption.[5] This motif invades the birth narratives,[6] the body of the Gospel and the account of the Resurrection.[7] What is not often realized is that the championship of Galilee in Matthew inevitably involves it in a rivalry older than Christianity, that between Galilee of the Gentiles and the

[1] In *The Background of the New Testament and its Eschatology*, ed. W. D. Davies and D. Daube, pp. 261 ff.; also *R.B.* (Paris, 1949), no. 1, p. 85; no. 2, p. 85.

[2] xvi. 21 has δεῖ αὐτὸν εἰς Ἱεροσόλυμα ἀπελθεῖν. Contrast Mark viii. 31: δεῖ... πολλὰ παθεῖν, so Luke ix. 22 (with modifications).

[3] xxi. 10, καὶ εἰσελθόντος αὐτοῦ εἰς Ἱεροσόλυμα ἐσείσθη πᾶσα ἡ πόλις, has no parallel in Mark and Luke. Compare R. H. Lightfoot, *Locality and Doctrine in the Gospels* (1938), p. 129.

[4] The Passion evokes 'emotion' in Luke as it does not in Mark and Matthew: for example, Luke xxii. 43; xxiii. 27.

[5] R. H. Lightfoot (*op. cit.* p. 126) recognizes this fully, even though he concludes that the distinctive choice of Galilee is not so consistently upheld as by Mark (p. 130).

[6] This has been emphasized by K. Stendahl, 'Quis et Unde? An analysis of Matt. 1–2', in *Z.N.W.* xxvi, 94 ff., in a way which escaped Lightfoot and Lohmeyer (*Galiläa und Jerusalem*, 1936).

[7] R. H. Lightfoot, *op. cit.*

'establishment', if we may so express it, both Pharisaic and Sadducaic, at the Holy City. We saw that the leader of Jamnian Judaism was especially in reaction against Galilean enthusiasms, so that the 'rivalry' to which we refer persisted into Jamnia. Over against the *Schwärmerei* and apocalyptic of the Galileans, and of others, the Sages placed their own sanity and sobriety. From the rabbinic point of view early Christianity shared in the *Schwärmerei* of Galilee. If Matthew was concerned to set a more radical ethic against that of Pharisaism, he may also have opposed to it his 'enthusiasm', especially, as we noted above, in such passages as vi. 25–34. Is the Matthaean formulation of the teaching of Jesus in the *SM*, characterized in some parts by attempts at the regulation of the radical, marked in others, as in vi. 25–34, by conscious criticism of the caution of the Sages? Certain it is that such words as vi. 34, which are absent from Luke, would strike them as irresponsible. Historically, much in the *SM* is illumined when understood in terms of the enthusiasm of a Galilean movement over against the realism of the Jamnian.

The 'rabbinic' habits of Matthew in the formal, detailed construction of his Gospel have frequently been pointed out.[1] Certain passages have even evoked the figure of Rabbi Johannan ben Zakkai,[2] and again Matthew has been called a 'converted Rabbi'.[3] The evidence for all this need not be repeated here. What has not been sufficiently recognized is the extent to which, as we have taken pains to make clear above, the period when Matthew emerged was one of the codification of Law in Judaism and of the reformulation or reformation of worship. The origins of the Mishnah are traceable to Jamnia: codification and liturgical reform was in the air. Has this a bearing on Matthew and particularly on the *SM*? In the next few pages we shall examine this question. We emphasize at the outset that what emerges is very tentative and, indeed, merely exploratory: the living contacts between Church and Synagogue are so little known in the Jamnian period that, at this stage, we can speak, not of assured results, but only of possibilities and probabilities. With this precaution, we proceed with the examination.

First, we turn to the antitheses in v. 22–48. The view that these, in their sixfold form, preceded the formation of M,[4] usually dated about

---

[1] See commentaries.

[2] B. W. Bacon, *op. cit.* pp. 71 ff., who not only refers to Von Dobschütz, 'Matthäus als Rabbi und Katechet' in *Z.N.W.* (1928), but refers to the striking parallel between xxii. 11–14 and a parable ascribed to R. Johannan b. Zakkai.

[3] Von Dobschütz, *op. cit.* p. 344; see also W. Trilling, *op. cit.* pp. 95 f.

[4] So T. W. Manson, *The Sayings of Jesus* (1949), pp. 23 f.

A.D. 65, is unlikely. Had they so existed, then it would be improbable that they were directed in any way towards Jamnia. Probably, in their present form, however, the antitheses are a Matthaean construction. But why their sixfold form? The arrangement of materials in groups of six is not usual in Matthew, who prefers groups of two, five, seven and, especially, three items. Since the antitheses draw upon the Decalogue,[1] their natural number might have been expected to be ten. Thus the use of sixfold antitheses raises a question. The suggestion has been made that 'criticisms made by Jesus of the Law may at a later time, when their origin was forgotten, have played some part in the development of the Jewish code as it took shape in the Mishnah and Talmud'.[2] But may not the reverse have also been the case? The Mishnah is divided into six *sedarim*, or orders, as are the two Talmuds, the Babylonian and the Palestinian, hence the name '*shas*' for the Talmud (six *sedarim*). The early history of the Mishnah is unknown,[3] but, as we saw, Finkelstein assumes that six orders of a Mishnah, though not in the present sequence, had been collected at the end of the first century. These orders represented the essentials of the Law. Was Matthew concerned in his six antitheses to provide a parallel to the Mishnaic sixfold division? Daube has shown how we have in v. 17–48 what is essentially an example of 'Principle and Cases', that is, 'the proclamation of a general principle, "I am not come to destroy, your righteousness shall exceed that of the Scribes and Pharisees", followed by a series of illustrations, "Ye have heard, thou shalt not kill..." and so on'.[4] Examples of this form are provided from the Mishnah. Is it possible that the choice of six illustrations may have been motivated by the fact that the Scribes and Pharisees mentioned in v. 20 divided their civil law into six essential orders?

There are obvious difficulties in the way of this view. First, where Matthew uses his material in a way which is numerically significant, he makes this clear by specific reference to the number concerned.[5] Any such is missing in the antitheses. Secondly, by no stretch of the imagination can the contents and order of the antitheses be compared with those of the Mishnah. We do not certainly know the 'Mishnaic' order in the first century, if with Finkelstein we assume that such existed. But a comparison with the present orders, which cannot be very different from the

---

[1] For example at v. 21, 27, 30. [2] T. W. Manson, *op. cit.* p. 12.
[3] See H. L. Strack, *Introduction to the Talmud and Midrash* (1931), pp. 8 ff.
[4] *Op. cit.* pp. 63 ff.
[5] As in the genealogy in chapter i.

earlier, reveals at once that only at points do the antitheses deal with Mishnaic themes. Thus the orders are as follows:

The Mishnah	The Antitheses
Zeraim (Seeds)	Murder and Anger
Moed (Set fasts)	Marriage and Sex
Nashim (Women)	Divorce
Nezikin (Damages)	Swearing
Kodashim (Hallowed things)	Revenge
Tohoroth (Cleannesses)	Love of Enemies

A glance at these columns is enough to reveal at once how the Mishnah, a detailed compendium of laws, cannot really be compared with the antitheses, which on the whole set forth absolute norms. There would seem, therefore, to be no justification for thinking of the latter as a little Mishnah. That there were six orders in the Mishnah and six antitheses would seem to be purely accidental, unless there be support for relating them elsewhere. Is there such? Can we connect Matthew in any way with Mishnaic activity?

That the strictly codal activity at Jamnia was of interest to Matthew, perhaps, emerges in two places. The first possibility is a very unexpected one: it is the genealogy in i. 1 ff. We emphasize again the emphatic division of the genealogy into a triad of fourteen generations. There is reason to believe that such a division would particularly impress Pharisaic readers. This emerges from the work of Finkelstein.[1] Pharisaism came to be concerned to provide itself with a reliable ancestry. Not a bloodlist of progenitors, however, but a succession of teachers through whom its tradition had been transmitted from the past. The necessity to guarantee the validity of this tradition, under circumstances into which we need not enter here,[2] compelled Pharisaism to produce its credentials, as it were. These are preserved for us in two forms, an earlier one in the Aboth de Rabbi Nathan and a later one in the Mishnah. These forms are as follows:

ARN

Moses was sanctified in the Cloud, and received the Torah from Sinai, as it is written, 'And the glory of the Lord abode on Mt. Sinai (and the Cloud covered it six days, and the seventh day He called unto Moses out of the midst of the Cloud)' (Exod. xxiv. 16). (This was in order) to purify him.

Joshua received the tradition from Moses, as it is written, 'And Joshua the son

---

[1] *Mabo le Massekot Abot ve Abot d'Rabbi Nathan*, pp. x ff.

[2] See E. J. Bickerman, *R.B.* LIX (1952), 44–54 on 'La Chaîne de la Tradition Pharisienne'.

of Nun was full of the spirit of wisdom; for Moses had laid his hands upon him'
(Deut. xxxiv. 9).

The elders received the tradition from Joshua, as it is written, 'And the people
served the Lord all the days of Joshua, and all the days of the elders that outlived
Joshua, who had seen the great work of the Lord that He had wrought for
Israel' (Judg. ii. 7).

The judges received the tradition from the elders, as it is written, 'And it came
to pass in the days when the judges judged' (Ruth i. 1).

The prophets received the tradition from the judges, as it is written, 'And
though I sent upon you all My servants the prophets, sending them daily betimes
and often' (Jer. vii. 25).

Haggai, Zechariah, and Malachi received the tradition from the prophets. The
men of the Great Synagogue received the tradition from Haggai, Zechariah, and
Malachi. And they said three things: 'Be patient in judgment; build a fence
about your words; and raise many sages.'[1]

M. Aboth

Moses received the Law from Sinai and committed it to Joshua, and Joshua to
the elders, and the elders to the Prophets; and the Prophets committed it to the
men of the Great Synagogue. They said three things: Be deliberate in judgment,
raise up many disciples, and make a fence around the Law.

The older form from the ARN traces the transmission down to Hillel
and Shammai. The most likely time for its composition, after the deaths
of these two figures, was during the period when codification was proceeding at Jamnia. Originally it was attached to the 'Manifesto of
Pharisaism' as it has been called, that is, Mishnah Sanhedrin 10, and so is
to be understood in the context of the struggle of Jamnian Judaism for
consolidation and conservation. It expresses the intention of Judaism to
preserve its identity in a manner that would impress its opponents. Later
on, when Judah the Prince included the 'professorial genealogy', if we
may so term it, in the present Mishnah, he introduced certain changes. In
order to make the chain of tradition complete, he added references to
Rabban Gamaliel and his son Rabban Simeon. But it is significant that
in order to keep the items in the 'genealogy' at the number fourteen, he
omitted two members of the older series preserved in ARN. Thus both
the younger and older lists present fourteen steps in the tradition.

The words of Finkelstein commenting on this deserve quotation:

The number, 'fourteen', is not accidental. It corresponds to the number of high
priests from Aaron to the establishment of Solomon's Temple; the number of

[1] *Op. cit. ad rem.*

high priests from the establishment of the Temple until Jaddua, the last high priest mentioned in Scripture. It is clear that a mystic significance attached to this number, in both the Sadducean and the Pharisaic traditions. Each group maintained that it was no accident that the number of links in the chain of what it considered the authoritative tradition, from Moses and Aaron until the time of Alexander the Great, was a multiple of the mystic number, 'seven'. This may seem a weak argument for the authenticity of a tradition; but antiquity was apparently prepared to be impressed by it. So impressive indeed was this argument, that in the Gospel of Matthew, the early Christian apologist, directing his argument against the Pharisees (and also the Sadducees) adopted a similar claim for Jesus, and traced his genealogy back to Abraham in a series of three chains of fourteen links each. (Matt. i. 17.)[1]

In the above quotation we may ignore the words in brackets '(and also the Sadducees)', because, on our view of Matthew's date, it was to Pharisaism in particular, and not to Sadduceanism, that the Gospel addressed itself. Does the Matthaean genealogy look to Jamnia? Like the important first section in Pirqe Aboth and ARN, it is governed by the mystic 'fourteen'. To Pharisaic readers it would at once suggest that section, except that it would also suggest a contrast—that between the genealogy of a person and of a succession of 'schools' or 'teachers', the one beginning with Abraham, the Father of Jewry, the other with Moses, their teacher (the 'Abraham begat' of i. 1 corresponding to the 'Moses received' of Mishnah Aboth i. 7 and ARN i. 1). In one thing the genealogy in i. 1 and the succession in the rabbinic sources are alike: they both begin at the ultimate human source of the 'tradition' or 'person'. Contrast with this the genealogy in Luke, who begins with Joseph and proceeds back to Adam. Luke shows a historical interest in the actual genealogy, Matthew in the nature and the antiquity of the genealogy. In other words, Matthew is presenting credentials as are the Aboth and ARN. If such an understanding of the Matthaean genealogy, as a counterpart to the beginning of the Aboth, be acceptable, then it provides added justification for thinking that Matthew was engaged with Jamnia.

Is there other evidence for this? So far we have ignored the structure of the *SM* itself. But, if we omit the Beatitudes and the concluding material after vii. 12, the body of the *SM* reveals a sequence which can be connected with a theme which *may* have especially occupied the Sages at Jamnia. The force of this suggestion has to be considered in the light of the comparison with Pharisaism drawn in v. 17–20; vi. 2, 5, 16, where the

---

[1] *Op. cit. ad rem.*

references to the Synagogue are clear and where the 'hypocrites' are almost certainly the Pharisees. True in v. 47; vi. 7, 32, Matthew sets the Christian 'way' also over against the ways of Gentiles. In the first two instances there are variant readings: in K Θ al at v. 47 we find not ἐθνικοί, but τελῶναι; at vi. 7 in B sy^c we have ὑποκριταί for ἐθνικοί. The manuscript support for these variants is not, however, impressive; but, in any case, the references to the Gentiles only intensify a comparison already made with the Pharisees in both v. 47 and vi. 7, and in all the passages, including vi. 32, which has τὰ ἔθνη not ἐθνικοί, the references to the Gentiles are more illustrative than determinative of Matthew's purposes. What then is the theme to which we refer?

Immediately following the statement of the credentials of Pharisaism in Mishnah Aboth i. 1, there occur in Mishnah Aboth i. 2 words that have been of fundamental significance in Judaism. They are:

שמעון הצדיק היה משירי כנסת הגדולה. הוא היה אומר על שלשה דברים העולם עומד על התורה ועל העבודה ועל גמילות חסדים.

These are usually translated as follows:

Simeon the Just was of the remnants of the Great Synagogue. He used to say: By three things is the world sustained: by the Law, by the (Temple) service, and by deeds of loving kindness.

This understanding of the Hebrew has recently been challenged in a significant article by Goldin[1] whose position we now state. The meaning of the phrase גמילות חסדים for Simeon the Just was not 'deeds of loving kindness', but any act of piety of a social or a cultic character; גמילות חסדים were, in short, simply acts in which the commandments (מצוות) were observed. In addition, a distinction should be rigidly made between the anarthrous תורה, which signifies not the Written Law, which is designated by the arthrous התורה, but the Oral Law. Finally, the term עולם, which in the Old Testament mostly bears a temporal connotation, such as 'age', is usually assumed to mean 'world' for the first time in Simeon the Just. But is it necessary to make this assumption? May he not have preserved the old meaning for it? In view of all this, the meaning of Simeon's words is: 'The Age, that is to say, your whole future, is supported by three pillars—the Works of the Torah, the Temple-cult, and acts of *pietas*' (that is, loyalty and obedience to God). The circumstances under which they were formulated, in the crisis of the Maccabaean period, made such a meaning peculiarly appropriate.

[1] J. Goldin, in *P.A.A.J.R.* xxvii (1958), 52 ff.

The position we have outlined is not convincing in all its details. It is not clear that עולם in the dictum by Simeon the Just should not mean 'world'.[1] On the other hand, the evidence supplied by Goldin in favour of the meaning he ascribes to גמילות חסדים seems to us convincing.[2] If so, his further suggestion deserves serious consideration. It is this. With the destruction of the Temple one element in Simeon's triad ceased to be a possibility, namely, Temple service. Moreover, the tragic circumstances of the period following upon the fall of Jerusalem demanded a new emphasis on piety, that is, on גמילית חסדים. Thus Johannan b. Zakkai faced a situation which called for a re-interpretation of traditional positions, including that of Simeon the Just. It is this that explains his insistence that mercy (חסד) had replaced Temple worship (עבודה) in the following passage:

ON ACTS OF LOVING-KINDNESS: how so? Lo, it says, *For I desire mercy and not sacrifice* (Hos. vi. 6).

From the very first the world was created only with mercy, as it is said, *For I have said, The world is built with mercy; in the very heavens Thou dost establish Thy faithfulness* (Ps. lxxxix. 3).

Once as Rabban Johanan ben Zakkai was coming forth from Jerusalem, Rabbi Joshua followed after him and beheld the Temple in ruins.

'Woe unto us!' Rabbi Joshua cried, 'that this, the place where the iniquities of Israel were atoned for, is laid waste!'

'My son,' Rabban Johanan said to him, 'be not grieved; we have another atonement as effective as this. And what is it? It is acts of loving-kindness, as it is said, *For I desire mercy and not sacrifice*' (Hos. vi. 6).[3]

In this passage חסד has replaced עבודה in the sense of Temple service. In another passage from the same source we read of the meeting of R. Johannan ben Zakkai with the Emperor:

'Art thou Rabban Johanan ben Zakkai?' Vespasian inquired; 'tell me, what may I give thee?'

'I ask naught of thee,' Rabban Johanan replied, 'save Jamnia, where I might go and teach my disciples and there establish a prayer [house] and perform all commandments.'[4]

---

[1] J. G. Weiss, *J.J.S.* x, 3, 4 (1959), 170, n. 8.

[2] *Op. cit.*; his references to Daniel are forceful.

[3] J. Goldin's translation, *The Fathers According to Rabbi Nathan* (1955), pp. 34 f.

[4] *Ibid.* p. 36.

Here *the* Torah has become the pillar of studying and teaching Torah; sacrificial worship has been replaced by prayer, and גמילית חסדים, acts of piety, by the performance of all the commandments. In this way, Rabbi Johannan ben Zakkai met the challenge of reconstruction by the re-interpretation of the pillars on which the world stood. It may be objected to all this that we have no means of pinning such a re-interpretation to the Jamnian period. This is to be admitted, except that the re-interpretation emerges with force in the account of the meeting between Johannan and Vespasian, so that, in the tradition, it is connected with the fall of Jerusalem. Moreover, historical probability favours the tradition at this point. Great crises seem to have a tendency to evoke certain significant aphorisms which sum up their essential challenge—in politics such phrases as 'Blood, Sweat and Tears' and 'The New Frontier' emerge, and in religion, for example, 'The Evangelization of the World in this Generation'. The Jamnian period, we may reasonably conjecture, in the light of the above, found its rallying point in an ancient triad reformulated by Johannan ben Zakkai.[1]

Turning to the *SM*, it is a striking fact that the teaching of Jesus is there presented in a roughly parallel triadic way. In v. 17–48 we find the Torah of Jesus set forth; in vi. 1–18 the true עבודה or worship, and in vi. 19–vii. 12 what corresponds to גמילות חסדים, the culmination, in vii. 12, expressing the true piety or obedience in terms of the Golden Rule. On these three elements is the house of the new Israel to be built: they alone enable it to stand in the eschatological trial. Matthew's neat division of his material suggests that he is working under the influence of a traditional arrangement. He confronts the Synagogue with a triadic formulation which would not be alien to it. At the same time, it differs significantly from Johannan's re-interpretation. Matthew remains nearer to Simeon the Just. He has no reference to the study and teaching of the Law; and עבודה he defines explicitly in terms of almsgiving, prayer and fasting, not of prayer only. His treatment of the Temple, however, is strangely reminiscent of R. Johannan ben Zakkai: he too desires חסד not sacrifice (ix. 13; xii. 7).

Within the triad, the section on worship is again triadic: in vi. 1 ff. 'religion' (δικαιοσύνη, צדקה, עבודה) is treated under almsgiving, prayer,

---

[1] B. W. Bacon, *loc. cit.* I frequently discussed this with the late T. W. Manson and he has pointed to the triadic structure of the *SM* and compared it with the saying of Simeon the Just in a posthumous volume *Ethics and the Gospel* (1961). He does not there note the point made above that the threefold pillars were being re-interpreted at the same time in Judaism.

20-2

fasting. This collocation, though not completely and not exactly in this order, is a common one in Judaism. Thus we have:

Ecclus. vii. 8–10:

'Be not impatient in thy prayer
And in righteousness be not behindhand.'

Tobit xii. 7–9:

'Better is prayer with truth and alms with righteousness. . . .'

T. J. Taanith ii. 1:

א״ר לעזר ג׳ דברים מבטלין את הגזירה קשה ואלו הן תפלה וצדקה ותשובה

This is rendered by Schwab (vol. 6, p. 153) thus:

R. Eleazar dit: il y a 3 moyens de modifier les décrets que la Providence a rendus contre nous, savoir la prière dite avec ferveur, l'exercice de la charité, l'amendement de notre conduite.

R. Eleazar bases all these on 2 Chron. ii. 14.

In the present-day service of the Day of Atonement, we find the order Repentance, Prayer, Charity (צדקה, תפלה, תשובה), where repentance is taken to denote especially 'fasting'.[1] Has the priority given by Matthew to almsgiving in vi. 2 ff. any significance? For obvious reasons, arising out of post-war conditions, almsgiving was given a special prominence in Jamnian Judaism: its regulation was of serious concern to the Sages. It may be objected that, ideally at least, concern for the poor had always been a mark of Judaism, and that it is, therefore, illegitimate to insist upon it as characteristic of the Jamnian period. Nevertheless, although the depression of Jewry after A.D. 70 has sometimes been over-emphasized,[2] the economic condition of most was such that only an extraordinary effort at philanthropy on the part of the more fortunate ones could avail to preserve the nation. The first of the six divisions of the Mishnah (Zeraim (Seeds)) was devoted to the regulations concerning the poor, along with the priests and levites. The system of public charity which emerged from the distress of the times, and which is described in Tosefta Peah, can only be carried back to the period immediately following the Hadrianic war, but there is evidence that that system arose out of the reorganization of a previously existing one which was of much concern to the Sages.[3] Possibly in the Matthaean community similar factors were at work.

---

[1] I owe this to J. Israelstam.

[2] See A. Büchler, op. cit., who makes this clear while doing full justice to the poverty: see pp. 14, 30, 34, 41 f., 63 ff.

[3] J. Goldin, The Period of the Talmud, p. 152; Mishnah Peah viii. 7 ff.

When we turn to the second element in the treatment of worship, namely, prayer, great caution is necessary. It should not be overlooked that it was customary for Jewish teachers to provide forms of prayer for their followers, and the Lord's Prayer originally doubtless emerged in accordance with this tradition.[1] Again, the indigenous needs of the Christian community would demand concern with prayer, so that external influences need not necessarily be postulated to account for the treatment of prayer in vi. 7–14. The reference to the Gentiles in vi. 7 might also be taken to suggest that comparison with strictly synagogal forms is not directly pertinent here. Nevertheless, the Matthaean form of the Lord's Prayer occurs in the context of a Christian community set over against Pharisaism. Are there indications that synagogal influences have helped to shape it? In particular, was the Matthaean version of the prayer formulated deliberately as a counterpart to the Shemoneh Esreh? We may first contrast the Matthaean with the Lucan form of the Lord's Prayer. The latter occurs in the context of the private prayer of Jesus (Luke xi. 1), while it was evoked by the prayer taught by John the Baptist to his disciples. The way in which it is introduced (εἶπε δὲ αὐτοῖς, ὅταν προσεύχησθε, λέγετε, Πάτερ...) and the absence of liturgical elaborations or cadences do not suggest any intent to set up a liturgically appropriate form. Despite all this, it has been claimed that the Lucan prayer was devised in the light of the demands of the Synagogue. The question of the disciples in Luke xi. 1 'Lord teach us to pray, as John taught his disciples' has been taken to mean, 'Teach us how we should pray when we are called upon to say the brief prayer in the sabbath service in the Synagogue'.[2] This claim is exceedingly unlikely for the Lucan form. But what of the Matthaean? This, we reiterate, is set in a total context which contrasts Christian and synagogal worship. (Pagan worship is also included in the contrast, secondarily, unless the reading of BSy^c, that is, ὑποκριταί, be accepted instead of ἐθνικοί in vi. 7; but this last is textually unjustifiable perhaps.)[3] The impartation of a standardized or

[1] See P. Fiebig, *Das Vaterunser* (1927), p. 37.

[2] See Heinrich Schürmann, *Das Gebet des Herrn* (Freiburg, 1957), p. 142, n. 142, who cites C. Steuernagel ('Die ursprüngliche Zweckbestimmung des Vaterunsers', Leipzig, *Gesellschaft- und sprachwissenschaftliche Reihe*, III (1953/4), 217–20), as holding this view.

[3] It is possible to find an anti-liturgical note in the verses preceding the Lord's Prayer in vi. 7–9 but this should not be allowed to prejudice our approach to the Prayer itself. While Matthew places the Lord's Prayer over against the customs of Jews and Gentiles (vi. 5 f., 7 f.), it is also clear that he does not thereby merely mean to give general directions for prayer. The total context is one in which Matthew deals

fixed form of prayer is possibly suggested in the words οὕτως οὖν προσεύχεσθε ὑμεῖς, where the ὑμεῖς is emphatic, setting off the Christian community from the Synagogue (and from Gentile usage). The liturgical elaborations of the prayer in Matthew are marked thus:

Luke	Matthew
(1) Father	*Our* Father, *which art in heaven,*
(2) Thy Kingdom come	Thy Kingdom come,
	Thy will be done on earth
	As it is in heaven.
(3) And lead us not into temptation	And lead us not into temptation,
	But deliver us from evil
(4)	*For thine is the Kingdom and the Power and the*
	Glory for ever and ever. Amen.

In the address in (1), the increased items of parallelism in (2) and (3) and, in later MSS, in (4), the liturgical intent of the Matthaean form is evident: it is a prayer designed for the new community.

Can we go further? At least the question may be posed whether the Matthaean Church was, in part at least, prompted to set forth its own prayer as a counterpart to the main prayer of the Synagogue, the Shemoneh Esreh, which was being formulated anew at Jamnia. On the basis of his retranslation of the Lord's Prayer into Aramaic, Kuhn[1] has suggested certain similarities in its structure and form to the Shemoneh Esreh.

(1) In both the Palestinian and Babylonian versions, the Shemoneh Esreh consists of three introductory and three concluding items, in between which there is a core of twelve benedictions.[2] These twelve are in two parts, the first dealing with the present and the second with 'eschatology'. The Lord's Prayer is similarly divided, except that eschatological petitions precede those for the present. The transition from part one to part two in the Lord's Prayer, as in the central core of the Shemoneh Esreh, occurs with the petition for daily bread (vi. 11): in the latter this is the end of the first part (Benediction 9) and in the former the beginning of the second part.

(2) The rhyme in the Lord's Prayer provided by the second personal singular suffix (אך) in the first part and by the first personal plural suffix

with the piety of the new community—its almsgiving, prayer, fasting, its attitude towards wealth, that is, he is thinking 'institutionally', so that the Lord's Prayer is to be understood here as a 'form' of prayer to be used by the New Israel. Compare Heinrich Schürmann, *op. cit.* pp. 106 ff. [1] *Op. cit.*

[2] On the Tefillah, see I. Elbogen, *op. cit.*; S–B, Exkurs iv, 1 ff. The first three Benedictions are of an introductory hymnic character, the last three consist of thanksgivings. For a convenient text, see C. W. Dugmore, *op. cit.* pp. 114–27.

in the second part (נא), is similar to that which occurs in the Shemoneh Esreh. Compare, for example, the rhyme in Berakoth 7[1] of the Shemoneh Esreh and the second part of Matthew's prayer, that is:

וְרִיבָה רִיבֵנוּ	רְאֵה בְעָנְיֵנוּ	that is,	a	a
לְמַעַן שְׁמֶךָ	וּגְאָלֵנוּ		b	a

and

לְיוֹמָא הַב לָנָא	לַחְמָנָא	that is,	a	a
חוֹבֵינָא	וּשְׁבֵק לָנָא		a	a

(3) Not only the rhyme but the rhythm in the Jewish and Christian prayers are significant. Compare, for example, Benediction 5[2] with the first petition in Matthew, that is,

לְתוֹרָתֶךָ	הֲשִׁיבֵינוּ	with	מַלְכוּתָךְ	תֵּאתֵא
לַעֲבוֹדָתֶךָ	וְקָרְבֵנוּ	with	רְעוּתָךְ	תִתְעֲבֵד

(4) The doxology in vi. 13 can be loosely compared with the three closing benedictions of the Shemoneh Esreh, which supply an ending of praise.[3]

(5) While their public use is not excluded, the intention of both the Shemoneh Esreh and the Lord's Prayer is individual.[4]

Having pointed out the above similarities, Kuhn emphasizes the theological differences between the two prayers. Such differences as he refers to are to be expected; they reflect those between the two faiths.[5] As such, do they stem from a conscious effort on the part of the Christian community to differentiate itself even in and through its prayers? This cannot be the case, because at whatever date Matthew formulated the Lord's Prayer, its substance, we must claim, goes back to Jesus himself, before a conscious opposition between the Church and the Synagogue, as two

---

[1] Palestinian Version.　　[2] Babylonian Version.　　[3] See Appendix VIII.

[4] In its Matthaean context and form the Lord's Prayer is doubtless designed for the New Israel as such. But its individual character must not be overlooked. Just as the New Israel and the individual Christian are addressed in the admonition to almsgiving, so in the call to the Lord's Prayer he is also addressed. The plural in 'Our Father' and in the body of the prayer does not make the prayer merely communal: rather does it unite the individual, in his prayer, with the community. The Didache viii. 3, which possibly gives us a glimpse into a Church like that of Matthew, shows how Christians took over the custom of the Synagogue which demanded prayer thrice daily by the individual; compare Acts ii. 15; x. 9; Mishnah Berakoth iv. 3. (See H. Schürmann, *op. cit.* pp. 111–14.)

[5] *Op. cit.* The eschatological emphasis in Christianity determines the structure of the Lord's Prayer.

institutions, had been set up. And this brings us to the caution necessary in dealing with the Lord's Prayer. As Kuhn himself admits, the re-translation of that Prayer into Aramaic presents very real difficulties, particularly since the exact nature of the language spoken by Jesus has not been determined.[1] On the other hand, the reconstruction he offers has sufficient probability to justify a cautious use of it. For our purposes the question remains, therefore, whether Matthew's *formulation* of the prayer, originally taught by Jesus in a form more like the Lucan, was in conscious reaction to Jamnian concern with prayer and particularly with the Shemoneh Esreh.

At first sight, the Lord's Prayer, even in the Matthaean form, is so brief that any comparison with the extended Shemoneh Esreh would seem to be immediately ruled out. But the Mishnah refers to 'an abbreviated Eighteen'. In Mishnah Berakoth iv. 3 we read:

Rabban Gamaliel says: Every day a man should say the Eighteen Benedictions. R. Joshua says: An Abbreviated Eighteen (מעין). R. Akiba says: If he knows it fluently he says the original eighteen, and if not an Abbreviated Eighteen. (The Soncino translation.)

or

Rabban Gamaliel says: A man should pray the Eighteen [Benedictions] every day. R. Joshua says: The substance (מעין) of the Eighteen. R. Akiba says: If his prayer is fluent in his mouth he should pray the Eighteen, but if not, the substance of the Eighteen. (Danby's translation.)

In the Gemara on Mishnah Berakoth iv. 3 in TB Berakoth 29a we find a discussion of these Abbreviated Eighteen, that is, the מעין (substance) of the Eighteen, as follows:

R. JOSHUA SAYS: AN ABBREVIATED EIGHTEEN. What is meant by 'AN ABBREVIATED EIGHTEEN'? Rab said: An abbreviated form of each blessing; Samuel said: Give us discernment, O Lord, to know Thy ways, and circumcise our heart to fear Thee, and forgive us so that we may be redeemed, and keep us far from our sufferings, and fatten us in the pastures of Thy land, and gather our dispersions from the four corners of the earth, and let them who err from Thy prescriptions be punished, and lift up Thy hand against the wicked, and let the righteous rejoice in the building of Thy city and the establishment of the temple and in the exalting of the horn of David Thy servant and the preparation of a light for the son of Jesse Thy Messiah; before we call mayest Thou answer; blessed art Thou, O Lord, who hearkenest to prayer.

---

[1] Thus a comparison of the translations offered by C. F. Burney, *The Poetry of Our Lord* (1925), C. C. Torrey, *The Translations Made from the Original Aramaic Gospels* (1912), and by K. G. Kuhn, *Achtzehngebet und Vater Unser*, is instructive.

The PT has a shorter abbreviation (see O. Holtzmann, *Berakot*, p. 62). Was the Lord's Prayer in Matthew's understanding of it an equivalent for an Abbreviated Eighteen? This would be more likely than that it was designed as an equivalent for the full Shemoneh Esreh.[1]

Finally, in the Matthaean triad on worship we have fasting. It may not be purely a coincidence that this was also much in the Jamnian air. As a result of the distress following the war, a tendency to excessive fasting frequently manifested itself. The Jamnian Sages, while recognizing that fasting had a certain value, opposed its excessive indulgence. This emerges in the following passage from TB Bathra 60*b*.

Our Rabbis taught: When the Temple was destroyed for the second time, large numbers in Israel became ascetics, binding themselves neither to eat meat nor

---

[1] Compare H. Schürmann, *op. cit.* who speaks of the Lord's Prayer as a 'Kerngebet', although he does not specifically regard it in terms of the Shemoneh Esreh. See also I. Elbogen, *op. cit.* chapter IX, 1; K. G. Kuhn, *op. cit.* p. 10; P. Fiebig, *Das Vaterunser* (1927), pp. 19 f. Precision in terminology is difficult here. If the Lord's Prayer be regarded as wholly the creation of the Church, it might be possible to think of the Matthaean form of it as the quintessential, liturgical *abbreviation* of a large body of primitive Christian prayer. But it is most likely that the Lord's Prayer in Matthew is an *enlargement* of a simple form of a prayer taught by Jesus himself to his disciples and more truly preserved in Luke xi. 2–4. In this case it should not be thought of as an *abbreviation*, but rather as a '*short prayer*' (for this term, see M. Berakoth iv. 2). The point we make above is unaffected by this. In either case, the Lord's Prayer in Matthew may be thought of as the counterpart of the Shemoneh Esreh or an Abbreviated Eighteen.

R. Gamaliel demanded that the Shemoneh Esreh should be recited *becol iôm wiôm* (M. Berakoth iv. 3). Holtzmann translated this simply as 'jeden Tag' (*Berakoth*, p. 61). But he commented on the phrase as follows: 'es klingt, als ob die 18 Bitten auf die 3 Gebete verteilt würden' (*ibid.*). He also pointed out that the daily recitation of the Shemoneh Esreh was demanded only of males (M. Berakoth iii. 3). In these two ways the use of the Shemoneh Esreh in Judaism differed from that of the Lord's Prayer in the Church. Matthew does not discuss who is to say the Lord's Prayer or when. But in the Didache viii. 3 Christians are to say it three times daily. Holtzmann contrasts with this the Jewish custom of reciting the three parts of the Shemoneh Esreh once a day—as he understands the text. If Holtzmann's interpretation of M. Berakoth iv. 3 be correct, may it be that this recital of the three *divisions* of the Shemoneh Esreh suggested the threefold daily *recital* of the whole of the shorter Lord's Prayer to the Church? Unfortunately, Holtzmann's interpretation of M. Berakoth iv. 3 is conjectural, and nothing can be built upon it.

It may be urged that all that the evidence allows us to claim is that there were parallel movements at Jamnia and in the Matthaean Church in the direction of the fixation of liturgical forms of prayer. We suggest that the cumulative force of all that we have written above demands that these movements were not only parallel but interacting. But it is to be admitted that, as compared with the sophisticated Rabbinism of Jamnia, that with which Matthew reacted to it is 'Rabbinism'—*formally*, though not otherwise—in a lower key.

to drink wine. R. Joshua got into conversation with them and said to them: My sons, why do you not eat meat nor drink wine? They replied: Shall we eat flesh which used to be brought as an offering on the altar, now that this altar is in abeyance? Shall we drink wine which used to be poured as a libation on the altar, but now no longer? He said to them: If that is so, we should not eat bread either, because the meal offerings have ceased. They said: [That is so, and] we can manage with fruit. We should not eat fruit either, [he said,] because there is no longer an offering of firstfruits. Then we can manage with other fruits [they said]. But, [he said,] we should not drink water, because there is no longer any ceremony of the pouring of water. To this they could find no answer, so he said to them: My sons, come and listen to me. Not to mourn at all is impossible, because the blow has fallen. To mourn overmuch is also impossible, because we do not impose on the community a hardship which the majority cannot endure, as it is written, *Ye are cursed with a curse, yet ye rob me [of the tithe], even this whole nation.* (Soncino translation.)

We know from the Didache that Christian fasting was compared with and contrasted to synagogal. Didache viii. 1 reads: 'Let not your fasts be with the hypocrites, for they fast on Mondays and Thursdays, but do you fast on Wednesdays and Fridays.' Here the aim appears to be the avoidance of Jewish usage. Like the Didache, the later Didascalia v. 14, 18–21 enjoins Wednesday and Friday as days for fasting and adds: 'But fast not after the custom of the former people, but according to the New Testament which I have appointed you.' In a passage in TB Taanith 27*b*, however, we read the following:

Our Rabbis have taught: The men of the *Mishmar* prayed over the sacrifice of their brethren that it may be favourably accepted, whilst the men of the *Ma'amad* assembled in their synagogues and observed four fasts, on Monday, Tuesday, Wednesday and Thursday of that week. On Monday [they fasted] for those that go down to the sea; on Tuesday for those who travel in the deserts; on Wednesday that croup may not attack children; on Thursday for pregnant women and nursing mothers, that pregnant women should not suffer a miscarriage, and that nursing mothers may be able to nurse their infants; on Friday they did not fast out of respect for the Sabbath; and certainly not on the Sabbath. Why did they not fast on Sunday?—R. Johanan said: Because of the Nazareans. R. Samuel b. Nahmani said: Because it is the third day after the creation of Man. Resh Laḳish said: Because of the additional soul. For Resh Laḳish said: Man is given an additional soul on Friday, but at the termination of the Sabbath it is taken away from him, as it is said, *He ceased from work and rested [shabat wa-yinafash]* that is to say, Once the rest had ceased, woe! that soul is gone. (Soncino translation.)

This raises two points, namely, that, apparently, despite what the Didache claims, there were Jewish fasts on Wednesdays and Fridays during the period of the Temple and that Christian custom influenced Jewish in this matter. Unfortunately the R. Johanan mentioned in the text is not explicitly characterized. It is unlikely that R. Johannan ben Zakkai is meant but rather Rabbi Johanan of the late third century. We cannot be sure therefore that in the Jamnian period Judaism adapted its fasting to Christian usage; and this must be regarded as unlikely. But it may be that Matthew was concerned to regulate the latter with an eye to what was going on among Jews. If so, while the rabbis were concerned to avoid extremes—if we can judge from the passage cited above, which cannot, however, be regarded as necessarily typical—Matthew was most concerned with the avoidance of hypocrisy.

We are now able to sum up our treatment of the structure of the *SM*. We cannot certainly connect it with the discussion and activity at Jamnia, but the possibility is a real one that the form of the *SM* was fashioned under their impact. It is our suggestion that one fruitful way of dealing with the *SM* is to regard it as the Christian answer to Jamnia. Using terms very loosely, the *SM* is a kind of Christian, mishnaic counterpart to the formulation taking place there. It is not our intention to deny other formative influences on Matthew. But neither Gnostic nor 'sectarian' pressures are sufficient to account for the massive elevation of the teaching of Jesus in the *SM*. Apart from the internal demands of the Christian community, it was the necessity to provide a Christian counterpart to 'Jamnia' that best illumines this. A reviewer of Mary Moorman's massive work on Wordsworth, after praising her factual thoroughness, warns her that 'only a thrust in the dark [in her case into the poet's life and thought] can give a biography permanent interest'. The same is true for the understanding of Matthew. The juxtaposition of it with Jamnia is not a leap into the dark, but into the twilight of available sources. But this juxtaposition, it seems to me, best explains the emergence of Matthew's manifesto. It was the desire and necessity to present a formulation of the way of the New Israel at a time when the rabbis were engaged in a parallel task for the Old Israel that provided the outside stimulus for the Evangelist to shape the *SM*. That that body of material is not only to be understood in terms of such a pressure—an external one—but also in terms of interests indigenous to the Church will appear from the next chapter.[1]

[1] For a wealth of bibliographical and other support for much in the above, see *Studies in the History of the Sanhedrin*, by Hugo Mantel (Harvard University Press, 1961).

V. THE SETTING IN THE EARLY CHURCH

So far we have examined factors originating outside the Church which may have played some part in the emergence and formulation of the Gospel of Matthew. We have considered the possible significance for its understanding of Jewish Messianic expectations, Gnostic, Essene or quasi-Essene sectarian influences, and rabbinic Judaism itself. In varying degrees, each of these elements has contributed to our understanding of some aspects of the Sermon, but no single one of them, nor all of them together, has proved to be decisively illuminating; they all point beyond themselves. And since our examination of its background has been thus inconclusive, it is necessary to look next at the foreground of the Gospel, that is, at the life of the early Church itself, within which it arose. Is his emphasis on the words of Jesus, as the law of the Messiah, an innovation, which indicates a difference between Matthew and the other members of the Christian community, or were there forces in the Church which prepared the way for this? Did Matthew impress a 'Christian legalism', peculiar to himself, upon Jesus or was he merely making more explicit than did others what the Church in general accepted? In short, what precisely is the setting of the Sermon in the early Church? Does the Christian movement reveal indigenous currents which illumine Matt. v–vii?

I. *Anti-Paulinism*

First, we have to deal with the frequently asserted view that Matthew 'composed' the *SM* in order to combat the influence of Paul on the Church. Put briefly, it is held that the Apostle to the Gentiles had so strongly emphasized the doctrine of grace, of salvation as a free gift of God rather than as a reward for good works, that many Christians, less subtle than he, who misunderstood him, had come to think of the Christian life as divorced from morality, faith in God's grace alone being necessary. Paulinism had become a menace to the good life. This it was that led Matthew, it is sometimes claimed, to emphasize the need for good works in the Sermon.[1]

[1] See, for example, Hans Windisch, *Der Sinn der Bergpredigt* (1929), p. 96. The relation between Matthew and Paul has further been dealt with by C. H. Dodd, *E.T.* LVIII (1947), 293 ff.; and especially by W. Joest, *Gesetz und Freiheit* (1951), pp. 155–60.

The position outlined, rarely thus boldly stated, draws upon certain well-defined supports. They can, for convenience, be treated under two heads. First, the cross-currents of the historical situation during the period when Matthew was written have been variously claimed to point to the view indicated, and, secondly, direct polemic against the teaching and person of Paul has been detected in the Gospel itself. Let us examine each of these alleged supports in turn.

The historical situation when Matthew emerged has been re-examined recently by Brandon, and his work provides a convenient starting point.[1] Pertinent to our purpose is the connexion he discovers between Matthew and what he considers to have been a rehabilitation of Paul, related closely to the fall of Jerusalem in A.D. 70. Like many before him, Brandon argues that the early Church was deeply divided. On the one hand, Palestinian Jewish-Christians did not recognize any essential break between Christianity and Judaism. During the period when the war against Rome was brewing, they were closely associated with the nationalist Jewish rebels. On the other hand stood Paul, and those who followed him. Called to be a missionary to the Gentiles by the Risen Christ alone, Paul was uninterested in the 'Jesus of History', knowledge of whom gave to the leaders of Jewish-Christianity their importance, and impatient with their 'particularism'. In a situation of such tension, the death of Paul at the hands of Rome was an event of potentially momentous significance. The leaders of Palestinian or Jewish-Christianity were left without a serious rival. Nor did they fail to exploit their advantage. The real possibility emerged that the 'particularistic', Palestinian version of the Gospel would prevail in all the churches, and, thereby, reduce Christianity to a mere adjunct of Judaism. That this did not in fact happen was due to one event, the Fall of Jerusalem in A.D. 70. This it was that broke the growing stranglehold of Jewish-Christians on the Christian movement.[2]

But, paradoxically enough, one of the first results of this was the appearance of literature among Gentile churches to perpetuate the traditions about the 'Jesus of History' derived from Jewish-Christianity. This was so because during the period, after the death of Paul, when it was in the ascendant, Jewish-Christianity had fostered among Gentile Churches an interest in the traditions mentioned. These last had appealed to Gentile Christians, and when the sources from which they were derived were threatened, by the fall of Jerusalem, the need was felt to preserve them.

[1] *The Fall of Jerusalem* (London, 1951): for polemic against Paul, pp. 231–6.
[2] *Op. cit.* pp. 31–153.

This explains the writing of the Gospel of Mark, an event which was a new departure in world literature.[1] However, Mark, writing in Rome after A.D. 70, could not simply reproduce the received tradition. In the Graeco-Roman world it had to be so presented that the connexion between the Christian movement, from its very inception, and the Jewish revolt, had to be clarified, that is, Christianity had to be disentangled from Jewish nationalism. But precisely this was what Paul had done. And thus it came about that Mark's concern to present the tradition about Jesus without giving offence to Rome on political grounds came to be bound up with his understanding of Paul, and that part of the result of the Fall of Jerusalem was the vindication of Pauline Christianity. Even though born of it, the Gospel was now shown to be independent of Judaism, as Paul had always insisted. The deepened realization of this truth was the germ from which sprang the rehabilitation of Paul.[2] This process was already at work in Mark and characterized the work of Luke. On the other hand, it is important for the understanding of Matthew because of the opposition it aroused.

With Brandon's claim that Matthew represents the point of view of an early Jewish-Christianity in the city of Alexandria, which was reinforced during the war with Rome by refugee Palestinian Christians, and closely associated with Peter, who, when it became too dangerous for him, left Jerusalem for Alexandria—with all this conjectural and improbable claim we need not stay.[3] But we can separate this from what particularly concerns us, namely, the connexion which Brandon asserts between Matthew and the rehabilitation of Paul, which, as we saw, he relates closely to the fall of Jerusalem. Can his reconstruction of the historical situation be substantiated?

Let us first consider his emphasis on the fall of Jerusalem. Whatever the exact date of the writing of Mark, and many would place it about A.D. 65 and even earlier, it must be insisted that the decisive 'leap' whereby the Palestinian Gospel had entered the Graeco-Roman world had taken place long before A.D. 70.[4] To judge from Acts, and, in view of the Hellenized character of first-century Judaism, this agrees with his-

---

[1] *Op. cit.* pp. 185–205. [2] *Op. cit.* pp. 200–1.

[3] For a review of S. G. F. Brandon, see C. F. D. Moule, *J.T.S.* new series, III, 106. The interpretation of 'to another place' in Acts xii. 17 by Brandon, as referring to Alexandria, is conjectural. The earliest history of Christianity in Alexandria eludes us, but what we do know of it does not recall Matthew.

[4] See, especially, G. Dix, *Jew and Greek* (London, 1953), pp. 51 ff. He describes the period A.D. 50–60 as 'the leap of the Church from the Syriac to the Greek world'.

torical probabilities, Jews and Gentiles co-existed in the Church from the earliest days. But the 'leap' to which we have referred was taken in part under the pressure of persecution. After the martyrdom of Stephen, the Hellenists left Jerusalem; and after the persecution under Herod Agrippa, Peter and possibly other Jewish-Christians left Jerusalem also and became missionaries at large. With the scattering of the Hellenists the new faith inevitably began to confront the Gentile world. One of 'the seven', Philip, evangelized Samaria. True, the people of Samaria were circumcised, but the Jews had no dealings with them. Philip also appears on the road from Jerusalem to Gaza, at Azotus and Caesarea. Hellenists went to Jews in Phoenicia, Cyprus and Antioch, and there may have been missions to Alexandria and Rome also. Though their activity seems to have been confined to Jews, some Hellenists from Cyprus and Cyrene preached at Antioch to the Gentiles and that with remarkable success. The 'leap' to the larger world had been taken. The term 'leap', however, suggests too deliberate a movement. The first preaching to the Gentiles was not a conscious policy, but the inevitable concomitant of any preaching in such a cosmopolitan centre as Antioch. Gentiles already attracted to Judaism heard the Gospel preached in synagogues and, possibly, elsewhere. They believed, and were not turned away by the Church. And, as at Antioch, so in other cities. The activity of most of the Hellenists is unknown to us, but, from scattered references in the New Testament, we must conclude that the Gospel took root in many cities through their labours and those of others. Although these references do not always make it clear that the groups of Christians called into being in various places were always composed of Gentiles, it is probable that some at least of the latter were included among them, especially in view of the frequent presence of Gentiles in synagogues, which were the usual points of departure for Christian missionaries. Barnabas and Mark worked in Cyprus; the brothers of the Lord and the other apostles were active in missionary work: that they were accompanied by their wives suggests that their periods of labour were protracted. By A.D. 49 Christianity had reached Rome: that the Church there survived the expulsion of the Jews under the Emperor Claudius in A.D. 49 probably means that it must have been composed of some Gentiles. In A.D. 42–3 there were disturbances in Alexandria, possibly caused by opposition to Jewish-Christian missionaries who had come from Syria. Apollos, a Christian from Alexandria, is found in Ephesus before Paul arrived there. According to 1 Peter there were churches in an area including Pontus, Galatia, Cappadocia, Asia and

Bithynia, the date and manner of whose foundation we do not know. The ascription of the Epistle to Peter *may* point to the fact that the Apostle himself perhaps did labour in these parts. There is some evidence that he visited Rome. But very many others who spread the Gospel have left no memorial. That Paul drew a sharp distinction between churches that he himself had founded, and those that he had not, points to a wide growth of churches other than the Pauline. Paul's activity took place within the context of a vast missionary expansion. Because, at first, not many wise and noble were converted (a fact which, however, must not be exaggerated in view of figures like Barnabas, Paul, Erastus, the city treasurer, Gaius, who entertained Paul and allowed the Church to meet in his house), the exact steps in the spread of Christianity could pass unnoticed, not only by secular historians, but also by those who came to positions of authority in the Church itself. Moreover, Acts has so elevated Paul that others who laboured have been dwarfed, and any assessment of the rise of Gentile Christianity must allow for the possible distortion introduced by this concentration of Acts on Paul. For example, we must somewhere find in a non-Pauline milieu a piety profound enough to produce the Epistle to the Hebrews. Paul was doubtless the best known first-century missionary, but not the only one. Besides him other missionaries, great and small, 'authorized' and 'unauthorized', had carried Christianity to Asia Minor, Macedonia, Greece, Italy and Egypt. In a few years' time we know that Gentile Christianity was in a position to offer material aid to the Jerusalem Churches. We may assume that so firmly was it established that even the great Apostle himself was not essential to its perpetuation. It is extremely unlikely that his removal would have delivered over the Gentile Churches a helpless prey to Jewish-Christianity, as Brandon holds.[1]

[1] For explicit references to points in the above paragraph, I refer to my treatment in the new *Peake's Commentary* (1962). S. G. F. Brandon's position is there stated. H. Chadwick, in his inaugural lecture, 'The Circle and the Ellipse' (Oxford, 1959), shows that Paul both stressed the solidarity of the Gentile Christians with the Church of Jerusalem through the collection for the saints and had a 'deep instinctive respect for Jerusalem' (page 13) and asserted his independence of it. He may in fact be regarded as having so established the importance of the Gentile Church and hence of Rome, that Christendom, which was first a 'circle' centred in Jerusalem, became an ellipse between that city and Rome. 'The apostle Paul is the creator of the idea of a quasi-independent Gentile-Christendom within the one Church of Jewish and Gentile believers' (page 15), so that 'if there is one man who more than any other one man may be regarded as founder of the papacy, that man is surely Paul' (page 17). If one may venture to do so in a field which is so much Professor Chadwick's own,

So too that the fall of Jerusalem radically influenced the history of early Christianity must remain highly questionable. The paucity of references to that event in the New Testament is probably due, not to the fact that the main sources which we possess are of a tendentious 'Pauline' character, but to the actualities of history. The fall of the city in A.D. 70, in the light of what we have written above, could, at best, only place the seal on what had already emerged, namely, the predominance of Gentile Christianity. Christianity reacted to that event much as did Judaism itself. Although it is possible to exaggerate this, already before A.D. 70 Judaism had really found an effective centre for its life in the Law and the Synagogue; already, possibly and even probably, the significance of the Temple had become secondary, so that, despite the despairing sorrow it caused to many at first, its fall was soon surmounted. It was for a school not for a temple that Rabbi Johannan b. Zakkai prayed when Jerusalem was falling.[1] So one might suggest that the marked *Christian* veneration of Jerusalem is a phenomenon later than the first century. Galilee not Jerusalem, if we follow much in the Synoptics, was the honoured place for Christians. Most of the evidence that Chadwick cites is later than the first century. It was later Christian generations who succumbed to the veneration of the old city, much as, in modern America, it is the third generation of emigrants that rediscovers Europe. Moreover, as Chadwick shows, the mystique of Rome itself emerges early (page 9).

[1] See *P.R.J.*[2] pp. 256 ff. See on this H. J. Schoeps, *Aus frühchristlicher Zeit* (1950), *ad rem*; M. Simon, *Verus Israel* (1948), pp. 20 ff., who points out concerning the passing of the Temple that 'le passé immédiat la prépare et la facilite' (p. 27). In the *J.Q.R.* L, 2 (October 1959), 97 ff., and 3, 229 ff., H. Nibley has argued that even Brandon, who gives to Jerusalem laurels that rightly belong only to the Temple, has underestimated the significance of the destruction of the latter for Christians. But the evidence to which he appeals in support of the view that the fall of the Temple *as such* was a crippling blow to the Church is in any case much later than the period of our concern; and where it is pertinent to his purpose, merely reinforces what we wrote above in connexion with Chadwick's views: following N. Leclercq in *Diction-naire d'archéologie chrétienne et de liturgie*, VII, 2311, he urges that 'Even the learned doctors of the second and third centuries "were unable to resist the fascination of the holy places", and came with the rest to see the spot where the Lord had left the earth and where he would return to his Temple' (p. 111). K. W. Clark, in an excellent article on 'Worship in the Jerusalem Temple after A.D. 70' in *N.T.S.* VI, 4 (July 1960), 269 ff., has urged that sacrificial worship did not cease in A.D. 70 but only in A.D. 135. If his view be accepted, the impact of the Fall of Jerusalem religiously would be to a certain degree softened and this would tend to support our position. But much of the argument is based upon silence; it may also be asked whether the uses of the present tense to which reference is made in Josephus, *Antiquities*, III, 224–36 and elsewhere do imply the present existence of the Temple cultus or merely what is present in the memory only (compare H. Hemmer, *Clément de Rome* (1926), pp. 85 f.); and, finally, there are rabbinic passages which seem to imply that the *significant* Temple worship had ceased in A.D. 70. See *P.R.J.*[2] p. 258. Clark has however drawn attention to an area that cries to be re-examined.

too was it with Christians. The role of Jerusalem and its Church in the early days of Christianity was an important one. But, however much the practice of frequenting the Temple was continued, almost from the very beginning the centre of Christian life had moved from the Temple to Christ himself. 'Now Hagar', writes Paul in Gal. iv. 25, 'is Mount Sinai in Arabia; she corresponds to the present Jerusalem, for she is in slavery with her children. But the Jerusalem above is free, and she is our mother....' These are the words of one who had broken the strings binding him to the earthly Jerusalem, and this was as true, in the last resort, as we might perhaps not too readily expect, of Palestinian as of Gentile Christianity. James, the brother of the Lord, despite his apparent conformity, was finally unacceptable to Judaism.[1] There is evidence that a catechism expressing the replacement of the old order at Jerusalem was early developed among Christians.[2] Sorrowful as it must have been to many Christians no less than to Jews, the fall of Jerusalem did not, as far as we can judge from our sources, deeply influence the development of the Church. For them the fall of the city was doubtless a vindication of their faith and a sign of the end, but deep reflection on it as a punishment for the incredulity of Jewry only came later.[3] The only arguments which Brandon can muster for the importance of the fall of Jerusalem in Christian history are, of necessity, conjectural. The silence of our sources is not accidental: it is the true measure of the impact of the events of A.D. 70 on the Church—so we must assume—so that Brandon has to make bricks without straw.

But, even if it be admitted that the fall of Jerusalem did in fact break the stultifying power of the Jerusalem Church in primitive Christianity, can it be claimed that there was a rehabilitation of Paul after A.D. 70? Certain considerations make this dubious. The view, once common, that

---

[1] See P. H. Menoud, *L'Église naissante et le Judaïsme* (1952), *ad rem.*

[2] See C. F. D. Moule, *J.T.S.* I, new series (1950), 29 ff. He argues for a definite body of apologetic along the lines that Christians *have* a temple and an altar in the Body of Christ, a Sacrifice in our offering of ourselves to him, a circumcision in the putting off of selfishness. To judge from Moule's treatment, this material was taught to catechumens before A.D. 70.

[3] On this, see Marcel Simon on 'Retour du Christ et reconstruction du Temple dans la pensée chrétienne primitive', in *Aux Sources de la Tradition Chrétienne: Mélanges offerts à M. M. Goguel* (Paris, 1950), pp. 247 ff. Simon distinguishes between the attitude of Gentile Christians, who saw in the final collapse of Jerusalem the abrogation of the old law and the rejection of Israel (p. 248), and that of Jewish Christians, who shared in the Jewish hope for the restoration of the city and its Temple (p. 249).

Paul was a solitary colossus in the early Church, either not understood or misunderstood, has long been questioned and, by many, abandoned. The recognition has grown that Paul shared much in common with that Church.[1] If we may so express it, Paulinism was not a peculiarity in primitive Christianity but a profundity. Paul shared his faith with his predecessors, his contemporaries, and, we may add, in the light of evidence to which we shall refer below, with his successors. While, on the one hand, it is erroneous to draw a sharp distinction between Paul and the Church, either in his day or later, on the other hand, it is equally erroneous to claim that after A.D. 70, through a 'rehabilitation' of the Apostle, what is generally understood under the term Paulinism became dominant in it. There is no evidence that such was the case. What unites Paul with the Church after A.D. 70 are not those peculiar emphases of his teaching which set him apart from other lesser Christians in his own day and in opposition, as Brandon claims, to Jewish-Christianity, but the common core of Christian conviction which informed much of the Christian movement. There is no evidence of a triumphant progress of Paulinism after A.D. 70, which necessitated a protest from a Matthew. Indeed there is some evidence in Acts that the kind of Judaizers who had dogged his footsteps during his lifetime continued to resist Paul's influence after his death. That the Ephesian elders are forewarned may reflect anti-Pauline activity after the death of the Apostle;[2] and anti-Pauline invective continued into the second century.[3]

The rehabilitation of Paul, as Brandon understands it, therefore, must be rejected. The probable place which the Apostle held in the Church after his death and during the last decades of the first century has been clarified for us by Goodspeed,[4] and rehabilitation is too misleading a word for the process that he has in mind. According to the Chicago scholar, Paul's letters did not from the time of their composition circulate freely and generally among the churches. To Paul himself and to his readers, his epistles were *parerga*, and there was no pressing motive for their preserva-

[1] A. M. Hunter, *Paul and His Predecessors* (London, 1940), *passim*.

[2] Acts xx. 39. See E. Haenchen, *Apostelgeschichte* (1956), p. 531—the reference is to the period after Paul's death; and Dibelius, *Studies in the Acts of the Apostles* (1956), p. 3.

[3] J. Wagenmann, *Die Stellung des Apostels Paulus neben den Zwölf* (Giessen, 1926), pp. 111 ff.

[4] E. J. Goodspeed, *The Meaning of Ephesians* (1933), and other writings of his. For a discussion of his contribution, see C. L. Mitton, *The Epistle to the Ephesians* (Oxford, 1951), pp. 45 ff.

tion, so that, for the most part, they would be carelessly kept and little used. Moreover, they were issued separately, and consequently could not have produced the massive impact which they did, and do, as a collection. In Goodspeed's view, it was only with the publication of Acts that the full magnitude of the achievement and significance of Paul broke upon the churches and eventually led to the formation of a Pauline corpus. Immediately relevant to Brandon's view is Goodspeed's insistence that the recognition of Paul followed the publication of Acts, and since he dates Acts after Matthew, it is clear that the latter, in Goodspeed's judgement, was not directly aimed at counteracting any rehabilitation of Paul. But, even more important, Goodspeed insists that the temporary eclipse of Paul, up to the publication of Acts, was due to certain inevitable circumstances. Not any deliberate anti-Pauline activity by Palestinian Christianity necessarily caused this, so much as the natural vagueness which would overtake the memory of a great man, whose work was little understood in its subtleties and, perhaps, little known. We may add that, as with Queen Elizabeth I after her death, and Sir Winston Churchill in 1945, so there may have been with Paul also what we may call a kind of 'surfeit of greatness'[1] among his contemporaries which led them to a natural neglect of him for a time after his death. In any case it is precarious on the considerations so far produced to connect Matthew with any 'rehabilitation' of Paul, as if Paul had once been under a cloud and then, after A.D. 70, emerged from this in bright glory.

And this last sentence brings us to the main assumption which underlies Brandon's work. His use of the term 'rehabilitation' implies a previous conscious 'dehabilitation' of Paul in the primitive Church and an unrelenting struggle between Pauline Christianity and the Jewish-Christianity centred in Jerusalem, a struggle carried to Alexandria and reflected in a Matthaean anti-Paulinism. Thus Brandon revives the Hegelian characteristic of the Tübingen school which will be familiar. But the precise relation of Paul to the early Church has been recently much re-examined, chiefly by Munck, Dix, Goppelt and Daniélou, and they are all, in different ways, unfavourable to any revived 'Tübingenism'. Schoeps also, who has emphasized the anti-Paulinism of second-century Jewish-Christianity very strongly, has endorsed the now customary

---

[1] This possibility came home to me in listening to Sir J. E. Neale lecturing on Elizabeth I. The point is valid even though that Queen, like Paul, had critics in abundance during her lifetime; see, for example, Hesketh Pearson on criticism of the monarchy in Shakespeare, *A Life of Shakespeare* (1942), pp. 76 ff.

suspicion of the Tübingen school, because it attempted a reconstruction of early Christianity before it had sifted its sources, and thus transferred to the first century conflicts that, in their developed form, belonged only to the second.[1] Suffice it here to note that while there were differences in the early Church between Paul and 'the Judaizers', which cannot be ignored, the fundamental fact remains that according to Galatians and Acts the Jerusalem leaders accepted the Gentile mission of Paul with few conditions. The missionary activity of Paul and Barnabas went under way with the full consent of the Jewish-Christian leaders at Jerusalem, so that Paul's practice of admitting Gentiles into the Church without insistence on circumcision or observance of the Law, was under no cloud of disapproval from the pillars of the Church. Paul was more at one with Peter and James, the brother of the Lord, than Brandon allows.[2] On broad historical considerations, therefore, it is unlikely that there was a 'movement' to 'rehabilitate' Paul immediately after the Fall of Jerusalem and a resulting counterblast against this on the side of an Alexandrian Jewish-Christianity from which Matthew emerged, such as Brandon has argued for.

But we have, in the second place, to examine those supports which have been found within Matthew itself for an anti-Pauline motif in its making. We have to consider three questions: (i) the general character of Matthew; (ii) the specific, thinly veiled, anti-Pauline references that are alleged; (iii) the elevation of Peter in an attempt to discredit Paul that has often been traced in the Gospel.

(i) Apart from a minority of American scholars, notably E. F. Scott[3] and K. W. Clark,[4] the Jewish-Christian character of the Gospel of Matthew has been, probably too easily, assumed in most modern scholarship. Although this has recently been radically questioned,[5] in order to

[1] H. J. Schoeps, *Theologie und Geschichte des Judenchristentums* (1949); see also Gregory Dix, *Jew and Greek*; Goppelt, *Christentum und Judentum* (Gütersloh, 1954); J. Daniélou, *Theologie du Judéo-Christianisme* (Tournai, 1958). J. Munck, *Paulus und die Heilsgeschichte* (1954), has gone too far in minimizing and even denying any gulf between Paul and the Jerusalem Church. See my *Christian Origins and Judaism* (1962).

[2] On the relation of Peter and Paul, see E. Hirsch, 'Petrus und Paulus', in *Z.N.W.* XXIX, 63 ff., a critique of Hans Lietzmann's claim that there was a sharp cleavage between the two apostles. On Peter, C. H. Turner, *Catholic and Apostolic*, ed. H. N. Bate (London, 1931), p. 214; T. G. Jalland, *The Church and the Papacy* (London, 1944), pp. 47 ff.

[3] *Introduction to the Literature of the New Testament* (New York, 1955), p. 67.

[4] *J.B.L.* LXVI (1947), 165 ff., on 'The Gentile Bias in Matthew'.

[5] See Nepper-Christensen, *Das Matthäusevangelium* (Aarhus, 1958).

argue from the same premises as Brandon, we shall not here examine this assumption as such, but rather concentrate on those elements in Matthew which seem to set it in opposition to Paul, and, in this section, on its so-called 'particularism'.

There are in Matthew passages peculiar to it which assert that the ministries of the disciples and of Jesus himself were confined to Jews. These are:

x. 5 f.:

These twelve Jesus sent out, charging them, 'Go nowhere among the Gentiles, and enter no town of the Samaritans, but go rather to the lost sheep of the house of Israel'.

x. 23:

When they persecute you in one town, flee to the next; for truly, I say to you, you will not have gone through all the towns of Israel, before the Son of man comes.

xv. 24:

I was sent only to the lost sheep of the house of Israel.

Appeal has also been made to his choice of twelve disciples in confirmation of Jesus' restriction of his ministry to Israel, as such, the twelve representing the people of God, that is, Israel in the ultimate restoration.[1] But this is not a peculiarity of Matthew, and cannot be allowed to indicate any particularism in that Gospel as such. So too the claim that the Gentile mission is forbidden in vii. 6 is not convincing. This is best taken as a kind of *gemaric* addition designed to modify the preceding prohibition of judgement probably within the community itself, where also discretion and discrimination are necessary.[2] But it does agree with x. 5, 23 and xv. 24 that in xxiii. 15 Jesus makes a violent attack on Jewish proselytizing. These passages it has been urged are all to be understood as reflecting a current or currents in primitive Christianity opposed to the Gentile mission, whose especial champion was Paul. Here the attitude of the Jewish-Christianity, to which Matthew belonged, has surely coloured his gospel.

[1] See, for example, C. H. Dodd, *History and the Gospel* (1938), p. 137; R. Newton Flew, *Jesus and His Church* (1938), p. 52: see especially Matt. xix. 28. On the historicity of the Twelve, which has been denied, see J. Wagenmann, *Die Stellung des Apostels Paulus neben den Zwölf*, pp. 6 f.

[2] See W. D. Davies, *H.T.R.* xlvi, 3 (July 1953), 117.

But there can be little question that such an explanation of these sayings is erroneous, and that for several reasons. The whole of the ministry of Jesus is set by Matthew within a framework which suggests not 'particularism' but 'universalism'. The beginning and end of the Gospel make this evident. In the first two chapters we find the story of the Magi, which may be intended to symbolize the submission of the Gentile world to Christ,[1] while, in the same story, the whole of Jerusalem along with Herod, that is, the Jewish world, opposes him. Moreover, the immediate introduction to the ministry of Jesus in iv. 15 is a quotation from Isa. viii. 23–ix. 1: the light has come to the Gentiles—'The land of Zebulun and the land of Naphtali, towards the sea, across the Jordan, Galilee of the Gentiles....'[2] A comparison of Matt. iv. 23–5 and Mark vii. 10 reveals to Jeremias the same emphasis: he suggests tentatively that the inhabitants of Syria, that is, Gentiles, brought their sick to Jesus who healed them, Matt. iv. 24 being an addition to the Marcan material. The response to the initial activity of Jesus transcended Israelite boundaries.[3] Similarly, at the close of the ministry, it is the Gentiles who recognize Jesus as the Son of God (xxvii. 54), while the Old Israel can only mock (xxvii. 41), and the Risen Lord in xxviii. 16–20 is made to sanction a Gentile mission 'to all nations'.

More pointed even than this is it that alongside the 'particularistic' utterances noted above, there are many others in Matthew which express the opposite, 'universalistic', point of view. There is no justification for regarding these last as less representative of Matthew and his Church than the former. The following passages, in which the ministry of Jesus himself and of the Church includes the Gentile world, are pertinent: the passages from Matthew are given first.

[1] See above, p. 66.

[2] See E. Lohmeyer, *Galiläa und Jerusalem* (Tübingen, 1936), pp. 30 ff., for the criticism of the Scribes and Pharisees, that is, of Jerusalem, in the Birth Narratives in Matthew. Recently this has been emphasized by K. Stendahl in *Judentum, Urchristentum, Kirche*, ed. W. Eltester (Berlin, 1960), pp. 94 ff., on 'Quis et Unde: an analysis of Matt. 1–2'.

[3] J. Jeremias, *Jesus' Promise to the Nations*, Eng. trans. (1958), p. 34. The term 'Syria' in Matthew is difficult to assess. Commentators have been divided. Some, for example Schlatter, Loisy, take it to refer to the whole province of Syria, others, for example Zahn, B. Weiss, Lagrange, Klostermann, understand by it parts to the North and North-east of Palestine. For passages dealing with Syria in the Mishnah, see Demai vi. 11; Shebiith vi. 1–6; Maaseroth v. 5; Hallah iv. 7, 11; Orlah iii. 9; Rosh ha Shanah i. 4; Baba Kamma vii. 7; Eduyoth vii. 7; Abodah Zarah i. 8; Oholoth xviii. 7. For the importance of these passages for the understanding of Matthew, see above, p. 296.

v. 13 ff.:

You are the salt of the earth....You are the light of the world....Let your light so shine before men. [Most of these verses are M; certainly v. 14*a* and v. 16 and, in its present Matthaean form, v. 13 are peculiar to Matthew, though there is a loose parallel in Luke xiv. 34.]

x. 18:

...and you will be dragged before governors and kings for my sake, to bear testimony before them and the Gentiles. [This 'universalistic' reference occurs in the middle of Matthaean material in Matt. x which has many parallels elsewhere in Luke and Mark, but is itself probably from M.]

In xii. 18 ff. is a quotation from Isa. xlii. 1–4 concerning the Suffering Servant. It includes two references to the Gentiles:

xii. 18*d*:

'...and he shall proclaim justice to the Gentiles';

xii. 21:

'...and in his name will the Gentiles hope'.

The quotation from Isaiah occurs as a pendant upon the healing ministry of Jesus: in parallel passages in Mark iii. 7–12 and Luke vi. 17–19 there is no such quotation.

xiii. 38:

[In the explanation given in xiii. 36 ff. of the parable of the Tares the universalist note occurs in xiii. 38]: 'The field is the world' (ὁ κόσμος).

xv. 29–31:

And Jesus went on from there and passed along the Sea of Galilee. And he went up unto the hills [So RSV: Greek: εἰς τὸ ὄρος], and sat down there. And great crowds came to him, bringing with them the lame, the maimed, the blind, the dumb, and many others, and they put them at his feet, and he healed them, so that the throng wondered, when they saw the dumb speaking, the maimed whole, the lame walking, and the blind seeing; and they glorified the God of Israel.... [The last sentence probably indicates that the crowds referred to are Gentiles.][1]

In xxi. 43 is an addition of Matthew's—either the composition of the Evangelist or derived from M. It cannot be claimed to add any peculiar universalist note to the material, but only to make more explicit this

[1] B. W. Bacon, *op. cit.* p. 227.

emphasis which was already present in Mark xii. 9; Luke xx. 16; Matt. xxi. 41. The verse reads:

xxi. 43:

Therefore I tell you, the kingdom of God will be taken away from you and given to a nation producing the fruits of it.

xxiv. 14:

And this gospel of the kingdom will be preached throughout the whole world, as a testimony to all nations; and then the end will come.

While this note is present in Mark xiii. 10 and by implication in Mark xiii. 13 and Luke xxi. 17 as in Matt. xxiv. 9, the peculiar Matthaean addition in xxiv. 14 does characterize the universalism of the Gospel with a new force.

xxv. 32:

Before him will be gathered all the nations....

xxv. 40:

the least of these my brethren. [This is possibly a reference to Gentiles, although it may refer to Christians.]

xxviii. 19 ff.:

...make disciples of all nations, baptizing them....

In addition to the above material from M, the universalist motif breaks through in material from Q or Mark used by Matthew at viii. 11 ff.: 'I tell you, many will come from east and west and sit down at table with Abraham, Isaac and Jacob in the kingdom of heaven, while the sons of the kingdom will be thrown into the outer darkness...'; and at xxii. 9 f.: '"Go therefore to the thoroughfares, and invite to the marriage feast as many as you find." And those servants went out into the streets and gathered all whom they found, both bad and good; so the wedding hall was filled with guests'; and again at xxvi. 13: 'Truly, I say to you, wherever this gospel is preached in the whole world, what she has done will be told in memory of her.' The future envisaged in viii. 11 f. must be referred to the final consummation, so that, while it can be claimed to reveal an ultimate concern for the salvation of Gentiles, it cannot be used to establish Matthew's insistence on a Gentile mission before that event, so that it falls into a large category of sayings, isolated by Jeremias, to refer to the eschatological incursion of Gentiles to God's Holy Mountain, namely, xxv. 21, 23, 32 ff.; xiii. 32 (= Luke xiii. 19); xix. 28; xvi. 28; xx. 21; v. 14, 35; xvi. 18; and Mark xiv. 58 and parallels.[1] But in the other two passages, xxii. 9 f.; xxvi. 13, despite Jeremias's insistence that originally both had reference to an apocalyptic event and not to a mission on earth, it is natural to find a specific reference to this last, as it is also in xii. 18 ff.; xiii. 38; xv. 29–31; xxi. 43, and certainly in xxviii. 16–20.[2] There can be no question in the light of all the above that 'universalistic' no less than 'particularistic' sayings were congenial to Matthew; the former no less than the latter were an expression of his interests.[3]

This last point militates against regarding the 'particularistic' sayings of Matthew as inserted in and created for the Gospel in a Jewish-Christian milieu, because it is difficult to concede that Matthew, who so clearly accepts the Gentile mission, should have deliberately either invented or desired to preserve material which contradicted so sharply his own convictions. Far more natural is it to assume that Matthew found this material in the tradition about Jesus that had come down to him, and handed it on faithfully. Moreover, apart from any native conservatism or loyalty to his sources that may have characterized him, there is a tangible reason why Matthew should have preserved this particularistic tradition, namely, the simple fact that it represented the historical realities of Jesus' ministry, which was confined to Israel. The 'particularism' of Matthew is not a sign of a Jewish-Christian, anti-Pauline current, but of his loyalty to the historic tradition of Jesus' ministry and of the early Church.[4]

In fact, on closer examination, the way in which Matthew has presented this tradition, so far from pointing to an anti-Pauline or un-Pauline position, itself suggests universalism. The ministry of Jesus had been

---

[1] Jeremias, *op. cit.*, pp. 63 ff.

[2] J. Jeremias, *op. cit.* pp. 22–4. See review by J. A. T. Robinson, *J.B.L.* LXXVIII (1959), 101 ff.

[3] E. Lohmeyer, *Kultus und Evangelium* (1942), has gone too far in his claims for universalism in Matthew. He holds that the latter's consciousness that the ministry of Jesus broke the bounds of Judaism is strikingly expressed by his choice and arrangement of the first three miracles in viii. 1–17. In viii. 1–4 a leper, that is, one who was 'unclean', is healed; in viii. 5–13, a centurion's servant, that is, a Gentile; and in viii. 14–17, a woman, Peter's mother-in-law. That is, Jesus blessed three categories which Judaism had placed in an inferior religious state. But such a view breaks down at the slightest consideration. As Professor Daube reminded me, a Gentile leper was healed in the Old Testament and the son of a Shunammite woman restored to life (2 Kings iv–vi). Lohmeyer's interpretation of the three pericopae must be dismissed outright: they have no cultic or specifically 'religious' significance for Matthew, as he urges. See also S. Zeitlin, *R.E.J.* vol. LXXXVII (1929), 79 ff.

[4] See C. H. Dodd, *History and the Gospel*, p. 131; J. Jeremias, *op. cit.* pp. 19 ff.

mainly confined to Jews, and the early Church likewise regarded its primary duty to lie with Jewry. The Gentile mission, as such, had to be justified. The attempt to come to terms with the rival claims of missions to Jews and to Gentiles is reflected in both Mark and Matthew, as elsewhere in the New Testament. In Mark vii. 24–30 the view is presented that while the Jews are to be fed first, afterwards the Gentiles deserve attention. This we cannot doubt, for reasons we can variously present, was the approach of Jesus and the primitive community. Matthew's presentation of the same material in xv. 21–8 differs in that the question is not expressly raised whether there should first be a mission to Jews and then to Gentiles. The position is tacitly assumed that there should be no mission to Gentiles. Nevertheless, Matthew no less than Mark finally accepts the Gentile mission, and Jesus is made to heal the daughter of the Canaanite woman.[1] No anti-Gentile or anti-Pauline interests are here at work, but merely the faithful preservation of the impact of the debates which agitated the early Church in this field. Just as Jesus confined his mission to Israel, and at the same time looked forward to the salvation of the Gentiles, so the early Church turned first to Israel. And the attitude of Paul was not fundamentally different. He too regarded the Gospel as for the Jew first,[2] and acted on this belief. It was partly the failure of Israel to respond to the Gospel that provoked the Gentile mission. Thus those elements in the primitive Church who favoured concentration on the Jewish mission did not exclude a concern for and mission to the Gentiles. So too Paul, and those like him, who came to devote their foremost labours to the Gentiles, did not forsake or forget 'Israel'. It might even be argued that Paul conducted the Gentile mission as much for the sake of Israel as for the Gentiles: the conversion of the latter he came to conceive as the means for the conversion of the former.[3] In sum, it is not possible to set Matthew in opposition to Paul on the Gentile question. Indeed it has been claimed that Matthew takes a more harsh attitude to Jews than does Paul, and reveals a distinct bias in favour of the Gentiles and an emphasis on the

---

[1] On this see B. W. Bacon, *op. cit.*, *ibid.* 'To Matthew the Canaanite woman is as typical an example of the stranger adopted among the people of God as Rahab the Canaanite harlot and Ruth the Moabitess, whom he specially mentions in his genealogy of Christ. Along with the believing Centurion, she is to Matthew the type of many who are to come from the East and from the West to "sit down with Abraham, Isaac and Jacob" at the messianic feast (viii. 1)' (p. 227).

[2] The testimony of Acts no less than the Epistles bears this out: Acts xiii. 5 14; xiv. 1; xvii. 1, 17; xviii. 4, 24 ff. See *P.R.J.*[2] pp. 68 ff.

[3] Rom. xi. 13 ff.

positive rejection of the old Israel. This has been especially urged by K. W. Clark[1] who finds that the very theme of the Gospel is the definite and final rejection of Israel by her God: he refers to viii. 12; xii. 21; xxi. 39 ff.; xxviii. 16 ff. ('Go and make disciples of all the gentile peoples...') and to the parables peculiar to Matthew: the Two Sons (xxi. 28–32); the Vineyard Tenants (xxi. 33–43); the Wedding Feast (xxii. 1–14); the Ten Virgins (xxv. 1–13); the Talents (xxv. 14–30), and the Judgement of the Son of Man (xxv. 31–46). But this is to ignore other elements in Matthew which point to an 'adherence' to Judaism, for example xxiii. 1 ff., and suggests that the struggle between Judaism and Christianity was still for him a struggle *intra muros*, as we have already pointed out above.[2]

But before we leave this section we have further to note certain claims made by Brandon. The latter has to admit, in the light of such facts as we have presented above, that Matthew recognized the right of Gentiles to admission into the Church. But he goes on to claim that circumstances alone compelled him to do this and that he did so only with a very bad grace. He illustrates this. In Matthew's treatment of the healing of the centurion's son, which is taken by Clark to assert the final rejection of Jewry, 'The children of the kingdom will be cast out' (viii. 12), Brandon insists that these true sons of the kingdom are still the Jews, although they have been cast out of their inheritance. To the parable of the Wedding Feast (xxii. 1–10) Matthew has added verses 12–14, the story of the guest who comes without a wedding garment. Brandon connects this with the fall of Jerusalem. 'The allusion to the destruction of Jerusalem [in xxii. 6 f.] naturally led Matthew on to think of its consequences, and in particular of one of its great problems: that of the personal preparedness of Gentiles for the privilege of Church membership.'[3] He finds here a grudging attitude to the Gentiles, a critical scrutiny of their right to membership in the people of God. This begrudging attitude re-emerges in the description of the Gentiles in the parables of the Labourers in the Vineyard (xxi. 33–43) as people who have stood idle in the market-place: they show little promise of good service, and, so we are to understand, do not really deserve entry into the Church. Apart from the rigidity of Brandon's approach, this last point needs no refutation. The ministry of Jesus *was* to the undeserving alike for Paulinist and for Jewish-Christian. Did

[1] *J.B.L.* XLVI, 165 ff.
[2] G. Bornkamm, *op. cit.* p. 248. Contrast E. P. Blair, *Jesus in the Gospel of Matthew* (1960), pp. 42, 113 n. 4.
[3] *The Fall of Jerusalem*, pp. 230–1. The quotation is on p. 231.

Matthew object to the grace of God in the way that Brandon here implies, then surely he would have had to object to the very Gospel itself. Similarly, Matthew was not alone in his concern for the moral rectitude of converts. Paul himself was continually exercised by the same problem. Such a concern in itself does not bespeak anti-Gentile tendencies. Moreover, the description of Jews as the 'sons of the kingdom' in viii. 12 would be thoroughly congenial to Paul. The whole section betrays, not a tardiness in allowing the same privileges to Jew and Gentile in the Church, as Brandon holds, but the duality of the early Christian attitude towards Jewry, which was at the same time one of condemnation and yet of respect. And, finally, to dismiss the universalism of Matt. xxviii. 16–20 by making 'the nations' in xxviii. 19 exclude the Jews, as does Clark, is unwarranted.[1] And Brandon is justified in referring the commandments to which it points, not only to the precepts of the *SM*, but also to 'undisguisedly Judaistic ones like v. 17–19; xxiii. 2, 3'.[2] Nevertheless, in the light of all the evidence presented above, while it would be to go too far to describe Matthew as pro-Gentile, it is not Jewish-Christian in its attitude to the Gentiles.

In other ways than those indicated above the anti-Paulinism of the general character of Matthew has recently been critically re-examined, and the conclusion drawn that it has been grossly exaggerated. To pursue all aspects of this theme here would carry us too far afield. Suffice it to note that the 'character' of Matthew can no longer be used in support of any anti-Paulinism it may be claimed to contain. We have above concen-

---

[1] *J.B.L.* XLVI, 166. Karl Barth's interpretation of 'all that I have commanded you' (in 'An Exegetical Study of Matt. xxviii. 16–20', in *The Theology of the Christian Mission*, ed. G. H. Anderson (1961), pp. 55–71) is untenable. He writes: '...*all that I have commanded you*. What did Jesus command them to do? To follow him, in order "to be with him" (Mark iii. 14)' (*sic*). Is it *exegetically* legitimate to expound a Matthaean passage by a reference in Mark which is explicitly omitted by Matthew? See the Matthaean parallel in x. 1.

[2] *Op. cit.* p. 230. Following Goppelt, Daniélou distinguishes three types of what we might call Jewish-Christianity: (1) the legalistic, represented by the Ebionites and the other Jewish 'extremists', who accepted Jesus as the Christ or a prophet but not as the Son of God: they are mid-way between Judaism and Christianity; (2) that which, while it remained true to certain forms of Judaism, never imposed these on Gentile converts and itself was in the main stream of the 'Christian' movement: to this belong the Nazarenes—they were probably strong in Syria; (3) a form of Christianity which continued to be dominated by the traditional thought-forms of Judaism, although it had no connexion with the Jewish communities. Matthew belongs not to the first group but, if not to the second, then somewhere between the second and third. (J. Daniélou, *Théologie du Judéo-Christianisme*, I, 17 ff.; L. Goppelt, *Christentum und Judentum* (Gütersloh, 1954).)

trated on Matthew's attitude to the Gentiles because in this sphere was it most likely that any neo-legalism he may have imposed upon the words of Jesus would have emerged to set him over against Paul.

(ii) But even though on the ground of its general character Matthew cannot be claimed to be anti-Pauline, what of those passages where specific reference of a polemic kind to the Apostle have been traced? We begin with Matt. v. 17–19:

17 Think not that I have come to abolish the law and the prophets; I have come not
18 to abolish them but to fulfil them. For truly, I say to you, till heaven and earth pass away, not an iota, not a dot, will pass from the law until all is accomplished.
19 Whoever then relaxes one of the least of these commandments and teaches men so, shall be called least in the kingdom of heaven; but he who does them and teaches them shall be called great in the kingdom of heaven....

Taken in isolation, at least, the first verse, v. 17, hardly expresses anything which contradicts Pauline teaching on the Law. As for v. 18, three broad interpretations (each with internal modifications) are possible. Two of these provide no ground for reading an anti-Pauline motive into the verse. The one finds v. 18 to be a word of Jesus himself in which the full validity of the Law is recognized, but only 'until all things come to pass', that is, only until the death of Jesus inaugurates finally the New Covenant.[1] The other sees in v. 18 an attempt at combining the Jewish-Christian point of view on the validity of the Law with Pauline speculation on the role of the Law in the Messianic Age or the Age to Come, that is, it is not anti-Pauline but even pro-Pauline in its intent.[2] It is the third interpretation alone which might be understood to justify the detection of an anti-Pauline motive in v. 18, namely, that which sees the verse as the creation of the unadulterated legalism of the Jewish-Christian Church which could be expected to have an anti-Pauline tradition. On this view the phrase 'until all be accomplished' refers to the complete fulfilment of the demands of the Law.[3]

If we reject this third interpretation of v. 18, then in two out of the three verses in v. 17–19 no anti-Paulinism appears. But does it not do so in

[1] See W. D. Davies, in *Mélanges Bibliques*, on 'Matt. v. 17, 18', pp. 428 ff. The NEB translates ἕως ἂν πάντα γένηται in v. 18 as 'until all that must happen has happened' (page 8); as an alternative it gives 'before all that it stands for is achieved' (p. 8, n. *b*).
[2] H. J. Schoeps, *Revue d'Histoire et de Philosophie religieuses*, XXXIII (1953), on 'Jésus et la loi juive', pp. 1 ff.
[3] R. Bultmann, *op. cit.* p. 146.

v. 19, and does not v. 18, read in the light of v. 19, almost certainly become anti-Pauline in its nuance? Many have answered these questions in the affirmative, and, following J. Weiss,[1] have found in v. 19 a tacit attack upon the work and teaching of Paul. And especially is it claimed that the use of the term 'least' (ἐλάχιστος) recalls how Paul described himself in 1 Cor. xv. 9 as the 'least of the apostles, unfit to be called an apostle, because I persecuted the church of God'. The term 'the least' could not but have gained anti-Pauline undertones and perhaps have become a cryptic designation of the Apostle himself.[2]

Nevertheless, the anti-Paulinism of v. 19 is not to be taken as so obvious as, on first impact, it seems. We cannot certainly appeal to an anti-Pauline context for it in v. 17, 18, because it is unjustifiable to discover anti-Paulinism in v. 19, and then to read it back into v. 18, in view of the clearly disjointed nature of the passage, a disjointedness caused by the absence of any expressed antecedent for the term 'these' (τούτων) in the phrase 'the least of these commandments' (τῶν ἐντολῶν τούτων). This led Kilpatrick[3] to suggest that originally v. 19 followed v. 41, so that the phrase concerned in v. 19 referred to the commandments as revised by Jesus in v. 21, 27, 33, 38. If so we are to find no trace at all in v. 19 of any anti-Paulinism, because there was none in the source from which Matthew drew the verse. This is, however, to cut the Gordian knot too drastically. Strangely enough, Goguel's suggestion is the exact opposite, namely, that, while the tradition from which he derived v. 19 *may* have been anti-Pauline, Matthew was unaware of this. 'Matthew may quite well have reproduced this saying somewhat mechanically without perhaps seeing its anti-Pauline prejudice.' The view is bound up with Goguel's understanding of the evangelists as manipulating their sources almost mechanically on purely literary grounds, with little if any 'theological' awareness. For reasons which we have touched upon above, we must reject this understanding of the evangelists, particularly in the case of Matthew. In the case of v. 19 it asks us to deny to Matthew that understanding of his

[1] *The History of Primitive Christianity* (1947), II, 753. Weiss holds the position indicated even if the word 'least' is not an allusion to the Apostle's designation of himself in 1 Cor. xv. 9. But it is against this last also that the ἐλάχιστος of Matt. v. 19 may not be superlative. See J. Wellhausen, *Das Evangelium Matthaei* (Berlin, 1904), p. 19, and A. H. McNeile, *The Gospel According to St Matthew* (1915), pp. 59 f. T. W. Manson (*The Sayings of Jesus*, p. 154) recognizes that the Aramaic might mean 'little' quite as much as 'least', though he favours the latter sense. He finds polemic against Paul in v. 19: see *op. cit.* p. 25.

[2] That the Latin *paulus* meant 'small' is pertinent here.

[3] *The Origins of the Gospel According to St Matthew* (Oxford, 1946), pp. 25 f.

sources which we claim for ourselves even at this remove in time and space. It is hardly credible that Matthew was unaware of a motif in his source which we can now detect after he himself has used it in innocence. Safer is it to give full weight to the absence of any certain anti-Pauline motif in its immediate context and to inquire afresh whether after all the saying itself does, in fact, point to anti-Paulinism.[1]

Apart from the assumptions, derived from the history of the controversies of Paul and Jewish-Christians, which we bring to the text, it is, as we saw, the use of the term 'least' which most strongly suggests anti-Paulinism. But this may merely have been suggested by the previous use of 'the least of these commandments', that is, if there is such at all, the play on words is on the immediately preceding 'least of these commandments' not on the remote 'least' in 1 Cor. xv. 9. That Paul's influence and significance would have been known to Matthew we can assume, but not that he knew Paul's letters, and 1 Cor. xv. 9 in particular, while it must not be overlooked that the view that 'the least' was used to describe Paul is purely conjectural. The outcome of all the above is that while v. 17–19 *may* have been directed against Paul, unless there is evidence elsewhere in Matthew for anti-Paulinism it would be unwarranted to claim that it certainly was so.[2] Is there such evidence?

Appeal is often made to the Parable of the Tares in xiii. 24–30, where the term 'An enemy' (xiii. 25; ὁ ἐχθρὸς ἄνθρωπος, xiii. 28) has been taken to be a cryptic reference to Paul. But in the explanation of the parable which Matthew gives in xiii. 36–43, 'the enemy' is identified explicitly with the devil. Brandon struggles to escape from this dilemma by dismissing xiii. 36–43 as a later interpolation, but, as he himself admits, there is no manuscript evidence for this, and xiii. 36–43 is of a piece with much other material in Matthew which probably points to Essene influence. The passage need be discussed no further: there is no justification for finding in it an anti-Pauline intent.[3]

(iii) Finally, we have to examine the claim that Matthew elevates Peter in order to depreciate Paul. Two classes of material in Matthew have prompted this: first, those passages which introduce Peter where he is absent in parallel passages in the Synoptics, as in xv. 15; xviii. 21; xix. 27. These, however, cannot be regarded as significant because they are cancelled out by passages in Mark and Luke which give prominence to

[1] M. Goguel, *La Naissance du Christianisme*, p. 360.
[2] So A. H. McNeile, *op. cit.*   [3] See S. G. F. Brandon, *op. cit.* pp. 234 ff.

Peter where Matthew fails to do so, as in Mark xi. 21 (contrast Matt. xxi. 20); xiii. 3 (contrast Matt. xxiv. 3); xiv. 37 (contrast Matt. xxvi. 40, here the directness of the address to Peter is lost), and again in Luke viii. 45 (contrast Mark v. 31, omitted by Matthew); Luke xxii. 8 (contrast Matt. xxvi. 17 ff.; Mark xiv. 13); Luke v. 1–11 (contrast Matt. iv. 18–22; Mark i. 16–20); Luke xxiv. 34 (no parallel in Matthew); so xxii. 24–32, contrast Matt. xxvi. 30–5. Secondly, and more important, are three passages peculiar to Matthew in which Peter is given prominence, namely, xiv. 28–31, 33, the Walking on the Sea; xvi. 17–19, the blessing of Peter; xvii. 24–7, the discussion of the Temple tax. These have been urged to reflect the concern of the early Church to point to Peter over against Paul as the 'rock' on which the Church is built, and especial attention has been given, in this connexion, to xvi. 17–19.

The three Petrine additions may be claimed to occur within the same total context, namely, within the unit referred to as the Fourth book (xiii. 53–xvii. 23; xvii. 24–xviii. 35), that is, the section which deals mainly with the Church, and they are to be understood in the light of Matthew's understanding of this. In xiv. 28–31, 33, which reads:

And Peter answered him, 'Lord, if it is you, bid me come to you on the water'. He said, 'Come'. So Peter got out of the boat and walked on the water and came to Jesus; but when he saw the wind, he was afraid, and beginning to sink he cried out, 'Lord, save me'. Jesus immediately reached out his hand and caught him, saying to him, 'O man of little faith, why did you doubt?'...And those in the boat worshipped him, saying, 'Truly you are the Son of God',

the intention seems to be to point to Peter as the one who, having begun to follow the Lord, despaired and failed, and, yet, nevertheless, turned again. After the feeding of the five thousand (xiv. 13–21), which is probably understood by Matthew as a foreshadowing of the founding of the Church, the Evangelist presents us with a 'pictorial' representation of Peter's prominent place in the history of the early Church. Although his participation in the increasing reverence, noticeable in the New Testament, for the Twelve, does not prevent Matthew from showing Peter 'warts and all', nevertheless, he is still for him the foundation of the Church.[1] It was the courage of Peter, chequered as it was by failure, which helped to turn the fear of the disciples (xiv. 26: the fear is more emphasized in Matthew

---

[1] See, for example, J. Wagenmann, *op. cit.* p. 61: 'Das Bild, das in diesen beiden Evangelien (Matthäus und Lukas) von den Zwölf entworfen wird, sieht erheblich anders aus. Alle Mängel, die ihnen bei Markus noch anhaften, sind beseitigt.' In the same way the great rabbis became types for Jews, see reference on p. 338, n. 1, below.

than in Mark vi. 45 ff.) to a paean of worship (xiv. 33: omitted in Mark). It is the 'foundation' character of Peter in the Church which is expressed in xvi. 17–19 and in xvii. 24–7 Peter is given instruction by Jesus in the matter of binding and loosing, that is, in the interpretation of Christian conduct promised as his prerogative in xvi. 19. The pre-eminence of Peter is unmistakably emphasized.[1] Can this be connected with anti-Paulinism?

There is no explicit indication of any polemic against Paul in any of the Petrine additions, and certain considerations make it exceedingly un-likely that there is any such implicit. The pre-eminence here accorded to Peter is undisputed both in the Gospels and in Paul,[2] so that it could not of itself suggest anti-Paulinism. The views with which Peter is here associated cannot be characterized as anti-Pauline. Thus the attitude towards the payment of taxes urged upon Peter in xvii. 24 ff. is similar to that recommended by Paul in 1 Cor. x. 23–xi. 1 in other matters, that is, the avoidance of unnecessary offence to both Jew and Gentile (so too Paul and Matthew are alike anxious to avoid offence within the Christian community itself, see Matt. xviii. 6 ff.; Rom. xiv. 21; 1 Cor. viii. 13; 2 Cor. xi. 29). Peter shares a truly Pauline sensitivity in such matters, which is far removed from the roughshod insensitivity of both Judaizers and 'Libertines'. When we turn to the material which follows xiv. 28–31, 33, we find questions discussed which would have allowed the Evangelist, had he so desired, to castigate the Pauline attitude to the Law. Instead, so Bacon has claimed,[3] in Matt. xv. 15 Peter (who is not mentioned in the parallel passage in Mark) is specifically instructed in what is virtually an attitude similar to that taken by Paul: he who is the founder of the Church, with power to declare what is and what is not obligatory, is to disavow the food laws. But, here, even Bacon nods. He fails to notice

[1] On the use of Apostolic figures as types to be imitated in the early Church, see J. Wagenmann, op. cit. pp. 52–76. (A similar idealizing of a first generation of leaders emerged in New England Puritanism, as in other movements—for example, Russian Communism. See Wertenbeker, The Puritan Oligarchy (1947), pp. 80 f. The Pilgrim Fathers also compared the crossing of the Atlantic to the Exodus, ibid. p. 74.) On the whole section above, see in addition to Wagenmann, B. W. Bacon, Studies in Matthew, pp. 223 ff.; J. Weiss, op. cit., ibid. Although there is an emphasis on Peter in Matthew, Cullmann rightly warns us against thinking of the Petrine priority as a peculiarity of Matthew's. This is rooted in all our sources, including the Fourth Gospel, despite its tendency to emphasize the Beloved Disciple (O. Cullmann, Peter: Disciple–Apostle–Martyr (London, 1953), pp. 23 ff.; C. H. Turner, op. cit. p. 214).

[2] O. Cullmann, op. cit. p. 39.

[3] Studies in Matthew, pp. 400–3; see also pp. 223–30.

what we have indicated previously, that the last clause in xv. 20 ('but to eat with unwashed hands does not defile a man') has the effect of confining the whole of the preceding discussion to the oral rather than the written law. Peter is not advised to go as far as does Mark in vii. 19 ('Thus he declared all foods clean'). Nevertheless neither is he urged to oppose Paul. The verse 'These are what defile a man; but to eat with unwashed hands does not defile a man' compared with the explicitness of Mark vii. 14–23 reveals not Paulinism, as Bacon holds, but a position of mediation. Peter is urged, if we may so put it, to lean to Paulinism but not to embrace it: in short, it reveals what Peter's role in history turned out to be. The ambiguity which marked Peter's career has here invaded Matthew's text.

To examine the ambiguity to which we have referred is not possible here. The Tübingen School, which drew a sharp distinction between the position of Peter and James, on the one hand, and Paul on the other, the former two representing a Jewish-Christianity still attached to the Mosaic Law and the latter Gentile-Christianity freed from its shackles, today finds few adherents. Between Paul and extreme Judaizers in the early Church, of a Pharisaic origin, there was an unbridgeable cleavage. But neither James nor Peter belonged to these. While James held the reins of power in Jerusalem Christianity, and Peter devoted his energies mainly to Jewish–Christians, there is no justification for Lietzmann's contention that Peter led an opposition of a Judaistic kind in Paul's churches.[1] Differences of emphasis and of tenacity there would be between Peter and Paul, but Peter's defection at Antioch to the side of the Judaizers was a momentary failure: in principle he was at one with Paul. Indeed it is more than probable that Peter was nearer to Paul than he was to James, and it has been possible to see in Matt. xvi. 18 f. a defence of Peter not against Paul but against James.[2] But it is not necessary to see in that passage either a polemic against Paul or against James. There is here merely an indication of a widespread recognition of the significance of Peter in the early Church. Three further considerations confirm us in this position. First, at no point does Paul himself fail to acknowledge Peter's importance,[3]

---

[1] See E. Hirsch, *Z.N.W.* xxix; J. Munck, *Paulus und die Heilsgeschichte, passim* (but see my review in *N.T.S.*); see also J. N. Sanders, *N.T.S.* ii (1956), 133–43, on 'Peter and Paul in Acts'.

[2] J. Weiss (*op. cit.* p. 753) recognizes this, although he also sees a rejection of Paul in Matthew. A. Loisy (*La Naissance du Christianisme*, 1933, p. 126) takes Matt. xvi. 17–19 as anti-Pauline. For bibliography on this, see O. Cullmann, *op. cit.* pp. 158 ff.

[3] O. Cullmann, *loc. cit.*

22-2

secondly, the extent to which Paul himself could compromise has become increasingly recognized so that Peter's vacillation would not be incomprehensible to him,[1] and, thirdly, the tradition of the early Church sets Paul and Peter not in rivalry but in mutual honour.[2] Without enlarging on the details, we can safely assert that it is not necessary to discover any anti-Pauline polemic in Matthew's Petrine additions. These last are sufficiently accounted for both by the role which Peter actually played in the history of the early Church and by the significance his history came to have in the moral exhortation of the Church.

The above treatment has probably prompted the question why we should have spent so much time in disputing the anti-Paulinism of Matthew. The answer is twofold. First, to regard the *SM* as primarily a counterblast against the influence of Paul, nurtures the temptation to interpret it as merely an emphasis on the part of Matthew, a corrective or polemic called forth by passing circumstances, which reveals an insight into the meaning of the Gospel less profound than that possessed by his opponents. The anti-Pauline interpretation of the Sermon might carry with it the implication that Matthew was a 'mere moralist', whose emphasis on the ethical teaching of Jesus was secondary and not of essential significance for the faith of the early Church. And with this goes our next point. Secondly, and, more important, if Matthew is in opposition to Paul, he stands over against one of the most creative and influential figures in the early Church, and over against the earliest figure that we extensively know in the life of that Church, because the Pauline epistles are earlier than any other New Testament documents. With Paul we are near the fountain-head of the Christian movement, so that if Matthew is far removed from Paul he is likely to be outside one of the main forces at work from the earliest days of the Church.

In the light of our examination, however, we can be fairly certain that the *SM* is not to be explained as a reaction against Paulinism, and we can proceed to inquire whether it can be placed not in opposition to forces operative in the early Church but in agreement with them. Was Matthew's concern with the teaching of Jesus rooted in an understanding of Jesus which he shared, in various ways, with the rest of the Church? At this juncture our method will be to set the *SM* over against or in comparison

---

[1] See the excellent study of Paul by H. Chadwick, *N.T.S.* I (1954–5), 261–75, on 'All things to all men'.
[2] For example, I Clement 5; Ignatius, 'Romans iv. 2'; Irenaeus, *Against Heresies*, CXI, I, 2; CXI, III, 2.

with other documents in the New Testament, both Gospels and Epistles. That Jesus in the New Testament appears as a teacher, that his relations to his disciples resembled in many ways those of a rabbi to his *talmidim*, that the content no less than the form of his teaching finds not only much of its antithesis but also much of its counterpart in that of Judaism, all this is generally accepted and need not detain us. Our concern here is not with the form and content of the ethical teaching ascribed to Jesus, as such, but rather with the various attitudes which were adopted towards it in the early Church. How did the various elements in the primitive community understand the teaching of Jesus, its role or significance? To answer this question, were it only by way of contrast, may help us to comprehend more fully the meaning of the Sermon. We shall deal with the Synoptic Gospels in the light of the generally accepted view that behind them lie the sources Q, M, and L. The existence of these has been questioned, but while the insistence that Matthew, like Luke, is not to be regarded as merely a mosaic of sources is salutary, as we have previously indicated, the suggested abandonment of the Q hypothesis and with it the 'nameless chimeras', as Farrer expresses it, of the 'documents' M and L, demands the most cautious scrutiny.[1] We shall here follow the consensus of scholarship, because, without prejudging their existence as written sources, we can use M, L and Q as symbols which conveniently isolate material for our examination according to its occurrence in the Synoptics. But before we turn to Synoptic material we must first further examine what is still earlier, namely, the epistles of Paul.

2. *Paul and Tradition*

At this point, therefore, we ask whether Paul and Matthew, who have so often been placed in opposition to each other, are far removed in their understanding of the Christian life and of the role of the words of Jesus in that life. Of all the figures of the New Testament Paul perhaps is the best known, but he is none the less difficult to understand. And, in particular, it is hard to grasp how Paul understood the ethical or moral life of Christians in its relation to his theology. His own life he seems to have divided clearly into two parts: there was, first, his life under the Law, when he was a Jew; and then, secondly, his life 'in Christ'. These two parts were distinctly separated by his experience on the road to

[1] See A. M. Farrer, *St Matthew and St Mark* (London, 1954); and 'On Dispensing with Q', in *Studies in the Gospels: Essays in memory of R. H. Lightfoot* (Blackwell, Oxford, 1955), pp. 55 ff. Contrast V. Taylor, *J.T.S.* IV (1953), 27 ff.

Damascus. The act by which a man acknowledged his faith and really began to live 'in Christ' was equally distinct, it was baptism,[1] an act which symbolized for Paul a death to the old life under the Law, a death once and for all, and a rising to a newness of life 'in Christ', or 'in the Spirit'. By baptism the Christian man through faith had died, had risen, had been justified; he was a new creation who had already passed from death to life, for whom the final judgement of God himself was past.

Was there room in such a man's life for anything more? Did he now need any law to guide him? Could he not now simply live, in spontaneous response to the Spirit that was in him, free from legal restraint of any kind? At first sight, at least, the contrast between the life before and the Life after faith seems to be a contrast between a life under law and a life under grace, and it has often been stated that there is no room for 'law' in the Christian life as Paul understood it: it was for him a life of freedom in the Spirit.[2] But, nevertheless, two factors complicated the new life 'in Christ', as Paul recognized. First, although he was a new creation the Christian man was still in the flesh and, therefore, still open to the attacks of sin. Secondly, because he was still in the flesh he was also still subject to the hostile supernatural forces which were arrayed against man; the prince of the power of the air, the elements of this world, these were still active, and had to be opposed. Saved and justified and even sanctified as he already was, the Christian was still living between the time of the first appearance of Christ and the End. Thus Paul was inevitably faced with the question of Christian behaviour. How was a Christian to conduct himself 'betwixt the times' in this world? Was Paul at all influenced by the ethical teaching of Jesus in answering this question?[3] There are many strands in his ethical exhortation which, while important, are not for our purpose of crucial significance,[4] but the two

---

[1] Gal. ii. 21; Rom. vi.

[2] The documentation for the above passages is familiar: see, for example, the excellent treatment in R. Schnackenburg, *Die sittliche Botschaft des Neuen Testaments* (München, 1954), pp. 183–209, and my article in *The Interpreter's Dictionary* on 'Ethics in the New Testament', vol. II, pp. 167–76.

[3] This question is a corollary to a wider one, that of the relation between Paul and the 'historical Jesus' and the early Church. See C. A. A. Scott, *Christianity according to St Paul* (1932), pp. 11 ff.; H. J. Schoeps, *Paulus* (1959), pp. 48–51 (he rejects any preoccupation of Paul with the historical Jesus, so also A. Schweitzer, *The Mysticism of Paul the Apostle, ad rem*); R. Bultmann, *Theologie*, I, 185.

[4] For example, Paul appeals to 'conscience', but only in a secondary way. See my article on 'Conscience' in *The Interpreter's Dictionary* for bibliography, vol. I, pp. 671–76. In a recent study, *Die Tugend- und Lasterkataloge im Neuen Testament* (Berlin,

most characteristic emphases in the Epistles—namely, the rooting of the imperative in the indicative[1] and the concept of the good life as the fruit of the Spirit—present us with a real problem in estimating the place of the words of Jesus in Paul's thought. With these we must now deal.

(i) When Paul exhorts Christians to the good life there can be no question that he most commonly appeals to the reality and character of the new life which they possess 'in Christ', with all that this implies. He urges them to live in accordance with their calling, their sanctification, their freedom, their sonship, their life 'in Christ' or 'in the Spirit'. To consider these realities makes sin intolerable. As, for example, in 1 Thess. ii. 10 ff.:

> You are witnesses, and God also, how holy and righteous and blameless was our behaviour to you believers; for you know how, like a father with his children, we exhorted each one of you and encouraged you and charged you to lead a life worthy of God, who calls you into his own kingdom and glory.

In response to a call to participate in God's kingdom and glory the Christian goes forward: the word of exhortation is at the same time a word of encouragement.

1959), Siegfried Wibbing has dealt with Paul's use of lists of virtues and vices in his paraenesis. (Gal. xiii–xxi, etc.) The closest parallels to these he finds in the DSS (e.g. 1QS iv. 9–11; iii. 13–iv. 26) where, as in Paul, the lists are set in a context of ethical dualism and of eschatology. (See W. D. Davies, 'Flesh and Spirit', in *The Scrolls and the New Testament*, ed. K. Stendahl, pp. 169 ff.) Paul's use of such lists Wibbing explains in terms of the relation between the indicative and the imperative in his thought (pp. 117 ff.). Whereas the DSS connect the lists of vices and virtues with man's very creation by God, it is with baptism that Paul connects the virtues. Through this the Christian man has become a new creation. But he has to express this fact in deeds. These are enumerated in the lists of virtues, which, however, do not constitute a new law, their items being too generalized for this (p. 117). 'Sie bieten Kasuistischen Gebots- oder Verbotsreihen, um bestimmte Situationen des Lebens zu erfassen und zu regeln. Es sind zum größten Teil abstrakte Begriffe, die hier nebeneinander gestellt werden' (p. 123). Wibbing may well be right in his understanding of Paul's use of the ethical lists, but his work prompts us to emphasize one point. That is, that even though Paul does use generalized directions in the lists referred to, without formulating them into a law, where he uses the words of Jesus directly, he treats them as 'law'. The instances of these are few, but they are sufficient to establish that Christ for Paul was Lawgiver as well as Redeemer (see pp. 387 f.).

[1] The best statement of this problem known to me is a brief one by W. Joest, *Gesetz und Freiheit: Das Problem des Tertius Usus Legis bei Luther und die neutestamentliche Parainese* (Göttingen, 1951), pp. 134 ff. The German discussion can be traced in his footnotes. See especially R. Bultmann, *Theology of the New Testament*, vol. 1. M. Goguel, *L'Église Primitive* (Paris, 1947), pp. 441 ff., contains a brilliant discussion of the problem.

Again in 1 Thess. iv. 7, 8 we read:

For God has not called us for uncleanness, but in holiness. Therefore whoever disregards this, disregards not man but God, who gives his Holy Spirit to you.

The previous verses also, iv. 3 ff., make it clear that God's call implies sanctification:[1] the Christian is to accept the 'lead' given to him by God's call, maintained by God's Spirit: he is 'to live out' his new existence. 1 Cor. vi. 15 is equally explicit. The 'bodily' relation of the Christian with his Lord makes relations with a prostitute unthinkable. Similarly marriage with an unbeliever is incompatible with the relationship of the Christian with God, in 2 Cor. vi. 15 f., where again the metaphor of the temple employed in 1 Cor. vi. 15 f. emerges. In Rom. vii. 4 ff. a new life is naturally regarded as the outcome of the new relationship in which the Christian lives. Even where Paul makes use of ethical commonplaces familiar to Hellenistic Judaism he still appeals to the nature of the Christian man in his exhortations. In this connexion 1 Cor. xi. 2 ff. is instructive. In 1 Cor. xi. 2–3 reference is made to the relation of men and women to Christ, but in 1 Cor. xi. 13, 14 (cf. Eph. v. 32, 33) there is a reference to what is natural, Paul making use possibly, though not certainly, of a Stoic concept at this point. But as Dahl has pointed out: 'This and similar appeals to "natural law" are not due to any lack of consistency; they are in full harmony with the Apostle's fundamental conviction, that what is realized in the Church, the new creation, is in harmony with the original will of God, the Creator. Sin corrupts creation; deification of the creature in the end leads to unnaturalness (Rom. i); but in the Church all natural human virtues should be in high esteem (Phil. iv. 8).'[2]

In the passages to which we have referred Paul grounds his imperative in an indicative: he urges Christians to become what they are. The following passages are also pertinent in illustration of this:

1 Cor. v. 7:

Cleanse out the old leaven that you may be fresh dough, as you really are unleavened.

---

[1] By this is meant that no sharp distinction is to be made, as in later Reformation theology but not in Luther himself (see W. Joest, *op. cit.*), between justification and sanctification.

[2] N. A. Dahl in *The Background of the N.T. and its Eschatology*, ed. W. D. Davies and D. Daube, pp. 439 f.

Gal. v. 1:

For freedom Christ has set us free; stand fast therefore, and do not submit again to the yoke of slavery.

Gal. v. 25:

If we live by the Spirit, let us also walk by the Spirit.

1 Thess. v. 5 ff.:

For you are all sons of light and sons of the day; we are not of the night or of
6 darkness. So then let us not sleep, as others do, but let us keep awake and be sober. [Compare Rom. xiii. 12–13; Eph. v. 8–10.]

2 Cor. viii. 7:

Now as you excel in everything—in faith, in utterance, in knowledge, in all earnestness, and in your love for us—see that you excel in this gracious work also.

Rom. vi. 2 ff.:

3 How can we who died to sin still live in it? Do you not know that all of us who have been baptized into Christ Jesus were baptized into his death? We were buried therefore with him by baptism into death, so that as Christ was raised from the dead by the glory of the Father, we too might walk in newness of life.

Col. iii. 1:

If then you have been raised with Christ, seek the things that are above, where Christ is, seated at the right hand of God.

We have already suggested above that this rooting of the imperative in the indicative is found also in Matthew,[1] who is no stranger to the Pauline profundity at this point.

---

[1] The evidence for this is not only what we produced above on pp. 98 f. It is not to be overlooked that the demand presented by Matthew in the *SM* as elsewhere is the demand of Jesus, who came to the lost. For Matthew 'das Kommen Jesu zu den Verlorenen und Verworfenen ist doch mehr als ein vorläufiger Amnestieakt, der nur die Grundlage schafft für ein neues Gesetz. Es ist endgültige Gottestat. Die synoptische Gerichtsparainese, die auf den kommenden Gerichtstag, die noch ausstehende Entscheidung, die Gefahr des Versagens und Fallens hinweist, wird begrenzt von der Verkündigung des in Jesus schon gegenwärtigen Reiches und Sieges. Das Reich Gottes ist zu euch gekommen, der Starke ist gebunden von dem Stärkeren (Matt. xii. 28 ff.)': so W. Joest, *op. cit.* p. 167. See also p. 157, 'auch die synoptische Parainese ist indikativisch begründet in der Zuwendung Gottes zu dem Sünder, die in der Person und dem Handeln Jesu leibhaftig wird'. Joest (*op. cit.* pp. 155 ff.) has attempted to show how Luther's understanding of Law (*Gesetz*) compares with those attitudes towards it which are found in the New Testament documents. Paul's understanding of Christ as the end of the Law, he asserts, affords

But the precise significance of this connexion between the imperative and indicative in Paul is important. It has been claimed that the point of reference for Paul in the indicative is not the character or the life of the Jesus of history as such, and certainly not his moral teaching, but the pivotal elements in the kerygma, the facts of the incarnation as therein presented, namely, that Christ was born a Jew, under the Law (Gal. iv. 4), of Davidic descent (Rom. i. 1), was betrayed (1 Cor. xi. 23), was crucified (1 Cor. ii. 2; Gal. iii. 1; Phil. ii. 6), was buried and rose again (1 Cor. xv. 4; Rom. vi. 4): these Paul refers to but not to the biographical details of Jesus' career. References to the character of Jesus do not serve Paul's central theological concepts but subserve his paraenetic purposes, that is, they are peripheral and not central. While the data given above reveal that the Apostle was concerned with Jesus as a historical and not a mythological figure, it is also clear that he does not call for any imitation of the life of Jesus, in its words and works, but only in its character as the act of God. The imperative of the Christian life is not attached to the deeds and teaching of Jesus but rather to the essential fact of his self-giving. On this view both the details of what Jesus did on earth and his teaching are largely irrelevant to Paul's understanding of the Christian faith.[1]

(ii) The same conclusion would seem to follow from the second emphasis in Pauline ethical teaching, namely, on the Christian life as the fruit of the Spirit. The passage in Gal. v. 16–24 is crucial:

But I say, walk by the Spirit, and do not gratify the desires of the flesh. For the desires of the flesh are against the Spirit, and the desires of the Spirit are against the flesh; for these are opposed to each other, to prevent you from doing what

a real parallel to Luther's doctrine of justification by faith, which he takes to be also the inbreaking of a 'new aeon' for Paul and the indicative in which the Pauline imperative is grounded. But Joest is compelled to recognize that, as in Matthew and James, so in the Pauline epistles, particularly in the paraenetical sections, there is another attitude which is difficult to reconcile with that of Luther. Thus Paul, as we indicate above, retains the concept of a future judgement in which man is judged according to his works, as do Matthew and James. There is no single Pauline understanding of the Christian life: justification by faith is only one aspect of it. It is possible not only to appeal from Matthew and James against Paul but from Paul against Paul. Just as Matthew ends his 'Sermon' with a reference to the 'End', in which obedience to the words of Jesus is the criterion for judgement, so too Paul looks forward to a judgement seat of Christ where, we may believe, the same criterion applies. For Paul and James, see the excellent study by J. Jeremias, *E.T.* LXVI (1954–5), 368 ff.

[1] J. Weiss, *op. cit.* II, 555; Bultmann, *Theologie*, I, 185. See the discussion in G. S. Hendry, *The Gospel of the Incarnation*, pp. 32–41, on 'The Jesus of History', and H. J. Schoeps, *Paulus* (1959), pp. 48 ff.

you would. But if you are led by the Spirit you are not under the law. Now the works of the flesh are plain: immorality, impurity, licentiousness, idolatry, sorcery, enmity, strife, jealousy, anger, selfishness, dissension, party spirit, envy, drunkenness, carousing, and the like. I warn you, as I warned you before, that those who do such things shall not inherit the kingdom of God. But the fruit of the Spirit is love, joy, peace, patience, kindness, goodness, faithfulness, gentleness, self-control; against such there is no law. And those who belong to Christ Jesus have crucified the flesh with its passions and desires.

A contrast is drawn between the *works* of the flesh, and the *fruit* of the Spirit, the implication being that the Christian life has the character of spontaneity. And in Gal. v. 18, 23 it is explicitly stated not to be bound by law. Similarly in 1 Cor. ii. 12–16 the Spirit apparently of itself assures to the Christian the possession of the mind of Christ, an illumination which is autonomous. Thus again the ethic of Paul in its concentration on the Spirit would seem to relegate the character of teaching of Jesus to insignificance.

To judge, then, from the two most familiar emphases in Pauline ethics, as interpreted above, unlike Matthew, who combines with 'the imperative rooted in the indicative' a very marked concentration on the words of Jesus, as the law of the Messiah, Paul would seem to have been, if not ignorant of, at least indifferent to the teaching of Jesus. Kümmel has expressed this with forceful clarity: 'Paulus fühlt sich nicht als Schüler des geschichtlichen Jesus, sondern als Beauftragter des Auferstandenen. Und darum ist es nicht seine Aufgabe, weiterzugeben was er über den geschicht-lichen Jesus und seine Worte gehört und überliefert erhalten hat, sondern Christus zu verkündigen.'[1] But before accepting such an evaluation of Paul certain factors are to be considered.

And, before we proceed, two preliminary correctives to what we have written on the indicative-imperative and on the Spirit in Paul are necessary. There is, in the first place, an apparent contradiction, which may even amount to an antinomy, in Paul's treatment of the moral life. One side of this we have above indicated, namely, its rooting of the imperative in the indicative. But while this must be accorded its due prominence, another side emerges clearly, if not so persistently, what might be called the 'vigilatory'. Paul retains three concepts, the last of which amounts to an emphasis, which stand in uneasy juxtaposition with the claims he makes that the Christian has been saved, justified, sanctified, is now, in short, a new creation, who is merely called upon to be what he is. These are :

[1] W. G. Kümmel cited by H. J. Schoeps, *op. cit.* p. 51.

(*a*) The idea that, however much the justification which he has already experienced anticipates it or may be regarded as 'final' in principle, the Christian still awaits a judgement yet to come, the last judgement.

(*b*) The idea that at this last judgement each will be rewarded, not according to his faith, but according to his works.

(*c*) The idea that in preparation for this final judgement obedience to the will of God is necessary, so that the Christian life turns out to be an ἄσκησις and a call to vigilance.

All this means that for Paul Christianity is a 'way' to be walked.

So, in the second place, while the spontaneity of life in the Spirit is to be acknowledged, it has also to be recognized that Paul knows the Spirit as a kind of 'law'. The reader is referred to our treatment of the evidence[1] elsewhere. Suffice it here to add the words of Goguel:

Il faut maintenir que la justification, la possession de l'Esprit, l'appel au salut, la promesse de ce salut jouent dans la vie du Chrétien le rôle d'une loi, une loi, il est vrai, qui est intérieure.

For our purposes, the question how this 'vigilatory' note in Paul and his understanding of the Spirit in terms of a law are to be reconciled with the 'indicatives' of the Epistles or whether there is an antinomy to be recognized at the heart of Paulinism, need not be faced. Suffice it that the evidence reveals Paul as occupied with obedience and works. Our concern is to discover whether the words of his Lord provided him with a reservoir of ethical tradition and even with a 'law' (a law not merely within, as Goguel writes) upon which he drew for the moral education of his converts.

To begin with, neither 'the indicative-imperative' emphasis nor that on the Spirit in Paul is to be divorced, as has been claimed above, from the actualities of the life and teaching of Jesus. [The reasons for our insistence on this we have presented elsewhere: the reader is referred to *Paul and Rabbinic Judaism*, pp. 136 ff., 195 ff.] Here a general consideration is pertinent. To be convincing as kerygma the content of the life and teaching of Jesus must have been consistent with the nature of the kerygma: the appeal of Paul to the Incarnation was of necessity also an appeal to the life and teaching of Jesus which had exhibited the quality of the Incarnation in the actuality of history. There is no antithesis to be set up or implied between the idea of the Incarnation and the facts of the life and teaching of

---

[1] *P.R.J.*[2] *ad rem.* The evidence for all this is treated by my pupil N. Watson in a dissertation on 'Justification by Faith and Eschatology', Princeton University, 1959.

Jesus as its actualization. To appeal to the kerygma was necessarily to appeal to the works and words of Jesus. Similarly the Spirit, whose fruit Paul describes in Gal. v. 16 ff. and elsewhere is, if not identified with Jesus himself, at least closely related to him: it is the Spirit *of Jesus* which informs Paul about the nature of the good life. These considerations make it difficult to agree with those who would belittle, if not dismiss, the place of the Jesus of history, his deeds and words, from the mind of Paul.[1]

But these general, though very real, considerations apart, there are others which reinforce our insistence on the re-examination of the role of the words of Jesus in Paul's thought. These are roughly of two kinds. On the one hand, (a) there are those which arise from the general conceptual world of Paul or from categories which he seems often to have employed in clarifying the nature of the Christian Dispensation. On the other hand, (b) there are those which rest upon evidence which can be very precisely isolated in the Epistles themselves. Let us deal with each group in turn.

(a) There is much to indicate that a very significant part of the conceptual world in which Paul moved, *as a Christian*, was that of the Exodus. It is clear that, as for Matthew and other New Testament writers, so for Paul, there was a real correspondence between the Christian Dispensation and the Exodus of Israel from Egypt. The redemption of the Old Israel from Egypt was the prototype of the greater redemption from sin wrought by Christ for the New Israel. This has been much recognized in recent scholarship.[2]

---

[1] C. H. Dodd, *The Evolution of Ethics*, ed. Sneath, p. 301. This is, indeed, the focal point in much of the recent discussion on the 'Quest of the Historical Jesus'. See J. M. Robinson, *A New Quest for the Historical Jesus* (1959); R. Hepburn, *Christianity and Paradox* (1958); for a useful essay J. D. McCaughey in *The Reformed Theological Review*, xx (1961), 1 ff.

[2] See, for example, *Moïse l'Homme de l'Alliance* (Paris, 1954); W. D. Davies, *P.R.J.*[2]; J. Jeremias in *T.W.Z.N.T.* vol. iv, Μωυσῆς; E. Sahlin on 'The New Exodus of Salvation', in *The Root of the Vine*, ed. A. Fridrichsen (Dacre Press, Westminster, 1953); C. F. Evans, 'The Central Section of St Luke's Gospel', in *Studies in the Gospels*, ed. D. E. Nineham (Blackwell, Oxford, 1955); J. Manek, on 'The New Exodus and the Book of Luke', *Novum Testamentum* (January 1957), 8 ff.; A. M. Farrer, *A Study in St Mark* (1951); E. C. Hoskyns and N. Davey, *The Fourth Gospel* (1931), p. 147 *et al.*; H. M. Teeple, *The Mosaic Eschatological Prophet* (1957); F. L. Cross, *1 Peter, a Paschal Liturgy* (Mowbray, London, 1954) (see review by C. F. D. Moule, *N.T.S.* (November 1956)); P. Dabeck, in *Biblica*, xxiii (Rome, 1942), 175–89, on 'Siehe, es erschienen Moses und Elias, Matt. xvii. 3'; C. Chavasse, *Theology*, liv, no. 374 (August 1951), 289 ff., on 'Jesus Christ and Moses'; H. J. Schoeps, *Theologie und Geschichte des Judenchristentums*, pp. 88 ff.; L. Goppelt, *Typos* (Gütersloh, 1954); J. Daniélou, *Sacramentum Futuri* (1950), pp. 131 ff. on 'La Typologie de l'Exode dans l'ancien et le Nouveau Testament'; J. Guillet, 'Le

1 Cor. x. 1 ff. reads as follows:

I want you to know, brethren, that our fathers were all under the cloud, and all passed through the sea, and all were baptized into Moses in the cloud and in the sea, and all ate the same supernatural food and all drank the same supernatural drink. For they drank from the supernatural Rock which followed them, and the Rock was Christ. Nevertheless with most of them God was not pleased; for they were overthrown in the wilderness.

Now these things are warnings for us, not to desire evil as they did. Do not be idolaters as some of them were; as it is written, 'The people sat down to eat and drink and rose up to dance'. We must not indulge in immorality as some of them did, and twenty-three thousand fell in a single day. We must not put the Lord to the test, as some of them did and were destroyed by serpents; nor grumble, as some of them did and were destroyed by the Destroyer.

The interpretation of the Christian life as a counterpart of the Exodus is here made quite explicit; note especially that the experience of the New Exodus, like that of the first, demands the forsaking of immorality (1 Cor. x. 8), that is, the taking up of the yoke of Christ, although this is not expressly so stated. Again, Paul's understanding of the Eucharist is largely covenantal: it is for him the institution of the New Israel, the counterpart of the Old (1 Cor. xi. 20–34).[1] This is reinforced in 1 Cor. v. 7, where Christ is referred to as a Passover lamb slain for Christians, and in 1 Cor. xv. 20, where Christ is the firstfruits. This last contains a side-glance at the ritual of the Passover; Christ is the firstfruits of a new redemption. Out of the six passages noted on pp. 343 ff. above in illustration of Paul's rooting of the imperative in the indicative, two certainly, and a third possibly, are influenced by the thought of the Christian as having undergone a new Exodus. This is so as we saw in 1 Cor. v. 7 and the motif of freedom in Gal. v. 1[2] owes something to the motif. Moreover, if our argument elsewhere be accepted that the Pauline concept of dying and rising with Christ is to be understood in terms of a New Exodus,[3] then another third passage, Rom. vi. 2 ff., from the six referred to, also

thème de la marche au désert dans l'Ancien Testament', *R.S.R.* (1949), 164 ff. For a criticism of the position advocated in the text, see Paul Neuenzeit, *Das Herrenmahl, Studien zur paulinischen Eucharistieauffassung* (München, 1960), pp. 148 ff. He finds an over-emphasis in *P.R.J.*[2] on the New Exodus motif in Paul. Compare R. Schnackenburg, 'Todes- und Lebensgemeinschaft mit Christus. Neue Studien zu Röm. vi. 1–11', *Th.Z.* vi (München, 1955), pp. 32 ff.   [1] *P.R.J.*[2] pp. 250–4.

[2] On this, see D. Daube, *The New Testament and Rabbinic Judaism* (1956), p. 282.

[3] *Ibid.* pp. 102 ff. See W. C. van Unnik, 'La conception paulinienne de la nouvelle alliance', in *Recherches Bibliques*, v, *Littérature et Théologie Pauliniennes* (Louvain, 1960), pp. 109–26.

contains this idea of the Christian Dispensation as a counterpart to the first Exodus. Among the metaphors used by Paul to expound his experience in Christ is that of 'redemption', which, we cannot doubt, was intimately bound up in his mind with the thought of the emancipation of the Old Israel from Egypt (Exod. vi. 6; xv. 13; Deut. vii. 8; xv. 15).[1] In 2 Cor. vi. 16 the presence of God in the temple of the New Israel, the Church, is expressly understood, we may assume, as the realization of the promise made to Moses, as for example in Exod. xxv. 8: 'And let them make me a sanctuary that I may dwell in their midst', or again in Exod. xxix. 43–5: 'There will I meet with the people of Israel, and it shall be sanctified by my glory; I will consecrate the tent of meeting and the altar...and I will dwell among the people of Israel, and will be their God.' This is in agreement with the view that in 2 Corinthians the thought of Paul is largely governed by the understanding of the Christian life in terms of a new covenant (2 Cor. iii. 1–18) and of the sojourn in the wilderness (2 Cor. v. 1 ff.). Moreover, the reference in 2 Cor. vi. 14 'Or what fellowship has light with darkness?'[2] reminds us that Christians for Paul are children of the day. Thus in Col. i. 12, 13, we read: 'giving thanks to the Father, who has qualified us to share in the inheritance of the saints in light (εἰς τὴν μερίδα τοῦ κλήρου τῶν ἁγίων ἐν τῷ φωτί). He has delivered us from the dominion of darkness and transferred us to the kingdom of his beloved Son, in whom we have redemption, the forgiveness of sins.' It is possible that here the Exodus motif is again apparent in the use of the term 'inheritance'. In Deuteronomy this term is closely connected with the deliverance from Egypt,[3] and it may be that for Paul also it suggests the eschatological redemption, through the death and resurrection of Christ, parallel to that wrought at the Exodus. Certainly the motif of 'light and darkness' which occurs in the same passage suggests this. In 1 Pet. ii. 9, 10 this motif occurs in a context which recalls the Exodus, and especially Exod. xix. 4–6. In Mishnah Pesahim x. 5 we read that in the Passover service: 'Therefore are we bound to give thanks, to praise, to glorify, to honour, to exalt, to extol, and to bless him who wrought all these wonders for our fathers and for us. He brought us out

---

[1] On this see D. Daube, *op. cit.* pp. 268–75.

[2] The use of the 'darkness and light' motif in Paul can be connected perhaps also with the kind of dualism we find in the DSS: see Wibbing, *op. cit.* pp. 61 ff., *et passim*. On 2 Cor. iii. 1–18; v. 1 ff., see *P.R.J.*[2]

[3] κληρονομέω and its corresponding substantives κλῆρος, κληρονομία have a long association with the Exodus, the land of Canaan being the 'inheritance' of Israel, for example Deut. iv. 20, 21, etc.

from bondage to freedom, from sorrow to gladness, and from mourning to a festival day, *and from darkness to great light* and from servitude to redemption; so let us say before him the *Hallelujah*' (our italics). Specific references to darkness and light are clear in the Exodus story itself. In Exod. x. 21 ff. we read:

21 Then the Lord said to Moses, 'Stretch out your hand toward heaven that there
22 may be darkness over the land of Egypt, a darkness to be felt'. So Moses stretched out his hand toward heaven, and there was thick darkness in all the
23 land of Egypt three days; they did not see one another, nor did any rise from his place for three days; but all the people of Israel had light where they dwelt.

The parallelism between Old and New Israel here may not be pressed, however, because the Old Israel did not strictly pass from darkness, although they were surrounded by it (Exod. x. 23). Nevertheless, the symbol of a passage from darkness to light was taken up by Deutero-Isaiah and employed to describe redemption (Isa. xlii. 16)—'I will turn the darkness before them into light, the rough places into level ground', a redemption which was a New Exodus. Paul in Col. i. 12, 13 f. may be governed by the same concept.

So far, however, we have only pointed to passages where the concept of the Exodus, as the type of the Christian redemption, has been employed by Paul in a general sense. In many of the passages cited above as containing the New Exodus motif, while there is an appeal, implicit or explicit, to its consequences in good conduct, there is none to any specific commandment as such which characterizes the New Exodus. Are we then to conclude that it was in the character of the Exodus almost solely as deliverance, rather than as also imposing a demand, in the giving of the Law, that Paul found it pertinent for the interpretation of the Gospel? In other words, did anything in his understanding of the New Exodus 'in Christ' correspond to those events in the total complex of the Exodus that transpired *particularly* at Sinai? It is our contention that there was, and that on grounds which may not be equally cogent but which are all worthy of attention. They constitute the second category of considerations which we mentioned above as specifically suggesting that the words of Jesus were important for Paul.

(*b*) We begin with the assertion that it has been insufficiently recognized how frequently the Epistles of Paul echo the Synoptic Gospels, even as it has been too readily assumed that the Apostle was indifferent to the Jesus of history, his works and, especially for our purpose, his words. Two factors are relevant: first, there is clearly traceable in the epistles a process whereby reminiscences of the words of the Lord Jesus himself are interwoven with traditional material, and, secondly, there is strong evidence that there was a collection of sayings of the Lord to which Paul appealed as authoritative; in this connexion 1 Cor. vii. 25 is particularly instructive. The data we have provided in detail elsewhere; we here merely reiterate that the tables presented by Resch in his work *Der Paulinismus und die Logia Jesu* (1904) demand serious evaluation.[1]

With the echoes of the teaching of Jesus in his epistles it agrees that Paul refers to a law of the Messiah.[2] This is not a mere overhang from a pre-Pauline Jewish-Christian legalism unrelated to the essentials of Paul's thought. In addition to what we have noted in *P.R.J.*[2], the evidence seems to suggest that the interpretation of the teaching of Jesus as a New Law was not necessarily aboriginal in primitive Jewish-Christianity but only comes into prominence in later Jewish-Christianity after the fall of Jerusalem in A.D. 70.[3] Nor again is the phrase 'the law of Christ' to be explained away as a vague equivalent to an immanent principle of life like the Stoic law of nature.[4] Moreover, though there are places where Paul seems to understand the law of the Messiah as fulfilled in the law of love, this last also does not exhaust the meaning of the phrase. Almost certainly it is a comprehensive expression for the totality of the ethical teaching of Jesus that had come down to Paul as authoritative. Paul's vocabulary at several points makes it clear that he regarded himself as the heir of a tradition of ethical, as of other, teaching, which he had received and which he had to transmit. He was the servant of one who had criticized the tradition of the fathers as obscuring the true will of God; he himself violently attacked the same tradition. Nevertheless, he turns out on examination to be the steward of a new tradition.[5]

---

[1] *P.R.J.*[2] pp. 136 ff.

[2] 1 Cor. ix. 21; Gal. vi. 2. See *P.R.J.*[2] pp. 142; C. H. Dodd, "Ἔννομος Χριστοῦ', in *Studia Paulina in honorem J. de Zwaan* (Haarlem, 1953), pp. 96–110.

[3] See M. Simon, *Verus Israel* (1948), pp. 100 ff., whose treatment, however, also shows that there were anticipations of the later interpretation of Christianity as a New Law in the New Testament itself, for example Jas. i. 25; Gal. vi. 2; Heb. vii. 12. The notion of a New Law is closely associated with that of a new people (pp. 102 f.); J. Daniélou (*Théologie du Judéo-Christianisme* (1957), 1, 216 ff.) notes how Christ became not only a New Law but the New Covenant.

[4] C. H. Dodd, *The Bible and the Greeks*, p. 37; the view is retracted in *Studia Paulina, op. cit. ad rem.*

[5] For what follows, see these pivotal works: O. Cullmann on *The Tradition*, now published in English in *The Early Church*, ed. A. J. B. Higgins (London, 1956),

The *content* of this tradition can be broadly divided into two groups:

(i) That which deals with Christian preaching where the tradition is identified with the Gospel or the Apostolic message itself. The chief passages are:

1 Thess. ii. 13:

And we also thank God constantly for this, that when you *received* (παραλαβόντες) the word of God which you heard from us, you *accepted* (ἐδέξασθε) it not as the word of men but as what it really is, the word of God, which is at work in you believers.

1 Cor. xv. 3 ff.:

For I *delivered* (παρέδωκα) to you as of first importance what I also *received* (παρέλαβον), that Christ died for our sins in accordance with the scriptures, that he was buried, that he was raised on the third day in accordance with the scriptures, and that he appeared to Cephas, then to the twelve. Then he appeared to more than five hundred brethren at one time, most of whom are still alive, though some have fallen asleep. Then he appeared to James, then to all the apostles. Last of all, as to one untimely born, he appeared also to me. For I am the least of the apostles, unfit to be called an apostle, because I persecuted the church of God. But by the grace of God I am what I am, and his grace toward me was not in vain. On the contrary, I worked harder than any of them, though it was not I, but the grace of God which is with me. Whether then it was I or they, so we preach and so you believed.

Gal. i. 11 f.:

For I would have you know, brethren, that the gospel which was preached by me is not man's gospel. For I did not *receive* (παρέλαβον) it from man, nor was I taught (ἐδιδάχθην) it, but it came through a revelation of Jesus Christ.

Col. ii. 6-8:

As therefore you *received* (παρελάβετε) Christ Jesus the Lord, so live in him, rooted and built up in him and established in the faith, just as you were taught (ἐδιδάχθητε), abounding in thanksgiving.

See to it that no one makes a prey of you by philosophy and empty deceit, according to human *tradition* (τὴν παράδοσιν), according to the elemental spirits of the universe, and not according to Christ.

pp. 59–104; L. Cerfaux, in *Recueil Lucien Cerfaux* (Gembloux, II, 1954), 253–82, on 'La Tradition selon Saint Paul'; and H. Riesenfeld, *The Gospel Tradition and its Beginnings* (London, 1957). See also P. Neuenzeit, *op. cit.* pp. 77–88; J. Wagenmann, *op. cit.* pp. 44 ff. *et passim*; Bultmann, *Theologie des Neuen Testaments*, pp. 464–73.

(ii) Tradition concerned strictly with rules or orders for the Christian life, as in

1 Cor. xi. 2:

I commend you because you remember me in everything and maintain the *traditions* even as I have *delivered* them to you.

2 Thess. ii. 15:

So then, brethren, stand firm and hold to the *traditions* which you were taught by us, either by word of mouth or by letter.

See also 1 Cor. vii. 10, 12, 40; xi. 14; 1 Thess. iv. 15.

The *forms* of the terminology employed to describe the reception and transmission of the traditions in both (i) and (ii), while they appear in Hellenistic sources,[1] almost certainly have their origin for Paul in a Jewish milieu. Note the following: 'hold to the tradition' (τὰς παραδόσεις κατέχετε, 1 Cor. xi. 2; xv. 2, compare Mark vii. 18); 'stand in the Gospel which you have received' (ἐν ᾧ καὶ ἑστήκατε, 1 Cor. xv. 1; 'to the traditions', 2 Thess. ii. 15).[2] Most striking, however, is the use of 'receive' (παραλαμβάνω) and 'deliver' (παραδίδωμι) (1 Cor. xi. 2, 23; xv. 3; 1 Thess. ii. 13; 2 Thess. ii. 15; iii. 6; Gal. i. 9, 12; Phil. iv. 9; Col. ii. 6, 8), which translate the Hebrew *qibbel min* and *masar le* respectively.

Thus the *terminology* used by Paul was customary in Judaism. Are we to conclude from this that he regarded the Christian tradition as similar in its nature to that handed down in Judaism, or was there an essential difference between them? In other words, is there a 'rabbinic' element in the Pauline understanding of tradition, that is, the conception of a tradition of a prescribed way of life transmitted from 'authority' to 'authority'? The question revolves around Paul's understanding of the source of the Christian tradition with which he was concerned. And in the first group of materials, mentioned above, the tradition is explicitly stated to have been derived, not from men, but directly from God. In 1 Thess. ii. 13 it constitutes the message *of God*; and, while in 1 Cor. xv. 1–11 its exact source is not described, both in Gal. i. 11–12 and Col. ii. 6–8 the tradition is deliberately, and very forcefully, set over against the tradition of men. Thus, so far as the content of his Gospel as such is concerned, that is, if we may so express it, as kerygma, Paul insists that it was given of God himself, who was its sole source. However, while in 1 Cor. xv. 1–11 Paul does not describe the source of the tradition, he clearly presents it in

---

[1] J. Dupont, *Gnosis* (1949), pp. 59 f., 293 f.
[2] See also Appendix IX, pp. 453 ff. below.

23-2

non-Pauline terms,[1] in a form moulded by the Church probably at Jerusalem, so that in one sense he can be claimed to have received it from men. But this is true for him only of the form: the substance of the tradition was of God, as his call was from God. While Paul could not but be aware of human agencies who had been at work in the precise formulation of the tradition containing his Gospel, his emphasis was not on this aspect of the matter, which was entirely secondary. What intermediaries there were in themselves were not significant. Paul's emphasis was on the Gospel as born of the divine initiative in Christ. As far, then, as what we may call the primary content of the kerygma was concerned, the tradition was not understood by Paul in a rabbinic manner. This is as true of 1 Cor. xv. 1–11, as of Gal. i. 11–12. Even though in 1 Cor. xv. 1–11 he might seem at first sight to be quoting authorities, as does Pirqe Aboth i. 1 f., this is, in fact, not the case. The authorities in 1 Cor. xv. 1–11 are not teachers transmitting an interpretation of a primary deposit, the one to another, but witnesses severally of a primary event. In Aboth i. 1 f. we find a chain of successive authorities; in 1 Cor. xv. 1–11 a series of 'original' witnesses. The chronological sequence in Aboth denotes authorities increasingly removed from contact with the original deposit, and increasingly dependent on the preceding secondary authorities, but the chronological sequence in 1 Cor. xv. 1–11 is intended merely to describe the order (τάξις) in which the 'immediacy' of the event was experienced by each witness: that is, it is not a rabbinic sequence. The source of Paul's Gospel is God himself, who took the initiative in revealing himself in Jesus Christ, and, through his Resurrection, created witnesses to Jesus Christ in the world. Thus Jesus Christ is not strictly the source of the kerygmatic tradition but its content: Jesus of Nazareth, crucified, buried and risen, is the primary deposit of the Christian tradition, given by God himself. In 2 Corinthians Paul contrasts the Christian ministry with that of the Old Covenant, and it is of the highest significance that it is Paul himself, not Jesus, who is set in parallelism with Moses: Jesus is rather parallel to the Law, that is, the revelation granted to Moses. Jesus is not the first link in a chain of teachers, no new Moses, but rather a new 'Law'.[2]

As far, then, as those passages which deal with the kerygma as a tradition are concerned, Paul does not think of himself as a Christian rabbi dependent upon teachers, the first of whom was Jesus. But what of those

---

[1] J. Jeremias, *The Eucharistic Words of Jesus*, Eng. trans. (Oxford, 1955), pp. 128 ff.
[2] *P.R.J.*[2] pp. 148 ff.

in the second group, isolated above, concerned with a tradition of teaching? Is there here another emphasis in which Jesus is thought of as a New Moses? In 1 Cor. x the implication is unmistakable that Jesus is such: incorporation into Christ, the Rock, who is distinguished from the first Moses, is, nevertheless, parallel to that into Moses and here the moral reference of the incorporation is made clear. The passages in which Paul cites the words of the Lord as authoritative would seem to support this implication. But here there is a complication. Paul in 1 Cor. x. 1 ff. uses the term, not Jesus, but Christ: elsewhere he speaks neither of a law nor of a word 'of Jesus', but 'of Christ' and 'of the Lord'.[1] Is this significant? Cullmann thinks that it is. While recognizing that there were words *of Jesus* in the tradition, by concentrating his attention on a passage which we omitted from our classifications above, because it demands separate treatment, Cullmann comes to a striking conclusion. The passage concerned is the following in 1 Cor. xi. 23 f.:

For I received from the Lord what I also delivered to you, that the Lord Jesus on the night when he was betrayed took bread, and when he had given thanks, he broke it, and said, 'This is my body which is for you. Do this in remembrance of me'.

Here the source of a particular tradition—not an ethical one, however—is declared to be 'the Lord', which refers, so Cullmann maintains, neither to God, the ultimate source of the kerygma, nor to the Jesus of history, but to the Risen Lord. This can only be reconciled with the fact, that we have previously noted, that Paul had received tradition from others, by claiming that the Lord, the exalted Christ, was himself the transmitter of his own words and deeds. Thus in 1 Cor. vii. 10, 'Unto the married I command, yet not I but the Lord', '*it is the exalted Lord who now proclaims to the Corinthians, through the tradition, what he had taught his disciples during his incarnation on earth*'.[2] Elsewhere in Col. ii. 6 the Lord is the content of the tradition. The Lord is, therefore, both author and content of the tradition: the genitive in the phrase 'the Gospel of Christ', in Rom. xv. 19 and elsewhere, is a subjective genitive: 'the exalted Christ is Himself originator of the Gospel of which He is also the object'.[3] While, as we noted above, the tradition is connected with the Jesus of history,

---

[1] In Gal. vi. 2, ὁ νόμος τοῦ Χριστοῦ. In 1 Cor. xiv. 37, ἐντολή is possibly not part of the original text: see C. H. Dodd in *Studia Paulina*, p. 105, although it is found in 𝔓⁴⁶ H ℵ*. In 1 Cor. ix. 21 we have ἔννομος Χριστοῦ.
[2] O. Cullmann, *op. cit.* p. 68. His italics.
[3] *Ibid.* p. 69.

Cullmann insists that we owe the tradition really to the exalted Lord. On 1 Cor. xi. 23 he writes: 'The designation *Kyrios* not only points to the historical Jesus as the chronological beginning of the chain of tradition as the first member of it, but accepts the exalted Lord as the real author of the whole tradition developing itself in the apostolic Church. Thus the apostolic *paradosis* can be set directly on a level with the exalted Kyrios.'[1] The use of the aorist (διέταξεν) in 1 Cor. ix. 14 indicates how the exalted Lord who *now* commands in 1 Cor. vii. 10 (τοῖς δὲ γεγαμηκόσι παραγγέλλω, οὐκ ἐγώ, ἀλλ' ὁ κύριος) and probably in 1 Thess. iv. 15 (τοῦτο γὰρ ὑμῖν λέγομεν ἐν λόγῳ κυρίου), is the same as the Jesus who walked on earth. 'The exalted One Himself after His resurrection delivers the words which He has spoken.' In this way, although Cullmann does not ignore the historical Jesus in this matter, he virtually relegates him to the background and elevates the Kyrios to supreme significance. It agrees with this that it is necessary for the exalted Lord to repeat what he had declared on earth. Moreover, Cullmann is thus able to connect the tradition with the activity of the Spirit, because the Kyrios is closely related to, if not identified with, the Spirit in Paul.[2] The conclusion is that tradition in Paul is opposed to the rabbinic principle of tradition in Judaism in two ways: 'Firstly, that the mediator of the tradition is not the teacher but the *Apostle* as the direct witness; secondly, the principle of succession does not operate mechanically as with the rabbis, but is bound to the Holy Spirit';[3] Cullmann refuses to treat the two groups of material distinguished on pp. 354f. above as different kinds of tradition: they are both to be understood as derived, as an undifferentiated whole, from the Lord, so that not only the kerygmatic tradition that Paul received and transmitted, but also the didactic is to some extent removed from the historical Jesus, and any analogy between Christian and Jewish tradition is obviated. Jesus as teacher, or Jesus as counterpart of Moses, has little significance for the tradition, but only Jesus as Lord. The Christ of Paul is not easily recognizable as the Jesus of the Mount, as Matthew understood him.

But is Paul so to be interpreted? Is the sharp distinction between the exalted Lord and the Jesus of history which Cullmann finds really present in Paul? Certain considerations are pertinent.

(*a*) The exegesis of certain texts suggested by Cullmann is questionable. Thus in 1 Cor. vii. 10, 12, is it correct to interpret the verse to mean that the exalted Lord is now commanding (verse 10) or refusing to

---

[1] O. Cullmann, *op. cit.* p. 62.   [2] *Ibid.* pp. 70 ff.; see *P.R.J.*[2] pp. 182, 196.
[3] O. Cullmann, *ibid.*

command (verse 12)? In 1 Cor. ix. 14 the past tense is used of a command of the Lord and it is probable that the reference in the former two passages is also to a commandment given by Jesus in the past, which is in force in the present. When Shakespeare wrote of the pound of flesh, he did not mean Shylock to imply that the particular law referred to was there and then enacted, although he used the present tense. So too Paul in 1 Cor. vii. 10, 12 merely claims that a past commandment of Jesus' is still in force. (See *The Merchant of Venice*, iv, i, 297.)

Again the very passage on which Cullmann leans most, 1 Cor. xi. 23–6, points not to a distinction between Jesus and 'the Lord', but to their identity. In xi. 26 we read: 'For as often as you eat this bread and drink this cup, you proclaim (καταγγέλλετε) the Lord's death until he comes.'[1] Clearly the 'Lord's' death can only refer to the death of the historical Jesus, which probably takes the place in the 'Christian Passover' or Eucharist of the historical event of the Exodus in the Haggadah of the Passover. The Jesus remembered and proclaimed is also the present Lord and the Lord to come. Past, present and future meet in the name 'Lord', because 'the Lord' is 'Jesus'. That very Holy Spirit to which Cullmann appeals in support of his position testifies to this very truth. While 'no one speaking by the Spirit of God ever says "Jesus be cursed"', it is equally true that 'no one can say "Jesus is Lord"', except by the Holy Spirit' (1 Cor. xii. 3).

(*b*) It has been claimed that Paul never refers to a word of Jesus as a commandment. But in 1 Cor. vii. 25 he does use ἐπιταγή[2] of a word of the Lord. The verbal form ἐπιτάσσειν in the LXX translates צָוָה. In 1 Cor. ix. 14 we read: οὕτως καὶ ὁ κύριος διέταξε τοῖς τὸ εὐαγγέλιον καταγγέλλουσιν ἐκ τοῦ εὐαγγελίου ζῆν, and the verb is used in Acts vii. 44 of a command of God to Moses, and in Matt. xi. 1 of Jesus' commands to his disciples.[3] In any case, the claim might be countered by the statement that nowhere does Paul regard the Spirit, the connexion of which with 'the Lord' Cullmann rightly emphasizes, as the source of ethical com-

---

[1] The force of 'proclaim' here is 'to make a haggadah of it'—as was the Exodus 'proclaimed' in the Passover Haggadah. See *P.R.J.*[2] pp. 252 f.; G. Buchanan Gray, *Sacrifice in the Old Testament* (1925), p. 395; and for another approach, P. Neuenzeit, *op. cit.* pp. 128 ff.

[2] D. Daube(*J.J.S.* x, 1–2, 12) claims that Paul's use of συγγνώμη and ἐπιταγή in 1 Cor. vii. 6 is exceedingly technical: the former denotes permission, indulgence, concession, the latter, commandment, duty: 'the Rabbinic antithesis is *reshuth* (concession, permission) over against *miswah* or *ḥobbah* [duty]'.

[3] See C. H. Dodd in *Studia Paulina, ad rem.*

mandments, although it is that of moral power. The term 'law' in Rom. viii. 2 ('For the law of the Spirit of life in Christ Jesus has set me free from the law of sin and death') denotes not so much commandments as 'principle'.

(c) A factor which is not clear in Cullmann's discussion is the exact meaning which he ascribes to the term 'Lord'. Does he mean the 'Risen Lord' and the 'Exalted Lord' to refer to the same phenomenon? He uses the two terms apparently interchangeably and rather sharply separates both the Risen Lord and the Exalted Lord, whom he seems not to distinguish, from the historical Jesus. The improbability that this separation should be accepted appears when we set Paul's understanding of the didactic role of the Lord, as Cullmann understands it, over against the data in the rest of the New Testament. Mark's conception of the activity of the Risen Lord we cannot certainly determine, either because the end of his Gospel has been lost, or, if he did finish it at xvi. 8, because he does not tell us anything about this activity. If we follow R. H. Lightfoot and others, and find in Mark xvi. 8 the expectation of an almost immediate Parousia to be enacted in Galilee, then no didactic activity of the Risen Lord can have been contemplated by Mark.[1] Clearly Mark cannot help us in our quest into the functions of the Risen Lord. Matthew, however, is rich in significance just at this point. It is probable that for Matthew the Resurrection is coincident with the glorification of Jesus as Lord. 'All authority in heaven and on earth *has* been given to Him': the aorist tense in xxviii. 18 is to be taken seriously—ἐδόθη μοι. Jesus as Risen Lord is in heaven, that is, glorified. But the ethical instructions which he issues are identified with those which he had given to his own while on earth, and, we may assume, particularly those recorded in the *SM*.[2] The Jesus of history had initiated an ethical paradosis which the glorified Christ reaffirms: the latter neither initiates the Christian paradosis nor repeats what, as the historical Jesus, he had previously delivered on earth: he needs merely to refer to the tradition of the latter. When we turn to Luke there is a significant change. The Risen Christ instructs his own (Luke xxiv. 27, 44 ff.; Acts i. 6 ff.), although no explicit reference is made to any moral teaching he may have given. After forty days, however, the Risen Christ ascended into heaven, where he was glorified. Contact with him, of a direct kind such as had been theirs hitherto, is now denied his disciples

---

[1] *Locality and Doctrine in the Gospels* (London, 1938), pp. 1–48.

[2] R. H. Lightfoot, *op. cit.* pp. 66 ff., on xxviii. 16–20. He does not do justice to the didactic factor in the passage.

until he comes again 'in the same way as you saw him go unto heaven' (Acts i. 11 ff.). The Risen Christ taught the things concerning himself (Luke xxiv. 44 ff.) and gave commands (Acts i. 2 ff.) and spoke of the Kingdom of God (Acts i. 3)—all of which possibly[1] *implies* ethical instruction—with a reference to what he had taught on earth. But the impression given is that the *glorified* Christ did not teach. This is the emphasis in Acts ii. 32–6; iii. 13–21, which reflect perhaps the earliest Christian preaching, and, by implication possibly, in Acts xiii. 30 f. On the other hand, in Acts x. 40 f. the Resurrection alone is to the fore, there being no emphasis on any Ascension. A didactic function is ascribed to the Risen Christ. Luke would seem to confine teaching whether ethical or other to the latter. The Lord of Glory is not directly available for such.[2] In the Fourth Gospel there is a reference to the Ascension implied in xx. 17, but emphasis is laid most on the Risen Christ. Moreover, for John the real glorification of Jesus had already occurred in the crucifixion.[3] It follows that there is nothing in the Fourth Gospel comparable to Matt. xxviii. 16–20 because, essentially, the resurrection could add nothing to the glory of the crucifixion. For John it is neither the Risen Jesus nor the Exalted Lord who exercises the task of teaching in the Church, but the Holy Spirit, to which this function is not thus directly applied in Paul. The content of the teaching of the Spirit, however, is rooted in teaching already given by the historical Jesus. 'But the Counsellor, the Holy Spirit', so we read, 'whom the Father will send in my name, he will teach you all things, and bring to your remembrance all that I have said to you' (John xiv. 26).

For our purpose what is significant in all the above is that, however the relation between the Risen Christ and the glorified or exalted Lord be conceived, whether in terms of ascension or not, the teaching ascribed to both figures always has reference to the teaching of the historical Jesus, both in ethical and other matters. The presumption, therefore, is that Paul also, unless he was quite removed from the main currents of the Church, intended the same reference. This is particularly reinforced by the fact that Paul's understanding of the Risen Christ seems to be closest

---

[1] The exact content of the teaching in Acts i. 2 f. is difficult to assess. Lake and Cadbury (*Beginnings*, IV, 3) write: 'The content of the ἐντολή is either not defined at all or not until verse 4.' It is too precarious to claim on the basis of Acts i. 2 f. that the Risen Lord gave ethical instructions. But this does not invalidate the distinction we make in the text between the Risen and the Glorified Lord in Acts.

[2] In Matthew there is no statement on the Ascension as such.

[3] John xvii. 1.

to that of Matthew. He does not mention any ascension, but only appearances of the Risen Christ, who becomes the object of worship of the Church. The resurrection would appear to be for him the glorification.[1] That the glorified one was the Risen Jesus would therefore have been central to Paul. That he called him the Lord does not mean that he was removed from the Jesus of history, with whom he is indeed identical.

(*d*) This last leads us to what should never have been questioned, namely, that the term 'Lord' stands in Paul for the historical Jesus in 1 Cor. xi. 23. The last phrase, 'you proclaim the Lord's death until he comes' in 1 Cor. xi. 26 *must* refer to the historical Jesus, and any distinction between 'the Lord' and 'the Lord Jesus' in 1 Cor. xi. 23 is unlikely. In Acts ix. 5, 13, 17, 27; xxii. 8, 19; xxvi. 15 the Risen Lord is made to refer to himself as Jesus, and 'Lord' is used of Jesus 80, 18, 103, 52 times respectively in Matthew, Mark, Luke, John. Early Christianity thought of the historical Jesus as 'Lord', and so did Paul.[2]

Paul then inherited and transmitted a tradition which has two elements, a kerygmatic and a didactic. How are these elements related in his thought? Were they sharply differentiated, as Cerfaux holds, one being conceived as from God and the other having its *point de départ* in the historical Jesus, so that there are two sources for the tradition? Or is Cullmann[3] justified in claiming that both elements issue from the Risen or Exalted Lord, who took the place of all Jewish paradosis? Cullmann makes too sharp a distinction between the Lord, as the source of all paradosis, and the historical Jesus as, at least, the source of the didactic paradosis. Cerfaux makes too rigid a distinction between the two kinds of paradosis. But he does greater justice to the texts by giving due place to the historical Jesus as an initiator of one aspect of the tradition. Jesus as Lord and Jesus as teacher were both one for Paul. He may have dwelt more in his epistles on the former, but this is not because he did not recognize the significance of the teaching of Jesus, which to him was authoritative.

And this brings us to the final point in this attempt to understand how

---

[1] It agrees with this that the resurrection of Christ is the inauguration of the New Age, not of an Age preliminary to this, see *P.R.J.*[2] pp. 285 ff.

[2] For a balanced statement, see L. Cerfaux, *Christ in the Theology of St Paul*, Eng. trans. (1959), pp. 179–89, especially pp. 187 f.

[3] On Cullmann's understanding of 'the Lord', see *The Christology of the New Testament*, Eng. trans. (1959), pp. 195 ff. Surprisingly he does not develop his understanding of the Lord as a designation of 'the tradition' in this volume.

the Apostle compares with Matthew, the possibility that for Paul the Person and the Words of Jesus had assumed the significance of a New Torah. In addition to the evidence for this supplied above, we refer to our treatment elsewhere.[1] The objections to this view have been many. But too much weight should not be accorded to the claim that, since Paul was indifferent to the life of Jesus, he was also indifferent to his moral teaching. Nor need the absence of an explicit claim that Jesus is the New Torah be taken as decisive.[2] The same motives which may have led Paul to avoid the use of the term Logos, the fear of being misunderstood by Hellenists, may have led him to avoid the description of Christ as the New Torah, which might have been misleading, in discussions with Jewish-Christian and Jewish opponents. Most serious is the objection that the concept of Christ as the New Torah contradicts Paul's radical criticism of the Law and his insistence on salvation as a free gift of grace in the epistles. The Law is there conceived of as a preliminary, provisional discipline, whose term the coming of Christ has closed.[3] Indeed does not the Law for Paul come to fulfil functions ascribed by Judaism to Satan himself?[4] Thus that Paul thought of Christ in terms of the Law is unlikely: more likely was he to view the Law in terms of Christ.

Full force must be given to these objections. But while, in ascribing to Paul the concept of Christ as the New Torah we are going outside Paul's *explicit* words or formulae, we are hardly going beyond his implicit intention, if we can judge this from his use of Jesus' words and life in his ethical exhortations, and his application to Jesus of those categories that Judaism had reserved for its highest treasure, namely, the Torah, that is, pre-existence, agency in creation, wisdom. To be 'in Christ' was for Paul to have died and risen with him in a New Exodus, and this in turn meant that he was to be ἔννομος Χριστοῦ, that is, subject to the authority of the words and Person of Christ as a pattern. The historical circumstances of Paul's ministry, set as it was in a conflict against Judaizers, has given to this aspect of his interpretation of the Christian Dispensation a secondary place, a fact further accentuated by the violence of Paul's personal engagement with the Law in Judaism not strictly as 'Law' in the

---

[1] See *P.R.J.*[2] pp. 147–76.

[2] Contrast at this point L. Cerfaux, *op. cit.* p. 274, n. 36; and W. Manson, *S.J.T.* (September 1948), 218 f.

[3] I have summarized this in an article in the *Interpreter's Dictionary of the Bible*, on 'Law in the New Testament', vol. III, pp. 95–102.

[4] G. B. Caird, *Principalities and Powers* (1956), p. 41.

sense of moral demand only but as a whole cultural or social system which had the effect of cutting him off from the fascinating Gentile world.[1] But, though Paul attacked Judaizers and avoids referring to himself or to Christians as 'disciples', at no point is he free from the constraint of Christ's example: he has as a Christian 'learnt Christ',[2] and this we may understand in a twofold way. He has learnt his words as formerly he did those of the Torah,[3] and he has become an imitator of Christ,[4] as formerly he had doubtless been an imitator of Gamaliel. The process of learning in Judaism had a twofold aspect—the learning of teaching and the imitation of a life, that of the rabbi.[5] The concept of the rabbi as living Torah and, therefore, as the object of imitation would be familiar to Paul, as it would have been to Philo,[6] who regards the Patriarchs as living the Law before it was given. When Paul refers to himself as an imitator of Christ he is doubtless thinking of Jesus as the Torah he has to copy—both in his words and deeds. A passage in Romans vi. 15 ff. suggests the formative power of the teaching of Jesus in Paul's conception of the Christian life, and reveals his understanding of this teaching in relation to grace. It reads:

What then? Are we to sin because we are not under law but under grace? By no means! Do you not know that if you yield yourselves to any one as obedient slaves, you are slaves of the one whom you obey, either of sin, which leads to death, or of obedience, which leads to righteousness? But thanks be to God, that you who were once slaves of sin *have become obedient from the heart to the standard of teaching to which you were committed*, and, having been set free from sin, have become slaves of righteousness. (RSV.)

The precise meaning of the words 'have become obedient from the heart to the standard of teaching to which you were committed...' (ὑπηκούσατε δὲ ἐκ καρδίας εἰς ὃν παρεδόθητε τύπον διδαχῆς) in Rom. vi. 17 has been

---

[1] See C. H. Dodd, *New Testament Studies* (1953), pp. 72 f. That Luther's struggle over Law and Gospel was also sociologically conditioned is noted by W. Joest, *op. cit.* p. 135, and E. Benz, *Z.R.G.* 4 (1951), 289 ff., on 'Das Paulus-Verständnis'.

[2] On the expression 'to learn Christ' (Eph. iv. 21), see W. Manson, *Jesus the Messiah* (1943), p. 54.

[3] This is implied in his use of the citations to which we have already referred.

[4] 1 Cor. xi. 1; 1 Thess. i. 6; Phil. ii. 5.

[5] See Appendix X.

[6] *T.M.* p. 94, n. 11. It is not irrelevant also to restate the fact that the Law itself has a 'personal' character for Philo: see J. Daniélou, *op. cit.* p. 217. For Judaism, see my 'Law in first-century Judaism', in the *Interpreter's Dictionary*, vol. III, pp. 89–95.

disputed. F. W. Beare's comment, however, is to be treated seriously. Taking τύπος here to mean 'a die or form or pattern, made for the purpose of giving its shape to something else—for instance, an intaglio seal...', he finds Paul to be claiming that 'the Christian Didache, when it is followed with a wholehearted obedience, imparts to our lives a specific character and pattern, moulding them into the likeness of Christ. St Paul speaks more often, it is true, of the power of the Spirit as the transforming influence in the Christian life; but it is quite wrong to imagine that he thinks of the leadings of the Spirit as a succession of formless impulses or vagrant illuminations. Here, in correlation with the call for obedience, he thinks naturally enough of the specific moral instruction in which the guiding of the Spirit is given concrete expression (Phil. iv. 8–9). For all his faith in the Spirit, the Apostle thinks of the Christian life as disciplined and ordered in keeping with clear and concrete instruction given by precept and example. Such teaching is here conceived as the die or pattern which shapes the whole of the life which yields to it, in conformity with the will of God. No antithesis with the Law or with other (non-Pauline) "forms" is implied or suggested. He is thinking simply of the Didache which belongs to the Gospel, the teaching concerning the way of life which is worthy of the Gospel of Christ, considered as a mould which gives to the new life its appropriate shape or pattern.'[1] The Christian life as Paul understood it was lived within a formative ethical tradition. This tradition is not an isolated deposit, however, but part and parcel of what Paul understands by the Christian Dispensation, and, therefore, seen, not in opposition to grace, but as a concomitant of it. At no point is Paul ἄνομος; he is always ἔννομος. To this extent Paul is at one with Matthew who also places the law of Christ in a context of the grace of Christ. This is nowhere clearer than in a section which is usually quoted in proof of the succour of Christ, but which also contains within itself the demand of Christ. 'Come to me, all who labour and are heavy-laden, and I will give you rest. Take my yoke upon you, and learn from me; for I am gentle and lowly in heart, and you will find rest for your souls. For my yoke is easy and my burden is light' (xi. 28–30). The 'yoke of Christ' stands over against the yoke of the Law. The upshot of all this is that Paul, who is usually set in antithesis to Matthew,

---

[1] *N.T.S.* v (April 1959), 206 ff., 'On the interpretation of Rom. vi. 17'. We should emphasize, as Beare does not, the role of the words of Jesus in the tradition. Beare refers to the other interpretations that have been suggested. We find his the most plausible, with the qualification mentioned.

would probably not have found the Matthaean emphasis on the 'law of Christ' either strange or uncongenial. He too knew of the same law, although the circumstances of his ministry demanded from him greater concentration on other aspects of the Gospel.[1]

We may now sum up. In the light of the above, it can be urged that Paul had access to a tradition of the words of Jesus. This he had 'received' and this he 'transmitted': to this, whenever necessary and possible, he appealed as authoritative, so that this tradition constituted for him part of the 'law of Christ'. Caution is, however, necessary in making this claim. Out of the epistles as a whole, the passages where this emerges are few and the use that the Apostle made of a catechesis derived possibly from a non-Christian Hellenistic–Jewish tradition, into which he introduced few, if any, express words of Jesus, makes it doubly clear that he did not formulate a 'Christian–rabbinic' casuistry on the basis of the words of Jesus that he had received. Whether the reason for the paucity of evidence in this matter is due to the historical fact that Paul during his ministry had to contend with 'judaizing' tendencies, as was suggested above, is uncertain. Nevertheless, it is not going too far to claim that part of the being 'in Christ' for Paul was standing under the words of Jesus. Paul, like Matthew, appealed to these as authoritative. As for Matthew, so for Paul there was a real correspondence between the Christian Dispensation and the events of the Exodus. The redemption of Israel from Egypt was the prototype of the greater redemption from sin wrought by Christ. Thus Christ for Paul also had the lineaments of a new and greater Moses. He shared with Matthew a common understanding of Christ and his words. Thus the *SM* would not have appeared to Paul as an alien importation into the faith. Like Matthew, Paul too can speak of a law of Christ, partly, at least, composed of Jesus' words.[2]

3. *Q and Crisis; Catechesis; the Pastorals*

But, turning away from Paul, can we trace the same reverence for the words of Jesus elsewhere before Matthew's time? Let us look at the two sources upon which the Sermon has drawn. The first is generally entitled Q, which, whether in written or oral form we need not decide (the distinction between these forms should not, in any case, be exaggerated in the first-century milieu), goes back probably to about A.D. 50, and stands

[1] Compare O. Cullmann, *op. cit.*
[2] See further J. R. Geiselmann on 'Die Tradition', in *Fragen der Theologi Heute* (Zürich, 1957), pp. 69–108.

for the material in the tradition which was common to Matthew and Luke. It is not difficult to find what appear to be obvious reasons for its preservation, either orally or in written form. Christians would naturally be eager to recall what Jesus had done and said, because he had become the Lord for them. The same words they would also naturally want to use for hortatory purposes in the Church, at baptism and in sermons. Moreover, in its confrontation with Judaism the Church would have found the impressive ethical teaching of Jesus a powerful weapon, as it was also for apologetic purposes in dealing with those elements in the Gentile world which were casting about for a moral and spiritual basis for society. It is when we inquire further as to what specific factors determined the process, and in what varying degrees, that caution is required.

T. W. Manson[1] regarded as the chief factor the first mentioned above, namely, the need of imparting to Christians a knowledge, not only of the life of Jesus, but also of his words as 'the standard and norm of Christian behaviour'. In this he was preceded by Harnack,[2] and recent form-critics have reinforced his contention. Dibelius[3] pointed out how in various epistles of the New Testament (Rom. xii. 13; Gal. v. 13 ff.; vi. 1 ff.; Col. iii. 4; 1 Thess. iv. 1 ff.; v. 1 ff.; James) in hortatory sections the words of Jesus seem to constitute a source of direct moral guidance. As we saw above, these words are sometimes specifically cited as such, while at other times they appear without differentiation along with other hortatory material. There can be no question that before the time of Paul words of Jesus were used as hortatory and regulatory material. So too in Q, although he is constrained to recognize that there is a Christological motive active in its preservation, Dibelius urges that the interest is centred in the teaching of Jesus, not in the narrative, and that this teaching was 'originally gathered together for a hortatory end'.[4] Taylor[5] equally emphatically regards Q as a catechetical document: he defines it as 'an innovation prompted by the needs of catechetical instruction'. 'The times demanded', he writes, 'a compend of the Lord's oracles, similar in form to the wise sayings of the Book of Proverbs. Such a collection could take its rise only out of that which already existed and it was compiled from Pronouncement stories, sayings-groups and words of Jesus in free circulation.' According to Harnack, T. W. Manson,

---

[1] *The Sayings of Jesus* (London, 1949), p. 11.
[2] *The Sayings of Jesus*, Eng. trans. pp. 168, 229.
[3] *From Tradition to Gospel*, Eng. trans. (1934), pp. 238 ff.; see *P.R.J.*[2] pp. 136 ff.
[4] *Op. cit.* pp. 243 ff.
[5] *The Formation of the Gospel Tradition* (London, 1935), p. 182.

Dibelius and Taylor, then, it was primarily as a quarry for direct moral guidance for catechetical and similar hortatory purposes that the ethical and other teaching in Q was preserved. And, both in the light of historical probability and of the express witness of the Pauline and other epistles, we need not cavil at the thought that catechetical and hortatory factors entered into the preservation of ethical teaching in Q as elsewhere. Exhortation breaks through expressly in Q at Luke xi. 35; xii. 40; xiv. 35. But before we agree that the early Church first preserved the teaching of Jesus because it discovered its hortatory and catechetical value, or, to put it in other words, because it was useful for the moral instruction of converts, so that its significance is primarily, if not wholly, utilitarian, certain facts have to be pondered. These are:

(i) Form-critics have isolated in the Gospel tradition certain short units or pericopae variously called *Apophthegmata* (Bultmann), Paradeigmata (Dibelius) and, more illuminatingly, Pronouncement-Stories (Taylor), which were useful for preaching purposes in that they supplied answers to difficulties which confronted the early Church.[1] These Pronouncement-Stories were eminently hortatory, so that if Q was intended to be such, we should expect it to contain a fair sprinkling of such stories. But out of all the pronouncement-stories listed by Dibelius, Bultmann and Taylor, only 4 or 5 are found in Q. The total number listed by the first scholar mentioned was 46 and by the last 44. One of the Pronouncement-Stories which is ascribed to Q, that of the Centurion's Servant (Luke vii. 2–10; Matt. viii. 5–13) is rejected by Taylor[2] and regarded by him as merely a story about Jesus. To claim that Q was intended as a sayings-source, as does Albertz,[3] and therefore naturally avoided narratives, is not convincing, because, as Dibelius and Taylor are compelled to admit in the light of the treatment of the Baptist and of the Temptation in it and of its Christological interest, it is not strictly correct to treat Q as a 'mere' sayings-source. Moreover, Taylor's[4] insistence, in explanation of the paucity of pronouncement stories and other factors in Q, that it was not a static entity throughout its history, but, on the contrary, a growing one, which began as a sayings-source pure and simple, but gradually took to itself pronouncement-stories and other elements, makes the comparative absence of such stories still more surprising. In a source designed to be exhortatory and catechetical, we should expect hortatory stories.

[1] See V. Taylor, *op. cit.* for a useful introduction.   [2] *Op. cit.* pp. 75 f.
[3] *Die synoptische Streitsgespräche* (1921), *ad rem.*
[4] *Op. cit.* pp. 182 ff.

(ii) An examination of those passages to which Dibelius[1] appeals in maintaining the hortatory character of Q and other sayings of Jesus does not substantiate his claim in the case of Q. In the first place, most of the passages to which he refers do not belong to Q. This is true of Matt. vi. 2; v. 29; xviii. 1; v. 16 (this is the only directly hortatory verse in the complex v. 13–16); xxi. 11–19; Luke xvi. 1; xiv. 7–11; xii. 57. All these belong either to M or L (Mark ix. 43 ff. is not pertinent to a discussion of Q). Thus, in the second place, we are left with Matt. v. 44 ff. (=Luke vi. 27 ff.); vi. 25 ff. (=Luke xii. 22 ff.), the former concerned with the imitation of the love of God, the latter with freedom from anxiety. In a very generalized sense, it is permissible to classify these two passages as exhortation, but it will also be readily agreed that their content is so exalted that their meaning, no less than their form, does not suggest the pedestrian purposes we usually associate with catechetical instruction and exhortation, or of the kind of prudential maxims we find in the book of Proverbs. But, in the third place, Dibelius[2] treats the story of John the Baptist as hortatory: its intention is to urge Christians to avoid the Baptist sect. But there is hardly polemic against that sect in Q. Commenting on Luke iii. 16, T. W. Manson writes: 'The original Q form...had no reference to the Spirit. It ran "He will baptize you with fire". So long as the Holy Spirit is retained John's words are a promise: my baptism is a prelude to a better. When the reference to the Spirit is dropped the true nature of the saying is apparent....The sense of the saying is not that John's baptism is the preliminary to something better; but that it is the last chance of escaping something very much worse, namely, the coming of judgement.'[3] Q was not concerned with polemic against John's followers but with the crisis which he announced to be impending. Similarly, there is a striking absence in Q of conflict stories, illustrating the confrontation of Judaism and Christianity. Again, Dibelius's[4] very improbable interpretation of the Matthaean Beatitudes as hortatory need not concern us because he accepts the Lucan form as original, that is, as from that nearest to that which they assumed in Q, and apparently does not regard the original Beatitudes in this light. In the fourth place, it is remarkable that only one of the parables to which Dibelius refers as having a hortatory influence, comes from Q, and it is quite clear that in its Q form the eschatological rather than the ethical interest predominated (Luke xix. 12–27 = Matt. xxv.

---

[1] *From Tradition to Gospel*, pp. 233 ff.
[2] *Op. cit.* p. 244, also *Die Urchristliche Überlieferung v. Joh. d. Täufer*, pp. 13 ff.
[3] *Op. cit.* p. 41.   [4] *Op. cit.* p. 247.

14–20). Jeremias[1] has brilliantly illustrated how parables were pressed into the service of catechesis and exhortation: but Q itself does not much reveal this process.

(iii) Taylor, like Harnack before him, found in Q a catechetical document. If this was the case, then we should be able to assume that much of the tradition of the words of Jesus has come down to us along catechetical channels, and that the formulary marks of those channels should be discoverable in Q. Fortunately, we can put this assumption to the test. In addition to the works of Seeberg[2] and Klein,[3] which were largely ignored until fairly recently, we now have those of Carrington[4] and Selwyn.[5] These have isolated much of the catechetical material which has found its way into the New Testament. They have both, Selwyn perhaps especially, probably too much systematized what was often fluid and amorphous, but their data do at least reveal clearly what the main body of that teaching was which was transmitted through the medium of catechesis. A comparison of these data with the material in Q should, therefore, help to determine whether Q is best understood in catechetical terms or not. And, since it is his that presents the catechetical material most fully and conveniently, we shall use Selwyn's treatment as the basis of a comparison of New Testament catechesis with Q.

First, as to the substance of the catechetical material: does it reveal a marked identity with what is found in Q? Selwyn tabulates his data as follows:

Table 1. Traces of a first baptismal catechism (B[1]) *based on a Christian Holiness Code*

Mostly found in 1 Thess. iv. 1–v. 15; 1 Pet. i. 2, 13–16, 22; ii. 11 f.; iii. 10–12; iv. 2, but with echoes in Acts xv. 29; Rom. xii. 2, 9, 17, 19; xiii. 9, 13; 1 Cor. iii. 16 f.; iv. 5; v. 9 f.; vi. 9 f.; Gal. v. 14; Col. iii. 5–7; Eph. iv. 17–19; v. 5; Jas. ii. 8; iii. 13.

In all this material we find no parallel to anything in Q. If the latter were hortatory or catechetical in intention, it would presumably almost certainly recall material such as is found, for example, in 1 Thess. iv. 1 ff.

---

[1] *The Parables of Jesus*, Eng. trans. (1954).
[2] A. Seeberg, *Der Katechismus der Urchristenheit* (1903).
[3] *Der älteste christliche Katechismus* (Berlin, 1909).
[4] *The Primitive Christian Catechism* (Cambridge, 1940).
[5] *The Epistle of St Peter* (London, 1946). See especially pp. 363–488, which include D. Daube's essay on 'Participle and Imperative in 1 Peter'.

Table 11. *Further catechetical material: the children of light*

1 Thess. v. 1–9, 17; 1 Pet. i. 1, 13, 14; ii. 8, 9, 12; iv. 1–3, 7; Acts i. 7; xx. 28; xxvi. 18; Rom. xiii. 11–14; xvi. 15; 1 Cor. xvi. 3; Phil. ii. 15; Col. i. 13; iv. 2, 3, 5; Eph. i. 14; v. 8, 18; vi. 14, 18; Heb. vi. 4; Jas. v. 8; Rev. iii. 2.

In the whole of this material Selwyn finds parallels to Q only in three places:

(i) Mark xiii. 32 (compare Acts i. 7). 'But of that day or that hour no one knows, not even the angels in heaven, nor the Son, but only the Father.' Selwyn assumes that this is from Q as well as in Mark, but it is not found in Luke, and, as Streeter[1] and Taylor[2] have urged, it is best not to regard the verse as derived from Q: its omission from Luke on this assumption is difficult to account for.

(ii) Luke xii. 39 (compare xxiv. 43. Selwyn draws attention to this). 'But know this, that if the householder had known at what hour the thief was coming, he would have been awake and would not have left his house to be broken into.' There is almost an exact parallel in Matt. xxiv. 43. The verse deals with the necessity to be prepared for a sudden crisis.

(iii) Luke xxi. 34 (compare Luke xii. 45; Mark iv. 19; 1 Thess. v. 6–7). 'But take heed to yourselves lest your hearts be weighed down with dissipation and drunkenness and cares of this life, and that day come upon you suddenly like a snare.' This verse, however, is not universally accepted as from Q. Selwyn[3] refers to Hawkins,[4] who, however, only takes the Q origin of xxi. 34–6 as conjectural. Creed[5] would favour, apparently, ascribing the complex to L. There are no parallels to it in Mark or Matthew. As the vocabulary of the complex reveals, we have here a late composition, although based on early material. It is certainly precarious to take this warning against unpreparedness as a part of Q.

Of the above three passages therefore, to which Selwyn refers, only the second can be seriously contemplated as from Q. Moreover, the sense in which we can claim even this for the catechetical tradition and for Q must be carefully assessed. Luke makes the passage refer to the apostles themselves, that is, the responsible leaders of the community (xii. 41); Matthew applies it to the disciples. Any catechetical reference in the strict sense, therefore, that is, to new adherents to or beginners in the faith, is

[1] *The Four Gospels, ad rem.*
[2] *The Gospel According to St Mark, ad rem.*
[3] *Op. cit.* p. 456, n. 1. He cites *Oxford Studies*, ed. W. Sanday (1911), p. 135 n.
[4] In *Oxford Studies*, p. 135. [5] *St Luke's Gospel, in loc.*

excluded. Again, it occurs in Matthew in a different context, in xxiv. 43–51, but with the same force. It probably, therefore, suggests a floating tradition, which illustrates the process whereby the early Church applied the parables of Jesus to its own situation as it awaited the Parousia, and presupposes a considerable history of transmission. Thus it is tempting to regard Luke xii. 39 f. as belonging to a secondary stage in the history of Q rather than to its fundament, as it were. Noteworthy in any case is it that the passage deals not with ethical questions as such but with a situation of crisis.

Table III (does not directly concern us).

Table IV (*Further catechetical material: baptism*—its basis in the Word, Truth, Gospel).

Table v. *Baptism: its nature described.* These two tables IV, v are best taken together. The passages concerned are:

1 Pet. i. 3, 14, 22, 23, 25; ii. 1, 2; Rom. vi. 4–7, 17; Col. i. 5 f.; iii. 1–3, 8, 10, 16; Jas. i. 18, 21; Eph. i. 13; ii. 15; iv. 22–4; John iii. 5 f.; vii. 17; 1 Thess. i. 5 f., 8; ii. 10–12; Gal. vi. 15; 2 Cor. v. 17; Tit. iii. 5; Mark x. 15.

To all these passages no parallel is offered from Q, although, in his discussion of them, Selwyn points out their relation to certain words of Christ. Thus the metaphors of 'rebirth' and 'bringing forth' or 'bearing' were suggested by the position of Christians as (1) like new-born children, (2) as the firstfruits of a harvest springing up from the sowing of the Word. 'These two aspects of conversion, which are traceable to the *verba Christi*, give rise respectively to the more developed ideas of regeneration and of new creation found in 1 Peter and St Paul respectively.'[1] Selwyn probably has in mind here such passages as the following:

Luke xvi. 8:

The master commended the dishonest steward for his prudence; for the sons of this world are wiser in their own generation than *the sons of light*.

Matt. xviii. 3:

Truly, I say to you, unless you turn and become like children, you will never enter the kingdom of heaven.

Matt. xix. 14:

Let the children come to me, and do not hinder them; for to such belongs the kingdom of heaven.

[1] *Op. cit.* p. 392.

Matt. xix. 28:

Truly, I say to you, in the new world, when the Son of Man shall sit on his glorious throne. . . .

But the first of these passages is from L and the other two are not from Q. Similarly teaching concerning Christians as the children of light which Selwyn[1] traces to *verba Christi* can only be connected with Matt. v. 14 ff. (in addition to Luke xvi. 8), which is from M, at least chiefly so.

Table VI. *The New Life: its negative implications or renunciations*

1 Pet. ii. 1, 2; iv. 1; Jas. i. 21; Rom. xiii. 12, 14; Col. iii. 5, 7, 8, 9, 10, 12; Eph. iv. 17–19, 22, 24, 25, 26, 29, 31, 32; 1 John ii. 15; Heb. xii. 1; 1 Thess. v. 8; Gal. iii. 27.

Again in his tables Selwyn notes no parallel to Q, although to the warning against revelry, intemperance and sensuality he finds a parallel in Matt. xxiv. 49 and Luke xxi. 34. These are legitimate parallels but they are not sufficiently cogent or extensive to suggest direct dependence. Moreover, the Lucan passage xxi. 34 is only doubtfully from Q.

Table VII. *The New Life: its faith and worship*

1 Pet. i. 14, 17; ii. 4, 9; Jas. i. 27; Rom. xii. 1, 2; Col. iii. 16, 17; Eph. v. 17–20; John iv. 23 f.; Heb. xiii. 15–16; Phil. ii. 10, 11; 1 Cor. iii. 16 f.; 2 Cor. vi. 16 f.; 1 Thess. v. 16–18, 20.

No parallel to Q material is offered here.

Table VIII (*a*). *Catechumen virtues: Love's Sincerity*

1 Thess. iv. 1–12; v. 12–22; Gal. v. 14; Jas. ii. 8; v. 7 f.; Heb. x. 30; Eph. iv. 26; Rom. xii. 1–20; xiii. 7–10; 1 Pet. i. 11; ii. 3, 4, 16; iii. 8 f., 11 f.; iv. 8–11, 13, 14.

As containing parallels to this material from the Synoptics, Selwyn refers to Mark xii. 31 (= Matt. xxii. 39; Luke xx. 27); Matt. xix. 18 f. which has partial parallels in Mark x. 19; Luke xviii. 20; Matt. xxii. 39 f. All these passages refer to Lev. xix. 18, but cannot be regarded as Q. The parallels to them in the catechetical material are due not to the direct dependence of the latter on *verba Christi*. They merely reveal that the primitive Church used material based on the Law of Holiness in Lev. xvii–xxvi, which was marked by special emphasis on Lev. xix. 18 as the highest expression of holiness. There is in Table VIII (*a*), therefore, little if any connexion with

[1] *Op. cit.* p. 393.

material from Q. Again, according to Selwyn,[1] Rom. xiii. 8–10 is almost a conflation of two words of Jesus, which interpreted the Jewish Law, but it is difficult to agree. The phrases in question in these verses suggest not so much direct dependence on words of Jesus as a tradition of catechesis possibly instigated by a word of Jesus which was not peculiar to Q. So is it also in Table VIII (b): *Catechumen Virtues: Another Version.*

Table VIII (c). *Teaching on Church Unity and Order*

The main passages are: 1 Thess. v. 12 f.; 1 Tim. v. 17; Heb. xii. 9; xiii. 17; Jas. iv. 6, 7, 10; Rom. xii. 3–8; 1 Pet. i. 12; iv. 8–11; v. 1, 2, 5; Col. iii. 14 f.; Eph. iv. 1–4, 7 f., 11 f.

To these Selwyn offers no parallel from Q. He is constrained to point out that Paul handles his traditional materials with greater freedom than 1 Peter, 'importing distinctive metaphors of his own and impressing his marked personality upon the earlier forms which he uses'.[2] But to judge from 1 Cor. vii this would hardly have been the case had he regarded those materials and forms as *verba Christi*. That the catechetical material can be so freely manipulated implies that it was hardly of dominical origin in the main.

Table x. *A Code of Subordination.* This and Table IX are not pertinent.

Table XI. *A Code on Civil Obedience*

To the former belong the following: 1 Pet. ii. 13–17, 18–25; iii. 1–8; v. 5 f.; Rom. xiii. 1, 7; Col. iii. 12, 18, 19–21, 22–5; iv. 1; Eph. v. 22–33; vi. 1–9; 1 Tim. ii. 1–15; vi. 1 f.; Tit. ii. 4–6, 9 f.; iii. 1; Jas. iv. 6–10; Heb. xii. 9; xiii. 7 and to the latter 1 Pet. ii. 13–17; Rom. xiii. 1–7; 1 Tim. ii. 1–3, 8; Tit. iii. 1–3, 8.

It is noteworthy that in the sections from 1 Peter the obedience of slaves to masters is buttressed not by reference to *verba Christi* but to the *imitatio Christi*, while the obedience of wives to husbands is based on Prov. iii. 25 and other quotations from the Old Testament, for example Prov. xxxi. 10 ff., 39; Gen. xii. The issue of obedience to the civil authority had arisen during the lifetime of Jesus and had called forth notable pronouncements by him, in Mark xii. 13–17 (see also Matt. xvii. 24–7), yet no appeal is made to this section even when the catechesis explicitly deals with its theme. Similarly the words used by 1 Pet. ii. 13 can hardly be made to refer to a *verbum Christi* and the particular verse[3] to which

---

[1] *Op. cit.* pp. 410, 414.   [2] *Op. cit.* p. 419.

[3] *Op. cit.* p. 428. It is difficult to know precisely to which word of Jesus Selwyn here refers; presumably it is to Mark xii. 13–17, but this is not Q.

Selwyn appeals is certainly not from Q. So too the *verbum Christi* in Matt. v. 14–16, to which Selwyn refers the motif that Christian obedience should be practised in order to create a favourable impression on pagan society, is not from Q but from M in the main; v. 15 alone is from Q in this complex.[1]

Table XII. *A Code on Slaves and Masters.* This appears from 1 Pet. ii. 18–25; Col. iii. 22–iv. 1; Eph. vi. 5–9; 1 Tim. vi. 1–2; Tit. ii. 9 f., where again, in sections dealing with the need for meekness and submission under injury, there is no appeal to *verba Christi*, but only to *imitatio Christi*. Apart from what must, however, be conceded to be a vague parallel between 1 Pet. ii. 19 and Luke vi. 32–4, no parallel to Q in Selwyn's judgement occurs; and he surely goes too far in trying to connect the emphasis on the duties of slaves in 1 Pet. ii. 18–25 with words of Christ.[2]

Table XIII. *A Code on Wives and Husbands.* The material is found in 1 Pet. iii. 1–7; Col. iii. 18, 19; Eph. v. 22–33; 1 Tim. ii. 9–15; Tit. ii. 4 f., but there is no suggestion of any dependence on Q. (In an added section on pp. 435–7 Selwyn suggests that a *verbum Christi* not Q may be behind regulations dealing with parents and children, order among members of the community.)

The conclusion seems inevitable that in dealing with the Code of Subordination we are dealing with essentially a Christian version of a code or codes previously in circulation. But the specifically Christian manipulation of such codes is not particularly marked by any large dependence on Q. Selwyn's words that the teaching has kept close to the *verba Christi* are hard to accept.

Before proceeding to the next group of materials it is well to note our conclusion on the Tables last dealt with, that is, XI, XII, XIII—'The Subordination Codes'. Any specifically Q material in all these is hard to find and the same applies to the previous groups of material studied. We must, therefore, reject Selwyn's view that the catechetical material so far isolated has kept close to words of Jesus. Is it different with the next Table?

Table XIV. *Teaching Called out by Crisis: Traces of a Persecution-Form.* The material under this heading is the most extensive so far treated: it occurs in the following:

1 Thess. i. 6; ii. 4, 14; iii. 2–5; v. 1–3, 4–11, 17–19; iii. 8; 2 Thess. i. 4–7, 10; ii. 15; 1 Pet. i. 6–7, 10–11, 13, 21; ii. 4–5, 8–9, 12, 20–1, 24; iii. 14–15; iv. 3, 5, 7, 12–13,

[1] *Op. cit.* p. 431.   [2] *Op. cit.* pp. 439 ff.

17–19; v. 4, 8–10, 12; Acts i. 7; v. 41; xiv. 22; xx. 28; 1 Cor. i. 7–9; iii. 13; vii. 29; xvi. 13; 2 Cor. viii. 2; Heb. x. 23, 30, 32–3; Jas. i. 2–3, 12; iv. 7; v. 8; Rom. ii. 5–11; v. 2, 3–4; xiii. 11, 13–14; Phil. i. 27–9; iv. 1; 2 Pet. iii. 10; Rev. xvi. 15; Col. iv. 2–3, 12; Eph. i. 14; vi. 14 ff.

Parallels to the above material are found according to Selwyn in the following passages from Q [*P*=possibly from Q]: (1) Matt. v. 10–12 (=Luke vi. 22); (2) Luke xx. 35; (3) Luke vi. 32 f.; (4) Luke xxii. 28; (5) Mark xiii. 13 (*P*); (6) Matt. xiii. 7 (*P*); (7) Mark xiii. 11 (*P*); (8) Matt. x. 28 (=Luke xii. 45); (9) Mark xiii. 32 f. (*P*); (10) Luke xii. 39–40 (compare Matt. xxiv. 43 f.) (*P*); (11) Luke xxi. 34 (*P*); (12) Mark xiii. 8 (=Matt. xxiv. 8) (*P*); (13) Matt. x. 32 f. (=Luke xii. 8, 9) (*P*); (14) Luke xxi. 36 (=Matt. vi. 13) (*P*); (15) Luke xii. 35 (*P*); (16) Mark xiii. 33, 35–7 (*P*); (17) Matt. xxv. 13 (*P*). (There are also parallels to Synoptic material from Matt. x. 25; Luke xvii. 7; Mark xiii. 27; viii. 38.)

Not all the above items can be accepted as Q material, however. Thus (2) (Luke xx. 35) is only doubtfully pertinent. While the substance of the passage from which it comes is found in Mark and Matthew, the specific phrase to which Selwyn refers, that is, οἱ δὲ καταξιωθέντες τοῦ αἰῶνος ἐκείνου, 'but those who are accounted worthy to attain to that age' is peculiar to Luke. So (4) (Luke xxii. 28) cannot certainly be regarded as Q. It may be L. The parallel in Matt. xix. 28 is only partial. Moreover, most of the items in (5) to (17) are placed by Selwyn only as probably from Q. There is inevitably here a considerable measure of uncertainty. (Passages marked by *P* above, indicating those that are only possibly from Q, are numerous.) Selwyn,[1] however, has found in the material isolated in Table xiv what he regards as a 'persecution code' formulated by teachers and prophets in the early Church, in times of persecution when Christians especially needed exhortation and support. This exhortation was closely intertwined, as we might expect, with the eschatological hope, as appears both in 1 Peter and in 1, 2 Thessalonians. The inevitability of persecution was a regular part of the Apostolic teaching from the beginning and a pattern for this existed which was largely based on *verba Christi*. Selwyn claims that 'the references to the "eschatological discourse" recorded in Mark xiii, Matt. xxiv, Luke xxi, and to similar passages in the *SM*, in Matt. x and Luke xii show how closely the primitive teaching stuck to the *verba Christi* and particularly to the *verba Christi* as they stood in Q'.[2] We may certainly agree with Selwyn that it is in this section that

[1] *Op. cit.* p. 451.
[2] We have been able to extricate from Selwyn's treatment the following passages

the catechetical material draws closest to the Synoptic tradition of the words of Jesus, but in the light of the evidence it is doubtful if we should be too confident that even here it can be specifically connected with Q. In any case, apart from Table XIV there is very little to suggest that the catechesis of primitive Christianity drew to any considerable extent on Q. Certainly this was not the main substance of catechetical instruction.

At this point it is not irrelevant to turn to documents of a later date than the catechesis we have so far dealt with. In the Pastoral Epistles, which are paraenetic in character, we should expect an appeal to the words of Jesus, had these been especially transmitted along catechetical and hortatory channels. But, in fact, the only echoes of the Synoptics in 1, 2 Timothy, and Titus, are the three following:

(*a*) 1 Tim. i. 15:

The saying is sure and worthy of full acceptance, that Christ Jesus came into the world to save sinners.

This recalls Mark ii. 17; the words of Jesus there recorded may have become a kind of watchword in the early Church.

where he finds parallels, of a catechetical kind, to the *SM* itself. They are not to be regarded as exhaustive:

Epistles	Synoptics
1 Pet. ii. 12	Matt. v. 14–16 (see Selwyn, *op. cit.* pp. 97 f.)
1 Tim. ii. 13	Matt. v. 14–16
Tit. iii. 8	Matt. v. 14–16
Col. iii. 8–15	A good *summary* of much in the Sermon (see Selwyn, *op. cit.* pp. 410–11)
Col. iii. 12	Matt. v. 3, 5, 7
Col. iii. 13	Matt. vi. 12
Col. iii. 14	Matt. v. 6, 9, 48
1 Thess. v (see Selwyn, *op. cit.* p. 379)	Matt. v. 14
1 Thess. iv. 7	Matt. v. 43
1 Pet. i. 15 ff.	Matt. v. 43
1 Pet. ii. 12	Matt. v. 16 (Selwyn, *op. cit.* p. 373)
1 Pet. iv. 3	Matt. vi. 34
1 Pet. iii. 15	Matt. v. 10
1 Pet. iii. 11	Matt. v. 9
1 Pet. iii. 9 f.	Matt. v. 44
1 Pet. ii. 20	Matt. v. 39
1 Pet. iii. 19 (Selwyn, *op. cit.* p. 176)	Matt. v. 43–8
1 Pet. v. 19, 20	Luke vi. 32–5

(*b*) 1 Tim. ii. 6:

Jesus Christ, who gave Himself as a ransom for all . . . .

Compare Mark x. 45.

(*c*) 1 Tim. v. 18:

The labourer deserves his wages.

Compare Luke x. 7.

The reference in 1 Tim. vi. 3 to 'the sound words (λόγοις) of our Lord Jesus Christ' cannot be to the explicit words of Jesus as such: the term 'words' here has the meaning of 'truths'. Similarly the reference to the commandment in 1 Tim. vi. 14 ('I charge you to keep the commandment (ἐντολήν) unstained . . .') is not to a word of Jesus: it either looks back to the whole content of 1 Tim. vi. 11–12 or, possibly, to the 'commandment' given at baptism. Baptism would be normally accompanied by a charge to live according to the commandments, as in Hippolytus, *Treatise on the Apostolic Tradition*, XXXII, 12 we read, at the close of the baptismal ceremony: 'And when these things are completed, let each one hasten to do good works, and to please God and to live aright, devoting himself to the church, practising the things he has learned, advancing in the service of God.' It has been plausibly claimed that 1 Pet. i. 3–iv. 11 was written to supply a baptismal exhortation. But it is striking that in such baptismal contexts there is no direct appeal to words of Jesus.[1]

Even more striking is it that there is no such appeal in contexts which clearly invite a reference to the Synoptic tradition of the teaching of Jesus. In 1 Tim. iv. 4 f. (compare Tit. i. 15: 'To the pure all things are pure, but to the corrupt and unbelieving nothing is pure; their very minds and consciences are corrupted'), a reference might be expected to Mark vii, but there is none. Similarly 1 Tim. ii. 1 ff., which deals with prayer for 'the ruling powers', omits any appeal to the well-known discussion of the things that belong to Caesar in Mark xii. 13–17 (and parallels), while in 1 Tim. ii. 8 ff. a reference to the Lord's Prayer, which might have been expected, is missing. 2 Tim. iv. 17 might have recalled such passages as Luke xxi. 15, and Mark xiii. 9–10, but shows no indication of having done so. The problem dealt with in 2 Tim. ii. 14–26, that is, the treatment of unworthy members in the Church, which had

---

[1] See F. L. Cross, *1 Peter: A Paschal Liturgy* (London, 1954). The association of commandments with baptism in early Christianity continues the tradition in Judaism, if Christian baptism is to be directly connected with proselyte baptism.

elsewhere been explicitly dealt with in terms of the Parable of the Tares and of the Dragnet in Matt. xiii. 24–30, 36–43, 49–50, reveals no side-glance towards these, although the position of tolerance urged in them is precisely that maintained in the Pastorals (2 Tim. ii. 24—6 'The Lord's servant must not be quarrelsome but kindly to every one, an apt teacher, forbearing, correcting his opponents with gentleness. God may perhaps grant that they will repent and come to know the truth, and they may escape from the snare of the devil...'). When we turn to Titus the same phenomenon meets us. Even passages which recall the words of Jesus do not directly appeal to them, for example Tit. i. 15, which might suggest Mark vii, and Tit. ii. 12, which might look back to Mark x. 45.

Moreover, another fact points in the same direction. One of the marks of Pauline paraenesis was that, by the addition of the phrase 'in Christ' or 'in the Lord' its content was Christianized, even when there was no direct appeal to the words of Jesus as such. Pauline paraenesis has, there-fore, an unmistakable Christocentric reference. In the Pastorals, how-ever, the ethical material employed is not thus Christified by the addition of any formula, but is presented neat. The result is that the ethical commonplaces of the Hellenistic world emerge in the Pastorals without any attempt being made to give them any specifically Christian orienta-tion. This it is that has led to the view that the 'Christian' ethic in the Pastorals is domesticated and 'bourgeois' in character.[1] The 'good conscience'—a phrase never used by Paul and described by Albert Schweitzer as 'an invention of the devil'—has become in the Pastorals a mark of the Christian man, who has found 'the world' a comparatively soft pillow. The absolute demand of Jesus is here replaced by the request for 'decency'. Thus, although in 1 Tim. i. 5 the author declares that 'the aim of our charge is love...', in fact, 'love' does not play a central part in the Pastorals, rather the more 'pedestrian' virtues of sobriety, serious-ness, temperance are praised. And, in any case, it is noteworthy that in 1 Tim. i. 5 the love desiderated is described not in terms of him who loved us and gave himself for us but of a 'pure heart, a good conscience and sincere faith'. And, while it is possible to exaggerate the extent to which the Pastorals present a 'domesticated' ethic, because the Christian motives for obedience constantly emerge,[2] it is true that the paraenesis they

[1] See my article on 'Conscience' in *The Interpreter's Dictionary*.

[2] See, for example, B. S. Easton, *The Pastoral Epistles* (1948), p. 98. For 'con-science' in the Pastorals, see M. Dibelius, *Die Pastoralbriefe*, II (1931), 11–12; C. Spicq, 'La Conscience dans le N.T.', in *R.B.* XLVII (1938), 50–80; *Les Épîtres Pastorales* (1947), pp. 29–38.

present lacks the penetrating radicalism which we connect with the words of Jesus. The Pastorals, therefore, confirm that it is unlikely that those words are to be especially connected with the paraenetic and catechetical tradition of the early Church.

Secondly, what can we learn from the structure of primitive Christian catechism? Can it be claimed that the structure of Q, as we can rediscover it, reveals a catechetical intent?

The outcome of our discussion so far is to render it questionable whether Q was primarily preserved because of its hortatory and catechetical value and to reveal that little of the teaching preserved in it was originally transmitted along hortatory lines or catechetical channels. Without entering into details in a field where the ground is well trodden, we may note that for the purposes indicated by these two terms the Church largely drew upon the paraenetic resources of Judaism which had much in common with those of the Graeco-Roman world. The view of Dibelius, T. W. Manson and Taylor that it was paraenesis and catechesis that chiefly influenced the preservation and collection of Q cannot be endorsed. Some factor or factors other than these must be given priority.[1]

Perhaps a clue to this may be found in one fact which has emerged in our comparison of Q and the catechesis. At one point only was there any marked parallelism noted between these two elements: the note of crisis sounded in both. Selwyn carefully distinguishes between the kind of crisis against which warning is given in Q, which centred in the imminence of the Parousia, and the mainly ethical provenance of the admonitions in the catechesis. But the necessity for this distinction—which, however, should not always be too rigidly pressed—is itself significant: it suggests

---

[1] Wibbing, *Die Tugend- und Lasterkataloge im Neuen Testament*, has attempted to deal with the lists of vices and virtues in the NT and in doing so gives a very useful survey of catechetical studies on the NT. It is, however, a serious weakness of his treatment that he does not relate his understanding of the lists to Carrington's work, which was not available to him. It is interesting to note that Selwyn despite his claim that '*verba Christi* lie just below the surface of (1 Peter)', nevertheless is uneasy as to why '1 Peter, despite his partiality for *verba Christi*, so often drives home a point by quoting from the Old Testament when a word of the Lord would have seemed more telling'. The answer he supplies is that 'the OT passage was already linked in Jewish tradition with the injunctions he was making, and was therefore more familiar to those Christians who had been accustomed to the Synagogue' (pp. 366–7). Is it not simpler to admit that the words of Jesus most often fulfilled another purpose than exhortation and catechesis?

that the distinctiveness of Q resides not chiefly in any hortatory or catechetical character which it may possess but in its 'crisis' significance, a crisis which, as we will argue, is to be understood Christologically.

But this view of Q at once encounters the difficulty raised by Bultmann, who has claimed that much of the material in Q is derived for purposes of edification, exhortation and catechesis from the contemporary wisdom. He therefore regards Q as not exclusively a collection of *Herrenworte* but as a combination of these with late Judaistic sayings, rules and predictions. The Church quite consciously drew upon these last, and at first used them with full awareness that they were not *Herrenworte*. The process by which such sayings, etc., came to be taken as such was a simple one. Bultmann notes how naturally a sentence such as 'love covers a multitude of sins' (1 Pet. iv. 8) came to be quoted as a word of the Lord. Clearly, if Bultmann is to be followed, much of the material in Q cannot have a crisis significance rooted in the coming of Jesus, but must be regarded as in the nature of general wisdom.[1]

The following are the passages from Q which Bultmann[2] regards as 'profane-proverbs' (*profanen Meschalim*) which were introduced into the tradition as words of Jesus:

Luke xii. 2 f. (=Matt. x. 26); ix. 58 (=Matt. viii. 20); xiv. 34 f. (=Matt. v. 13). Luke xi. 33 (=Matt. v. 15); xi. 23 (=Matt. xii. 30); vi. 39 (=Matt. xv. 14). Luke vi. 40 (=Matt. x. 24); xvii. 37 b (=Matt. xxiv. 28); xii. 25 (=Matt. vi. 27). Luke vi. 30 (=Matt. v. 1); x. 16b (=Matt. x. 10b); vi. 31 (=Matt. vii. 21). Luke xviii. 14 (=Matt. xxiii. 12); xix. 26 (=Matt. xxv. 39).

The relation between the ethical teaching in the Gospels and Jesus Himself we shall discuss in the next chapter. Here let it merely be claimed that, however much reminiscent of the profane wisdom of the period, the sayings which Bultmann here traces[3] to the creativity, born out of catechetical and paraenetic necessities, of the primitive Christian community, at least equally well fit into the setting of Jesus' own ministry. The passages which Bultmann regards as having been generalized wisdom sayings were probably applied by Jesus to illuminate the crisis constituted by his coming. They are indeed in most cases precisely what we might expect on the lips of Jesus, this whatever their original derivation (and, of course, it is not to be ruled out that Jesus' own words naturally often reflected sayings that had previously been current). The reader is referred

---

[1] For Bultmann's understanding of Q, see *op. cit.* pp. 194 ff.   [2] *Op. cit.*
[3] See the discussion in W. Manson, *Jesus the Messiah*, pp. 56 ff.

to the extended footnote[1] for a defence of this understanding of the passages concerned. Moreover, an examination of all the material in Q, as far as we can reconstruct it or in so far as it is preserved, reveals that it brings into prominence two things, that the coming of Jesus was a crisis of the old order and the inauguration of a new and that this crisis, as this implies, centres in the figure of Jesus himself.[2]

Q begins with the teaching of John the Baptist, which at once introduces a note of crisis. The wrath of God is about to break forth; repentance, the final repentance before the Day of the Lord, is called for. A crisis has come upon the Old Israel, 'the Sons of Abraham', and the suggestion is clear (Luke iii. 17) that a New Israel is to be gathered. Then, just as the baptism of Jesus sets him forth as the Son of God, so too the temptations are those of the Son of God. It is difficult not to think that the temptations are Messianic; they are those of the Christ. Thus Q opens on a note of crisis arising out of his Christology (Luke iii (2b), 3a, 7b–9, 16, 17; iv. 1b–12: compare Matt. iii. 1–10, 11, 12; iv. 1–11).

Dibelius, as previously noted, would have us regard the next section in Q (Luke vi. 20–49: compare Matt. v. 3–12, 39–48; vii. 12; x. 24, 25; xii. 33–5; xv. 14), the Beatitudes, as exhortatory. Safer is it to regard them as setting forth the nature of the crisis inaugurated by Jesus in its aspect of promise. The Lucan form of the Beatitudes, which probably best preserves that of the original Q, is highly eschatological: we need not understand the contrast between 'now' and 'then' as secondary.[3] And while it is possible that the reference to persecution, in Luke vi. 22, may have a catechetical interest, the Beatitudes are, otherwise, declaratory. Leaving aside the express ethical teaching in Luke vi. 27–45 we note that it is given an eschatological reference by the addition in Luke vi. 46–9 of the parable of the Two Builders. It is to be admitted that the phrase 'on that day' used in Matt. vii. 22, which gives to the whole Matthaean complex an unmistakable eschatological intent (vii. 21–7), is missing in Luke vi. 46 ff., but Luke xiii. 22–30, which is also largely Q, makes the eschatological reference clear.

The next material, the story of the centurion's boy (Luke vii. 2, 6b–10), the dialogue of which alone belongs to Q, has as its chief point the contrast between the unbelief of Jewry and the faith of the Gentile world: the crisis has fallen upon the Old Israel to its discredit but to the credit of 'the many'. That the crisis expected by Judaism, the new order, has

---

[1] See Appendix XI.   [2] See Appendix XII.
[3] See J. M. Creed, *The Gospel According to St Luke, ad rem.*

arrived in Christ is the burden of the reply of Jesus to emissaries sent by John the Baptist (Luke vii. 18*b*, 19, 22–8, 31–5: compare Matt. xi. 2–6, 7–19). This section has both an eschatological and a Christological reference. The crisis is not in doom only but in grace also, over against that predicted by the Baptist. (Notice that T. W. Manson regarded this as the close of the first part of Q, which deals with the relation between the Baptist and Jesus.)[1]

But the note of crisis, which has already been struck, continues into the next section (Luke ix. 57–62 = Matt. viii. 19–22), which deals with 'would-be' disciples of Jesus. Doubtless this material could be and was used in exhortation, but its immediate impact is to evoke a sense of total emergency: it points to the inexorable demand laid upon men by the coming of Jesus. Similarly, in Luke x. 1–16 (compare Matt. ix. 37, 38; x. 7–16, 40; xi. 21–3), the instructions given to the seventy, who are sent forth on a mission, are coloured by the conviction that the Kingdom of God has drawn near: the End is imminent. Such instructions we should not expect to be suitable for catechetical purposes, at least in 'normal' times, and they do not appear in the catechetical material of the Epistles: they are orders for veterans in a crisis not for neophytes. This same note of crisis is intensified in Luke x. 17 ff.: the coming of Christ has the aspect of wrath not only on unbelieving Israel but also on the unseen powers of evil, on Satan himself. The high Christology implied in Luke x. 17 ff. then reaches its climax in Luke x. 21–8, where the unique sonship of Jesus is asserted. The following verses in Luke x. 23 f. unmistakably endorse the critical significance of Jesus' ministry. The sections Luke xi. 2–4 (the Lord's Prayer), and xi. 5–8 (the Parable of the friend at midnight) recall us again to the urgency of the hour. Disciples are to pray that they may not be led into 'temptations', which here probably refer to the 'fiery trial' of the End (xi. 4), while in Luke xi. 9–13 the reference is equally eschatological. 'The door to be knocked is the door which gives entrance into the Kingdom of God', and the section ends by stressing the grace of God.

The next material in Q begins with the controversy over 'Beelzebub' in Luke xi. 14–23 (Matt. xii. 22–30). This is eschatological and Christological in its significance. The war between Satan and the Messiah has begun in earnest: the section closes with the implicit demand of Jesus that men should be with him: not to be with him is to be for Satan. This also is the purport of Luke xi. 24–6 (Matt. xii. 43–6); it also demands a whole-hearted committal to Christ. The crisis of his coming is reiterated in

[1] *The Sayings of Jesus*, pp. 62–6.

Luke xi. 29 ff. where Christ himself is represented as the critical sign, like Jonah of old in his generation. The significance of this verse for the eschatology of the New Testament is familiar. The very difficult verses in Luke xi. 33–6 (Matt. v. 15; vi. 22 f.) may also be claimed to have a Messianic significance. Those who have the light inherit the task of the Servant of the Lord: they have a Messianic task.

Next comes the controversy with the Scribes and Pharisees in Luke xi. 39*b*, 42, 43 (44), 46–52 (compare Matt. xxiii. 4–36): the judgement of his coming falls heavily upon them. The conclusion of this section may rightly be understood to be in Luke xii. 2–3. 'Nothing is covered up that will not be revealed'—a time is at hand when actions will be exposed. The things that are said and done in secret are not concealed from God, and in the judgement that is at hand all will be brought to light. There follow in Luke xii. 4–12 a series of exhortations to the disciples, concerning their behaviour in the face of this situation, which have an eschatological reference: the ultimate condemnation of God is that which is to be feared (Luke xii. 4 ff.). In the final consummation acceptance of or rejection of the Son of Man becomes the norm for judgement. Christ demands final loyalty. This is also the burden of Luke xii. 22–31 (Matt. vi. 25–33), because it ends with a claim for complete commitment to the Kingdom of God, which we are assured in Luke xii. 32 f. is God's gift—a treasure indestructible, for which no sacrifice is too great. Luke xii. 33–40 are the expression of an utterly radical demand in response to that which is given (Luke xii. 32) and a warning to be awake, which is reinforced by the parables in xii. 41–6. Here it seems not unlikely that catechetical instruction has coloured the formulation of Q, but the note of crisis continues in Luke xii. 41–6 unmistakably. He 'came to cast fire upon the earth' (Luke xii. 49). The passage in Luke xii. 57–9, which in Matt. v. 25, 26 is paraenetic, may be so also in Luke: its position in Luke is suggested by the reference to judging the signs of the times in the previous section xii. 54–6. It may, therefore, have had an eschatological reference originally, although this is not clear in its present form. The parables in Luke xiii. 18–21 (the mustard seed and the leaven: the steady growth of the Kingdom despite opposition (compare Matt. xiii. 31–3)) deal with the mysteriously active presence of the Kingdom of God. In Luke xiii. 23–30 the need is urged for striving to respond appropriately to this fact and a prediction of the 'breadth' of the coming Kingdom is made (xiii. 28 ff.) and of the crisis that awaits the Holy City (xiii. 34 f.). So, too, the solitary verse from Q, appended to the parable of the marriage feast in

Luke xiv. 7–10, in xiv. 11 (=Matt. xviii. 14) on self-exaltation, has an eschatological reference: it looks forward to the *peripeteia* which the End will bring. In the parable of the Great Supper in Luke xiv. 16–23 (compare Matt. xxii. 1–10) stress is laid upon the immediate and radical response required of those upon whom the Kingdom of God has come, and the same is set forth with penetrating force in Luke xiv. 26–33, 34, 35, a motif which re-emerges later on in Luke xvi. 13 in the saying on the two masters (compare Matt. xviii. 12–14). In Luke xvi. 16–17 we find at the same time an assertion of the perpetuity of the Law of Judaism (xvi. 17) and an assertion of the newness of the situation caused by the advent of Jesus (xvii. 16): Luke xvii. 1 f. underlines the seriousness of opposing or hindering the salvation now available and xvii. 3–4 again emphasizes the radicalism of God's demand, and xvii. 5–6 belong to the same world of total commitment which Jesus introduced. The remainder of the material in Q deals with the coming Parousia (Luke xvii. 23, 24, 26–30, 34, 35, 37*b*): and this is the reference in the Parable of the Talents (xix. 12, 13, 15*b*–26). In addition xxii. 28–30 (the Apostles' thrones) may also be from Q.

The outcome of such a rough survey of the material in Q as we have sketched above is to confirm what we previously noted. Q sets forth the crisis constituted in the coming of Jesus, and it is as a part of this crisis that it understands the ethical teaching of Jesus: it is itself an expression of this crisis. That teaching emerges directly in very few places only. (On the widest possible interpretation of the term 'ethical' it includes only Luke vi. 20–49, the Sermon on the Plain; xii. 22–31, on freedom from care; xii. 33*b*–34, on treasure; xii. 57–9, the duty of speedy reconciliation; xiii. 24–9, the narrow way; xiv. 11 (=xviii. 14), on self-exaltation; xiv. 26 f., on hating one's next of kin and on bearing the cross; xvi. 13, on serving two masters; xvi. 16–18, on divorce; xvii. 3–4, on forgiveness.) It is never presented as a statement of general ethical principles, but always as the demand made upon those who have encountered the crisis of his coming: the teaching is *his* teaching. Can we characterize it further as it emerges in Q?

Three things would seem to be clear. First, the sound of the axe of crisis is heard throughout Q, and the ethical teaching it contains expresses the total, final demand that God lays upon men in Christ. Thus one word to describe the ethical teaching preserved in Q would be *radical*. It presents an absolute ethic concerned to register the immediate impact of the divine demand, uninfluenced by the contingencies of experience or the crippling realities of circumstance. Q attests the uncompromising character of the claim of the words of Jesus in their nakedness. But, secondly, it follows, almost necessarily, that the teaching of Jesus in Q cannot with justice be characterized as catechetical, if by catechetical is meant elementary instruction given to candidates for admission into the Church at baptism. The words of Jesus in Q point not as much to the normalities of catechetical instruction as to the moral enthusiasm of the earliest Christians, the 'first fine careless rapture' of a community which confronted and dared the impossible, as the experiment of communism in Acts reveals. Q doubtless preserves 'the way' demanded by Jesus and often attempted by the earliest Christians under his initial, unsullied influence. To squeeze the ethical teaching of Jesus in Q into a merely catechetical mould is to underestimate its unprecedented intensity and its extraordinary thrust, an intensity and a thrust that later catechetical usage had to tame. True, as we now have it, it reveals traces of such usage. But neither the origin of this ethic nor the initial impulse to its preservation was catechetical. Interest in the words of Jesus both antedates and transcends the need for catechesis. It seems clear from Q that, before and apart from the catechetical usage of the primitive Church, which did draw upon the words of Jesus along with other material for its purposes, the Church had preserved a tradition of the ethical teaching of Jesus which it regarded as in itself part of the crisis wrought in his coming. To put it yet more forcibly, this teaching itself helped to constitute that crisis. Q sets the ethical teaching of Jesus in its utterly radical or critical context as part of the drawing near of the Kingdom, that is, that teaching is not primarily a catechetical necessity or an addendum to the Gospel but itself part of the Gospel. This helps us to appreciate, in the third place, that the ethical teaching of Jesus in Q was preserved not merely as catechetically useful, and not only as radical demand, but as *revelatory*: it illumines the nature and meaning of the coming of the Kingdom as demand, which is the concomitant of the coming of the Kingdom as grace. It is, therefore, not the case that the words of Jesus were handed down, at first, in isolation from the kerygma and later were found to be necessary in catechetical work and so introduced alongside the kerygma. To judge from Q, concentration on them antedates any catechetical concerns because, from the first, they were included within the kerygma. In Q, crisis and commandment are one.[1]

[1] See my 'Ethics in the New Testament', in *The Interpreter's Dictionary of the Bible.* For the radicalism of the teaching of Jesus, see J. Knox, *The Ethic of Jesus in the Teaching of the Early Church* (1961), *passim.*

4. *M and* Gemara

The time was not long, however, before the harsh reality had to be faced that the crisis inaugurated by Jesus had not issued in a new heaven and a new earth. The advent of the Lord, when he was finally to introduce a new order, was delayed. The enthusiasts of the Day of Pentecost had to go out into a cold world to face again on an old earth the light of common day. Enthusiasm proved not to be enough. The primitive experiment in 'communism', so-called, was short-lived; soon it became necessary to send money to the 'poor' of Jerusalem who had used their capital unwisely.[1] And the same necessity to be true to 'earth', as well as 'heaven', emerges in the earliest Pauline epistles. Christians at Thessalonica,[2] thinking that the Day of the Lord, which would wind up all things, was at hand, had come to the conclusion that to labour was superfluous. But, with what has been called his 'robust common sense',[3] Paul issued an injunction that those who did not work should neither eat: he calls upon Christians to recognize the actualities of existence in this world. The ethic of crisis had to be adapted to the humdrum affairs of life. The contemplation of the lilies of the field that toiled not nor spun had to be reconciled with the maintenance of life. The teaching of Q had to be applied. And the process whereby this application of an 'impossible ethic' was at work in the early Church can be seen most clearly, outside the catechesis with which we have dealt above, in the other material which we found behind the *SM* which is designated as M.

In two ways the teaching of Jesus as presented in M, although it too preserves the crisis character of the words of Jesus, in the intensity of their demand, nevertheless, shows how these *radical* words begin to take on a *regulatory* character, that is, they became used as guides for the actual business of living, the *point d'appui* for an incipient Christian casuistry.

In the first place, whereas the teaching of Jesus in Q is set out in relation to the ministry of John the Baptist, that is, in a context of crisis, M relates the teaching of Jesus to the Scriptures of Judaism and compares it with that of the ancient Jewish worthies.[4] This comparison antedates M itself.

---

[1] C. H. Dodd, *Interpreter*, XVIII, no. 1 (1921).

[2] 2 Thess. iii. 6–12. Here again Paul acts in true rabbinic fashion to become the *type* to be followed by the flock, as the rabbi is to be imitated by his *talmidim*.

[3] C. H. Dodd, *N.T.S.* (1953), 114. The questions which R. Niebuhr has forced us to face in *The Interpretation of Christian Ethics* and other volumes are thus already raised in the New Testament itself.

[4] This is the force of the antitheses in v. 21 ff.

Luke vi. 27 suggests that the antitheses of Matt. v. 21 ff. had their parallel in a source behind Q: the verse 'But I say to you that hear...' naturally implies a contrast, although it is unexpressed. The comparison goes back to the earliest days of the Church, if not to Jesus himself.[1] Significant is it here that the antithetical form of M's presentation of the words of Jesus over against Judaism has the effect of characterizing them as a new law which has fulfilled the old. It is so that Matthew may have understood the antitheses, as we saw before, and at this point therefore he did not innovate. There can be little doubt that the confrontation of the words of Jesus with Judaism in M did provide for the possibility of the legal understanding of the words of Jesus, that is, their use in a regulatory fashion.

But, in the second place, certain passages reveal that M treated the words of Jesus in a regulatory manner. As a starting point, we turn to a familiar passage: Matt. xix. 3–9 (compare Mark x. 1–12). The former introduces an exceptive clause into Mark x. 11, and reads 'Whoever divorces his wife *except for unchastity* (μὴ ἐπὶ πορνείᾳ), and marries another, commits adultery'. The total prohibition of divorce, which both Mark and Luke (xvi. 18) ascribe to Jesus, Matthew rejects. He makes of Jesus' prohibition a principle to be applied in a regulatory fashion: he makes it practicable and thus 'legalizes' it. The word of Jesus on marriage, in its neat form, has been modified.[2] And the New Testament reveals that from two directions at least it was necessary for the primitive community to 'interpret' the commandment of Jesus on marriage. First, Gentile Christians, living under Roman law, had to ask the question whether Jesus' refusal to allow husbands to divorce their wives, which dealt with the usage of Judaism, in which wives could not divorce their husbands, carried with it as a corollary a refusal to countenance the divorce of husbands by wives, which was permitted under Roman law. Here the geographic expansion of Christianity probably created a need for interpretation. And in Mark x. 12 Mark extends the prohibition of divorce to include the right of wives to do so, so Paul, while he does not allow a wife to divorce an unbelieving husband, does permit separation from him while a wife is not even to separate from a believing husband (1 Cor. vii. 10–16). But whereas Mark adds x. 12 without any indication that he is interpreting his Lord's words as he thinks fit, Paul is careful in

---

[1] A. H. McNeile, *The Gospel According to St Matthew, ad rem.* The antitheses have figured prominently in recent discussion.

[2] See J. Bonsirven, *Les Enseignements de Jésus-Christ* (1946), pp. 144 ff., and references there given.

1 Cor. vii. 12 ff. to make it clear that it is not the precise words of the Lord that he is quoting (see further below, pp. 397 f.). However, that in extending the words of Jesus to include divorce and separation from husbands by women, Mark and Paul were being true to the intention of their Lord few would deny. Notice that Matthew, a Palestinian Gospel, does not have to face this particular kind of interpretation, that is, that governed by the change in the geographic incidence of Christians.[1]

But, secondly, there was also an ubiquitous factor which called for an interpretative encounter with the words which, in the light of the End, Jesus had uttered with terrible and unambiguous clarity. From one point of view at least, that light could blind as well as illumine. That the way-faring disciples found it so is clear. The context of the discussion of divorce in Mark x. 2 ff. and Matt. xix. 3 ff., to which we have already referred, is significant. In Mark, after the confession at Caesarea Philippi the followers of Jesus appear in a bad light. Peter resents the necessity that Christ should suffer (Mark viii. 32), and in ix. 32 the disciples as a whole are equally uncomprehending. In ix. 28 they confess their inability to cast out a dumb and deaf spirit; and this is due to their lack of prayer. Mark x. 10 reveals them incapable of understanding Jesus' interpretation of Gen. i. 27; ii. 24. They have to be enlightened in a private interview. There follows, in Mark x. 17–22, the story of the rich young ruler who leaves Jesus sorrowfully 'because he had great possessions'. The demands of Jesus appear to be impossible. Even after the third prediction of the Passion in x. 32–4 James and John, the sons of Zebedee, are still unable to read the mind of Jesus (x. 35–45). Not by accident does Mark x close with the story of a blind beggar demanding his sight: the author sees the disciples themselves as 'blind' (x. 46 ff.).

Matthew has followed Mark's treatment faithfully, except that, at certain points, he has introduced new material; and this reveals a greater emphasis than is found in Mark on the moral perplexity of the disciples, as over against their moral obtuseness, that is, Jesus is revealed not merely as having exposed the moral inadequacy of the disciples, but as having created moral confusion which he has to dispel by offering explicit guidance. Pertinent to our purpose are the following passages.

(i) Let us begin with xvii. 24–7:

When they came to Capernaum, the collectors of the half-shekel tax went up to Peter and said, 'Does not your teacher pay the tax?' He said, 'Yes'. And when he came home, Jesus spoke to him first, saying, 'What do you think, Simon?

[1] See Appendix XIII.

From whom do kings of the earth take toll or tribute? From their sons or from others?' And when he said, 'From others', Jesus said to him, 'Then the sons are free. However, not to give offence to them, go to the sea and cast a hook, and take the first fish that comes up, and when you open its mouth you will find a shekel; take that and give it to them for me and for yourself.'

The exact provenance of this pericope is uncertain. Does it reflect or record an actual occurrence during the ministry of Jesus?[1] Many scholars have deemed this unlikely because, despite the incident of its cleansing, the attitude of Jesus to the Temple seems to have been one of acceptance, so that he would naturally have paid the tax for its maintenance, and any question on this score would, therefore, have been superfluous. The pericope must be regarded as reflecting a setting, not in the ministry, but in the life of the early Church. This view must not be too readily endorsed, however; the precise position that Jesus took on Temple worship is still open to doubt.[2] There may have been words of Jesus, as there was one act,[3] which may have confused both his opponents and his followers, so that the latter would need guidance during the ministry itself. But, on the other hand, the pericope itself reveals no such confusion in the mind of Peter: and it is not the disciples themselves that raise the issue, although, once being raised, it would naturally exercise them, as is implied in xvii. 25.

If we turn away from the ministry itself, two possibilities are open. The pericope is either concerned with the duties of Jewish-Christians in relation to the half-shekel levied by Judaism on all Jews, which would best fit the reference to avoiding offence (Christians being enjoined to avoid provoking Jewry) or with their duties in relation to the half-shekel tax levied by Rome on all Jews after A.D. 70. This would suit the reference to the kings of the earth in xvii. 25, but does not so well, perhaps, comport with the necessity to avoid offence. 'Offending', it might be argued, is too weak a word for the refusal to pay an enforced Roman tax, though it might not be so in describing the refusal to pay a religious due to Jews.

[1] See the various commentaries; Bultmann, *op. cit. ad rem*; B. W. Bacon, *op. cit.* pp. 228 ff.—an excellent discussion. He rightly notes that 'the story would be as easy to date under Domitian or Trajan as under Claudius or Nero' (p. 229). F. V. Filson seems to date it without question in the ministry of Jesus (*The Gospel According to St Matthew*, pp. 195 f.). There is no need to see in the story an anti-cultic motif as such, as does Lohmeyer (*Kultus und Evangelium* (1942), *ad rem*).

[2] See R. H. Lightfoot, *The Gospel Message of Mark* (1950), *ad rem*; E. F. Scott, *The Crisis in the Ministry* (New York, 1952).

[3] On the words of Jesus on the destruction of the Temple, see C. F. D. Moule, *J.T.S. op. cit.*; E. Lohmeyer's work, referred to above, is brilliant but to be very carefully scrutinized.

Klostermann[1] also argues that a date before A.D. 70 is implied because the tax concerned was thought of as paid to God by his children, and not to the kings of the earth. But this is to introduce an unsuitable scientific precision into a midrashic pericope. It may be suggested that, while the whole section in Matt. xvii. 24–7 appears at first sight to be unrelated to what precedes, on examination, it turns out to be an explanatory addition to xvii. 22–3. There the powers of this world are predicted to kill the Son of Man: the 'hands of men' kill the 'Son of Man'. What precisely does the phrase 'hands of men' mean? In the other two predictions of the Passion in xvi. 21; xx. 17–19, Matthew, like Mark and Luke, makes explicit reference to elders, chief priests and Scribes by whom Jesus is to suffer, and, in xx. 17–19, a reference to the Gentiles, who mock and scourge and crucify, is made. Matt. xvii. 23, however, only refers to the hands of men that kill, that is, the reference is to Rome only. Thus Matt. xvii. 22–3 was likely to raise the question what the attitude of Christians should be to Rome. Should it be one of rejection, non-co-operation or tolerance? In xvii. 24–7 we are given the answer. Offence is to be avoided. A practical problem is here given a practical answer.

For our immediate purpose, however, it is not the exact setting in life of the pericope that is important, but rather the fact that Matthew alone has included in his Gospel precise moral guidance on the payment of taxes. This guidance conforms to that given by Paul, and the motive appealed to is also consonant with what we find in 1 Cor. viii. 9–13: the same verb σκανδαλίζω occurs in both contexts. Both Paul and Matthew recognize the necessity to avoid giving offence. Matthew cites words of Jesus to justify the payment of taxes on this ground. With the role of Peter at this point we shall be concerned later: xvii. 24–7 belongs to a Petrine stratum in M in which Peter assumes what we may call a rabbinic role, that is, issues Halakah delivered to him by Jesus, either in a midrashic context, as here, or more simply, as in xviii. 21 f., Jesus is the source of a Christian Halakah, transmitted here to Peter.

(ii) Matt. xviii. 15–17. These read:

If your brother sins against you, go and tell him his fault, between you and him alone. If he listens to you, you have gained your brother. But if he does not listen, take one or two others along with you, that every word may be confirmed by the evidence of two or three witnesses. If he refuses to listen to them, tell it to the Church; and if he refuses to listen even to the Church, let him be to you as a Gentile and a tax collector.

[1] *Matthäusevangelium, ad rem.*

It is instructive to compare with this what is a partial parallel in Q. Luke xvii. 3 reads: 'Take heed to yourselves; if your brother sins, rebuke him, and if he repents, forgive him.' The Q passage is content to state the demand for forgiveness. To this Q material—in a modified form—M material has been added by Matthew which gives regulations on the *practice* of reconciliation. Not enough for Matthew the injunction: he provides details of the process for its execution. Matt. xviii. 15 really annuls the too literal understanding of Matt. vii. 1, which had forbidden all judging of others. Matthew spells out how an absolute prohibition is to work in the practical life of the Church. The same cautionary motif had previously emerged within the *SM* itself, where in vii. 6, following the unambiguous rejection of all 'judgement', we find a bit of *gemara* warning against the misuse of this principle. Pearls are not to be cast before swine.

But Matt. xviii. 21–2 follows in order to safeguard, this time, against strict adherence to caution:

Then Peter came up and said to him, 'Lord, how often shall my brother sin against me, and I forgive him? As many as seven times?' Jesus said to him, 'I do not say to you seven times, but seventy times seven'.

Again the Q parallel in Luke is illuminating: 'And if he sins against you seven times in the day, and turns to you seven times, and says, "I repent", you must forgive him' (Luke xvii. 4). Matthew's concern is clearly twofold: to avoid an indiscriminate benevolence, and, at the same time, to guard against a forgiveness governed by any careful calculus of 'less and more'. So he goes further than Q, and insists on forgiveness without limit, which is here the force of seventy times seven. But this in turn caused much heart-searching in the early Church. How can Christians be sure that they have so forgiven? Again Matthew supplies *gemara*, this time in the form of a parable from M in xviii. 23–35: the forgiveness demanded essentially is that which comes from the heart: this alone is limitless.

Matt. xviii as a totality, it should be noted, constitutes what may be described as an incipient manual of discipline. Material from Mark illustrating the *disposition* of those who receive the Kingdom (Mark ix. 36 ff.; x. 15: compare Luke ix. 46–8; xviii. 17), becomes, in Matt. xviii. 1–6, descriptive of the Church members; the little ones in xviii. 10 are such, and a parable in Luke xv. 3–7 is modified in its light; in Luke the parable of the Lost Sheep illustrates the joy in heaven over the repentant sinner, in Matt. xviii. 14 the eagerness of the Father to preserve those in the Church. The strictly ecclesiastical reference in Matt. xviii. 10 has been clarified for us by the DSS.[1]

(iii) Matt. xix. 10–12. Following what we may regard as an attempt to provide the Church with a guide to the conduct and ordering of its own life, in chapter xix, as indicated, Matthew turned to more directly ethical problems. In xix. 2–10 he modified the absolute character of Jesus' teaching. But he is not content with this and introduces from M, in xix. 10–12, a treatment of the renunciation of marriage as follows:

The disciples said to him, 'If such is the case of a man with his wife, it is not expedient to marry'. But he said to them, 'Not all men can receive this precept, but only those to whom it is given. For there are eunuchs who have been so from birth, and there are eunuchs who have been made eunuchs by men, and there are eunuchs who have made themselves eunuchs for the sake of the Kingdom of heaven. He who is able to receive this, let him receive it.'

These words form what we might call a bit of Christian *gemara*—whether going back to Jesus himself we can discuss later—an explanatory addition or comment. They cannot be said to arise naturally out of the content of xix. 2–9. The reaction of the disciples to the proclamation in xix. 9 reflects no credit on them: they virtually make the attractiveness of marriage contingent upon the possibility of divorce, and that on easy terms. Such an attitude as they express is historically possible, if not probable. Divorce was treated very lightly in some high Jewish circles, even though others rejected it outright,[2] as did Jesus. Nevertheless, it might be expected that Jesus would have reacted violently against such an attitude as the disciples here display, castigating their low appreciation of the marriage state. But this we do not find. Two possibilities for the interpretation of xix. 10–12 are open. (*a*) We may refer the words τὸν λόγον τοῦτον, rendered by the RSV 'this precept', to the saying of Jesus in xix. 9. Although Matthew in xix. 9 has cast the words of Jesus in the form of a solemn pronouncement ('And I say unto you'), the Lord takes the point of view of the disciples seriously and proceeds to temper his demand, modified as it already is by the exceptive clause treated above, still further. The words on marriage are not to be applied absolutely and indiscriminately to all alike: in their utterly radical form (and this includes for Matthew the exceptive clause, be it repeated) they can only apply to

[1] See above, pp. 221 ff.
[2] See J. Bonsirven, *Textes Rabbiniques des deux Premiers Siècles Chrétiens pour servir à l'intelligence du Nouveau Testament* (Rome, 1954), index under 'divorce'.

him 'who is able to stand it' or 'to those to whom it is given to do so'.[1] On this view those are to accept marriage on Jesus' terms who alone are capable of it: his prohibition of all divorce, except on the ground of adultery, cannot be made a fixed law for all. Did Matthew close his *gemara* at verse 11, this would be a legitimate interpretation of xix. 9–11. But the addition of xix. 12 opens up another possibility, namely (*b*), that the phrase τὸν λόγον τοῦτον may apply to the comment of the disciples, not to the words of Jesus, that is, to the phrase οὐ συμφέρει γαμῆσαι, 'it is not expedient to marry'. To this statement, the reply is that not all are capable of living up to this principle, but only those 'to whom it is given'. There follows a reference to three types of eunuchs: to two of these types, at least—those who are by nature not called upon to marry and those who voluntarily renounce marriage—the principle 'it is not expedient to marry'

---

[1] The point of view of Matthew has a well-defined parallel in Rabbinic law. There was a well established decree that demands which the public could not fulfil should not be imposed. The following is taken from TB Abodah Zarah 36*a*: 'The following articles of heathens are prohibited but the prohibition does not extend to all use of them: Milk which a heathen milked without an Israelite watching him, their bread and oil—Rabbi [that is, R. Judah II, the grandson of R. Judah who compiled the Mishnah] and his court permitted the oil—stewed.' The prohibition of oil rested on Dan. i. 8. How could rabbi and his court permit what Daniel had forbidden? Rab came out of the difficulty by saying that Daniel forbade it for himself but not for all Israel. Hillel and Shammai followed Daniel. The position of R. Judah II and his court was justified as follows: 'they relied upon the dictum of Rabban Simeon b. Gamaliel and R. Eliezer b. Zadok who declared: "We make no decree upon the community unless the majority are able to abide by it"' (וסמכו רבותינו על דברי רבן שמעון בן גמליאל ועל דברי רבי אלעזר בר צדוק שהיו אמרין אין גוזרין גזירה על הצבור אלא אם כן רוב צבור יוכלין לעמד בה). Oil was one of the staple products of Palestine and the trade in it was of vital importance, so that it became difficult to keep the laws (see W. A. L. Elmslie, *The Mishnah on Idolatry*, '*Aboda Zara*' (1911), p. 38), and, in fact, the prohibition concerning oil did not spread through all the people: it was probably economically impossible for them to observe this. The rule quoted from Rabban Simeon b. Gamaliel and R. Eliezer b. Zadok was accordingly supported by R. Adda b. Ahaba as follows: 'What Scriptural verse supports this rule? *Ye are cursed with the curse; for ye rob Me, even this whole nation* (Mal. iii. 9)—that is, when the whole nation has (accepted an ordinance then the curse which is the penalty of its infraction) does apply, otherwise it does not.' (Soncino translation, p. 175.) Compare TB Horayoth 3*b* where the same principle is enunciated. In TB Baba Kamma 79*b* it is appealed to in connexion with the trade in cattle, and in TB B. Bathra 60*b* in connexion with fasting after the fall of the Temple, where R. Joshua b. Hananiah cites it. This passage is interesting also because it includes the reference to marriage. Should conditions under Roman rule dictate disobedience to the commandment to marry and beget children? Marriage is allowed here not for the same reason as it is allowed by Matthew. See also Midrash Psalms on cxxxvii. 5. Related to all this is the insistence that the Law was given that men might 'live' by it and not die (Jer. vii. 23; Deut. xxx. 15–19; xxxii. 45–7).

applies. But this must not be demanded of all. He alone should forswear marriage who can do so. If this be the meaning of xix. 10–12, then Jesus would here seem to accept the desirability, for those who can do so, of giving up marriage.

The addition of xix. 10–12 to xix. 3–9 is confused and confusing. As it stands, the second interpretation is most plausible, namely, that Jesus here commends the unmarried state to those who are fitted for it and whose 'call' demands it. 'The strong'[1] (ὁ δυνάμενος) can practise that state, and it is difficult to resist the claim that, by implication at least, the celibate is exalted above the married. Similar is the position of Paul in 1 Cor. vii. 7 where his reason for enjoining abstention from marriage, wherever possible, is not that the married state is necessarily sinful, nor merely that the distress of the End impends (1 Cor. vii. 28 f.), but that he regards the unmarried state as superior, because it permits a more undivided devotion to the things of the Lord than does the married.[2]

Pertinent to our purpose is the attempt made in Matthew to come to terms with the actualities of marriage: the material from M in xix. 10–12 reflects the same kind of concern, to make the ethic of Jesus practicable, as we find in Paul. Radicalism is tempered to the generality.

(iv) Similarly in xix. 16–22 Matthew is concerned with the same problem. Apart from changes in Mark x. 17–31 which at the moment do not concern us, he has substituted for Mark's 'You lack one thing' (Luke xviii. 22, 'One thing you still lack') the sentence 'If you would be perfect',[3] that is, Matthew has introduced the idea that there are grades of achievement in the Christian life. The counsel to sell all and give to the poor is designed only for the perfect: it is not meant to be applied to all. It has been possible to find in this verse the introduction into the Church of the concept of two orders of morality. More likely is it that what is intended is the claim that the commandment of Jesus discriminates; it respects individual differences among men. The story of the Rich Young Man in Mark and Luke reveals an intensification of the demands of Jesus or their radicalism: Matthew by introducing the concept of 'perfection' has, indirectly, softened this radicalism.

---

[1] On the derivation of this category, see J. Dupont ('Syneidesis: aux origines de la notion chrétienne de conscience morale', in *Studia Hellenistica*, v (1948), pp. 119–53), who finds the distinction between the 'strong' and the 'weak' in Hellenistic sources. But we see from the previous note how such a category could have evolved in Judaism itself.

[2] See, however, H. Chadwick, *N.T.S. loc. cit.*, on Paul and marriage.

[3] On this, see above, pp. 209 ff.

(v) Again in Matt. xix. 13–15, which, however, has an almost exact parallel in Mark, we find the same concern to understand what the moral demands of Jesus implied. Did they allow for the bringing up of children? Could one who was to make as his aim the kind of indifference to toil and labour that we find in the lily of the field—could he assume the responsibilities of fatherhood? The disciples were tempted sometimes perhaps to a negative answer. Their Lord takes the opposite view.

The process which we have traced appears also in the *SM* itself. In its present context in Matthew the Lord's Prayer itself may be regarded as broadly gemaric and we have already referred to vii. 6.[1] For even more clear gemaric elements, see above, pp. 235 ff.

In the passages from M with which we have dealt above there is traceable, then, a tendency to present Jesus as a practical legislator, who has his feet on the ground. The radicalism of his absolute ethic, as revealed in Q, is softened. With this it agrees that the Church, as it emerges in Matthew, is a society in which a tradition is handed on which has to be interpreted. Scribes[2] are to be found in it and there is constantly going on a process of 'binding and loosing',[3] that is, of allowing certain things

[1] A parallel to this emerges in the instructions in DSD ix. 21 ff. 'Now these are the rules of the way for the wise man in these times, with regard to his love as well as his hate. Let there be eternal hatred toward the men of the Pit in *the spirit of secrecy* (ברוח הסתר)'. On other parallels to the DSS, see pp. 235 ff.

[2] xxiii. 34; xiii. 52. ἑταῖρος: occurs only three times in the New Testament and always in Matthew. It translates the Hebrew חבר (see M. Aboth i. 6; M. Yebamoth xvi. 7; 'Erub. ii. 6). Particularly in xxvi. 50 (the NEB renders 'friend') the implication is that Judas is one of the school, of the same position as Jesus, as is made clear by his use of 'rabbi' in the previous verse. In xi. 16 there is a difficulty in the reading: some manuscripts have ἑτέροις and others ἑταίροις: the former is to be preferred. It may be significant that in xx. 13 and xxii. 12 those called into the Christian vineyard and feast are designated by a term which suggests the rabbinic חבר, although this should not be pressed, as in xxvi. 50. The term also should be read in Didache xv. 3, where the same conception of the 'Church member' appears as in Matthew, although in xvi. 18 and xviii. 15–17, where the term ἐκκλησία emerges, the term used is ἀδελφός, as in Didache iv. 8. See J.-P. Audet, *La Didachè* (1958), p. 468. Christians are still thinking of themselves, to some degree, in Matthew as members of a *ḥaburah*. The following is H. Loewe's treatment of a *Ḥaber*: it is used especially 'in contradistinction to Am ha Aretz, a member of a brotherhood, scrupulous in tithing and other religious observances. Sometimes the *Ḥaber* was not a learned man, for example, 'Ye are sages, I am but a *Ḥaber*' (Ḳid. 33 b)', *A Rabbinic Anthology* (1938), p. 354. The whole note should be consulted.

[3] xviii. 16. G. Bornkamm's words are strictly correct: 'Die zwischen Jesus und seinen Jüngern einerseits und den jüdischen Gegnern andrerseits strittige Frage ist damit die Frage nach der rechten Auslegung des Gesetzes. Schriftgelehrten Auslegung muß es auch in der christlichen Gemeinde geben, daher wird der Titel des γραμματεύς auch für die Jünger verwendet (xxiii. 34), nur ist der Jünger ein γραμματεύς

to be done and of forbidding others. Peter emerges particularly as the Christian counterpart of a Jewish rabbi, who has to interpret the words of his Lord.[1] As we have seen this tendency to 'rabbinize' Christianity is not peculiar to M. It appears even in Paul. In addition to the passages in his epistles previously referred to, in Rom. xii, in a section which contains many echoes of the absolute standards of the *SM*, we read in xii. 18 'If it be possible (εἰ δυνατόν), as much as lieth in you (τὸ ἐξ ὑμῶν), live peaceably with all men' (KJV). This is the spirit of M.

The casuistry of M—if we may so express it—poses two problems, which arise from the nature of the material it contains. First, how much of it can we ascribe to Jesus himself? This question must be asked, because in the ethical material with which we have dealt, two factors are noticeable: (1) the words of Jesus were changed to give them practicality. This appears particularly in Matthew's treatment of divorce, and we have seen that even in Q, dominated as it is by crisis sayings, and certainly in the parables, whose manipulation in the interests of paraenesis in the early Church Professor Jeremias has so illumined for us, and to a far greater extent in M, there is concern not merely to reproduce the words of Jesus but to apply them to problems of personal, ecclesiastical and social conduct, so that words of crisis on the lips of Jesus himself came in the course of time to have a regulatory significance. But (2) there is a process at work far more difficult to assess than this. Material of a regulatory kind is ascribed in M *in toto* to Jesus himself. We know from Mark that material of this nature has been wrongly so ascribed. As we saw above, in 1 Cor. vii. 10 ff., Paul distinguishes carefully between words of the Lord and his own opinion, however valuable. The section reads:

> To the married I give charge, *not I but the Lord*, that the wife should not separate from her husband (but if she does, let her remain single or else be reconciled to her husband)—and that the husband should not divorce his wife. To the rest *I say, not the Lord*, that if any brother has a wife who is an unbeliever, and she consents to live with him, he should not divorce her. If any woman has a husband who is an unbeliever, and he consents to live with her, she should not divorce him.

1 Cor. vii. 13 disallows divorce of a husband who is an unbeliever by a wife, but this prohibition is advanced by Paul as his own judgement

---

μαθητευθεὶς τῇ βασιλείᾳ τῶν οὐρανῶν (xiii. 52).' See *Studies in Honour of C. H. Dodd*, ed. W. D. Davies and D. Daube, pp. 232 ff.

[1] See B. W. Bacon on the Petrine supplements in Matthew, *op. cit.* p. 222. The pertinent passages are xvi. 17–19; xvii. 24–7; we might add xviii. 21–35. These Bacon regards as 'parasitic growths' on the tradition, of the nature of targums, p. 230.

(under the need not only, perhaps, to apply Jesus' teaching to Roman usage but also to further the missionary work of the Christian (1 Cor. vii. 16)). The Apostle knew that Jesus did not specifically utter any pronouncement on the express duties of wives in such matters, otherwise he would not have made the distinction he does in the above passage. Mark, however, under the same need to which we referred above, adds verse x. 12, which expresses the same position as 1 Cor. vii. 13, without any indication that he is adding to the words of his Lord or innovating in any way. That the intention of Jesus is honoured by Mark is clear, but this is not, at present, the point of interest, which is that the evangelist has felt free to ascribe to Jesus words which, we may presume almost beyond any doubt, he never uttered. To put the matter in this way may be misleading. Mark has not so much deliberately made his own addition to his Lord's words as relied on a tradition in which this ascription had already been made. At what precise point this took place we cannot discover, but it may be taken to have been probably post-Pauline. What concerns us is that the regulatory material peculiar to M may be of the same kind. The parallels to it from sectarian and other sources might suggest that it is a secondary accretion, an imposition on Jesus. Here we state a problem which is dealt with at length in the next chapter. We can, however, here issue the caveat that it should not be too readily assumed that Jesus may not in fact have given directions for the actualities of life as well as words of crisis. Or, again, is it quite unthinkable that Jesus had two kinds of ethical teaching, one radical, critical, kerygmatic to 'the crowds' and another, more applied, to those who had already responded to his appeal?

The second question which the regulatory material peculiar to M prompts is that of its transmission. The transmission of Q along catechetical channels we found highly questionable; is the same true of M? The material we have had to deal with occurs mostly in Matt. v–vii; xviii, xix. It has suggested to many a catechetical matrix, as follows:

(i) *Matt. v–vii*

Isolating the structure of the primitive Christian catechism as it emerges in 1 Thess. ii. 13; iv. 1–8; 2 Thess. ii. 15; iii. 6; 1 Thess. i. 9–10; ii. 12; iv. 2, 11 (compare 2 Thess. iii. 6, 10, 12); iv. 3–9; v. 2, 12–22; 2 Thess. iii. 7–10; 1 Thess. v. 15; 1 Thess. v. 3–10 (compare Rom. xii. 3–8), Dodd finds the following parallelism with the *SM*:

(*a*) The Holiness of the Christian calling = the Beatitudes.

(*b*) The repudiation of pagan vices

(*c*) The Law of charity (ἀγάπη including φιλαδελφία) } =Matt. v. 17–48.

(*d*) Eschatological motives=Matt. vii. 22 ff.

(*e*) The order and discipline of the Church=Matt. vi. 1–18; vii. 6, 15–20.

The parallelism is not rigid: (*d*) follows (*e*) in the Sermon and the repudiation of pagan vices is replaced by the 'repudiation' of the Jewish tradition in v. 17 ff. As contrasted with the Lucan Sermon on the Plain, the over-all structure of Matt. v–vii may be taken to suggest a Jewish-Christian catechetical background, although, as we have seen,[1] other approaches to the structure of the Sermon are possible. We may claim that the correlation of M and Q material in Matt. v–vii has been cast into a catechetical mould, but this reveals nothing about the transmission and use of the material in Matthew before this correlation took place. The character of the M material in Matt. v–vii makes it unsuitable for catechesis: it is too detailed in its application for this last and suggests more the casuistry of the school than the directness of catechesis. This at least is the case to judge from the catechetical material in the epistles: but the Jewish-Christian catechetical tradition may have differed.

(ii) *Matt. xviii, xix*

With Matt. xviii we need not at first tarry: unless we stretch the term catechesis to include guidance both to long established Christians, and to leaders of the Church, then the contents of Matt. xviii, which are largely directed to such, cannot be taken as strictly catechetical.[2] The case with Matt. xix is more to the point. Here we have sections dealing with marriage and divorce (xix. 3–9), celibacy (xix. 10–12), children (xix. 13–15), riches (xix. 16–22). This sequence of subjects has prompted the comment that here Matthew, like Mark, upon whom he is largely dependent, draws upon a simple catechetical tradition such as emerges in a more developed form in Col. iii. 18–iv. 1; 1 Tim. ii. 8–iii. 13; v. 1–vi. 2; Eph. v. 22–vi. 9; Tit. i. 5–9; ii. 2–10; 1 Pet. ii. 13–18; iii. 1–7; v. 1–5.[3] But here again while the structure of the material in Matt. xix may suggest such a tradition, the content points to another than a catechetical transmission.

[1] See C. H. Dodd, *New Testament Essays: Studies in Memory of T. W. Manson* (1959), 107 ff.; J. Jeremias, *Die Bergpredigt* (Stuttgart, 1959), pp. 17 ff.

[2] G. D. Kilpatrick (*op. cit.* pp. 78 ff.), who minimizes the catechetical element in Matthew. His position is endorsed, with modification of the reasons he gives for it, by K. Stendahl, *The School of Matthew*, pp. 22 f.

[3] V. Taylor, *The Gospel According to St Mark, ad rem.*

Neither in Jewish nor Gentile catechesis is the narrative element introduced as here:[1] the substance of Matt. xix points to reflection on the Christian life by 'casuists', not so much to the more formulated conclusions handed to converts or neophytes.

In view of all this while a catechetical imprint on the structure of the material from M may be allowed, the origin of that material is elsewhere to seek. And, at this point, we may profitably turn to Matt. xviii. Here there is a construction, far removed from the direct, apodictic usages of catechism, revealing developed reflection on the Christian community which we can best account for in terms of a Christian casuistry, implying probably a Christian school in which the words of Jesus had been the object of study and comment.[2] Here Matthew has gathered together passages from Mark ix. 33–7, 42–8; Luke xv. 3–7; xvii. 3 f. and from M to produce a statement of the discipline of the life of the Christian community. The materials he took from Mark had, in part at least, previously been used in such an 'ecclesiastical' context, as Mark ix. 42 makes clear, but the omission by Matthew of Mark ix. 38–41 in this section shows how the material in Matt. xviii is intended to deal exclusively with intra-mural relations among Christians: Mark ix. 38–42 deals with the activities and attitudes of non-Christians, and so is not pertinent. Similarly Mark ix. 48–50 is passed by because it deals not so much with discipline itself as with the character or nature of the Christian community as 'salt'. Only what is directly related to order and discipline in the Church is here taken over from Mark. Similarly passages taken from Q (see xv. 3–7 and xvii. 3 f.) are manipulated and enlarged by Matthew for his own purposes. Thus the parable of the Lost Sheep, which in Luke xv. 3–7 denotes the joy in heaven over a repentant sinner, becomes in Matt. xviii. 12–14 a comment on the joy over the preservation of the Church member: and Luke xvii. 4 is expanded into Matt. xviii. 15–20. Not catechism but casuistry lies behind all this: in this casuistry a Christian gemaric element is noticeable: words of Jesus from some sources become the occasion for the insertion of related material by way of enlargement or comment, and in the material peculiar to Matthew the rabbinization of the Church is seen

[1] C. F. D. Moule has urged that parables and sayings were used as *illustrative* (our italics) material in Christian catechism (*J.T.S.* III, new series (1952), 75–9). If so, they were not structurally important for catechesis, but secondary.

[2] K. Stendahl, *The School of Matthew* (1954). The more one enters into the spirit and detail of Matthew the more convincing does the main thesis of this work appear to be, even though one may question the specific parallel drawn with Qumran.

at work. And in Matt. xviii the very arrangement of the material can be understood as rabbinic.[1]

We have surveyed above the two sources upon which the *SM* chiefly draws. While the distinction between them must not be made into a hard and fast one, they do roughly reveal a twofold approach to the words of Jesus. In the first block, Q (although it is not wise to define the material too precisely in terms of specific sources), it is the absolute character of the words which is most marked, their radical impact. It presents the teaching of Jesus as it came to his disciples, perhaps in its utter nakedness, during his actual ministry when he called his own to forsake all and to follow him. Q expresses not a catechism but a cataclysmic crisis. It would not be too misleading to think of it as reflecting the pre-Easter and immediately post-Easter period of the Church. In the second block of material, designated M, there is an attempt made to make applicable these words to the problems of daily living. There is a recognition of what is possible and impossible, absolute and relative. M more than Q, we may claim, reflects, among other things, the experience of the early Church sometime after Easter, when the blinding light of the ministry and Resurrection was past and the Church had emerged as a community in the world, which had to take the words of Jesus not merely as historically interesting but as valid for its own life. The Church had to consider what this validity meant. In the process it took what was radical, modified it, and made it regulatory. The process wherein this happened is contained and continued in the Christian-rabbinism of Matthew, where we see slowly emerging a neo-legalistic society.

5. *The Epistle of James and the Johannine Sources*

On the other hand, we now have to recognize another different development. This was concerned not with the elaboration of any kind of casuistry, but rather with subsuming the ethical teaching of Jesus under one all-embracing norm or principle.[2] This co-existed with the tendency

---

[1] See above, pp. 221 ff.

[2] In two ways there is a parallel in Judaism. Philo regarded the Decalogue as the κεφάλαια νόμων (*Decal.* 18 f.; *Leg. Spec.* I, I, I), so too R. Ishmael, TB Hagigah 6 *a*. See D. Daube, *op. cit.* pp. 63 ff., on *Principle and Cases*, where he notes how rabbis distinguished between a general principle and its applications in specific laws. 'The word *'abh*, literally "father", "ancestor", is used in technical language to denote a comprehensive notion: *toladha*, literally "descendant", signifies a narrower notion falling under it' (p. 65). Again, *guph* is used of a fundamental principle of the Torah; for example, Mishnah Horayoth i. 3, where an incorrect decision against

to make of the words of Jesus a new law, but is to be distinguished from, although not altogether opposed to, it.

The development referred to is apparent even in Matthew itself. At the climax of his treatment of the Christian interpretation of the Law, Christian worship and Christian loving-kindness, Matthew has placed vii. 12, which is known as the Golden Rule. Similarly the love of God and of the neighbour is made the summation of the Law in Mark xii. 28. Paul also knows the law of love as the essence of God's demand, as in Rom. xiii. 9. 'For he that loveth another hath fulfilled the Law'..., 'love is the fulfilling of the Law', and again in Gal. v. 14, 'for all the Law is fulfilled in one word, even in this, thou shalt love thy neighbour as thyself', and in Col. iii. 14, 'And above all these things put on charity which is the bond of perfection'.

But it is in the Epistle of James that the words of Jesus break through more often than in any other document outside the Synoptics, while at the same time they are subsumed under a single principle, the law of love. The following parallels between James and the Synoptics have been suggested:

James	Matthew	Mark	Luke
v. 12*	v. 34 ff.	—	—
i. 2†*	v. 11 f.	—	(vi. 23)
v. 10*	v. 12	—	—

a fundamental principle of the Law is treated as godlessness, whereas such a decision on a point of detailed application was not so regarded. Again *kelal*—'the universal' is used of a basic commandment of the Law and *perat* of a detailed rule. It is not such uses of general principles, however, that we here have in mind, but rather the use of certain basic concepts as containing the whole Law. The idea that the Decalogue was the substance of the moral law is not peculiar to Philo. This was symbolized by the recital of it, along with the Shema, by the priests in the Temple (TB Berakoth 11*b*: so Boaz Cohen, *Law and Tradition in Judaism*, p. 221; but the force of the passage cited is not clear). In TB Shabb. 31*a* Hillel asserts that the essence of the Law is contained in Lev. xviii. 18; Akiba found this in the commandment 'to love one's neighbour as oneself' (Genesis Rabbah xxiv. 7; *P.R.J.*[2] p. 55). The insistence that the Law was given that men might live by it, so that except under the most extreme circumstances, obedience to it should not involve death, rests ultimately on such passages as Deut. xxx. 15–19, 11–14; xxxii. 45–7; Jer. vii. 23. Thus in Siphre on Deuteronomy, Shofetim 107*b*; TB Yebamoth 90*b*, certain exigencies might demand the suppression or cancellation of the Law, '"A prophet...shall the Lord raise up... to him shall ye hearken" (Deut. xviii. 15). Even though he bid thee transgress one of the commands ordained in the Torah, as did Elijah on Mt. Carmel, *yet according to the need of the hour listen to him.*' We should connect with this the recognition that in the future the Law would have to be modified, this because of its difficulty for life. See above, pp. 161 ff.

James	Matthew	Mark	Luke
i. 4	v. 48	—	—
i. 5†*	vii. 7	—	xi. 9
i. 6	—	xi. 23 f.	—
i. 20	v. 22	—	—
i. 22†	vii. 24, 26	—	(vi. 46 ff.)
ii. 5*	v. 3, 5	—	—
ii. 8	xxii. 39 f.	xii. 31	—
ii. 11	(v. 21 f.)	—	—
iv. 2 ff.	(vii. 7)	—	—
ii. 13*	v. 7	—	—
ii. 15*	(vi. 25)	—	—
iii. 12*	vii. 16	—	—
iii. 18*	v. 9	—	—
iv. 3*	vii. 7, 8	—	—
iv. 3	xii. 39	—	—
iv. 9	—	—	vi. 25
iv. 10†	xxiii. 12	—	(xiv. 11; xviii. 14)
iv. 11 f.†*	vii. 1	—	(vi. 37)
v. 1	—	—	vi. 24 f.
v. 2†*	vi. 19	—	vi. 37
v. 6	—	—	vi. 37
v. 9	xxiv. 33	—	—

The items in the above lists that are most convincing are those marked by an asterisk.[1] Many other items, taken in isolation, might be regarded as highly questionable. But the cumulative effect of the parallels is impressive. James has clearly drawn upon a tradition of the sayings of Jesus for his paraenetic purposes. It is significant in the light of our insistence that Q was not primarily catechetically or paraenetically oriented, that the parallels between James and Q are very few, being confined to the items marked by a dagger above, that is, Q has again turned out to be a tradition not particularly drawn upon for paraenetic purposes. It is not necessary

[1] On this, see H. Riesenfeld, *op. cit.* p. 15. The force of the above 'parallels' has been variously assessed; see especially M. Dibelius, *Der Brief des Jakobus*[8], revised by H. Greeven (1956), pp. 27 f. He finds a similarity of form, style and of 'sentiment' between much in James and the words of Jesus in Matthew and Luke. While many of the parallels can be explained as a common inheritance from Judaism, there are others which demand a close relationship—they are derived from a tradition of paraenesis which contained the words of Jesus, although there is no proof that James drew upon our Gospels. (For a full list of parallels, see J. B. Mayor, *The Epistle of James* (1897), pp. lxxxiv–lxxxvi.) So also F. Hauck, *Der Brief Jakobus* (1926): '[JK] scheint einer Zeit zuzugehören, wo es nicht selbstverständlich war, daß man sich auf schriftlich festgelegte Herrenworte berief, sondern man scheint noch in stromlebendiger mündlicher Überlieferung zu stehen. Von Gedanken Jesu ist jedoch der ganze Brief durchtränkt.' Spitta, *Der Brief des Jakobus* (1896), rejected any dependence on Jesus. (W. L. Knox, *J.T.S.* xlvi, 10 ff.)

26-2

to assume that James has drawn upon the written Gospels as such. Apart from the unsettled question as to the date of the Epistle, the parallels do not demand this. Moreover, the attempt to distinguish distinct stages in the use of the sayings of Jesus, on the basis of the above parallels, must be regarded as questionable. This attempt was made by Kittel,[1] who distinguished three stages in the use made of the *logia*. In the first stage, they were used without differentiation or acknowledgement, that is, without any direct citation. This stage is revealed in James, where words of Jesus occur without being ascribed to him, and it is reflected also in those passages in the Pauline epistles where reminiscences of the words of Jesus occur. The second stage is revealed particularly in Paul where the words of Jesus are occasionally cited directly as his, as we showed above, especially in 1 Cor. vii. This stage is not represented in James. The third stage, in which the words have assumed written form and are cited as Scripture, occurs in the Apostolic Fathers.[2] This schematization agrees with Kittel's view of James as derived from a Palestinian milieu and ascribed to an early date.

Dibelius[3] has rightly objected that Kittel's scheme ignores the fact that in paraenetic documents, such as James, the material used is necessarily presented without citation, so that the 'informal' way in which James incorporates words of Jesus without direct citation is no indication that the epistle should be relegated to any early stage. But be this as it may, Kittel is surely to be followed in the view that, in the milieu from which James drew its materials, the words of Jesus were in the air, so that, as a living and formative tradition, they moulded the life of the Christian community both directly by supplying, on occasion, specific halakah, as at Jas. v. 12, and indirectly by supplying a climate of and a norm for a 'Christian' moral awareness.[4]

But we may go further than this. The Epistle of James reveals that out-

---

[1] G. Kittel, *Z.N.W.* XLI (1942), 71–105, especially pp. 88 ff. on 'Der Geschichtliche Ort des Jakobus-brief'.

[2] H. Koester, *Synoptische Überlieferung bei den Apostolischen Vätern* (1957), which is indispensable. Does the fact that the Fathers do not show a direct dependence on the Gospels mean that the tradition preserved in the Gospels in a written form was not authoritative or that the oral form of the tradition continued to enjoy authority also? See also A. J. Bellinzoni, *The Sayings of Jesus in the writings of Justin Martyr* (unpublished diss. Harvard University, 1962).

[3] *Der Brief des Jakobus*, p. 28; *From Tradition to Gospel*, Eng. trans. pp. 240 ff.

[4] So Hauck, *Der Brief Jakobus*. Note that Jas. v. 12, though parallel in a close manner to v. 34–7, does not suggest direct dependence on the Matthaean text. Compare Bellinzoni, *op. cit.* pp. 105–9.

side the Matthaean, there were other communities where the words of Jesus not merely constituted a reservoir of moral cultivation in a generalized way, but also a new law. In i. 25 we read: 'But he who looks into the perfect law, the law of liberty (νόμον τέλειον τὸν τῆς ἐλευθερίας) and perseveres, being no hearer that forgets but a doer that acts, he shall be blessed in his doing' (KJV). And again in ii. 8: 'If you really fulfil the royal law (νόμον τελεῖτε βασιλικόν), according to the scripture, "You shall love your neighbour as yourself", you do well' (KJV). The royal law is the law of the Messiah here summed up in terms of *agape*.[1] To those who ascribe James to a Palestinian milieu such an understanding of the Gospel occasions no difficulty. On the other hand, this is also explicable if James emerged in communities of Hellenistic-Jewish Christians or even of purely Hellenistic Christians. There were many communities in Antioch, Rome, Tarsus, Alexandria and other cities where there would be both kinds of Christians. Among these also there would have been influences both Hellenistic and Jewish tending to the interpretation of the Gospel in terms of law. For many of them the acceptance of Jesus as Messiah would have involved no rejection of Law, but merely the substitution of the New Law of the Messiah for the Old. Influences from the Stoics and from Philo, as well as from Judaism, would have contributed to the understanding of the Gospel as 'the perfect law of freedom', which is found in Jas. i. 25.[2] What is significant for our purpose is that the subsuming of the teaching of Jesus under the one principle of love was apparently widespread and it emerges especially, as we shall see below, in the Fourth Gospel.[3]

But one striking point is to be noticed in all these extra-Synoptic references. They refer to the love of neighbour *but not to the love of God*. Only in 1 John iv. 21 is this conjunction made with specific reference to

---

[1] On the perfect law of i. 25, see M. Dibelius, *Der Brief des Jakobus*, pp. 110–13. In his exegesis of the verse he defines the content of the 'perfect law' as the 'implanted word' (ἔμφυτος λόγος) of i. 21, which is further clarified in i. 27, but, in his discussion of its background, Dibelius fully recognizes that outside Pauline circles, especially when there was no longer any danger from Judaizers, it was quite congenial to interpret Christianity in terms of a new law. But within Paulinism, while he takes ὁ νόμος τοῦ πνεύματος τῆς ζωῆς in Rom. viii. 2 to be merely a rhetorical antithesis to ὁ νόμος τῆς ἁμαρτίας καὶ τοῦ θανάτου and so too does not press ἔννομος Χριστοῦ in 1 Cor. ix. 21, he has to recognize the force of Gal. vi. 2; v. 14, 23. He places special emphasis on the significance in this connexion of the actual formulation of the *SM* as a rule of life (p. 113).

[2] This is documented fully in Dibelius, *op. cit.*

[3] For the Fourth Gospel, see J. Dupont, *Agape*, III, 125 ff.

the teaching of Jesus. It reads: 'And this commandment have we from him, That he who loveth God, love his brother also.' Why is it that, apart from 1 John iv. 21, the law of love, outside the Gospels of Matthew, Mark and Luke, has no reference to the love of God but only to the love of neighbour? The context of the verse in 1 John iv. 21 supplies the answer. In 1 John iv. 7–12 we read:

7 Beloved, let us love one another; for love is of God, and he who loves is born
8 of God and knows God. He who does not love does not know God; for God
9 is love. In this the love of God was made manifest among us, that God sent his
10 only Son into the world, so that we might live through him. In this is love, not
11 that we loved God but that he loved us and sent his Son to be the expiation for
12 our sins. Beloved, if God so loved us, we also ought to love one another. No man has ever seen God; if we love one another, God abides in us and his love is perfected in us.

Here the love of God has been defined in terms of the life of Jesus. The act whereby God sent his son into the world to die for sinners has become the pattern, the paradigm, of his love. For the early Church in general, since the death of Jesus, the connotation of the phrase 'the love of God' had been historically conditioned or illumined. The nature of God's love is to be understood in the same terms—in the love of the brother. 'If a man say, I love God and hateth his brother, he is a liar: for he that loveth not his brother, whom he hath seen, how can he love God whom he hath not seen?' This does not mean that love of God and love of man are equated: this would be to empty the love of God of all its numinous, awful nature.[1] But it does mean that love of the brother is the sure test of the true love of God.[2]

But to return again to our theme. The same orientation is found in Paul. He too seldom speaks of the love of God or of loving God. He speaks of loving the neighbour in terms of God's act in Christ. This is now for Paul also the pattern of love and of life.

[1] On this see H. R. Niebuhr, *Christ and Culture* (1950), pp. 15 ff. The rabbis also were shy of expressly conjoining the love of God and the love of man, as do the Synoptics and the Testament of the Twelve Patriarchs (Test. Dan. v. 3; also Test. Isa. v. 2). The reason Boaz Cohen gives for this is that the 'Rabbis felt that it would be giving equal honor, so to speak, to the Master and the servant'. (*Op. cit.* p. 224. But see M. Aboth iv. 15.)

[2] C. H. Dodd, *The Johannine Epistles* (1945), pp. 81 ff., especially p. 86, where he speaks of 'the downright concreteness, almost crudity, in stating the moral requirements of religion (in 1 John, which) belongs to the genius of New Testament Christianity in general'.

Rom. v. 6 ff.:

While we were yet helpless, at the right time Christ died for the ungodly. Why, one will hardly die for a righteous man—though perhaps for a good man one will dare even to die. But God shows his love for us in that while we were yet sinners Christ died for us. (RSV.)

Rom. viii. 32:

He who did not spare his own Son but gave him up for us all, will he not also give us all things with him? (RSV.)

Eph. v. 1:

Therefore be imitators of God, as beloved children. And walk in love, as Christ loved us and gave himself up for us.... (RSV.)

The most striking example of Paul's Christocentric understanding of love, however, occurs in 1 Cor. xiii, the hymn to love, which is probably to be understood as based upon a kind of character sketch of Jesus himself.[1]

We can therefore claim that, like 1 John, Paul also urges us not so much to love our neighbour and to love God as to look at Jesus and then to love our neighbour in His light. Although the words of Jesus, as we have previously seen, are important for Paul, nevertheless, this reference to Jesus means, primarily, participation in his life of self-giving: not listening to his words only or chiefly, but appropriating his life, death and resurrection is most emphasized. This emphasis comes out most clearly, however, in the Fourth Gospel. While concentration on the act of God in Christ co-exists in Paul with reverence for his words, and while in Matthew the words of Jesus are given a prominence at least equal to his acts, when we turn to the Fourth Gospel we seem to be in a different world! Although John presents Jesus as a prophet, and is careful to explain that the title rabbi as applied to Jesus was not a mere honorific but bore the connotation of 'teacher', nevertheless his attitude to the words of Jesus needs careful scrutiny.[2] In the Fourth Gospel the title rabbi is applied freely to Jesus by disciples and 'outsiders'; even the Risen Lord is addressed as Rabboni.[3] That the Johannine Christ envisages his relation to his disciples somewhat after the manner of a rabbi emerges clearly, and possibly, if not probably, underlies John xiii. 1 ff.[4] Moreover, the verb

---

[1] *P.R.J.*[2] p. 147.   [2] John iii. 2.

[3] John xx. 16; see also John i. 38, 49; vi. 25.

[4] The precise point of contrast in the footwashing in John xiii. 1–17 cannot be determined. Jesus has taken on himself the role of a slave, and a Gentile slave at that, in order to give an example (ὑπόδειγμα) to his disciples. Is there here a deliberate contrast intended, or at least a side-glance, at the usages of rabbinic scholars in

διδάσκειν (to teach) is used of Jesus in the same absolute way as in the Synoptics, without any indication being given as to the content of his teaching.[1] In the Synoptics, and especially Matthew, it would appear that διδάσκειν refers frequently to the ethical teaching of Jesus; but what is its reference in the Fourth Gospel?

In John xii. 24 f. we find an outcrop of the kind of ethical teaching which we encounter in the Jesus of the Synoptics: it inculcates self-sacrifice and reads: 'Truly, truly, I say to you, unless a grain of wheat falls into the earth and dies, it remains alone; but if it dies, it bears much fruit.' But here the ethical teaching does not stand on its own feet: it is a kind of exegetical pendant designed to unfold the meaning of the hour which has come at which the Son of Man is to be glorified (xii. 23). It is thus not introduced primarily for its intrinsic worth, but merely as explanatory of an event, the work of Jesus, his death. Apart from vii. 14–24, where we find a conflict story about Jesus and 'the Jews', reminiscent of the kind which occurs in Mark, turning on the moral issue of healing on the sabbath, xii. 24 f. is the only passage in the Fourth Gospel, outside the Farewell discourses, where the ethical teaching of Jesus *as such* breaks through; and, as we saw, even here it is not neat.

relation to their disciples? This is not to be ruled out. In verses 13, 14, Jesus is teacher (διδάσκαλος = רַב) and in verse 5 it is the feet of his disciples (μαθητῶν) that he washes. On the other hand, the disciples address Jesus, so he himself asserts, as 'Lord' (κύριε, מַר) in verses 7, 8, 9 (see S–B, II, 558), and the application of his action is proffered in terms of the master–slave relationship, verse 16. The probability is that John thinks in terms both of pupil–teacher and of master–slave relationships. These were, in fact, very close. A pupil or שַׁמָּעָא was required to perform *all* the duties of a slave to his rabbi, except that of washing his feet, which was reserved for the slave. Is the point of John xiii, that here, Jesus, the rabbi, performs *for his pupils* a duty which even a pupil was not expected to do for his rabbi? Judaism was careful to distinguish the duties of Jewish slaves from those of Gentile slaves and pupils of rabbis were to be careful, even in the fulfilment of their service to the rabbi, not to allow themselves to be confused with slaves. The difficulty of deciding on the exact reference in the foot-washing is acknowledged by Rengstorf in *T.W.Z.N.T.* II, 156, where details on the duties of scholars to teachers are given: in II, 281, he leans to the 'master–slave' emphasis. S–B, II, 557, do not emphasize this. The pertinent rabbinic passages are given by the latter. D. Daube (*op. cit.* p. 182) regards the foot-washing as 'a gesture' performed 'in order to bring about question and interpretation'. He contrasts such an action which is performed not for its own sake but for the meaning it conveys, with those which have their *raison d'être* in themselves, for example the healing miracles. The foot-washing approaches the form which he calls a 'mystifying gesture' (pp. 170–83). It is peculiar to John. Rabbis were accustomed to expressing sentiments not unlike those found in John xiii by Jesus, the rabbi.

[1] See G. Kittel, *T.W.Z.N.T.* I, 140.

Similarly the application of the term *prophet* to Jesus does not connote any moral passion such as we usually associate with the term: it is his divinatory prowess in iv. 19, and in vii. 41 the mystery of his claims, rather than their ethical demand that provokes the use of the term, while in vi. 14 and ix. 17 it is a 'sign' that calls forth the reference to a prophet.

And this last, like the subordination of ethical teaching to an event in John xii. 24 f., is typical, because, until we come to the Passion Narrative, where the ethical demand of Jesus emerges unmistakably but in a peculiarly Johannine manner, it is the acts or signs of Jesus that are significant, not his ethical exhortation. In ii. 23 many believed because of the 'signs': there is no mention of the 'teaching'; in iii. 2 it is the signs which authenticate the divine origin of the teacher. So in chapter v the ethical teaching is not mentioned. What provokes opposition to him is the alleged claim of Jesus to be equal with God (v. 19). It is given to the Son not to teach, but to do and to judge. The teaching of Jesus is not listed among those things which authenticate or bear witness to his claims. So in vi. 31 it is a work of Christ to which appeal is made, and in ix. 5 the important thing is to work the 'works of him that sent me'. In x. 32 Jesus assumes that it is not his teaching but one of his acts that has caused Jewry to persecute him, just as it is his works that bear witness to him in x. 26, and that instigate faith in xi. 45 and opposition in xii. 37. The ethical teaching of Jesus, it would appear, does not constitute for the Fourth Gospel a *sign* of the Messiah as it does for Matthew and to a lesser degree for Mark.

This would seem to be reinforced when we ask what is the exact content of that teaching which is ascribed to Jesus in the Fourth Gospel. In chapter iii entry into the Kingdom of God is not to be made a disciple unto it, as in Matt. xiii. 52, but to be born anew of water and the Spirit, and the content of the teaching of Jesus is conceived to be concerned with the revelation of 'the things above' (iii. 12, 27, 31). In vii. 28 f. the content of the teaching turns out to be not an ethical demand, but a revelation of his own origins, just as in viii. 29, 34, 47 the content is 'what his father has taught him'.

And this leads to another emphasis in the Johannine presentation: the teaching of Jesus is markedly derivative. Waiving for the moment the meaning of the phrase 'But I say unto you' in the *SM*, the teaching of Jesus in the Synoptics is stamped with his own authority. The Johannine Christ, on the other hand, is careful to insist that he teaches only what has been given him to teach by the Father. In chapter vii Jesus disclaims that his teaching is his: it is that of him who sent him. So in xiv. 10 the teaching of Jesus (his ῥήματα) leads to knowledge of the Father and is not his own (xiv. 24; xvii. 8, 14; xv. 10). In iv. 41 the phrase 'they believed on account of his word' does not help us to fix precisely what the 'word' of Jesus meant; and again in v. 24 it is difficult to ascertain exactly what hearing the word of Christ means. The phrase is parallel to 'to believe in him that sent me' so that it is probable that the 'word' connotes the revelation of God which Jesus has brought.[1] Enough has been written to indicate that the words of Jesus on matters of conduct do not play in John the part they play in the Synoptics and especially in Matthew.[2]

How is this fact to be interpreted, that the Fourth Gospel is apparently not concerned to indicate the moral teaching of Jesus as are the Synoptics? The suggestion is to hand that it had no need to do so because that teaching, by the time the Fourth Gospel came to be written, had become part and parcel of the Christian community. To recount the teaching was redundant. It is, therefore, perhaps because it assumes the awareness of that teaching that the Fourth Gospel 'ignores' it. But this is hardly a sufficient account of the matter, because the Fourth Gospel does assert the ethical seriousness of Jesus quite as strongly as Matthew, albeit in its own way.

In the first place, the Fourth Gospel sets Jesus *over against* Moses more explicitly than does Matthew, who sets the two figures, as we saw, in parallelism. In the very first chapter the Law which had come through Moses is contrasted with the grace and truth which came through Jesus, who is the exegesis of God, so to put it. And elsewhere in John, Jesus appears not as the interpreter of the old Torah but as, in his own person, the Word, the Torah: important is it to note that it is in the *person* and *acts* of Jesus more than in any synopsis of his words such as we find in Matthew that John finds Jesus as the Light, the Truth, the Way and the Word.

And, in the second place, John has summed up for himself the whole of the ethical teaching of Jesus in a 'new commandment' (καινὴ ἐντολή). This new commandment, however, finds its meaning not in any words that Jesus uttered so much as in the love showed by Christ. It is the possession of this love rather than any training in the words of Jesus which constitutes discipleship.

As the Father has loved me, so have I loved you; abide in my love. If you keep my commandments, you will abide in my love, just as I have kept my Father's

---

[1] On the meaning of 'the Word', etc., in John, see C. H. Dodd, *The Interpretation of the Fourth Gospel* (Cambridge, 1953).
[2] See Appendix XIV.

commandments and abide in his love. These things I have spoken to you, that my joy may be in you, and that your joy may be full. This is my commandment, that you love one another as I have loved you. Greater love has no man than this, that a man lay down his life for his friends. (John xv. 9–13.)

The new commandment corresponds with the commandment which Jesus had himself received from the Father (x. 18), which was that he should lay down his life; and it is this commandment which includes all the commandments which Jesus has to give (xiv. 15; xv. 20). It is significant that the 'new commandment of love' occurs in the context of the Passion. This is fitting because the Passion itself is for John the most signal pattern of the new commandment. But not only so. Although there is no account of the taking of the bread and drinking of the cup at the Last Supper in John, the phrase 'the new commandment' may be taken to indicate that he too like the Synoptics thinks of the death of Jesus in covenantal terms: it inaugurates a new commandment for his own, illumined by his death.

The Johannine writings, therefore, set forth the ethical demand of Jesus as the lofty one of love, after the pattern of the love of God revealed in Christ's giving of himself, a love as absolute as any directly commanded in the *SM* in v. 43 ff. From this point of view we may roughly compare the Johannine literature with Q, which, as we saw, set forth the absolute demand of Jesus. But there is also present in it an element which can, at least roughly, be compared with M's concern with the practicality or 'earthiness' of that demand. This may perhaps be seen in the Fourth Gospel itself, where in John xiii the absolute demand of Jesus is spelt out in terms of the menial task of footwashing, and in John xxi the love for Christ as Lord is interpreted as the will to feed his sheep.[1] But it is in 1 John that the motif with which we are concerned emerges most forcibly. Thus in the passage quoted above in 1 John iv. 21, reference is made to the commandment of love as given by Jesus. But lest this commandment become too 'high falutin' it is pinned down in 1 John iv. 19–21 and defined concretely. The whole verses read:

We love, because he first loved us. If any one says, 'I love God', and hates his brother, he is a liar; for he who does not love his brother whom he has seen, cannot love God whom he has not seen. And this commandment we have from him, that he who loves God should love his brother also.

[1] In addition to the above passages which contain specifically moral teaching, C. H. Dodd has pointed out an impressive number of reminiscences of the Synoptic tradition in 1 John, which do not directly concern us. (See *The Johannine Epistles*, pp. xxxviii–xlii.)

Here in 1 John iv. 20 is a qualifying comment on 1 John iv. 19. The same concern to tie down what might become too etherealized emerges in 1 John iii. 17, which brings 1 John iii. 16 down to earth:

We know that we have passed out of death into life, because we love the brethren. He who does not love remains in death. Any one who hates his brother is a murderer, and you know that no murderer has eternal life abiding in him. By this we know love, that he laid down his life for us; and we ought to lay down our lives for the brethren. But if any one has the world's goods and sees his brother in need, yet closes his heart against him, how does God's love abide in him?

In all this there is no halakic development such as we found incipient in M, which issued in specific practical directions, but there is concern to be 'realistic'. In addition it is pertinent to note further that, while in the Fourth Gospel itself the ethical teaching of Jesus seldom emerges directly, nevertheless in the First Epistle of John, which many ascribe to the author of the Gospel and is at any rate deutero-Johannine, so that it emerges from the same milieu as the Gospel, the words of Jesus frequently find an echo. A comparison of the following passages reveals this:

With Mark xii. 29–31	compare	1 John iv. 21
With Matt. xviii. 23	compare	1 John iv. 11
With Matt. v. 44–5	compare	1 John iv. 7
With Matt. v. 21–2	compare	1 John iii. 15
With Matt. vii. 21	compare	1 John ii. 17
With Matt. v. 48 (compare Luke vi. 36)	compare	1 John iii. 17
With Matt. v. 8–9	compare	1 John iii. 1–3
With Luke vi. 22	compare	1 John iii. 13
With Matt. vii. 8 (Luke xi. 10)	compare	1 John iii. 22
With Matt. vi. 22–3 (Luke xi. 34–6)	compare	1 John i. 5–6; ii. 9–11

Here again the wish can be the father to the thought, and the parallels are not always obvious. Nevertheless, they are sufficiently cogent to enable us to claim that in the community of the Fourth Gospel also the words of Jesus did play their part as in other communities in the primitive Church. While the *emphasis* of the Gospel falls where we have indicated above it would be precarious, particularly in the light of 1 John, to divorce it from the tradition of the ethical teaching of Jesus in his words.

Our survey of the various approaches to the words of Jesus in the documents of the New Testament can now be recapitulated. Behind both

Matthew and Paul we detected strata in which the commandments of Jesus can be characterized as *radical*, *regulatory* and *revelatory*. The demands of Jesus were initially preserved not merely because of their striking and unforgettable absoluteness, nor for their practical usefulness in catechesis and paraenesis, but because they constituted an indispensable part of the Gospel itself without which it could not be adequately comprehended in its moral seriousness. In other words, they were essential as revelatory of the nature of the Gospel. The demands of Jesus are part of the givenness of the Gospel. What we find in Matthew, and to a lesser degree in Paul, is that the revelatory and radical demands are used in what we may loosely call a regulatory, rabbinic manner, that is, they come to constitute a base, or given ground, from which halakoth are deduced or to which they are attached. For both Matthew and Paul the commandments of Jesus came to constitute a law of the Messiah and the same was true for James. As far as we can judge, however, there did not develop in primitive Christianity an intricate method for the exegesis or casuistic development of the commandments such as we find in rabbinic exegesis, although there is an incipient casuistry in both Matthew and Paul.

Outside Matthew and Paul the development was different. For the author of the Fourth Gospel the words of Jesus do not, explicitly at least, constitute a court of appeal. Rather they are summed up in one commandment—prominent also in Matthew and Paul, as elsewhere—which finds its connotation, primarily at least, not in what Jesus said, but in what he did, and especially in the Cross. Particularly noteworthy is it that in the moral education of the Gentile Christians, revealed to us in the catechetical elements preserved in the epistles and in the paraenesis of the Pastorals, the Church turned to Jewish and Hellenistic sources for its material, sometimes, as in the Pastorals, without attempting to root this in the Gospel in any obvious manner, that is, it took over much of the ethical tradition of Judaism and Hellenism for its own preliminary ethical teaching with no sense of incongruity at all.[1]

The inference is natural, in the light of this, that only in those documents which emerged within a milieu where the tradition of Judaism was markedly present did the demands of Jesus come to be understood as the Law of the Messiah. This, however, in the light of what we discovered in Paul and of the Johannine emphasis on the new commandment should not be pressed. Moreover, even though the demands laid upon Christians in catechesis and paraenesis in the Epistles lack the direct 'heroism' of those

---

[1] Compare C. H. Dodd, *Gospel and Law*, pp. 22 ff.

413

of Jesus, their significance should not be overlooked. Nowhere, even when the Church had become preponderantly Gentile, was the Gospel presented without its demand, and the Synoptic tradition of those demands, we may assume, was always presupposed. In sum, there is no reason to believe that Matthew's presentation of the teaching of Jesus as the Law of the Messiah would have been alien even to the Gentile Churches.

Finally, it is pertinent to point out that the understanding of the Gospel in terms of law, which we have traced in various forms in the New Testament, provides a bridge between the first century and the second which has too often been ignored. As has been frequently emphasized, in the Apostolic Fathers the interpretation of the Faith as a new law emerges without ambiguity, whereas in the New Testament itself, even in Matthew, we found a certain reserve or tentativeness at this point. It is possible that the more the Church broke away from the Old Israel and became aware of itself as the *New*, the more easily did it arrogate to itself a New Law. As the necessity to conciliate and to understand Judaism at close quarters, which made Matthew hesitant of making *explicit* claims about the New Moses and the New Law, gradually ceased to exist, what was implicit in the New Testament could become explicit in the Fathers. Not for us is it to minimize the differences between the Christianity of the New Testament and that of the second and later centuries, but at least we have provided sufficient evidence that any rigid characterization of the former as a religion of grace over against that of the Apostolic Fathers as one of law must be rejected. In leaving the first-century Church for that of the second, we experience no μετάβασις εἰς ἄλλο γένος, however clear-cut the break that separates the one from the other appears to be.[1] Rather, as historical probability should lead us to expect, we can already trace the beginnings of things to come in the primitive communities. Here we can only indicate this, without elaboration, because we have still to face a prior question, namely, how the understanding of his words, as the Law of the Messiah, in Matthew, was related to the ministry of Jesus himself.

[1] This is over-emphasized by T. F. Torrance, *The Doctrine of Grace in the Apostolic Fathers* (1948). Werner Jaeger, *Early Christianity and Greek Paideia* (Harvard University Press, 1961), shows how the Church came to receive Greek paideia and press it into its services. But, before it did this, it had already used a paideia—if we may so express it—based upon the words of Jesus and the moral tradition of Judaism. In this way also the second and subsequent centuries were prepared for by the first. That Jewish and Greek paideia had largely merged in many circles by the first century appears from such passages as TB Pesahim, 112*a*, where Akiba quotes a Greek proverb deriving from Aristophanes. See S. Lieberman, *Greek in Jewish Palestine* (New York, 1942), pp. 144–60, on 'Greek and Latin Proverbs in Rabbinic Literature'.

VI. THE SETTING IN THE MINISTRY OF JESUS

As we have seen in the preceding pages, Matthew drew around the figure of Jesus the mantle of a lawgiver. Certain elements in the primitive Church would have found this quite natural, and certain factors both outside and inside the Christian communities, anti-Paulinism, perhaps, Gnosticism of an incipient kind, sectarian infiltrations and the challenge of Judaism, may have stimulated this understanding of the Lord in Matthew. There remains to ask the question whether in thus rabbinizing Jesus, to use a loose term, Matthew has decked his Lord in an alien garb which falsifies the 'Jesus of history', that is, Jesus in so far as we can know him as he actually lived. Can we define the relation in which the Christ of the Mount stands to Jesus himself?

1. *Transmission of his words*

Here those difficulties arise which we mentioned at the beginning of chapter I. During the last two centuries we have witnessed the quest for 'the historical Jesus'. The motive behind this quest, which has largely dominated much NT scholarship both consciously and unconsciously for many decades, was the desire to be able to see Jesus of Nazareth behind and apart from the incrustations of Church tradition and dogma. But the labour devoted to it has had a very unexpected dénouement. Paradoxically enough, the outcome of the source- and form-criticism which it inspired has not been to lead us away from the 'traditional' Christ of the Church to a simpler, more probable and credible Jesus of history, as was often intended, but to engender the awareness that the very documents which are available for the quest are themselves so fashioned by the Church or Churches within which they arose that, in fact, it is only the Christ of the Church or the Jesus interpreted by the Church that we can know. To put it in other words, the Christ of the stained glass windows of tradition and dogma, to the destruction of whom so many books and sermons have been devoted, persistently re-emerges behind the dust of scholarship. The only changes in the picture seem to be confined to the background effects. These have recently taken on a far more Jewish colouring because we now know so much more about first-century Judaism. But the Jesus of history himself—so it is claimed—eludes us: we can only touch the hem of his garment. More pertinent to our immediate task is it that we can also only hear, so it is asserted, the whisper of his voice. The majority of the sayings ascribed to Jesus are sometimes stated to be the creation of the primitive Church. Hence it is not possible to discover what Jesus himself actually taught, but only what the early Church credited to him. And in this case, the *SM* cannot fruitfully be discussed in its relation to the teaching of Jesus, since there can be no clear statement of this.

But the extreme scepticism which has often marked modern study of the life and teaching of Jesus is now being questioned. In connexion particularly with the teaching of Jesus, certain facts and probabilities should not be overlooked. First, the milieu within which Jesus appeared was conditioned for the faithful reception and transmission of tradition. The phenomenon of the retention and repetition of sayings and speeches by worthy men in the Semitic world of the first and other centuries is familiar. To note one example, the laws now codified in the Mishnah were long preserved orally.[1] Secondly, the technical formulae describing the

---

[1] On all the above, see Lucien Cerfaux, *Recueil Lucien Cerfaux*, I (1954), 353 ff., and now, especially, B. Gerhardsson, *Memory and Manuscript* (1961). The following words attributed by Plato to Socrates are illuminating on an ancient attitude: 'I heard, then, that at Naucratis, in Egypt, was one of the ancient gods of that country, the one whose sacred bird is called the ibis, and the name of the god himself was Theuth. He it was who invented numbers and arithmetic and geometry and astronomy, also draughts and dice, and most important of all, letters. Now the king of all Egypt at that time was the god Thamus, who lived in the great city of the upper region, which the Greeks call the Egyptian Thebes, and they call the god himself Ammon. To him came Theuth to show his inventions, saying that they ought to be imparted to the other Egyptians. But Thamus asked what use there was in each, and as Theuth enumerated their uses, expressed praise or blame, according as he approved or disapproved. The story goes that Thamus said many things to Theuth in praise or blame of the various arts, which it would take too long to repeat; but when they came to the letters, "This invention, O king", said Theuth, "will make the Egyptians wiser and will improve their memories; for it is an elixir of memory and wisdom that I have discovered". But Thamus replied, "Most ingenious Theuth, one man has the ability to beget arts, but the ability to judge of their usefulness or harmfulness to their users belongs to another; and now you, who are the father of letters, have been led by your affection to ascribe to them a power the opposite of that which they really possess. For this invention will produce forgetfulness in the minds of those who learn to use it, because they will not practise their memory. Their trust in writing, produced by external characters which are not part of themselves, will discourage the use of their own memory within them. You have invented an elixir not of memory, but of reminding; and you offer your pupils the appearance of wisdom, not true wisdom, for they will read many things without instruction and will therefore seem to know many things, when they are for the most part ignorant and hard to get along with, since they are not wise, but only appear wise."' (Fowler's translation, *Phaedrus*, 274 C–275 A.)

reception and transmission of tradition emerge so clearly in the New Testament documents that we must believe that the early Christian communities handed on a tradition. That this tradition included ethical teaching and not merely doctrinal truths appears clearly. Moreover, that this ethical teaching contained specific directions from Jesus himself is rendered certain for an early period by the fact that Paul used collections, oral or written, of the words of Jesus, which he sharply distinguished from his own opinions; and it is a fair assumption that Paul was not alone in making this distinction.[1] Thirdly, the claim that Jesus spoke most probably in Aramaic, and that, therefore, since the tradition of his acts and words has come down to us in Greek, there is inevitably a certain falsification in the tradition, because translation is notoriously interpretation, if not misinterpretation, must not be denied. But apart from the possibility that Jesus *may* have been familiar with Greek, there were from the earliest days of the Church bilingual Christians to whom the translation of words from Aramaic to Greek would present no serious difficulty, so that the loss in authenticity incurred in translation should not be exaggerated.[2] Fourthly, it is highly pertinent to note that there was frequent intercourse between figures such as Peter, and other apostolic guardians of the tradition, and Christian communities in various places, so that the transmission and development of the tradition was not unchecked. It is not a vague, folk tradition, developing over vast stretches of time, that lies behind the NT, but an ecclesiastical one, which developed intensively in a brief period.[3] And, finally, there were specific interests at work in the early Church which would have naturally fostered the preservation of Jesus' words.[4]

[1] See above treatment, particularly of Paul, on pp. 341 ff.

[2] On the language of Jesus, see the bibliography in W. F. Stinespring, 'History and present state of Aramaic studies', in *The Journal of Bible and Religion*, XXVI (October 1958), 298 ff. To which add A. Dupont-Sommer, *Les Araméens* (Paris, 1949); W. F. Unger, *Israel and the Aramaeans of Damascus* (London, 1957); also Morton Smith, in *The Journal of Bible and Religion*, XXVI (October 1958), 304 ff. on 'Aramaic studies and the study of the New Testament'. Particularly important is E. Y. Kutscher, 'The language of the Genesis Apocryphon', in *Scripta Hierosolymitana*, IV (1958), pp. 1–34; and the work referred to by M. Black, *N.T.S.* III (1957), 305 ff. on 'The recovery of the language of Jesus'. On Jesus and Greek, R. O. P. Taylor, *The Groundwork of the Gospels* (1946), pp. 91 ff. It is probably impossible to go back to a point when the Church was not bilingual.

[3] On this see H. Riesenfeld, *The Gospel Tradition and its Beginnings*, pp. 18 ff. On the danger of applying to the New Testament methods appropriate to the Old, see W. F. Howard, *The Fourth Gospel in Recent Criticism and Research* (1931).

[4] See above, pp. 366 f. In addition special attention should be paid to the inaugural address of N. A. Dahl, 'Anamnesis', in *Studia Theologica* (Lund, 1948), I, 69–95, with which I find myself in much agreement.

While, therefore, it is idle to ignore that the tradition was influenced by the preaching, teaching, apologetic propaganda, catechism and liturgy of the Church as the form-critics have made luminously clear, and furthermore, that the Church did ascribe to the Jesus of history words uttered under the influence of the Spirit, nevertheless, the actual words of Jesus had a fair chance of survival. Indeed, the very fact that the words uttered in the Spirit were ascribed to the Jesus of history, if such indeed were the case, is itself testimony to the seriousness with which the Church deemed it necessary to anchor its tradition in him.[1] That there was a wholesale creation of sayings by the primitive communities, which were foisted on to the earthly Jesus, we should not assume. Far more likely is it that the Church inherited and preserved sayings of Jesus which floated in the tradition, modified them for its own purposes, and then again ascribed them to Jesus in a new form. The recognition of the original form may not be easy, but is also not always impossible.

So far, however, we have merely adduced general considerations to maintain that it is not unreasonable to claim that we may, after much sifting, be able to speak of the ethical teaching of Jesus and not merely of the early Church. Can we go further?

2. *The Teacher*

Let us begin by insisting upon what may appear banal, namely, that Jesus of Nazareth was a teacher. That he was such is attested beyond dispute by the Fathers of the Church, extra-canonical sources, and, particularly, by the New Testament itself. We begin with the early Fathers of the Church. The view is sometimes expressed that the weight of Christian devotion to Jesus soon proved too heavy to be expressed in terms of a pupil–teacher relationship and that as soon as Christianity encountered Hellenistic forces on any direct front the terms 'teacher' and 'disciples' proved inadequate: the name 'Christian' emerged at Antioch and the 'teacher' became a 'Lord'.[2] But this is to overlook the fact that in the early centuries of the Church Jesus appears as the 'illuminator' and is frequently designated as 'teacher'. The plenteous evidence for this is familiar.[3]

Of course, it is possible to argue that it was the Church that fabricated for itself the teaching that the Fathers ascribe to Jesus. But this would not

[1] G. Bornkamm, *Jesus of Nazareth*, Eng. trans. (1960), pp. 13–26.

[2] Vincent Taylor, *The Names of Jesus* (1959), pp. 12–14.

[3] H. E. W. Turner, *The Patristic Doctrine of Redemption* (1952); D. Van Den Eynde, *Les Normes de l'enseignement chrétien dans la littérature patristique des trois premiers siècles* (Paris, 1933).

invalidate their evidence as to the *propriety* of regarding Jesus as a teacher. Again it is possible to dismiss the didactic emphasis in the Patristic understanding of Jesus, with which we are here concerned, as the intellectualizing of Christianity under the impact of Graeco-Roman culture and to claim, for example, that when Clement of Alexandria speaks of Christ as teacher the term connotes not so much a source of ethical instruction as that of a saving mystery or gnosis.[1] But that the Hellenization of the tradition in Clement never went so far as to divorce it from its ground in Judaism appears from Clement's expectation of his Lord at his epiphany as 'teacher': that means that he is 'teacher' as judge: the ethical seriousness of the title is thus retained.[2] It is quite unnecessary to account for the Patristic emphasis by any extraneous influences: it is the natural continuation of an element already present in the New Testament itself. That it became more marked in the Fathers is to be readily granted, but not that it indicates any peculiarity of theirs or, in itself, their decline.[3]

The same understanding of Jesus as teacher emerges in the Jewish sources that refer to Jesus. When these are sifted they reveal Jesus as a crucified false-teacher who had his disciples (*talmidim*).[4] In one passage an actual word of his is cited[5] and it is possible that Christian emphasis on Jesus as an ethical teacher who had his own interpretation of the Law, because he was the Messiah, led to the suppression of much Jewish speculation on the Messiah as the inaugurator of a New Law.[6]

Apart from such secondary sources, the evidence of the NT itself is unambiguous. He was addressed as teacher by his own disciples,[7] by the public,[8] and by the learned themselves.[9] He called 'disciples' to himself.[10]

3. *The eschatological Preacher*

At this point caution is necessary. Are we to think of him as a rabbi or as some other kind of teacher? There were certainly many things which set him apart from the rabbis. The Synoptic tradition emphasizes the

---

[1] H. E. W. Turner, *op. cit.* pp. 39 ff.   [2] *Ibid.*

[3] Contrast T. F. Torrance, *The Doctrine of Grace in the Apostolic Fathers.*

[4] See references given by T. W. Manson, *Bulletin of the John Rylands Library*, vol. XXVII, no. 2 (June 1943). He concludes from a survey of all the non-canonical Jewish evidence that it suggests a 'crucified false-*teacher*'.

[5] TB Shabbath 116 *a–b*, although in the light of K. G. Kuhn's work this is now seen to be late.   [6] See above, pp. 185 ff.

[7] See on all this K. H. Rengstorf, *T.W.Z.N.T.* III, 138 ff., on διδάσκω, etc.

[8] *Ibid.*   [9] *Ibid.*

[10] *Ibid.* But, to preserve a balanced picture, see E. Stauffer, *op. cit.* pp. 13 ff.

authority of his teaching: it differed from that of the scribes.[1] Usually Jewish teachers had been the pupils of teachers from whom they had learnt faithfully that which they in turn had transmitted to their own pupils. While they exercised great ingenuity in the exegesis of their Scriptures, their greatest respect was reserved for the virtue of faithfulness in handing on what had been received.[2] But, as far as we know, Jesus had not been the pupil of 'teachers' other than those who may have taught him in the village school at Nazareth.[3] And the 'authority' with which Jesus spoke constituted a problem to his hearers. He spoke with the *reshuth*, the authority, of a rabbi, though he had not been taught or ordained:[4] his authority was therefore not derivative but autonomous. How could this be, that an unlettered man (ἀγράμματος) should know?[5] The source of his authority in teaching, therefore, differs from that of the rabbis. It agrees with this that he expresses his teaching in the imperative, not in the participial form customary among rabbis,[6] as does also the fact that, according to the tradition,[7] he used Scripture as a witness to himself which a rabbi would not normally do.[8] And here it is that the content of Jesus' teaching perhaps most radically differs from that of the rabbis. If the tradition of scriptural exegesis which emerges so forcibly in the documents of the New Testament, whereby certain blocks of passages from the Old Testament were applied to the life, death and resurrection of Jesus to illumine them, owes its initial impetus to Jesus himself, then it is clear that his attitude to exegesis was not altogether or even chiefly rabbinic. It is closer to that found in the Dead Sea Scrolls where also Scripture is applied for the interpretation of historical events. It implies a more directly *personal* involvement with the meaning of Scripture than was the case with the rabbis. This is explicable in the light of the understanding of his own ministry that Jesus possessed, that in his coming the Rule of God had drawn near. To this we shall return later. And just as this eschatological awareness demanded of Jesus an exegetical orientation

[1] Mark i. 28; vii. 28.
[2] For example, M. Aboth ii. 8, where R. Eliezer b. Hyrcanus is praised as 'a plastered cistern which loses not a drop', that is, retains what has been taught.
[3] On the school system of Palestine in the first century, see N. Drazin, *The History of Jewish Education from 515 B.C.E. to 220 C.E.* (1940); N. Morris, *The Jewish School* (1937). H. I. Marrou, *A History of Education in Antiquity*, Eng. trans. (1956), pays hardly any attention to Jewish education.
[4] See D. Daube, *op. cit.* pp. 206 ff.   [5] John vii. 15; Jesus is ἀγράμματος.
[6] D. Daube, *op. cit.* pp. 90 ff.
[7] C. H. Dodd, *According to the Scriptures* (1952), p. 110.
[8] Mark xii. 35 ff.

different from that of the haggadic fancy and casuistry of rabbinism, so it also dictated the external features of his teaching activity. Jesus not only taught in synagogues but also in the open air by the sea and on the hills.[1] His audiences consisted not only of pupils, members of his circle or 'school',[2] though he had such perhaps, but also of the people of the land, publicans, and sinners with whom he freely consorted. The nature of discipleship to Jesus has to be carefully noted, because it involved certain elements which differentiated it from the life of rabbinic *talmidim*. Discipleship arose in response to a call from Jesus to follow him, a call directed to the individual in isolation or to hearers at large. By its very origin, therefore, it involved commitment of a personal kind to Jesus himself and to his service. It frequently meant the forsaking of home, kith and kin, wealth, comfort and security, and readiness to share in the way of Jesus himself, which was the way of the Cross. Thus in Luke xxii. 28, Jesus can describe his disciples as those who have continued with him in his πειρασμοί, his trials.[3] How does all this compare with that of a Jewish *talmid*? There may be instances of rabbis choosing their own pupils or encouraging 'bright young students' to sit at their feet, and rabbis are urged to raise up many disciples,[4] but the Aboth advises an aspiring pupil 'to get him a teacher'.[5] Akiba[6] journeyed all the way from Babylon to Jerusalem to get him such a one in Hillel. The case of Akiba is also instructive in another way. For years during his student life he was dependent on his wife for support, and, normally, preoccupation with the Law did not involve the severance of natural human ties: many rabbis had secular callings as did also their students. To become a *talmid* involved not so much a crisis, as did the call of Jesus, as concentration in study.

---

[1] For example, Mark iv. 1 ff.; v. 1 ff.

[2] Does οἶκος in Mark sometimes have the meaning of school? Was there a 'beth Joshua' as well as a 'beth Hillel'? Jesus' disciples were certainly compared to those of the Pharisees (Mark ii. 18).

[3] See K. H. Rengstorf, *T.W.Z.N.T.* III on διδάσκω.

[4] M. Aboth i. 1. There is also the saying of Akiba that if the calf (that is, the pupil) craves for milk the cow (that is, the teacher) also yearns even more to give it, TB Pesahim, 112a. This reads: 'Five things did R. Akiba charge R. Simeon b. Yoḥai when he was immured in prison (during Hadrian's edict against practising and teaching Judaism, *J.E.* I, 305). He [the latter] said to him, "Master, teach me Torah". "I will not teach you", he replied. "If thou wilt not teach me", he said, "I will tell my father Yoḥai and he will deliver thee to the state." "My son", answered he, "more than the calf wishes to suck, does the cow desire to suckle." Said he to him, "Yet who is in danger? Surely the calf is in danger".' (Soncino translation.)

[5] *Ibid.* i. 6.

[6] L. Finkelstein, *Akiba, Scholar, Saint and Martyr, ad rem.*

And although the sacrifices made by the students of the rabbis for the sake of the Torah shine brightly, and although in times of persecution loyalty to their studies often meant death, nevertheless there was a marked difference between a life dedicated to study at the feet of a rabbi, in which the aim was an increasing knowledge of the Law which would eventually 'qualify' a student himself to become a rabbi, and the life of the Christian disciple (often, to judge from 'the Twelve', not markedly studious by nature!) called to personal loyalty to Jesus in his way. For the one the Torah is the ultimate concern, for the other Jesus himself, and it is this personalism also that made of the *talmid* of Jesus not another rabbi but an apostle or witness.

4. *The Rabbi*

We have tried to do justice to the eschatological character of Jesus as teacher. Nevertheless, when all the differences between him and a rabbi have been noted and if it be admitted that in many ways Jesus was like a wandering Cynic–Stoic preacher rather than a rabbi or, more accurately, like a preacher from Galilee, one of the '*ober Gᵃlila'ah*, this must not be allowed to pre-empt him of all affinity with rabbis. Because the rabbinic traits in Jesus are unmistakable also. He was called rabbi. While in his day the title did not have the exact connotation of one officially ordained to teach that it later acquired, it was more than a courtesy title: it did designate a 'teacher' in the strict sense. Evidence of a rabbinic colouring in the activity of Jesus emerges also in the terminology employed of the disciples. A distinction is recognizable between 'coming to Jesus' (προσέρχεσθαι πρός) and 'going after Jesus' (ὀπίσω ἐλθεῖν) (= הלך אחרי). The last phrase is the equivalent of 'to follow Jesus' = ἀκολουθεῖν. When Jesus addresses the multitudes he invites them 'to come to him' (προσ-έρχεσθαι πρός): it is only the disciples themselves who can be said to follow (ὀπίσω ἔρχεσθαι). But the terms προσέρχεσθαι πρός and ὀπίσω ἔρχεσθαι are probably to be understood as the equivalents of rabbinic technical terms for going to a rabbi for instruction (בא ל'), and following a rabbi as his 'servant' (הלך אחרי).[1] It agrees with this that in Mark xv. 41 (= Matt. xxvii. 55: compare Luke viii. 2 f.) ἀκολουθεῖν, which is the equivalent of ὀπίσω ἔρχεσθαι, is interpreted as διακονεῖν, which is an admirable translation of the rabbinic שמש, Piel שימש, which, as we have seen, is used of students being in attendance upon a scholar as a disciple.

[1] On all this, see E. Fascher on 'Jesus der Lehrer' in *Theologische Literaturzeitung*, LXXIX (1954), cols. 325–42.

The fact that in Mark xv. 41 those who serve are women does not make the terminology less significant, as we shall see below. The duties of a שַׁמָּשׁ are manifold. He brings his master's sandals, supports him at need, prepares his way for him, manages the ass on which he rides.[1] A late passage defines the duties of a שַׁמָּשׁ as those of a slave except that he is not to take off his teacher's sandals: this last is reserved for the slave. It will appear that the functions of the disciples in the Gospels are those ascribed to a שַׁמָּשׁ. The foot-washing scene in John xiii may have a side-glance at the rabbinic custom. There Jesus repudiates the need for a שַׁמָּשׁ for himself and inculcates the same spirit for his disciples. There is a rabbinic parallel to this scene which shows that rabbis also could share in this spirit.[2] Again in Mark x. 45 the reference to the διάκονος (שַׁמָּשָׁא or שַׁמָּשׁ) and the δοῦλος is instructive. Jesus seems here to be repudiating the reverential treatment meted out to the great: his terms may suggest rabbis. But this is unlikely, however, because the context quite clearly has reference not to rabbinic usage but to Gentile. Moreover, Jesus seems to have accepted the honour ascribed to him just as did the rabbis. Thus we are to understand in this light, probably, the service rendered to Jesus by Peter's mother-in-law[3] and others. The service rendered is more than that at table: it belongs to the category of that rendered to great teachers even by their mothers and fathers.

Finally, we note that when Jesus taught he sat,[4] as did Jewish teachers, and we may surmise that, despite the itinerary and 'crisis' character of his ministry, much of his time with his disciples went into the exposition of the Law. He was questioned in public about the Law and he was questioned in private. He was recognized by opponents as having the way of truth or at least as being able to discuss this; the reference in Mark xii. 14 f. is clearly sarcastic.[5] The problems which emerge in the Gospels as having been dealt with by Jesus, for example marriage, divorce, *lex talionis*, etc., are such as rabbis discussed. The extent to which the sources reveal an ability on the part of Jesus to use the rabbinic Hebrew of the schools must be a matter of conjecture.[6] That he could hold his own with the learned

[1] E. Schweizer deals with 'Following Jesus' with great insight in *Lordship ana Discipleship*, Eng. trans. (1960), pp. 11 ff.; but he ignores the element of 'receiving a tradition of words' with which we are here concerned. See especially pp. 21, 93 f.

[2] See S–B, *ad rem*.   [3] Mark i. 31; Luke x. 40.   [4] v. 1 *et al.*

[5] The private explanation is prominent in Mark; see, for example, Mark iv. 10 ff. *et passim.*

[6] See Morton Smith, *Tannaitic Parallels to the Gospels*, and T. W. Manson, *The Teaching of Jesus.*

emerges clearly and this, presumably, implies the ability to use their terms. On the other hand, it would appear that those technical terms which do emerge in the Synoptic accounts of discussions with learned opponents, for example the practice of Corban in Mark vii, reference to which by Jesus has been taken to imply acquaintance with scholarly techniques, may have been so well known that no inference should be drawn from Jesus' allusion to it that he was technically learned. Again, other rabbinic terminology of an obvious kind occurs in passages which may not be authentic, for example the phrase 'binding and loosing' in Matt. xviii. 18; xvi. 19. But the use of such terminology again demands no *particular* acquaintance with the methods of the schools. Subtlety, and a native wit, and awareness, the conflict of Jesus with his scribal, Pharisaic and other opponents, reveals, but not necessarily, the learning of the schools, although he could hold his own with scribal opponents, and must, therefore, have had a lively awareness of their method, if not an exact knowledge of it. The exegesis we find in Jesus' words is not casuistic in the rabbinic sense, but usually more direct.

Nevertheless, the evidence presented probably justifies us in thinking of the Jesus of history as having a kind of 'school' around him: not a strictly rabbinic school but yet one that had rabbinic traits. Later on there was much in the structure of the Church that recalls the transmission of tradition in Judaism: the impetus to this development was already present in the ministry of Jesus.[1] We need not doubt that those chosen to be with him learnt of him, treasured his words and passed them on. The emergence of the words of Jesus in so many of the documents of the early Church is not accidental: there was a Christian paradosis which had its point of departure in Jesus of Nazareth himself, and whose 'continuity' was preserved by the *talmidim* of Jesus and their successors, of various kinds, in the early Church. All of which makes it credible that the 'words' of Jesus were preserved and transmitted with some degree of faithfulness.[2]

If what we have written above be accepted, then Jesus of Nazareth appears in a twofold form, at least, as an eschatological figure and as a rabbi, a teacher of morality. As the oscillations in NT scholarship from Harnack to Schweitzer show, the temptation is always present to concentrate on the one to the neglect of the other: but the two belong to one person. They may seem uneasily yoked but the conjunction to which we

[1] See especially B. Gerhardsson, *Memory and Manuscript* (1961); H. Riesenfeld, *The Gospel Tradition and its Beginnings* (1957).
[2] See Appendix XV.

refer should not be unexpected, because, in the Jewish hope for the future, eschatology was never divorced from the ethical, the Messianic King was to be also a teacher or interpreter of the Law: the Messiah could be like Moses. And the same is true in the New Testament: Jesus as Servant-Messiah had also to define his attitude to the Law: *as the eschatological figure he was necessarily a teacher of morality*. This appears clearly in the Marcan summary of the message of Jesus: it reads: 'The time is fulfilled and the Kingdom of God is at hand; repent ye and believe the Gospel.' The proclamation of the eschatological event calls for repentance: the act of God in the Gospel constitutes an appeal to man for a better life: the gift and the demand are inseparable. And despite the modifications introduced into his words by the Church, in view of that transmission of a tradition from Jesus through his disciples which we have indicated above, it is a fair assumption that we can know what the ethical teaching of Jesus, in its main emphases and intention, was.

5. The demand of Jesus in its setting

To begin with we have seen that Jesus of Nazareth appeared as a preacher of repentance. How did he conceive this repentance? It is sometimes stated that his call to repentance was not in terms of the Law. Is this view justified? Or was it not natural for him as the New Moses to think of repentance in such terms? A comparison of Jesus with others who called for repentance in first-century Judaism may be instructive at this point. There were many such who thought of repentance in the light of the Law. The following factors are relevant.

The majority of Jews in the first century, we may assume, lived their lives in disregard of the claims of the Law. They constituted 'the people of the land' who were held in contempt by the religious. The circles from which Jesus emerged were not strictly speaking among 'the people of the land', the *'am haaretz*, in the technical sense.[1] The whole of his dialogue with the Scribes and Pharisees makes it clear that he took the Law seriously. Whether Jesus intended to reject the Law we shall discuss below, but even if he did, which is unlikely, it was not from indifference to it, such as prevailed among the *'am haaretz*. As we shall see, Jesus honoured the Law even while he struck it. For our present purpose, we merely have to note that the *'am haaretz* do not at least directly illumine for us his call to

[1] On these, see G. F. Moore in *The Beginnings of Christianity*, ed. Foakes Jackson and Kirsopp Lake, 1 (1920), 439 ff.

repentance, except in so far as his call was directed to them with a sorrow-ful compassion and passion unlike the passionate contempt often showed to them by other religious leaders.[1]

The second attitude to the Law in first-century Judaism is that asso-ciated with the Sadducees. This was to accept the written Law and the written Law only. They rejected the authority of the oral tradition which had grown like a fence around the Law itself. In one sense in his critical attitude towards the traditions of the fathers, Jesus is near to the Saddu-cees. But whereas their rejection of the oral tradition sprang from a rigid conservatism, which, by insisting on the written Law only, virtually relegated it to 'the museum for antiquities', Jesus rejected the tradition of the fathers only to replace it by his own tradition or interpretation, so that he is both near to Sadducean conservatism and far removed from it.[2]

Next we come to the liberal approach of the Pharisees. In their desire to make the Law relevant for the whole of life the Pharisees accepted both the written Law and the oral Law, which was its fence, as authoritative. Their loyalty to tradition was the condition of adaptability in a changing world. They were concerned to apply the Law to life (to judge from Finkelstein's treatment, at least in its spirit), much as Christian Socialists and Liberals in our time have been anxious to apply Christianity to life. There is much evidence that Jesus for some time sought to understand the Pharisees, and, in some ways, he cannot but have sympathized with them. Nevertheless, it was finally with the 'liberal' Pharisees that Jesus was most in conflict because the very tradition which they sponsored, as Jesus saw it, had ceased to express the spirit of the Law around which it had grown, and had, indeed, come even to annul its intention. This is the force of Jesus' criticism of the Pharisees in Mark vii. He rejected their kind of tradition. The call to repentance uttered by Jesus was not the same then as that sent forth by the Pharisees: his demand for righteousness was to be greater and more exacting than theirs.[3]

And, finally, we come to the group with which Jesus may have had, in one sense, much in common, and yet which he criticized, the sectarians,

[1] See on this especially J. Jeremias, *The Parables of Jesus* (1954), pp. 99 ff.
[2] For the view that Jesus was nearer the Sadducees than is generally realized, see R. Leszynsky, *Die Pharisäer und die Sadduzäer* (1912); his views are summarized by J. Jocz, *The Jewish People and Jesus Christ* (London, 1949), pp. 16 f.
[3] I have followed the consensus of scholarship on Pharisaism. L. Finkelstein's work is the most illuminating. For a brief summary, see my *Introduction to Phari-saism* (Brecon, 1954–5).

whose literary remains have been recently discovered near the Dead Sea. Their attitude to the Law can best be described as *radical*. One of the key words they employed was the word '*all*'. 'All' that the Law as interpreted in the tradition of the Sect demanded was to be observed. To this end, they forsook all, for a community 'in Torah and in wealth'. Here even more 'desperately'—a word which we use advisedly—than in Pharisaism the Law was interpreted and taken seriously. So seriously, indeed, that in no place do we find more agonized cries of unworthiness before the Law in pre-Christian Judaism than here: here is Judaism at its 'boiling point'.[1]

Can we understand Jesus' call to repentance better in the light of that of the sectarians? These are not mentioned by name in the New Testament, but that John the Baptist had been influenced by them is possible, and Jesus himself, we may assume, knew of them. Like the sectarians, Jesus issued a call to a radical repentance, for a decision in the light of an eschatological event, for obedience which was essentially moral and not cultic. Nevertheless, there is evidence that he criticized the Sect. As we saw, we can probably pin down this criticism explicitly to v. 43 ff.: 'Ye have heard that it was said, Thou shalt love thy neighbour and hate thine enemy: but I say unto you, Love your enemies', etc. This criticism occurs in that section where Jesus is giving his interpretation of the will of God and contrasting it with the understanding of '*those of old*'. And it is precisely at this point—in the interpretation of the will of God—that Jesus differs from the sectarians. As we have seen, his 'personal' approach to the Scriptures of the Old Testament was in a certain way like theirs, because the sectarians also applied the Scriptures directly to themselves. But whereas their understanding of the Law led them to an insistence on total, literal, obedience to their own understanding of the Law, which in turn meant entry into a closed community, governed by a rule which was uniform for all, and which demanded hatred of those outside, Jesus had his own interpretation. He too demanded obedience to the will or Law of God, but as he understood it this was not an iron discipline equally applicable to all in a closed community but an all-inclusive love of the brethren and of those outside. Thus the difference between Jesus and the sectarians was not in the intensity of the obedience they demanded: Jesus and the sectarians are both 'totalitarians'. The difference between them lies in their interpretation of the Will of God which demands this total obedience. They are alike in their radicalism but not in

[1] See *Christian Origins and Judaism*, p. 176, n. 86.

their understanding of the essential nature of the obedience demanded by God.[1]

Can we reveal further the nature of this demand for Jesus?

Let us begin with the assertion that the Law and the Prophets of the OT remained valid for Jesus as the expression of the will of God: there is no complete break in Jesus with the ethical teaching of Judaism.[2] The conflict stories at the beginning of Mark have given the impression that Jesus from the very beginning of his ministry was at daggers drawn with the teachers of his day. But this impression is to be resisted. There is much evidence that, for a time at least, Jesus and the Pharisees were not so opposed.[3] The sources we possess for the ministry of Jesus emerge from a period when the Church and the Synagogue were increasingly diverging. But Jesus in his conduct seems to have been conservative. He appears in the Synagogue on the sabbath day, he joins pilgrims on feast days in Jerusalem, he is found in the Temple, he celebrates the Passover, he accepts the sacrificial rites, and religious customs such as fasting, prayer and alms-giving. He wears the traditional dress of the pious: he is careful to recognize the rightful authority of the priest. With this it agrees that the early Church does not appeal to his practice to defend its freedom from legal observance. Rather even for Paul Jesus is a minister of the circumcision born under the Law.[4]

Thus Jesus was no iconoclastic revolutionary; nor was he contemptuously withdrawn from the people of his day. He came not to destroy. On the other hand, he did come to fulfil. And there is much in his activity in the Gospels which suggests an attitude of sovereign freedom towards the Law. For example, his attitude to the sabbath appears to have been very free, as does his treatment of things clean and unclean. It is highly doubtful whether at any point Jesus specifically annuls the Law. Thus in the discussions on the sabbath and on divorce he remains within the framework of the Law. At one point only can he be considered to annul the Law, in Mark vii, and on examination even this point is doubtful.[5]

We shall, then, hold that the Law and the Prophets remained valid for

---

[1] See the indispensable and thorough work of H. Braun, *Spätjüdisch-häretischer und frühchristlicher Radikalismus*, 2 vols. (Tübingen, 1957), where he deals with the *Toraverschärfung* of Qumran; especially pp. 3 ff. See also above, p. 216.

[2] For Jesus and the Law, see my article in *Mélanges Bibliques, op. cit.*

[3] *Mélanges Bibliques*, pp. 441 ff.

[4] *Ibid. passim.* Contrast the repudiation of the customary usage of Judaism by Qumran.

[5] *Ibid.*

Jesus as the expression of the will of God. At this point, he was at one with Sadducee, Pharisee and sectarian. Not his estimate of the Law as the revelation of the will of God set him apart from these but his interpretation of this revelation. In this sense there is a real continuity between his ethical teaching and that of the Law.

How then, did Jesus regard the Law? In the Synoptic Gospels the moral teaching of Jesus is presented in at least three contexts: in a context of doom, in a context of creation, and in a context of Law. First, in a context of doom. The Gospels present Jesus as labouring under the conviction that the present order was to pass away either immediately or soon. In any case he lived his life in the conviction that the End was at hand. And it has been claimed that it was this imminence of the End that enabled Jesus to shed all inessentials in his ethical teaching and to concentrate on the absolutely necessary demands of God: it was the light of the End that lent radicalism to his words and lit up for him the moral plight of man and his duty. Some have gone further and have said that it is only to the comparatively brief period that remained for him before the End of all things that his words were meant to apply.[1] But there is much in the teaching of Jesus which does not bear this character, but is clearly applicable to all times. Moreover, it is important to remember that it is highly questionable whether in fact an impending crisis does illuminate our present duty. The awareness of an imminent doom in itself may as much confuse as illumine, as we who face possible nuclear catastrophe know only too well. The sectarians at Qumran lived in the awareness of an impending crisis, but this led them to an increasingly rigid and narrow ascetic and withdrawn rigorism very different from the radicalism of Jesus. Thessalonian Christians who thought that the End of all things was at hand promptly concluded that it was foolish to work. Those who calculated the times before the End both in Judaism and Christianity are not necessarily those most marked by ethical sensitivity. Even if Jesus did contemplate the End of all things soon, this in itself was not the secret of his illumination.

Next we noted that his ethic is related to creation.[2] We find in Jesus an appeal to the order of creation itself as a ground for morality, that is, an

---

[1] The detailed references I have supplied in my essay on 'Ethics in the NT' in *The Interpreter's Dictionary*.

[2] Mark x. 2–9; xii. 13–17; Matt. v. 44–8; vi. 19–20; vii. 24; x. 29; xiii. 24 ff.; xxiv. 27 ff., etc. Jesus, a poet, had the 'spirit of the beginning of things'; he knew 'the roots of the world'. See Edith Sitwell, *The Atlantic Monthly* (New York. Feb. 1954), pp. 42–3, on 'Dylan Thomas'.

appeal to what was prior to the Law of Moses in time and rooted in the act of creation. Two sections in particular suggest this. There is first Mark x. 1 ff. Here Jesus' view of marriage and divorce is grounded in the very act of God in the creation of male and female. The purpose of God in creation is an indissoluble marriage but the Law of Moses slipped in later owing to the hardness of men's hearts to allow divorce. Again, the appeal to the natural order as a guide to the good life appears also in v. 45 ff.; vi. 20 ff. The same appeal is implied also in the parables of Jesus where a real correspondence is assumed between the natural and the spiritual world. This principle also played a prominent role in the early Fathers. Are we to conclude that it was Jesus who introduced this method of thinking about moral problems? This has been claimed, but there is the same appeal to the created order in the CDC in a passage which though written in Hebrew strongly recalls Mark x; it reads:

although the principle of nature is: 'a male and a female He created them' (ויסוד הבריאה זכר ונקבה ברא אותם) (CDC iv. 21.) (Rabin's translation.)

And again in the Book of Jubilees laws are constantly based on the history of creation.[1] Moreover, the Old Testament itself finds a congruity between Nature and Man: for it too the good life is the 'natural' life as for much in Stoicism—τὸ κατὰ φύσιν ζῆν is appropriate to the Old Testament, as to Hellenistic sources.[2]

Here again we must be careful, therefore, not to derive the peculiarity of the teaching of Jesus from any single principle such as 'the natural' or 'the created' to which we have just referred. This principle is employed elsewhere without producing that moral illumination which we find in Jesus. Thus the Dead Sea Sect appealed to the principle of creation, but did not escape its terrible rigorism for that reason.

So we come to the third element detectable in the teaching of Jesus: he sets his teaching in the context of Law. Let us begin with the fact that we shall assume, namely, that Jesus of Nazareth thought of himself as the Messiah.[3] But to say Messiah is also to say 'Moses': the Messiah is Lawgiver, and Jesus, if he thought of himself as Messiah, had to come to his own terms with the Law. Both as Jew and as Messiah, the category of Law was not alien to him, as it is to us modern Protestants, but native and congenial.[4] And although there can be little doubt that the antitheses of

[1] Jubilees ii. 1 ff., et passim　　[2] Isa. i. 2 f.; Ps. viii, xix, etc.
[3] I am fully aware of the magnitude of this assumption, but plead indulgence for not discussing it in detail here because of the length of the treatment.
[4] Contrast E. Stauffer in his *Die Botschaft Jesu, passim.*

v. 22 ff.[1] are the formulation of Matthew, there can be equally little doubt that Jesus himself set his own teaching in relation to the Law of his people. A good starting point is v. 43 which gives us an antithesis which, I think, goes back to Jesus himself. Here the understanding of the love of neighbour is taken radically by Jesus over against the tradition of Qumran, which allowed, and indeed demanded, hatred of those outside. The centrality of love in the teaching of Jesus appears elsewhere in the Synoptics in Mark xii. 28–34; Matt. xxii. 34–40; Luke x. 25 ff. And while the commandment of love cannot be found frequently on the lips of Jesus himself, nevertheless the NT as a whole makes it a justifiable assumption that this was a central theme of his teaching. The evidence for this I have given elsewhere.[2] The concept of love is undoubtedly the best summation of the ethical teaching of Jesus. It is customary to state that Jesus enlarged the understanding of the demand of love in three ways: (1) by inseparably conjoining the love of God and man; (2) by reducing *the whole* of the demand of God to the twofold commandment of love of God and of neighbour he gave to these two commandments an unmistakable priority; (3) by extending the term neighbour to include everybody he universalized the demand of love.[3] All this is true; but more important is it to recognize that Jesus revealed the nature of 'love' itself. I do not refer at this point to the use of the word *agape* rather than *eros* in the New Testament, because the distinction usually insisted upon between these two terms cannot always be rigidly maintained. Rather do I think of the revelation of the nature of *agape* vouchsafed to us in the pure, unlimited self-giving which is exemplified by Jesus. 'Thou shalt love thy neighbour as thyself'—where the norm is the life and word of Jesus himself—is the commandment of the Messiah. And, as Jesus radicalized love, so he radicalized the other demands of the Law, as is made clear in the Antitheses.

But we still have not answered the question as to how Jesus came to this penetrating understanding of God's will. Let us retrace our steps. As summarized in Mark, we saw above that the message of Jesus had two facets, the declaration that the Kingdom of God had drawn near and the

[1] Here I agree with H. Braun, *op. cit.* part 2, p. 5. The antitheses in our form are 'secondary'. Contrast E. Käsemann, *Zeitschrift für Theologie und Kirche*, LI (1954), 144–8.

[2] *The Interpreter's Dictionary*, on 'Ethics in the New Testament'; see also above, pp. 401 ff.

[3] R. Schnackenburg, *Die sittliche Botschaft des Neuen Testamentes* (1954), p. 59; also George F. Thomas, *Christian Ethics and Moral Philosophy* (1953), pp. 42 ff.

call to radical repentance.[1] And it is here, we suggest, that the secret of the radicalism of Jesus' demand lies. Not any imminent end of the universe, not any principle of creation, not any casuistry, led Jesus to his understanding of God's will. He passed beyond all principles he had inherited, beyond the light of Law and Prophet, to what we can only call an intuitive awareness of the will of God in its nakedness. This awareness he expressed in terms of the imminence or presence of the Kingdom of God. We find in the DSS an awareness of the imminence of the End, but it is not expressed in terms of the Rule or Kingdom of God. The term the 'Kingdom of God'[2] does not occur in the Scrolls, whereas in the Gospels it is ubiquitous. 'If I by the finger of God cast out demons, then has the Kingdom of God come upon you.' Whatever the actual teaching of Jesus about the future, the distinctive element in his teaching and activity was the realization that, in his ministry, the Kingdom of God was actively at work. It is this that illumined him—his awareness of the Sovereign Rule of God in and through himself. This meant that whereas for Judaism the Law expressed the will of God, for Jesus his immediate awareness of the will of God became 'Law'.

And this awareness, which lies behind his ethical demand, raises the question as to who Jesus was that he had this awareness. This is another point at which the DSS are distinguished from the New Testament. They know no person who connected the Kingdom with himself, as did Jesus, and thus no ethic that passes beyond Scripture to the absolute will of God revealed to a Person and in a Person. Thus the expression of the absolute demand of God in the *SM*, as elsewhere in the New Testament, drives us back to the mystery of the person of Jesus himself. He himself in his own intuitive awareness of the will of God is the source of the radical ethic. His very words, therefore, point beyond themselves to himself, as their source: they too become witnesses to the 'King-Messiah'.

We find here a reconciling principle. We noted previously that several strands co-exist in the ethical tradition enshrined in the NT. The indicative strand, pointing to the life, death and resurrection of Jesus, to the act of God in Christ, as the root and pattern of all Christian living, appears in Paul, John and elsewhere. Similar to it is the emphasis on the imitation of Jesus, which also emerges in several places. These two strands, the

[1] The texts which omit 'Repent' in iv. 17 are Sy^{sc} Ju Cl Or Eus h. The overwhelming weight of evidence favours its retention. Notice how Matthew places 'Repentance' first, while Mark puts it almost last, i. 15.

[2] See K. G. Kuhn, *Konkordanz zu den Qumrantexten* (1961), *ad rem.*

indicative and the imitative, bid us look essentially to the fact of Christ, as the Epistle to the Hebrews puts it—'unto Jesus the author and perfector of our faith' (xii. 1). But alongside these two emphases, we have also traced a fairly ubiquitous emphasis on the significance of the words of Jesus as such. But in the last resort these very words also compel us to ask: 'Who is this person who thus speaks?': they too witness to him. The acts and words of Jesus compel the same question. They belong together as part of the ethic of Jesus and the mystery of his person: his words themselves confront us with him who utters them.

We are now in a position to answer the question, whether Matthew in concentrating on the words of Jesus as a 'new law' has departed from the mind of Jesus. The answer is both yes, and no. In so far as he thereby recognizes that there is a demand, as well as succour, at the heart of the Gospel, he remains true to Jesus. By gathering together the words of his Lord and concentrating them into an impressive frontispiece to his Gospel, he has presented them, to some extent, as a unified collection, constituting a 'law' in an external or independent sense. He has thus made it possible, and even easy, for many to separate the moral demand of Jesus from its total setting, as part of the Rule of God which Jesus proclaimed. In this sense, Matthew has helped to generate an isolated understanding of his commandments which has often prompted, on the one hand, a shallow moralism, and, on the other, what sometimes appears to be a kerygmatic amoralism, which, in its despair before the utter radicalism of his words, evacuates them of any real significance for the understanding of Jesus himself or for the business of living. But all this Matthew certainly never intended. We read the *SM* in isolation contrary to its purpose. It occurs after iv. 23–25, which reveal the compassion of the ministry of Jesus, how he went about not only preaching and teaching but 'healing every disease and every infirmity among the people', and 'how they brought him all the sick, those afflicted with various diseases and pains, demoniacs, epileptics and paralytics', and how 'he healed them'. The same emphasis on the mercy of his acts re-emerges in miracles in viii–ix, which follow the *SM*.[1] Before and after the demand of the *SM* stands the compassion of the Messiah. The infinite demand is embedded in infinite succour: they both belong together: his acts and his

---

[1] That Matthew has so placed the *SM* is not due only to his own insight; the collocation of grace or compassion and demand is given in the actualities of Jesus' ministry. Here I find W. T. Stace's insistence on 'sympathy' as a peculiarly Christian contribution to ethical thinking essentially true to the New Testament.

words are congruous. The words of Jesus the Messiah bring us to the climax of God's demand, but they do this in the context of a ministry which is the expression of the ultimate mercy. There can be little question that what is peculiarly characteristic of Jesus, as a teacher of morality, is the absoluteness of his words. Whether in attempting, however tentatively, to make of Jesus' expression of the ultimate demand, which seems so little governed by any consideration of historical contingency, a way of life, that is, halakah, and the basis for it, Matthew wholly departed from Jesus, it is not possible to decide categorically owing to the extreme complexity of our sources. But we may well ask whether Jesus was always merely concerned with proclaiming the eschatological demand and not also, sometimes, with the contingencies of existence. Did he not perhaps teach on two levels: for the uncommitted, the imminent judgement and absolute demand of God, and, for the committed, precise rulings as on divorce, and mutual concern in xviii? Can we not conceive that radicalism and legislation coincided sometimes in his ministry? Can we not trace the mark of the Sage in him as well as the Eschatological?[1]

That Jesus called men to radical decision as Bultmann has insisted is true. But the bare category of 'decision' does not do justice to the *content* of the teaching of Jesus, which calls not only for a decision *in vacuo*, but to a way of life illumined by his words. So too the claim that, given the courage to decide for the Rule of God, sufficient insight into the right conduct to be followed in any given situation is furnished by that situation itself, ignores the *revelatory* force of the words of the Messiah. The words of Jesus are proclaimed by him as authoritative: for him it is not their self-authenticating character that is significant but their source in God's will, which he reveals.[2] Apart from him, the teaching of Jesus as the demand of God could not be derived from the essential requirement of any given situation.[3] Precisely the ability or insight to define this requirement as the essential will of God was the role of Jesus as teacher. Similarly any attempt to understand the words of Jesus merely as a hammer, to use

[1] On his 'wisdom', see W. A. Curtis, *Jesus Christ the Teacher*, pp. 159 f. *et al.*

[2] R. Schnackenburg, *op. cit.* p. 48. He deserves quotation: 'Eine aus dem Geist der Neuzeit gegebene, aber durch kein Wort Jesu zu begründende Erklärung ist die Auskunft Bultmann, daß es dem Menschen zugetraut und zugemutet werde, selbst zu sehen, was von ihm gefordert ist. "Gottes Forderungen gelten also als einsichtig. Damit aber ist der Gedanke des Gehorsams erst radikal gedacht" [Bultmann, *Jesus*, p. 68]. Nein, Jesus stellt dem alten Gesetzeswortlaut sein: *"Ich* aber sage euch..."* entgegen.' For a criticism of Bultmann, see also E. Percy, *Die Botschaft Jesu*, p. 164.

[3] See, for example, S. Kierkegaard, *Fear and Trembling* (Oxford, 1939), p. 106, where duty is divorced from love.

Luther's phrase,[1] to reduce us to despair and thus prepare us for the Gospel is alien to the purpose of Jesus—his words are a light for our way, they are the Law of the Messiah to guide. The precise sense in which they are 'Law' we cannot define, because in our sources the mind of the Church has been at work upon them. What we can be certain of is this: that Jesus displayed the utmost ἀγάπη to 'the Lost' and demanded the utmost ἀγάπη of his own. His words as Messianic 'law' lie between these two poles and are themselves congruous with them: it was this insight that made Matthew set the Antitheses after the Beatitudes and close them with the demand for watchfulness before a 'threat', implied at least,[2] but embed the whole of the *SM* in a context of his Lord's ministry of compassion.

Thus the words of the *SM* ultimately lead us back to him who uttered them. Its imperatives thus become themselves indicatives. And, we may go further, they are *necessary* to every indicative in the New Testament. This is why nowhere in the New Testament is the Gospel set forth without moral demand, and nowhere is morality understood apart from the Gospel. In the *SM* we are confronted primarily not with the question, who can perform these commandments or are they practicable or sound, or, taken seriously, would they not spell the end of social, national and international life as we know it? Rather the *SM* compels us, in the first place, to ask who he is who utters these words: they are themselves kerygmatic. But emphasis on the act and person of Christ in life, death and resurrection, central and essential though it be, is never wholly free from the danger of abstraction from life. The meaning of the kerygma for life has to become concrete. And it is the penetrating precepts of Jesus as they encounter us in the *SM*, and elsewhere, that are the astringent protection against any interpretation of that person, life, death and resurrection in other than moral terms. In this sense the very words of Jesus are part of the Gospel and Matthew a true interpretation of his Lord's intention. This is what the Scriptures fulfilled in Jesus would lead us to expect. Jesus was the Mediator of a New Covenant. But a covenant always implied gracious initiative and demand. And as the King-Messiah, the Covenant Mediator of the End, Jesus also issued his demand. And despite the pattern that Matthew for his own purposes gave to it, this demand in its grace and terror still confronts us in the *SM*.

[1] See J. S. Whale, *The Protestant Tradition* (1955), p. 37.
[2] J. Jeremias related Paul with the beginning of the *SM* and the Epistle of James with its end, and thus reconciles them; see an illuminating article in *E.T.* LXVI (1954–5), 368 ff., on 'Paul and James'. It is the glory of Matthew that it contains in itself both justification by faith and justification by works.

VII. CONCLUSION

Our examination of the historical setting of the *SM* is over, and it is well to record certain reflections which it has provoked, because, although there are substantial signs of change, it might be claimed that such a strictly historical concern as we have above pursued stands outside the main stream of New Testament studies in recent decades, and that for obvious reasons.

On the one hand, literary disciplines have established for many that the Gospel tradition preserves only the whisper of the voice of Jesus. And, since to acquiesce in such a position is to imply that what that voice uttered is dispensable, a decline of interest in such passages as the *SM* was to be expected. On the other hand, with a few notable exceptions, interpreters of the New Testament have been largely absorbed in kerygmatic or strictly theological questions. The moral teaching of Jesus, although acknowledged, has been sharply distinguished from the kerygma of the Church and often treated as a Cinderella. Scholars have sometimes been even self-consciously anxious to relegate his teaching to a markedly subordinate place in the exposition of the faith of the New Testament.[1] In particular, under the impact of a general revival of dogmatic interests, emphasis on Paulinism, often understood in terms of 'Justification by Faith Alone', as the most profound element in the New Testament, has made it difficult to do justice to other elements in which the demand of

[1] This comes to concentrated and superb expression in Paul Tillich, *Systematic Theology*, vol. II, *Existence and the Christ* (Chicago, 1957), pp. 64, 80 f., 105, 119 ff. He rejects both 'legalist liberalism' which makes of the sayings of Jesus a 'law' and Bultmann's 'existentialist liberalism', which reduces them to a call to decision. Similarly *imitatio Christi*, except as participation in Christ, is dismissed. 'Jesus as the Christ is the bearer of the New Being in the totality of his being, not in any special expressions of it' (p. 121). Any radical separation of his 'words' from Jesus as 'The Word' we must, with Tillich, abhor (the evidence presented above demands this), and with his view that the words are the expression of the New Being we cannot but agree. We must only ask whether his fear of 'law' (as on p. 80, where he writes of a 'continuous flight from law to chaos and from chaos to law') does justice to all the elements in the New Testament. The 'words' must not be separated from 'The Word', but neither can they be so absorbed in 'The Word' as to lose their positive significance. Part of that significance in the New Testament is that they serve as the 'law' of Christ. This applies to the treatment of this theme by E. Schweizer, *Lordship and Discipleship*, pp. 93 ff., where the ethics of Jesus are rigidly separated from 'Jesus Christ himself'. But is such a separation possible? To separate 'The Word' from the 'words' is as undesirable as it is to separate 'the words' from 'The Word'.

the Gospel, no less than its gift, emerges. The proper assessment of the relationship between Kerygma and Didache, Gospel and Law, has been jeopardized.[1]

While our study has not presumed to deal with the theological problems raised by the relation of Gospel and Law, its pursuit could not but stir up the ghosts of these problems, and it has inevitably reshuffled the data in terms of which they must be approached within the New Testament. Historical as is its intention, therefore, it is hoped that it may not be without significance theologically. At least it prompts the question whether history can sometimes be called in to redress the balance of theology. To examine the setting of the *SM* is to be compelled to recognize that 'these sayings of mine', 'the law of Christ', 'the new commandment' played a more significant part in the New Testament as a whole than is often recognized. The faith of early Christians rested, not on a mime,[2] but on a drama, and in this drama the words of the chief protagonist on morality, as on other subjects, were essential to the action. For some in the primitive Church, if not for all, the penetrating demands of Jesus, no less than the great kerygmatic affirmations about him, were part of 'the bright light of the Gospel', that is, they were revelatory.

And not only so. However spontaneous its life in the Spirit and 'revolutionary' its ardour, the stern realities which confronted the infant Christian community, both within its own ranks and in its encounter with Judaism and the larger world, soon involved it in problems of law and order. At this point, an instructive parallel with the experience of the early Christian community is provided by that of modern Russia. Parallels between Communism and Christianity have frequently been drawn, but it has seldom been noted how similar is their dealing with the question of 'law'. Marx, and other socialist theorists, approached this in two ways. First, they regarded the traditional Russian legal system, like all existing legal systems, as a cloak for class interest, a device which reflected the claims of the bourgeoisie over against the propertyless

[1] See, for example, T. F. Torrance, *The Doctrine of Grace in the Apostolic Fathers* (London, 1948), and the comments on it by J. Lawson, *A Theological and Historical Introduction of the Apostolic Fathers* (New York, 1961), pp. 15 ff.

[2] Kierkegaard's words are famous: 'If the contemporary generation had left behind them nothing but the words, "We have believed that in such and such a year God appeared among us in the humble figure of a servant, that he lived and taught in our community; and finally died", it would be more than enough' (*Philosophical Fragments* (Princeton University Press, 1936), p. 87). This is to reduce Christianity to a mime: it fails to do justice to the Synoptic Gospels and much else in the New Testament, as we have seen.

masses. 'The economic structure of society', wrote Engels, 'always forms the real basis from which, in the last analysis, is to be explained the whole superstructure of legal and political institutions, as well as of the religious, philosophical, and other conceptions of each historical period.' And again, 'The jurist imagines that he is operating with *a priori* principles, whereas they are really only economic reflexes'.[1] But, secondly, in consonance with this, the same theorists looked forward to a future in which law, like the state, would vanish. In the new classless society, in which the proletariat would play a Messianic role, property relations would cease to exist, and thus the law and the state, which were designed to serve these, would no longer be necessary. There would be 'a glorious transition to a new order of equality and freedom *without* law'.[2] Communism would be the end of law: it reveals on the question of law what a historian has referred to as a 'kind of New Testament foolishness'.[3] It is not surprising, therefore, that Soviet Russia, after 1917, passed through a period of legal nihilism. As late as 1930 a Soviet jurist was looking forward to 'the withering away of law in general, that is, the gradual disappearance of the juridical element from human relations',[4] and in 1927 a president of the Soviet Supreme Court wrote: 'Communism means not the victory of socialist law, but the victory of socialism over any law, since with the abolition of classes with their antagonistic interests, law will disappear altogether.'[5] And at first, after the Revolution, in accordance with Communist theory, law did tend to die out. But not for long could such a position be held. Already, before the above statements were written, under the brute actualities of Soviet life, there had begun a rehabilitation of law; the New Economic Policy adopted in the period 1921–8 meant, in effect, the restoration of 'bourgeois law'. The nihilism and apocalypticism which had sought for a society without law proved to be bankrupt, and a 'strategic retreat to law' the only possible policy.[6]

To compare the emergence of a vast modern state with that of the Christian Church may seem unrealistic. The parallel cannot be pressed

[1] Both quotations are taken from an unpublished work, by H. J. Berman of the Harvard Law School, *Comparison of Soviet and American Law* (1961), pp. 9 f. There is a brief bibliography in another work, *Soviet Law in Action*, by Boris A. Konstantinovsky, edited by Harold J. Berman (Harvard University Press, 1953), p. v n.

[2] H. J. Berman, *op. cit.* p. 24.   [3] So H. J. Berman, *op. cit.* p. 17.

[4] Cited by Berman, *op. cit.* p. 21.

[5] Cited by Berman, *ibid.* I was introduced to Professor Berman's work by another Harvard lawyer, Mr C. Wadsworth.

[6] H. J. Berman, *op. cit.* p. 21.

because at no point in the Church, not even in Paul, who coined the phrase 'Christ is the end of the law', is there a radical rejection of the traditional law of Judaism but rather the recognition of its fulfilment in the 'law of love' and in the words of Jesus. The early Church was not iconoclastic: it refused to recognize legal nihilism. This was the only course possible for it, because, unlike Communism, it rooted the authority of the law, not in passing social structures, but in God, who could not be mocked.[1] Nevertheless, within our immediate purpose, the parallel is illuminating. That the Church found it increasingly necessary to make the revelatory, radical, eschatological demands of Jesus the source of regulations is apparent. Convinced that they were living in the Messianic Age and yet compelled to recognize that that Age had not reached its consummation, Christians had to face moral problems which demanded a Christian way to meet these.[2] Some did this, not only by grounding imperatives in a kerygmatic indicative, but also by turning to the words of Jesus as their 'law' and the ground of a new casuistry. The fullness of the time had indeed come, but law was not dispensable. It is the reality of this state of affairs in its many ramifications that this study has revealed. To interpret the faith of the New Testament only, or even mainly, in terms of a rigid understanding of the Pauline antithesis of Grace and Law is to ignore not only the tumultuous, tortuous nature of Paul himself (a fact which alone should make us chary of making his experience in any

[1] Cf. G. Bornkamm, *Jesus of Nazareth*, Eng. trans. (New York, 1960), pp. 100 ff.
[2] M. Goguel urges that in this situation Paul and, by implication, other Christians faced a problem which was alien to Judaism. He writes: 'Il a posé un problème nouveau qui ne pouvait pas exister pour le judaïsme; celui de la sanctification, c'est-à-dire des relations entre la religion et la morale, l'Évangile et la Loi.... Pour le judaïsme, l'acte rédempteur, l'intervention du Messie, devait se situer à la fin des temps, au moment même où le monde ancien, celui de la chair, serait anéanti, et où le monde nouveau, celui de l'Esprit, serait réalisé. Le problème de la sanctification ne peut trouver place dans le cadre d'une telle conception; car justification et rédemption... coïncident dans le temps et ne forment qu'un seul et même acte.' But in the light of chapter III we may question this sharp view: there was 'law' also, in some form, in the Messianic Age and the Age to Come of Judaism. See *Revue d'Histoire et de Philosophie Religieuses* (Strasbourg, 1937), pp. 25 f. This contains important discussions of 'L'Évangile et la loi' by M. F. Ménégoz, M. Goguel, Auguste Lecerf, André Jundt, A. W. d'Aygalliers, C. Hauter, on pp. 1–57. See also G. Salet on 'La Loi dans nos cœurs', in *Nouvelle Revue Théologique*, LXXXIX (Paris, 1957), 449 ff. and 561 ff.; M. Villey, *Leçons d'histoire de la philosophie du droit* (Paris, 1957); J. Ellul, *Le Fondement théologique du droit* (Paris, 1946); S. E. Stumpf, J. Ellul, M. Villey on 'La Théologie chrétienne et le droit' in *Archives de Philosophie du Droit*, no. 5 (Paris, 1960), pp. 1–61; B. Häring, *Das Gesetz Christi* (Freiburg im Breisgau, 1954).

way normative), and not only the exaggerations engendered by the historical controversy out of which that antithesis arose, but, even more, much evidence pointing to a 'law' which remains in the new covenant of grace, and, indeed, especially there, and which is rooted in the words of Jesus Christ himself.[1]

A historical approach, such as we have attempted above, therefore, spurs the question anew whether, in the matter of Gospel and Law, the gulf fixed in the subsequent life of the Church between Protestant and Roman Catholic, Lutheran and Calvinist, cannot be bridged in terms of the wholeness of the New Testament, the fragmentation of Christian history being healed there. Certain it is that the *SM* in its setting spans the arch of Grace and Law, conjoins demands such as those of 'the right strawy Epistle' of James with the Pauline profundities. Its opening, the Beatitudes, recognizes man's infinite need for grace, his misery; its absolute demand recognizes man's infinite moral possibilities, his grandeur. Thus it is that our effort to set the *SM* historically in its place finally sets us in our place. And the place in which it sets us is the Last Judgement, before the infinite succour and the infinite demand of Christ.

[1] I am fully aware of difficulties in this theme which are here silently passed by: for a judicious survey of these, see G. F. Thomas, *Christian Ethics and Moral Philosophy* (New York, 1955), pp. 105 ff. My aim has been merely to reopen discussion on it in the light of the *SM* and other New Testament evidence: failure to take this evidence seriously has exposed the faith of the New Testament to the charge of 'romanticism' levied against it by Leo Baeck in his masterly essay 'Romantic Religion' in his work *Judaism and Christianity*, Eng. trans. by Walter Kaufmann (Philadelphia, 1958), pp. 189–292. As much of the New Testament reveals it, the Christian life is freedom 'in the Spirit'. But it is freedom informed by a moral tradition stemming from the words of Jesus himself, enshrined in the Gospels and especially in the *SM*. It shuns both the rootless licence of antinomianism and the Messianic licence of perfectionism (a phrase which I borrow from an unpublished paper by Dr Stendahl) and follows 'the way' of a tradition of the words of Jesus which is living: it renews itself, not by departing from that tradition, but by a deeper apprehension and application of it, so that it is a continuity and a casuistry. Those who heard the above in lecture form may recall my concluding reference to the words of two Welsh poets—to those of the sagacious Elfed:

> *Hyfryd eiriau'r Iesu!*
> *Bywyd ynddynt sydd...,*

and to those of the more radical Gwenallt

> *Gwae inni wybod y geiriau*
> *Heb adnabod Y Gair.*

In the proper apprehension of these two truths (of 'the Word' and 'the words') lies the true balance between Gospel and Law.

APPENDICES

APPENDIX I

Mekilta on Exod. xiv. 13

Stand Still and See the Salvation of the Lord. The Israelites asked him: 'When?' Moses said to them: 'Today the Holy Spirit rests upon you.' For the expression 'standing' (*yeẓibah*) everywhere suggests the presence of the Holy Spirit, as in the passages: 'I saw the Lord standing beside the altar' (Amos ix. 1). 'And the Lord came, and stood, and called as at other times: "Samuel, Samuel"' (1 Sam. iii. 10). And it also says: 'Call Joshua and stand in the tent of meeting that I may give him a charge' (Deut. xxxi. 14). To what were the Israelites at that moment like? To a dove fleeing from a hawk, and about to enter a cleft in the rock where there is a hissing serpent. If she enters, there is the serpent! If she stays out, there is the hawk! In such a plight were the Israelites at that moment, the sea forming a bar and the enemy pursuing. Immediately they set their mind upon prayer. Of them it is stated in the traditional sacred writings: 'O my dove that art in the clefts of the rock', etc. (Cant. ii. 14). And when it further says: 'For sweet is thy voice and thy countenance is comely' (*ibid.*), it means, for thy voice is sweet in prayer and thy countenance is comely in the study of the Torah. Another Interpretation: For thy voice is sweet in prayer and thy countenance is comely in good deeds.

Another Interpretation: *Stand Still and See*, etc. The Israelites asked Moses: 'When?' He answered them: 'Tomorrow!' Then the Israelites said to Moses: 'Moses, our Master, we have not the strength to endure.' At that moment Moses prayed and God caused them to see squadrons upon squadrons of ministering angels standing before them, just as it is said: 'And when the servant of the man of God was risen early, and gone forth, behold, a host with horses and chariots was round about the city. And his servant said unto him: "Alas, my master! how shall we do?" And he answered: "Fear not: for they that are with us are more than they that are with them." And Elisha prayed, and said: "Lord I pray Thee, open his eyes, that he may see." And the Lord opened the eyes of the young man; and he saw; and, behold, the mountain was full of horses and chariots of fire round about Elisha' (2 Kings vi. 15–17). And so also here Moses prayed at that moment and God caused them to see squadrons upon squadrons of ministering angels standing before them. And thus it says: 'At the brightness before Him, there passed through His thick clouds, hailstones and coals of fire' (Ps. xviii. 13)—'His thick clouds', as against their squadrons; 'hailstones', as against their catapults; 'coals', as against their missiles; 'fire', as against their naphtha. 'The Lord also thundered in the heavens' (*ibid.* verse 14)

—as against the clashing of their shields and the noise of their trampling shoes. 'And the Most High gave forth His voice' (*ibid.*), as against their whetting the swords. 'And He sent out His arrows and scattered them' (*ibid.* verse 15), as against their arrows.

MEKILTA ON EXOD. XIV. 14

The Lord Will Fight for You. Not only at this time, but at all times will He fight against your enemies. R. Meir says: *The Lord Will Fight for You.* If even when you stand there silent, the Lord will fight for you, how much more so when you render praise to Him! Rabbi says: *The Lord Will Fight for You and Ye Shall Hold Your Peace.* Shall God perform miracles and mighty deeds for you and you be standing there silent? The Israelites then said to Moses: Moses, our teacher, what is there for us to do? And he said to them: You should be exalting, glorifying and praising, uttering songs of praise, adoration and glorification to Him in whose hands are the fortunes of wars, just as it is said: 'Let the high praises of God be in their mouth' (Ps. cxlix. 6). And it also says: 'Be Thou exalted, O God, above the heavens; Thy glory be above all the earth' (*ibid.* lvii. 12). And it also says: 'O Lord, Thou art my God, I will exalt Thee' (Isa. xxv. 1).

At that moment the Israelites opened their mouths and recited the song: 'I will sing unto the Lord, for He is highly exalted', etc. (Exod. xv. 2).

MEKILTA ON EXOD. XIV. 15

And the Lord Said unto Moses: 'Wherefore Criest Thou unto Me? Speak unto the Children of Israel that They Go Forward.' R. Joshua says: The Holy One, blessed be He, said unto Moses: 'Moses, all that Israel has to do is to go forward.' R. Eliezer says: The Holy One, blessed be He, said to Moses: 'Moses, My children are in distress, the sea forming a bar and the enemy pursuing, and you stand there reciting long prayers; wherefore criest thou unto Me?' For R. Eliezer used to say: There is a time to be brief in prayer and a time to be lengthy. 'Heal her now, O God, I beseech Thee' (Num. xii. 13). This is an instance of being brief.

(Lauterbach's translation, *Mekilta*, XVII, 210 ff., 216.)

APPENDIX II

MEKILTA ON EXOD. XV. 1

And Spoke Saying. R. Nehemiah says: The holy spirit rested upon Israel and they uttered the song in the manner in which people recite the *Shema*. R. Akiba says: The holy spirit rested upon Israel and they uttered the song in the manner in which people recite the *Hallel*. R. Eliezer the son of Taddai says: Moses would first begin with the opening words. Israel would then repeat them after him and finish the verse with him. Moses began, saying: 'I will sing unto the

Lord, for He is highly exalted.' And Israel repeated after him and finished with him: 'I will sing unto the Lord, for He is highly exalted. The horse and the rider hath He thrown into the sea.' Moses began, saying: 'The Lord is my strength and my song.' And Israel repeated after him and finished with him: 'The Lord is my strength and my song. And He is become my salvation.' Moses began, saying: 'The Lord is a man of war.' And Israel repeated after him and finished with him: 'The Lord is a man of war, the Lord is His name.'

Mekilta on Exod. xv. 2

Another Interpretation: *My Strength.* Thou art a helper and a supporter of all who come into the world, but of me especially. *And Song is the Lord.* Thou art the subject of song to all who come into the world but to me especially. He has proclaimed me of special distinction and I have proclaimed Him of special distinction. He has proclaimed me of special distinction, as it is said: 'And the Lord has avouched thee this day' (Deut. xxvi. 18). And I have proclaimed Him of special distinction, as it is said: 'Thou hast avouched the Lord this day' (*ibid.* verse 17).—But behold, all the nations of the world declare the praise of Him by whose word the world came into being! Mine, however, is more pleasing, as it is said: 'But sweet are the songs of Israel' (2 Sam. xxiii. 1)—Israel says: 'Hear, O Israel! The Lord our God, the Lord is One' (Deut. vi. 4). And the Holy Spirit calls aloud from heaven and says: 'And who is like Thy people Israel, a nation one in the earth' (1 Chron. xvii. 21). Israel says: 'Who is like unto Thee, O Lord, among the mighty' (Exod. xv. 11). And the Holy Spirit calls aloud from heaven and says: 'Happy art thou, O Israel, who is like unto thee' (Deut. xxxiii. 29). Israel says: 'As the Lord our God is whensoever we call upon Him' (Deut. iv. 7). And the Holy Spirit calls aloud from heaven and says: 'And what great nation is there, that hath statutes and ordinances so righteous?', etc. (*ibid.* verse 8). Israel says: 'For Thou art the glory of their strength' (Ps. lxxxix. 18). And the Holy Spirit calls aloud from heaven and says: 'Israel in whom I will be glorified' (Isa. xlix. 3).

(Lauterbach's translation, *Mekilta*, xi, 7 ff., 23 ff.)

APPENDIX III

The Character of Matt. i and ii

See J. Moffatt, *Introduction to the Literature of the NT* (1922), pp. 249 ff.; V. Taylor, *The Historical Evidence for the Virgin Birth* (1920). Did Matthew originally circulate without i and ii, it is clear that they could throw little light on the rest of the Gospel. Textual support for this, however, there is none; and since the consensus of scholarship is also against it, we can safely dismiss it. But there is a more serious difficulty to be noted. Assuming that Matt. i and ii were always part of the Gospel, what is their character? Do they constitute merely a number of separate pericopae, which, like marbles in a box, have no essential connexion or unity? If so, while the individual pericopae may throw light on separate aspects of the Gospel, the chapters as a whole are probably not very significant for our quest. And the genealogy, the account of the Virgin Birth and the story of the Magi, have all in turn been regarded by different scholars as later interpolations (see Moffatt, *op. cit.*) so that the essential unity of the chapters has been denied. Similar in effect are the views of K. L. Schmidt (*Der Rahmen der Geschichte Jesu* (1919), *ad rem*) and Bultmann (*Die Geschichte der synoptischen Tradition, ad rem*), although they do not subscribe to the theory of interpolation. Schmidt urged that the various elements in i and ii were taken by Matthew from the tradition and strung together without any attempt being made at changing them in the interests of chronological and topographical unity. He points out that the time and place of the birth of Jesus are not mentioned till ii. 1, which shows that no proper biographical concern governs the chapters as a whole. Such a concern only crops up at the very end in ii. 23. Schmidt contrasts the *inconsequence* of the material in i and ii with the element of continuity in that in the Passion Narrative. His treatment, however, is brief and leaves the impression that he regarded the two chapters as rather ill-digested complexes which should not receive our serious consideration. Bultmann treats the chapters in greater detail. i. 18–25 is a legend that grew around a simple core in which an angel promised to Joseph that his son would be the Messiah. This legend Matthew has joined on to ii. 1–23 with which it originally had no connexion. Bultmann traces the hand of Matthew in i. 21, 22, and recognizes that the present literary form of ii. 1–23 is his. Here he has joined together the Story of the Magi and that of the Massacre of the Innocents which were originally distinct. But despite his recognition of Matthew's hand in i and ii Bultmann fails to enlarge upon any underlying motif or motifs in the chapters, so that, though richer, the essential impact of his treatment is similar to that of Schmidt's. The reason for this probably is that both Schmidt and Bultmann have failed to recognize what was forcibly insisted upon by V. Taylor in his book *The Virgin Birth*. A detailed examination of their style, vocabulary and contents convinced Taylor of the unity of i and ii as part of the Gospel from the first. On several grounds both the genealogy and i. 18–25, so far from being interpolations, are shown to be integral parts of the Gospel. Box came to the same conclusion (*The Virgin Birth of Jesus Christ* (1916)). Taylor submits convincingly that while, as Bultmann asserts, Matt. ii may originally have been quite independent of i. 18–25 'it is quite congruous with what is told in that passage, and, indeed, agrees better with the supposition of the Virgin Birth'. Similarly, to claim, as does Bultmann, that the Massacre of the Innocents did not originally belong to the story of the Magi, even if acceptable, has no bearing upon the essential unity which underlies both stories for Matthew.

APPENDIX IV

Isaiah XLI. 2 and the Pre-existent Messiah

Interesting is the ascription of Isa. xli. 2 to Abraham. It reads:

Who stirred (הֵעִיר) up one from the east
whom victory meets at every step?

By the substitution of הֵאִיר for הֵעִיר it could be translated 'Who gave forth light from the east'. The association of 'light' with the advent of significant personages may have a bearing on the appearance of the 'star' from the east in Matt. ii. The same play on הֵעִיר appears in Gen. Rabbah xliii. 3 (Soncino translation, p. 354). 'It is written: Who hath raised up (הֵעִיר) one from the east, Zedek (Righteousness) calling him to his feet (Isa. xli. 2) (this alludes to Zedek—the Righteous One), the Life of all the worlds, who illumined (מֵאִיר) his path wherever he went.' On the association of 'Light' with the birth of the righteous, see R. Mach, *Der Zaddik in Talmud und Midrasch* (1957), pp. 68 ff., 78 ff. It is interesting, in the light of all this, to speculate on the connotation of the term ἀνατολή in Matt. ii. 1, 2, 9. In accordance with the emphasis of the Scandinavian School, Bentzen (*King and Messiah* (1955), p. 17) has urged that for Judaism the advent of the Messiah, like the enthronement of the King, would be the re-enactment of the enthronement of that primitive king who gained mastery over the chaos in the *Urzeit*, the beginning of all things. Thus it is that Micah v, 'But you, O Bethlehem Ephratah, who are little to be among the clans of Judah, from you shall come forth for me one who is to be ruler in Israel, *whose origin is from of old, from ancient days*' (MT: וּמוֹצָאֹתָיו מִקֶּדֶם מִימֵי עוֹלָם [v. 1]; LXX: καὶ οἱ ἔξοδοι αὐτοῦ ἀπ' ἀρχῆς ἐξ ἡμερῶν αἰῶνος), which is partially quoted in Matt. ii. 6, speaks of the מוֹצָאוֹת, the outgoings, of the Messiah, which are connected with the Sun. The coming of the Messiah is the coming out from an age-old kind of pre-existence. This concept of a pre-existent Messiah who has to 'come forth' is also found by Windisch in Ps. cx. 1–3 (RSV cx. 3*b*—'From the womb of the morning like dew your youth will come to you' (MT: מֵרֶחֶם מִשְׁחָר לְךָ טַל יַלְדֻתֶךָ; LXX cix. 3: ἐκ γαστρὸς πρὸ ἑωσφόρου ἐξεγέννησά σε). (*Die Weisheit und die Paulinische Christologie*, in *Texte und Untersuchungen* (Leipzig, 1904), pp. 227 f.; see *P.R.J.*[2] p. 159.) The term ἀνατολή does not occur in the LXX at either of these places to describe the coming forth of the Messiah. But Bentzen compares the ἔξοδοι of Micah v. 1 (LXX) with the ἀνατολή of Luke i. 78, and suggests thereby that the ἀνατολή of Luke i. 78 has the same cosmic undertone as the ἔξοδοι of Micah v. 1, that is, the coming of the Messiah is linked with the creation itself. Burney long since saw in Luke i. 78 the concept of a new creation. In the LXX ἀνατολή is a designation of the Messiah in Zech. iii. 8; vi. 12; compare also Jer. xxiii. 5. As Benoit points out, this use of ἀνατολή messianically was prepared for in the LXX use of ἀνατέλλειν in connexion with the Messianic Age. He refers to Isa. xliii. 19; xlv. 8; lxi. 1; Ezek. xxix. 21; Ps. lxxi. 7; lxxxiv. 12; xcvi. 11, and in particular to Num. xxiv. 17; Mal. iv. 2 (LXX xiii. 20); Isa. lx. 1—passages which deal with the rise of the Messianic Star or Light. ('L'enfance de Jean-Baptiste selon Luc i', *N.T.S.* III, 3 (May 1957), 186, n. 1, where a bibliography is given.) In addition note Ps. xcvii. 11 (LXX xcvi. 11), 'Light dawns (ἀνέτειλεν) for the righteous'. In Midrash Tehillim this is associated with the light that shone at creation. See also 2 Sam. xxiii. 4; Isa. lviii. 10; lxi. 11. The term ἀνατολή clearly has Messianic nuances, which connect the appearance of the Messianic deliverer with creation itself. Perhaps the term ἐν τῇ ἀνατολῇ in Matt. ii. 3, 9 should not be emptied of such significance. The suggestion is made very hesitatingly. Schlier in *T.W.Z.N.T.* I, 354 f. does not connect Matt. ii. 9 with Messianic speculation.

APPENDIX V

'¿Cesará la Tora en la Edad Messiánica?'

I owe the full awareness of this to Alejandro Díez Macho, M.S.C., who, in two issues of *Estudios Bíblicos*, XII, 2 (April–June 1953), 115–18 and XIII, 1 (January–March 1954), 5–51, under the title, '¿ Cesará la Tora en la Edad Messiánica?', subjects my monograph on this theme to the most exhaustive and excellent criticism. He draws attention to the following sources:

(1) The *Pugio fidei* of Fr Raimundo Martí, which deals with the question of the abolition of the Torah in chs. XI, XII, XX of the Distinctio III, Pars III (pp. 774–817). Many of the sources which he uses are also discussed above, but the conclusions are the opposite. (The last edition of the book was made by Josef de Voisin in 1687. Díez Macho discusses the authenticity of the materials used by Martí in *Sefarad* IX (1949), pp. 165–96. The authenticity of his materials has also been defended by Saul Lieberman in *Historia Judaica*, V (1943), 87–102, in English.)

(2) The Protocols of the Controversy of Tortosa between Jews and Christian theologians (particularly Jerome of Santa Fe) in 1413–14. (The original manuscript is in the Vatican. A summary is offered by Poznansky in *R.E.J.* LXXIV–LXXVI. Also Card. Ehrle, *Martin de Alparzil, Chronica Actitatorum . . .* (Paderborn, 1906); and F. Baer, 'Die Disp. von Tortosa', *Spanische Forschungen* III, 307–36.) In the discussion many of these same passages are used (especially sess. 24, 26, 37).

(3) *Hieronimi de Sancta Fide, Judaei ad Christianismum conversi*, libri duo, quorum prior fidem et religionem (judeorum) impugnat, alter vero Talmud (ed. Gesner, Zürich, 1557). Summarized by Poznansky (*op. cit.* LXXIV, 17–39, 160–8). It was composed in 1412. Chapter 12 discusses our problem, coming to the conclusion that the Messiah comes to give a new law, and to abolish sacrifices

and the prohibition of certain foods. Compare also Cecil Roth, 'The Disputation of Barcelona, 1263', *Harvard Theological Review*, XLIII (1950), 137 ff. Josef Albó de Daroca, *Sefer ha-'Iqqerim*, ed. Isaac Husik (Philadelphia, Jewish Publication Society of America, 1929), 4 vols. Compare especially I. I, ch. 25; I. III, chs. 14–16, 25, pp. 217–45.

His conclusions are: (i) the OT not only does not predict the permanence of the Mosaic Torah in the Messianic Age, but it also predicts positively its substitution by a new law; (ii) Jer. xxxi. 31–4 predicts a new law; (iii) Isa. xlii. 1–4 does not predict that the Messiah will proclaim the Law of Moses; (iv) nothing can be positively concluded from Isa. ii. 1–4; (v) the early Christians, although they had been won by the dominant pharisaic conviction of the permanence of the Torah, were led to change this idea through the teaching of the Apostles and the support of the OT; (vi) much rabbinic material was weakened, ignored, modified or suppressed by Judaism; (vii) even though the largest part of such material as was preserved upholds the perpetuity of the Torah, there is convincing testimony of a belief in the partial or total abrogation of the law in the Messianic Age; (viii) the relevant passages admit an interpretation in the sense of affirming, negatively, the abolition of the Torah, and positively, the New Law.

Unfortunately I have been unable to examine the Jewish-Christian controversies of the Middle Ages, and it is to be emphasized that this field is still to be examined for light on our theme. The weight of Díez Macho's criticism is that I have been excessively cautious in finding the expectation of a new Torah. It is clear to me now that the probability of my understanding of Matthew as presenting a Messianic Torah in the *SM* is certainly not weakened and indeed much strengthened by the Spanish scholar's treatment.

APPENDIX VI

THE ROLE OF TORAH IN THE MESSIANIC AGE

Before we proceed to discuss it, it will not be irrelevant to ask why this question has not attracted more attention. Apart from the comparative ignorance of rabbinic Judaism among Christians in general, the first answer probably lies in an insufficient understanding of the nature of apocalyptic thinking. Too often it has been assumed that apocalyptic was the outcome of a mere escapism, and it was often possible to dismiss it with the condescension, if not contempt, with which moderns usually dismiss the more bizarre forms of the Second Advent Hope. In view of this, allied to the sharp distinction which was usually drawn between the sober Pharisee and the fiery, day-dreaming Apocalyptist, it was not recognized that apocalyptic was the outcome of a profound ethical seriousness, which was usually no less concerned with the observance of the Torah than was Pharisaism, and that the Messianic hope was relevant for ethics. Fortunately we have now been recalled to the ethical ground of apocalyptic thinking (see A. N. Wilder, *Eschatology and Ethics in the Teaching of Jesus*, pp. 30 f.; H. H. Rowley, *The Relevance of Apocalyptic*, p. 162), and the climate is therefore congenial to a more favourable approach to the relation of Messianism or apocalyptic to the Torah.

The second answer, possibly, is to be sought in that too marked antithesis which it has long been customary to draw in the Old Testament between the Law and the prophets. Modern critics have been dominated by the view that the Law was inferior to the prophets, or, as H. H. Rowley has recently described it, 'that the prophets were the advocates of a purely spiritual religion that had no use for the sacrificial cultus, while the creators of the Law were reactionaries who triumphed over the teaching of the Prophets, and fastened the yoke of ceremonial observances firmly upon the Jews' (*Bulletin of the John Rylands Library*, XXIX, 2, 327). This attitude has, perhaps unconsciously, been carried over into the study of the New Testament, and it has been customary, and consequently easy, to show that Jesus is best understood in the light of the prophetic tradition, as the fulfilment of the prophets' hope, while, at the same time, he has often been represented as the opponent of the legalistic tradition in all its forms; thus, for example, a recent exponent of the intention of Jesus has isolated the prophetic tradition as that which is most relevant for the understanding of Jesus. (See J. W. Bowman, *The Intention of Jesus* (1945), pp. 63 ff.; also C. H. Dodd in *Mysterium Christi*, ed. A. E. J. Rawlinson, pp. 60 f. It should, however, be noted that J. W. Bowman also finds it possible to apply the term Torah to Christ himself, *op. cit.*) As long as this attitude prevailed, despite the express words particularly of Matt. v. 17–20, and many other passages, it is unlikely that justice should be done to Jesus as the fulfilment of the Torah as well as of prophecy: and it is this attitude which possibly accounts for the fact that, while the prophetic antecedents and characteristics of Jesus have been amply recognized, the possibility that he was consciously fulfilling the expectation of a Messianic Torah, as surely as he fulfilled other elements in the Messianic expectation, has not been the object of sufficient interest.

It is still the dominant view that there is a sharp cleavage between the Law and the prophets, but that it is not the only possible view has been shown convincingly by H. H. Rowley (in the article to which we have already referred). He reminds us that there were prophetic groups within the cultus, that within the prophetic canon the priestly attitude is given expression, that it was not the cultus as such that the prophets condemned but its misuse, and that while there was undoubtedly a difference of emphasis between prophets and priests there was no fundamental conflict. This reconciling tendency in Old Testament studies has a bearing upon the study of the New Testament. It prompts the question whether Law and prophecy, if they are not sharply opposed in the Old Testament, are not both fulfilled in the New Testament. Certain it is that if, as

I think we should, we follow H. H. Rowley in a new evaluation of the legal portions of the Old Testament, we should also be more prepared to set Jesus not so much in iconoclastic opposition to the Torah as in critical fulfilment of it, and hence more anxious to inquire as to the role ascribed to it in the Messianic Age. (See especially A. R. Johnson, *The Cultic Prophet in Israel* (1944); for references, p. 62.)

In the third place, it is possible that the theological atmosphere within which New Testament, like other biblical, studies were pursued until recently has had much to do with the neglect of the problem with which we are concerned. That interpretation of the teaching of Jesus which saw in it an ethic that was meant to be applied directly in this world by the aid of the Holy Spirit tended to produce, quite naturally, an impatience with the patient minutiae of legalism in all its forms. 'To love God and do what one liked'—phrases such as this expressed an attitude which made it difficult to appreciate that there might be any relevance for Christianity in the legal tradition of Judaism: and it was phrases such as this that what we shall call (for want of a better term) Liberal Christianity employed to describe the ethical life 'in Christ'; and it is not surprising that it very often dismissed the casuistry of legalism as mere pettifogging—a pettifoggery that was swept away by Christ. (It is relevant to point out here that some recent scholars, for example T. W. Manson, *The Teaching of Jesus*[2], p. 48, and R. Bultmann, have increasingly recognized rabbinical elements in Jesus' teaching: see *Jesus and the Word*, Eng. trans. pp. 55 f.; K. H. Rengstorf, *T.W.Z.N.T.* II, 155 ff.)

But the temper of the theological scene has changed; not only has life in this 'time of the breaking of nations' sobered us, but the increasing recognition in recent scholarship of the eschatological character of the teaching of Jesus and of the absolute nature of his ethical demand has also made acute the problem of its application to life in this world. This in turn has made it impossible for us to be wholly contemptuous of the so-called 'casuistry' of legalism. We now have painfully to confess, as T. W. Manson has expressed it, 'that it is much easier to denounce the scribal system than to do without it'. (*The Teaching of Jesus*[2], p. 296. The whole chapter on 'Religion and Morals' in this book brings the problem we are discussing to a focus: we are, however, inclined to doubt Manson's too sharp distinction between the moral teaching of Jesus (at least as it came to be understood in the early Church) and that of the Scribes.) 'The relevance of an impossible ethic' (see, for example, R. Niebuhr, *An Interpretation of Christian Ethics* (1936))—it is phrases such as this that are now in the air, and they are indicative of our dilemma. But it was this very dilemma, in a less agonizing but no less real form, which gave birth to Jewish legalism. That legalism was the mint of prophecy: essentially, its intention was to make relevant the prophetic ethic. Hence it should be easier for us now to do justice to that 'casuistry' which has too often been the object of our contempt. It may not be a new 'casuistry' that modern Christendom needs, but it does need to make relevant to its life an ethic that is eschatological, and may therefore learn from that development of the Law which attempted to meet a similar need. (Compare, for example, E. Robertson in *Law and Religion*, ed. E. I. J. Rosenthal (1938), pp. 74 f.; L. Finkelstein, *The Pharisees* (1940).) We have mentioned above those factors in the contemporary theological situation which should make it possible, and necessary, for us to appreciate more fully the significance of the Torah for the Christian dispensation, and with this end in view we have been concerned to discover what part, if any, the expectation of a new Torah in the Messianic Age or in the Age to Come had in the eschatological speculation of Jewry in the first century. In our endeavour we have drawn upon the material used by the scholars named above, but tried to assess it for ourselves.

APPENDIX VII

GALILEAN AND JUDAEAN JUDAISM

Galilean Judaism can be differentiated from Judaean Judaism even among the rabbis. Those in Galilee, if we may judge from R. Hananiah ben Dosa (A.D. 80–120), were marked by 'faith healing', asceticism, and miracle (TB Berakoth 34*b*, TB Taanit 24*b*). R. Johannan b. Zakkai, for example, found the spiritual climate in Galilee much less congenial than in Jerusalem: Sages of his kind were few in Galilee and infrequently consulted. Learning was not as highly prized there as in Jerusalem. This may be the significance of the difference in emphasis found in words ascribed to R. Hananiah b. Dosa and R. Johannan ben Zakkai. According to the former: 'He in whom the spirit of his fellow man takes delight, in him the spirit of the Omnipresent takes delight, and he in whom the spirit of his fellow creatures takes no delight, in him the spirit of the Omnipresent takes no delight' (Aboth iii. 11); and again: 'He whose fear of sin takes precedence over his wisdom, his wisdom shall endure, but he whose wisdom takes precedence over his sin, his wisdom shall not endure, as it is said, "The fear of the Lord is the beginning of wisdom" (Ps. cxi. 10).' He used to say: 'He whose works exceed his wisdom, his wisdom shall endure, but he whose wisdom exceeds his works, his wisdom shall not endure, as it is said, "We shall do and we shall hearken" (Exod. xxiv. 7)' (Aboth iii. 12). Contrast with these words, as revealing a different temper, those of R. Johannan b. Zakkai: 'If one is wise and fears sin, what is he like? Lo, he is a craftsman with the tools of his craft in his hand. If one is wise and does not fear sin, what is he like? Lo, he is a craftsman without the tools of his craft in his hand. If one fears sin, but is not wise, what is he like? He is not a craftsman, but the tools of his craft are in his hand' (*A.R.N.* xxii). In *A.R.N.* xxii the juxtaposition of the above passages suggest that R. Johannan's words are a kind of commentary on those of R. Hananiah. See S. Schechter, *A.R.N.* p. 34*a*. The difference between a

APPENDICES

Galilean rabbi and one destined to lead in Jerusalem was perceived by R. Johannan's wife:

Our rabbis taught: Once the son of R. Gamaliel fell ill. He sent two scholars to R. Haninah b. Dosa to ask him to pray for him. When he saw them he went up to an upper chamber and prayed for him. When he came down he said to them: Go, the fever has left him; They said to him: Are you a prophet? He replied: I am neither a prophet nor the son of a prophet, but I learnt this from experience. If my prayer is fluent in my mouth, I know that he is accepted: but if not, I know that he is rejected. They sat down and made a note of the exact moment. When they came to R. Gamaliel, he said to them: By the temple service! You have not been a moment too soon or too late, but so it happened: at that very moment the fever left him and he asked for water to drink.

On another occasion it happened that R. Haninah b. Dosa went to study Torah with R. Johanan ben Zakkai. The son of R. Johanan ben Zakkai fell ill. He said to him: Haninah my son, pray for him that he may live. He put his head between his knees and prayed for him and he lived. Said R. Johanan ben Zakkai: If ben Zakkai had stuck his head between his knees for the whole day, no notice would have been taken of him. Said his wife to him: Is Haninah greater than you are? He replied to her: No; but he is like a servant before the king, and I am like a nobleman before a king. (TB Berakoth 34b.)

On Galilee in this period: S. W. Baron, *A Social and Religious History of the Jews*, I–II (1952), 278 f.; L. E. Binns, *Galilean Christianity* (1956), pp. 17–22, which gives a useful statement of the mixed character of Galilee; R. Otto, *The Kingdom of God and the Son of Man*, Eng. trans. (1943), pp. 13 ff.; he relies on W. Bauer, *Jesus, der Galiläer*. The difference between Galilee and Judaea in language is also to be noted: see, for example, M. Black, *An Aramaic Approach to the Gospels and Acts* (1946), p. 3; A. Edersheim, *The Life and Times of Jesus the Messiah*, I, 224–34. M. Black, *The Scrolls and Christian Origins* (New York, 1961), p. 81 follows E. Lohmeyer, *Galiläa und Jerusalem* (1956).

APPENDIX VIII

The Doxology in Matt. VI. 13

The doxology in vi. 13, 'For thine is the Kingdom and the Power and the Glory for ever and ever. Amen', has caused difficulty. It is missing in most manuscripts (for example, א B Dpm it vg^codd), but occurs, with variations, in 17, vg^scl k θ f g¹ k q sy sa Did hʳ. If there was no doxology in the original text, then the above fourth point of comparison fails. On manuscript evidence alone it should be rejected as a late insertion as by the NEB, for example. But certain factors should be considered. First, Professor James Muilenburg, from his detailed knowledge of the forms of Old Testament psalms and prayers, urged upon me that it is antecedently unlikely that Matthew and, for that matter, Jesus himself should finish a prayer without a doxology, expressed or assumed (compare Ps. xli. 13; lxxii. 18; lxxxix. 52; cvi. 48; cxv. 18; cl. 6; 1 Chron. xvi. 36). Secondly, it was the rule at Jamnia that every benediction had to be responded to with the full doxology, which was once permitted only in the Temple: 'Praised be His Name whose glorious Kingdom is for ever and ever' (TB Berakoth 62*b*–63*a*), and not with the simple 'Amen', the typical response of the Synagogue. H. Schürmann, *op. cit.* p. 140, n. 449, writes: 'Es war zur Zeit Jesu jüdische Sitte, daß die Gemeinde Gebete ihres Vorbeters mit derartigen Doxologien beantwortete (vgl. ähnlich 1 Chro. xxix. 11 f.; Offb. xii. 10; Did. viii. 2; ix. 4). Wenn schon die ersten Jünger Jesu das Vater Unser hier und da auch einmal gemeinsam gebetet haben sollten, hat wohl ein Vorbeter es vorgesprochen und alle haben so oder sehr ähnlich geantwortet—und Jesus wird es ihnen dann gewiß nich verwertet haben.' Such enlargements to the 'Kern' (see note 293) were natural (H. Schürmann, *op. cit.* pp. 141 f., n. 464). May the explanation of the Doxology in the many manuscripts be that it was *assumed*, and so sometimes included and sometimes omitted? The influence of Temple and Synagogue liturgical forms on the practice of the Church needs to be re-examined. A third point to notice is that Matthew—if we take the doxology seriously—has avoided offence to Pharisaism. The doxology in vi. 13 combines the Synagogue and Temple tradition—containing a doxology proper and the Amen. The kind of doxology found in vi. 13 would attract the attention of Pharisaic leaders. In Mishnah Berakoth ix. 5 we read: 'At the close of every Benediction in the Temple they used to say, "From everlasting (מן העולם)"; but after the heretics [some MSS: Sadducees: see *J.Q.R.* VI (1915), 314] had taught corruptly and said that there is but one world (אין עולם אלא אחד) it was ordained that they should say "From everlasting to everlasting" (מן העולם ועד העולם).' Matthew's use of εἰς τοὺς αἰῶνας, 'for the ages', is significant: *this would not offend the Pharisees.* Eric Werner, *op. cit.* (1959), pp. 273 ff., 42 n. 6, 44 n. 22, shows how the Synagogue was sensitive to the doxologies of the Church (as their importance increased in the latter, they decreased in the former). He thinks that the later Church fashioned some of its liturgical ceremonies after the pattern of the sects, like the Samaritans, Sadducees, and Karaites, which were always hostile to Pharisaism. But there is nothing in the Matthaean doxology to indicate or create hostility to Pharisaism. C. F. D. Moule, *Worship in the New Testament* (1961), p. 72, notes how amazing it is that the Matthaean doxology 'is totally devoid of the Christian formula "through Christ Jesus"'. His work came into my hands after I had written the above. I am glad to note that he recognizes the possibility (*op. cit.* p. 77) that Jesus himself did use some sort of doxology.

Over against the *possibility* suggested here, that the doxology in vi. 13 be treated as part of the Lord's Prayer, are two considerations. First, as Werner points out (*op. cit.* pp. 298), the Gospels are markedly lacking in liturgical passages because they reflect 'the poor and the meek', rural society opposed to the priests and rabbis who were liturgically conscious. 'The small local synagogues', he writes, 'with their unceremonious, almost intimate, attitude toward prayer and God were the birthplaces of Christian liturgy. There was no room in these communal houses of worship for rigid and solemn formulas, such as the Temple doxologies of the hierarchical cult of Jerusalem' (p. 298). Secondly, he notes that the theocratic ideal expressed in most of the Church's doxologies, explicitly or implicitly, is by and large alien to the early Christian concept of prayer (p. 310, n. 108). But to the first point we may reply that Matthew or/and his school were not untutored people, but articulate and liturgically conscious. This much, at least, has emerged from the work of K. Stendahl (*op. cit.*); P. Carrington (*The Primitive Christian Calendar*); and G. D. Kilpatrick (*op. cit.*). And, secondly, while intimacy did mark the prayer of Jesus and of early Christians, especially if we follow J. Jeremias, 'Kennzeichen der ipsissima vox Jesu', in *Synoptische Studien* (München, 1953), pp. 87 ff.; *Theologische Literaturzeitung*, LXXIX (1954), 213 f., the notion of God's sovereignty is also expressed in the Lord's Prayer as in early Christian prayer generally. (A study of the prayers in Acts is illuminating from this point of view: see P. H. Menoud, *La Vie de l'église naissante* (1952).) On the prayers of Jesus, see R. Bultmann, *Jesus*, pp. 158–9, 188 ff., who objects to any consideration of them because of the historical uncertainty surrounding them. Contrast F. Heiler, *Das Gebet*, Eng. trans., pp. 280, 401; T. W. Manson, in *Christian Worship*, ed. N. Micklem, p. 42; *The Teaching of Jesus* (1951), pp. 89–93. Heiler notes how in Jesus, as in the prophets, a filial relationship co-exists with that of a subject to a king. Note that in xxvi. 39 Matthew avoids the 'familiar' Abba of his Marcan source (Mark xiv. 36 f.): Matthew has softened the Marcan form (on this see V. Taylor, *Mark*, p. 551). In xi. 27–30 'the father' is also 'Lord of Heaven and earth'.

APPENDIX IX

The Use of the Term ἱστορῆσαι in Gal. i. 18

At this point it is pertinent to refer also to the use of the term ἱστορῆσαι in Gal. i. 18, which reads: ἔπειτα μετὰ ἔτη τρία ἀνῆλθον εἰς Ἱεροσόλυμα ἱστορῆσαι Κηφᾶν [Πέτρον K D G pl latt syʰ]. The RSV translated 'to visit Cephas': the NEB is stronger and better, and renders 'to get to know Cephas'. But even this is perhaps not strong enough. The Aramaic 'Cephas' prompts us to seek for an Aramaic word behind ἱστορῆσαι. Does this translate, in Paul's thought, an Aramaic term denoting to seek after a tradition or to inquire after a tradition or to visit an authoritative teacher? We read, for example, in TB Yebamoth 42 *b*: 'Said R. Jeremiah to R. Zerika: When you visit R. Abbahu point out to him the following contradiction' (Soncino translation). The Hebrew for 'When you visit' is 'כי עיילת לקמיה דר. The term קמיה can be rendered 'in the presence of', but it also has the meaning of going before a person 'to procure his decision' on a matter of Law (see Jastrow, *ad rem*). The phrase עלה לקמיה, however, does not readily suggest ἱστορῆσαι. But a passage in TB Yom Tob 27*a* may offer a parallel. In connexion with a disputed point of Law we read: 'A certain person explained: May it fall to my lot to go thither (Palestine) *and learn this teaching from the mouth of the master*' (Soncino translation). The words italicized read ואגמרא לשמעתא מפומיה דמרה: does Paul have such a phrase in his mind? That the translation of ἱστορῆσαι in the RSV and NEB is too weak would also seem to be supported by the use of the verb in the papyri for consulting an oracle.

The evidence for finding in the verb the meaning 'to consult over tradition', while not beyond question, is accepted by G. D. Kilpatrick in *New Testament Essays: Studies in Memory of Thomas Walter Manson*, ed. A. J. B. Higgins (1959), pp. 144–9. He favours the translation 'to get information (about Jesus) from Cephas'. He overcomes the difficulty of the context for such a translation by claiming that Peter, to whom alone the verb is applied, possessed information about the teaching and ministry of Jesus which James could not supply. But the context makes it unnecessary to argue in this manner because clearly Paul was especially sensitive about his relationship to Peter (Gal. ii. 11–14), and J. Weiss, in *Primitive Christianity*, Eng. trans. I, 201, held that the verb ἱστορῆσαι was chosen deliberately by Paul for precisely the opposite reason, namely, to explain that 'the visit was only to satisfy a purely personal, though actually unnecessary, curiosity to become acquainted with this great personage among the Twelve'. It is, however, possible that J. Weiss does not allow sufficient force to the term ἱστορῆσαι which, if we follow the meaning suggested by Liddell and Scott, gains all the more significance in that it is used in a context precisely designed to deny Paul's dependence on a human tradition. Certainly Paul and Peter did not spend their time 'talking about the weather'. Can it be that 'reception of tradition' *will* break through Paul's account because of the nature of his encounter with Peter even though the context demands that the nature of that encounter, as a means of learning about the tradition, should be discounted? Professor S. Lieberman informs me that he takes the term ἱστορῆσαι to mean simply 'to see', as it is rendered in the oldest Palestinian Syriac Christian versions—דיחמא לקיפס (*Horae Semiticae*, VIII, 146). (He also pointed out to me the exact equivalent of τὰς παραδόσεις κατέχετε in את המסורות אתם תופשים. He refers to *Sifra, Beḥukothai*, ed. Weiss, 112*b* (viii. 2),

שהם תפוסי מעשה אבותם

'The verb תפס', he writes, 'means to hold fast, to stick to. It has also a legal meaning of possession. As for ἑστήκατε it is correctly translated in the Palestinian Syriac texts: אתין קימין (קאמין) (*Horae Semiticae*, VIII (1909), 128).') H. Riesenfeld, *op. cit.* p. 19, takes ἱστορῆσαι to have for its purpose 'that Peter should test whether he, Paul, during his term of preparation, had really made the tradition of the words and deeds of Jesus his own'. J. Wagenmann, *op. cit.* pp. 34 ff., has a helpful approach. He distinguishes between Paul's desire to learn from and about Peter (ἱστορῆσαι) and any acknowledgement on Paul's part that he was seeking recognition from Peter. The issue must be regarded as an open one; and we must be content with relegating ἱστορῆσαι to those terms which only possibly suggest a 'rabbinic' connotation.

APPENDIX X

Rabbis and their Pupils

Just as Catholicism speaks of a great nun as a 'living rule' (see, for example, K. Hulme, *The Nun's Story*), so Judaism knew of rabbis as examples of living Torah. And the imitation of Christ in Paul is not to be wholly divorced from the imitation of the rabbi as the 'living Law' in Judaism. The life of the rabbi was itself Torah. It was not enough to learn the words of a rabbi, but necessary to live with him, so as to absorb his thought and copy his every gesture. Like Paul in 1 Cor. vii, the disciple, when he expressed his own opinions, had to be careful to distinguish these from those of his teacher (S. Schechter, *Some Aspects of Rabbinic Theology*, pp. 123, 126; J. Bonsirven, *Le Judaïsme palestinien*, I, 281 ff.). The verb used to describe the service of a student שִׁמֵּשׁ to the rabbi, his teacher, was שִׁמֵּשׁ and learning by serving a rabbi was שִׁמּוּשׁ חֲכָמִים or שִׁמּוּשָׁהּ שֶׁל תּוֹרָה. To follow after a rabbi (הלך אחרי) was to become his pupil (ἀκολουθεῖν, δεῦτε ὀπίσω κ.τ.λ.). S–B, I, 187, write: 'Das Schülerverhältnis forderte persönlichen Anschluß an den Lehrer; denn der Schüler lernte nicht bloß aus den Worten seines Lehrers, sondern vielmehr noch aus dessen praktischer Gesetzesübung.' On this, see *A.R.N.* IV. For the duties of the student, Tos. Negaim viii. 2, TB Yebamoth 42 b, TB Ketuboth 63 a, Tos. Chagigah ii. 1; particularly interesting in the light of John xiii is the following passage (c. A.D. 219) from TB Ketuboth 96 a: it reads:

R. Joshua b. Levi ruled: All manner of service that a slave must render to his master a student must render to his teacher, except that of taking off his shoes. [Only a Canaanite slave performs this menial service, and a student performing it might be mistaken for such a slave.] Raba explained: This ruling [that a student should not assist his teacher in taking off his shoes] applies only to a place where he is not known but where he is known there can be no objection. R. Ashi said: Even where he is not known the ruling applies only where he does not put on tefillin [as slaves also do not wear tefillin (TB Gittin 40 a) his status might well be mistaken], but where he puts on tefillin, he may well perform such a service.

A rabbi might have more than one attendant, as in the obviously legendary story of TB Ketuboth 63 a, where R. Akiba was accompanied by 12,000 disciples! From TB Yebamoth it is clear that the שַׁמָּעָא often fulfilled the role of pupil and scholar. We may suggest that the custom of having the שַׁמָּעָא has its roots in the Old Testament. The biblical equivalent to שִׁימֵשׁ is שֵׁרֵת. This is the term used to

455

describe the relationship of Joshua to Moses (Exod. xxiv. 13; xxiii. 11; Num. xi. 28; Josh. i. 1) and of Elisha to Elijah (1 Kings xix. 21). The learning and transmission of Torah seems to have been involved in these relationships. Significantly Moses, Joshua and the Prophets are in the chain of tradition in Aboth i. 1. Particularly interesting is 1 Kings xix. 21 where the later terminology of following after a teacher emerges.

It is not suggested that this parallel exhausts the significance of the imitation of Christ in Paul, but its rabbinic character is not to be wholly excluded. Certain it is that Judaism paid great attention to 'imitation'. Some passages assert that one who has not served a rabbi, in the sense indicated above, has not really learnt Torah (see TB Berakoth 47b: 'But it has been taught (a phrase which points to an old tradition): Others say that even if one has learnt scripture and Mishnah but has not ministered to the disciples of the wise, he is an *am ha-arez*' (see the Soncino translation, p. 287)).

It is interesting to speculate how Paul regarded Titus, Timothy and even more Mark. In 2 Tim. iv. 11 Mark 'is very useful in serving me' (εὔχρηστος εἰς διακονίαν: διακονεῖν is the LXX translation for שרת): he probably did for Paul what the שַׁמָּשָׁא did for his rabbi. This does not emerge so clearly in the cases of Titus and Timothy who are perhaps more 'colleagues' than 'pupils', although in 2 Cor. xii. 18 Titus goes in Paul's steps (οὐ τοῖς αὐτοῖς ἴχνεσιν;). Timothy is a μαθητής in Acts xvi. 1. In Acts xvii. 15 (ἐντολή) Paul commands Silas and Timothy. In 1 Cor. iv. 17 he is to remind the Corinthian Church of Paul's ways in Christ, 'as I remind them everywhere in every church' (ὃς ὑμᾶς ἀναμνήσει τὰς ὁδούς μου τὰς ἐν Χριστῷ Ἰησοῦ, καθὼς πανταχοῦ ἐν πάσῃ ἐκκλησίᾳ διδάσκω). The 'ways' are Paul's *halakoth*. Notice how, as in Judaism, the 'talmid' is careful to give his teacher's 'ways'. Structurally, Paul's relation to Silas, Timothy and Titus was rabbinic although the content of the tradition with which they dwelt was more than rabbinic.

There is a wide background to this question of learning by precept and example; see D. Daube, *op. cit.* pp. 67 ff., who shows how Jesus appeals to the *example* of David in Mark ii. 23 ff.; Luke vi. 1 ff., and Matthew also refers to the *conduct* of priests (xii. 1 ff.) which was based on the rules, precepts, governing the Temple service. Daube holds that while a historical event could be used as an *example*, nevertheless, 'any detailed rule, any *halakha*, must rest, directly or indirectly, on an actual precept promulgated in Scripture' (p. 68). 'Historical data...might serve to inculcate moral lessons, general religious truths, wisdom; they might also serve to illustrate and corroborate a *halakha*. But they could not form its primary source' (p. 69). The emphasis in the New Testament has changed: Jesus—his work as well as his words—has become normative, that is, he takes the place of the Torah, although (if we follow Daube) Matthew, by referring to an activity based on definite precepts (that of the priests), has here presented a rabbinically more technical and, therefore, more forceful argument than Mark and Luke who have only made use of the example of David. This is another indication of the 'scholarly' *Herkunft* of Matthew. Since the above was written there has appeared the important study by Gerhardsson, *Memory and Manuscript*; see pp. 242 ff.

APPENDIX XI

'Wisdom' Sayings of Jesus

(i) Luke xiv. 34 f. (=Matt. v. 13: compare Mark ix. 50): 'Salt is good; but if salt has lost its taste, how shall its saltness be restored? It is fit neither for the land nor for the dunghill; men throw it away.' Luke addresses this to the multitudes (xiv. 25), and it is legitimate to consider that he has either 'everyman' or, more likely, Israel, in mind. The old Israel is here warned that the chosen may become outcast. Matthew, on the other hand, clearly refers the saying as he understands it to the disciples, the nucleus of the new Israel. The saying probably came down both to Luke and Matthew in an unattached form. There is a parallel in Mark ix. 50 where it is applied, as in Matthew, to the disciples. J. Jeremias, *The Parables of Jesus*, p. 30, thinks that Luke's application of the parable to Israel is correct 'since according to TB Bekh. 8 b, the Jews interpreted the proverb about salt as a threat against Israel (S–B, I, 236)'. The reason that Jeremias gives for his application of the parable to the old Israel must be regarded as questionable; it is perhaps best to think of the parable as originally spoken with the challenge to Qumran in mind. Qumran, and indeed, if we will, all who hear Jesus, must choose whom they will serve and for good or for ill abide by their choice. The saying is a crisis saying that easily fits into Jesus' ministry from more than one point of view. There is no reason why Jesus himself could not have uttered these words. (Compare p. 250 above.)

(ii) Luke xi. 33 (=Matt. v. 15): 'No one after lighting a lamp puts it in a cellar or under a bushel, but on a stand, that those who enter may see the light.' (See also Mark iv. 21; Luke viii. 16.) In Luke viii. 16 the words are addressed to the disciples but in xi. 33 to the crowds: Matthew clearly has the same ambiguity. Like the rest of the *SM*, v. 15 in Matthew is addressed both to the crowds (v. 1 a and vii. 28) and to the disciples. In Mark the words in iv. 21 are related to the Gospel itself (it has attracted to itself iv. 22), on which see above for a parallel in Luke viii. 17. Luke applies the parable to Jesus himself, as is clear from the preceding verses in xi. 29 ff., Matthew to the disciples and Mark to the Gospel itself. The Lucan context suggests that the putting of the lamp in a cellar or under a bushel may have reference to the possibility that the light of Jesus' ministry would be put out by 'this evil generation' (xi. 29). In any case, the pertinency of this saying to the actualities of Jesus' ministry or to the nature of the new community he had called into being or to the function of the Gospel itself is clear. (Compare pp. 251 f. above.)

(iii) Luke xi. 23: 'He who is not with me is against me, and he who does not gather with me scatters.' This verse admirably expresses the situation in the ministry of Jesus where no man can be neutral: his 'crisis' divides men according to their response to himself, a motif familiar elsewhere in the New Testament. The verse is in apparent conflict with Luke ix. 50 'for he that is not against you is for you'. But this conflict must not be exaggerated, because 'he that is not against you' (Luke ix. 50) actually refers to one who does cast out demons in Jesus' name, so that he is in a real sense with Christ, although not among his own. Mark's version in ix. 38–41 makes this doubly clear. If the conflict be emphasized then it has to be admitted that Jesus takes more seriously men's tepid attitude to himself than to his disciples. It is the response to him not to his followers that constitutes the crucial test (compare Matt. x).

(iv) Luke vi. 39, 40 (compare Matt. xv. 14; x. 24–5): 'He also told them a parable: "Can a blind man lead a blind man? Will they not both fall into a pit? A disciple is not above his teacher, but every one when he is fully taught will be like his teacher."' Luke has inserted the saying on the blind leading the blind in the Sermon on the Plain so that he refers it to the disciples. Matthew on the other hand directs it to the Pharisees, in their refusal to judge properly in the matter of things clean and unclean. The precise setting in life of the parable has been lost: it may well have been a proverbial saying used by Jesus either in connexion with his followers or his opponents. T. W. Manson regarded vi. 39 as a statement in 'general terms of a principle which is presently to be more particularly applied in vi. 46–9'. The connexion between these is not clear. In this case, however, Matthew, we may hazard the opinion, has preserved the more likely historical context: the castigation of the Pharisees as blind is well established in Matt. xxiii. 16 ff. In any case, there is no inherent improbability that Jesus himself employed the proverbial usage, if it was such.

(v) Luke xvii. 37b (=Matt. xxiv. 28): 'He said to them, "Where the body is, there the eagles will be gathered together".' Again, we are probably to admit the use of a proverbial saying. It is, however, perfectly natural for Jesus himself to emphasize in this way the speed and suddenness with which the day of the Son of Man was to come, and its accompaniments.

(vi) Luke xii. 25 (=Matt. vi. 27): 'And which of you by being anxious can add a cubit to his span of life?' Whether this rendering be accepted or that which Jeremias (see *op. cit.* p. 148), following Bornhäuser and Schlatter, has preferred, namely, 'And which of you *by putting forth effort* can add', etc., the essential reference of the saying is clear and fits perfectly into the ministry of Jesus himself. Not the thought of anxiety as such, on the one view, nor of labour as such on the other, is predominant but the need, in the light of the crisis that is at hand, for total commitment, which allows neither the debilitating effect of anxiety nor the diverting effects of labouring after the things which, however necessary, in the crisis of the ministry are secondary.

(vii) Luke vi. 30: 'Give to everyone who begs from you; and of him who takes away your goods, do not ask them again.' To classify such a startling demand as traditional, prudential exhortation is surely inadmissible: it belongs to that absolute demand which Jesus so clearly laid upon his own.

(viii) Luke x. 16: 'He who hears you hears me, and he who rejects you rejects me, and he who rejects me rejects him who sent me.' This verse is so rooted in Hebrew concepts of solidarity which everywhere break forth in the NT that its provenance must certainly be Jewish; moreover, it so fits into the idea that Jesus and his own belong to one another that it is not difficult to ascribe it to Jesus himself.

(ix) Luke xix. 26: 'I tell you, that to every one who has will more be given; but from him who has not, even what he has will be taken away.' The point of the parable in Luke xix. 11–27 is to indicate that the judgement of God is now about to be revealed upon the stewardship of the spiritual leaders of the Jewish nation, to whom much has been entrusted. To those who have added something of their own to what has been entrusted to them, more shall be entrusted. On the contrary, to those who have not done so, the judgement will be strict. While T. W. Manson (*The Sayings of Jesus*, p. 248) finds no difficulty to ascribing the words to Jesus himself, Jeremias (*op. cit.* pp. 85 ff.) has argued that they constitute a generalizing explanatory comment which changes the outlook of the whole parable since the insertion of the comment immediately before the final sentence makes it an interpretation of the whole parable, instead of that of a single verse (Matt. xxv. 28): it makes the whole parable an exposition of the nature and manner of divine grace. The term παντί 'all' or 'everyone', in particular, makes the sense a general one. On the whole one must agree with Jeremias that here, as so often elsewhere, we are to trace the activity of the Church. But it can hardly be claimed that the thought of Luke xix. 26 is, in any way, a serious item for the understanding of Q.

(x) Luke vi. 31: 'And as you wish that men would do to you, do so to them.' There is no difficulty in ascribing this to Jesus: it is a kind of rule of thumb for his followers.

(xi) Luke xii. 2: 'Nothing is covered up that will not be revealed, or hidden that will not be known.' There can be little doubt that Jesus himself may have uttered this *logion*, although the precise context in which he did so has been lost to us. Mark iv. 22 refers it to the secret of the kingdom: Luke xii. 3 (compare viii. 17) relates it to the preaching of the disciples, Matthew uses it for exhortation: no hostility can frustrate the preaching. Here in Luke xii. 2 it is a warning against the hypocrisy of the Pharisees. There is a parallel in *Oxyrhynchus Pap.* xi, 5. In any case, the words point to a coming reversal of existing conditions: they are words of 'crisis', pointing to the coming consummation.

(xii) Luke xviii. 14=xiv. 11 (=Matt. xviii. 4; xxiii. 12): 'I tell you, this man went down to his house justified rather than the other; for every one who exalts himself will be humbled, but he who humbles himself will be exalted.' This verse perfectly fits into the context in Luke xiv. 11. Some have found that xviii. 14 smacks too much of popular morality. Nevertheless, if full force be given to its future tenses, the eschatological reference becomes unmistakable. It is possible that Jesus used the words on different occasions with a different application, or, again, that the original application has been lost, while the two applications now suggested are secondary.

(xiii) Luke ix. 58 (= Matt. viii. 20): 'And Jesus said to him, "Foxes have holes, and birds of the air have nests; but the Son of Man has nowhere to lay his head".' Whatever proverbial force be found in this saying, its relevance to the actualities of Jesus' own ministry are unmistakable.

Bultmann refers in all to 26 passages from Q as belonging to profane proverbs, but we have dealt with the chief instances that he adduces above. His view cannot be substantiated. While it is not to be deemed unlikely that Jesus may have used such proverbs, nevertheless almost all the passages which Bultmann regards as generalized wisdom sayings can be understood as having been applied by Jesus himself to illumine the crisis constituted by his coming. Moreover, it will have emerged that few of those passages belong strictly to the ethical teaching of Jesus as such. In those that do, the note of crisis is evident. Further, our conclusion concerning the passages isolated by Bultmann agrees with the nature of the material in Q in its totality, as is pointed out above.

APPENDIX XII

The Influence of Catechisms on the Gospels

Two recent discussions came into our hands too late for discussion in the body of the text, one in an article by C. H. Dodd, in *Studies in Memory of T. W. Manson* (1959), on 'The Primitive Catechism and the Sayings of Jesus', pp. 106 ff. and another by Siegfried Wibbing, *Die Tugend- und Lasterkataloge im Neuen Testament* (1959). Dodd argues that catechetical patterns have influenced the Gospels at two stages: first, *directly*, in their final composition, so that the Gospels themselves partake of the nature of catechisms, and secondly, *indirectly*, in so far as much of the material which they incorporate had previously been arranged for catechetical purposes. To illustrate the first point, he refers to the incidence of the eschatological discourses in the Synoptic Gospels, which have a parallel in the Farewell Discourses of the Fourth Gospel. The second point is supported by appeal to the structure of the *SM* in Matthew which also culminates with an eschatological reference. So too, although the Sermon on the Plain in Luke does not reveal a catechetical pattern such as is apparent in the Matthaean *SM*, in Luke xii. 22–34, which leads on to the eschatological material in xii. 35–46, Dodd finds a sequence in it, determined by the fact that the material had previously been used for catechetical purposes. (See our treatment of this section above.) The contention that in Luke xii. 22–46 the tradition has been influenced by catechetical usage is convincing. And it is also possible to endorse the parallelism drawn between the structure of Matthew's *SM* and catechesis, although another interpretation of it would seem to be equally, if not more, illuminating (see pp. 304 ff. above), while it is significant that neither Dodd nor Carrington can account for all the material in the Sermon on the Mount in catechetical terms (see P. Carrington, *op. cit.*). We may, however, question whether the structures of the Gospels have been so influenced. Thus, does the incidence of eschatological material at the end of the Gospels necessarily demand a catechetical explanation? To close documents on an eschatological note was natural and traditional. Eccles. xii. 14 ends with the words 'For God will bring every deed into judgement, with every secret thing, whether good or evil'. The eschatological discourses in Isa. xxxv and lxvi are natural conclusions to collections of material. 'But go your way till the end; and you shall rest, and shall stand in your allotted place at the end of the days'— this is equally to be expected at the end of Daniel; while Hosea, Joel, Amos, Obadiah, Micah, Zephaniah, Haggai, Zechariah and Malachi—all these Old Testament documents find it fitting to end on an eschatological note. Moreover, in two ways Dodd confirms the position which we have taken in our text above. He finds that the substance of the Gospel tradition about the words of Jesus was not primarily transmitted along catechetical channels, and it is of the utmost interest, in view of our treatment, that it is at one point only that he draws any considerable parallels in substance between the catechesis, isolated by Carrington, Selwyn and others, and the words ascribed to Jesus in the Synoptics, namely, at the point where the awareness of crisis emerges, that is, the very point which we also insisted upon above. What we may call more normal, ethical catechesis does not supply so obvious a parallel.

Our fundamental position is also confirmed by the treatment of the lists of virtues and vices used in the New Testament by Wibbing, *op. cit.* On pp. 87 f. he lists the vices most frequently found in the New Testament. In the Pastoral Epistles 30 terms for vices occur which have no parallel elsewhere in the New Testament, a fact which suggests that the lists bear especially upon the problems facing the Pastorals in the period to which they belonged, when traditional lists of vices were not adequate or pertinent. This alone shows that the words of Jesus were not normative for such purposes and could not be. More significant is it that out of 65 vices listed outside the Pastorals, only 14 occur in the Synoptic Gospels, and, what is still more striking, *all* the parallels occur in a single passage in Mark vii. 21–2 and its parallel in Matt. xv. 19. The lists, however, correspond closely with those of the DSS (see Wibbing, *op. cit.* pp. 92 ff.). The conclusion is inevitable. The lists of vices draw not upon words of Jesus but upon a Jewish tradition.

APPENDIX XIII

The Textual Problem of Mark x. 12

See on this D. Daube, *The New Testament and Rabbinic Judaism*, pp. 362 ff.;
Mark x. 12 presents a textual problem. Three forms of the text emerge:

(1) אB, etc.
    καὶ ἐὰν αὐτὴ ἀπολύσασα τὸν ἄνδρα
    αὐτῆς γαμήσῃ ἄλλον, μοιχᾶται

(2) (with few modifications) A, the Byzantine text f 1, it (some MSS) vg syᵖʰ:
    ἐὰν γυνὴ ἀπολύσῃ τὸν ἄνδρα αὐτῆς
    καὶ γαμηθῇ ἄλλῳ

(3) D θ f 13 al it syˢ (with few modifications):
    ἐὰν γυνὴ ἐξέλθῃ ἀπὸ τοῦ ἀνδρὸς
    καὶ γαμήσῃ ἄλλον μοιχᾶται

(1) and (2) present no significant difference in meaning, but (3) contemplates not
divorce but separation and marriage to another man. Wellhausen, *Das Evangelium Matthaei*, p. 84, follows (3) and so does V. Taylor, *St Mark, ad rem.* If (3) be
accepted, there is no reference to Roman legal practice in the passage but possibly
a side-glance at Herodias. But the best manuscripts support (1) and (2), in which
case Mark has adopted the teaching of Jesus to a Gentile situation, unless, of
course, it be contemplated that Jesus himself had referred to Gentile practice
(C. E. B. Cranfield, *St Mark* (1959), p. 322, mentions this possibility). Against the
latter view is that Matthew has no such reference. The whole subject has been dealt
with exhaustively by Daube, *op. cit.* pp. 362–8. He regards the text (3) above,
reading ἐξέρχομαι, and other texts, not hitherto mentioned, that is, Bob., Colb.;
Holm, giving ἀπολείπειν, as the more original. He explains the change from
ἐξέρχομαι or ἀπολείπειν to ἀπολύειν in א B, etc., as due to: (i) assimilation to Mark
x. 11 where ἀπολύειν is used; and (ii) adaptation such as we have suggested above
when Mark x. 12 fell into Hellenistic hands. Daube, however, also points out
that, while under rabbinic law a wife could not divorce her husband, there were
Jewish circles where this happened in violation of the law. See for example the
cases of Salome and Herodias (Josephus, *Ant.* xv, vii, 10; xviii, v, 5). In any case
we are justified in finding here adaptation to Roman custom, even though the
original reference may have been directed against Herodias who, in any case,
like Salome, was an 'assimilated lady', who had been impressed by Roman law
(Boaz Cohen, *Law and Tradition in Judaism* (1959), p. 105; his chapter on
'Concerning Jewish law on domestic relations' (pp. 100–18) shows how
rabbinic Judaism was 'sensitive to the inequality of women with respect to the
right to sue for divorce' (p. 106) and took measures accordingly by establishing the doctrine of 'compulsory consent', etc., allowing mad husbands to

divorce their wives in 'lucid' moments, etc. (pp. 109 f.)). The problem of divorce was particularly acute in Judaism after the fall of Jerusalem not only as a result of the dislocation caused by the war but because of the general conditions in the first two centuries of the Common Era (Boaz Cohen, *op. cit.* pp. 104, 108). See J. Muirhead, *Historical Introduction to the Law of Rome* (1916), pp. 223 f., 274 f.

APPENDIX XIV

Echoes of Synoptic Words in John

There are echoes of Synoptic words in John, as C. H. Dodd has shown in *N.T.S.* II, 2 (November 1955), 75 ff., 'Some Johannine "Herrnworte" with parallels in the Synoptic Gospels'. He refers to (1) John xiii. 16, compare Matt. x. 24, 25; (2) John ii. 25, compare Mark viii. 35; Luke ix. 24; x. 39; xvi. 25; xvii. 33. With xii. 24 we dealt above. (3) John xiii. 20 (compare John xv. 23), compare Matt. x. 40; Mark ix. 37; Luke ix. 48; x. 16; (4) John xx. 23, compare Matt. xviii. 18. Only John xii. 25 can be regarded as *strictly* ethical in its provenance. A. Schlatter dealt with the problem in *Die Parallelen in den Worten Jesu bei Johannes und Matthäus* (Gütersloh, 1898). He rightly recognizes how in Matthew and John the commandment of love is the summation of the ethical demand. Compare vii. 12; v. 43–8; xxii. 34–40 with John xiii. 34; xiv. 21–4; xviii. 23 ff. Schlatter comments on xiv. 21–4: 'Wer meine Gebote hält, der ist der mich liebende. Seine Gebote sind aber befaßt in die Weisung einander zu lieben' (*op. cit.* p. 63). The commandment of love is raised to centrality in Matthew in terms of the struggle with Judaism, in John in the context of the Christian community itself (*op. cit.* p. 55). The similarity between the Matthaean and Johannine understanding of the Church emerges when we compare xxviii. 20 with John xiv. 18 f.: in both the Christ gives his own his commandment and spirit and also himself. But, apart from the commandment of love, as we have indicated above, John does not emphasize the strictly ethical teaching of Jesus. Of the 101 parallels between the two Gospels that Schlatter lists, only the following can be claimed to deal with ethical teaching and that only in a broad sense (the majority of the items he isolates are only very indirectly ethically concerned):

Matthew vi. 1–6	John v. 44
v. 18	x. 36
vii. 24	xii. 47 f.
xviii. 23	xiii. 34 (but this is hardly a clear parallel)

Schlatter's 'parallels' have to be coaxed or forced out of the texts he presents. Most of them do not suggest the use of a rich tradition of the words of Jesus such as emerges in Matthew but a common treasury of understanding of the Christian life, which belongs to the same conceptual world as that tradition, but can only be verbally or directly connected to it by tortuous exegesis. Neither the treatment of Dodd nor of Schlatter compels us to change the position taken in the text. Schlatter writes: 'Johannes lag es daran, daß wir in Jesus Gott als den gegenwärtigen offenbaren, redenden, liebenden, gebenden haben, daß wir in unserer Kenntnis Jesu unsere Religion haben, daß unser Blick auf Jesu Blick auf Gott sei und bleibe. Damit hängen auch die Vereinfachungen zusammen, die seine Darstellung den älteren Evangelien gegenüber zeigt, sowohl die Weglassung der konkreten ethischen Stoffe im Kampf Jesu mit der Judenschaft, wie in der Unterweisung der Jünger, als auch die Entfernung derjenigen Sätze aus der Weissagung Jesu, die auf das Ende des Geschichtslauf und das Geschick der Welt hinübersehen. Weder diese noch jene sind geleugnet oder bezweifelt, stehen aber dem Evangelisten hinter dem einen Hauptsatz, den er betont, zurück, hinter der für ihn fundamentalen Überzeugung, daß in Jesu Gott unserem Erkennen und Lieben zugänglich geworden ist' (*op. cit.* pp. 71 ff.).

APPENDIX XV

REFLECTIONS ON A SCANDINAVIAN APPROACH TO 'THE GOSPEL TRADITION'

The question of the origin and transmission of the tradition of the works and words of Jesus has recently especially occupied New Testament scholars and theologians. An examination of it here is therefore both timely and apt. And in order to set our present discussion in true perspective, we first recall the main answers that have hitherto been given to it. Apart from the non-critical, these are three: (i) that which separates Jesus of Nazareth radically from his world and time and finds in the tradition presented in the New Testament a misunderstanding of him born of 'Qumranizing' and 'Judaizing' tendencies in the primitive church;[1] (ii) that which derives that tradition mainly from the primitive communities which created and formed it to meet its own needs. On this view the tradition is from the Church, by the Church, for the Church: it reveals primarily, not Jesus of Nazareth, but the faith of the Church in him, and the degree to which he is represented or can be discovered through the Gospels is tentatively and variously assessed;[2] (iii) that which finds the origin of the tradition in the life, teaching, death and resurrection of Jesus himself, as these were remembered and preserved by the Church. The tradition was not created by the latter and, although in the course of its preservation and transmission it could not but be modified, it was never made wholly subservient to the needs of the

[1] E. Stauffer, *Die Botschaft Jesu* (1959), pp. 9 ff.

[2] This position is particularly associated with R. Bultmann. His followers seem to be moving away from extreme scepticism, for example G. Bornkamm, *Jesus von Nazareth* (1956). Important also is the work of Professor J. Knox.

community but remained true to its initial impulse in Jesus himself. Thus, on this view, however much they represent the Church, the Gospels preserve the authentic figure of Jesus of Nazareth, whose act we can see and voice hear in them.[1]

We are here concerned with a major contribution recently made to this discussion. The third view represented above has been taken much further by Professor Harald Riesenfeld in a now famous monograph entitled *The Gospel Tradition and its Beginnings: A Study in the Limits of 'Formgeschichte'* (London, 1957), and by Dr Birger Gerhardsson in *Memory and Manuscript, Oral Tradition and Written Transmission in Rabbinic Judaism and Early Christianity* (Uppsala, 1961). Their respective positions are so similar that they can be dealt with together. The latter, we may surmise, has presented in great detail the pertinent elements in the Jewish milieu of primitive Christianity and in the New Testament itself upon which Riesenfeld had based his case, although the two Scandinavian scholars do not always speak with the same voice. They both recognize the valuable contribution of form-criticism but claim that the emphasis on preaching, by Dibelius, and on teaching, catechism, apologetics, polemics, discipline, organization and study of the Scriptures in the Church, by Bultmann, do not adequately account either for the origin or for the transmission of the Gospel tradition. At bottom, this is so because they fail to do justice to indications in the New Testament that Christianity from the first was a guaranteed tradition 'involving a deliberate didactic activity on the part of definite doctrinal authorities: the formulation of definite sayings and the methodical delivery and reception of such sayings'.[2] As Riesenfeld and Gerhardsson interpret the evidence, behind the tradition preserved in the New Testament stands a 'Holy Word'. This was accorded a status similar, in sanctity, to that of the Old Testament and, as such, was or may have been solemnly recited in the early Christian assemblies for worship.[3] In the first place Jesus himself, as Messiah, had taught the 'Holy Word' to his disciples, who learnt it *by heart* at his feet. It is this that accounts for the rhythmic, mnemonic character of so much in the Gospels. Gerhardsson closes his treatment thus:

When the Evangelists edited their Gospels . . . they worked on a basis of a fixed, distinct tradition from, and about, Jesus—a tradition which was partly memorized and partly written down in notebooks and private scrolls, *but invariably isolated from the teachings of other doctrinal authorities.*[4]

How shall we assess this position? At two points the Scandinavian scholars command assent. First, on grounds which will appear from what I have written elsewhere and which need not be repeated here, it seems historically probable that the essentials of the tradition find their ultimate origin in Jesus. In the

---

[1] British scholars such as C. H. Dodd, W. Manson, T. W. Manson, V. Taylor are the most typical representatives of this position. [2] Gerhardsson, *op. cit.* p. 14.

[3] Riesenfeld, *op. cit.*; Gerhardsson is not so emphatic, *op. cit.* p. 335.

[4] *Op. cit.* p. 335 (our italics).

nature of the case, because of their attitude towards Jesus, the earliest Christians, especially the disciples who constantly accompanied him during his ministry, would have treasured the memory of his works and words with reverent tenacity.[1] Thus a 'traditionalist' emphasis was present from the very beginning of the Christian movement, a fact which our earliest sources, the Pauline Epistles, abundantly attest.

Secondly, we can no longer doubt that the process whereby the Christian tradition was transmitted is to be largely understood in the light of Pharisaic usage in dealing with Oral Tradition (תורה שבעל פה), a usage which was not without Hellenistic parallels.[2] At this point, full recognition must be given to Gerhardsson's work. An indispensable task—that of gathering together what could be known of the oral and written transmission of tradition in rabbinic Judaism and showing its relevance for the understanding of primitive Christian usage—has at last been fulfilled. This is not the place to expound or examine his treatment, which covers the bulk of his volume on pp. 19–192; we merely note that this alone makes his contribution of primary importance. To illustrate by one example only, which we have elsewhere independently urged, the concept of the imitation of Christ and of the Apostles, Gerhardsson shows, can only be appreciated in its full significance in terms of 'the service of the Torah' (שמושה של תורה).[3] In recalling us to an emphasis in the New Testament too often ignored, that on the responsible reception and transmission of tradition and their *Mutterboden* in Judaism, Riesenfeld and Gerhardsson have rendered an important, salutary, distinguished service.

It is when we inquire what precisely is to be understood by 'the tradition' that we enter into difficulty, and our purpose here is not to offer a criticism of the Scandinavians' position so much as to indicate points where there is need for greater clarification and certainty before it can be endorsed.

The Scandinavian scholars include in what Riesenfeld, in the title of his monograph, calls 'The Gospel Tradition', not only the ethical teaching of Jesus, but the total kerygmatic and didactic substance of primitive Christianity. Within this 'Gospel Tradition' both he and Gerhardsson distinguish three items:

(1) 'The Word' (ὁ λόγος), that is, the Gospel as the recognition that Jesus was the Son of God. This was 'revealed'.[4]

(2) 'The Word of the Gospel' (ὁ λόγος τοῦ εὐαγγελίου), that is, the core of the Gospel tradition,[5] a corpus containing sayings of and about Christ. This

---

[1] Gerhardsson, *op. cit.* p. 258, writes: 'All historical probability is in favour of Jesus' disciples, and the whole of early Christianity, having accorded the sayings of one whom they believed to be the Messiah at least the same degree of respect as the pupils of a Rabbi accorded the words of *their* master!' I find this reasonable: its consequences are, of course, significant for one's approach to 'The Tradition'.

[2] See E. J. Bickerman, *Revue Biblique*, LIX (1952), 44–54, on 'La chaîne de la tradition pharisienne'.

[3] Gerhardsson, *op. cit.* pp. 242 ff.   [4] *Op. cit.*   [5] *Op. cit.*

both Riesenfeld and Gerhardsson term 'the Holy Word' (ἱερὸς λόγος) (although Gerhardsson also refers to it as 'the Gospel tradition'). This was carefully safe-guarded and authoritatively transmitted intact. To use Riesenfeld's phrase, this 'Holy Word' was not to be 'bandied about', but treated with the kind of reverence accorded to the Old Testament.[1]

(3) This tradition of a 'Holy Word' was not merely transmitted intact but 'used', and out of this 'use' arose the totality of the primitive tradition, the tradition 'undifferentiated' as it were. (Again Gerhardsson's usage does not seem always consistent: he sometimes calls 'the Word of the Gospel', that is, item (2) above, simply 'the Word'; compare pp. 295 and 296.)

Thus, for both Riesenfeld and Gerhardsson the Synoptic Gospels (they do not treat the Fourth Gospel extensively) preserve the veritable activity and teaching of Jesus 'uncontaminated'. Can the dissection of the tradition which they propose be accepted? The following considerations are pertinent.

I

In presenting his case for a fixed 'Holy Word', Gerhardsson begins with the Fathers of the Church, in whom the fact of tradition and the recognized vocabu-lary of its transmission emerge clearly. For the Fathers, Christianity was indubitably a tradition transmitted, and that primarily orally, from authentic witnesses. But we are left with a question. Did this tradition constitute an unmistakable, well-defined entity, which would correspond to the postulated 'Holy Word'? Gerhardsson appeals to the following passages:

(1) 'Irenaeus relates that he carries in his memory many traditions which he received from his childhood from Polycarp', as follows:

I can even name the place where the blessed Polycarp sat and taught (καθεζό-μενος διελέγετο), where he went out and in. I remember his way of life (τὸν χαρακτῆρα τοῦ βίου), what he looked like, the addresses (τὰς διαλέξεις) he delivered to the people, how he told (ἀπήγγελλε) of his intercourse with John and with the others who had seen the Lord, how he remembered their words (ἀπεμνημόνευε τοὺς λόγους αὐτῶν) and what he heard from them about the Lord, about his miracles, and about his teaching (τῆς διδασκαλίας). As one who had received this from eye-witnesses of the word of life (ὡς παρὰ αὐτοπτῶν τῆς ζωῆς τοῦ Λόγου παρειληφώς) Polycarp retold everything in accordance with the Scriptures (σύμφωνα ταῖς Γραφαῖς). I listened to this then, because of the grace of God which was given me, carefully, copying it down, not on paper, but in my heart (ὑπομνηματιζόμενος αὐτά· οὐκ ἐν χάρτῃ ἀλλ' ἐν τῇ ἐμῇ καρδίᾳ). And I repeat it (ἀναμαρυκῶμαι) constantly in genuine form by the grace of God.

(2) Papias expressed his reverence for those who speak of 'commandments which are given *by the Lord* for faith and which derive *from the very truth*' (Gerhardsson's italics), and then we find:

And then whenever someone came who (as a disciple) had accompanied the elders (εἰ δέ που καὶ παρηκολουθηκώς τις τοῖς πρεσβυτέροις ἔλθοι) I used to search

---

[1] *Op. cit.*

for (ἀνέκρινον) the words of the elders: what Andrew or what Peter had said (εἶπεν) or what Philip or what Thomas or what James or what John or what Matthew or any other disciple of the Lord, or what Aristion or what John the Elder, the disciples of the Lord, say (λέγουσιν).

Into the meaning of πρεσβύτερος here we cannot enter; the passage, however, clearly asserts transmission by 'authorities' and that orally.

(3) The *Clementine Recognitions*, XI, 1, records Peter's habit of memorizing:

I have adopted the habit of recalling in my memory (*revocare ad memoriam*) the words of my Lord which I heard from himself, and because of my longing for them I force my mind and my thoughts to be roused, so that, awaking to them, and recalling and repeating each one of them, I may keep them in memory (*ut evigilans ad ea et singula quaeque recolens ac retexens possim memoriter retinere*).

To this Gerhardsson rightly offers rabbinic parallels.[1]

All these passages can rightly be claimed to attest among the Fathers the reliance on authorities, oral transmission, the imitation of teachers, the desire for a pure tradition. But do they demand the recognition of any single, clearly defined, 'Holy Word'? The first and second passages referred to imply, not a single fixed tradition, but one having many a source, and, therefore, many a form. Thus Polycarp remembered 'his intercourse with John *and with the others who had seen the Lord*' (our italics). Papias clearly had many streams of tradition upon which to draw. This is recognized by Gerhardsson, who notes that in the passage on Papias 'the Apostles do not stand as traditionists *en bloc*, but individually'. He goes on to state: 'Here we may glimpse a terminology—and method—of transmission of the same type as that used by the Rabbis: Rabbi A. said in Rabbi B.'s name'.[2] But is this precisely the force of the passage in Papias? It seems to demand not the transmission of a single tradition from A. to B., but, at least, several forms of the same tradition derived from different sources. The tradition which the above-mentioned Fathers knew was already multiform. Other Fathers show an even greater confusion.[3] They know no definitely delineated 'tradition', no 'Holy Word' undefiled, but a more fluid, living tradition than such a phrase suggests. While the appeal to the Fathers does support Riesenfeld and Gerhardsson in their interpretation of the mode of

---

[1] See for the first passage Eusebius, *Hist. Eccl.* v, 20 [*M.P.G.* xx, 485]; for the second Eusebius, *Hist. Eccl.* III, 39 [*M.P.G.* xx, 297]. Gerhardsson's treatment is on pp. 202–7. On πρεσβύτερος, see especially J. Munck, *Harvard Theological Review*, LII (1959), 233 ff., who takes 'presbyters' to include 'Apostles'.

[2] *Op. cit.* p. 206.

[3] See R. P. C. Hanson on 'The Church and Tradition in the Pre-Nicene Fathers', in *The Scottish Journal of Theology*, XII (1959), 21 ff. Gerhardsson does not deal at length with the question why, if there were a 'Holy Word' preserved intact, there was such textual variation. H. Köster's work, *Synoptische Überlieferung bei den apostolischen Vätern* (1957), he does not regard as serious for his thesis; see *op. cit.* p. 198. Both these matters demand more adequate discussion.

the transmission of the tradition, it does not seem to us to corroborate their insistence on a fixed 'Holy Word'. Had such existed in so tangible a form as they suggest, it is hardly credible that the struggle with Gnosticism would have been so crucial: that agonic struggle arose partly because the appeal to 'the tradition' was ambiguous.

II

Next uneasiness arises over Gerhardsson's broad understanding of the early Christian movement. This he largely interprets in terms of three closely related concepts—the Temple at Jerusalem, the Twelve, centred there, and the Torah, teaching, emanating thence through these. In order to support his position he concentrates attention first of all on Luke–Acts. But even granting, without discussion, that Acts contains early sources, questions insinuate themselves in connexion with all these terms.

First, Gerhardsson[1] ascribes great importance to Jerusalem and its Temple in the life and thought of the primitive Church. In this, early Christian thinking was governed by that which it had inherited from Judaism. The latter not only recognized the central role which the City of David had played in the past history of the People of God, but also cherished the expectation that in the Messianic Age it would continue to have special significance, among other ways, as the point of departure for a Messianic Torah. And just as in the past the Torah had been closely associated with the Temple, so in the ideal future that sanctuary would be the centre of teaching. To these expectations early Christianity fell heir. Gerhardsson claims, as we shall see further below, that in the activity of Jesus in the Temple during the last days of his ministry, as well as in the abiding of the disciples in the Holy City and their attendance at the Temple, Luke saw the fulfilment of these Messianic expectations. From Holy Temple, in the Holy City, the Holy Word was to go forth; the Christian community conceived of itself as a new Jerusalem and a new Temple where this Word was preserved and applied and whence it was disseminated.

The evidence in favour of this position, produced by Gerhardsson, is impressive. Jesus did set his face to die in Jerusalem at the national centre in an appeal to Israel as a people. In doing so he inevitably and, we must believe, deliberately became involved with the Temple. Similarly there can be no shadow of doubt that the Church *at Jerusalem* was the real centre of the early movement. But is the evidence such as to allow us to go further?

Does Luke, in fact, ascribe to Jerusalem the significance that Gerhardsson asserts? As he himself notes, there co-exist in Luke two attitudes to the Holy City, a positive one, which Gerhardsson strongly emphasizes, to which we have already referred, and a negative, which breaks out in the weeping over Jerusalem

---

[1] *Op. cit.* pp. 214 ff. In this section we are reminded much of J. Munck's emphasis on Jerusalem in his *Paulus und die Heilsgeschichte* (1954), on which see chapter VIII in my *Christian Origins and Judaism* (1962).

(Luke xix. 41–4) and in the eschatological discourse where judgement upon Jerusalem is predicted (Luke xxi. 5–36, and especially verses 20–4). Gerhardsson escapes from this dilemma by drawing a distinction between the actual Jerusalem, especially as represented by High Priests, Scribes and Elders, and the Christian community, which has itself become the true Jerusalem. To reinforce this he holds that all the people of Jerusalem 'are favourably inclined both to Jesus and the Young Church', 'so that the Apostles and the original congregation around them are presented as—shall we say?—"the true Jerusalem"'.[1]

But the significance ascribed by Gerhardsson to Luke's references to 'the people' of Jerusalem is not to be too easily endorsed. Those references are indeed striking. They occur at Luke xix. 47–8, which depict 'the people' hanging on Jesus' words and preventing the leaders from acting against him; xx. 1 f., which merely indicates that 'the people' were addressed by Jesus; xx. 19, where their favourable attitude is contrasted with the leaders' hostility; xx. 45, where a condemnation of the Scribes is uttered in the presence of 'the people', the two groups being, by implication, sharply distinguished; xxi. 38, strong evidence of Jesus' popularity with 'the people' as such, as is xxii. 2. But Gerhardsson omits two significant passages from Luke which run counter to his view. In xxiii. 1–5 there is no emphasis on the people of Jerusalem as such: the case against Jesus is that 'His teaching is causing disaffection among the people through all Judaea. It started from Galilee and has spread as far as this city' (xxiii. 5) (NEB). Moreover, in xxiii. 13–25 'the people' of Jerusalem are included among those who call for Jesus' crucifixion. At the crucial point they too, no less than their leaders, failed him. With this agrees xxiii. 27, where it is explicitly stated that many (not all) of the people sympathetically followed Jesus to Golgotha. Similarly, while in Acts i. 4 the disciples are commanded not to leave Jerusalem, their witness in i. 8 is to be 'all over Judaea and Samaria, and away to the ends of the earth' (NEB). The 'universalist' intention of Acts ii, which probably is meant to evoke the story of the Tower of Babel in reverse, needs no emphasis.[2] Pentecost is a sign not primarily to Israel but to all the world.[3] Neither here nor in Acts v. 13–16 is there any exclusive concentration on Jerusalem. There seems to be little justification for the claim that the Christian community constituted for Luke–Acts a new Jerusalem, and still less a new Temple. Gerhardsson's references to the latter are vague.[4] Certainly Stephen's radicalism in rejecting even the idea of a Temple, as the place of God's abode, is against any such a conception. If it be urged that he was an exception, there is still no tangible evidence for Gerhardsson's position. It should be noted that

---

[1] *Op. cit.* p. 217.

[2] Kirsopp Lake, *The Beginnings of Christianity*, v (1933), 114 f.

[3] *Ibid.*; the reading 'Ιουδαῖοι, in Acts ii. 5, should probably be omitted.

[4] *Op. cit.* pp. 219 f.

neither in the Dead Sea Sect nor in the early Church does the notion of a new Temple necessarily imply a geographic location at Jerusalem. The community *at Qumran*[1] is a Temple; Christians *at Corinth* constitute a Temple.[2] Not only in the Fourth Gospel but in the Synoptics the old Temple at Jerusalem is suspect. The 'new Temple' is not to be confined to the old city.[3] Moreover, if the primitive community, in Luke's understanding of it, interpreted itself as the new Jerusalem, constituting the new Temple, then Gerhardsson is involved in an inner contradiction. On the one hand he insists on the significance of the *geographic* Jerusalem as such for the early Church, but, on the other, on the *spiritual* Jerusalem, the Church. It is difficult to see how the primitive community could both spiritualize its understanding of 'Jerusalem' and, at the same time, retain its actual geographic centrality for the Messianic Age.[4]

But apart from its status in Luke–Acts, Gerhardsson has re-opened the question of the importance of Jerusalem in primitive Christianity in a more general way. As we saw, and as he himself admits, Luke–Acts itself reveals a negative as well as a positive approach to the Holy City, so that even Gerhardsson's primary source is ambiguous. But even if such were not the case and the eschatological centrality of Jerusalem for Acts could unequivocally be maintained, it would then be necessary to emphasize that there were currents in the early Church which regarded Jerusalem, not as the source of Messianic Torah, but of apostasy. To recount the arguments in favour of this is not necessary; suffice it to refer to the work of E. Lohmeyer, R. H. Lightfoot and others. While it may not be established that there existed a Galilean over against a Jerusalem Christianity, the evidence is at the least sufficient to suggest that among many Christians Jerusalem was not so much the seat of the Messiah as the place of his rejection. Two things should be clearly distinguished. On the one hand, the historical and geographical significance of Jerusalem in primitive Christianity has to be fully recognized. Thus Paul, our earliest witness, had to go up to that city to make sure that he had not run in vain.[5] On the other hand, a theological significance should not be too certainly derived from the historical and geographical role of the city—this despite the full force of Jewish expectation. To turn again to Paul, it is striking how soon he came to contrast the earthly Jerusalem with another. See Gal. iv. 21–7; the pertinent verses are verses 24–6: 'The two women stand for two covenants. The one bearing children into slavery is the covenant that comes from Mount Sinai: that is Hagar. Sinai is a mountain in Arabia and it represents the Jerusalem of today, for she and her children are in slavery. But the heavenly Jerusalem is the free woman; she is our mother' (NEB).

I have elsewhere supplied evidence that the dominance of Jerusalem in primitive Christianity was short-lived: the 'leap' into the Gentile world came

[1] DSD. viii. 5 ff.　　　[2] 1 Cor. iii. 16 (ναός).　　　[3] John iv. 21.
[4] See our criticism of J. Munck, *op. cit.*, reference in p. 469, n. 1.
[5] Gal. ii. 2.

early; and the glorification of the City of David in Christian circles belongs to a later period than that of the New Testament—to that of the *epigonoi*. Acts itself suggests all this. Its 'hero' is neither James nor Peter but Paul: its centre of interest quickly shifts from Jerusalem to the Gentile world. A case can even be made that the geographic centre for Acts is not Jerusalem but Rome. 'Paul at Rome', it has been said, is for Luke 'the climax of the Gospel'. Early Christianity soon became an ellipse not a circle.[1]

Coupled with the problem of Jerusalem is the role of 'the Twelve'. Gerhardsson points out that except at two places, where he follows a source without changing it at Acts xiv. 4, 14, Luke confines the term 'apostle' to 'the Twelve', and in Acts xv, in the so-called Apostolic Council, their doctrinal authority becomes evident. But the full evidence that is presented for the claim that 'the Twelve' constituted a collegium, a central doctrinal authority for the early Church at Jerusalem, and, specifically, at the Temple, cannot be repeated here. It prompts a negative and positive response.

On the negative side, certain factors must be mentioned. First, it might be argued that if Luke was so concerned to emphasize the identity of 'the apostles' with 'the Twelve' he would surely, wherever necessary, have manipulated his sources with this in view, so that the references to 'apostles' other than 'the Twelve' must be taken more seriously than by Gerhardsson. Secondly, it should never be overlooked that in Acts probably the greatest experiment in all the history of the Church, the Mission to the Gentiles, took place without the authority of 'the Twelve'.[2] Thirdly—a point which we have previously made in another connexion—the structure of Acts itself does not suggest the overwhelming primacy of 'the Twelve'. Had the latter been dominant, is it likely that Acts should so quickly have turned its attention away from them to Paul? All these factors compel us to temper Gerhardsson's enthusiasm in emphasizing the role of 'the Twelve'. But do they invalidate that emphasis?

On the positive side, although it can be exaggerated, the authority of 'the Twelve' in Luke–Acts is so marked that in the light of the evidence produced by Gerhardsson full significance must be given to it. The deliberateness with which the place of Judas was refilled and the clear statement of the necessary qualifications for the Apostolate are both indicative (Acts i. 9–12). And our other sources confirm the impression given there that 'the Twelve' were in a position of authority. In the Pauline Epistles the term 'apostle' has a wide range of application so that it is used of Andronicus and Junias (Rom. xvi. 7); James, the Lord's brother (Gal. i. 19: this is at least a possibility); Epaphroditus (Phil. ii. 25); Silas and Timothy (1 Thess. ii. 6); 2 Cor. xi. 13 suggests that Paul regarded 'apostles' as numerous. But, nevertheless, he clearly distinguished 'apostles' in general from 'the Twelve', a term which had already become technical before his day (1 Cor. xv. 3 ff.). And, although we can not enlarge on

---

[1] See above, pp. 317 ff.   [2] W. Telfer, *J.T.S.* XLVIII (1947), 226.

the problem here, one thing is clear—that Paul was anxious to be in agreement with 'the pillars' at Jerusalem, which in itself suggests that the authoritative position ascribed to 'the Twelve' by Gerhardsson is not inconsistent with what we find in the Pauline epistles (Gal. i. 18–ii. 10).[1] Similarly in the various strata in the Synoptics the significance of 'the Twelve' shines clear, as has been shown by R. R. Williams who has collected the necessary data on this point.[2] Much has been made of the discrepancies between the lists of the names of 'the Twelve' that have come down to us and of the traditions about their activity away from Jerusalem. But a distinction should be made between 'the Twelve' as an 'institution' or 'body' and its individual members. A modern parallel, though admittedly a loose one, may help here. Of the crucial importance of the Supreme Court of the United States there can be no question, yet few Americans could name more than three or four of the judges—only 'the pillars'—who serve on that body, nor would it be significant that individual members of the Court travelled as long as it remained, as a 'body', seated in Washington D.C. Or to use a more contemporary parallel, the authority of the Beth Din at Jamnia was not jeopardized by a visit of R. Gamaliel II to Rome, while of its members we only know such 'mighty hammers' and 'fiery pillars' as R. Johannan ben Zakkai and R. Joshua ben Hananiah, the majority being lost in obscurity. In view of all the above, while Acts may have heightened the role or sharpened the function of 'the Twelve' in the earliest days of the Church so that it over-emphasizes, except in this sense, it cannot be held to have falsified the history. This must be doubly recognized in the light of its milieu in first-century Judaism to which Gerhardsson so effectively draws attention.[3]

Granting, then, that 'the Twelve' did play a significant role at the emergence of Christianity, is Gerhardsson further justified in regarding them as constituting the chief doctrinal authority, a central collegium, concerned to preserve, transmit and apply (or 'use', as Gerhardsson puts it) a 'Holy Word'?

As over against Judaism which was Torah-centric, Gerhardsson fully recognizes that early Christianity was Christocentric.[4] The Word of the Lord had taken the place of the Torah. But although he does not express the point in precisely this way, he emphasizes that there was from the beginning what we may call a 'rabbinic' element in the Church, that is, the preservation and trans-

---

[1] See above, pp. 323 ff.

[2] *Authority in the Apostolic Age* (London, 1950).

[3] The quality of Luke's writing has been discussed in a masterly lecture by C. K. Barrett, *Luke the Historian in Recent Study* (1961), which came into my hands too late for use. He takes a more negative attitude to 'the Twelve' than we do, *op. cit.* p. 71. Luke had 'little knowledge of them, apart from their number...', and 'he had no intention of magnifying them into religious dictators'. Here it seems to us that Professor Barrett underestimates as much as Gerhardsson overestimates 'the Twelve' in Luke.

[4] *Op. cit.* p. 19 *et al.*

mission of a deposit of tradition by duly constituted authorities, the Twelve Apostles, with whom we have dealt above. He seeks to establish this by a cumulative argument which, for the sake of clarity, we present here in our own order.

As a preliminary, Gerhardsson refers to the close of the ministry of Jesus in Luke, where the emphasis on the teaching of Jesus in the Temple is remarkable. Much of this arose in response to attempts by his opponents to entrap Jesus,[1] but much he also *chose* to give, and that in the Temple. That the activity of Jesus at that period was majestically deliberate appears from the prophetic act of symbolism, the Cleansing of the Temple, and although at no point is there any explicit claim made to issue a Messianic Torah, there is sufficient evidence to indicate that, for Luke, we are here in the presence of a deliberate, Messianic, didactic activity. This was continued by the Risen Lord. In Luke xxiv and Acts ii he emerges as an interpreter of the Scriptures, who, like the Teacher of Righteousness, has brought their deeper meaning to light and is in fact a New Moses. Around this Risen Lord are the authorities who have received Torah from him as the first Moses received the old Torah from Sinai.[2] This is why Luke, as we have already indicated, almost entirely confines the term 'apostle' to the Twelve. Within a community dedicated to 'searching' the Scriptures, whose members are very significantly called 'disciples', these had the distinct role of preserving and transmitting 'the Holy Word'.[3] Their function of witnessing to Christ is to be understood mostly in terms of 'teaching', and the way in which reference is made to this teaching, as in the Name of Jesus, suggests that its transmission was understood in rabbinic terms.[4] The Twelve, in short, constituted a collegium,

---

[1] This Gerhardsson does not sufficiently note.   [2] *Op. cit.* p. 231.

[3] *Op. cit.* pp. 220–61. This must be read *in toto* to be appreciated.

[4] *Op. cit.* p. 223. Contrast C. K. Barrett, *op. cit.* pp. 71 ff. I have sought to argue on Gerhardsson's own premisses, but I am not at all convinced that the Lucan understanding of the Apostolate requires this marked *emphasis* on its teaching function in the strictest sense. There is clear evidence of the Apostles' teaching activity, see Acts iv. 2, 18; v. 21, 25, 28, 42. The name μαθηταί for Christians is significant. But note: (1) Nowhere do we read in Luke–Acts of 'teaching' or 'learning' Christ (contrast Eph. iv. 20); (2) wherever we examine the precise content of 'the Word of God', the emphasis lies on the Cross and Resurrection; in Acts iv. 8 ff. on healing; ii. 22 ff. has no reference to Jesus' teaching; iii. 12 emphasizes the Cross and Resurrection; in v. 29 ff. the Resurrection is to the fore. In x. 34 ff., where the ministry as a totality is referred to, there is no mention of Jesus' teaching. If Barrett ignores, Gerhardsson elevates too much the rabbinic character of the Apostolate. Both scholars agree that Luke is concerned to connect the Christian community and mission directly with the work of Jesus. Dr Barrett sees Luke's means of doing this as 'historical', that is, he introduces a 'connexion between each missionary development and the Jerusalem Church', for example Acts xi. 22 especially and also viii. 14. See his important footnote on p. 72. (But, we may ask, does not Luke's historical device in fact turn out to be an 'ecclesiastical' one?) Gerhardsson sees the connexion in terms of authoritative tradition. It is humbling and disturbing to realize how the

which had supreme doctrinal authority in the Church. On the basis of Acts, Gerhardsson describes both the 'exegetical' method and 'legal' procedure of this collegium, and does so in the light of the usage of the Dead Sea Sect and of Pharisaic Judaism. He points out that Pharisees had joined the Church, and discusses Acts xv. Here there is special reference to Christians who had been Pharisees, of the House of Shammai, as indeed had Paul himself been of the House of Hillel. It was natural that such would reproduce in the convocation of Christians customs that they had previously followed in Judaism. The brief, precise phraseology and the well-defined terminology (στάσις καὶ 3ήτησις, 3ήτημα, κρίνεσθαι) of Acts xv suggest traditional legal procedures; Luke is apparently following the regulation in Deut. xvii. 8 ff., the highest court of the Church had its judges in Jerusalem: Luke xxii. 29 was already being fulfilled. The three groups mentioned in the proceedings—the Apostles, the elders and the multitude—recall the three groups in the sessions at Qumran—the priests, the elders and all the people. But Gerhardsson considers that, did we have more information, the procedure followed at the Council was even more like sessions of the contemporary Sanhedrin. The method by which the assembly as a whole approved or adopted the decision proposed by the leaders, as Linton[1] had previously pointed out, conforms to the usage in Judaism, as does that of sending 'apostles' (שליחים) to communicate that decision to the communities.

There is an antecedent probability that the early Church borrowed from contemporary Jewish organizational usage, as Gerhardsson holds; Luke's presentation, we may agree with him, provides evidence for this. However, this parallel between early Christian practice and that of Judaism can be carried too far. But this can best be shown in conjunction with the discussion of the 'exegetical' activity of the Church, which Gerhardsson reconstructs from Luke–Acts.

The Scandinavian scholar points out that in Judaism the solution to any problem would be sought in the light of the following: (i) the Miqra, (ii) the Oral Tradition, (iii) the Interpretation of this, and (iv) Rationalization. There was a parallel to this in the life of the Church, which appealed to (i) Scripture, (ii) the Common Tradition which developed in the life of the Church, (iii) the

same evidence can be so differently interpreted. Has Dr Barrett's intense theological awareness led him unconsciously to minimize the didactic, 'traditionalist' elements in the material? Despite his anxiety to set Luke alongside contemporary historians both pagan and Jewish, is he in danger of reading Luke–Acts *in vacuo*, that is, without sufficient attention to the rich and subtle background of the reception and transmission of tradition to which Gerhardsson points? On the other hand, have the Scandinavian scholars unconsciously allowed their vivid awareness of the 'hinterland' of the early Christian movement in Judaism to dominate their interpretation of material which reveals both continuity and discontinuity, or, to express it differently, both its roots in Judaism and a radical, kerygmatic newness? To interpret Luke–Acts both the theological acuteness of Dr Barrett and the sensitivity of the Scandinavians to the contemporary actualities are necessary.

[1] *Das Problem der Urkirche* (1932), pp. 189 ff.

Words of Jesus, and (iv) Rational Arguments. In the case of any major decision the last item, 'rationalization', would not, by itself, have been deemed sufficiently cogent. In fact, when the Church had to define the conditions on which Gentiles were to be accepted, it found guidance neither in items (i), (ii), nor (iii), while item (iv) alone was not authoritative enough. It fell back, therefore, on what Gerhardsson calls a מעשה of Peter, that is, the account of Peter's experience when the Gentiles received the Holy Spirit (Acts x. 1 ff.).[1]

And this reference to a מעשה of Peter is a convenient point of departure for pointing out difficulties. Actually it is not to any activity of his own that Peter appeals in Acts xv, but to the coming of the Spirit which was not under his control but an invasive energy. Gerhardsson's understanding of the reference to Peter's experience as a מעשה may be taken as an indication of his failure to deal seriously enough with the role of the Spirit in Acts, to which we have previously referred. He is careful to point out, as we have done in another connexion, that as in the Qumran Sect,[2] so in the early Church, order co-existed with ardour, the Spirit with Law, charisma with office. But has he done sufficient justice to the special emphasis on the Spirit in Luke–Acts, an emphasis which goes beyond anything found at Qumran?[3] Discussions of this problem have been notoriously subjective. Thus the late J. Vernon Bartlet[4] was able, from his particular point of view, to claim of the early days of the Church that '[they] were marked by an inspired fervour or enthusiasm, a sense of "holy spirit" moving upon and in God's Messianic people...'; the Day of Pentecost 'brought a new sense of personal relationship with their Lord, as the exalted Head of God's own people, the nucleus of a converted and regenerate Israel'. Throughout Acts the Spirit is the authoritative source of guidance. Acts xv makes it clear that this was so no less in matters of teaching than in the vicissitudes of missionary journeys.[5] Thus the phrase ἔδοξεν γὰρ τῷ πνεύματι τῷ ἁγίῳ καὶ ἡμῖν ascribes the primary place in the decision reached by the Council to the Spirit, a fact which Gerhardsson recognizes but only tepidly. If Bartlet overlooked data to which Gerhardsson rightly appeals, the latter has also too much minimized the force of the evidence presented by the former.

Related to this is another factor. Gerhardsson, because he is concerned with the 'traditionalist' element, notes that Pharisees who had become Christians were present at the Council described in Acts xv and, of course, generally in the

[1] *Op. cit.* pp. 254 ff.

[2] *Op. cit.* p. 212; see my 'The Dead Sea Scrolls and Christian Origins' in *Christian Origins and Judaism*, pp. 97 ff.

[3] See my treatment of the Spirit in Paul, *ibid.* The emphasis on the Spirit in Acts needs no documentation. C. K. Barrett, *op. cit.* pp. 67 ff., does full justice to it. In some ways his emphasis recalls J. V. Bartlet, see next note.

[4] *Peake's Commentary* (1929), pp. 643 and 638.

[5] Acts viii. 29; xvi. 6 f.; the Spirit it is that empowers those who evangelize, for example Acts iv. 8; vi. 5; xiii. 9.

life of the primitive community. But, while this should be more fully acknowledged than is usually the case, is it not precarious to make their influence so powerful that they cast the life of the Church into a Pharisaic or rabbinic mould? Here it is pertinent to recall that 'the Twelve' were Galileans in Jerusalem, whose genius, apart from their Christian experience of the Spirit, usually ran counter to the Jerusalemite and Pharisaic. As I have written elsewhere,[1] the enthusiasm of the early chapters of Acts is 'Galilean' although it breaks out in Jerusalem. Here we cannot but feel that while Gerhardsson may be right in his 'facts', he may be wrong in his emphasis.

But more important than the difficulties already mentioned is that the precise nature of the teaching of 'the Twelve', as Gerhardsson describes it, does not favour his main position. He devotes much space to distinguishing two foci for the didactic activity of 'the Twelve', one in the words and works of Jesus and the other in Scripture. Not only Acts but the rest of the New Testament in part supports this. The Christian community was in some ways like a 'Bible Class', in which the Scriptures were searched for illumination on the life, death and resurrection of Jesus.

We have seen, however, that, at the one point in Acts where a major problem had to be solved, no appeal to the 'Christo-Pharisaic norms' (if we may so call them) was made, that is, there was no appeal to Scripture, to the words of Jesus, or to Christian usage. This means that the situation which confronted the primitive community could not be contained within even a neo-Pharisaism. This we have previously recognized by insisting on the need for a greater emphasis on the Spirit in the interpretation of Acts than is found in Gerhardsson. What we are more particularly concerned to note now is that the interpretative activity of the earliest communities, involving the setting of events and words in the light of the Old Testament, was likely to lend fluidity rather than fixity to the material transmitted, a fluidity in which event and meaning, *ipsissima verba* and their interpretation, would tend to merge.[2]

Gerhardsson, as we saw, distinguished between a 'Holy Word', which is apparently identified with the canonical gospels, and the rest of the primitive tradition. In the case of Paul it seems that a case could be made for such a distinction. Gerhardsson's words deserve quotation:

[1] See above, pp. 299 ff., 450 ff.

[2] The position of the Scandinavian scholars is more plausible in terms of the *moral* teaching of Jesus than in terms of their inquiry where *kerygma*, as well as *didache*, is included in the 'Holy Word', Jesus' deeds as well as his words. Thus it is easier, for example, to imagine that the 'words' attributed to Jesus preserved as a 'Holy Word', derived from himself, than that the stories of the miracles, etc., in their present form go back to Jesus himself. Moreover, while Gerhardsson recognizes that the concept of Christians as 'disciples' was more common in the Jerusalem than the Pauline Churches, has he sufficiently allowed for the variety of early Church life and thought? B. H. Streeter's *The Primitive Church* is still relevant.

We may make a comparison, though we do so fully aware of the dangers of using such a terminology, and say that this central corpus [what Gerhardsson calls 'the gospel tradition' and Riesenfeld 'the Holy Word] *is the mishnah to which the rest of the Apostle's preaching, teaching and legislation is the talmud* (our italics). At all events, this Christ-tradition seems to occupy a self-evident position as a basis, focus and point of departure for the work of the Apostle Paul. It is evident that he attempts to provide a firm basis in this centre even for what appear to be peripheral rules. But he does not pass on this focal tradition in his epistles. He *presupposes* (Gerhardsson's italics) it constantly since it has already been delivered.[1]

With Paul we are nearest the source of the tradition: fusion of *ipsissima verba* of Jesus with *gemara* upon them had not then proceeded far. Yet even in Paul reminiscences of Jesus' words already appear undifferentiated from his own.[2]

In the later canonical Gospels the process of fusion has gone further. Gerhardsson has not dealt exhaustively with these, and he does not note how difficult it is not to recognize that in them extraneous elements have crept into the tradition containing *ipsissima verba* of Jesus. There are in Matthew especially *gemaric* arrangements which at least contain secondary elements, so that we cannot regard the materials in the canonical Gospels as a sacrosanct 'Holy Word'.[3] If it be claimed that Luke reveals less *gemaric* material than Matthew, so that it can, more readily than Matthew, be claimed to preserve a 'Holy Word', then we are faced with an anomaly. If Luke is concerned to present the importance of the 'Pharisaic' didactic function of the Twelve, as Gerhardsson holds, it is in his Gospel that we should expect most *gemara*, whereas in fact we do not find this to be the case. But, even so, it can hardly be claimed with certainty that even the Lucan tradition is 'uncontaminated'; certainly that in Matthew and John is not.

Judaism, it is true, was never in danger of confusing its 'Mishnah' and its 'Talmud'. And Gerhardsson demands of us the view that the same was true in the primitive Church, that is, that the sacrosanct Gospels correspond to the Mishnah in Judaism. But if our understanding of the Gospels be correct, to use Gerhardsson's terms, it is precisely the confusion of 'Mishnah' and 'Talmud' that they reveal. The tradition originating in Jesus has become so merged with material which arose from its use in the Christian community that it can no longer always be easily isolated. A *gemaric* development took place, before the formation of the Gospels, which fused the original deposit with later materials.[4] But more important than this fact is another, which it implies, namely, that in the

---

[1] *Op. cit.* p. 295. [2] See my *P.R.J.*[2] *ad rem.*
[3] See above, pp. 387 ff.
[4] The manipulation of the 'tradition' in the primitive communities was far more complicated than even the above indicates. In addition to the *gemaric* activity, there was the *midrashic* also, pursued especially in the context of the Jewish festivals as these influenced Christians. See especially D. Daube on 'The earliest structure of the Gospels' in *N.T.S.* v, 3 (1959), 174–87.

Gospels themselves the necessity for so disentangling *ipsissima verba* of Jesus from the *gemara* of the churches does not emerge. The two items have become indistinguishable for the Evangelists, or, to express the matter more accurately, are not distinguished by them.

This fact prompts a question. Where was the centre of gravity for primitive Christianity? Was it in a transmitted body of words and works? If so, the transmitted deposit would surely have been more clearly distinguishable. Did it not lie in a living centre, capable of taking such a deposit and enlarging it? What that centre was we cannot doubt—it was Jesus Christ past, present and to come. We have seen that Gerhardsson fully recognizes the Christocentric character of early Christianity. But does he do this radically enough? He sees in the Christian tradition in the New Testament three strands: Scripture (that is, the Old Testament), the words and works of Jesus, the 'use' or application of these by the Christian community. These three strands correspond, on his view, to Scripture, Mishnah, Gemara in Judaism. But whereas in the latter the three strands are distinguished, in the Christian tradition the three corresponding items are merged. We suggest that they are so merged because the point of reference in the Church is Jesus Christ, who has become in himself Scripture, Mishnah, Gemara. It is significant that Gerhardsson allows Jesus Christ to fulfil in the Christian dispensation a role corresponding to that of the Oral Law in Judaism. He does not deal with a suggestion which we made in *Paul and Rabbinic Judaism*, which was endorsed by Dr Cullmann,[1] that Jesus had a function more than this: he fulfilled the role of the Torah in its totality. Gerhardsson is fully aware of the Christian Dispensation as a *New Exodus*. In connexion with Luke xxiv he writes:

In the introduction to Acts, Luke refers back to what he described in his previous work, although on that occasion one has the impression that the ascension took place immediately after the Risen Lord's appearance to the twelve (xxiv. 50 ff.). We read here that the Lord showed himself to his disciples for 'forty days' and spoke with them about the Kingdom of God (λέγων τὰ περὶ τῆς βασιλείας τοῦ θεοῦ). Just as Moses received the holy Torah in the course of forty days' fellowship with God on the mountain according to the Jewish tradition, so on this occasion the twelve receive the principle of eschatological logos in all its fulness in forty days.[2]

Gerhardsson does not note that, in terms of the parallel he draws, it is implied that Jesus has become more than Moses and more than Torah. If Gerhardsson is to be followed at this point, then his comparison of Jesus' role with that of the Oral Torah is inadequate. The fact that in the Christian movement, as revealed in the Gospels, no distinction is made between original deposit, be it expressed in *ipsissima verba* of Jesus or in his works, and enlargement upon this, means that

[1] *Revue d'histoire et de philosophie religieuses*, no. 1 (1950), pp. 12 ff.
[2] *Op. cit.* pp. 230 f.

its centre of gravity did not lie there. To ignore this is to miss the difference between Christianity and its mother Faith. This can be expressed somewhat as follows.[1] Whereas in the complex referred to as the Exodus, at which Israel's redemption was wrought, Judaism came to place more and more emphasis on the Torah, that is, the demand uttered on Sinai, which was itself a gift, the figure of Moses being a colossus because he mediated the Torah, the Church as it looked back to the New Exodus wrought in Christ, first remembered not the demand but the person of Jesus Christ, through whom the New Exodus was wrought, and who thus came to have for the Church the significance of Torah. This is why ultimately the tradition in Judaism culminates in the Mishnah, a code of *halakoth*, and in Christianity in the Gospels, where all is subservient to Jesus as Lord.

The above concentration on the difficulties and obscurities in the work of Riesenfeld and Gerhardsson could create the wholly erroneous impression that they have made no positive contribution. To avoid any such impression, it is necessary, finally, to state briefly where the importance of their studies consists. By bringing to bear the usages of contemporary Judaism, in a fresh and comprehensive manner, on the transmission of the Gospel Tradition they have forcibly compelled the recognition of the structural parallelism between much in Primitive Christianity and Pharisaic Judaism. This means, in our judgement, that they have made it far more historically probable and reasonably credible, over against the scepticism of much form-criticism, that in the Gospels we are within hearing of the authentic voice and within sight of the authentic activity of Jesus of Nazareth, however much muffled and obscured these may be by the process of transmission. And even though, in the light of the hesitations we have indicated, it may have been taken too boldly, this is a significant step forward.[2]

[1] In this formulation I owe much to Dr David Daube.

[2] I now realize that I have not sufficiently indicated in the above where Riesenfeld and Gerhardsson differ. Riesenfeld stresses that the Gospel tradition had its own *Sitz im Leben*, the recitation in the assemblies of the primitive community. He emphasizes the safekeeping and committal of the Gospel tradition to trustworthy persons. Gerhardsson regards this only as one possible context and emphasizes that the transmitted word was *used* and worked upon. See the last chapter of *Memory and Manuscript*. I regret that I did not point this out. Nevertheless, the intent of Riesenfeld and Gerhardsson is the same, and it is justifiable to speak of them as establishing a 'Scandinavian approach', despite their difference in emphasis.

BIBLIOGRAPHY

A. DICTIONARIES AND ENCYCLOPAEDIAS AND SOURCE BOOKS

The Ante-Nicene Christian Library, ed. A. Roberts and J. Donaldson, 12 vols. Edinburgh, 1867–72.

The Apocrypha and Pseudepigrapha of the Old Testament, ed. R. H. Charles, 2 vols. Oxford, 1913.

The Babylonian Talmud, Eng. trans. ed. by Rabbi Dr I. Epstein. London: Soncino Press, 1935.

The Babylonian Talmud [the ordinary pagination is followed]: *Jerusalem Talmud*, ed. Krotoschin, 1866.

The Bible in Aramaic, The Pentateuch according to Targum Onkelos, ed. Alexander Sperber, vol. 1. Leiden, 1959.

Biblia Hebraica, ed. R. Kittel, 2 vols. Stuttgart, 1925.

Cohn and Wendland, ed. of Philo Judaeus, 1896–8; index vol. by H. Leisegang, 1926; Eng. trans. by F. H. Coulson. Loeb, London and New York, 1929.

The Dead Sea Scrolls (see list of abbreviations, p. xv).

Dictionary of the Bible, ed. J. Hastings, 5 vols. Edinburgh, 1900.

Dictionary of the Targumim, the Talmud Babli and Yerushalmi and the Midrashic Literature, Marcus Jastrow, 2 vols. London and New York, 1903.

Dictionnaire d'archéologie chrétienne et de liturgie. Paris, 1907–53.

Dictionnaire de la Bible—Supplément, ed. Louis Pirot. Paris, 1928.

Encyclopaedia Biblica, ed. T. K. Cheyne and J. Sutherland Black. London, 1899.

Encyclopaedia Judaica, Das Judenthum in Geschichte und Gegenwart, 10 vols. Berlin, 1927.

Encyclopaedia of Religion and Ethics, ed. J. Hastings, 13 vols. Edinburgh, 1908.

Hatch, E. and Redpath, H. A., *A Concordance to the Septuagint and other Greek Versions of the Old Testament including the Apocryphal Books*. Oxford, 1897–1907.

The Interpreter's Bible. Nashville and New York, 1951–.

The Interpreter's Dictionary of the Bible, Nashville and New York, 1962.

Jewish Authorized Daily Prayer Book, Hebrew and English, 13th ed. London, 1925.

Jewish Encyclopedia, ed. Isidore Singer, 12 vols. New York and London, 1901.

Mekilta, Eng. trans. and Hebrew text, ed. by J. Z. Lauterbach. Philadelphia, 1933–5.

Midrash Rabbah. Wilna, 1876; *Midrash Rabbah*, Eng. trans. ed. by H. Freedmann and M. Simon, 9 vols. Soncino Press, London, 1939.

Midrash Tehillim, ed. Salomon Buber; German trans. by A. Wunsche. Trier, Mayer, 1892–3.

The Mishnah, Eng. trans. by H. Danby. Oxford, 1933.

The New Testament in Syriac, an edition of the Peshitta text prepared by W. Greenfield. Bagster, London, 1836.

Origenis Hexaplorum quae supersunt; sive, Veterum interpretum Graecorum in totum Vetus Testamentum fragmenta..., ed. Fridericus Field, 2 vols. Oxford, 1875.

Pesiqta de Rab Kahana, ed. Salomon Buber. Lyk, 1868; German trans. by A. Wünsche. Leipzig, 1885.

Pesiqta Rabbati, ed. M. Friedmann. Vienna, 1880.

Prophetas Chaldaicos e fide codicis reuchliniani edidit Paulus de Lagarde. 1872.

Die Religion in Geschichte und Gegenwart, hrsg. von Hermann Gunkel und D. Leopold Zscharnack, 5 vols. Tübingen, 1927.

Schwab, M., *Talmud Yerushalmi, Le Talmud de Jérusalem*, traduit pour la première fois. [No place of publication], 1871–90.

The Septuagint, ed. H. B. Swete. Cambridge, 1891, 1894; 3rd ed. Alfred Rahlfs (Stuttgart, 1949).

Sifra on Leviticus, ed. J. H. Weiss and J. Schlossberg. Wien, 1872.

Sifre debé Rab, ed. M. Friedmann. Wien, 1864.

Strack, H. L. and Billerbeck, P., *Kommentar zum Neuen Testament aus Talmud und Midrasch*. München, 1922–6.

The Targums: The Targum of Isaiah, ed. and trans. by J. F. Stenning. Oxford, 1949.

Theologisches Wörterbuch zum Neuen Testament, hrsg. von Gerhard Kittel, vols. I–III. Stuttgart, 1933.

The Tosefta, ed. M. S. Zuckermandel. Pasewalk, 1880.

The Vocabulary of the Greek Testament, J. H. Moulton and G. Milligan. London, 1914–29.

The Works of Flavius Josephus, Eng. trans. by W. Whiston. Edinburgh. Also the Loeb edition and translation [no date].

Wünsche, Aug., *Bibliotheca Rabbinica*. Leipzig, 1881.

Yale Judaica Series, vol. XIII, *Midrash on Psalms*. New Haven, 1959.

Yalqut.

B. BOOKS BY MODERN AUTHORS REFERRED TO IN THE TEXT

Abel, F. M., *Les Livres des Maccabées*. Paris, 1949.

Abrahams, I., *Studies in Pharisaism and the Gospels*, 2nd series. Cambridge, 1924.

Albeck, C., *Untersuchungen über die Redaktion der Mischna*. Berlin, 1923.

Albertz, D. M., *Botschaft des Neuen Testaments*. Zürich, 1947–52.

Albertz, D. M., *Die synoptischen Streitgespräche*. Berlin, 1921.

Albo de Daroca, Josef, *Sefer ha-'Iqqerim*, ed. Isaac Husik in 4 vols. Philadelphia, The Jewish Publication Society of America, 1929.

Allen, W. C., *A Critical and Exegetical Commentary on the Gospel according to St Matthew* (I.C.C.). Edinburgh, 1907.

BIBLIOGRAPHY

Altmann, A., on 'Gnostic themes in Rabbinic cosmology', in *Essays in Honour of J. H. Hertz*. London, 1942.

Anderson, G. H. (ed.), *The Theology of the Christian Mission*. New York, 1961.

Archambault, G., *Justin: Dialogue avec Tryphon*, 2 vols. Paris, 1909.

Audet, J. P., *La Didachè*. Paris, 1958.

Bacher, W., *Die Agada der Tannaïten*, 2 vols. Strassburg, 1884–90.

Bacher, W., *Die älteste Terminologie der Jüdischen Schriftauslegung*. Leipzig, 1889.

Bacon, B. W., *Studies in Matthew*. New York, 1930.

Baeck, Leo, *Judaism and Christianity*, Eng. trans. by W. Kaufmann. Philadelphia, 1958.

Baeck, Leo, *The Pharisees*, Eng. trans. from the German by author. New York, 1947.

Baltensweiler, H., *Die Verklärung Jesu*. Zürich, 1959.

Baron, S. W., *A Social and Religious History of the Jews*, 2nd ed. in 8 vols. Philadelphia, 1952.

Barrett, C. K., *The Holy Spirit in the Gospel Tradition*. New York, 1947.

Barrett, C. K., *Luke the Historian in Recent Study*. London, 1961.

Barthélemy, D. and Milik, J. T., *Qumran Cave I*. Oxford, 1955.

Bate, H. N. (ed.), *Catholic and Apostolic*. London, 1931.

Begrich, J., *Studien zu Deuterojesaja*. Stuttgart, 1938.

Bellinzoni, A. J., Jr., *The Sayings of Jesus in the Writings of Justin Martyr*. (Unpublished dissertation, Harvard University, 1962.)

Benoit, P., *L'Évangile selon St Matthieu*. Paris, 1950.

Bentzen, A., *Introduction to the Old Testament*. Copenhagen, 1949.

Bentzen, A., *King and Messiah*, Eng. trans. London, 1955.

Bentzen, A., *Messias, Moses redivivus, Menschensohn*. Zürich, 1948.

Bergmann, J., *Jüdische Apologetik im neutestamentlichen Zeitalter*. Berlin, 1908.

Berman, H. J. (ed.), *Soviet Law in Action*. Cambridge, Mass., 1953.

Bevan, Edwyn, *Hellenism and Christianity*. London, 1921.

Bewer, J. A., *The Literature of the Old Testament*. New York, 1922.

Beyerlin, W., *Herkunft und Geschichte der ältesten Sinaïtraditionen*. Tübingen, 1961.

Briggs, C. A., *Psalms*, 2 vols. (I.C.C.). New York, 1906–7.

Binns, L. E. Elliott-, *see* Elliott-Binns.

Black, M., *An Aramaic Approach to the Gospels and Acts*. Oxford, 1946.

Black, M., *The Scrolls and Christian Origins*. New York, 1961.

Blair, E. P., *Jesus in the Gospel of Matthew*. New York, 1960.

Bloch, J., *On the Apocalyptic in Judaism* (J.Q.R. monograph series no. 2). Philadelphia, 1952.

Bokser, B. Z., *Pharisaic Judaism in Transition*. New York, 1935.

Bonnard, P., 'La signification du désert selon le N.T.', in *Hommage et reconnaissance* (Recueil Karl Barth). Neuchâtel, 1946.

Bonsirven, J., *Les Enseignments de Jésus-Christ*. Paris, 1946.

Bonsirven, J., *Le Judaïsme palestinien*, 2 vols. Paris, 1934–5.

Bonsirven, J., *Textes rabbiniques des deux premiers siècles chrétiens pour servir à l'intelligence du Nouveau Testament*. Rome, 1954.

Bornhäuser, K. *Die Bergpredigt*. Gütersloh, 1923.

Bornkamm, G., *Jesus of Nazareth*, Eng. trans. by Irene and Fraser McLuskey with James Robinson. New York, 1960.

Bornkamm, G., Barth, G., Held, H. J., *Auslegung und Überlieferung im Matthäusevangelium*. Neukirchen, 1960.

Bowman, J. W., *The Intention of Jesus*. Philadelphia, 1943.

Box, G. H., *The Virgin Birth of Jesus Christ*. London, 1916.

Brandon, S. G. F., *The Fall of Jerusalem*. London, 1951.

Branscomb, B. H., *St Mark* (M.N.T.C.). New York and London [no date].

Braun, H., *Spätjüdisch-häretischer und frühchristlicher Radikalismus*, 2 vols. Tübingen, 1957.

Brownlee, W. H., *The Dead Sea Habakkuk Midrash and the Targum Jonathan*. Duke Divinity School (privately circulated), 1953.

Buber, M., *Two Types of Faith*, Eng. trans. by N. P. Goldhawk. London, 1951.

Büchler, A., *The Economic Conditions of Judea after the Destruction of the Second Temple* (Jews College Publication). London, 1912.

Buck, H. M., Jr., *The Johannine Lessons in the Greek Gospel Lectionary*. Chicago, 1958.

Bultmann, R., *Die Geschichte der synoptischen Tradition*, 2nd ed. Göttingen, 1931.

Bultmann, R., *Jesus*, 1st German ed. Berlin, 1929.

Bultmann, R., *Jesus and the Word*, Eng. trans. by L. P. Smith and E. Huntress. New York and London, 1934.

Bultmann, R., *Theologie des Neuen Testaments*. Tübingen, 1953.

Bultmann, R., *Theology of the New Testament*, Eng. trans. by K. Grobel in 2 vols. New York, 1951–5.

Burkitt, F. C., *The Church and Gnosis*. Cambridge, 1932.

Burkitt, F. C., *The Gospel History and its Transmission*. Edinburgh, 1906.

Burkitt, F. C., *Jewish and Christian Apocalypses* (Schweich Lecture). London, 1913.

Burney, C. F., *The Poetry of Our Lord*. Oxford, 1925.

Bussmann, W., *Synoptische Studien*, 3 vols. Halle, 1925–31.

Caird, G. B., *Principalities and Powers*. Oxford, 1956.

Carrington, P., *According to Mark*. Cambridge, 1960.

Carrington, P., *The Primitive Christian Calendar*. Cambridge, 1940.

Cazelles, H. (ed.), *Moïse l'Homme de l'Alliance*. Paris and New York, 1955.

Cerfaux, L. (ed.), *L'Attente du Messie*. Paris, 1954.

Cerfaux, L., *Christ in the Theology of St Paul*, Eng. trans. by G. Webb and A. Walker. New York, 1959.

Cerfaux, L., 'La Tradition selon St Paul' in *Recueil Lucien Cerfaux*, 2 vols. Gembloux, 1954.

Cerfaux, L. and Peremans, W. (ed.), *Studia Hellenistica*, vol. 5, Universitas Catholica Lovaniensis. 1948.

Chadwick, H., *The Circle and the Ellipse*. Oxford, 1959.

Charles, R. H., *The Book of Enoch or I Enoch*. Oxford, 1912.

Charles, R. H., *A Critical History of the Doctrine of the Future Life*. London, 1889.

Chavalier, M. A., *L'Esprit et le Messie*. Paris, 1958.

Cheyne, T. K., *The Prophecies of Isaiah*, 2 vols. London, 1884.

Clarke, K. W. L. (ed.), *Liturgy and Worship*. London and New York, 1932.

Cohen, Boaz, *Law and Tradition in Judaism*. New York, 1959.

Colpe, Carsten, *Die religionsgeschichtliche Schule*. Göttingen, 1961.

Condamin, A., *Le livre de Jérémie*. Paris, 1920.

Conzelmann, H., *Die Mitte der Zeit*. Tübingen, 1954.

Cook, S. A., *The 'Truth' of the Bible*. Cambridge, 1938.

Cornill, C. H., *Einleitung in das Alte Testament*. Tübingen, 1913.

Cranfield, C. E. B., *The Gospel according to St Mark*. Cambridge, 1959.

Creed, J. M., *The Gospel according to St Luke*. London, 1930.

Cross, F. L., *I Peter, A Paschal Liturgy*. London, 1954.

Cross, F. M., *The Ancient Library of Qumran and Modern Biblical Studies*. London, 1958.

Cullmann, O., *The Christology of the New Testament*, Eng. trans. by S. C. Guthrie and C. A. M. Hall. Philadelphia, 1959.

Cullmann, O., *The Earliest Christian Confessions*. London, 1949.

Cullmann, O., *Peter: Disciple–Apostle–Martyr*, Eng. trans. by F. V. Filson. London, 1953.

Curtis, W. A., *Jesus Christ the Teacher*. London and New York, 1945.

Dalman, G. F., *Jesus–Jeshua*, Eng. trans. by P. L. Levertoff. London, 1929.

Dancy, J. C., *A Commentary on I Maccabees*. Oxford, 1954.

Daniélou, J., *Les Manuscrits de la Mer Morte et les Origines du christianisme*. Paris, 1957.

Daniélou, J., *Sacramentum Futuri*. Paris, 1950.

Daniélou, J., *Théologie du Judéo-Christianisme*. Tournai, 1958.

Daube, D., *The New Testament and Rabbinic Judaism*. London, 1956.

Daube, D., *Studies in Biblical Law*. Cambridge, 1947.

Davies, W. D., *Christian Origins and Judaism*. London, 1962.

Davies, W. D., *Introduction to Pharisaism*. Brecon, 1954–5.

Davies, W. D., 'Matthew 5: 18', in *Mélanges Bibliques rédigés en l'honneur de André Robert*. Paris, 1957.

Davies, W. D., *Paul and Rabbinic Judaism*, 2nd ed. London, 1955.

Davies, W. D. and Daube, D., *The Background of the New Testament and its Eschatology* (Studies in Honour of C. H. Dodd). Cambridge, 1956.

Davis, M. (ed.), *Israel: Its Role in Civilization*. New York, 1956.

Descamps, A., *Les Justes et la justice*. Louvain, 1950.

Dibelius, M., *Der Brief des Jacobus*, 8th ed. rev. by H. Greeven. Göttingen, 1956.

Dibelius, M., *Die Pastoralbriefe*, 2nd ed. Tübingen, 1931.

Dibelius, M., *Studies in the Acts of the Apostles*, Eng. trans. by M. Ling. New York, 1956.

Dibelius, M., *From Tradition to Gospel*, Eng. trans. by B. L. Woolf. London, 1934.

Dibelius, M., *Die Urchristliche Überlieferung von Johannes dem Täufer*. Göttingen, 1911.

Dix, G., *Jew and Greek*. London, 1953.

Dodd, C. H., *According to the Scriptures*. London, 1952.

Dodd, C. H., *Apostolic Preaching and its Developments*. New York and London, 1949.

Dodd, C. H., *The Bible and the Greeks*. London, 1935.

Dodd, C. H., "ΕΝΝΟΜΟΣ ΧΡΙΣΤΟΥ', in *Studia Paulina in honorem Johannis de Zwaan*, pp. 96 ff. Haarlem, 1953.

Dodd, C. H., *Gospel and Law*. New York, 1951.

Dodd, C. H., *History and the Gospel*. New York, 1938.

Dodd, C. H., *The Interpretation of the Fourth Gospel*. Cambridge, 1953.

Dodd, C. H., 'Jesus as Teacher and Prophet', in *Mysterium Christi*, ed. by G. K. A. Bell and A. Deissmann. London, New York and Toronto, 1930.

Dodd, C. H., *The Johannine Epistles* (M.N.T.C.). New York and London, 1945.

Dodd, C. H., *New Testament Studies*. Manchester, 1953.

Drazin, N., *The History of Jewish Education from 515 B.C.E. to 220 C.E.* Baltimore, 1940.

Driver, S. R., *Deuteronomy* (I.C.C.). New York, 1902.

Driver, S. R., *The Book of the Prophet Jeremiah*. London, 1906.

Driver, S. R., *A Treatise on the Use of the Tenses in Hebrew and some other Syntactical Questions*. Oxford, 1892.

Dugmore, C. W., *The Influence of the Synagogue on the Divine Office*. London, 1944.

Duhm, B., *Israels Propheten*, 2nd ed. Tübingen, 1922.

Dunn, Bogard van, *Some Mythological and Cosmological Motifs in the Gospel according to Mark* (an unpublished dissertation, Duke University). 1954.

Dupont, J., *Agapè*, vol. 3. Paris, 1958–9.

Dupont, J., *Les Béatitudes*. Bruges, 1958.

Dupont, J., *Gnosis*. Bruges, 1949.

Dupont-Sommer, A., *Les Araméens*. Paris, 1949.

Easton, B. S., *The Pastoral Epistles*. New York, 1948.

Edersheim, A., *The Life and Times of Jesus the Messiah*, 2 vols. New York, 1896.

Ehrle, Card., *Martin de Alparʒil, Chronica Actitatorum*. Paderborn, 1906.

Eissfeldt, O., *Einleitung in das Alte Testament*. Tübingen, 1934.

Elbogen, I., *Der jüdische Gottesdienst*. Leipzig, 1913.

Elbogen, I., 'Die Überlieferung von Hillel', in *Festschrift für Leo Baeck*. Berlin, 1938.

Elliger, K., *Studien ʒum Habakuk-Kommentar vom Toten Meer*. Tübingen, 1953.

Elliott-Binns, L. E., *The Book of the Prophet Jeremiah* (Westminster Commentaries). London, 1919.

Elliott-Binns, L. E., *Galilean Christianity*. London, 1956.

Ellul, J., *Le Fondement théologique du droit*. Paris, 1946.

Elmslie, W. A., *The Mishnah on Idolatry 'Aboda Zarah'*. Cambridge, 1911.

Eltester, W. (ed.), *Judentum, Urchristentum, Kirche: Festschrift für Joachim Jeremias*. Berlin, 1960.

Etheridge, J. W., *The Targums of Onkelos and Jonathan ben Uʒʒiel on the Pentateuch*, 2 vols. London, 1865.

Farrer, A. M., *St Matthew and St Mark*. London, 1954.

Farrer, A. M., *A Study in St Mark*. Westminster, 1951.

Feine, P. and Behm, J., *Einleitung in das Neue Testament*. Heidelberg, 1950.

Fiebig, P., *Das Vaterunser*. Gütersloh, 1927.

Filson, F. V., *The Gospel according to St Matthew*. London, 1960.

Finkelstein, L., *Akiba: Scholar, Saint and Martyr*. New York, 1936.

Finkelstein, L. (ed.), *The Jews*, 2 vols. New York, 1960.

Finkelstein, L., *Mabo le Massekot Abot ve Abot d'Rabbi Nathan* (Introduction to the treatises Abot and Abot of Rabbi Nathan). New York, 1950.

Finkelstein, L., *The Pharisees*. The Jewish Publication Society of America, Philadelphia, 1940.

Flemington, W. F., *The New Testament Doctrine of Baptism*. London, 1948.

Flew, R. N., *Jesus and his Church*. New York, 1938.

Flusser, D., 'The Dead Sea Scrolls and pre-Pauline Christianity', in *Scripta Hierosolymitana*, IV (Jerusalem, 1958), 215–66.

Frame, J. E., *Thessalonians* (I.C.C.). New York, 1912.

Fridrichsen, A. J. (ed.), *The Root of the Vine*: chapter by E. Sahlin on 'The Exodus of Salvation'. Westminster, 1952.

Friedländer, M., *Der Antichrist*. Göttingen, 1901.

Friedländer, M., *Der vorchristliche jüdische Gnosticismus*. Göttingen, 1898.

Gärtner, B., *The Theology of the Gospel of Thomas*. London, 1961.

Gaster, T. H., *The Dead Sea Scriptures*. Garden City, New York, 1956.

Gemser, B., 'The importance of the motive clause in the Old Testament', in *Congress Volume Copenhagen 1953*, Leiden, 1953, pp. 50–66.

Gerhardsson, B., *Memory and Manuscript*. Uppsala, 1961.

Giesebrecht, F., *Das Buch Jeremia* (Handkommentar zum Alten Testament ed. by W. Nowack, zweiter Band, erster Teil). Göttingen, 1907.

Gils, F., *Jésus prophète d'après les évangiles synoptiques*. Louvain, 1957.

Ginzberg, L., *The Legends of the Jews*, Eng. trans. by H. Szold in 7 vols. Philadelphia, 1942.

Ginzberg, L., *Eine unbekannte jüdische Sekte*. New York, 1922.

Glatzer, N. N., *Hillel the Elder*. New York, 1956.

Goguel, M., *Jesus and the Origins of Christianity*, Eng. trans. by O. Wyon in 2 vols. for Harper Torch Books. New York, 1960.

Goguel, M., *Jésus et les origines du christianisme*, 3 vols. Paris, 1932–47.

Goldin, J., *The Fathers according to Rabbi Nathan*. New Haven, 1955.

Goldin, J., 'The Period of the Talmud', in *The Jews*, ed. by L. Finkelstein. New York, 1960.

Goldstein, M., *Jesus in the Jewish Tradition*. New York, 1950.

Goodenough, E. R., *Jewish Symbols in the Graeco-Roman World*, 8 vols. New York, 1953–8.

Goodspeed, E. J., *The Meaning of Ephesians*. Chicago, 1933.

Goppelt, L., *Christentum und Judentum*. Gütersloh, 1954.

Goppelt, L., *Typos*. Gütersloh, 1939.

Gore, C., Goudge, H. L. and Guillaume, A. (ed.), *A New Commentary on Holy Scripture including the Apocrypha*. London, 1928.

Graetz, H., *The History of the Jews*, Eng. trans. by B. Lowy in 6 vols. Philadelphia, 1893.

Grant, F. C., *The Gospels*. New York, 1959.

Grant, R. M., *Gnosticism and Early Christianity*. New York, 1959.

Grant, R. M. and Freedman, D. N., *The Secret Sayings of Thomas*. Garden City, New York, 1960.

Gray, G. B., *A Critical Introduction to the Old Testament*. London, 1913.

Gray, G. B., *Isaiah, I–XXXIX* (I.C.C.). New York, 1912.

Gray, G. B., *Sacrifice in the Old Testament*. Oxford, 1925.

Green, A. A., *The Revised Haggada*. London, 1897.

Green, F. W., *Saint Matthew* (The Clarendon Bible). Oxford, 1936.

Gressmann, H., *Moses und seine Zeit*. Göttingen, 1913.

Guillet, J., *Thèmes Bibliques*. Paris, 1951.

Gunkel, H., *Schöpfung und Chaos in Urzeit und Endzeit*. Göttingen, 1895.

Haenchen, E., *Apostelgeschichte*. Göttingen, 1956.

Harris, J. R., *Testimonies*, 2 vols. Cambridge, 1920.

Hauck, F., *Der Brief des Jakobus* (Kommentar zum Neuen Testament). Leipzig, 1926.

Hauck, F., *Das Lukasevangelium* (Theologische Handkommentar). Leipzig, 1934.

Hawkins, J. C., *Horae Synopticae*. Oxford, 1899.

Heaton, E. W., *Daniel* (Torch Commentaries). London, 1956.

Heiler, F., *Prayer*, Eng. trans. by S. M. McComb. London and New York, 1932.

Helfgott, B. W., *The Doctrine of Election in Tannaitic Literature*. New York, 1954.

Hemmer, H., *Clément de Rome*. Paris, 1926.

Hendry, G. S., *The Gospel of the Incarnation*. Philadelphia, 1958.

Hepburn, R., *Christianity and Paradox*. London, 1958.

Herford, R. T., *Christianity in Talmud and Midrash*. London, 1903.

Hertz, J. H., *The Sayings of the Fathers*. London, 1952.

Higgins, A. J. B. (ed.), *The Early Church*. London, 1956.

Higgins, A. J. B. (ed.), *New Testament Essays: Studies in Memory of T. W. Manson*. Manchester, 1959.

Hoenig, S. B., *The Great Sanhedrin*. New York, 1953.

Hoffman, D., *Die erste Mischna und die Controversen der Tannaïm*. Berlin, 1882.

Holl, K. (ed.), *Gesammelte Aufsätze*, vol. II. Tübingen, 1928.

Holtzmann, H. J. (ed.), *Handkommentar zum Neuen Testament*. Freiburg, 1889.

Holtzmann, O., *Berakot* (*Die Mischna*). Giessen, 1912.

Hooke, S. H. (ed.), *The Labyrinth*. New York, 1935.

Hooker, M. D., *Jesus and the Servant*. London, 1959.

Hoskyns, E. C. and Davey, F. N., *The Fourth Gospel*. London, 1939.

Howard, W. F., *The Fourth Gospel in Recent Criticism and Interpretation*. London, 1931.

Huber, H. H., *Die Bergpredigt. Exegetische Studie*. Göttingen, 1932.

Hunter, A. M., *Paul and his Predecessors*. London, 1940.

Jaeger, W., *Early Christianity and Greek 'Paideia'*. Cambridge, Mass., 1961.

James, M. R., *The Apocryphal New Testament*. Oxford, 1953.

Jellinek, A., *Beth ha-Midrash*, 3 vols. Leipzig, 1853–77.

Jeremias, J., *The Eucharistic Words of Jesus*, Eng. trans. by A. Ehrhardt from 2nd German ed. Oxford, 1955.

Jeremias, J., *Jerusalem zur Zeit Jesu*. Göttingen, 1958.

Jeremias, J., *Jesus' Promise to the Nations*, Eng. trans. by S. H. Hooke. Naperville, Ill., 1958.

Jeremias, J., 'Kennzeichen der *ipsissima vox* Jesu', in *Synoptische Studien Alfred Wikenhauser*. München, 1953.

Jeremias, J., *Die Kindertaufe in den ersten vier Jahrhunderten*. Göttingen, 1958.

Jeremias, J., *The Parables of Jesus*, Eng. trans. by S. H. Hooke. New York, 1955.

Jocz, J., *The Jewish People and Jesus Christ*. London, 1949.

Joest, W., *Gesetz und Freiheit*. Göttingen, 1951.

Johnson, A. R., *The Cultic Prophet in Ancient Israel*. Cardiff, Wales, 1944.

Johnson, A. R., *The One and the Many in the Israelite Conception of God*. University of Wales, Cardiff, 1942.

Johnston, G., *The Doctrine of the Church in the New Testament*. Cambridge, 1943.

Jonas, H., *The Gnostic Religion*. Boston, 1958.

Jost, I. M., *Geschichte der Israeliten*, 5 vols. Berlin, 1820–8.

Kierkegaard, S., *Philosophical Fragments*. Princeton, 1936.

Kilpatrick, G. D., *The Origins of the Gospel according to St Matthew*. Oxford, 1946.

Kirk, K. E. (ed.), *The Apostolic Ministry*. New York, 1946.

Kissane, E. J., *The Book of Isaiah*, 2 vols. Dublin, 1941–3.

Kistemaker, S., *The Psalms Citations in the Epistle to the Hebrews*. Amsterdam, 1961.

Klausner, J., *From Jesus to Paul*, Eng. trans. by W. F. Stinespring. New York, 1943.

Klausner, J., *Jesus of Nazareth*, Eng. trans. by H. Danby. New York, 1926.

Klausner, J., *Die messianischen Vorstellungen des jüdischen Volkes im Zeitalter der Tannaïten*. Berlin, 1904.

Klein, G., *Der älteste christliche Katechismus*. Berlin, 1909.

Klostermann, E., *Das Matthäusevangelium* (Handbuch zum Neuen Testament, vol. IV). Tübingen, 1927.

Knox, J., *The Ethic of Jesus in the Teaching of the Church*. New York, 1961.

Knox, W. L., 'St Luke and St Matthew', in *Sources of the Synoptic Gospels*, vol. II. Cambridge, 1957.

Köster, H., *Synoptische Überlieferung bei den apostolischen Vätern*. Berlin, 1957.

Kuhn, K. G., *Achtzehngebet und Vaterunser und der Reim*. Tübingen, 1950.

Kuhn, K. G., *Konkordanz zu den Qumrantexten*. Göttingen, 1961.

Kuhn, K. G., *Phylakterien aus Höhle 4 von Qumran*. Heidelberg, 1957.

Kutscher, E. Y., 'The Language of the Genesis Apocryphon', in *Scripta Hierosolymitana*, IV (1958), 1 ff.

Lagrange, M.-J., *Évangile selon S. Matthieu*. Paris, 1923.

Lake, K. and Jackson, F. J. F. (ed.), *Beginnings of Christianity*, 3 vols. London, 1920–6.

Lauterbach, J. Z., *Rabbinic Essays*. Cincinnati, 1951.

Lawson, J., *A Theological and Historical Introduction of the Apostolic Fathers*. New York, 1961.

Legg, S. C. E., *Novum Testamentum Graece, Evangelium secundum Matthaeum*. Oxford, 1940.

Leszynsky, R., *Pharisäer und Sadduzäer*. Frankfort, 1912.

Lieberman, S., *Greek in Jewish Palestine*. New York, 1942.

Lietzmann, H., *Beginnings of the Christian Church*, trans. by B. L. Woolf. New York, 1937.

Lightfoot, R. H., *The Gospel Message of Mark*. Oxford, 1950.

Lightfoot, R. H., *History and Interpretation in the Gospels*. London, 1935.

BIBLIOGRAPHY

Lightfoot, R. H., *Locality and Doctrine in the Gospels*. London, 1938.

Lofthouse, W. F., *Jeremiah and the New Covenant*. London, 1925.

Lohmeyer, E., *Das Evangelium des Markus*. Göttingen, 1958.

Lohmeyer, E., *Galiläa und Jerusalem*. Tübingen, 1936.

Lohmeyer, E., *Kultus und Evangelium*. Göttingen, 1942.

Lohse, E., *Die Ordination im Spätjudentum und im Neuen Testament*. Göttingen, 1951.

Loisy, A., *La Naissance du christianisme*. Paris, 1933.

Mach, R., *Der Zaddik in Talmud und Midrasch*. Leiden, 1957.

McNeile, A. H., *The Gospel according to St Matthew*. London, 1915.

Mann, J., *The Bible as Read and Preached in the Old Synagogue*. Cincinnati, 1940.

Manson, T. W. (ed.), *A Companion to the Bible*. Edinburgh, 1939.

Manson, T. W., *Ethics and the Gospel*. London, 1961.

Manson, T. W., *The Sayings of Jesus*. London, 1954.

Manson, T. W., *The Servant-Messiah*. Cambridge, 1953.

Manson, T. W., 'Some reflections on Apocalyptic', in *Aux Sources de la tradition chrétienne: Mélanges offerts à M. M. Goguel*, pp. 139 ff. Paris, 1950.

Manson, T. W., *The Teaching of Jesus*, 2nd ed. Cambridge, 1931.

Manson, W., *Jesus the Messiah*. London, 1943.

Marcus, R., *Law in the Apocrypha*. New York, 1927.

Marmorstein, A., *Studies in Jewish Theology*. London and New York, 1950.

Marriott, H., *The Sermon on the Mount*. London, 1925.

Marrou, H. I., *A History of Education in Antiquity*, Eng. trans. by G. Lamb. New York, 1956.

Marxsen, W., *Der Evangelist Markus*. Göttingen, 1959.

Mayor, J. B., *The Epistle of St James*. London and New York, 1897.

Menoud, P. H., *La Vie de l'église naissante*. Paris, 1952.

Menoud, P. H., *L'Église naissante et le Judaïsme*. Paris, 1952.

Messel, N., *Die Einheitlichkeit der jüdischen Eschatologie*. Giessen, 1915.

Meyer, R., *Jesus, der Prophet aus Galiläa*. Leipzig, 1940.

Michaelis, W., *Einleitung in das Neue Testament*. Bern, 1946.

Michaelis, W., *Das Evangelium nach Matthäus*, 2 vols. Zürich, 1948.

Micklem, N. (ed.), *Christian Worship*. London, 1938.

Milik, J. T., *Dix ans de découvertes dans le désert de Juda*. Paris, 1951.

Mitton, C. L., *The Epistle to the Ephesians*. Oxford, 1951.

Moffatt, J., *Introduction to the Literature of the New Testament*. New York, 1922.

Montefiore, C. G. and Loewe, H. (ed.), *A Rabbinic Anthology*. London, 1938.

Moore, G. F., *Judaism in the First Centuries of the Christian Era*, 3 vols. Cambridge, Mass., 1932.

Morgenthaler, R., *Statistik des neutestamentlichen Wortschatzes*. Zürich, 1959.

Morris, N., *The Jewish School*. London, 1937.

Moule, C. F. D., *Worship in the New Testament*. London, 1961.

Mowinckel, S., *He that Cometh*, Eng. trans. by G. W. Anderson. Oxford, 1956.

Mowinckel, S., *Prophecy and Tradition*. Oslo, 1946.

Mudge, L. S., *The Servant Christology in the New Testament* (an unpublished dissertation). Princeton University, 1961.

Muilenburg, J., *Isaiah, XL-LXVI* (The Interpreter's Bible). Nashville and New York, 1956.

Muilenburg, J., *The Way of Israel*. New York, 1961.

Muirhead, J., *Historical Introduction to the Law of Rome*. 1916.

Munck, J., *Paulus und die Heilsgeschichte*. Aarhus, 1954.

Neil, W., *The Epistle of Paul to the Thessalonians* (M.N.T.C.). New York and London, 1950.

Nepper-Christensen, P., *Das Matthäusevangelium*. Aarhus, 1958.

Neuenzeit, P., *Das Herrenmahl, Studien zur paulinischen Eucharistieauffassung*. München, 1960.

Neusner, J., *Rabbi Johannan ben Zakkai* (an unpublished Columbia-Union Ph.D. dissertation). New York, 1961.

Niebuhr, H. R., *Christ and Culture*. New York, 1950.

Niebuhr, R., *An Interpretation of Christian Ethics*. New York and London, 1935.

Nineham, D. (ed.), *Studies in the Gospels: Essays in Memory of R. H. Lightfoot*. Oxford, 1955.

North, C. R., *The Old Testament Interpretation of History*. London, 1946.

North, C. R., *The Suffering Servant in Deutero-Isaiah*. London, 1948.

Nötscher, F., *Das Buch Jeremias*. Bonn, 1934.

Oesterley, W. O. E. and Robinson, T. H., *An Introduction to the Literature of the Old Testament*. London, 1934.

Ortmann, H., *Der alte und der neue Bund bei Jeremia*. Berlin, 1940.

Ostborn, G., *Torā in the Old Testament*. Lund, 1945.

Ottley, R. R., *A Handbook to the Septuagint*. New York, 1920.

Otto, R., *The Kingdom of God and the Son of Man*, Eng. trans. by F. V. Filson and B. L. Woolf. London and Redhill, 1943.

Peake, A. S., *Jeremiah* (Century Bible). Edinburgh and London, 1929.

Peake, A. S. (ed.), *The People and the Book*. Oxford, 1925.

Pedersen, J., *Israel, Its Life and Culture*, 4 vols. London, 1926–47.

Percy, E., *Die Botschaft Jesu*. Lund, 1953.

Plummer, A., *An Exegetical Commentary on the Gospel according to St Matthew*. London, 1909.

Podro, J., *The Last Pharisee, The Life and Times of Rabbi Joshua ben Hananyah: A First Century Idealist*. London, 1959.

Preiss, T., *Life in Christ*, Eng. trans. by H. Knight. Chicago, 1954.

Procksch, O., *Jesaia*, 1. Leipzig, 1930.

Rabin, C., *The Zadokite Documents*, 2nd rev. ed. Oxford, 1958.

Radin, M., *Jews among the Greeks and Romans*. Philadelphia, 1915.

Ramsay, A. M., *The Resurrection of Christ*. London, 1945.

Richardson, A., *The Miracle Stories of the Gospels*. New York, 1941.

Riesenfeld, H., *The Gospel Tradition and its Beginnings*. London, 1951.

Riesenfeld, H., *Jésus Transfiguré*. København, 1947.

Rist, M., *Revelation* (Interpreter's Bible, vol. XII). Nashville and New York, 1957.

Robertson, E., *Law and Religion*, ed. by E. I. J. Rosenthal. New York, 1937–8.

Robinson, H. W., *Inspiration and Revelation in the Old Testament*. Oxford, 1946.

Robinson, J. M., *A New Quest for the Historical Jesus*. Naperville, Ill., 1959.

Robinson, T. H., *A History of Israel*, 2 vols. Oxford, 1951.

Robinson, T. H., *Matthew* (M.N.T.C.). Garden City, New York, 1928.

Rost, L., 'Die Vorstufen von Kirche und Synagoge im Alten Testament', in *Beiträge zur Wissenschaft vom Alten und Neuen Testament*, ed. G. Kittel. Stuttgart, 1929.

Rostovtzeff, M., *Dura-Europos and its Art*. Oxford, 1938.

Roth, C., *Judaism*. New York, 1954.

Rowley, H. H., *The Biblical Doctrine of Election*. London, 1950.

Rowley, H. H., *The Growth of the Old Testament*. London and New York, 1950.

Rowley, H. H., *Jewish Apocalyptic and the Dead Sea Sect*. London, 1957.

Rowley, H. H. (ed.), *The Old Testament in Modern Study*. Oxford, 1951.

Rowley, H. H., *The Relevance of Apocalyptic*. London, 1944.

Rowley, H. H., *The Servant of the Lord*. London, 1952.

Rowley, H. H. (ed.), *Studies in Old Testament Prophecy*. Edinburgh, 1950.

Rowley, H. H., *The Zadokite Fragments*. Oxford, 1954.

Rudolph, H., *Jeremia*. Tübingen, 1947.

Ryle, H. E. and James, M. R., *The Psalms of Solomon*. London and New York, 1891.

Sahlin, S., *see* Fridrichsen, A. J.

Sanday, W. (ed.), *Studies in the Synoptic Problem*. Oxford, 1911.

Schechter, S., *Aboth de Rabbi Nathan*. Wien, 1887; New York, 1945.

Schechter, S., *Some Aspects of Rabbinic Theology*. London, 1909.

Schlatter, A., *Der Evangelist Matthäus*. Stuttgart, 1948.

Schlatter, A., *Die Parallelen in den Worten Jesu bei Johannes und Matthäus*. Gütersloh, 1898.

Schmid, J., *Das Evangelium nach Matthäus*. Regensburg, 1956.

Schmidt, H., *Die Schriften des Alten Testaments* (zweite Abteilung). Göttingen, 1923.

Schmidt, K. L., *Der Rahmen der Geschichte Jesu*. Berlin, 1919.

Schnackenburg, R., *Die sittliche Botschaft des Neuen Testamentes*. München, 1954.

Schniewind, J., *Das Evangelium nach Mätthaus* (Das Neue Testament Deutsch). Göttingen, 1956.

Schoeps, H. J., *Aus frühchristlicher Zeit: religionsgeschichtliche Untersuchungen*. Tübingen, 1950.

Schoeps, H. J., *Paulus: die Theologie des Apostels im Lichte der jüdischen Religionsgeschichte*. Tübingen, 1959.

Schoeps, H. J., *Theologie und Geschichte des Judenchristentums*. Tübingen, 1949.

Schoeps, H. J., *Urgemeinde, Judenchristentum, Gnosis*. Tübingen, 1956.

Scholem, G., *Jewish Gnosticism, Merkabah Mysticism, and Talmudic Tradition*. New York, 5720–1960.

Schürer, E., *A History of the Jewish People in the Time of Jesus Christ*, 2nd and rev. ed. Edinburgh, 1885–96.

Schürmann, H., *Das Gebet des Herrn*. Freiburg, 1957.

Schweitzer, A., *The Mysticism of Paul the Apostle*, Eng. trans. by W. Montgomery. London, 1931.

Schweitzer, A., *The Quest of the Historical Jesus*, Eng. trans. by W. Montgomery, 1st Eng. ed. New York, 1910.

Schweizer, E., *Lordship and Discipleship*, Eng. trans. with revisions by the author. London, 1960.

Scott, C. A. A., *Christianity according to St Paul*. Cambridge, 1932.

Scott, E. F., *The Crisis in the Life of Jesus*. New York, 1952.

Scott, R. B. Y., *The Book of Isaiah, Chapters I–XXXIX* (Interpreter's Bible). Nashville and New York, 1956.

Seeberg, A., *Der Katechismus der Urchristenheit*. 1903.

Sellin, E., *Introduction to the Old Testament*, Eng. trans. by W. Montgomery. New York, 1923.

Selwyn, E. G., *The First Epistle of St Peter*. London, 1946.

Silver, H., *The History of Messianic Speculation in Israel*. 1927.

Simon, M., *Verus Israel*. Paris, 1948.

Skinner, J., *A Critical and Exegetical Commentary on Genesis* (I.C.C.). Edinburgh, 1930.

Skinner, J., *Isaiah XL–LXVI* (Cambridge Bible for Schools). 1911.

Skinner, J., *Prophecy and Religion*. Cambridge, 1922.

Smith, C. R., *The Biblical Doctrine of Sin*. London, 1953.

Smith, G. A., *Jeremiah* (Baird Lectures). London, 1923.

Smith, Harold, *Ante-Nicene Exegesis of the Gospels* (8 vols.). London, 1925.

Smith, J. M. P., *Micah* (I.C.C.). New York, 1911.

Smith, Morton, *Tannaitic Parallels to the Gospels*. Philadelphia, 1951.

Smith, N., *Jesus in the Gospel of John*. Nashville, 1959.

Snaith, N. H., *The Distinctive Ideas of the Old Testament*. London, 1944.

Snaith, N. H., *The Jewish New Year Festival*. London, 1947.

Sneath, E. H. (ed.), *The Evolution of Ethics*. London, 1927.

Soiron, Th., *Die Logia Jesu, Neutestamentliche Abhandlungen*. Münster, 1916.

Spicq, C., *Les Épîtres pastorales*. Paris, 1947.

Spitta, F., *Der Brief des Jakobus*. Göttingen, 1896.

Stauffer, E., *Die Botschaft Jesu, damals und heute*. Bern, 1959.

Stauffer, E., *Jerusalem und Rom im Zeitalter Jesu Christi*. Bern, 1957.

Stauffer, E., *Jesus, Gestalt und Geschichte*. Bern, 1957.

Stauffer, E., *Jesus and his Story*, Eng. trans. by D. M. Barton. London, 1960.

Stendahl, K., *The School of Matthew*. Lund, 1954.

Stendahl, K. (ed.), *The Scrolls and the New Testament*. New York, 1957.

Stenning, J. F., *The Targum of Isaiah*. Oxford, 1949.

Stonehouse, N. B., *The Witness of Matthew and Mark to Christ*. Philadelphia, 1944.

Strack, H. L., *Introduction to the Talmud and Midrash*. Philadelphia, 1931.

Streane, A. W., *The Double Text of Jeremiah*. Cambridge, 1896.

Streeter, B. H., *The Four Gospels*. London, 1926.

Sutcliffe, E. F., *The Monks of Qumran*. London, 1960.

Tasker, R. V. G., *The Old Testament in the New Testament*. London, 1946.

Taylor, R. O. P., *The Groundwork of the Gospels*. Oxford, 1946.

Taylor, V., *The Formation of the Gospel Tradition*. London, 1933.

Taylor, V., *The Gospel according to St Mark*. London, 1953.

Taylor, V., *The Historical Evidence for the Virgin Birth*. Oxford, 1920.

Taylor, V., *The Names of Jesus*. London, 1959.

Teeple, H. M., *The Mosaic Eschatological Prophet (Journal of Biblical Literature: monograph series, v, 10)*. Philadelphia, 1957.

Thomas, G. F., *Christian Ethics and Moral Philosophy*. New York, 1953.

Tillich, Paul, *Systematic Theology*, 2 vols. Chicago, 1957.

Torrance, T. F., *The Doctrine of Grace in the Apostolic Fathers*. Edinburgh, 1948.

Torrey, C. C., *The Translation made from the Original Aramaic Gospels*. New York, 1912.

Trilling, W., *Das wahre Israel*. Leipzig, 1959.

Turner, H. E. W., *The Patristic Doctrine of Redemption*. London, 1952.

Unger, M. F., *Israel and the Aramaeans of Damascus*. London, 1957.

Van Den Eynde, D., *Les Normes de l'enseignement chrétien dans la littérature patristique des trois premiers siècles*. Paris, 1933.

Van Der Woude, A. S., *Die messianischen Vorstellungen der Gemeinde von Qumran*. Assen, 1957.

Venetianer, L., *Ursprung und Bedeutung der Propheten-Lektionen*. Leipzig, 1909.

Via, D. O., *The Church in Matthew* (an unpublished dissertation). Duke University, 1955.

Villey, M., *Leçons d'histoire de la philosophie du droit.* Paris, 1957.

Vischer, W., *Die evangelische Gemeindeordnung.* Zürich, 1933.

Vischer, W., *Die evangelische Gemeindeordnung; Matthäus 16, 13–20, 28.* Zürich, 1946.

Volz, P., *Eschatologie der jüdischen Gemeinde.* Tübingen, 1934.

Volz, P., *Der Prophet Jeremia* (Kommentar zum Alten Testament). Leipzig, 1922.

Volz, P., *Studien zum Text des Jeremia.* Leipzig, 1920.

von Rad, G., *Das Formgeschichtliche Problem des Hexateuchs.* Stuttgart, 1938.

Wade, G. W., *The Book of the Prophet Isaiah* (Westminster Commentaries). London, 1929.

Wagenmann, J., *Die Stellung des Apostels Paulus neben den Zwölf.* Giessen, 1926.

Weiss, J., *The History of Primitive Christianity,* Eng. trans. by F. C. Grant and four friends in 2 vols. New York, 1947.

Welch, A. C., *Jeremiah: his Time and his Work.* Oxford, 1928.

Wellhausen, J., *Das Evangelium Matthaei.* Berlin, 1904.

Wernberg-Møller, P., *The Manual of Discipline translated and annotated with an Introduction.* Leiden, 1957.

Werner, E., *The Sacred Bridge.* London and New York, 1959.

Wertenbeker, T. J., *The Puritan Oligarchy; The Founding of American Civilization.* New York, 1947.

Westcott, B. F. and Hort, F. J. A., *The New Testament in the Original Greek,* 2 vols. Cambridge and London, 1882.

Whale, J. S., *The Protestant Tradition.* Cambridge, 1955.

Wibbing, S., *Die Tugend- und Lasterkataloge im Neuen Testament.* Berlin, 1959.

Widengren, G., *Sakrales Königtum im Alten Testament und im Judentum.* Stuttgart, 1952.

Wilder, A. N., *Eschatology and Ethics in the Teaching of Jesus.* New York and London, 1939.

Wilson, R. McL., *The Gnostic Problem.* London, 1958.

Windisch, H., *Der Sinn der Bergpredigt.* Leipzig, 1929.

Windisch, H., *Die Weisheit und die paulinische Christologie* (Untersuchungen z. Neuen Testament). Leipzig, 1912.

Wood, H. G. (ed.), *Amicitiae Corolla.* London, 1923.

Workman, G. C., *The Text of Jeremiah.* Edinburgh, 1889.

Wright, A., *A Synopsis of the Gospels in Greek,* 3rd rev. ed. London, 1906.

Zunz, L., *Die gottesdienstlichen Vorträge der Juden.* Berlin, 1832.

BIBLIOGRAPHY

C. PERIODICALS REFERRED TO IN THE TEXT

Abstracts of Proceedings (Oxford Society of Historical Theology for 1953).
(B. J. Roberts, 'The DSS and Apocalyptic literature', pp. 29 ff.)

The American Journal of Semitic Languages and Literature (Jan.–Oct. 1938),
vol. LV. (J. Morgenstern, 'A chapter in the history of the high-priesthood',
pp. 1 ff.)

Archives de Philosophie du Droit (1960), no. 5. (S. E. Stumpf, J. Ellul, M. Villey,
'La théologie chrétienne et le droit', pp. 1 ff.)

Biblica
(1942), vol. XXIII. (P. Dabeck, 'Siehe, es erschienen Moses und Elias,
Matt. 17: 3', pp. 175 ff.)
(1958), vol. XXXIX. (A. Feuillet, 'Les perspectives propres à chaque
évangéliste dans les récits de la Transfiguration', pp. 281 ff.)

Bulletin of the John Rylands Library
(June 1943), vol. XXVII. (T. W. Manson, 'The life of Jesus: a study of the
available material', pp. 3 ff.)
(1946), vol. XXIX, no. 2. (H. H. Rowley, 'The Unity of the Old Testament',
pp. 327 ff.)
(1948), vol. XXXI, no. 1. (I. Engnell, 'The Ebed Yahweh Songs and the
Suffering Messiah in Deutero-Isaiah', pp. 54 ff.)
(1951–2), vol. XXXIV. (B. J. Roberts, 'The Dead Sea Scrolls and the Old
Testament', pp. 366 ff.)
(1953–4), vol. XXXVI. (B. J. Roberts, 'The Dead Sea Scrolls and the Old
Testament', pp. 75 ff.)
(1958), vol. XL. (M. Smith, 'The image of God: notes on the Hellenization
of Judaism with especial reference to E. R. Goodenough's work on
Jewish symbols', pp. 473 ff.)

Cahiers Sioniens
(1954), viiie année, no. 2–3–4. (A. Gelin, 'Moïse dans l'Ancien Testament',
pp. 30 ff.)
(1954), viiie année, no. 2–3–4. (G. Vermès, 'La figure de Moïse au tournant
des deux Testaments', pp. 63 ff.)
(1954), viiie année, no. 2–3–4. (R. Bloch, 'Quelques aspects de la figure de
Moïse dans la tradition rabbinique', pp. 93 ff.)

The Canadian Journal of Religious Thought (1926), vol. III. (R. B. Y. Scott,
'The expectation of Elijah', pp. 490 ff.)

Ephemerides Theologicae Lovanienses
(1954), vol. XXX. (L. Cerfaux, 'Les sources scripturaires de Matt. xi, 25–30',
pp. 740 ff.)

(1955), vol. XXXI. (L. Cerfaux, 'Les sources scripturaires de Matt. xi, 25–30', pp. 238 ff.)

Estudios Bíblicos
(April–June 1953), vol. XII. (A. Diez Macho, '¿Cesará la Tora en la Edad Messiánica?', pp. 115 ff.)
(Jan.–March 1954), vol. XIII. (A. Diez Macho, '¿Cesará la Tora en la Edad Messiánica?', pp. 5 ff.)

The Expositor (1918), vol. XV, 8th series. (B. W. Bacon, 'The "Five Books" of Matthew against the Jews', pp. 56 ff.)

Expository Times
(1947), vol. LVIII, no. 11. (C. H. Dodd, 'Matthew and Paul', pp. 296 ff.)
(1948), vol. LIX, no. 10. (W. D. Davies, 'Apocalyptic and Pharisaism', pp. 233 ff.)
(1950), vol. LXII. (A. R. Johnson, 'Living issues in Biblical scholarship: divine kingship and the Old Testament', pp. 36 ff.)
(1954–5), vol. LXVI. (J. Jeremias, 'Paul and James', pp. 368 ff.)

Gesellschafts- und sprachwissenschaftliche Reihe (1953–4), vol. III. (C. Steuernagel, 'Die ursprüngliche Zweckbestimmung des Vaterunsers', pp. 217 ff.)

Gnomon
(1955), vol. XXVII. (A. D. Nock's review of E. R. Goodenough's 'Jewish Symbols', vols. 1–4, pp. 558 ff.)
(1957), vol. XXIX. (A. D. Nock's review of E. R. Goodenough's 'Jewish Symbols', vols. 5–8, pp. 524 ff.)

Harvard Theological Review
(Oct. 1931), vol. XXIV. (Sh. Spiegel, 'Ezekiel or pseudo-Ezekiel', pp. 245 ff.)
(Oct. 1937), vol. XXX. (R. Marcus, 'The "plain meaning" of Isaiah 42: 1–4', pp. 249 ff.)
(Jan. 1947), vol. XL. (R. M. Grant, 'The Decalogue in early Christianity', pp. 1 ff.)
(1950), vol. XLIII. (C. Roth, 'The Disputation of Barcelona, 1263', pp. 117 ff.)
(1952), vol. XLV. (M. Smith, 'Matt. 5: 43: "Hate thine enemy"', pp. 71 ff.)
(July 1953), vol. XLVI, no. 3. (W. D. Davies, '"Knowledge" in the Dead Sea Scrolls and Matthew 11: 25–30', pp. 113 ff.)
(1955), vol. XLVIII. (S. E. Johnson, 'Paul and the Manual of Discipline', pp. 157 ff.)
(Jan. 1958), vol. LI, no. i. (H. J. Cadbury, 'A Qumran parallel to Paul', pp. 1 ff.)

Hebrew Union College Annual

(1930), vol. VII. (S. H. Blank, 'The Septuagint renderings of the Old Testament terms for law', pp. 278 ff.)

(1937–8), vols. XII–XIII (J. Morgenstern, 'The sin of Uzziah, the festival of Jeroboam and the date of Amos', pp. 1 ff.)

(1947), vol. XX. (A. Guttmann, 'The significance of miracles for Talmudic Judaism', pp. 363 ff.)

(1957), vol. XXVIII. (A. Guttmann, 'Hillelites and Shammaites—a clarification', pp. 115 ff.)

(1961), vol. XXXII. (J. Muilenburg, 'The linguistic and rhetorical usages of the particle כִּי in the Old Testament', pp. 135 ff.)

Historia Judaica (ed. by G. Kisch) (Oct. 1943), vol. V. (S. Lieberman, 'Raymund Martini and his alleged forgeries', pp. 87 ff.)

Interpreter (1921), vol. XVIII, no. 1. (C. H. Dodd, 'Communism in the New Testament', pp. 1 ff.)

Jewish Quarterly Review

(1900), vol. XII. (S. Schechter, 'Some rabbinic parallels to the New Testament', pp. 415 ff.)

(Oct. 1951), new series, vol. XLII. (A review of M. Waxman, 'Taame Ha-Mitzwot', pp. 217 ff.)

(1959–60), new series, vol. L. (H. Nibley, 'Christian envy of the Temple', pp. 97 ff. and 229 ff.)

Journal of Bible and Religion

(Oct. 1958), vol. XXVI. (W. F. Stinespring, 'History and present state of Aramaic studies', pp. 298 ff.)

(Oct. 1958), vol. XXVI. (Morton Smith, 'Aramaic studies and the study of the New Testament', pp. 304 ff.)

Journal of Biblical Literature

(1922), vol. XLI. (L. Ginzberg, 'Some observations on the attitude of the Synagogue to the apocalyptic-eschatological writings', pp. 115 ff.)

(1935), vol. LIV. (C. Perry, 'The framework of the Sermon on the Mount', pp. 103 ff.)

(1940), vol. LIX. (C. C. McCown, 'The scene of John's ministry and its relation to the purpose and outcome of his mission', pp. 122 ff.)

(1947), vol. LXVI. (K. W. Clark, 'The Gentile bias in Matthew', pp. 165 ff.)

(1951), vol. LXX. (J. Bright, 'The date of the prose sermons of Jeremiah', pp. 15 ff.)

(1953), vol. LXXII. (S. S. Cohon, review of Morton Smith, *Tannaitic Parallels to the Gospels*, pp. 64 ff.)

(1955), vol. LXXIX. (H. G. May, 'Some cosmic connotations of Mayim Rabbim, "Many Waters"', pp. 5 ff.)

(1955), vol. LXXIV. (Y. Yadin, 'A Note on DSD iv. 20', pp. 40 ff.)

(1955), vol. LXXIV. (R. A. Harrisville, 'The concept of newness in the New Testament', pp. 69 ff.)

(1959), vol. LXXVIII. (Morton Smith, 'What is implied by the variety of Messianic figures?', pp. 66 ff.)

(1959), vol. LXXVIII. (J. A. T. Robinson, review of Joachim Jeremias, *Jesus' Promise to the Nations*, pp. 101 ff.)

(1959), vol. LXXVIII. (R. W. Funk, 'The Wilderness', pp. 205 ff.)

Journal of Jewish Studies

(1953), vol. IV. (N. Wieder, 'The "Law-Interpreter" of the sect of the Dead Sea Scrolls: the Second Moses', pp. 158 ff.)

(1956), vol. VII. (A review of B. W. Helfgott's 'The Doctrine of Election in Tannaitic Literature', signed Z.W., p. 238.)

(1959), vol. X, nos. 1–2. (D. Daube, 'Concessions to sinfulness in Jewish law', pp. 1 ff.)

(1959), vol. X, nos. 3, 4. (J. G. Weiss, 'On the formula melekh ha-'olam as anti-Gnostic protest', pp. 169 ff.)

(1959), vol. X, nos. 3, 4. (B. de Vries, review of H. Albeck, *Mavo' La-Mishnah*, pp. 173 ff.)

Journal of Religion

(Oct. 1944), vol. XXIV. (C. T. Craig, 'The identification of Jesus with the Suffering Servant', pp. 240 ff.)

(Jan. 1946), vol. XXVI. (N. N. Glatzer, 'A study of talmudic interpretation of prophecy', pp. 115 ff.)

Journal of Theological Studies

(1933), vol. XXXIV. (P. L. Couchoud, 'Notes de critique verbale sur St Marc et St Matthieu', pp. 113 ff.)

(1935), vol. XXXVI. (R. P. Casey, 'The study of Gnosticism', pp. 45 ff.)

(1938), vol. XXXIX. (D. Daube, 'ἐξουσία in Mark 1: 22 and 27', pp. 45 ff.)

(1945), vol. XLVI. (W. L. Knox, 'The Epistle of St James', pp. 10 ff.)

(1947), vol. XLVIII. (J. Y. Campbell, 'The origin and meaning of the term Son of Man', pp. 145 ff.)

(1950), vol. I, new series. (C. F. D. Moule, 'Sanctuary and sacrifice in the Church of the New Testament', pp. 29 ff.)

(1950), vol. I, new series. (T. W. Manson: review of *P.R.J.*, pp. 94 ff.)

(1952), vol. III, new series. (C. F. D. Moule, 'The use of parables and sayings as illustrative materials in early Christian catechesis', pp. 75–9.)

(1952), vol. III, new series. (C. F. D. Moule, review of S. G. F. Brandon, *The Fall of Jerusalem*, pp. 106 ff.)

(1960), vol. XI, new series. (J. Jeremias, review of M. D. Hooker's *Jesus and the Servant*, pp. 140 ff.)

Judaica (1952), vol. VIII. (G. Molin, 'Elijahu, der Prophet und sein Weiterleben in den Hoffnungen des Judentums und der Christenheit', pp. 65 ff.)

Monatschrift für Geschichte und Wissenschaft des Judentums
(1929), vol. LXXI. (A. Marmorstein, 'Mitteilungen zur Geschichte und Literatur aus der Geniza', pp. 24 ff.)
(1929), vol. LXXI. (A. Marmorstein, 'Eine apologetische Mischna', pp. 376 ff.)
(1932), vol. LXXIV. (V. Aptowitzer, 'Bemerkungen zur Liturgie und Geschichte der Liturgie', pp. 110 ff.)

New Testament Studies
(1954), vol. I. (Bo Reicke, 'Traces of gnosticism in the DSS', pp. 137 ff.)
(1954–5), vol. I. (H. Chadwick, 'All things to all men', pp. 261 ff.)
(1955–6), vol. II. (W. D. Davies, review of J. Munck, *Paulus und die Heilsgeschichte*, pp. 60 ff.)
(1955–6), vol. II. (C. H. Dodd, 'Some Johannine "Herrenworte" with parallels in the Synoptic Gospels', pp. 75 ff.)
(1955–6), vol. II. (J. N. Sanders, 'Peter and Paul in Acts', pp. 133 ff.)
(May 1956), vol. II. (L. Cerfaux, 'La connaissance des secrets du royaume d'après Matt. xiii. 11 et parallèles', pp. 238 ff.)
(1956–7), vol. III. (C. F. D. Moule, 'The nature and purpose of 1 Peter', pp. 1 ff.)
(1956–7), vol. III. (W. H. Brownlee, 'Messianic motifs of Qumran and the New Testament', p. 17.)
(1956–7), vol. III. (M. Black, 'The recovery of the language of Jesus', pp. 305 ff.)
(1956–7), vol. III. (P. Benoit, 'L'enfance de Jean-Baptiste selon Luc i', pp. 169 ff.)
(1957–8), vol. IV. (J. A. Fitzmyer, 'A feature of Qumran angelology and the angels of 1 Cor. xi. 10', pp. 48 ff.)
(July 1958), vol. IV. (B. Rigaux, 'Révélation des mystères et perfection à Qumrân et dans le Nouveau Testament', pp. 237 ff.)
(April 1959), vol. V. (W. Grundmann, 'Die νήπιοι in der urchristlichen Paränese', pp. 188 ff.)
(April 1959), vol. V. (F. W. Beare, 'On the interpretation of Rom. vi. 17', pp. 206 ff.)
(July 1959), vol. V. (G. Ogg, 'The age of Jesus when he taught', pp. 297 ff.)
(July 1959), vol. V. (B. M. Metzger, 'Seventy or seventy-two disciples?', pp. 303 ff.)
(July 1960), vol. VI. (K. W. Clark, 'Worship in the Jerusalem Temple after A.D. 70', pp. 269 ff.)
(July 1960), vol. VI. (S. Jellicoe, 'St Luke and the seventy-two', p. 319.)
(July 1961), vol. VII. (P. Benoit, 'Qumran et le Nouveau Testament', pp. 276 ff.)

(July 1961), vol. VII. (J. A. Fitzmyer, 'The use of explicit Old Testament quotations in Qumran literature and in the New Testament', pp. 297 ff.)

(July 1961), vol. VII. (M. Smith, 'The Dead Sea Sect in relation to ancient Judaism', pp. 347 ff.)

Nouvelle Revue Théologique (1957), vol. LXXXIX. (G. Salet, 'La loi dans nos cœurs', pp. 449 ff. and 561 ff.)

Novum Testamentum (Jan. 1958), vol. II. (J. Manek, 'The New Exodus and the book of Luke', pp. 8 ff.)

Nuntius (Uppsala), 1949, vol. I, no. I. (J. Jeremias, review of *P.R.J.*, pp. I ff.)

Proceedings of the American Academy for Jewish Research
  (1931–2), vol. III. (S. Zeitlin, 'An historical study of the canonization of the Hebrew scriptures', pp. 121 ff.)
  (1957), vol. XXVII. (J. Goldin, 'The three pillars of Simeon the Righteous', pp. 43 ff.)
  (1962), vol. XXX (J. Neusner, 'Studies on the problem of Tannaim in Babylonia', pp. 79 ff.)

Recherches Bibliques (1960), vol. V (W. C. van Unnik, 'La conception paulinienne de la nouvelle alliance', in *Littérature et théologie pauliniennes*, pp. 109–26).

Recherches de Science Religieuse (1949), vol. XXXVI. (J. Guillet, 'La typologie de l'Exode dans l'Ancien et le Nouveau Testament: le thème de la marche au désert dans l'Ancien Testament', pp. 16 ff.)

Reformed Theological Review (1961), vol. XX. (J. D. McCaughey, 'The question of the historical Jesus', pp. I ff.)

Review of Religion (Nov. 1956), vol. XXI. (S. S. Kayser, review of E. R. Goodenough, *Jewish Symbols*, pp. 54 ff.)

Revue Biblique
  (1938), vol. XLVII. (C. Spicq, 'La conscience dans le NT', pp. 50 ff.)
  (1953), vol. LX. (D. Barthélemy: review of *Torah in the Messianic Age and/or the Age to Come*, pp. 316 ff.)
  (1952), vol. LIX. (E. J. Bickerman, 'La chaîne de la tradition Pharisienne', pp. 44 ff.)
  (1955), vol. LXII. (A. Feuillet, 'Jésus et la sagesse divine d'après les évangiles synoptiques', pp. 161 ff.)

Revue des Études Juives
  (1895), vols. XXX–XXXI. (L. Blau, 'Origine et histoire de la lecture du schema', pp. 179 ff.)
  (1922–3), vols. LXXIV–LXXVII. (S. Poznansky, 'La colloque de Tortose et de San Mateo (7 février 1413–13 novembre 1414)', pp. 74 and 187 ff.)
  (1929), vol. LXXXVII. (S. Zeitlin, 'Un témoignage pour eux', pp. 79 ff.)

Revue d'Histoire et de Philosophie Religieuses
  (1937), vol. XVII. (M. Goguel, A. Lecerf, A. Jundt, A. W. d'Aygalliers and
  C. Hauter, 'L'évangile et la loi', pp. 1 ff.)
  (1950), vol. XXX. (O. Cullmann, 'Paradosis et Kyrios: le problème de la
  tradition dans le Paulinisme', pp. 424 ff.)
  (1953), vol. XXXIII. (H. J. Schoeps, 'Jésus et la loi juive', pp. 1 ff.)

Revue de Qumrân
  (Feb. 1960), vol. I. (W. Grundmann, 'Der Lehrer der Gerechtigkeit von
  Qumran und die Frage nach der Glaubensgerechtigkeit in der Theologie
  des Apostels Paulus', pp. 237 ff.)
  (1959–60), vol. II. (B. Hjerl-Hansen, 'Did Christ know the Qumran Sect?',
  pp. 495 ff.)
  (Nov. 1959), vol. II. (E. Ettisch, 'Eschatologisch-astrologische Vorstellungen
  in der Gemeinderegel, x. 1–8', pp. 3 ff.)

Revue des Sciences Religieuses (Oct. 1956), vol. XIX. (J. Schmitt, 'Les écrits du
  Nouveau Testament et les textes de Qumrân', p. 398, also vol. XXX, 1956,
  pp. 55 ff. and 261 ff.)

Revue de Théologie et des Questions Religieuses, 3ᵉ Année (Montauban, 1894
  (published as a pamphlet)). (M. Wabnitz, 'La charité et son organisation
  au temps de Jésus-Christ et des Apôtres'.)

Scottish Journal of Theology
  (1953), vol. VI. (M. Black, 'The Servant of the Lord and the Son of Man', p. 953.)
  (1957), vol. X. (J. J. Vincent, 'Didactic kerygma in the Synoptic Gospels',
  pp. 262 ff.)

Sefarad (1949), vol. IX. (A. Diez Macho, 'Acerca de los Midrashim falsificados
  de Raimundo Martini', pp. 165 ff.)

Spanische Forschungen (no date), vol. III. (F. Baer, 'Die Disp. von Tortosa',
  pp. 307 ff.) (Cited by A. Diez Macho, *op. cit.* vol. XII (1953), p. 121.)

Studia Catholica (1952), vol. XXVII. (W. Grossouw, 'The Dead Sea Scrolls and
  the New Testament', pp. 1 ff.)

Studia Theologica
  (1948), vol. I. (N. A. Dahl, 'Anamnesis', pp. 69 ff.)
  (1954), vol. VIII. (B. Gärtner, 'The Habakkuk Commentary (DSH) and the
  Gospel of Matthew', pp. 1 ff.)

Svensk Exegetisk Årsbok (1953–4), vols. XVIII–XIX. (M. Black, 'Theological
  conceptions in the Dead Sea Scrolls', p. 86.)

Tarbiz (1958), vol. XXIII. (E. Urbach, 'Law and Prophecy', pp. 1–25.)

Theologische Literaturzeitung
  (Dec. 1952), vol. LXXVII. (K. Stendahl, 'Kerygma und Kerygmatisch',
  pp. 715 ff.)

(1954), vol. LXXIX. (G. Gloege, 'Offenbarung und Überlieferung', cols. 213 ff.)

(1954), vol. LXXIX. (E. Fascher, 'Jesus der Lehrer', cols. 325 ff.)

(1954), vol. LXXIX. (H. Braun, 'Beobachtungen zur Tora-Verschärfung im häretischen Spätjudentum', cols. 347 ff.)

(1955), vol. LXXX. (C. H. Hunzinger, 'Die jüdische Bannpraxis im neu-testamentlichen Zeitalter', pp. 114 f.)

Theologische Studien und Kritiken (1911), vol. LXXXIV. (E. Wendling, 'Die Äußerung des Petrus in der Verklärungsgeschichte, Mark. 9, 5', p. 111.)

Theologische Zeitschrift

(1950), vol. VI. (E. Peterson, 'Das Schiff als Symbol der Kirche', pp. 79 ff.) (*B.T.Z.*)

(1955), vol. VI. (R. Schnackenburg, 'Todes- und Lebensgemeinschaft mit Christus: neue Studien zu Röm. 6: 1–11', pp. 32–53.) (*M.T.Z.*)

Theology (July–Aug. 1951), vol. LIV. (C. Chavasse, 'Jesus Christ and Moses' [in two parts], pp. 244 ff. and pp. 289 ff.)

Theology Today (Oct. 1950), vol. VII, no. 3. (P. Minear, 'The interpreter and the Nativity stories', pp. 358 ff.)

Wissenschaftliche Zeitschrift der Martin-Luther-Universität, Halle-Wittenberg (March, 1958), vol. VII. (E. Stauffer, 'Neue Wege der Jesusforschung', pp. 451 ff.)

Zeitschrift für die Alttestamentliche Wissenschaft (1931–2), vol. XLIX–L. (C. K. North, 'The religious aspects of Hebrew kingship', pp. 8 ff.)

Zeitschrift für Neutestamentliche Wissenschaft

(1900), Bhft. I. (M. Steffen, 'Das Verhältnis von Geist und Glauben bei Paulus', pp. 234 ff.)

(1928), Bhft. XXII. (Von Dobschütz, 'Matthäus als Rabbi und Katechet', pp. 11 ff.)

(1930), Bhft. XXIX. (E. Hirsch, 'Petrus und Paulus', pp. 63 ff.)

(1960), Bhft. XXVI. (K. G. Kuhn, 'Giljonim und Sifre Minim', pp. 24 ff.)

(1960), Bhft. XXVI. (K. Stendahl, 'Quis et Unde? An analysis of Mt. 1 and 2', pp. 94 ff.)

Zeitschrift für Religions- und Geistesgeschichte (1951), vol. IV (Ernst Benz, 'Das Paulus-Verständnis in der morgenländischen und abendländischen Kirche', pp. 289–309.)

Zeitschrift für Theologie und Kirche

(1951), vol. XLVIII. (E. Haenchen, 'Matthew 23', pp. 38 ff.)

(1954), vol. LI. (E. Käsemann, 'Das Problem des historischen Jesu', pp. 125 ff.)

(1956), vol. LIII. (G. Friedrich, 'Beobachtungen zur messianischen Hohe-priestererwartung in den Synoptikern', pp. 260 ff.)

INDICES

I. INDEX OF QUOTATIONS

A. *The Old Testament*

Genesis	PAGE	Exodus (*cont.*)	PAGE
i	70, 71, 91	viii. 19	79, 91
i. 1	70, 71 n. 3	ix. 11	79
i. 1–ii. 23	68 (LXX)	x. 21 f.	84
i. 2	71 n. 3	x. 21 ff.	84, 352
i. 4	80	x. 23	352
i. 26 ff.	71	xii. 2	73
i. 27	105, 389	xiii. 1–10	281
ii. 2	70	xiii. 11–16	281
ii. 4 ff.	71	xiv	84
ii. 4*a*	67 (LXX) (Aquila)	xiv. 13	441
	(Symmachus), 68, 70	xiv. 14	442
ii. 4*b*	68 (LXX)	xiv. 15	442
ii. 24	389	xiv. 19 ff.	84
v. 1	67 (LXX), 70	xv. 1	442
v. 1 ff.	72	xv. 2	442, 443
v. 9 ff.	72	xv. 11	443
v. 24	68	xv. 13	351
x. 1 ff.	72	xv. 26	260
xi. 10	72	xix	99
xi. 27	72	xix. 4–6	351
xii	374	xix. 16	84
xiv. 14	75	xix. 16–20	85
xxv. 12	72	xx. 1	117
xxv. 19	72	xx. 7	245
xxxi. 3	76	xx. 14	252
xli. 8	79 (Symmachus)	xx. 21	84
		xxii. 30	286 n. 3
Exodus		xxiii. 11	456
i. 15	81	xxiv. 7	450
ii. 11	80 n. 3	xxiv. 8	83
ii. 15	81	xxiv. 13	456
ii. 25	81	xxiv. 16	302
iv. 18	78	xxv. 8	351
iv. 20	60 (LXX)	xxvi. 31	84
iv. 22	78	xxix. 43–5	351
vi. 6	351	xxxii	117
vii. 11	79	xxxii. 31 ff.	117
vii. 11 f.	79	xxxii. 32	117
vii. 12	79	xxxiii. 22	113
viii. 7	79	xxxiv. 3	117
viii. 18	79	xxxiv. 8	117

Exodus (*cont.*)   PAGE
  xxxiv. 29–35   51 (LXX)

Leviticus
  i. 1   75 n. 3
  xvii–xxvi   373
  xix. 12   245 (LXX)
  xix. 18   245 (LXX), 373
  xix. 22   210
  xxiii. 40   269

Numbers
  v. 18   75
  v. 21   243
  xi. 28   456
  xii. 13   442
  xvi. 1   75
  xxiv. 17   446
  xxviii. 9 f.   103
  xxx. 3   240, 245

Deuteronomy
  i. 37   117
  iii. 26   117
  iv. 1   117
  iv. 7   443
  iv. 13   117
  iv. 20   351 n. 3
  iv. 21   351 n. 3
  iv. 26   117
  vi. 4   443
  vi. 4–9   281
  vi. 7   128
  vi. 8   443
  vi. 20–4   112
  vi. 32–4   112
  vii. 8   351
  vii. 11–12   117
  viii. 3   195
  ix. 17–20   117
  ix. 25–9   117
  x. 4   117
  x. 16   126
  xi. 13–21   281
  xi. 19   128
  xv. 15   351
  xvii. 8 ff.   475
  xvii. 18–19   121 n. 5, 121 n. 6
  xvii. 19   127
  xviii. 13   210

Deuteronomy (*cont.*)   PAGE
  xviii. 15   53 (LXX), 117, 144 (LXX),
          190 n. 2, 402 n. 2
  xix. 15   223
  xxi. 18 ff.   287 n. 5
  xxiii. 22   245
  xxiii. 22 ff.   240
  xxv. 7–9   265
  xxvi. 5 ff.   111
  xxvi. 7   81
  xxvi. 17   443
  xxvi. 18   443
  xxx. 6   126
  xxx. 11–14   402 n. 2
  xxx. 14   127
  xxx. 15–19   394 n. 1, 402 n. 2
  xxxi. 10–13   121 n. 5
  xxxi. 14   441
  xxxi. 15   55 (LXX)
  xxxii. 45–7   394 n. 1, 402 n. 2
  xxxii. 47   239 (LXX)
  xxxiii. 29   443
  xxxiv. 9   55 (LXX), 303
  xxxiv. 10–12   117

Joshua
  i. 1   456
  i. 8   127
  xxiv. 26–31   112

Judges
  ii. 7   303

Ruth
  i. 1   303
  iv. 18–22   76

1 Samuel
  iii. 10   441
  x. 18   113
  xxvii. 1–7   103

2 Samuel
  v. 2   77
  v. 8   227 n. 2
  vi. 12–19   121 n. 5
  vii. 6   113
  vii. 23   113
  xxiii. 1   443
  xxiii. 4   446

1 Kings	PAGE
viii. 1–6	121 n. 5 (LXX)
viii. 7–11	121 n. 5
viii. 14	121 n. 5
ix. 7 f.	298
xii. 33	121 n. 5
xix. 9	113
xix. 21	456

2 Kings	
iv–vi	330 n. 3
vi. 1	113
vi. 15–17	84, 441
viii. 16	113
viii. 21	113
xiv. 6	129 n. 1 (LXX)
xxiii. 2 f.	121 n. 5
xxiii. 21–3	114

1 Chronicles	
i. 1 ff.	68
i. 3–6	76
ii. 1–15	76
iii. 10–17	76
xvi. 36	451
xvii. 21	443
xxix. 11 f.	452

2 Chronicles	
ii. 14	308
xxvi. 16–20	121 n. 5
xxx. 2	114

Nehemiah	
v. 13	236

Job	
xxxi. 9	252 n. 3
xxxviii. 8–11	89

Psalms	
viii	430 n. 2
xviii. 13	441
xviii. 14	441
xviii. 15	442
xix	430 n. 2
xix. 3	234 (LXX)
xxix. 3	89
xxix. 10	89
xxxiii. 5	134 (LXX)

Psalms (cont.)	PAGE
xxxiii. 6	89
xxxvii. 31	127
xl. 8	127
xli. 13	451
xlii. 10	89
xlvi	89
l. 2	127
lvii. 12	442
lxv. 7 f.	89
lxxi. 7	446
lxxii. 18	451
lxxiii. 1	73
lxxiv. 12–15	120 n. 2
lxxv. 1	73
lxxvii. 11 f.	120 n. 2
lxxvii. 16	89
lxxvii. 19 f.	89
lxxviii. 2	234 (LXX) (Symmachus) (Aquila)
lxxxiv. 12	446
lxxxix. 3	306
lxxxix. 9	89
lxxxix. 18	443
lxxxix. 52	451
xciii. 3 f.	89
xcvi. 11	89, 446 (LXX)
xcvii. 11	446
xcviii. 7	89
ci. 11	134 (LXX)
civ. 5–9	89
cvi. 9	90
cvi. 48	451
cx. 1–3	445 (LXX)
cxi. 7	134 (LXX)
cxi. 10	450
cxv. 18	451
cxlix. 6	442

Proverbs	
iii. 25	374
viii. 22–31	89
xxxi. 10 ff.	374
xxxi. 39	374

Ecclesiastes	
xii. 14	461

Song of Solomon	
ii. 14	441

Isaiah	PAGE	Isaiah (cont.)	PAGE
i. 2 f.	430 n. 2	lxi. 1	251, 446
ii. 1–4	447	lxi. 11	446
ii. 3	137 (LXX)	lxiii. 11–14	114
vii. 14	72, 282 (LXX), 288	lxv. 17	121 n. 3
viii. 23–ix. 1	327	lxvi	461
xvii. 12–14	89	lxvi. 22	121 n. 3
xxx. 7	120 n. 2	lxxxvii. 4	120 n. 2
xxxv	461		
xl. 3	114	Jeremiah	
xli. 2	445	ii. 1–3	113
xli. 17–20	114	ii. 6	113
xlii. 1	52 (LXX)	iv. 4	126
xlii. 1–4	328, 447	v. 22*b*	89
xlii. 1–6	121 n. 6	vii. 7 ff.	125
xlii. 2	134 (LXX)	vii. 22–6	113
xlii. 4	117, 135 (LXX)	vii. 23	394 n. 1, 402 n. 2
xlii. 6	117	vii. 25	303
xlii. 10	114	xvi. 14 f.	113 f.
xlii. 14–xliv. 23	114	xxiii. 5	445
xlii. 16	352	xxvi. 4	129 n. 1 (LXX)
xlii. 23–xliii. 2	114	xxx. 35	89
xliii	31 (LXX)	xxxi. 15	83
xliii. 9–12	114	xxxi. 31 f.	114
xliii. 14–17	114	xxxi. 31 ff.	83, 121 n. 3, 128 (LXX),
xliii. 18–21	114		129 n. 1 (LXX)
xliii. 19	446	xxxi. 31–4	111, 122 ff., 125, 447
xliv. 27	114	xxxii. 17–23	113
xlv. 7	280	xliv. 10	129 n. 1 (LXX)
xlv. 8	446		
xlviii. 20	33 n. 1 (LXX)	Ezekiel	
xlix. 3	443	xi. 9	128
xlix. 5 f.	117	xx. 5–13	114
xlix. 6	117	xx. 36 f.	114
xlix. 8	117	xxix. 21	446
xlix. 8–12	117	xxx. 31 ff.	121 n. 3
l. 2	114	xxxvi. 26 ff.	128
l. 4	117	xli. 22	225
l. 7–8	117	xliv. 1 ff.	121 n. 3
li. 9–11	120 n. 2	xliv. 4	121 n. 3
li. 10 f.	114		
lii. 3 f.	114	Daniel	
lii. 11	33 n. 1 (LXX)	i. 8	394 n. 1
lii. 12	114	i. 20	79 (Theodotion)
liii. 12	117	ii. 2	79 n. 3
lv. 3	114	vii	85
lv. 6	225	vii. 1–13	198
lviii. 8	114	vii. 6	198 (LXX) (Theodotion)
lviii. 10	446	vii. 12	198 (LXX) (Theodotion)
lix. 15*b*–20	89	vii. 13–14	200
lx. 21	259	vii. 14	197 (LXX), 198
		vii. 15 ff.	200

Daniel (*cont.*)	PAGE		Micah	PAGE
vii. 23	198		v	445 (LXX)
vii. 24 ff.	198		v. 1	77
vii. 26	198		vi. 3–4	114
vii. 27	198 (LXX) (Theodotion)		vii. 15	87
xi. 16	202 n. 1		Nahum	
xi. 41	202 n. 1		i. 4	89
Hosea				
ii. 14–15	113, 114 n. 2		Habakkuk	
vi. 6	306		ii	218
ix. 10	113		iii. 15	89
xi. 1	78			
xi. 10	113		Zechariah	
xiii. 4–5	113		iii. 8	445
			vi. 12	445
Amos				
iii. 1–2	113		Malachi	
viii. 1–ix. 10	84, 85		iii. 1	32 (LXX)
ix. 1	441		iii. 9	394 n. 1
ix. 2 ff.	85		iv. 2	446

B. The Apocrypha and Pseudepigrapha of the Old Testament

1 Maccabees			1 Enoch	
iv. 41–6	143		xxxviii	140
ix. 27	143		xxxviii. 2	141
xiv. 25–49	144		xxxix	140
			xxxix. 6	141
2 Maccabees			xlvi. 2	141
vi. 8	36 n. 3		xlviii. 1 f.	140
			xlix. 1 f.	141
Ecclesiasticus			li. 3	141
v. 8	142		liii. 6	141
x. 5	153 n. 2			
xxiv. 3 ff.	141		Test. Levi	
xxiv. 23	141		ii. 6	36 n. 3
xlii. 1 ff.	142		v. 1	36 n. 3
xlviii. 1 f.	142		xviii. 6, 7	36, 36 n. 3
xlix. 1 f.	142		xviii. 9	160
xci. 10	142			
			Test. Judah	
Apoc. Baruch			xxiv. 2	36 n. 3
xvii. 2	120 n. 1			
xxii. 2	36 n. 3		Test. Benjamin	
xxxii. 6	120 n. 1		xi. 2	160
Jubilees	111 n.		2 Baruch	
i. 29	120 n. 1		xlii. 1 f.	142

2 Baruch (cont.)	PAGE	Zadokite Documents (cont.)	PAGE
xliv. 14	142	vi. 10	154 n. 4
xlix. 1	142 n. 1	vi. 10–11	155 n. 2
		vi. 11	154 n. 4
4 Ezra		vi. 14	148
vii. 75	120 n. 1	vii. 6	155 n. 1
		vii. 8	243
Asc. Is.		vii. 18	152, 154
vi. 9	36 n. 3	vii. 18–20	151
		ix	225
Psalms of Solomon		ix ff.	225
xvii. 29 f.	142	ix–xvi	223
xvii. 34	142	ix. 2 f.	222
xvii. 37	142 n. 2	ix. 9	243
xvii. 41	142	ix. 11	243
xvii. 42	142	xii. 23	152
xvii. 48	142	xiii. 1	115 n. 1
		xiii. 10	225
Zadokite Documents (CDC)		xiv. 3, 9	115 n. 1
i. 1 ff.	153	xiv. 19	151 f.
i. 1–12	216	xiv. 21	222
i. 10–12	148	xv–xvi	243
i. 11	217 n. 1	xv. 1	243
i. 16	149	xv. 1–13	242 f.
ii. 6	232	xv. 6	242
ii. 12–vi. 1	152	xv. 6–19	244
iii. 13	147 n. 2	xv. 8–10	147 n. 2
iii. 13–16	262 n. 2	xv. 9	243
iii. 18–21	218	xv. 12	243
iii. 19	147 n. 2	xvi. 1–6	244
iv. 3	33 n. 1	xvi. 6b–13	244
iv. 13 ff.	232	xvi. 13	225
iv. 21	430	xvi. 13–19	244
v. 18	80 n. 1	xvii. 3 ff.	228 n. 1
v. 18–19	80	xix. 2–3	115 n. 1
vi. 2–11	218	xix. 10	152
vi. 4 ff.	153	xix. 16	247 n. 3
vi. 5	33 n. 1	xx. 1	152
vi. 8 ff.	152	xx. 8 f.	149 n. 1

C. The New Testament

Matthew		Matthew (cont.)	
i	70, 71, 72, 78, 301 n. 5	i. 2 ff.	68, 69
i–ii	67 n. 1, 299 n. 6, 327 n. 2, 443, 444	i. 2–6	74, 76
		i. 2–16	67
i. 1	67, 68 ff., 72, 77, 83, 304	i. 7	73
i. 1 ff.	74 n. 1, 76, 288, 302	i. 7–12	76
i. 1–11	76	i. 8	73
i. 1–16	76	i. 10	73
i. 1–17	72, 74, 76	i. 13–16	76

Matthew (*cont.*)   PAGE

i. 17   72 n. 1, 77, 304
i. 18   68 f., 69
i. 18–25   70 f., 71, 72, 81, 444
i. 20   77
i. 21   444
i. 22   72, 444
i. 23   71, 85, 208
ii   66, 72, 77, 78, 79, 445
ii. 1   444, 445
ii. 1–2   77, 80
ii. 1–23   444
ii. 2   445
ii. 3   446
ii. 6   77, 208, 445
ii. 9   445, 446
ii. 13   78
ii. 14   82 n. 3
ii. 15   78, 208
ii. 16   78
ii. 17   71
ii. 18   83, 208
ii. 19 f.   80
ii. 19 ff.   78
ii. 19–21   78
ii. 20*b*   78
ii. 23   208, 444
iii. 1 ff.   83
iii. 1–10   382
iii. 7   291 n. 2
iii. 11   382
iii. 12   382
iii. 15   95, 96, 217 n. 3
iv   96
iv. 1–11   382
iv. 3 f.   194
iv. 15   327
iv. 15 ff.   96
iv. 15–16   208
iv. 17   432 n. 1
iv. 18–22   337
iv. 23   297
iv. 23 ff.   96
iv. 23–5   100, 327, 433
iv. 24   327
v–vii   93
v. 1   85, 93, 99, 381, 423 n. 4
v. 1–11   290
v. 1–vii. 28   90
v. 3   251, 377, 403
v. 3–8   289

Matthew (*cont.*)   PAGE

v. 3–11   96
v. 3–12   382
v. 5   377, 403
v. 6   377
v. 7   377, 403
v. 8–9   412
v. 9   377, 403
v. 10   289, 377
v. 10–12   376
v. 11   99, 249, 297
v. 11–12   289 n. 1, 290
v. 11 f.   402
v. 11 ff.   289
v. 12   251, 252, 292, 402
v. 13   249, 250, 290, 381, 457
v. 13 ff.   328
v. 13–16   249, 250, 290, 369
v. 14   249, 250, 330, 377
v. 14 ff.   373
v. 14–16   290, 292, 375, 377
v. 15   249, 250, 375, 381, 384, 457
v. 16   195, 249, 250, 251, 290, 369, 377
v. 17   88, 95, 101, 334, 335
v. 17 ff.   100, 217 n. 3, 399
v. 17–18   307
v. 17–19   333, 334, 336
v. 17–20   100, 249, 304, 448
v. 17–48   301, 399
v. 18   102, 334, 335, 463
v. 19   335
v. 20   96, 291, 301
v. 20–vii. 12   290
v. 21   236, 237, 290 n. 3, 301 n. 1, 335
v. 21 f.   93, 96, 103, 235, 536, 238, 239, 403
v. 21 ff.   387 n. 4
v. 21–2   412
v. 21–3   237
v. 21–48   101
v. 22   98, 403
v. 22 f.   249
v. 22 ff.   212, 431
v. 22–4   235
v. 22–48   300
v. 23   236
v. 23 f.   98
v. 25   384
v. 26   384

Matthew (*cont.*)	PAGE	Matthew (*cont.*)	PAGE
v. 27	301 n. 1, 335	vi. 19 f.	96
v. 28	85, 252	vi. 19–20	429 n. 2
v. 29	369	vi. 19–vii. 12	307
v. 29–30	227 n. 2	vi. 20	288
v. 30	301 n. 1	vi. 20 ff.	430
v. 31 f.	240	vi. 21	288
v. 33	245, 335	vi. 22 f.	384
v. 33–7	239, 240, 241	vi. 22–3	412
v. 34	244	vi. 25	403
v. 34–7	404 n. 4	vi. 25 ff.	369
v. 35	330	vi. 25–33	384
v. 35–6	244	vi. 25–34	300
v. 38	335	vi. 27	381, 458
v. 39	377	vi. 32	305
v. 39–48	382	vi. 34	300, 377
v. 41	335	vii. 1	247, 392, 403
v. 43	213, 245, 246, 247, 248, 290 n. 3, 377, 402	vii. 1 ff.	291
v. 43 f.	211	vii. 3–5	98, 249
v. 43 ff.	411, 427	vii. 6	326, 392, 396, 399
v. 43–8	245, 463	vii. 7	403
v. 44	377	vii. 8	403, 412
v. 44 ff.	369	vii. 12	95, 290, 304, 382, 402, 463
v. 44–5	412	vii. 13 f.	199
v. 44–8	429 n. 2	vii. 15	200, 201
v. 45	205	vii. 15 ff.	199, 203
v. 45 ff.	430	vii. 15–21	291, 399
v. 46–8	249	vii. 16	403
v. 47	98, 249, 305	vii. 21	230, 381, 412
v. 48	95, 209, 210, 211, 212, 213, 214, 215, 249, 283 n. 1, 377, 403, 412, 431	vii. 21 ff.	97, 200
vi. 1 ff.	283, 307	vii. 21–7	382
vi. 1–6	463	vii. 22	382
vi. 1–16	307	vii. 22 ff.	399
vi. 1–18	399	vii. 23	202, 205
vi. 2	304, 369	vii. 24	94, 203, 403, 429 n. 2, 463
vi. 2 ff.	250, 251, 308	vii. 26	403
vi. 5	304	vii. 28	100, 107, 457
vi. 5 f.	309 n. 3	vii. 29	291, 297
vi. 7	196 n. 3, 305, 309	viii–ix	100, 433
vi. 7 f.	309 n. 3	viii. 1	331 n. 1
vi. 7–9	309 n. 3	viii. 1 ff.	90
vi. 7–14	309	viii. 1–4	330 n. 3
vi. 11	310	viii. 1–15	87
vi. 12	377	viii. 1–17	330 n. 3
vi. 13	311, 376, 451, 452	viii. 1–ix. 32	90
vi. 16	304	viii. 1–ix. 34	86, 91, 92
vi. 16–18	292	viii. 2–4	86
vi. 19	403	viii. 4	88, 105
		viii. 5–13	86, 90, 330 n. 3, 368
		viii. 9	90
		viii. 10	95

INDEX OF QUOTATIONS

Matthew (*cont.*)	PAGE	Matthew (*cont.*)	PAGE
viii. 11	223	x. 18	328
viii. 11 ff.	329	x. 23	297
viii. 12	332, 333	x. 23 f.	326
viii. 13	90, 95, 218	x. 24	97, 381, 382, 463
viii. 14	90	x. 24 f.	97
viii. 14–17	86, 90, 91, 330 n. 3	x. 24–5	458
viii. 16	90	x. 25	376, 382, 463
viii. 17	208	x. 26	201, 381
viii. 18 ff.	91	x. 28	376
viii. 18–22	90	x. 29	429 n. 2
viii. 19–22	213 n. 3, 383	x. 32 f.	376
viii. 20	381, 460	x. 40	98, 383, 463
viii. 20–7	89	xi. 2	189 n. 2
viii. 23	90	xi. 2 ff.	207
viii. 23–7	86, 87, 90, 91	xi. 2–6	383
viii. 23–ix. 8	87	xi. 5	251
viii. 24–7	88	xi. 7–19	383
viii. 27	90	xi. 13	307
viii. 28–34	86, 87, 91	xi. 17	396 n. 2
viii. 29	90, 91	xi. 19	287
viii. 52	94, 106	xi. 21–3	383
ix. 1–8	87, 90, 91	xi. 25	207
ix. 2	95	xi. 25 ff.	199
ix. 2–8	86	xi. 25–30	206, 207, 214 n. 5
ix. 9 ff.	90	xi. 27–30	214, 292, 453
ix. 18 ff.	90	xi. 28–30	365
ix. 18–19	86	xi. 29	94
ix. 18–26	87, 88	xii. 1 ff.	456
ix. 18–34	87, 91	xii. 1–14	103
ix. 20–2	86	xii. 5	103
ix. 20–3	87	xii. 7	307
ix. 22	91, 95	xii. 9	297
ix. 23–6	86	xii. 11	104, 290 n. 3
ix. 25	91	xii. 15	96
ix. 27–31	86	xii. 18 ff.	328, 330
ix. 28 f.	95	xii. 18–21	208
ix. 29	91, 218	xii. 21	328, 332
ix. 32–4	86	xii. 22–30	383
ix. 33	91	xii. 28 ff.	345 n. 1
ix. 34	91	xii. 30	381
ix. 35	297	xii. 31–2	239
ix. 37	383	xii. 33–5	382
ix. 38	383	xii. 34	291 n. 2
x	98, 376, 458	xii. 36	238
x. 1	333 n. 1	xii. 36 f.	239
x. 5 f.	326	xii. 39	403
x. 7–16	383	xii. 43–6	383
x. 10	381	xiii. 7	376
x. 17	297	xiii. 10 ff.	214
x. 17 ff.	96	xiii. 11	207 n. 2, 214 n. 5

Matthew (*cont.*)   PAGE

xiii. 24 ff.   232, 233, 429 n. 2
xiii. 24–30   221, 230, 336, 379
xiii. 25   336
xiii. 31–3   384
xiii. 32   330
xiii. 34 f.   234, 235
xiii. 35   208, 234
xiii. 36   234
xiii. 36 ff.   234, 328
xiii. 36–43   232, 233, 336, 379
xiii. 36–50   234
xiii. 37–43   215
xiii. 38   232, 328, 330
xiii. 39   232
xiii. 41   204, 205, 232
xiii. 43   232
xiii. 44–5   215
xiii. 47   234
xiii. 47 f.   232
xiii. 47 ff.   233
xiii. 47–50   221, 230, 232
xiii. 49–50   379
xiii. 51   233
xiii. 51–2   234
xiii. 52   233, 396 n. 2, 409
xiii. 53–xvii. 23   337
xiii. 54   297
xiv. 13–21   337
xiv. 26   337
xiv. 28–31   337, 338
xiv. 33   215, 337, 338
xv. 1–20   103, 104
xv. 3 ff.   106
xv. 3–7   400
xv. 4   105
xv. 14   106, 292, 381, 382, 458
xv. 15   336, 338
xv. 15 ff.   225 n. 1
xv. 19   461
xv. 20   339
xv. 21–8   331
xv. 24   326
xv. 28   218
xv. 29–31   328, 330
xvi. 11–12   291
xvi. 13–16   189 n. 2
xvi. 13–20   228
xvi. 16   215
xvi. 17–19   221, 229, 337, 338, 339
                              n. 2, 397 n. 1

Matthew (*cont.*)   PAGE

xvi. 18   229, 330, 396 n. 2
xvi. 18 f.   339
xvi. 18 ff.   230
xvi. 19   229, 338, 424
xvi. 21   299 n. 2, 391
xvi. 24 ff.   96
xvi. 28   330
xvii. 1   85
xvii. 1 ff.   86
xvii. 3   349 n. 2
xvii. 3 f.   105, 400
xvii. 20   95
xvii. 22–3   391
xvii. 23   391
xvii. 24   228
xvii. 24 ff.   338
xvii. 24–7   337, 338, 374, 389, 391,
                                   397 n. 1
xvii. 24–xviii. 35   337
xvii. 25   390
xviii   392, 399, 400, 401, 434
xviii. 1   228, 369
xviii. 1 f.   96
xviii. 1–6   392
xviii. 1–15   226
xviii. 3   372
xviii. 4   459
xviii. 6   95, 98, 227 n. 2
xviii. 6 ff.   338
xviii. 7   227 n. 2
xviii. 8–9   227 n. 2
xviii. 10   98, 226, 227 n. 2, 392, 393
xviii. 10–14   226
xviii. 12–14   385, 400
xviii. 14   385, 393
xviii. 15   98, 225, 392
xviii. 15 f.   230
xviii. 15 ff.   223, 224, 228, 249
xviii. 15–17   222, 391, 396 n. 2
xviii. 15–20   221, 225, 400
xviii. 15–21   249
xviii. 16   396 n. 3
xviii. 17   224
xviii. 18   94, 225, 228, 229, 424,
                                        463
xviii. 18 ff.   224
xviii. 19 f.   224
xviii. 20   225
xviii. 21   98, 336
xviii. 21–2   226, 391, 392

Matthew (*cont.*)	PAGE	Matthew (*cont.*)	PAGE
xviii. 21–35	397 n. 1	xxii. 9 f.	329, 330
xviii. 23	412, 463	xxii. 11–14	300 n. 2
xviii. 23–35	392	xxii. 12	396 n. 2
xix	393, 398, 399, 400	xxii. 12–14	332
xix. 1–9	103, 104	xxii. 31	105
xix. 2–9	393	xxii. 34–40	431, 463
xix. 2–10	393	xxii. 39	373
xix. 3 ff.	389	xxii. 39 f.	373, 403
xix. 3–9	212, 388, 395, 399	xxii. 40	95
xix. 4	252	xxiii	291 n. 1
xix. 9	393	xxiii. 1–7	106
xix. 9–11	394	xxiii. 1–36	291
xix. 10–12	212, 393, 395, 399	xxiii. 2	106, 333
xix. 11	394	xxiii. 2–3	291
xix. 12	394	xxiii. 3	333
xix. 13–15	212, 396, 399	xxiii. 4	292
xix. 14	372	xxiii. 4–36	384
xix. 16 ff.	211	xxiii. 5–10	297
xix. 16–20	96	xxiii. 7 ff.	96
xix. 16–22	395, 399	xxiii. 8	94, 298
xix. 17	211	xxiii. 12	381, 403, 459
xix. 18 f.	373	xxiii. 13–36	291
xix. 19	212	xxiii. 15	326
xix. 21	210, 211, 212, 213, 214, 215	xxiii. 16	292
xix. 23 ff.	96	xxiii. 16 ff.	240, 458
xix. 23–30	212	xxiii. 23	95, 219, 290 n. 3
xix. 27	336	xxiii. 25–8	292
xix. 28	228, 229, 330, 373	xxiii. 28	205
xix. 29	228	xxiii. 29	200, 205
xx. 13	396 n. 2	xxiii. 31 ff.	96
xx. 17–19	391	xxiii. 33	291 n. 2
xx. 20 ff.	96	xxiii. 34	94, 106, 297, 396 n. 2
xx. 21	330	xxiii. 34–6	292
xxi. 10	299 n. 3	xxiii. 37	298
xxi. 11	189 n. 2	xxiii. 37–9	299
xxi. 11–19	369	xxiv	376
xxi. 14	227 n. 2	xxiv. 1–3	299
xxi. 20	95, 337	xxiv. 3	337
xxi. 28–32	332	xxiv. 4 ff.	202
xxi. 32	219	xxiv. 5	201
xxi. 33–43	332	xxiv. 8	376
xxi. 33–45	290	xxiv. 9	329
xxi. 39 ff.	332	xxiv. 9–13	201
xxi. 41	329	xxiv. 11	200, 201
xxi. 43	328, 329, 330	xxiv. 12	203, 204, 205
xxi. 46	189 n. 2	xxiv. 14	329
xxii. 1 ff.	298	xxiv. 24	200, 201
xxii. 1–10	332, 385	xxiv. 26	202
xxii. 1–14	332	xxiv. 27 ff.	429 n. 2
xxii. 7	298	xxiv. 28	381, 458

Matthew (*cont.*)	PAGE	Matthew (*cont.*)	PAGE
xxiv. 33	403	xxviii. 19	333
xxiv. 43	371	xxviii. 20	94, 463
xxiv. 43 f.	376		
xxiv. 43–51	372	Mark	
xxiv. 49	373	i. 1	70
xxv. 1–13	332	i. 4	83
xxv. 13	376	i. 15	432 n. 1
xxv. 14–20	369	i. 16–20	233, 337
xxv. 14–30	332	i. 21 ff.	100
xxv. 21	330	i. 21–8	100
xxv. 21 ff.	98	i. 22	100
xxv. 23	330	i. 27	100 n. 1
xxv. 28	459	i. 28	420 n. 1
xxv. 31–46	98, 215, 332	i. 29–34	86
xxv. 32	329	i. 31	423 n. 3
xxv. 32 ff.	330	i. 40–4	86
xxv. 37 ff.	98	ii. 3–12	86
xxv. 39	381	ii. 17	377
xxv. 40	249, 329	ii. 18	421 n. 2
xxvi. 1–xxviii. 20	83 ff.	ii. 18–20	283
xxvi. 13	329, 330	ii. 23 ff.	456
xxvi. 17 ff.	337	ii. 23–8	103
xxvi. 28	83	ii. 23–iii. 16	103
xxvi. 29	84	iii. 1–6	104
xxvi. 30–5	337	iii. 7–12	328
xxvi. 39	453	iii. 14	333 n. 1
xxvi. 40	337	iv. 1 ff.	421 n. 1
xxvi. 50	396 n. 2	iv. 19	371
xxvi. 52	84, 202	iv. 21	457
xxvi. 52–4	202	iv. 22	457, 459
xxvi. 64*b*	197	iv. 36–41	86
xxvii. 15–26	290	v. 1 ff.	421 n. 1
xxvii. 41	327	v. 1–20	86
xxvii. 42	95	v. 22–4	86
xxvii. 45	84	v. 25–34	86
xxvii. 45–56	84	v. 31	337
xxvii. 51	84	v. 35–43	86
xxvii. 51*b*–52	84, 85	vi. 45 ff.	338
xxvii. 53	299	vii	378, 379, 424, 426, 428
xxvii. 54	327	vii. 1–23	104
xxvii. 55	422	vii. 10	105, 327
xxvii. 62 ff.	287	vii. 14–23	339
xxviii. 11	299	vii. 18	355
xxviii. 15	286, 287, 297	vii. 19	104, 339
xxviii. 16	85	vii. 21–2	461
xxviii. 16 ff.	92, 197, 223, 329, 332	vii. 23	104
xxviii. 16–20	85, 86, 97, 327, 330, 333, 360 n. 2, 361	vii. 24–30	331
		vii. 28	420 n. 1
xxviii. 18	196, 197, 198, 199, 360	viii. 31	299 n. 2
xxviii. 18–20	221	viii. 32	389

Mark (*cont.*)	PAGE	Mark (*cont.*)	PAGE
viii. 35	463	xiii. 13	329, 376
viii. 38	376	xiii. 27	376
ix. 2 ff.	86	xiii. 32	371
ix. 28	389	xiii. 32 f.	376
ix. 32	389	xiii. 33	376
ix. 33–7	400	xiii. 35–7	376
ix. 36 ff.	392	xiv. 24	83
ix. 37	463	xiv. 33	337
ix. 38–41	400, 458	xiv. 36 f.	453
ix. 38–42	400	xiv. 37	337
ix. 41	98	xiv. 58	330
ix. 42	95, 400	xv. 32	95
ix. 43 ff.	369	xv. 41	422, 423
ix. 48–50	400	xvi. 8	360
ix. 50	457		
x	389, 430	Luke	
x. 1 ff.	430	i. 78	445
x. 1–12	388	iii. 2	382
x. 2 ff.	389	iii. 3	83, 382
x. 2–9	429 n. 2	iii. 7–9	382
x. 2–12	104	iii.. 16	369, 382
x. 10	389	iii. 17	382
x. 11	388, 462	iv. 1–12	382
x. 12	388, 398, 462	v. 1–11	337
x. 15	372, 392	vi. 1 ff.	456
x. 17–22	389	vi. 1–11	103
x. 17–31	395	vi. 17	99
x. 19	373	vi. 17–19	328
x. 35–45	389	vi. 20–49	382, 385
x. 45	378, 379, 423	vi. 22	376, 382, 412
x. 46 ff.	389	vi. 22–3	290 n. 1
xi. 21	337	vi. 23	402
xi. 23 f.	403	vi. 24 f.	403
xii. 9	329	vi. 24 ff.	289
xii. 13–17	374, 378, 429 n. 2	vi. 25	403
xii. 14 f.	423	vi. 27	388
xii. 26	105	vi. 27 ff.	369
xii. 27 ff.	91	vi. 27–45	382
xii. 28	402	vi. 30	381, 459
xii. 28–34	431	vi. 31	381, 459
xii. 29–31	412	vi. 32 f.	376
xii. 31	373, 403	vi. 32–4	375
xii. 35 ff.	420 n. 8	vi. 32–5	377
xiii	376	vi. 36	210, 412
xiii. 3	337	vi. 37	403
xiii. 6	201	vi. 39	381, 458
xiii. 8	376	vi. 40	381, 458
xiii. 9–10	378	vi. 46 ff.	382, 403
xiii. 10	329	vi. 46–9	382, 458
xiii. 11	376	vii. 2	382

Luke (*cont.*)	PAGE	Luke (*cont.*)	PAGE
vii. 2–10	368	xi. 46–52	384
vii. 6–10	382	xii	376
vii. 18	383	xii. 1	291
vii. 19	383	xii. 2	459
vii. 22–8	383	xii. 2 f.	381
vii. 31–5	383	xii. 2–3	384
vii. 34	287	xii. 3	459
viii. 2 f.	422	xii. 4 ff.	384
viii. 16	457	xii. 4–12	384
viii. 17	457, 459	xii. 8	376
viii. 45	337	xii. 9	376
ix. 22	299 n. 2	xii. 22 ff.	369
ix. 24	463	xii. 22–31	384, 385
ix. 41–4	470	xii. 22–34	460
ix. 46–8	392	xii. 22–46	461
ix. 48	463	xii. 25	381, 458
ix. 50	458	xii. 32	384
ix. 57–62	383	xii. 32 f.	384
ix. 58	381, 460	xii. 33–4	385
x. 1–16	383	xii. 33–40	384
x. 7	378	xii. 35	376
x. 16	98, 381, 459, 463	xii. 39	371
x. 17 ff.	383	xii. 39 f.	372
x. 21–8	383	xii. 39–40	376
x. 23 f.	383	xii. 40	368
x. 25 ff.	431	xii. 41	371
x. 39	463	xii. 41–6	384
x. 40	423 n. 3	xii. 45	371, 376
xi. 1	309	xii. 49	384
xi. 2–4	383	xii. 54–6	384
xi. 4	383	xii. 57	369
xi. 5–8	383	xii. 57–9	384, 385
xi. 9	403	xiii. 18–21	384
xi. 9–13	383	xiii. 19	330
xi. 10	412	xiii. 22–30	382
xi. 14–23	383	xiii. 23–30	384
xi. 19 ff.	91	xiii. 24–9	385
xi. 20	79	xiii. 28 ff.	384
xi. 23	381, 458	xiii. 31–3	298
xi. 24–6	383	xiii. 34	298
xi. 29	457	xiii. 34 f.	384
xi. 29 ff.	384, 457	xiv. 7–10	385
xi. 33	249, 381, 457	xiv. 7–11	369
xi. 33–6	249, 384	xiv. 11	385, 403, 459, 460
xi. 34–6	412	xiv. 16–23	385
xi. 35	368	xiv. 21	227 n. 2
xi. 39	384	xiv. 25	457
xi. 42	384	xiv. 25 ff.	250
xi. 43	384	xiv. 26 f.	385
xi. 44	384	xiv. 26–33	385

Luke (*cont.*)	PAGE	Luke (*cont.*)	PAGE
xiv. 33	250	xxi. 17	329
xiv. 34	250, 328, 385	xxi. 20	202 n. 1
xiv. 34 f.	381, 457	xxi. 20–4	470
xiv. 35	368, 385	xxi. 34	371, 373, 376
xv. 3–7	392, 400	xxi. 34–6	371
xvi. 1	369	xxi. 36	376
xvi. 1 f.	385	xxi. 38	470
xvi. 8	372, 373	xxii. 2	470
xvi. 13	385	xxii. 8	337
xvi. 16–17	385	xxii. 24–32	337
xvi. 16–18	385	xxii. 28	376, 421
xvi. 17	385	xxii. 28–30	385
xvi. 18	388	xxii. 29	475
xvi. 25	463	xxii. 43	299 n. 4
xvii. 3	392	xxiii. 1–5	470
xvii. 3 f.	400	xxiii. 5	470
xvii. 3–4	385	xxiii. 13–25	470
xvii. 4	392	xxiii. 27	299 n. 4, 470
xvii. 5–6	385	xxiv	474, 479
xvii. 7	376	xxiv. 27	360
xvii. 16	385	xxiv. 34	337
xvii. 23	385	xxiv. 43	371
xvii. 24	385	xxiv. 44 ff.	360, 361
xvii. 26–30	385	xxiv. 50 ff.	479
xvii. 33	463		
xvii. 34	385	John	
xvii. 35	385	i. 13	71 n. 3
xvii. 37	381, 385, 458	i. 17	95
xviii. 14	381, 385, 403, 459, 460	i. 22	189 n. 2
xviii. 17	392	i. 38	407 n. 3
xviii. 20	373	i. 49	407 n. 3
xviii. 22	395	ii. 23	409
xviii. 29–30	228	ii. 25	463
xix. 11–27	459	iii	409
xix. 12	385	iii. 2	71, 407 n. 2, 409
xix. 12–27	369	iii. 5	71 n. 3
xix. 13	385	iii. 5 f.	372
xix. 15–26	385	iii. 6	71 n. 3
xix. 26	381, 459	iii. 8	71, 71 n. 3
xix. 47–8	470	iii. 12	409
xx. 1 f.	470	iii. 27	409
xx. 16	329	iii. 31	409
xx. 19	470	iv. 19	409
xx. 27	373	iv. 21	471 n. 3
xx. 35	376	iv. 23 f.	373
xx. 45	470	iv. 41	410
xxi	376	v	409
xxi. 5–36	470	v. 10–18	283 n. 1
xxi. 8	201	v. 19	409
xxi. 15	378	v. 24	410

John (*cont.*)	PAGE	John (*cont.*)	PAGE
v. 44	463	xx. 16	407 n. 3
vi	189 n. 2	xx. 17	361
vi. 14	189 n. 2, 409	xx. 23	463
vi. 15	189 n. 2	xxi	411
vi. 25	407 n. 3		
vi. 30–4	116	Acts	
vi. 31	409	i. 1	70
vii	409	i. 2 f.	361 n. 1
vii. 14–24	408	i. 2 ff.	361
vii. 15	420 n. 5	i. 3	361
vii. 17	372	i. 4	470
vii. 28 f.	409	i. 6 ff.	360
vii. 41	409	i. 7	371, 376
viii. 29	409	i. 8	470
viii. 34	409	i. 9–12	472
viii. 47	409	i. 11 ff.	361
ix. 5	409	ii	470, 474
ix. 17	409	ii. 5	470 n. 3
x. 18	411	ii. 15	311 n. 2
x. 26	409	ii. 22 ff.	474 n. 4
x. 32	409	ii. 32–6	361
x. 36	463	iii. 2	189 n. 2
xi. 45	409	iii. 12	474 n. 4
xii. 23	408	iii. 13–21	361
xii. 24 f.	408, 409	iv. 2	474 n. 4
xii. 25	463	iv. 8	476 n. 5
xii. 37	409	iv. 8 ff.	474 n. 4
xii. 44 f.	98	iv. 18	474 n. 4
xii. 47 f.	463	v. 13–16	470
xiii	411, 423, 455	v. 21	474 n. 4
xiii. 1 ff.	407	v. 25	474 n. 4
xiii. 1–17	407 n. 4	v. 28	474 n. 4
xiii. 13	408 n. 4	v. 29 ff.	474 n. 4
xiii. 14	408 n. 4	v. 36 ff.	201
xiii. 16	463	v. 41	376
xiii. 20	98, 463	v. 42	474 n. 4
xiii. 34	463	vi. 5	476 n. 5
xiv. 10	409	vii. 37	189 n. 2
xiv. 15	411	vii. 44	359
xiv. 18 f.	463	viii. 14	474 n. 4
xiv. 21–4	463	viii. 29	476 n. 5
xiv. 24	410	ix. 5	362
xiv. 26	361	ix. 13	362
xv. 10	410	ix. 17	362
xv. 20	411	ix. 27	362
xv. 23	463	x. 1 ff.	476
xvii. 1	361 n. 3	x. 9	311 n. 2
xvii. 8	410	x. 34 ff.	474 n. 4
xvii. 14	410	x. 40 f.	361
xviii. 23 ff.	463	xi. 1	359

Acts (*cont.*)	PAGE	Romans (*cont.*)	PAGE
xi. 22	474 n. 4	xii. 1	373
xii. 17	318 n. 3	xii. 1–20	373
xiii. 5	331 n. 3	xii. 2	370, 373
xiii. 9	476 n. 5	xii. 3–8	374, 398
xiii. 14	331 n. 3	xii. 9	370
xiii. 30 f.	361	xii. 13	367
xiv. 1	331 n. 3	xii. 17	370
xiv. 4	472	xii. 18	397
xiv. 14	472	xii. 19	370
xiv. 22	376	xiii. 1	374
xv	472, 475, 476	xiii. 1–7	374
xv. 29	370	xiii. 7	374
xvi. 1	456	xiii. 7–10	373
xvi. 6 f.	476 n. 5	xiii. 8–10	374
xvii. 1	331 n. 3	xiii. 9	370, 402
xvii. 15	456	xiii. 11	376
xvii. 17	331 n. 3	xiii. 11–14	371
xviii. 4	331 n. 3	xiii. 12	373
xviii. 24 ff.	331 n. 3	xiii. 12–13	345
xx. 28	371, 376	xiii. 13	370
xx. 39	323 n. 2	xiii. 13–14	376
xxi. 20	206 n. 1	xiii. 14	373
xxii. 8	362	xiv. 21	338
xxii. 19	362	xv. 19	357
xxvi. 15	362	xvi. 7	472
xxvi. 18	371	xvi. 15	371
xxvii. 9 ff.	89		
		1 Corinthians	
Romans		i. 7–9	376
i	344	ii. 2	346
i. 1	346	ii. 12–16	347
i. 17	218 n. 1	iii. 13	376
ii. 5–11	376	iii. 16	471 n. 2
iv. 7	206 n. 1	iii. 16 f.	370, 373
iv. 10 ff.	73	iv. 5	370
v. 2	376	iv. 17	456
v. 3–4	376	v. 1 ff.	224
v. 6 ff.	407	v. 1–13	225 n. 1
vi	342 n. 1	v. 7	344, 350
vi. 1–11	350 n. 2	v. 9 f.	370
vi. 2 ff.	345, 350	vi. 9 f.	370
vi. 4	346	vi. 15	344
vi. 4–7	372	vi. 15 f.	344
vi. 15 ff.	364	vii	374, 404, 455
vi. 17	364, 365 n. 1, 372	vii. 6	359 n. 2
vi. 19	206 n. 1	vii. 7	395
vii. 1–6	183 n. 1	vii. 10	355, 357, 358, 359
viii. 2	360, 405 n. 1	vii. 10 ff.	397
viii. 32	407	vii. 10–16	388
xii	397	vii. 12	355, 358, 359

1 Corinthians (*cont.*)   PAGE

vii. 12 ff. — 389
vii. 13 — 397, 398
vii. 16 — 398
vii. 25 — 353, 359
vii. 28 f. — 395
vii. 29 — 376
vii. 40 — 355
viii. 9–13 — 391
viii. 13 — 338
ix. 14 — 358, 359
ix. 20 — 287
ix. 21 — 353 n. 2, 357 n. 1
ix. 27 — 203
x — 357
x. 1 ff. — 350, 357
x. 8 — 350
x. 23–xi. 1 — 338
xi. 1 — 364 n. 4
xi. 2 ff. — 344
xi. 2 — 355
xi. 13 — 344
xi. 14 — 344, 355
xi. 20–34 — 350
xi. 23 — 346, 355, 358, 362
xi. 23 f. — 357
xi. 23–6 — 359
xi. 26 — 359, 362
xii. 3 — 359
xiii — 203, 407
xiv. 37 — 357 n. 1
xv. 1 — 355
xv. 1–11 — 355, 356
xv. 2 — 355
xv. 3 — 355
xv. 3 ff. — 354, 472
xv. 4 — 346
xv. 9 — 335, 336
xv. 20 — 350
xvi. 3 — 371, 376

2 Corinthians

iii. 1–18 — 351
v. 1 ff. — 351
v. 17 — 68 n. 1, 372
v. 17*b* — 114 n. 2
vi. 14 — 206 n. 1, 351
vi. 15 f. — 344
vi. 16 — 351
vi. 16 f. — 373
viii. 2 — 376

2 Corinthians (*cont.*)   PAGE

viii. 7 — 345
xi. 13 — 472
xi. 29 — 338
xii. 18 — 456

Galatians

i. 9 — 355
i. 11–12 — 355, 356
i. 12 — 355
i. 14 — 206 n. 1
i. 18 — 453
i. 18–ii. 10 — 472
i. 19 — 472
ii. 2 — 471 n. 5
ii. 11–14 — 454
ii. 21 — 342 n. 1
iii. 1 — 346
iii. 11 — 218 n. 1
iii. 16 ff. — 73
iii. 27 — 373
iv. 4 — 346
iv. 25 — 322
v. 1 — 345, 350
v. 13 ff. — 367
v. 14 — 370, 373, 402, 405 n. 1
v. 16 ff. — 349
v. 16–24 — 346
v. 18 — 347
v. 23 — 347, 405 n. 1
v. 25 — 345
vi. 1 f. — 225 n. 1
vi. 1 ff. — 367
vi. 2 — 353 n. 2, 353 n. 3, 357 n. 1, 405 n. 1
vi. 15 — 372

Ephesians

i. 13 — 372
i. 14 — 371, 376
ii. 15 — 372
iv. 1–4 — 374
iv. 7 f. — 374
iv. 11 f. — 374
iv. 17–19 — 370, 373
iv. 20 — 474 n. 4
iv. 22 — 373
iv. 22–4 — 372
iv. 24 — 373
iv. 25 — 373
iv. 26 — 373

Ephesians (*cont.*)	PAGE	Colossians (*cont.*)	PAGE
iv. 29	373	iii. 13	377
iv. 31	373	iii. 14	377, 402
iv. 32	373	iii. 14 f.	374
v. 1	407	iii. 16	372, 373
v. 5	370	iii. 17	373
v. 8	371	iii. 18	374, 375
v. 8–10	345	iii. 18–iv. 1	399
v. 17–20	373	iii. 19	375
v. 18	371	iii. 19–21	374
v. 22–33	374, 375	iii. 22–5	374
v. 22–vi. 9	399	iii. 22–iv. 1	375
v. 32	344	iv. 1	374
v. 33	344	iv. 2	371
vi. 1–9	374	iv. 2–3	376
vi. 5–9	375	iv. 3	371
vi. 14	371	iv. 5	371
vi. 14 ff.	376	iv. 12	376
vi. 18	371		
		1 Thessalonians	
Philippians		i. 5 f.	372
i. 27–9	376	i. 6	364 n. 4, 375
ii. 5	364 n. 4	i. 8	372
ii. 6	346	i. 9–10	398
ii. 10	373	ii. 4	375
ii. 11	373	ii. 6	472
ii. 15	371, 472	ii. 10 ff.	343
iv. 1	376	ii. 10–12	372
iv. 8	344	ii. 12	398
iv. 8–9	365	ii. 13	354, 355, 398
iv. 9	355	ii. 14	375
		iii. 2–5	375
Colossians		iii. 8	375
i. 5 f.	372	iv. 1 ff.	367
i. 12	351, 352	iv. 1–8	398
i. 13	351, 371	iv. 1–12	373
i. 13 f.	352	iv. 1–v. 15	370
ii. 6	355, 357	iv. 2	398
ii. 6–8	354, 355	iv. 3–9	398
ii. 8	355	iv. 7	344, 377
iii. 1–3	372	iv. 8	344
iii. 1–5	345	iv. 11	398
iii. 4	367	iv. 15	355, 358
iii. 5	373	v	377
iii. 5–7	370	v. 1 ff.	367
iii. 7–10	373	v. 1–3	375
iii. 8	372	v. 1–9	371
iii. 8–15	377	v. 2	398
iii. 10	372	v. 3–10	398
iii. 12	373, 374, 377	v. 4–11	375
		v. 5 ff.	345

1 Thessalonians (*cont.*)

	PAGE
v. 6–7	371
v. 8	373
v. 12 f.	374
v. 12–22	373, 398
v. 15	398
v. 16–18	373
v. 17	371
v. 17–19	375
v. 20	373

2 Thessalonians

i. 4–7	375
i. 10	375
ii. 15	355, 375, 398
iii. 6	355, 398
iii. 6–12	387 n. 2
iii. 7–10	398
iii. 10	398
iii. 12	398

1 Timothy

i. 4	208
i. 5	379
i. 15	377
ii. 1 ff.	378
ii. 1–3	374
ii. 1–15	374
ii. 6	378
ii. 8	374
ii. 8 ff.	378
ii. 8–iii. 13	399
ii. 9–15	375
ii. 13	377
iii. 16	226
iv. 1 ff.	378
v. 1–vi. 2	399
v. 17	374
v. 18	378
v. 21	226 n. 4
vi. 1 f.	374 f.
vi. 3	378
vi. 11–12	378
vi. 14	378

2 Timothy

ii. 14–26	378
ii. 24–6	379
iii. 8	80
iv. 11	456

2 Timothy (*cont.*)

	PAGE
iv. 17	378

Titus

i. 5–9	399
i. 15	379
ii. 2–10	399
ii. 4 f.	375
ii. 4–6	374
ii. 9 f.	374, 375
ii. 12	379
ii. 14	206 n. 1
iii. 1	374
iii. 1–3	374
iii. 5	372
iii. 8	374, 377

Hebrews

i. 9	206 n. 1
vi. 4	371
vii. 11–14	257 n. 2
vii. 12	353 n. 3
x. 17	206 n. 1
x. 23	376
x. 30	373, 376
x. 32–3	376
xi. 38	218 n. 1
xii	84
xii. 1	373, 433
xii. 9	374
xii. 18 ff.	85, 93
xiii. 7	374
xiii. 15–16	373
xiii. 17	374

James

i. 2	402
i. 2–3	376
i. 4	403
i. 5	403
i. 6	403
i. 12	376
i. 18	372
i. 20	403
i. 21	372, 373, 405 n. 1
i. 22	403
i. 25	353 n. 3, 405
i. 27	373, 405 n. 1
ii. 5	403
ii. 8	370, 373, 403, 405
ii. 11	403

James (*cont.*)	PAGE	1 Peter (*cont.*)	PAGE
ii. 13	403	ii. 11 f.	370
ii. 14 ff.	218 n. 1	ii. 12	371, 375, 377
ii. 15	403	ii. 13	374
iii. 12	403	ii. 13–17	374
iii. 13	370	ii. 13–18	399
iii. 18	403	ii. 16	373
iv. 2 ff.	403	ii. 18–25	374, 375
iv. 3	403	ii. 19	375
iv. 6	374	ii. 20	377
iv. 6–10	374	ii. 20–1	375
iv. 7	374, 376	ii. 24	375
iv. 9	403	iii. 1–7	375, 399
iv. 10	374, 403	iii. 1–8	374
iv. 11 f.	403	iii. 8 f.	373
v. 1	403	iii. 9 f.	377
v. 2	403	iii. 10–12	370
v. 6	403	iii. 11	377
v. 7 f.	373	iii. 11 f.	373
v. 8	371, 376	iii. 14–15	375
v. 9	403	iii. 15	377
v. 10	402	iii. 19	377
v. 12	240, 402, 404	iv. 1	373
		iv. 1–3	371
1 Peter		iv. 2	370
i. 1	371	iv. 3	375, 377
i. 2	370	iv. 5	375
i. 3	372	iv. 7	371, 375
i. 3–iv. 11	378	iv. 8	381
i. 6–7	375	iv. 8–11	373, 374
i. 10–11	375	iv. 12–13	375
i. 11	373	iv. 13	373
i. 12	374	iv. 14	373
i. 13	371, 375	iv. 17–19	376
i. 13–16	370	v. 1	374
i. 14	371, 372, 373	v. 2	374
i. 15 ff.	377	v. 4	376
i. 17	373	v. 5	374
i. 21	375	v. 5 f.	374
i. 22	370, 372	v. 8–10	376
i. 23	372	v. 12	376
i. 25	372	v. 19	377
ii. 1	372, 373	v. 20	377
ii. 2	372, 373		
ii. 3	373	2 Peter	
ii. 4	373	iii. 10	376
ii. 4–5	375		
ii. 8	371	1 John	
ii. 8–9	375	i. 5–6	412
ii. 9	351, 371, 373	ii. 9–11	412
ii. 10	351	ii. 15	373

1 John (*cont.*)   PAGE

   ii. 17   412
   iii. 1–3   412
   iii. 4   206 n. 1
   iii. 13   412
   iii. 15   412
   iii. 16   412
   iii. 17   412
   iii. 22   412
   iv. 7   412
   iv. 7–12   406
   iv. 11   412
   iv. 19   412

1 John (*cont.*)   PAGE

   iv. 19–21   411
   iv. 20   412
   iv. 21   405, 406, 411, 412

Revelation
   iii. 2   371
   vi. 10   247
   xii. 10   452
   xiii. 18   74, 75
   xvi. 15   376
   xxi. 5   114 n. 1

D. The Targums

On Deut.
   xxi. 18 ff.   287 n. 5

On Song of Songs
   v. 10   175

On Is.
   xii. 1–3   173

E. The Dead Sea Scrolls

IQS or DSD   12, 115, 213 n. 2

   i. 1   147 n. 2
   i. 7 f.   247 n. 3
   i. 7 ff.   245
   i. 9   211
   i. 10 f.   247 n. 3, 248
   i. 11–12   211
   i. 13   211
   i. 14   262 n. 2
   i. 16 ff.–ii. 18   60 n. 4
   i. 24 f.   247 n. 3
   ii. 5–9   246
   iii. 13–iv. 26   342 n. 4
   iii. 17 f.   231
   iii. 17 ff.   232
   iii. 18   232
   iv. 2 ff.   207 n. 5
   iv. 3   251
   iv. 9–11   342 n. 4
   iv. 12   246
   iv. 17   232
   iv. 17–19   231
   iv. 18–26   149 f., 155
   iv. 24–6   231
   iv. 25   232
   iv. 26   232
   v. 2   211

IQS or DSD (*cont.*)

   v. 8   147 n. 2, 242
   v. 10   242
   v. 10–14   246
   v. 24   211
   v. 25–vi. 1   221 f.
   vi. 24   238
   vi. 24 ff.   237
   vi. 24–vii. 25   223
   vi. 27   242
   vii. 1   242
   vii. 3   238
   vii. 4   238
   vii. 5   238
   vii. 9   238
   vii. 14   238
   vii. 16 ff.   239
   viii. 1   211
   viii. 1 ff.   229
   viii. 4–8   229
   viii. 9   211, 229
   viii. 10   229
   viii. 10*b*   211
   viii. 12–16   115 n. 1
   viii. 13–14   147
   viii. 13–15   209 n. 1
   viii. 14   31

IQS or DSD (*cont.*)	PAGE	IQH	PAGE
viii. 23	223	v. 4	246
viii. 26	211, 223	vii. 8–9	230
ix. 2	211		
ix. 4	239	IQM	
ix. 5	211	iii. 7	246
ix. 6	211	iv. 1 f.	246
ix. 8	211	xiv. 7	251
ix. 9	211	xv. 6	246
ix. 9–11	147 f., 151 f., 154		
ix. 15 f.	246		
ix. 19	211	IQp Hab and IQp H	
ix. 21 f.	246	ii. 2–3	153, 217 n. 1
ix. 21 ff.	248, 396 n. 1	vi. 12	247 n. 3
x. 1–9	262 n. 2	vii. 4–5	235, 217 n. 1
x. 18	248	viii. 1–3	153, 217
x. 19	248		
x. 21	211	IQSa	149 n. 2
x. 22 ff.	239	i. 25–ii. 10	227
x. 24	239	ii. 8–9	227
xi. 4	230	ii. 11–22	151 f.
xi. 8 f.	226 f.	xi. 8	227
4 Q Flor.	151		
		IQSb	151, 227
4 Qp ISa Testimonia		iv. 25–6	227
x. 22–xi. 4	151, 154		

F. Rabbinical Sources

(Tractates are alphabetically arranged. The names of individual Rabbis
appear in Index IV)

(1) *The Mishnah*		Aboth (*cont.*)	
Abodah Zarah		iii. 13	248
i. 8	327 n. 3	iii. 15	285 n. 3
Aboth		iii. 19	74 n. 4, 75
i. 1	303, 305, 306, 356, 421 n. 4	iv. 15	406 n. 1
i. 2	305	Arakhin	240
i. 6	396 n. 2		
i. 7	304	Baba Kamma	
i. 8–16	268 n. 1	vii. 7	327 n. 3
ii. 8	174	Baba Metzia	
ii. 8	420 n. 2	i. 8	159
ii. 14	259 n. 1	iii. 4	159
iii. 3	225	iii. 5	159
iii. 6	285 n. 3	Berakoth	
iii. 11	450	iv. 2	313 n. 1
iii. 12	450	iv. 3	311 n. 2, 312 f.

	PAGE		PAGE
Berakoth (*cont.*)		Peah	
ix. 5	452	viii. 7 ff.	308
		Pesahim	
Demai		x. 5	351
vi. 11	327 n. 3		
		Rosh ha-Shanah	
Eduyoth		i. 4	294, 327 n. 3
i. 4	266	i. 6	294 n. 5
i. 5	266	ii. 8–9	269
iv. 8	265	iv. 1	261
v. 6	236	iv. 4	262
vii. 2	267		
vii. 7	295, 327 n. 3		
viii. 7	159, 160 172	Sanhedrin	
Erubin		iii. 4	267
ii. 6	396 n. 2	x. 1	259, 273
		Shabbath	
Gittin		xviii. 3	104
vi. 5	267	Shebiith	
		vi. 1–6	327 n. 3
Hallah		Shekalim	
iv. 7	327 n. 3	ii. 5	159
iv. 11	327 n. 3	Sotah	
Horayoth		ix. 12	145
i. 3	401 n. 2	ix. 15	204 n. 1
Kelim	267		
Ketuboth		Taanith	
v. 3	267	viii. 1	159
v. 6	267	Tamid	267
		Tebul Yom	
Maaseroth		iv. 5	267
v. 5	327 n. 3		
Maaser Sheni		Uktzin	
v. 2	263	iii. 12	75, 267
Makkoth			
iii. 16	285 n. 3		
Middoth	267	Yadaim	
		iv. 6	272
Nazir		Yebamoth	
vi. 1	267	iv. 13	68 n. 2, 287 n. 5
Nedarim	240	xii. 1 ff.	265 n. 1
ix. 6	267	xvi. 7	396 n. 2
xi. 12	267	Yoma	
Niddah		i. 6	73 n. 1
x. 6	267	viii. 6	104, 267
Oholoth			
xviii. 7	327 n. 3	Zebahim	
Orlah		i. 3	292 n. 2
iii. 9	327 n. 3		

(2) *The Babylonian Talmud*   PAGE

Abodah Zarah

9 *a*	180
16 *b*	42 n. 2, 277 n. 1
17 *a*	277 n. 1
27 *b*	288
36 *a*	264 n. 2, 394 n. 1
36 *b*	264 n. 2

Baba Bathra

60 *b*	260, 284 n. 2, 313, 394 n. 1

Baba Kamma

79 *b*	394 n. 1
82 *a*	267

Baba Metzia

59 *a*	284 n. 3
59 *b*	269

Bekhoroth

36 *a*	263 n. 1, 269

Berakoth

11 *a*	264
11 *b*	402 n.
12 *a*	281
27 *b*	269
28 *a*	269
28 *b*	270
29 *a*	269, 312
34 *b*	450, 451
35 *b*	159
47 *b*	456
62 *b*	452
63 *a*	452

Erubin

13 *b*	265

Gittin

40	455
42 *b*	159
45 *b*	274

Hagigah

6 *a*	401 n. 2
25 *a*	159

Horayoth

3 *b*	394 n. 1

Hullin

49 *a*	263 n. 1

Ketuboth

63 *a*	455

Ketuboth (*cont.*)   PAGE

96 *a*	455

Kiddushin

33 *b*	285 n. 3
	396 n. 2

Makkoth

24 *b*	260

Megillah

31 *b*	267

Menahoth

43 *b*	286 n.
45 *a*	159

Nedarim

22 *a*	240
28 *a*	241
41 *a*	267

Niddah

61 *b*	170, 181

Pesahim

13 *a*	159
70 *a*	159
112 *a*	414 n. 1, 421 n. 4

Rosh ha-Shanah

5 *a*	269
21 *b*	262
29 *b*	261, 294
31 *b*	262

Sanhedrin

32 *b*	292 n. 2
42 *a*	179 n. 1
43 *a*	287 n. 1
51 *b*	169
86 *a*	267
97 *a*	178, 178 n., 180
100 *b*	271

Shabbath

17 *a*	264 n. 2
31 *a*	402
32 *b*	263 n. 2
63 *a*	182
104 *a*	186
108 *a*	159
116 *a*	274
116 *a–b*	42 n. 2
151 *b*	148 n. 2, 170, 181, 182

Sotah

11 *b*	81

Sotah (*cont.*)   PAGE
   12*a*   80 n. 3
   48*b*   146
Sukkah
   20*a*   108 n. 2

Taanith
   8. 1   159
   24*b*   450
   27*b*   283 n. 3
   27*b*   314

Yebamoth
   35*a*   159
   41*b*   159, 293 n. 2
   42*b*   453, 455
   47*a–b*   43 n. 1
   90*b*   402 n.
   102*a*   159
Yom Tob
   27*a*   454
Yoma
   9*b*   284 n. 3
   23*a*   257 n. 3
   74*b*   81

(3) *The Jerusalem Talmud* (ed. Krotoschin, 1866)
Abodah Zarah
   ii. 2. 40*d*   288
   ii. 2. 41*a*   288

Berakoth
   i. 1. 2*c*   159
   i. 8. 3*c*   281
   ii. 4. 5*a*   62 n. 5
Betzah
   iii. 6. 62*a*   292 n. 2

Hallah
   i. 1. 57*c*   263
Horayoth
   iii. 7. 48*a*   295 n. 5

Megillah
   i. 7. 70*d*   161 n. 2

Pesahim
   ii. 7. 29*c*   295 n. 1

Sanhedrin
   i. 2. 19*a*   271

Shabbath   PAGE
   xiv. 4. 14*d*   288
Shekalim
   viii. 4. 51*b*   263

Taanith
   ii. 1. 65*b*   308

(4) *Extra-Canonical Tractates*
Aboth de Rabbi Nathan (ed. Solomon Schechter, Wien, 1887)
   i. 1 ff.   302 n. 1, 304
   iv   284 n. 2, 455
   xxii   450

(5) *Mekilta* (ed. J. Z. Lauterbach, Philadelphia, 1933–5)
On Exodus
   xiv   41, 84
   xiv. 13   40, 441
   xiv. 14   40, 442
   xiv. 15   40
   xv   41
   xv. 1   442
   xv. 2   40, 42, 443
   xvi. 11–15   46 n. 4
   xvi. 16–27   29 n. 2
   xvi. 28–36   49 n. 2
   xvi. 33   28
   xxii. 30   286 n.

(6) *Tosefta* (ed. M. S. Zuckermandel, Pasewalk, 1880)
Hagigah
   ii. 1   455
Hullin
   ii. 22   287
   ii. 23   287
   ii. 24   42 n. 2
   xi. 24   277
Negaim
   vii. 12   455

Peah   308

Sanhedrin
   ii. 13   264 n. 2
   iv. 4 f.   168
   iv. 7   168
Shabbath
   xiii. 5   274

Sotah   PAGE
   xiii. 2   146
   xiv. 1   174 n. 1

Yadaim
   ii. 13   274

(7) *Midrash Rabbah* (Wilna, 1876)
Genesis Rabbah
   xxiv. 7   402 n.
   xxxix. 11   76
   xcv–xvi   164 n. 1
   xcviii. 8 on xlix. 10   179
   xcviii. 9 on xlix. 11   179

Exodus Rabbah
   i. 13 on i. 15   81
   i. 20 on ii. 2   80 n. 3
   i. 25 on ii. 25   81
   v. 5 on iv. 20   60
   xv. 26 on xii. 2   72 n. 2, 73, 76
   xxi. 5 on xiv. 15   41 n. 1
   xlvii. 5 f. on xxxiv. 28 f.   52 n. 1

Leviticus Rabbah
   i. 3 on i. 1   75 n. 3
   ix. 7 on vii. 11–12   161
   xiii. 3 on xi. 2   165, 173 n. 1
   xv. 1 on xiii. 2   56 n. 2

Numbers Rabbah
   ix. 16 on v. 18   75
   xviii. 3 on xvi. 1   75
   xix. 6 on xix. 2   171, 172
   xix. 8 on xix. 2   172

Deuteronomy Rabbah
   vii. 6 on xxx. 11, 12   185, 186

Ecclesiastes Rabbah (or Midrash
    Qoheleth)
   on i. 8   278
   on ii. 1   174
   on vii. 26   277
   on xi. 8   174

Midrash Proverbs   PAGE
   ix. 2   162

Song of Songs Rabbah
   ii. 29 on ii. 13   178

(8) *Sifra on Leviticus* (ed. J. H. Weiss
    and J. Schlossberg, Wien, 1872)
   86*a*   171 n. 1
   112*b*   454

(9) *Sifre on Numbers and Deuteronomy*
    (Wilna, 1866)
on Numbers
   xv. 14 § 108   27
on Deuteronomy
   i. 1*b* § 17   269 n. 1
   vi. 8 § 35   281 n. 2
   xi. 18 § 45   285 n. 3
   xvii. 18 § 160   167
   xviii. 15 § 165   402 n. 3

(10) *Midrash Tehillim*
   on xcvii. 11   446
   cxxxvii. 5   394 n. 1
   cxlvi. 7   163, 170, 177

(11) *Pesiḳta Rabbati* (ed. Salomon
    Buber, Wilna, 1885)
   75*a*   178 n. 1

(12) *Tanḥuma* (ed. Salomon Buber,
    Wilna, 1885)
Eqeb
   7*b*   56 n. 2 (cited by H. J. Schoeps,
                  but unverifiable)

(13) *Yalqut*
on Zech.
   ix. 9. 575   60
on Proverbs
   ix. 2   162
on Is.
   xxvi. 2   176

II. INDEX OF REFERENCES TO CLASSICAL AND HELLENISTIC AUTHORS AND EXTRA-CANONICAL CHRISTIAN WRITINGS

Aristophanes   PAGE 414 n. 1

Clement of Alexandria   419
  Excerpta ex Theodoto
    3, 1   196 n. 2
    3, 2   196 n. 2
I Clement
    5   340 n. 2
Clementine Recognitions XI, 1   468

Didache   12, 281
  ii. 3   245
  iv. 8   296 n. 2
  viii. 1   284, 313
  viii. 3   311 n. 2, 313 n. 1
  xv. 3   396 n. 2

Epistle of Barnabas
  IX   75
Eusebius
  Hist. Eccl.
    III, 39, 15   270 n. 3, 468 n. 1
    V, 20   468 n. 1
    CXI, 39   19 n. 1

Gospel According to the Hebrews   30
Gospel of the Ebionites   29–30
Greek Fragment on Matthew   14 n. 5

Hippolytus
  Refutations of All Heresies
    VII, 21   194 n. 2
  Treatise on the Apostolic Tradition
    V, 14   314
    V, 18–21   314
    XXXII, 12   378

Ignatius   79
Ignatius of Antioch
  Romans
    iv. 2   340 n. 2
Irenaeus   281
  Against Heresies   14 n. 5
    I, 2   201
    I, 6, 1   196 n. 2

Irenaeus (*cont.*)   PAGE
    I, 26, 1 f.   194 nn. 1, 2
    III, 3, 4   194 n. 2
    V, 21, 2   195 n. 2
    VI, 37, 2   196 n. 2
    XXIII   193 n.3
    CXI, I, 2   340 n. 2
    CXI, III, 2   340 n. 2

Jason of Cyrene   16 n. 2
Josephus   115
  Against Apion
    I, 8, 41   143 n. 1
  Antiquities
    II, ix, 2   80
    II, ix, 3 ff.   81
    II, ix, 5   82
    II, ix, 7   80
    III, 224–36   321 n. 1
    XX, V, 1   118
  The Jewish War
    II, viii, 2   246 n. 1
    II, viii, 6   241
    II, viii, 7   241
    II, ii   246 n. 5
Justin   66
  Apology
    I, xxxiii   66 n. 4
    XXXI   202
  Dialogue with Trypho   278 f., 282
    I, 51 ff.   186 n. 1
    XVI, 4   278
    XVII, 1–3   279
    XLIII, 7   282
    L, 3   31
    LXVIII, 1   282
    LXXI, 1 f.   282
    LXXXIV, 3   282
    CVIII, 2   279
    CXVII, 3   279
    CXXXVIII, 1   279

Origen   79
Papias   16 n. 8

Papias (*cont.*) PAGE
Expositions of the Dominical Oracles
  18 f., 23
Philo of Alexandria 72, 187 n. 1, 293
  n. 1, 364, 405
De Decalogo
  18 f. 401 n. 2
De Somniis
  II, 189 40 n. 1
De Specialibus Legibus
  I, I, I 401 n. 2
De Virtutibus
  LI 40 n. 1
De Vita Mosis
  I 118 n. 4
  II, 3, 14–16 158 n. 2
  II, 6 40 n. 1
  II, 188–245 40 n. 1

Philo of Alexandria (*cont.*) PAGE
  II, 91 40 n. 1
Quod Omnis Probus Liber Sit
  83 246 n. 2
  89–91 246 n. 4
Plato
Phaedrus
  274 C–275 A 416 n. 1
Pliny 281
Naturalis Historia
  V, XV, 73 246 n. 3
Tertullian 79
On Baptism
  IX 45 n. 2
On Idolatry
  IX 66 n. 5

III. INDEX OF AUTHORS

Abel, F. M., 143 n. 1, 144 n. 1
Abrahams, I., 110, 147 n. 1
Abravanel, I., 164 n. 1
Albeck, C., 164 n. 1, 266 n. 2
Albertz, D. M., 101, 368
Allegro, J. M., 151
Allen, W. C., 14 n. 3, 22 n. 2, 62, 65 n. 3, 69 n. 4, 87, 160
Altmann, A., 193 n. 5
Anderson, G. H., 333 n. 1
Aptowitzer, V., 110, 158 n. 3, 161 n. 2, 165 n. 1, 179 n. 1, 283 n. 3
Archambault, G., 186 n. 1, 278 n. 2
Arndt, W., 55 n. 2
Audet, J. P., 245 n. 1, 284 n. 1, 396 n. 2

Bächer, W., 74 nn. 3, 4, 260 n. 1, 272 n. 1
Bacon, B. W., 14–24, 25 n. 3, 64 n. 2, 65 n. 2, 87 f., 93, 104 n. 2, 107, 193 f., 199 n. 1, 300 n. 2, 307 n. 1, 328 n. 1, 331 n. 1, 338 f., 390 n. 1, 397 n. 1
Baeck, Leo, 110, 148 n. 2, 180 f., 183 n. 1, 440 n. 1
Baer, F., 446
Bammel, E., 251 n. 3
Baltensweiler, H., 56 n. 1
Baron, S. W., 187 n. 1, 259 n. 1, 270 n. 2; 272 n. 3, 451

Barrett, C. K., 13 n. 1, 37 n. 1, 45 n. 3, 66 n. 1, 71 n. 2, 473 n. 3, 474 n. 4, 475 n. 3
Barth, G., 212 n. 1, 214 n. 1, 219 n. 1, 290 n. 3
Barth, K., 333 n. 1
Barthélemy, D., 120 n. 1, 167, 183 n. 1, 227
Bartlet, J. V., 476
Bate, H. N., 325 n. 2
Bauer, W., 451
Beare, F. W., 365
Begrich, J., 134, 135 n. 5
Behm, J., 17, 197 nn. 1, 2
Bellinzoni, A. J., 404 nn. 2, 4
Benoit, P., 16, 203, 207 n. 5, 445
Bentzen, A., 114 n. 2, 117, 120 n. 2, 121 n. 1, 123 n. 3, 126 n. 3, 132, 135 n. 5, 445
Bergman, J., 258 n. 4, 259 n. 1, 285 nn. 2, 3
Berman, H. J., 438 nn. 1–6
Bertholet, A., 134
Bevan, Edwyn, 193 n. 1
Bewer, J. A., 123 n. 2
Bickerman, E. J., 302 n. 2, 466 n. 2
Binns, L. E., 123 n. 2, 451
Black, M., 115 n. 1, 132, 153 n. 3, 154 n. 1, 254 n. 2, 417 n. 2, 451

Blair, E. P., 25 n. 1, 254 n. 1, 290 n. 3, 291 n. 1, 332 n. 2
Blank, S. H., 129 n. 1
Blau, L., 270 n. 5, 283 n. 1
Bloch, J., 73 n. 1, 140 n. 1
Bloch, R., 80 nn. 2, 3, 82 n. 3, 92 n. 1, 116, 118 nn. 3, 4
Bokser, B. Z., 259 n. 1, 295 nn. 1, 4, 5
Bonnard, P., 56 n. 2
Bonsirven, J., 110, 158 n. 1, 162 n. 1, 167 ff., 183, 186 f., 388 n. 2, 393 n. 2, 455
Bornhäuser, K., 72 n. 2, 236
Bornkamm, G., 13 n. 1, 44 n. 1, 95 n. 3, 96 n. 1, 106 n. 1, 212 n. 1, 214 n. 1, 290 n. 3, 332 n. 2, 396 n. 3, 418 n. 1, 439 n. 1, 464 n. 2
Box, G. H., 64 n. 2, 65, 66 n. 2, 72 n. 2, 75 n. 3, 444
Bowman, J. W., 448
Brandon, S. G. F., 317–20, 321 n. 1, 322–6, 332 f., 336
Branscomb, B. H., 14 n. 1
Braude, W. G., 163
Braun, H., 213 n. 2, 428 n. 1, 431 n. 1
Briggs, C. A., 127
Bright, J., 114 n. 2
Brownlee, W. H., 27 n. 2, 56 n. 2, 150 n. 2, 153 nn. 2, 3, 208, 226, 231 f., 237 ff.
Buber, M., 71 n. 3, 164 n. 1, 219
Büchler, A., 260 n. 1, 261 n. 1, 263 n. 1, 292 n. 2, 294 n. 1, 307 n. 2
Buck, H. M., Jr., 21 n. 2
Bultmann, R., 4, 5, 18, 21, 63, 65 n. 8, 88, 189 n. 2, 221, 229, 235, 334 n. 3, 342 n. 3, 343 n. 1, 346 n. 1, 368, 381, 390 n. 1, 434 n. 2, 444, 449, 453, 460, 464 n. 2
Burkitt, F. C., 65, 77, 139 n. 5, 192, 201 n. 3
Burney, C. F., 312 n. 1, 445
Burrows, E., 55 n. 1, 135 n. 5
Burrows, M., 115, 147, 149, 151, 211, 229, 230, 238, 242
Bussmann, W., 21 f.

Cadbury, H. J., 226 n. 3, 361 n. 1
Caird, G. B., 363 n. 4
Campbell, J. Y., 140
Carrington, P., 4 n. 2, 21, 45 n. 4, 195 n. 1, 370, 380 n. 1, 453

Casey, R. P., 192
Cerfaux, L., 207 n. 2, 214 nn. 5, 6, 353 n. 5, 362, 363 n. 2, 416 n. 1
Chadwick, H., 320 n. 1, 321 n. 1, 340 n. 1, 395 n. 2
Charles, R. H., 16, 139, 142, 182 n. 1
Chavasse, C., 117 n. 2, 349 n. 2
Chevalier, M.-A., 47 n. 2
Cheyne, T. K., 133, 137 f.
Clark, K. W., 260 n. 1, 290 n. 2, 321 n. 1, 325, 332
Clarke, K. W. L., 280 n. 3, 283 n. 1
Cobb, W. F., 127
Cohen, Boaz, 401 n. 2, 406 n. 1, 462, 463
Cohon, S. S., 9 n. 1
Colpe, C., 192 n. 4, 207 n. 1
Condamin, A., 123 n. 2, 131 n. 4
Conzelmann, H., 13 n. 1
Cook, S. A., 89 n. 2
Cornill, C. H., 123 n. 2
Couchoud, P. L., 100 n. 1
Craig, C. T., 133 n. 2
Cranfield, C. E. B., 39 n. 3, 44 n. 1, 45 n. 4, 70 n. 1, 105 n. 2, 462
Creed, J. M., 288 n. 3, 371, 382 n. 3
Cross, F. L., 349 n. 2, 378 n. 1
Cross, F. M., 148 n. 3
Cullmann, O., 43 n. 1, 47 n. 3, 254 nn. 1, 2, 338 nn. 1, 2, 339 nn. 2, 3, 353 n. 5, 357–62, 366 n. 1, 479
Curtis, W. A., 434 n. 1

Dabeck, P., 50 n. 1, 56 n. 2, 60 n. 3, 349 n. 2
Dahl, N. A., 344 n. 2, 417 n. 4
Dalman, G. F., 184
Danby, H., 16 n. 2, 74 n. 4, 145, 156 n. 3, 160, 172 n. 1, 259 n. 1, 265 n. 1, 266 n. 2, 267 f., 273, 312
Dancy, J. C., 143 n. 1, 144 n. 1
Daniélou, J., 41 n. 1, 45 nn. 1, 2, 48 n. 1, 50 n. 1, 56 n. 2, 193 n. 5, 255 n. 1, 324, 325 n. 1, 333 n. 2, 349 n. 2, 353 n. 3, 364 n. 6
Daube, D., 4 n. 2, 43 n. 1, 48 n. 1, 55, 63, 81, 82 n. 3, 101–3, 104 n. 1, 105, 107 f., 157, 163 n. 1, 174, 198, 220, 245, 272 n. 1, 299 n. 1, 301, 330 n. 3, 333 n. 2, 344 n. 2, 350 n. 2, 351 n. 1, 359 n. 2, 370 n. 5, 396 n. 3, 401 n. 1, 407 n. 4, 420 nn. 4, 6, 456, 462, 478 n. 4, 480 n. 1

Davey, F. N., 95 n. 1, 349 n. 2
Davies, W. D., 4 n. 2, 21 n. 3, 73 n. 1,
    103 nn. 2, 3, 150 n. 1, 299 n. 1, 326
    n. 2, 334 n. 1, 342 n. 4, 344 n. 2, 349
    n. 2, 396 n. 3
Davis, S., 157 n. 1
d'Aygalliers, A. W., 439 n. 2
de Boer, P. A. H., 132 n. 7
de Daroca, J. A., 447
Descamps, A., 252 n. 2
de Vries, B., 266 n. 2
Dibelius, M., 34 n. 2, 323 n. 2, 367 ff.,
    379 n. 2, 380, 382, 403 n. 1, 404, 405
    nn. 1, 2
Dix, G., 58 n. 2, 318 n. 4, 324, 325 n. 1
Dodd, C. H., 7 n. 2, 14 n. 2, 32 n. 2, 33
    n. 3, 71 n. 3, 98 n. 1, 138 n. 1, 218 n. 1,
    219 n. 4, 225 n. 1, 288, 292 n. 1, 316
    n. 1, 326 n. 1, 330 n. 4, 349 n. 1, 353
    nn. 2, 4, 357 n. 1, 359 n. 3, 364 n. 1,
    387 nn. 1, 3; 398, 399 n. 1, 406 n. 2,
    410 n. 1, 411 n. 1, 413 n. 1, 448, 460 f.,
    463, 465 n. 1
Döderlein, J. C., 131 n. 4
Drazin, N., 420 n. 3
Driver, S. R., 123 n. 2, 129 n. 1, 137
Dugmore, C. W., 260 n. 1, 275 n. 1, 280
    nn. 4, 5, 283 n. 1, 310 n. 2
Duhm, B., 122 f., 126 n. 3, 131 nn. 1, 4,
    133, 135, 137 f.
Dunn, Bogard van, 39
Dupont, J., 101 n. 1, 192 n. 4, 197 n. 1,
    213 n. 5, 251 n. 2, 289 n. 1, 290 n. 1,
    355 n. 1, 395 n. 1, 405 n. 3
Dupont-Sommer, A., 417 n. 2

Easton, B. S., 379 n. 2
Edelkoort, A. H., 131 n. 4
Edersheim, A., 42 n. 2, 109, 166, 180 n. 1,
    184
Ehrle, Card., 446
Eissfeldt, O., 123 n. 3, 271 n. 1
Elbogen, I., 108 n. 2, 270 n. 4, 276 n. 2,
    280 n. 5, 310 n. 2, 313 n. 1
Eliot, T. S., 191
Elliger, K., 233 n. 2
Ellul, J., 439 n. 2
Elmslie, W. A. L., 394 n. 1
Eltester, W., 327 n. 2
Emmet, D. M., 108 n. 2
Engnell, I., 117, 132, 135 n. 5

Epstein, I., 285 n. 3
Etheridge, J. W., 80 n. 1
Ettisch, E., 262 n. 2
Evans, C. F., 349 n. 2

Farrer, A. M., 9–13, 25 n. 1, 58 n. 2, 341
    n. 1, 349 n. 2
Fascher, E., 422 n. 1
Feine, P.–Behm, J., 17 n. 2
Feldmann, F., 131 n. 4
Feuillet, A., 16, 50 n. 1, 54 n. 1, 207 n. 2,
    214 n. 5, 299
Fiebig, P., 309 n. 1, 313 n. 1
Field, F., 67 n. 2, 79 n. 2
Filson, F. V., 25 n. 2, 201 n. 1, 207 n. 4,
    298 n. 3, 390 n. 1
Finkelstein, L., 164 n. 1, 257 n. 1, 258
    n. 1, 267 f., 283 n. 1, 292 n. 3, 294 n. 3,
    295 n. 1, 301–4, 421 n. 6, 426 n. 3, 450
Fischer, J., 131 n. 4
Fitzmyer, J. A., 208 n. 5, 226 n. 3
Flemington, W. F., 34 n. 3, 35 n. 2, 36
    n. 2, 39 n. 1
Flew, R. N., 209 n. 3, 326 n. 1
Flusser, D., 149 n. 2
Frame, J. E., 206 n. 1
Freedman, D. N., 95 n. 2, 196 n. 2
Freedman, H., 181
Fridrichsen, A. J., 349 n. 2
Friedländer, M., 286 n. 1
Friedmann, M., 178 n. 1
Friedrich, G., 7 n. 2, 161 n. 1
Füllkrug, G., 131 n. 4
Funk, R. W., 56 n. 2

Galling, K., 119
Gärtner, B., 196 n. 2, 208 n. 5
Gaster, T. H., 26 n. 2, 31, 115 n. 1, 148
    n. 1
Geiselmann, J. R., 366 n. 2
Gelin, A., 79 n. 1, 117 n. 1, 119 n. 2
Gemser, B., 172 n. 2
Gerhardsson, B., 137, 416 n. 1, 424 n. 1,
    457
Gesenius–Kautzsch, 177
Gfrörer, A. F., 74, 77
Giblet, J., 26 n. 1, 115 n. 2, 116, 118 n. 3,
    140 n. 1, 142, 143 n. 1, 144 n. 2, 160
    n. 2
Giesebrecht, F., 123 n. 2
Gils, F., 7 n. 2, 214 n. 6, 252 n. 2

Gingrich, F. W., 55 n. 2
Ginzberg, J., 154 n. 4
Ginzberg, L., 29 n. 2, 52 n. 1, 159 f., 177 n. 2, 182 n. 3, 189, 272 n. 2
Glatzer, N. N., 200 n. 1, 264 n. 1
Godet, F., 16, 18
Goguel, M., 62 n. 3, 335, 336 n. 1, 343 n. 1, 348, 439 n. 2
Goldin, J., 271, 284 n. 2, 294 nn. 3, 4, 295 n. 1, 305 f., 308 n. 3
Goldstein, M., 276 n. 1, 277 n. 1, 288 n. 1
Goodenough, E. R., 157, 293 n. 1
Goodspeed, E. J., 41 n. 2, 323 f.
Goppelt, L., 324, 333 n. 2, 349 n. 2
Gore, C., 27 n. 1
Goudge, H. L., 27 n. 1
Graetz, H., 202, 258 n. 2, 264 nn. 1, 2, 277 n. 3, 295 n. 1
Grant, F. C., 202 n. 1, 221 n. 1
Grant, R. M., 95 n. 2, 196 n. 2, 201 n. 3, 282 n. 1
Gray, G. B., 123 n. 2, 137 f., 359 n. 1
Green, A. A., 270 n. 1
Green, F. W., 16
Greeven, H., 403 n. 1
Gressmann, H., 114 n. 2, 131 n. 4
Grossouw, W., 150 n. 1
Grundmann, W., 150 n. 1, 207 n. 2, 214 n. 5
Guignebert A., 74
Guillaume, A., 27 n. 1
Guillet, J., 47 n. 2, 349 n. 2
Gunkel, H., 89 n. 2
Guttmann, A., 41 n. 2, 166 n. 1, 168 n. 1, 169 n. 1, 175, 266 n. 1, 285 n. 1

Haenchen, E., 106 n. 2, 291 n. 1, 232 n. 2
Haering, B., 429 n. 2
Hanson, R. P. C., 468 n. 3
Hare, D. R. A., 297 n. 3
Harnack, A., 367, 370
Harris, J. R., 14 n. 5
Harrisville, R. A., 189 n. 2
Hauck, F., 250, 403 n. 1, 404 n. 4
Hauter, C., 439 n. 2
Hawkins, J. C., 15–18, 20, 21 n. 4, 97 n. 1, 371
Heaton, E. W., 121 n. 2
Heiler, F., 453
Held, H. J., 212 n. 1, 214 n. 1
Helfgott, B. W., 285 n. 2

Hemmer, H., 321 n. 1
Hendry, G. S., 346 n. 1
Hepburn, R., 349 n. 1
Herford, R. T., 42 n. 2
Herntrich, V., 135 n. 1
Hertz, H. J., 285 n. 3
Higgings, A. J. B., 353 n. 5, 454
Hirsch, E., 325 n. 2, 339 n. 1
Hjerl-Hansen, B., 58 n. 1, 202 n. 2
Hoenig, S. B., 261 n. 1, 262 n. 1
Hoffmann, D., 266 n. 2
Holl, K., 253
Hölscher, G., 123 n. 3
Holtzmann, H. J., 85 n. 1
Holtzmann, O., 275 n. 1, 280 n. 6, 313 n. 1
Hooke, S. H., 37 n. 3, 55 n. 1
Hooker, M. D., 131
Hort, F. J. A., 69 n. 4
Hoskyns, E. C., 95 n. 1, 349 n. 2
Howard, W. F., 417 n. 3
Hüber, H. H., 236 f., 239
Hulme, K. C., 455
Hunter, A. M., 323 n. 1
Hunzinger, C. H., 224 n. 1, 277 n. 2, 297 n. 2

Israelstam, J. 162, 166 f., 173, 177, 308 n. 1

Jackson, F. J. F., 361 n. 1
Jaeger, W., 414 n. 1
Jalland, T. G., 325 n. 2
James, M. R., 29 n. 1, 30, 142 n. 2
Jastrow, M., 162 n. 1, 174, 197 n. 3, 259 n. 1
Jellicoe, S., 58 n. 2
Jellinek, A., 165 n. 1
Jeremias, J., 5 n. 1, 43 n. 1, 45 n. 4, 46 n. 4, 50 n. 1, 56 n. 2, 57 n. 2, 68 n. 2, 72 n. 2, 92 n. 1, 102 n. 2, 115 n. 1, 118, 131 n. 2, 132, 136, 153 n. 3, 160, 248 n. 2, 292 n. 2, 327, 329 f., 345 n. 1, 349 n. 2, 356 n. 1, 370, 397, 426 n. 1, 435 n. 2, 453, 457, 458
Jocz, J., 276 n. 1, 426 n. 2
Joest, W., 316 n. 1, 343 n. 1, 344 n. 1, 345 n. 1, 364 n. 1
Johnson, A. R., 37 n. 3, 38, 39 n. 1, 98 n. 2, 131, 132 n. 4, 449
Johnson, S. E., 150 n. 1, 217 n. 4
Johnston, G., 209 n. 3
Jonas, H., 192 n. 4, 193 nn. 2, 3

Jost, I. M., 269 n. 1
Jundt, A., 439 n. 2

Käseman, E., 431 n. 1
Kaufmann, W., 440 n. 1
Kayser, S. S., 293 n. 1
Kennedy, H. A. A., 146 f.
Kierkegaard, S., 434 n. 3, 437 n. 2
Kilpatrick, G. D., 2 n. 2, 16, 21, 69, 240, 297 nn. 1, 3, 335, 399 n. 2, 453, 454
Kirk, K. E., 58 n. 2
Kissane, E. J., 114 n. 2, 133 n. 4, 138 n. 3
Kistemaker, S., 208 n. 5
Kittel, G., 56 n. 2, 57 n. 1, 135 n. 1, 213 n. 3, 404, 408 n. 1
Klausner, J., 42 n. 2, 109 n. 1, 110, 121, 162 n. 5, 167 n. 3, 178 f., 181, 182 n. 1, 184 ff., 285 n. 3
Klein, G., 370
Klostermann, E., 18 n. 2, 21, 87 n. 3, 327 n. 3, 391
Knox, J., 386 n. 1, 464 n. 2
Knox, W. L., 2, 25 n. 3, 35, 298 n. 4, 403 n. 1
Kohler, K., 110
Konstantinovsky, B. A., 438 n. 1
Koster, H., 404 n. 2, 468 n. 3
Kraeling, C. H., 27 n. 2
Kuhn, K. G., 118 n. 1, 152, 275, 276 nn. 1, 2, 281 n. 1, 310 ff., 313 n. 1, 432 n. 2
Kümmel, W. G., 347
Kutscher, E. Y., 417 n. 2

Lagrange, M. J., 16 f., 62, 199 f., 236 n. 3, 327
Lake, K., 21 n. 1, 361 n. 1, 470 n. 2
Lake, S., 21 n. 1
Laue, L., 131 n. 4
Lauterbach, J. Z., 40 n. 3, 182 n. 3, 266 n. 2
Lawson, J., 437 n. 1
Lecerf, A., 439 n. 2
Leclercq, N., 321 n. 1
Légasse, S., 214 n. 5
Legg, S. C. E., 9 n. 3, 69
Leszynsky, R., 426 n. 2
Levertoff, P., 27, 28 n. 1, 34 n. 1, 280 n. 3, 283 n. 1
Ley, J., 131 n. 4
Lieberman, S., 109, 157, 182 n. 3, 240, 414 n. 1, 454

Lietzmann, H., 253 n. 1, 325 n. 2, 339
Lightfoot, R. H., 3 n. 2, 61 n. 1, 197 n. 2, 299 nn. 3, 5, 6, 7, 360, 390 n. 2, 471
Linton, O., 475
Loewe, H., 110, 162, 163 n. 2, 176, 281, 285 n. 3, 396 n. 2
Lofthouse, W. F., 123 n. 2
Lohmeyer, E., 17, 33 n. 1, 34 n. 2, 36 n. 3, 37 n. 1, 39, 49 n. 1, 70 n. 1, 88, 90 n. 1, 100 n. 1, 161 n. 4, 299 n. 6, 327 n. 2, 330 n. 3, 390 nn. 1, 3, 451, 471
Lohse, E., 55 n. 2
Loisy, A., 17, 64 n. 2, 88, 327 n. 3, 339 n. 2
Luria, D., 166 n. 1

Mach, R., 89 n. 1, 445
Macho, A. Díez, 134, 167, 446
Mäcklenburg, A., 131 n. 4
Manek, J., 349 n. 2
Mann, J., 282 nn. 3, 4
Manson, T. W., 17, 21 n. 6, 23 f., 33 n. 3, 91 n. 1, 132 n. 7, 139 n. 6, 182 n. 2, 195 n. 4, 240, 300 n. 4, 301 n. 2, 307 n. 1, 335 n. 1, 367, 369, 380, 383, 423 n. 6, 449, 453, 458 f., 460, 464 n. 1
Manson, W., 132, 363 n. 2, 364 n. 2, 381 n. 3
Marcus, R., 134 n. 3, 140 n. 2, 156 n. 2, 158 n. 3, 187 n. 1
Marmorstein, A., 110 n. 3, 258 n. 4, 280 n. 1
Marriott, H., 1, 2 n. 1
Marrou, H. I., 420 n. 3
Marxsen, W., 13 n. 1
May, H. G., 120 n. 2
Mayor, J. B., 403 n. 1
McCaughey, J. D., 349 n. 1
McCown, C. C., 56 n. 2
McNeile, A. H., 17, 18 n. 2, 65, 200, 335 n. 1, 336 n. 2, 388 n. 1
Ménégoz, M. F., 439 n. 2
Menoud, P. H., 322 n. 1, 453
Messel, N., 183 n. 3
Metzger, B. M., 58 n. 2
Meyer, R., 56 n. 2
Michaelis, W., 17, 62 n. 1, 65 n. 9, 66 n. 2, 87
Micklem, N., 453
Miegge, G., 70 n. 2

Milik, J. T., 115 n. 1, 147 n. 2, 227
Milik, P., 140 n. 4
Minear, P., 63 n. 1, 67 n. 1
Mishcon, A., 180 f.
Mitton, C. L., 323 n. 4
Moffatt, J., 62 n. 2, 443
Molin, G., 154 n. 3
Montefiore, C. G., 17, 43 n. 1, 73, 110,
    163 n. 2
Montgomery, W., 123 n. 2
Moore, G. F., 40 n. 3, 110, 155, 157, 158,
    184 n. 1, 185 n. 1, 187 n. 1, 264 n. 1,
    294 n. 2, 425 n. 1
Morgenstern, J., 37 n. 3
Morgenthaler, R., 97 n. 1
Morris, N., 420 n. 3
Moule, C. F. D., 283 n. 2, 318 n. 3,
    322 n. 1, 349 n. 2, 390 n. 3, 400 n. 1,
    452
Mowinckel, S., 121, 123 n. 3, 126 n. 3,
    132 n. 1, 134, 135 n. 4, 136 n. 2
Mudge, L. S., 131 n. 2
Muilenburg, J., 16 n. 2, 36 n. 5, 39 n. 2,
    46 n. 3, 114 n. 2, 117 n. 3, 172 n. 2,
    451
Muirhead, J., 463
Munck, J., 324, 325 n. 1, 339 n. 1, 468
    n. 1, 469 n. 1, 471 n. 4

Neil, W., 206 n. 1
Nepper-Christensen, P., 325 n. 5
Nestle, E., 18, 69 n. 1
Neuenzeit, P., 349 n. 2, 353 n. 5, 359
    n. 1
Neusner, J., 269 n. 3, 273 n. 1
Nibley, H., 321 n. 1
Niebuhr, H. R., 406 n. 1
Niebuhr, R., 387 n. 3, 449
Nineham, D. E., 349 n. 2
Nock, A. D., 293 n. 1
North, C. R., 37 n. 3, 114 n. 2, 117 n. 2,
    119 f., 120 n. 2, 131–4, 135 n. 1, 136
    n. 2, 139
Noth, M., 119 n. 2
Nötscher, F., 123 n. 2
Nowack, W., 123 n. 2
Nyberg, H. S., 132

Oesterley, W. O. E., 123 nn. 2, 3, 283
    n. 1
Ogg, G., 63 n. 1

Ortmann, H., 123 n. 3
Östborn, G., 122, 125, 126 ff., 130, 135,
    138 f.
Ottley, R. R., 129 n. 1, 282 n. 5
Otto, R., 451

Peake, A. S., 37 n. 3, 123 n. 2, 124, 137 f.
Pearson, H., 324 n. 1
Pedersen, J., 37 n. 3, 114 n. 1, 118 n. 4,
    125 n. 5, 128 n. 1
Percy, E., 103 n. 1, 237
Perry, C., 2
Peterson, E., 89 n. 1
Plummer, A., 66 n. 1
Podro, J., 269 n. 1
Powis-Smith, J. M., 138
Poznansky, S., 446
Preiss, T., 98 n. 2
Procksch, O., 131 n. 4, 138 n. 3

Quell, G., 125, 187 n. 1

Rabin, C., 148, 151 ff., 154 n. 1, 155 n. 2,
    218, 233, 240, 242 f.
Radin, M., 285 n. 3
Ramsay, A. M., 85 n. 1
Raven, C. E., 71 n. 1
Rawlinson, A. E. J., 448
Reicke, Bo, 207 n. 5
Rengstorf, K. H., 407 n. 4, 421 n. 3, 449
Resch, J. A., 353
Richardson, A., 89 n. 2
Riesenfeld, H., 13 n. 1, 55 n. 1, 117 n. 2,
    118 n. 4, 353 n. 5, 403 n. 1, 417 n. 3,
    424 n. 1, 454, 465 ff., 468, 480 n. 2
Rigaux, B., 210, 213 n. 1, 215, 217 n. 1
Rist, M., 75 n. 2
Roberts, B. J., 208, 233 n. 2
Robertson, E., 450
Robinson, H. W., 37 n. 3, 113 n. 1, 131
Robinson, J. A. T., 330 n. 2
Robinson, J. M., 349 n. 1
Robinson, T. H., 1, 17, 121 n. 1, 123
    nn. 2, 3, 125 n. 4
Rosenthal, E. I. J., 450
Rost, L., 58 n. 2
Rostovtzeff, M., 118 n. 4
Roth, C., 293 n. 1, 447
Rowley, H. H., 114 n. 2, 121 n. 1, 123
    n. 2, 125 n. 4, 126, 131 n. 1, 132, 140
    n. 3, 233 n. 2, 448

Rudolph, W., 123 n. 3
Ryle, H. E., 1 42n. 2

Sahlin, E., 349 n. 2
Salet, G., 439 n. 2
Sanders, J. N., 339 n. 1
Schechter, S., 72 n. 2, 182 n. 3, 275, 451, 455
Schelhaas, J., 131 n. 4
Schlatter, A., 16, 48 n. 1, 77, 194–9, 278 n. 1, 327 n. 3, 463 f.
Schlier, H., 445
Schmid, J., 17, 46 n. 1, 47 nn. 1, 2, 49 n. 1
Schmidt, H., 123 n. 2
Schmidt, K. L., 444
Schmitt, J., 115 n. 1.
Schnackenburg, R., 342 n. 2, 349 n. 2, 431 n. 3, 434 n. 2
Schneider, J., 244
Schniewind, J., 17, 46 nn. 1, 2, 47 n. 2, 49 n. 1, 70 n. 1, 73 n. 2, 203 n. 2, 235
Schoeps, H. J., 42 n. 2, 56 n. 2, 58 n. 2, 60 n. 1, 87, 103, 118 n. 4, 183 n. 1, 187 n. 1, 193 n. 5, 272 n. 4, 321 n. 1, 324, 325 n. 1, 334 n. 2, 342 n. 3, 346 n. 1, 349 n. 2
Scholem, G. G., 148 n. 2
Schubert, K., 251 f.
Schürer, E., 140 n. 1
Schürmann, H., 309 nn. 2, 3, 311 n. 4, 313 n. 1, 452
Schwab, M., 161 n. 2, 308
Schweitzer, A., 5, 49 n. 1, 98 n. 1, 342 n. 3, 379
Schweizer, E., 423 n. 1, 436 n. 1
Scott, C. A. A., 342 n. 3
Scott, E. F., 325, 390 n. 2
Scott, R. B. Y., 138 n. 3, 159 n. 1
Seeberg, A., 370
Sellin, E., 117, 123 n. 2
Selwyn, E. G., 370–6, 380
Silver, H., 181
Simon, M., 80 n. 2, 186 n. 4, 272 n. 4, 321 n. 1, 322 n. 3, 353 n. 3
Singer, S., 110 n. 3, 283 n. 1
Sitwell, E., 429 n. 2
Skinner, J., 36 n. 5, 71 n. 1, 123 nn. 1, 2, 126, 130, 133, 136
Smith, C. R., 206 n. 1
Smith, G. A., 123 n. 2, 124, 128, 129

Smith, Harold, 66 nn. 3, 5
Smith, Morton, 2 n. 4, 5–9, 13, 103 n. 1, 149 n. 3, 157, 180 n. 2, 245 n. 2, 257 n. 3, 293 n. 1, 417 n. 2, 423 n. 6
Smith, N., 287 n. 2
Smith, Robertson, 139
Snaith, N. H., 131 n. 1, 132 n. 4, 134
Sneath, E. H., 349 n. 1
Soiron, Th., 2 f., 227 n. 2
Souter, A., 69 n. 1
Spicq, C., 379 n. 2
Spiegel, Sh., 161 n. 2, 172 n. 1
Spitta, F., 403 n. 1
Stace, W. T., 433 n. 1
Stauffer, E., 63 n. 1, 103 n. 2, 217 n. 3, 262 n. 2, 287 nn. 3, 5, 430 n. 3, 464 n. 1
Steinespring, W. F., 162 n. 5, 417 n. 2
Stendahl, K., 3 n. 1, 7 n. 2, 16, 27 n. 2, 32 n. 1, 56 n. 2, 60 n. 2, 65, 67 n. 1, 94, 118 n. 1, 149 n. 2, 150 nn. 1, 2, 152 n. 1, 208 f., 219 n. 2, 222 n. 1, 227 n. 1, 234 f., 251 nn. 1, 4, 254 n. 1, 299 n. 6, 327 n. 2, 342 n. 4, 399 n. 2, 400 n. 2, 453
Stenning, J. F., 135 n. 1, 173 n. 2, 174
Steuernagel, C., 309 n. 2
Stonehouse, N. B., 17
Strack, H. L., 64, 157 n. 2, 177 n. 2, 266 n. 2, 301 n. 3
Strack, H. L. and Billerbeck, P., 68 n. 2, 72 n. 2, 74 n. 2, 80 n. 3, 82 nn. 1, 2, 110, 115 n. 1, 158 n. 3, 166, 171, 174 n. 2, 176, 184, 186, 226, 227 n. 2, 270 n. 4, 272 n. 1, 277 n. 2, 281 n. 1, 292 n. 2, 310 n. 2, 407 n. 4
Strauss, D. F., 56 n. 1
Streane, A. W., 129 n. 1
Streeter, B. H., 18, 20, 21 n. 4, 22, 371, 477 n. 2
Stumpf, S. E., 439 n. 2
Suggs, M. Jack, 185 n. 2
Sutcliffe, E. F., 151 n. 1, 153 n. 1, 242, 247 f.
Swete, H. B., 128

Tasker, R. V. G., 82 n. 3
Taylor, R. O. P., 417 n. 2
Taylor, V., 3 n. 2, 33 n. 1, 36 nn. 3, 7, 37, 39, 49 n. 1, 62 n. 2, 65, 77n. 3, 100 n. 1, 195 n. 1, 202 n. 1, 283n. 2,

Taylor, V. (*cont.*)
  341 n. 1, 367 f., 370 f., 380, 399 n. 3,
  418 n. 2, 443 f., 453, 462, 464 n. 1
Teeple, H. M., 115 n. 1, 147 n. 2, 148
  n. 1, 153 nn. 2, 3, 349 n. 2
Telfer, W., 472 n. 2
Thomas, G. F., 431 n. 3, 440 n. 1
Thomas, D. O., 108 n. 2
Tillich, Paul, 436 n. 1
Torrance, T. F., 414 n. 1, 437 n. 1
Torrey, C. C., 312 n. 1
Trilling, W., 290 n. 2, 297 nn. 1, 3, 300 n. 3
Turner, C. H., 325 n. 2, 338 n. 1
Turner, H. E. W., 418 n. 3

Unger, M. F., 417 n. 2
Urbach, E., 200 n. 1

Van Den Eynde, D., 418 n. 3
Van Der Flier, A., 131 n. 4
Van Der Ploeg, J. S., 131 n. 4
Van Der Woude, A. S., 148, 149 nn. 1, 2,
  150 n. 2, 152 n. 2, 154
Van Hoonacker, A., 131 n. 4
Venetianer, L., 282 n. 3
Vermès, G., 27 n. 2, 56 n. 2, 115 n. 1,
  118 n. 4, 147 n. 2, 153 nn. 2, 3
Via, D. O., 98 nn. 1, 2, 99 n. 2
Villey, M., 439 n. 2
Vincent, T. J., 7 n. 2
Vischer, W., 24 n. 2, 253
Volz, P., 114 n. 2, 118 n. 4, 123 n. 2,
  125 f., 129 n. 1, 155 n. 1, 157 n. 3, 183
von Dobschutz, E., 300 nn. 2, 3
von Rad, G., 113 n. 1, 125 f.

Wade, G. W., 133, 137 f.
Wadsworth, C., 438 n. 5

Wagenmann, J., 203 n. 1, 323 n. 3, 326
  n. 1, 337 n. 1, 338 n. 1, 353 n. 5, 454
Watson, N., 348 n. 1
Waxman, M., 171 n. 1
Weis, P. R., 163 n. 2
Weiss, B., 17, 327 n. 3
Weiss, J., 238, 306 n. 1, 335 n. 1, 338
  n. 1, 339, 346 n. 1, 454
Weiss, W., 42 n. 2
Welch, A. C., 123 n. 2
Wellhausen, J., 17, 210, 335 n. 1, 462
Wendling, E., 56 n. 1
Wernberg-Møller, P., 248
Werner, E., 214 n. 6, 258 n. 3, 263 n. 1,
  452
Wertenbeker, T. J., 338 n. 1
Westcott, B. F., 69 n. 4
Whale, J. S., 435 n. 1
Wibbing, S., 342 n. 4, 351 n. 2, 380 n. 1,
  460 f.
Widengren, G., 121 n. 5
Wieder, N., 115 n. 1, 153 n. 3
Wilder, A. N., 99 n. 1, 448
Williams, R. R., 473
Wilson, R. McL., 192 n. 4
Windisch, H., 316 n. 1, 445
Wood, H. G., 21 n. 1
Workman, G. C., 129 n. 1
Wright, A., 65
Wünsche, A., 162, 166 n. 1

Yadin, Y., 150 n. 2
Young, F. W., 189 n. 2

Zahn, T., 64 n. 2, 327 n. 3
Zeitlin, S., 272 n. 2
Ziemer, E., 131 n. 4
Zunz, L., 64

IV. INDEX OF SUBJECTS

Abbahu, R., 453
Abin b. Kahana, R., 165
Adda b. Ahaba, R., 394 n. 1
Age to Come, *see* Messianic hope
Akiba, R., 108 n. 2, 260 n. 1, 267 f.,
  271, 273, 280, 292 n. 2, 295, 442,
  455
almsgiving, 305 ff.

Amidah, 270 f., 275
  contrasted with Christian prayer,
  309 ff.
ἀνατολή, 445 f.
angels
  as aids to Jesus, 84; and Matt. xviii.
  10, 226; as viewed by Qumran,
  226 f.

INDEX OF SUBJECTS

anger, 235 ff.
ἀνομία, 202 ff.
Antitheses, of *SM*, 101 ff., 235 ff., 300 f.
apocalyptic, 139 f.; *see also* Messianic hope
Aquila, 67, 234, 282 n. 5
Ashi, R., 455
authority
    of Jesus Christ, 90 f., 102, 107 f., 196 ff., 224, 409 f., 420 f.; of church, 224 f.; of rabbis, 261 f., 302 f., 276 ff., 262, 294; of Torah, 157 f.; ἐξουσία, 197

baptism
    by John, 34 f., 369; and Exodus, 40 ff.; according to Paul, 342
Bar Kokba, 201 f.
bath qôl, 36, 41, 285
Beatitudes, 9 ff.
    related to blessings in Deut., 60; related to Qumran, 251 f.; related to rabbinic Judaism, 288 f.; in Q as depicting crisis, 382
Birkath ha minim, 275 f., 278 f.
birth narratives
    of Moses, 81 f.; of Jesus, 61 ff., 67 ff., 72 ff., 287 f., 302 ff., 443 f., 445 f.

calendar, authority of rabbis over after A.D. 70, 261 f.
canon, establishment of by rabbis, 271 ff.
catechesis
    and Q, 370 ff., 380; and *SM*, 376 n. 2, 460; in Pastoral Epistles, 377 ff.; and Gospels, 460 f.
Cerinthus, 194
Church
    as the Body of Christ, 98 f.; authority invested in, 224 f.; development of toward 'Catholicism', 253 f., 414, 419; division of early church, 317 f., 324 f.; spread of early church, 318 ff.; significance of fall of Jerusalem for, 321 f.; understanding of teaching of Jesus in, 340 f.; accuracy of tradition in, 416 f., 464 ff., 473 ff.; involvement in problems of law and order, 437; understanding of by Gerhardsson, 469 ff.; importance of Jerusalem and

Temple for, 469 ff.; centrality of the Twelve in, 472 f.
Communism, as compared with early Christianity, 437 f.
Covenant
    the New, 83, 113; Jeremiah's view of the New, 122 ff.; replaced by Torah as centre of Jewish life, 186 f.
creation
    of man, 71 f.; new, 36, 67 ff., 90 f., 120 f.; in teaching of Jesus, 429 f.; and Messiah, 445 f.

darkness, at death of Jesus, 84 f.
Dead Sea Sect, *see* Qumran
Decalogue, removal from Synagogue service, 281 f.
disciples
    choosing of, 58 f., 421; referring to all Christians, 94; life of, 94 ff., 248 ff.; as servants, 96; identification with Christ, 97 ff.; relation to Christ, 407 f.; of rabbis, 455 ff.; retention of words of Jesus by, 465 ff.; as the Twelve, 58 f., 472 f.; the Twelve as possessing doctrinal authority, 474 f.
divorce
    according to Matthew, 104 f.; according to M, 388 f.; according to Mark x. 12, 462 f.
dove, in account of Jesus' baptism, 36

Eleazar, R., 308
Eleazar b. Azariah, R., 260 n. 1, 264
Eleazar b. Dama, R., 277 f., 288
Eleazar of Modiim, R., 285 n. 3
Eliezer, R., 42, 162, 261, 271, 277 f., 280, 284, 295, 442
Eliezer b. Taddai, R., 442
Eliezer b. Zadok, R., 394 n. 1
Eliezer the Great, R., 292 n. 2
Elijah
    herald of Messiah, 28 f.; belief in return of, 154 f.; return of according to rabbis, 158 ff.; as future interpreter of Torah, 159 f.
Eucharist
    relation to Sinai, 24 f.; relation to Exodus, 59, 83 ff.; according to Paul, 350
evil *yetzer*, 233

541

excommunication, by rabbis, 236, 276 ff.
Exodus
  (a) of Old Testament: 26, 40 f.; and
    views of Paul, 36; as kerygma,
    111 ff.; and Moses, 116; and co-
    venant obligations, 119 f.; (b) New
    Exodus: 25 ff., 78 ff., 114 f.; in Old
    Testament, 114; in Qumran, 115;
    relation to motif of creation, 120 f.;
    in Paul's thought, 349 ff.
ἐξουσία, 197; see also authority

faith
  as loyalty to Christ, 95; in Qumran,
    217 f.; according to Matthew, 218 f.
fasting
  conflict between Jews and Christians
    over, 283 f.; in SM, 313 f.
feeding of the five thousand, 48 ff.
  and motif of the New Moses, 48
festivals
  in Messianic Age, 162; control over
    by Jamnia, 261 f.
form-criticism
  of SM, 2; forms isolated by, 368;
    results of, 415 f.; scepticism of
    questioned, 416 f., 460, 480

Galilee
  contrast of with Judean Judaism,
    299 f., 450 f.; as scene of redemp-
    tion for Matthew, 299
Gamaliel I, R., 271
Gamaliel II, R., 258, 260 n. 1, 269 f.,
    273, 275 f., 295 f., 312, 451, 473
gematria, in prologue of Matthew, 74 ff.
Gentiles
  righteous of included in blessings of
    Messianic Torah, 156, 177, 179 f.;
    as Christians, 317, 319 ff., 329 ff.,
    338 ff.
Gnosticism, 192 f.
  relation to Matthew, 193 ff.; rejection
    of view that Matthew is anti-
    Gnostic, 194 ff., 199 ff.

Hananiah, R., 277
Hananiah b. Akashya, R., 285 n. 3
Hananiah b. Dosa, R., 450 f.
Hellenists, in Acts, 254
Hillel, 108 n. 2, 256, 264 ff., 271, 401 n. 2

ἱστορῆσαι, 453 ff.
Hiyya, R., 267
Huna, R., 146, 172

Imitatio Christi, 95 f., 346, 364 f., 455 ff.
Ishmael, R., 264, 288, 401 n. 2
Issi of Caesarea, R., 277

Jacob of kefar-Nibbuyara, 277
Jacob of kefar-Sama, 277, 288
James, Epistle of
  teaching of Christ subsumed under
    law of love, 402; use of words of
    Jesus, 403 f.
Jamnia
  founding of Beth Din at, 256 f.;
    problems confronting, 258 f.; au-
    thority of Beth Din at, 262, 294;
    and codification of Torah, 266 ff.;
    and liturgy, 269 ff.; and canon, 271;
    and conflict with Christianity,
    272 f.; reaction of Matthew toward,
    292 ff.; city of 293 f.; see also rabbis
Jeremiah
  scholarly views of ch. xxxi, 122 ff.;
    relation of to Deuteronomic re-
    formation, 125 f.
Jeremiah, R., 453
Jerusalem
  fall of, 298 f.; significance of fall of for
    church, 321 f.; importance of for
    church, 469 ff.
Jesus Christ
  as Servant, 38 f., 96; as New Adam,
    68 ff.; as Son of David, 74 ff.; as
    Messiah, 430, 432 f.; as Son of Man,
    85; as New Moses, 25 ff., 51 ff., 61,
    78 ff., 85 ff., 357, 366, 410, 430; as
    transcending motif of New Moses,
    96 ff., 410; as giver of New Torah,
    94 ff., 106 f., 363, 412 ff., 456, 474;
    relation to Old Torah, 101 ff.;
    relation to New Torah, 189; identi-
    fication with Israel, 39 ff., 45;
    authority of, 90 f., 102, 107 f.,
    196 ff., 224, 409 f., 420 f.; birth of,
    62 ff.; as Lord, 97, 102, 357 ff.,
    361 f.; knowledge of, 206 f., 214;
    relation to Qumran, 252, 255;
    teaching of as understood by
    Church, 340 f.; teaching of as found

Jesus Christ (*cont.*)

in Paul, 348 f.; as source of Christian tradition, 357 ff.; as causing crisis in old order, 382; attitude toward Temple tax, 289 f.; teaching subsumed under one principle, 401 ff.; love of God defined in terms of life of, 406, 410 f.; as New Torah a means of transition to second-century Christianity, 414; as teacher, 418 f., 422 ff.; as demanding commitment, 419 ff.; as rabbi with a school, 422 ff.; as preacher of repentance, 425 f.; view of Jewish Torah, 425 ff.; as preacher of judgement, 429; view of creation as ground for morality, 429 f.; teaching as related to kingdom of God, 432; teaching as demanding infinite succour and demand, 433 ff.; and wisdom sayings, 457 ff.; as fulfilling role of Oral Law for the Church, 478 f.; *see also* Messiah

Johannine Epistles, love of God and man in, 406 f., 411 f.

John, Gospel of

feeding of five thousand, 49; treatment of love, 407; relation of Christ to disciples, 407 f.; place of teaching of Jesus in, 408 ff.; Jesus as contrasted with Moses, 410; Jesus as the New Commandment, 410 f.; relation to Synoptic words of Jesus, 463 f.

John the Baptist, 26 ff.

understood in terms of Exodus, 29 ff., 43 f.; preparation for Messiah, 29 f.; as ethical teacher, 32 f.; baptism of, 34 f., 369

Joḥanan, R., 161, 170 f., 283

Joḥannan b. Zakkai, R., 156, 159 f., 171, 256 ff., 261 f., 269 ff., 283 f., 293, 300, 306 f., 321, 450 f., 473

Jose, R., 263

Jose b. Hanina, R., 169, 172

Joseph, R., 169

Joshua b. Hananiah, R., 159, 260 n. 1, 267, 271, 278, 280, 284 f., 306, 310, 313, 394 n. 1, 442

Joshua b. Karha, R., 262

Joshua b. Levi, R., 455

Josiah, R., 80 n. 3

Judah (Rabbi), 80 n. 3, 159, 267 f., 442

Judah II, R., 394 n. 1

Judah b. Nakosa, R., 278

Judah b. Simeon, R., 165

kerygma

and *SM*, 7 f.; Exodus account as, 111 ff.; relation to works and words of Jesus in Paul, 348 f., 354; Q as, 386; words of Jesus as part of, 413; as Torah, providing transition to second-century Christianity, 414; over-emphasis upon, 436 f.

king, ideology of, 37 f.

ideology of as source of doctrine of Messiah, 121

Kingdom of God, *see* Messianic hope

knowledge

possessed by Jesus Christ, 206 f., 214; taught by Jesus Christ, 214; as true interpretation of Torah, 215

Last Supper, *see* Eucharist

Law, *see* Torah

lectionaries, Matthew as, 21

Levi, R., 161

literary form, of *SM*, 5 ff.; of Tannaitic materials, 6

liturgical influence on *SM*, 4

Lord

Christ as, 97, 102, 357 ff., 360 ff.; exalted Lord related to risen Christ, 360 f.

Lord's Prayer

form in Matthew and Luke, 4 f., 11 f.; doxology of, 451 ff.; and Judaism, 309 ff.

love

of enemies, 245 f.; of God explained in terms of Christ, 405 ff.; Jesus' view of, 431 ff.; as summation of Gospel, 402, 405

Luke

Gospel of, account of Transfiguration, 52 ff.; beatitudes in, 288 f.; view of Jerusalem, 469 f.; view of Spirit in Luke and Acts, 467 f.

M, 23 f., 387 ff.

as adapting radical demand to daily life, 387 ff., 396; and the tax on the

M (*cont.*)

Jews, 390 f.; and church regulations, 391 f.; and marriage regulations, 393 ff.; relation of to Jesus, 397 f.; as casuistry rather than catechism, 398 ff.

Magi, 63, 78 ff., 327

manna, 45 f., 48 f.

Mark, Gospel of

use by Matthew, 26 ff.; view of John the Baptist, 27 f.; view of Transfiguration, 50 f.; and Gnosticism, 193 f.; as vindication of Paulinism, 318

marriage, 393 ff.

Matthew, Gospel of

arrangement in five books, 14 ff., 107; Caesarea Philippi as pivotal point of, 17; conclusions to five discourses, 17 f., 20; five discourses derived from sources, 18, 21 ff.; division into narrative and legal parts, 19; description of John the Baptist, 27 f.; view of Transfiguration, 51 f.; Prologue of, 61 ff., 287 f.; genealogy of, 72 ff., 302 ff.; Epilogue of, 83 ff.; Last Supper, 83 f.; Miracles, 86 ff.; avoidance of title 'rabbi' for Jesus, 96 f.; view of teaching as related to Torah, 99 ff.; use of *qal waḥomer*, 103 f.; attitude towards Scribes and Pharisees, 106, 290 f.; relation of to Jewish speculation about Messianic Torah, 187 ff.; *Sitz im Leben* of, 191 ff.; relation to Gnosticism, 193 ff.; view of 'false prophets', 199 f.; interpretation of Old Testament, 208 f.; relation of ecclesiology to Qumran, 209 ff., 221 ff., 254 ff.; meaning of τέλειος, 209 ff.; meaning of faith, 218 f.; views of eschatology, 215 ff., 220; relation of ethic to Qumran, 221 ff.; authority of Church in, 224 f.; rank of Church members in, 228 ff.; and separation of wheat and tares, 230 ff.; relation of *SM* to Qumran, 235 f.; views of anger, 235 ff.; views of slander, 238 f.; view of oaths, 239 ff.; view of love for enemies, 245 f.; reaction to rabbinic Judaism,

286 ff., 452 f.; report of empty tomb, 287; reaction to Jamnia, 292 ff.; and persecution of Christians, 297; and desire for titles of honour, 297 f.; view of fall of Jerusalem, 298 ff.; *SM* interpreted in light of Jamnia, 300 ff., 304 f., 314 f.; Antitheses of, 300 f.; structure of *SM* as triadic, 307; view of almsgiving, 307 f.; prayer in contrasted with Amidah, 309 ff.; view of fasting, 313; view of as anti-Pauline, 316, 325 f., 334 ff.; universalism of, 327 ff.; not opposed to Gentile church, 330 ff.; view of as exalting Peter at expense of Paul, 336 ff.; view rejected, 338 ff.; and Jesus' own intent, 433

Meir, R., 80 n. 3, 168, 267 f., 271, 441

Mekilta, view of Exodus, 40 ff., 441 ff.

Menahem of Gallia, R., 161

Messiah

and Spirit, 36; and Servant, 37 ff., 131 f., 136 f.; community of, 98; origin of belief in, 121; according to Qumran, 147 ff., 151 ff.; false messiahs, 201 f.; Jesus as, 430, 432 f.; Law of, *see* Torah; view of as pre-existent, 445 f.

Messianic hope

and New Exodus, 26; and New Israel, 73; and Torah, 109 ff., 122 ff., 150 f., 158 ff., 446 ff.; and Exodus, 111 ff.; and the Prophet, 117 f.; and Moses, 45, 117 ff.; as New Creation, 36, 67 ff., 90 f., 120 f.; and Wisdom, 142; in Qumran, 147 ff., 215 ff., 220; relation between Messianic Age and Age to Come, 182 f.; Age to Come, is and is yet to come, 181 f.; according to Matthew, 215 ff., 220, *see also* Matthew; in Paul, 342 ff.; and Spirit according to Paul, 342 ff.; and future judgement according to Paul, 348; Kingdom of God and teaching of Jesus, 431 f.; *see also* Jesus Christ *and* Messiah

minim

books of, 273 f.; benediction against, 275 ff.

miracles
  Jesus and Moses related with respect to, 86 ff.; healing of paralytic, 88; stilling of sea, 88 ff.; feeding of five thousand, 48 ff.
Mishnah
  order of, 268, 301 f.; relative to Jesus, 478
Moses, 26
  identification with Israel, 44; and Messianic Age, 45, 117 ff.; birth of, 81 f.; miracles of, 86 ff.; attitude of Matthew toward, 105; treatment of in Old Testament, 116 f.; and Servant of Yahweh, 117; New Moses, 25 ff., 51 ff., 61, 78 ff., 85 ff., 117 ff., 152 ff., 357, 366, 410, 430
mountain, place of giving of *SM*, 99

Nahman, R., 146, 169
Nehemiah, R., 442

oaths, 239 ff.
obedience, 203, 419 ff.
ordination, by Jesus of disciples, 54 f.

parables
  of wheat and tares, 230 ff.; teaching of Jesus in, 234
Passover
  relation to Last Supper, 59, 83 f.; Haggadah of, 270
Paul
  views of Exodus, 36; relation of to Matt. xviii. 15 ff., 224; polemic against, 285; *SM* as opposed to, 316 f.; view of rehabilitation of after fall of Jerusalem, 317 f.; view refuted, 318 ff.; Goodspeed's view of formation of Pauline corpus, 323 f.; life 'in Christ', 342; ethic of, 342 f.; sanctification of life of Christians, 344; imperative and indicative in, 344 ff.; life in the Spirit, 342 f., 346 f., 348, 358 f.; view of future judgement, 348; Christian life as New Exodus, 349 ff.; words of Jesus as New Torah, 348 f., 352 f.; person of Jesus as New

Torah, 363, 366; tradition passed on by, 354 f.; source of tradition for Paul, 355 ff.; view of Christ as risen Lord, 361 f.; rarity of references to love of God, 406 f.; antitheses of law and grace overstressed by Church, 436, 439 f.; and relation to Peter, 453 ff.
Peter
  importance of to Matthew and Qumran, 228 ff.; in relation to Paul, 336 ff., 453 ff.
Pharisees
  attitude of Matthew toward, 106, 290 f.; view of Torah by, 426; *see also* rabbis
Phinehas, R., 161, 175
priest
  rejection of as Messianic figure, 145 ff.; attitude of rabbis toward, 257 f., 260 ff., 269 f.
prophecy
  fulfilment of, 72 f., return of in future, 143 f., 151
prophet
  as eschatological figure, 117 f., 154; view of in 1 Maccabees as non-eschatological, 143 ff.; false prophets, 199 ff.; in sharp contrast with Torah, 448 f.
purity, laws of, attitude of Matthew toward, 104

Q, 23 f.
  use by Matthew, 26 ff.; reason for, 366 f.; as more than sayings source, 368 ff.; view of as catechetical source, 370 ff.; rejection of view, 380, 403 f.; as having crisis significance, 380 ff.; as radical demand, 385 f.; as kerygma, 386; relation of to Johannine literature, 411; *see also* Matthew
qal waḥomer, use by Matthew, 103 f.
Qumran
  influence on Matthew, 208 ff.; methods of Scriptural interpretation, 208 f.; ecclesiology of, 209 ff.; view of knowledge, 207, 215; view of faith, 217 f.; eschatology of, 215 ff., 220 ff.; discipline of, 221 ff.; view

Qumran (*cont.*)
    of angels, 226 f.; rank of members, 228 ff.; relation to *SM*, 235 ff.; view of anger, 237 f.; view of oaths, 241 ff.; hatred of enemies, 245 ff.; influence of ecclesiology on Matthew, 253 f.; and Jesus, 252, 255

Rab, 169, 312
Rab Judah, 281
Raba, 455
Rabbah b. Abbuha, 169
rabbis
    variety of views among, 156 f.; views on Torah in Messianic Age, 158 ff.; conflict against Christianity, 185 f., 272 f.; views of reflected in Matt. xviii, 224 ff., 230; views of evil *yetzer*, 2 33; excommunication by, 236, 276 ff.; views of oaths, 240 f.; and period of Jamnia, 256 ff.; relation to Priesthood, 257, 260 ff., 269 f.; conflict with Sadducees, 259 f., 272 f.; authority in calendrical matters, 261 f.; disunity among, 263; differences between House of Hillel and House of Shammai, 264 ff.; and codification of oral law, 266 ff.; and development of synagogue service, 269 ff., 275 f., 279 ff.; and canon, 271 f., 273 f.; institution of rabbinate, 271; and desire for titles of honour, 298 f.; opposition to enthusiasms of Galilean Judaism, 299 f.; chain of tradition of, 302 f.; pillars of world according to Simeon the Just, 305 f.; pillars as reinterpreted by Johannan b. Zakkai, 306 f.; and fasting, 313 f.; accuracy of tradition among, 416, 455, 466; and view of Jesus, 419; contrast of Judean with Galilean, 450 f.; and pupils, 455 ff.; exegetical methods of, 475 f.; *see also* Jamnia
Roman Catholic scholarship, 2 f.

sabbath, attitude of Matthew toward, 103 f.
sacrifice, and Messianic Age, 161 f.

Sadducees
    disappearance of after A.D. 70, 259 f.; conflict of with rabbis, 272 f.; view of Torah, 426
Samuel, R., 147, 169, 312
Samuel b. Nahman, R., 281, 314
Samuel the Small, 275 f.
Sermon on the Mount
    relation to Exod. xx–xxiv, 9 f.; unity of, 1, 13; and Jesus, 5; and literary form, 5 ff.; in opposition to Jamnia, 292 ff., 300 ff., 314; structure of, 304 ff.; as opposed to Paul, 316 f.; as catechetical, 398 f.; *see also* Matthew
sermonic form, of Sermon on the Mount, 5 ff.
Servant of Yahweh
    and Jesus, 37 ff., 96; and Moses, 117; scholarly views of, 131; as teacher of Torah, 133 ff.
Shammai, 264 ff., 271
Shekinah, 52
Shema, 279 f.; benedictions of, 282 f.
Shemoneh Esreh, *see* Amidah
Simeon b. Eleazar, R., 169
Simeon b. Gamaliel, R., 170
Simeon b. Gamaliel II, R., 267
Simeon the Just, 305 ff.
Simeon b. Laqish, R., 161 n. 2, 314
Simeon ha-Pakuli, 270
Simeon (b. Yohai), R., 159, 271
Simeon b. Zabdai, R., 174
Simon Magus, 193, 201
slander, as viewed by Qumran and New Testament, 238 f.
Son of Man, 51, 85, 140, 142
    and Servant, 132; enthronement of, 197
source-criticism, of *SM*, 1 ff.
Spirit, the, 36, 70 ff., 150
    life in according to Paul, 342 f., 346 f., 348, 358 f.; view of in Luke–Acts, 467 f.
Symmachus, 67, 79, 234
Synagogue
    transference of Temple ritual to, 262 f., 269 f.; standardization of service in, 270 f.; changes in liturgy of by rabbis, 275 f., 279 ff.; liturgy contrasted to Christian by Matthew, 309 f.

Syria
 influenced by Gnosticism, 193; influence upon by rabbinic decrees, 295 f.

Teacher of Righteousness, 148 f.
 as New Moses, 118, 152 f.; as eschatological, 152 f.; possible relation to interpretation by Matthew of Christ, 215 ff.
τέλειος, in Matthew, 209 ff.
Temple
 transference of liturgy from, 262 f., 269 f.; tax of, 389 f.; importance of for Jesus, 469 ff.; attitude of rabbis toward, 257 f., 260 ff.; importance of for Church, 469 ff.
Temptation of Jesus, 45 ff.
 and Mosaic motifs, 45 ff.; Matthew's account not anti-Gnostic, 194 f.
Theodotion, 79, 198
Theudas, 115, 118, 201
time, fulfilment of, 73
tomb, of Jesus, 287
Torah
 role of in Messianic Age, 109 ff., 119 f., 122 f., 161 ff., 173 ff., 446 ff.; New Torah according to Jeremiah, 124 ff.; Messianic Torah in Apocrypha and Pseudepigrapha, 140 ff.; Messianic Torah and Qumran, 147 f.; rabbinic views of Messianic Torah, 158 ff., 172 ff., 176 f.; to be interpreted in future by Elijah, 159 f.; some parts of to cease in Messianic Age, 161 ff., 180 f.; some parts of to change in Messianic Age, 163 f.; to be explained fully in Messianic Age, 170 ff.; inclusion of Gentiles in Messianic Torah, 179 f.; date of rabbinic sources which speak of New Torah, 185 ff.; ambiguity of Jewish views on New Torah, 188; New Torah and Matthew, 187 ff.; New Torah and Paul, 363; and Servant, 130 ff.; and Qumran, 147 f.; centrality of in Judaism of first century A.D., 157; considered eternal, 157 f.; obedience to Torah of Christ, 203 ff.; codification of Oral Torah, 266 ff.; attitude of Pharisees and Sadducees toward, 426; attitude of Sectarians toward, 426 f.; attitude of Jesus toward, 425 ff.; need for re-emphasis of in Christianity, 436 ff.; view of put in sharp contrast with prophets, 448 ff.
tradition
 and Paul, 354 ff.; transmission of according to a Scandinavian approach, 464 ff.; content of in Gospels, 466 f.; among Church Fathers, 467 f.; authoritative transmission of by early Church, 473 ff.; Church and rabbis related in regard to transmission of, 465 ff.; Jesus as source of Christian tradition, 357 ff.
Transfiguration, 50 ff.

Wilderness, 30 ff.
 as related to motif of Exodus, 50 ff., 56 ff.; in relation to eschatology, 58; see also Exodus
Wisdom
 and Torah, 141 f.; as mark of Messianic existence, 142; sayings of Jesus and, 457 ff.

Zerika, R., 453